PERSPECTIVES ON GUSTAV MAHLER

For Julie, Georgina, Samuel and Harry

Perspectives on Gustav Mahler

Edited by
JEREMY BARHAM
University of Surrey, UK

ASHGATE

Published by
Ashgate Publishing Limited
Gower House
Croft Road
Aldershot
Hants GU11 3HR
England

Ashgate Publishing Company
Suite 420
101 Cherry Street
Burlington, VT 05401-4405
USA

Ashgate website: http://www.ashgate.com

British Library Cataloguing in Publication Data
Perspectives on Gustav Mahler
   1. Mahler, Gustav, 1860–1911 – Criticism and interpretation
   I. Barham, Jeremy
   780.9'2

Library of Congress Cataloging-in-Publication Data
Perspectives on Gustav Mahler / edited by Jeremy Barham.
     p. cm.
   Includes bibliographical references and index.
   ISBN 0-7546-0709-7 (alk. paper)
    1. Mahler, Gustav, 1860–1911 – Criticism and interpretation. I. Barham, Jeremy, 1963–

   ML410.M23P47 2003
   780'92–dc22

                            2003060498

ISBN 0 7546 0709 7

Typeset by Express Typesetters Ltd, Farnham
Printed and bound in Great Britain by MPG Books, Bodmin, Cornwall

In Memoriam

Vladimír Karbusický

1925–2002

and

Herta Blaukopf

1924–2005

Contents

List of Plates

List of Tables

List of Music Examples

List of Figures

List of Contributors

JEREMY BARHAM studied music at the Universities of Durham and Surrey, writing his doctoral thesis (1998) on the relationship between Mahler's music and late nineteenth-century German philosophy. He was formerly Lecturer and Research Fellow at Trinity College of Music in London, and is now Lecturer in Music at the University of Surrey. He has written on Mahler's early compositions in *The Mahler Companion* (OUP, 2002), contributes regularly to *Music & Letters* and is editor of *The Cambridge Companion to Mahler* (forthcoming, 2005). His other research interests include music and nineteenth-century psychological theory, film studies and jazz.

HERTA BLAUKOPF was born in Vienna, studied at the University of Vienna and was active for over fifty years as a writer on the musical and literary culture of her native city. Together with her late husband, Kurt Blaukopf, she published *Die Wiener Philharmoniker. Welt des Orchesters – Orchester der Welt* (Vienna, 1986 & 1992) and *Mahler: His Life, Work and World* (London, 1991). She was the editor of several volumes of Mahler's letters, including *Gustav Mahler–Richard Strauss: Correspondence 1888–1911* (London, 1984), *Mahler's Unknown Letters* (London, 1986) and *Gustav Mahler Briefe* (Vienna, 1996). She continued throughout her life to write regularly on topics relating to Mahler and the history of Austrian literature.

FRANS BOUWMAN studied piano with Gerard Hengeveld and Geoffrey Madge at the Royal Conservatory of The Hague, and musicology with, among others, Marius Flothuis at the University of Utrecht. He has been closely associated with Mahler's Tenth Symphony since the late 1960s, and has produced arrangements of the work for two pianos based on the scores prepared by Deryck Cooke and Remo Mazzetti. In 1986 he was involved in organizing the 'Mahler X Symposium' in Utrecht, at whose opening he performed the Mazzetti reduction with his wife. He has written several articles on the Symphony, and is the editor of a comprehensive bibliography relating to the work (The Hague, 1996). He was responsible for proofreading the performing versions by Remo Mazzetti and the revised performing version by Joe Wheeler, and was in close contact with Rudolf Barshai during the preparation of his score. He is currently working on a scholarly edition of all existing manuscripts of the Tenth Symphony.

JAMES BUHLER is Assistant Professor of Music Theory in the School of Music at the University of Texas at Austin. He is editor, with Caryl Flinn and David Neumeyer, of *Music and Cinema* (Wesleyan University Press, 2000). He is currently working on two projects: *Music in Film*, a study of the relation of music to sound design with particular attention to how the technical advances in cinematic sound reproduction have altered the place and function of music in the soundtrack; and *Especially for You*, a collection of essays on music, mass culture and the dialectic of enlightenment.

SUSAN M. FILLER earned her PhD in 1977 from Northwestern University with a dissertation on the sources of Mahler's Third and Tenth Symphonies. She has lectured widely in the USA, France, Italy, the Netherlands and China, and has contributed to periodicals including the *Journal of Musicological Research*, *Music and Letters*, *College Music Symposium* and *News About Mahler Research*, as well as the books *Fragment or Completion? Proceedings of the Mahler X Symposium* and *Neue Mahleriana: Essays in Honour of Henry-Louis de La Grange on his Seventieth Birthday*. She co-edited *Essays in Honor of John F. Ohl: A Compendium of American Musicology*, and her first book, *Gustav and Alma Mahler: A Guide to Research* (Garland, 1989) is now in revision for a new edition planned by Routledge. She is also writing a source book of musicological research at the time of the Third Reich, to be published by Indiana University Press. She has edited songs of Alma Mahler for Hildegard Publishing and G.K. Hall, and has made performing versions of Gustav Mahler's little-known Scherzo in C minor and Presto in F major. Recently she was named editor of *Naturlaut*, the newsletter of the Chicago Mahler Society.

ROBERT G. HOPKINS graduated from Oberlin College before pursuing graduate study in musicology and music theory at the University of Chicago and the University of Pennsylvania, where he was a protégé of Leonard B. Meyer. He is the author of *Closure and Mahler's Music* (1990). He has special interests in the psychology of music and in nineteenth-century music, and is currently Associate Professor of Music at Hamilton College, New York.

JULIAN JOHNSON is a Lecturer in Music at the University of Oxford and Tutorial Fellow in Music at St Anne's College. His publications include *Webern and the Transformation of Nature* (Cambridge, 1999) and *Who Needs Classical Music?* (New York, 2002) as well as a number of contributions to edited volumes. His articles on nineteenth- and twentieth-century music, particularly Mahler and Webern, and Adorno and *Aesthetic Theory*, have appeared in *19th-Century Music*, *Music Analysis*, *Journal of the American Musicological Society*, *The Musical Times*, *Music & Letters*, *Journal of the Arnold Schoenberg Center*, *Repercussions* and *The British Journal of Aesthetics*. He is also a composer, his works having been performed in Europe and North America and in BBC Radio broadcasts. He is currently working on a new book on Mahler.

GILBERT KAPLAN is the author and editor of the award-winning volume *The Mahler Album* (1995) and has published facsimile editions of the autograph manuscripts of Mahler's Second Symphony (1986) and the Adagietto movement of the Fifth Symphony (1992). His writings on Mahler and performance practice have appeared in publications ranging from *The Musical Times* to *The New York Times*. He is regarded as a leading interpreter of Mahler's Second Symphony, a work that he has conducted to wide acclaim with more than fifty orchestras around the world. His recording of the work with the London Symphony Orchestra has become the best-selling Mahler recording in history. He has lectured extensively at universities and conservatoires throughout the USA and Europe and currently presents the classical music radio programme 'Mad About Music'. A member of the faculty of the Juilliard School, he is the recipient of an honorary degree of Doctor of Humanities from Westminster Choir College and the George Eastman Medal for distinguished musical achievement from the Eastman School of Music. He serves on the boards of several musical institutions including Carnegie Hall, the South Bank Centre (Royal Festival Hall, London) and the Visiting Committee to the Department of Music at Harvard University.

RICHARD KAPLAN, Associate Professor of Music Theory at Louisiana State University, is a graduate of Cornell University and the University of Michigan. His work on harmony, tonality, and form in late nineteenth- and early twentieth-century music (particularly that of Gustav Mahler) has appeared in major journals including *Music Theory Spectrum*, *19th-Century Music* and *The Journal of Musicology*. He served as Program Chair for the 1996 Annual Meeting of the Society for Music Theory, and has presented numerous papers to national meetings of both the Society for Music Theory and the American Musicological Society. He is currently engaged in a large-scale study of cyclic organization in the instrumental music of Brahms.

The late VLADIMÍR KARBUSICKÝ studied musicology, aesthetics and philosophy at the Charles University in Prague. After leaving Czechoslovakia in 1968 he held research and teaching posts in Cologne, Wuppertal and Kassel before being appointed Professor of Systematic Musicology at the University of Hamburg in 1976. His principal fields of research included the ethnological and sociological study of Eastern European music, aesthetics, semiotics, and the music of Mahler and Martinů. His work has been published extensively throughout the world, and in addition to such theoretical and historical volumes as *Widerspiegelungstheorie und Strukturalismus* (1973), *Grundriß der musikalischen Semantik* (1986), *Sinn und Bedeutung in der Musik* (1990) and *Wie deutsch ist das Abendland? Geschichtliches Sendungsbewußtsein im Spiegel der Musik* (1995), his output includes the specialist studies *Gustav Mahler und seine Umwelt* (1978) and *Mahler in Hamburg. Chronik einer Freundschaft* (1996).

REINHOLD KUBIK was born in 1942 in Vienna and studied at the University of Erlangen-Nuremberg, writing his doctoral thesis on Handel's opera *Rinaldo*. He has been active in the field of music publishing for over twenty years, producing numerous critical editions of works by Bach, Handel, Zelenka, Zelter, Schubert and Mahler, as well as teaching at the Vienna Conservatoire, the Nuremberg Music Academy and Yale University. As a specialist in baroque stage works he is director of the ensemble L'Azione Teatrale, dedicated to the authentic performance of this repertoire, and has given masterclasses at, for example, the International Handel Academy in Karlsruhe, King's College London and the Royal Conservatoire in Antwerp. Since 1993 he has been Vice President of the Internationale Gustav Mahler Gesellschaft and Chief Editor of the society's Complete Critical Edition, his most recent publication being the Fifth Symphony (2002). From 1998 to 2000 he was involved in producing performance editions of the complete church cantatas of J.S. Bach for John Eliot Gardiner's 'Bach Cantata Pilgrimage' project.

VERA MICZNIK's doctoral dissertation at the State University of New York at Stony Brook, 'Meaning in Gustav Mahler's Music: A Historical and Analytical Study Focusing on the Ninth Symphony' (1989), dealt with problems of understanding musical meaning through reception, genre and topic theory, as well as through analytical approaches borrowed from semiotics and literary criticism. Her work on Mahler, presented at several musicological conferences, has been published in *Revue Mahler Review*, *The Journal of Musicology*, *19th-Century Music*, and the *Journal of the Royal Music Association*. She has also published on Alban Berg in *In Theory Only*, on Liszt and programme music in *Music & Letters*, and on Berlioz's *Roméo et Juliette* in *19th-Century Music*. At present she is working on a book-length study of nineteenth-century 'music textualities'. She teaches historical musicology as Associate Professor at the University of British Columbia School of Music, in Vancouver, Canada.

KAREN PAINTER, Associate Professor of Music at Harvard University, specializes in musical thought, aesthetics and ideology from the late eighteenth to the twentieth century. She studied piano, philosophy and musicology at Yale, and received her PhD from Columbia University. After teaching for two years at Dartmouth, she joined the Harvard faculty in 1997. In 1999–2000 she was resident in Berlin as a Humboldt fellow and as the recipient of a Berlin Prize from the American Academy in Berlin. She is currently completing a book entitled *Symphonic Aspirations: German Ideology and Musical Thought, 1900–45* for Harvard University Press, and has recently edited *Mahler and his World* (Princeton, 2002). She has published in *Archiv für Musikwissenschaft*, on the ideology of counterpoint in the reception of Mahler, Richard Strauss and early Schoenberg, as well as in *The Musical Quarterly* on the idea of 'symphonic ambitions' in the Third Reich. Her forthcoming article in the same journal discusses bourgeois musical culture and analyses the role of 'work' and 'pleasure' in aesthetic thought within early biographies of Mozart.

DAVID PICKETT was born in Yorkshire (1946), plays the harpsichord and organ and is a conductor, Tonmeister and musicologist. He was a recording engineer for EMI (1969–79), has taught recording arts and sciences at the University of Surrey (1979–83) and Indiana University (1983–99) and is the producer of many recordings. A pupil of Igor Markevitch, he founded the Bushey Symphony Orchestra, and has been Music Director of two Indiana orchestras. His PhD thesis (University of Surrey, 1990) studied Mahler's 'Retuschen', including his re-scorings of the symphonies of Beethoven, Mozart, Schumann and Schubert. He is currently editing scores of these for publication in the Internationale Gustav Mahler Gesellschaft's Complete Critical Edition.

A native of Hungary, ZOLTAN ROMAN studied at the Universities of British Columbia and Toronto, gaining his PhD in 1970 with a dissertation on Mahler's songs. He joined the Department of Music at the University of Calgary in 1966, was appointed Professor of Musicology in 1976, and retired in 1992 as Professor Emeritus; he now makes his home in Victoria, BC. His scholarly work has been devoted chiefly to the biographical, analytical, editorial and bibliographic study of Mahler and Anton von Webern, and to interdisciplinary studies focussing on the turn of the twentieth century. He is a regular speaker at meetings of the International, American and Australian Musicological Societies, the Gesellschaft für Musikforschung, the Canadian University Music Society and the Hungarian Academy of Sciences. He has edited several fascicles of Mahler's songs for the Complete Critical Edition, and is the author of numerous books and articles. In recognition of his contribution to musical scholarship he has been elected to the governing bodies of the American Musicological Society (Council, 1991–94), the International Musicological Society (Council, 1982–92, 1997–2002), the International Webern Society (Board, from 1978) and the Internationale Gustav Mahler Gesellschaft (Executive Committee, and the Academic Advisory Board, from 1976).

ELISABETH SCHMIERER studied musicology at the University of Kiel, producing her doctoral thesis on Mahler's orchestral songs (1989). In 1996 she habilitated at the Technical University of Berlin with a study of the *tragédies lyriques* of Niccolò Piccinni. She has been the recipient of a grant from the Deutsche Forschungsgemeinschaft, and has worked in the Musicological Institutes of the Universities of Kiel, Marburg and Erlangen, as well as in the Hochschule der Künste in Berlin. Currently she teaches at the Technical University of Berlin and at the Musikhochschule Essen-Werden. She has published on the history of the Lied, opera, French music and the works of classical modernism.

A native of Norway, MORTEN SOLVIK grew up and received his education in the USA before moving to Vienna in 1990. He earned his PhD at the University of Pennsylvania with a dissertation on the cultural setting of Mahler's Third

Symphony, and continues to pursue the tantalizing connections between music and culture in his research, especially in relation to Vienna. Recent projects include a study of Mahler's concept of nature and its impact on his musical thinking, an investigation of song manuscripts which led to the uncovering of an unknown Liederspiel by Schubert, and an examination of Bruckner reception during the Nazi regime and its influence on the compilation of the composer's Critical Edition in the 1930s and 1940s. He has participated in productions for radio and television, organized innovative concerts, and lectured on a wide variety of topics. His writing has appeared in numerous books and in journals including *The Musical Quarterly*, *Notes* and the *Österreichische Musikzeitschrift*. He holds teaching positions at the University of Music and Performing Arts in Vienna and at the Institute of European Studies.

JAMES L. ZYCHOWICZ is a musicologist with experience in teaching and publishing. He received a PhD in musicology from the University of Cincinnati with a thesis on the sources of Mahler's Fourth Symphony (1988) and has undertaken research in Vienna through a Fulbright Scholarship. He has lectured in the USA and Europe on various aspects of Mahler's music, and has published articles in *The Journal of Musicology* and elsewhere. Among his recent publications is the monograph *Mahler's Fourth Symphony* (OUP, 2000) in the series 'Studies in Musical Genesis and Structure', and the two-volume critical edition of Mahler's score for Weber's opera *Die drei Pintos* (A-R Editions, 2000) in the series 'Recent Researches in the Music of the Nineteenth and Early Twentieth Centuries'.

Introduction

JEREMY BARHAM

There is more than one Gustav Mahler: victim of musical incomprehension and anti-Semitic ideological vilification, yet cultural icon of postmodern generations; marginalized in performance to varying degrees until the 1960s, yet staple diet of the late twentieth- and early twenty-first-century orchestral repertoire, and modern-day conductors' rite of passage; formerly the preserve of only the most prestigious performing institutions, yet increasingly embraced by non-professionals;[1] musically innovative but intellectually conservative; Czech-Bohemian as well as Austro-German; Central European Jew and assimilated Jew; Jew and 'Catholic'; 'Catholic' and pantheist; lifelong conductor of opera but composer of none; ruthlessly practical theatre director and creator of impractical, idealistic symphonic worlds; seeker of artistic 'truth' but derider of 'realism' in art; *volkstümlich* sophisticate; Wagnerian and post-Wagnerian, Nietzschean and anti-Nietzschean; to Schoenberg a 'saint', dismissed by Debussy as the representative of an outmoded Germanic tradition; reputed personal ascetic but extravagant structural and sonic architect; programmatic and non-programmatic composer; respecter but determined manipulator of formal and generic convention, reconfiguring the symphonic terrain as an ambiguous – and to some analytically recalcitrant – interplay of tone poem, abstract instrumental form, orchestral song cycle, dramatic cantata, 'suite' of character pieces, 'grand opera'; the embodiment of a melancholic resignation to death and the greatest affirmation of existence; deeply sensitive thinker but arguably naive husband.

The contours of Mahler's reception history as traced by some of these dualities, though readily explicable, are none the less striking. The remaining multiple contradictions seem to fissure more severely Mahler's biography and accounts of his music and musical activity, suspending any definitive understanding of his cultural position. The situation is complicated further by the unravelling of some of these problematic distinctions. For example, Mahler was not unsuccessful as a composer during his lifetime, and the early twentieth-century body of aesthetic and political anti-Semitic criticism was by no means blind to the powerful and novel qualities of his music, as Karen Painter reveals in her contribution to this volume, which explores both this literature and the

---

[1] For example, the UK's National Youth Orchestra performed the Eighth Symphony, and the European Union Youth Orchestra the Sixth Symphony, respectively, at the 2002 and 2003 London Promenade Concerts.

problems involved in reconstructing Mahler's response to Jewish culture and the changing historical conditions of his Jewish identity. Similarly the ambiguities of Mahler's doctrinal affiliations have underpinned conflicting readings of the religiosity of his works. For various political and institutional reasons a Teutonic-Christian hermeneutic context for such readings has tended to prevail. The voice of Vladimír Karbusický as represented in this book, has been one of a minority which has attempted to reposition Mahler more accurately in the light of neglected aspects of his musical language and his early Jewish and non-Germanic cultural experience. Karbusický provides not just an alternative view but a corrective to assumptions regarding the Judaeo-Christian and Austro-German/Eastern European significance of Mahler's music.

As one of his most idiosyncratic and contentious traits, Mahler's musico-poetic intermingling of disparate genres and their attendant structural principles has spawned much critical confusion, misreading and disagreement. Rather than tease out the analytical minutiae of such intergeneric migration in synchronic fashion, Zoltan Roman's essay begins this volume with a broad-based appraisal of the dynamics of Mahler's unfolding compositional aesthetic. Recognizing the primary issue to be the diverse infiltration of real or 'abstract' vocal categories into Mahler's symphonic conception, Roman uncovers the cyclical yet regenerative nature of this conception across the broad span of the composer's output, invoking the archetypal beginning-and-end paradigm through which Mahler revisited and reinterpreted points of departure in the trajectory of his creative life. Arguably Mahler's musical innovation did not, however, extend as far in terms of absolute chromatic density and extreme tonal subversion as it did in areas such as the one just discussed,[2] and by the time of his final three works Schoenberg had already crossed the Rubicon of atonality. Despite both this and Mahler's lifelong preference for pre-modern literature and philosophy, he was often labelled as a self-indulgent modernist by his fiercest contemporary critics. The paradox of his relationship with the culture of modernism is addressed here by Morten Solvik in the context of the sensuous preoccupations of *fin-de-siècle* Viennese thought and the realism of contemporaneous theatrical drama, for which Mahler professed profound dislike and which he viewed as incompatible with a belief in the notion of art as a source of metaphysical 'truth'.[3] Given the highly allusive qualities of his own artworks – both with and without texts – it is not surprising that commentators have long been concerned to situate them

---

[2] This is not to say that other aspects of Mahler's harmonic language and long-term tonal planning, as evident in passages of tonal dissolution and in the manipulation of fields of diatonicism and chromaticism, were not strikingly original and distinct from the work of many of his contemporaries.

[3] An irony in light of the composer's apparent enthusiasm for elements of the realist nineteenth-century novel, to whose narrative techniques his symphonic idiom has frequently been compared.

within an identifiable intellectual milieu. In order to shed new empirical light on the range of Mahler's experience of this literary culture, Jeremy Barham presents the results of archival investigation into what was one of the last unexplored collections relating to the composer: the Alma Mahler-Werfel Collection at the University of Pennsylvania, Philadelphia, which houses the remains of Mahler's library. While such threads of Mahler's interaction with surrounding culture continue to be traced with increasing precision, his allusions to questions of nature both in his music and in written correspondence, though well known, are seldom explored beyond the level of clichéd, late-romantic oppositions constructed between the urban and the rural, the sophisticated and the *volkstümlich*. Julian Johnson addresses in his chapter the deeper complexities of Mahler's interiorization of the nature topic, seen here in terms of a critical dialogue with the very substance and function of art itself.

The fact that Mahler's prophecy of the future acceptance of his music was to a significant extent fulfilled through the economic and technological agency of mass communication, entertainment and the film soundtrack is an irony that the composer might well have grudgingly appreciated, and one which is symptomatic of a critical problem: the high-principled and unworldly becomes the subject of popular appropriation, balletic choreography, cinematic commodification and even jazz adaptation – the modern becomes postmodern.[4] This widespread late twentieth-century consumption of his music may appear to have occurred largely at the expense of a multi-levelled understanding of its historical significance. Elements of disturbing 'otherness', de-centredness and negation have tended to be subsumed within the comforting voice of psychological and emotional panacea projected by performers no longer challenged by the music. David Pickett examines the extent to which historically and technically the recording medium in particular has both served Mahler by disseminating his music more widely than he could ever have thought possible, and undermined his cause through negligence and misunderstanding on the part

---

[4] For example Antony Tudor's ballet *Dark Elegies* (1937) is set to the *Kindertotenlieder*, and Maurice Béjart's *Le Chant du compagnon errant* (1971) to the *Lieder eines fahrenden Gesellen*. The year 1971 also saw the release of Luchino Visconti's film *Death in Venice* (*Morte a Venezia*), which employs the fourth movements of the Third and Fifth Symphonies as its soundtrack, and Ken Russell produced his controversial 'biopic', *Mahler*, in 1974. The years following the centenary in 1960 were ones of rapid expansion in the availability of Mahler's music on disc, and, as David Pickett shows in Chapter 13 of this book, the period 1960–75 saw the first complete recorded cycles of the symphonies. More recently Uri Caine has developed jazz and klezmer 'interpretations' of movements from *Das Lied von der Erde* and the First, Second and Fifth Symphonies, as well as songs from *Lieder eines fahrenden Gesellen*, *Des Knaben Wunderhorn*, *Kindertotenlieder,* and the *Rückertlieder* (*Gustav Mahler/Uri Caine: Urlicht/Primal Light*, Winter & Winter, New Edition CD 910004–2, 1997, *Gustav Mahler in Toblach*, Winter & Winter, New Edition CD 9100462, 1999, and *Uri Caine/Gustav Mahler: Dark Flame*, Winter & Winter, CD 910095–2, 2003).

of certain interpreters. In so doing, Pickett re-establishes the importance of discographical studies as an indispensable tool in understanding traditions of performance practice and broader configurations of reception history. In other respects the rapid expansion in Mahler studies of recent years has neither adequately contextualized the composer within the history and theoretical understanding of nineteenth- and early twentieth-century performance practice – expanding areas of current scholarly interest – nor sufficiently addressed the conflicting mindsets of performers who project exceptionally divergent readings of, for example, the melancholic and affirmatory qualities of certain works. The essays by Gilbert Kaplan and Reinhold Kubik suggest complementary approaches to these neglected issues. In an updated account of his seminal work on the Fifth Symphony Adagietto, Kaplan invokes the authorial and anecdotal (in the true sense of unpublished or 'secret' history) alongside manuscript study, while Kubik – in relation to his recent revised critical edition – takes a closer look at notational variants in a range of sources of the same Symphony in order to locate Mahler's practice more precisely within a historical context that extends back to classical and baroque conventions. Opening the themed section 'Mahler in Performance', Herta Blaukopf's chapter provides further insight into the autocratic nature of his directorial approach, which has since become the stuff of legend. With reference to contemporary newspaper criticism and other Viennese archival records, Blaukopf underscores the composer's remarkable aptitude for the practicalities of operatic direction – an activity which, in his highly successful first year in Vienna, prevented him from composing but nevertheless paved the way for his transformational period of office at the Hofoper. Enforced attention to the realities of music-making combined with the unrelenting struggle towards an imagined ideal were qualities common to Mahler's re-creative *and* creative endeavours, suggesting the need for continued re-evaluation of traditional accounts which have tended to emphasize the discreteness of their domains.

Related to the study of performance practices, as both sources of evidence and medium for the concrete realization of its findings, are the activities of sketch analysis and publication. With experience in both fields, James Zychowicz is well placed to give a summative and revisionary account of the complexities of Mahlerian source study and their relation to editorial philosophy and the preparation of critical texts – an account that is all the more timely in view of Mahler's ever deeper consolidation within the scholarly canon via the Gustav Mahler Gesellschaft's current revision of the Gesamtausgabe. Until recently the Gesellschaft had been wary of engaging openly with Mahler's unfinished works. From their differing perspectives the final two chapters of this book attempt to strip away the layers of protective ownership and saintly auras of death-obsessed mythology with which the Tenth Symphony and the middle-period Scherzo and Presto fragments have been encrusted. Susan Filler reinterprets medical and biographical data to account for, and censure, the more prolonged suppression of the two lesser-known fragments in comparison with the remains of the Tenth

Symphony, and to argue for their increased recognition. Frans Bouwman, the leading authority on the manuscripts of the Tenth Symphony, takes the dispassionate and salutary view that any ethical evaluation of the Symphony's reconstruction must be based on full knowledge of the status and content of all the associated autograph material. He therefore reviews in detail eight previously unpublished manuscript pages housed in the Bayerische Staatsbibliothek, Munich (formerly in the collection of Hans Moldenhauer), the Österreichische Nationalbibliothek and the Internationale Gustav Mahler Gesellschaft as a prelude to discussing anew issues of compositional chronology, interrelations of the Symphony with Alma Mahler's songs and the music of Josef Suk, and the relative merits of all the existing 'performing versions'. Bouwman's prospective collaboration with the Mahler Gesellschaft in the production of an annotated scholarly transcription of the complete autograph materials of the Symphony will help ground the seemingly unstoppable flow of 'completions' within a more pragmatic and informed editorial environment, and will provide a valuable complement to the findings of the present chapter.

There has always been a degree of tension in the Mahlerian analytical project, whose roots can be traced to the relative weight and differing level of semantic importance writers have attached to elements of tonal language, thematic and textural processes, form, genre and intrinsic or extrinsic factors involving the written word. The old and rather oversimplified question of whether or not Mahler wrote 'programme music' has often underpinned analytical and critical propensities, but the conflicting contemporaneous views of the programmaticists Arthur Seidl ([1900] 1920) and Constantin Floros (1981, 1987a & 1991) and the non-programmaticists Guido Adler ([1916] 1982) and Christopher Lewis (1984) demonstrate that there has been no clear-cut historical progression from hermeneutics to 'pure' analysis or vice versa. Recent institutionalized developments in musicology have admittedly provided a fertile environment for attempted rapprochements between issues of 'text' and 'context' – and indeed the dissolution of this distinction altogether in view of developments in critical theory – which utilize interdisciplinary methodologies traditionally associated with manifestly conceptual–semantic art forms,[5] but this should be set against the continuing work of John Williamson, Kofi Agawu, Richard Kaplan and others.[6] If Mahlerian analysis is to thrive, then it will clearly do so at the expense of unreflective dogma and in conditions where reductive, cultural and hybrid analyses coexist, and at times interact. The characterization of Mahler's output as

---

[5] The special Mahler issue (20/2, Fall 1996) and steady influx of articles on the composer in the leading organ of 'new musicology', *19th-Century Music*, together with the appearance of like-minded chapters or whole books on Mahler (for example, Abbate, 1991, Newcomb, 1992, Samuels, 1995, Monelle, 2000, Franklin, 2002), are indicative of this trend.

[6] See for example Williamson, 1986 & 1997, Agawu, 1986 & 1997, Kaplan, 1981 & 1996, Lewis, 1984 & 1996, and Bruns, 1989.

gedankenmusikalisch (Eggebrecht, 1982b, p. 233)[7] may, for example, provide a useful tool in dismantling the artificial 'programmatic'–'absolute' critical divide, since any kind of analytical engagement with Mahler's music will sooner or later encounter, and be compelled to account for, the composer's historically self-conscious and knowingly manipulative approach to his materials. Chapters 7–11 analyse the multi-layered constructive and communicative dimension of Mahler's music, tracing, in a pattern of increasing extrinsicality, aspects of its technical, formal, generic, historical, cultural and emotional 'physiognomy' evoked by Eggebrecht's term.

Richard Kaplan demonstrates Mahler's liberating exploitation of the sonata-form paradigm in terms of unusually piecemeal expositional techniques displayed in the First, Second, Third and Tenth Symphonies. Just as Mahler reveals in this process both an indebtedness to, and a determination to adapt, his nineteenth-century symphonic legacy, so, Kaplan argues, an approach which is flexible enough to engage with this interlacing of traditional sonata functions with unprecedented, dynamic formal and tonal configurations is the only appropriate analytical response. The multi-functionality of Mahler's structuring elements has been highlighted in Robert Hopkins's unique focus on parameters of structural articulation other than tonality and rhythm. Identifying Mahler's control of intensities of dissonance and his registral, dynamic and textural strategies in the generation of closure and continuity enables Hopkins to reconsider the complex form of the Fifth Symphony's opening movement in the light of a long tradition of analytical disagreement. Elisabeth Schmierer elaborates the structural dimension of Zoltan Roman's earlier discussion of the aesthetic lineages of *Das Lied von der Erde* by exploring the sophisticated mechanics of the first movement's synthesis of instrumental and vocal genres. Taking into account the strophic nature of the text and the symphonic tendencies of the whole vocal–instrumental complex, Schmierer outlines the movement's intimate dialectic of conformity to, and deviation from, the dual expectations yielded by the generic models – a process of expressive intensification which distinguished Mahler from many other contemporary composers of orchestral songs. In a paean to the essential untidiness of analysis, and in homage to Adorno – a pivotal figure in Mahler studies around whom analytical programmes have hovered with varying degrees of frustration and veneration – James Buhler seeks to elucidate in his chapter the delicate subversion of rondo form and celebration of non-identity in the Sixth Symphony's Andante moderato. The dream world of an anti-rondo which assimilates itself to a sense of radical 'otherness' through the

---

7   The related term *Gedankenlyrik* – usually translated somewhat prescriptively as 'philosophical poetry' – referring to verse characterized by an underlying conceptual theme, has often been applied to the works of several of Mahler's favourite writers including Angelus Silesius, Schiller, Goethe, Hölderlin, as well as Hebbel, whose collected works are found in the remains of the Mahlers' library (see Chapter 3 of this book).

agency of the thematic variant and by focussing on elements at the imagined periphery, may be less amenable to the reductive language of graphic analysis, but is none the less one that for Buhler speaks of a profound humanity and deserves to be articulated in glowing terms. Resisting both the kind of one-dimensional mapping of 'extra-musical' concept on to musical event, and the overemphasis on a documented history of origins characteristic of some earlier traditions of Mahlerian semantic exegesis, Vera Micznik's chapter engages in a strongly theorized, narratological discussion of structural processes in the first movement of the Third Symphony. Notions of 'story' and 'discourse', the semiology of connotation, intertextuality and topic theory are called upon in order to examine the ways in which Mahler's *music* encodes layers of meaning, and to stress the need for a reintegration of musical functions as a primary resource in cultural analysis.

The essays brought together in this volume are intended neither to serve a particular agenda nor to provide comprehensive coverage of Mahler's output. Instead their diverse topics and methodologies aim to address certain neglected areas in the current scholarly understanding of the composer, and to provide contexts for a continuing discourse receptive to differing musicological concerns, including those whose emergence ironically coincided with the period of the wider late twentieth-century Mahler renaissance. If the collection is unified by a single theme then it is paradoxically one distinguished by those concepts of pluralism and heterogeneity so evident in Mahler's own creative practice. Whether the larger project of Mahler studies should therefore be regarded in terms of some archetypal deconstructive process of managing an unending radical relativism, or whether, for example, the apparent oppositions and incongruities listed at the beginning of this introduction will ever be susceptible to meaningful degrees of cultural unification and ideological closure, is difficult to say. Perhaps the distinction between these two positions is itself to be dissolved through the presence of some greater kind of binary interdependence between critical programmes. After all, this book also suggests that reconstructive, documentary, theoretical, analytical, discursive and interpretative impulses can, and should, coexist to mutual advantage in the scholarly domain. At the very least these essays reinforce the fact that the process of historical contextualizing does not negate the need for – and indeed gains its identity through – an independent, evolving, and hence historically contingent, critical sensibility; and conversely that a radical, particularized form of interpretation is founded on the perceived existence of those 'objective' contexts it seeks to unravel. Recognizing and addressing the gap or 'shifting and elusive slide' (to borrow Pierre Boulez's phrase)[8] between life and artistic creativity, and, by extension, between the results of artistic creativity and the analytical–

---

[8] 'Curseur mobile et insaisissable', preface to La Grange, 1979, p. 3.

interpretative process are problems particularly pertinent to Mahlerian critical practice. If this volume enriches these perceptions and, in turn, the understanding of Mahler's life and work, then it will have fulfilled its purpose.

Note
Where appropriate, the following pitch referencing system is adopted in this book: C4 = middle C; D4 = the D above middle C; higher-octave Cs are C5, C6, and so on; lower-octave Cs are C3, C2, and so on.

Acknowledgments

I would like to express my gratitude to the following individuals and institutions who have assisted directly or indirectly in the preparation of this volume: Jennifer Barnes at Trinity College of Music, London; Antony Beaumont; Herta Blaukopf; Susan Filler; Steve Goss; Erik Hense; Reinhold Kubik; Henry-Louis de La Grange; Stephen McClatchie; John Rink; Renate Stark-Voit; Polly Fallows; Julie Barham for advice on translations; Matthew Downey for help in the preparation of plates; Ingvo Clauder for painstaking work in producing the musical examples; my editor Rachel Lynch for her patience in awaiting the completion of the text; and all the authors for their commitment to this project; the Department of Music, University of Surrey; the Annenberg Rare Book & Manuscript Library, University of Pennsylvania, Philadelphia; Oxford University Press; the Department of Special Collections at the library of the University of California at Los Angeles; the Pierpont Morgan Library, New York; Peter Petersen of the Musikwissenschaftliches Institut of the University of Hamburg; the Archive of the University of Vienna; the Regents of the University of California; the Haus-, Hof- und Staatsarchiv, Vienna; the Kaplan Foundation, New York; the Bibliothek der Universität für Musik und darstellende Kunst, Vienna; the Wiener Stadt- und Landesbibliothek (Universal Edition archive); the Internationale Gustav Mahler Gesellschaft, Vienna; Universal Edition A.G., Vienna; the Department of Special Collections of the Stanford University Libraries, Stanford, California; the Arnold Schoenberg Institute, Vienna; Collection Netherlands Music Institute/Willem Mengelberg Archive Foundation, The Hague; C.F. Peters, Frankfurt; Musiksammlung, Staatsbibliothek Preußischer Kulturbesitz, Berlin; G. Henle Verlag, Munich; Music Division, the New York Public Library for the Performing Arts, Astor, Lenox and Tilden Foundations; the Bayerische Staatsbibliothek, Munich; and the Österreichische Nationalbibliothek. Finally I owe the greatest debt of thanks to my family for living with this project for so long.

Jeremy Barham
2005

PART ONE

Nature, Culture, Aesthetic

Chapter One

'Vocal' Music in the Symphonic Context: From *'Titan'*, *eine Tondichtung in Symphonieform* to *Das Lied von der Erde*, or the Road 'Less Traveled'[1]

ZOLTAN ROMAN

'Ma fin est mon commencement, et mon commencement ma fin': so sang the celebrated medieval French poet-musician Guillaume de Machaut (c. 1300–74), the outstanding innovator and consummator of the French Ars Nova.[2] Some 600 years later, T.S. Eliot (1888–1965) framed the second part of his *Four Quartets* with a subtle metaphrase of the same riddle: 'In my beginning is my end', and about 200 lines on, 'In my end is my beginning'.[3] In the fourth and last part of this ingeniously 'musical' work the conundrum is elaborated by a process akin to developing variation: 'What we call the beginning is often the end/And to make an end is to make a beginning'; eventually this culminates in the grand peroration:

> We shall not cease from exploration
> And the end of all our exploring

---

[1] An earlier version of this essay was read at the international symposium which formed part of the MahlerFest XI, January 1998, Boulder, Colorado.

[2] This rondeau, composed some time between 1349 and 1363, is one of the earliest examples of a musical palindrome (Paris, Bibliothèque Nationale, MS f. fr. 1584). Published as No. 14 of Machaut's 22 rondeaux by Friedrich Ludwig in *Guillaume de Machaut – Musikalische Werke* 1 (Publikationen älterer Musik, 1. Jahrgang, 1. Teil, 1926; [repr. Leipzig: Breitkopf & Härtel, 1954, pp. 63–64].

[3] 'East Coker' (1940), lines 1 & 209 in *Four Quartets* (London: Faber & Faber, 1959), pp. 23 & 32. The author is indebted to Donald Mitchell's article 'The World was Mahler's Symphony', *Muziek & Wetenschap*, 5 (3), (1995/1996), 207–23, for pointing to these lines from Eliot (see p. 207).

Will be to arrive where we started
And know the place for the first time.[4]

If one great contemporary poet's vision of the interconnectedness of time and place is able to capture and reflect so strikingly the inherent continuity that binds the *oeuvre* of Gustav Mahler – the quintessential 'transitional' composer on the threshold of our own 'ars nova' – the intuitive self-perception of another can assist us with the tracing of that line of continuity in terms of his personal and musical development. The subtitle of this essay is of course a play on a proverbial line from a well-known poem by Robert Frost (1874–1964) – a poem that has been linked with Mahler at least once before in musical scholarship (see Hefling, 1983). But whereas in that instance only the negative connotations of the poem's title were educed, thus stripping it of its Aristotelian irony, the purpose of the present author in reaching inside Frost's verses for an alternative formulation is to bring out the positive, dynamic aspects of an unfolding creative journey. For that reason, a brief excursus over the writer and the poem is in order before we explore our main topic: the beginning-and-end relationship between Mahler's First Symphony in its original guise and *Das Lied von der Erde*.

It might be fitting to begin with a silent apology to the poet, as much for forcing him into a seemingly spurious association as for tampering with his typography and conflating his title with the line of verse which is of particular importance to this study. The image that 'The Road Not Taken' raises is framed thus in the poem:

Two roads diverged in the wood, and I –
I took the one less traveled by,
And that has made all the difference.[5]

What, then, is the relevance of a sadly underrated American poet to a transcendental master whose relatively recent rise to prominence has been so spectacular? Free association, perhaps; fortuity, certainly. In fact, though, the seemingly haphazard coupling of these two creative figures is not as far-fetched as it may appear at first sight – certainly no more so than the juxtaposition of Mahler and Ives seemed to some just twenty years ago.[6] Like Mahler, Frost

---

4   'Little Gidding' (1942), lines 214–15 & 239–42 in *Four Quartets*, pp. 58 & 59.

5   'The Road Not Taken' (1915), lines 18–20, in *The Poetry of Robert Frost*, ed. Edward C. Lathem (New York: Holt, Rinehart and Winston, 1969), p. 105. This piece makes for a good example of the occasionally striking disagreements between a poem's literal–popular understanding and its 'professional' exegeses. Most literary commentators interpret Frost's poem as an ironic – if not actually satirical – gloss on the conceit of choosing one's course through life. As the 'sound' of the image is just as important for the purposes of this essay as its sense, however, a literal reading of the pertinent lines suits present needs well enough.

6   The earliest sizeable scholarly study devoted to Mahler and Ives known to the author is Robert P. Morgan's 'Ives and Mahler: Mutual Responses at the End of an Era', *19th-Century Music*, 2 (1), (1978), 72–81.

generated creative tension by combining the simple, rustic and ingenuous with the complex, sophisticated, ironic and ambiguous. For the brief time their creative paths ran parallel, both mirrored a complex and changing age faithfully and uncompromisingly. Frost's achievement is not significantly diminished by his lack of that ultimate spark of innovation that we recognize today as the essential element in Mahler's genius.

Although the verses of Eliot and Frost will be returned to later, it is now necessary to elucidate the multiple layers of signification that are embedded in the title of this chapter. This will be best achieved through an introductory synopsis of the study's premises and conclusions.

To begin with, the First Symphony and *Das Lied von der Erde* are regarded by the author as the first and last stations on the developmental curve which centres Mahler's *oeuvre*. (See Fig. 1.1 for a mapping of all strands of his creative development.) Secondly, the aim is to show that both the nature and the course of that central channel of development were determined largely by Mahler's unprecedented expansion of the place and function of 'vocal' music in the symphonic context.[7] Finally, it was his choice of this particular road – one that was decidedly 'less traveled', not only by his predecessors but also by his contemporaries – that added up to an overall achievement that is widely recognized as groundbreaking in its consistency and concentration. Moreover, it is precisely this choice that enables us to look on him as the great synthesizer of the main symphonic trends at the end of the nineteenth century (see Fig. 1.2 for a somewhat simplified schematic illustration of Mahler's music-historical position as a symphonist).

In the course of the 1900–1901 winter season, Natalie Bauer-Lechner, faithful companion and amanuensis to Mahler in his middle years, recorded in her diary an exceptionally rich and wide-ranging series of conversations with him concerning his symphonic firstling. Looking back from a distance of a dozen turbulent years (and – coincidentally for us – from a time that has come to be seen as the end of his first creative 'period'), the composer recalled his own impression of the work – both as process and as product – in a quasi-nostalgic, quasi-enigmatic sentence that continues to puzzle: 'It was still composed in a most carefree and bold manner' ['Sie ist noch am unbekümmertsten und kecksten geschrieben'] (Killian, 1984, p. 176).[8] As the rest of his comments on that occasion dealt chiefly with the aftermath of the 1889 première in Budapest, the

---

[7] The quotation marks around the adjective 'vocal' in the title and elsewhere indicate that in this study the term is used both in its literal and in its transferred epithetical sense.

[8] Unless otherwise indicated, the translations are the author's own. Another translation – 'free' to be sure, but feasible nevertheless – might be: 'It remains my most carefree and bold work.' Indicative of the need to regard all such evidence of Mahler's creative enthusiasms with caution is this – on the surface very similar – sentence: 'It is the most carefree [piece] I have ever written' ['Es ist das Unbekümmertste, was ich je

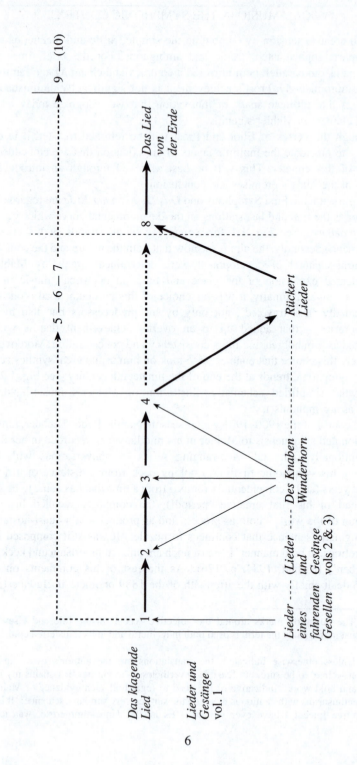

Fig 1.1 Schematic illustration of Mahler's creative development

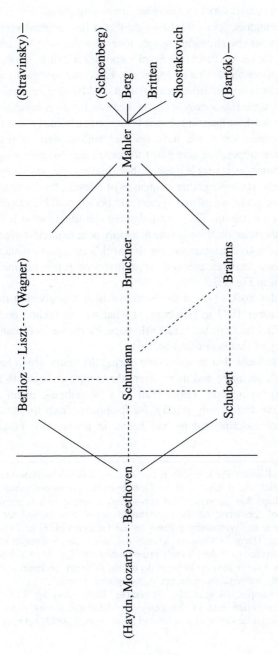

etc.

Fig 1.2 Schematic illustration of Mahler's music-historical position as a symphonist

'it' of the foregoing sentence unquestionably refers to the five-movement 'symphonic poem' rather than to the four-movement work that was eventually published as the First Symphony.

The same set of remarks includes another interesting phrase that is invariably ignored by commentators: 'Naively, I thought that it [the original version of the First Symphony] would be childishly simple for performers and listeners [alike]' ['Ich meinte naiv, die sei kindleicht für Spieler und Hörer'] (ibid.). Assuming that both Mahler's recollection of what he apparently had come to regard some twelve years after the event as a youthful miscalculation, and Bauer-Lechner's record of their conversation, were reasonably accurate, here we have yet another pointer to the identity of the work in question. For it is altogether unlikely that this young but experienced conductor would have been incautious enough (even in his excitement over the impending première) to regard any modern, unperformed 'absolute' symphony as 'simple' for either players or audiences. But a picturesque, loosely strung-together sequence of 'descriptive' movements (in other words a large-scale articulated symphonic poem) could conceivably have been open to such a reception.[9] This misjudgment – if that is what it was – may also explain his otherwise baffling failure to supply both explicit movement titles and a detailed descriptive programme for the work's first performance. On that occasion the advance press releases and the printed concert programme presented the work as shown in Fig. 1.3.[10]

We first meet the work's title in the form in which it is given at the head of this chapter in October 1893 in Hamburg, at what was its second performance. Yet curiously Mahler had created a full title page for the revised manuscript as recently as January of that year (see Fig. 1.4).

This seems to indicate that at some time during the years which had elapsed between the work's première and its revision, the composer began to think of it as a (programme) 'symphony' rather than as a 'symphonic poem'. But this situation could have lasted only briefly, for it appears from the dates Mahler entered into the manuscript that he had begun to revise it in January 1893,

---

geschrieben habe'] (Killian, 1984, p. 49). It too was noted down by Bauer-Lechner, but some four years earlier, and it referred to the Third Symphony's second movement.

[9] It was perhaps this 'looseness' (or non-narrative nature, in a non-modern, non-fashionable sense of the term) of the 'symphonic poem' that caused the otherwise inexplicable reference to 'symphonic poems' by La Grange (1973, p. 746). Probably building on this error, Hermann Danuser actually discussed the implication of the plural usage in an article devoted to Mahler's early programmes (1975, p. 14). Curiously, as will be seen later, Mahler had the idea at one time, according to Bauer-Lechner, of entitling the Third Symphony's six movements collectively 'Symphonic Poems'.

[10] In, for example, *Nemzet*, 14 November 1889, evening edition, [1] (in Hungarian). The Hungarian text of the concert programme shows some small but significant differences; a facsimile of it is printed in La Grange, 1973, between pp. 486 & 487, as Plate 32.

2. *Mahler.* "Symphoniai költemény" két részben [Symphonic poem in two parts]
I. rész [part]: 1. Bevezetés és [Introduction and] Allegro commodo.
2. Andante. 3. Scherzo.

II. rész [part]: 4. A la pompes funebres; attacca. 5. Molto appassionato.

Kézirat, *első előadás* a szerző vezénylete alatt. [Manuscript, *first performance* under the composer's direction.]

Fig. 1.3 Excerpt from the Budapest Philharmonic concert programme for 20 November 1889

completing the task in August. Presumably, then, it was during the time between the period of revision (January to August) and the performance in October that he both crossed out the original title page *and* invented a new title for the (revised) work. This title brought back the idea of a 'tone poem' – but this time combining it with a reference to the 'form' of a symphony (see Fig. 1.5). Such an intensive revisiting of the work undoubtedly brought back memories of the painful lessons of the first performance in Budapest four years earlier. Was Mahler trying to please everyone this time by proffering a 'hybrid', as it were? Perhaps so; yet the subsequent history of the work makes this doubtful.

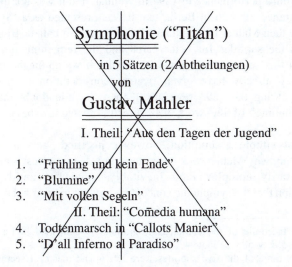

Symphonie ("Titan")

in 5 Sätzen (2 Abtheilungen)

von

Gustav Mahler

I. Theil "Aus den Tagen der Jugend"

1. "Frühling und kein Ende"
2. "Blumine"
3. "Mit vollen Segeln"
    II. Theil: "Comedia humana"
4. Todtenmarsch in "Callots Manier"
5. "D'all Inferno al Paradiso"

Fig. 1.4 Original title page of the First Symphony, crossed out by the composer[11]

[11] The manuscript is in the Yale University Library. A facsimile of the title page was published as Plate III in Diether, 1969, between pp. 80 & 81. Aside from the inevitable changes in a few facts brought about by new discoveries, Diether's fine study of the early history of the First Symphony (pp. 76–100) has stood the test of time.

7. **"Titan"**, eine Tondichtung in Symphonieform (Manuscript) .... *Mahler*.

1. Theil.
"Aus den Tagen der Jugend", Blumen-, Frucht- und Dornstücke.
I.   **"Frühling und kein Ende"** (Einleitung und Allegro comodo). ...
II. **"Blumine"** (Andante).
III. **"Mit vollen Segeln"** (Scherzo).

2. Theil.
"Commedia humana"
IV. **"Gestrandet!"** (ein Todtenmarsch in "Callot's Manier"). ...
V. **"Dall' Inferno"** (Allegro furioso) ...

Fig. 1.5   Excerpt from the Laube Orchestra concert programme for 27 October 1893 in Hamburg[12]

If we accept the crossed-out title from early 1893,[13] with its singular emphasis on 'symphony', as a mere detour (even if not an unimportant one) along the evolutionary road of the work we know today as the First Symphony, it becomes clear that the idea of a 'symphonic poem' remained in Mahler's mind for most of the first seven or eight years of the work's existence. For he reused the Hamburg title at the third performance in 1894 in Weimar, and it was not until the work's next appearance in 1896 in Berlin that it was presented as a 'Symphony in D major'. By then Mahler had eliminated the second, so-called 'Blumine' section, as well as the subtitles for both 'parts' and the remaining four movements. Looking at this sequence of events (especially if we admit the possibility that Mahler may already have given fleeting consideration to the omitting of 'Blumine' during the 1893 revisions[14]), there is little doubt that this drastic 'de-programming' of the work was directly related to the removal of that movement.

But that simple assumption, however justified, gets us no closer to understanding why Mahler took these steps. For that, we must seek an answer in the necessarily complex (and inevitably somewhat untidy) process of reformulation that the symphonic concept underwent in his mind during the years

---

[12] A facsimile of the complete programme is published in La Grange, 1973, between pp. 582 & 583, as Plate 47.

[13] As three of the five subtitles were left in the music, it seems reasonable to suggest that Mahler's main purpose in crossing out the title page was to get rid of the overall title, rather than that he had thought better of the subtitles.

[14] Musing over the physical appearance and numbering of the 1893 manuscript pages which contain the music for 'Blumine', as well as on the considerably later date given by the composer for the revision/completion of those pages, Diether (1969, p. 83) came to the conclusion that Mahler had actually decided to eliminate this movement in 1893, then changed his mind and reinserted it into the revised manuscript.

in question. These years included the completion of the evolving First Symphony and of the fully formed Second, the composition of the Third, and the series of performances of various versions of the first two; these culminated (in a most important sense of the word) in the 1896 Berlin performance of the 'Symphony in D major'. Roughly speaking, then (for, regrettably, we continue to lack precise, documented dates for some of these events), this span of time takes in the years from c. 1887–88 to c. 1896.

The available evidence suggests that in 1889 (and presumably during the years he had worked on his 'symphonic poem') Mahler's conception of a 'symphony' continued to correspond by and large to that inherited from his immediate predecessors and older contemporaries. This was the large-scale, multi-movement, aesthetically and musically integrated instrumental piece for orchestra (Beethoven's Ninth, and one or two other, more or less anomalous works notwithstanding). Thus a suite-like work consisting of an 'irregularly' invented (or perhaps better, derived) and constructed first movement, an ambiguous song-and-dance section (labelled as a Scherzo in that first set of subtitles, probably thought up only in 1889), a mock (though not necessarily mocking) 'funeral march' and a recognizable (though none the less 'misformed') symphonic 'finale' well nigh had to be tagged with that less exalted generic label 'symphonic poem'. The case gains added credibility if we allow for the possibility that 'Blumine' had been an accretion rather than an integral part of the original design (whatever that may have been).[15]

Some time between 1894 (the Weimar performance of the *Tondichtung in Symphonieform*) and 1896 (the presentation of the *Symphonie in D-Dur für grosses Orchester* in Berlin), Mahler had reached the point at which he was ready to elevate his erstwhile 'symphonic poem' to the status of a fully fledged 'symphony'. Already a large step for a young composer at the end of the nineteenth century, it is unimaginable that he would have taken it without doing everything possible technically (and even musico-poetically) to ensure that the work he so designated satisfied the expectations of his time for large-scale formal integrity. While one of the means by which he was able to achieve 'compliance'

---

[15] I have little doubt that this movement was added to the work after March 1888 when the composer wrote his well-known letter to Löhr announcing the completion of what he then referred to simply – but not accidentally – as his 'work' (Blaukopf, 1996, p. 92). Perhaps the movement was given as a separate score to the delegation of the Budapest Philharmonic's musicians who had come to ask him for a new work for their forthcoming season. Mahler possibly wished to take advantage of a prestigious occasion, or he needed to supply them with a certain amount of music. Fanciful as such speculation may appear, it is not altogether without support in the available documents: both the absence of this movement from a recently surfaced putative copy of the Budapest manuscript (see McClatchie, 1996) and another, complementary, interpretation of the physical nature of this part of the revised 1893 score (see n. 11) may be seen as pointing in this direction.

(that is, tonal coherence) may still have been a given at the time, the other was not; and this was the pervasive use of real or transmuted 'vocal' music in the symphonic context.

The first movement was clearly song-inspired: even to those who were not familiar with the source of the main thematic material, its character and its treatment bespoke its vocal origins.[16] In addition to those sections which utilized the transgeneric evocative capabilities of the late nineteenth-century Ländler/waltz, the 'Scherzo' incorporated material which was related to the composer's folkish dance-song 'Hans und Grete', as it had been known to many since the publication of the *Lieder und Gesänge* in 1892. The third movement's three main sections were absolutely dominated by vocal music: the outer sections incorporated the well-known student song 'Bruder Martin' transmogrified into a dirge, while the central section introduced – in a straightforward and thus inevitably jarring manner – the lullaby from the closing song of the *Gesellen-Lieder*. Finally, the last movement returned material from the first and augmented this with implicitly 'vocal' matter in the guises of a chorale and a cantabile 'aria' for instruments.

This left 'Blumine' as the odd movement out. Its origins were picayune: it was probably lifted whole from the incidental pieces Mahler had been obliged to compose for *tableaux vivants* during his time in Kassel. Though he was pleased with them at first, he soon came to deprecate both the effort and the result.[17] Clearly it was merely a matter of time – time that gave his evolving conception a chance to firm and mature – before he had to recognize this purely 'instrumental' (and truly incidental) piece as an alien presence in the midst of an abstract-vocal symphony.

The extent to which Mahler may have comprehended this 'inherent' reason for removing 'Blumine' from the First is discernible only vaguely from his correspondence and from the recollections of his memoirists. On the other hand he seemed to place undue emphasis on the stylistic problem, as he evidently perceived it, caused by the presence of this movement in the symphonic cycle. Conversing with Bauer-Lechner in October 1900 about the need to balance tonal relationships correctly in a symphony, he remarked: 'I had removed the Andante

---

16 In the absence of any direct or anecdotal evidence about the matter, it would be interesting to know whether there was more than simply an exploiting of fortuitous circumstances behind Mahler's pairing of the première of the *Lieder eines fahrenden Gesellen* and the first performance of the First Symphony as a 'symphony'.

17 Mahler first reported his work-in-progress on this music (for a staging of Joseph Viktor von Scheffel's verse narrative, *Der Trompeter von Säkkingen*) to Friedrich Löhr on 22 June 1884: 'I must confess that it gives me much pleasure' ['ich muß gestehen, daß ich eine große Freude daran habe']. Six months later, in the famous New Year letter to Löhr, he was downplaying his interest in the widespread success his 'Trompetermusik' was enjoying just then: 'you know how little precisely this work concerns me' ['Du weißt, wie wenig mich gerade dieses Werk in Anspruch nimmt'] (Blaukopf, 1996, pp. 53 & 57).

"Blumine" from the First chiefly because of excessive similarities among the keys of the adjacent movements' (see Killian, 1984, p. 169).[18]

On 2 March 1896 Mahler wrote to a new and valued correspondent: 'My entire nature is oriented towards the symphony' (Blaukopf, 1983, p. 123); he expanded and focussed this remark by referring to his First Symphony as 'that in D major'.[19] As the letter was written just two weeks before the work's performance in Berlin, it is reasonable to assume that he had by then completed the spiritual and material journey he had had to undertake in order to rethink and recast the old five-movement 'symphonic poem' as the (at least aesthetically) new four-movement 'symphony'. Had he also come to recognize then his true (but perhaps still obscured) creative 'nature' by realizing what this 'new' symphony signified? The available facts are too few to support a definite answer but there is a sufficient number of pointers to encourage us to indulge in some informed speculation.

It is appropriate to recall here the chronological juxtapositions which were referred to earlier. It seems that even before he had completed the then untitled (four- or five-movement) symphonic poem in March 1888, Mahler began to compose another large symphonic work. Though in time this piece became the first movement of the Second Symphony, its evolution, changes of nomenclature and series of successive performances add up to a work history that is quite as convoluted as that of the First Symphony. The following facts are the most relevant to this study.[20]

Mahler completed the large single movement for orchestra in September 1888. Soon thereafter he gave it the title 'Todtenfeier'. Although it had apparently been inscribed initially as the first movement of a symphony, he offered the manuscript for publication to B. Schott's Söhne of Mainz in 1891 as a (presumably independent) 'symphonic poem'. It was rejected, together with the *Gesellen-Lieder* and that earlier, five-movement 'symphonic poem'.

---

[18] Given the fact that the tonal order of the first three movements (with 'Blumine') was D–C–A, Sander Wilkens is probably right when he suggests that Mahler's reasons for removing the Andante were in fact stylistic rather than tonal (see 'Allgemeine Werkgeschichte' in *Symphonie Nr. 1, Verbesserte Ausgabe, Gustav Mahler, Sämtliche Werke, Kritische Gesamtausgabe, Bd. I* (Vienna: Universal Edition, 1992), p. vi). Of course the question remains whether Mahler acted because he came to see that 'Blumine' was simply inferior music, or whether this signalled his growing awareness of the new concept of symphonic cyclicity, realized in this work for the first time precisely through the removal of the 'alien' movement.

[19] The new correspondent – to remain an erudite and faithful friend to Mahler until at least 1901 – was the painter, journalist and pianist Annie Sommerfeld-Mincieux. The sentences in question are in a biographical sketch the composer included in the letter.

[20] The history of the evolution of the Second Symphony presented here is a composite of the information culled from Mitchell, 1975, Martner & Becqué, 1977, and Stephan, 1979b.

'Todtenfeier' began to metamorphose in 1893: that summer Mahler wrote the second, third and fourth movements of what at that point may be called the Second Symphony. Approximately one year later he completed the work with the grandiose finale we know today.

The first public performance of the Second Symphony in March 1895 in Berlin was an incomplete one. It is an indication of the curious, interlocking work histories of the First and Second Symphonies that on this occasion Mahler styled the latter 'Symphonie Nr. 2' – a full year before he introduced the First as a 'symphony' at a public performance. Moreover the printed programme included a note to the effect that the three movements presented constituted 'Part I' of the Second Symphony. Were we to surmise from this that the composer may not have been as free of the symphony/symphonic poem quandary as the evolution of the Second between 1893 and 1895 might lead us to believe, the aforementioned performance in 1896 in Berlin would surely prove the case. For on that occasion the concert opened with a piece titled 'Todtenfeier'. Hedging his bets in a way that is familiar by now, Mahler parenthetically identified the work as '(I. movement from the Symphony in c-minor for large orchestra)' (see the facsimile of the programme in La Grange, 1974, between pp. 678 & 679, Plate 50). This already convoluted history becomes even more tangled when we learn that at its first complete performance in December 1895, the Second was presented simply as 'Sinfonie C-moll für Soli, Chor u. Orchester' without a number.[21]

One of the reasons 1896 is a suitable *terminus ad quem* for a tracing of Mahler's evolving (and often, it seems, temporizing) conception of his new symphony is the need to include the developmental history of the Third Symphony. For what we observed about the composer's struggles with the generic designation and large-scale structure of his first two symphonic works would continue (if not actually increase) with the Third.

Once again the histories overlap. As far as we can determine, Mahler began to draft plans for the Third even before the nomenclature and shape of the First Symphony had been finalized, or the Second had had its first full performance. But equally importantly, while the evolution of the Third was subject to the same indecision with regard to its genre as that of the preceding works, this one also released an unprecedented flood of comment by the composer. Much of it was either aimed at or ended up serving the process of clarifying his new concept of the symphony. In what follows we shall look at a few of the comments that are especially important.

By all accounts Mahler composed the Third Symphony during the summers of 1895 and 1896. Though he was to sketch a bewildering variety of plans (in effect attenuated programmes) for the work during that time, as early as August 1895

---

[21] Both the lack of a number and this spelling of the generic title occur as late as October 1900, at a performance of the work in Munich.

he reported quite accurately to his friend Löhr: 'My new symphony will last about one and a half hours – it is all in *large* symphonic form' (see Blaukopf, 1996, p. 150). It is, then, so much more surprising to find him fretting about the overall length of the piece ('a total duration of two hours') in a conversation with Bauer-Lechner (dated 4 July 1896) which had taken place only a month before he wrote to the critic Max Marschalk on 6 August 1896: 'My work is completely finished.' Moreover, in the same talk with Bauer-Lechner Mahler had added (in all likelihood because of the work's length) that he planned to perform the first movement as 'Part I' and to title the whole 'Pan, Symphonic Poem*s*' (Killian, 1984, p. 60; Blaukopf, 1996, p. 196).

In the end all titles were dropped. But one related, and important, feature remained. Having omitted any reference to 'parts' in the published scores of his first two symphonies, in the Third Mahler allowed the division into Part I (1st movement) and Part II (2nd–6th movements) to stand. As with several other facets of his evolving symphonic conception and practice we note the burgeoning of this means of large-scale formal demarcation over the later works in which he chose to employ it: the five movements of the Fifth Symphony are grouped in three parts, headed only by roman numerals, while the monumental, in themselves continuous, sections of the Eighth are labelled solely as Parts One and Two.[22]

Programmes issued for performances of the Third Symphony in Mahler's lifetime fail to yield information which would advance our understanding of his growth as his own kind of symphonist. On occasion some of the original subtitles were printed in the programme. Thus, at an early performance in Budapest (why would Mahler return to the scene of his first disappointment with a new and untried work?), the second movement's subtitle was printed in both German and Hungarian; it was also identified as the 'Menuett' from the Third Symphony (see

3. *Mahler*. "Mit susognak a mezei virágok" (Was mir die Blumen auf der Wiese erzählen)/"Menuett" a III. Symphoniából (*Először*)
[What the flowers in the meadow tell me/Minuet from the Third Symphony (first performance)]

Fig. 1.6   Excerpt from the Budapest Philharmonic concert programme for 31 March 1897[23]

---

   [22] Without going into details that lie beyond the limits of the present study, it may be noted here that this apparent progression is unrelated to size: whereas the playing time of the Third Symphony is c. 90 minutes, the Fifth takes under 70 and the Eighth about 80 minutes to perform.
   [23] A facsimile of the programme is published in Roman, 1991, as illustration 40. This is the only post-completion instance known to the author where the movement is specifically labelled as a Minuet; the score has only the performance direction 'Tempo di Menuetto'.

Fig. 1.6). At other times only the generic label and the performing forces were given, while now and then the full sectional layout of the work was printed.[24]

Thus it would appear that by 1896 at the latest Mahler had settled the matter of nomenclature in his own mind. Together with the histories of the Second and Third Symphonies – especially as they parallel and overlap each other – and with the process of generic reformulation that had been ongoing with the First, his labelling of the latter as a 'symphony' in that very year is clear evidence of this. We must now ascertain whether these concrete developments, connected with specific symphonic works, were at the same time generating an overall (and increasingly coherent and conscious) evolution of the concept itself.

In addition to specific remarks about the Third Symphony, the 'flood of comments' generated by this work also contained others that had a more general import. Two of these are especially meaningful in the process of creative self-analysis that Mahler seemed to be undertaking at the time, and are thus particularly important to our understanding of his evolution as a symphonist after the First Symphony. In the summer of 1895 (that is, at a relatively early stage in the writing of the Third), he declared to Bauer-Lechner:

> That I call [the Third] a symphony is actually incorrect, for it does not keep
> to the traditional form in any respect. But to me symphony means simply to
> erect a universe with all means of the available technique. The ever new and
> changing content itself determines its own form.
>
> (Killian, 1984, p. 35)

The same diary entry includes another 'emotional and excited' comment: 'It was just the thing that I hit upon with the word and the human voice in my Second Symphony, where I needed them to make myself clear' (ibid.).

Here we can mark two stages of the generic–conceptual evolution beyond the formal and musico-poetic jelling of the First Symphony (even if such chronological locators as 'beyond' have little more than symbolic meaning at this juncture in Mahler's creativity). What was described earlier as the 'abstract-vocal' nature of this work began to undergo a process of metamorphic expansion in the Second. The agent of change was the 'word'. Importing it into the type of symphonic entity that had been created in the earlier work caused its expansion as well as a further concretizing of certain of its constituent units. What is more, these two interrelated processes accelerated (in a conceptual rather than physical sense) in the course of the piece, giving rise to a musico-poetic curve which was the reverse of that which we had observed in the preceding work. Whereas in the First Symphony the 'vocal' nature of the opening movement was the most pronounced and that of the finale the least so, in the Second the curve ascends

---

[24] For example on 27 March 1904 in Cologne and on 1 February of the same year in Heidelberg. Facsimiles of the programmes are published in Martner, 1985, pp. 82 & 80 respectively.

from the first two movements, through the abstract-vocal Scherzo and the miniature, concrete-vocal 'Urlicht', to the oratorical Finale.

The Third Symphony failed to continue the overall developmental curve which so closely links the first two symphonies. To be sure, here too there are three clearly vocal movements (one abstract and two concrete). Moreover, the pattern of 'acceleration' observed in the Second is duplicated (or rather imitated) here in the succession of movements three to five. But the sheer weight of the decidedly non-vocal Finale unavoidably breaks down the process. Of course, there are other 'secondary' traits in both the planning and the execution of this sprawling work which signal an ongoing, if somewhat diminished, evolutionary ferment. It is sufficient to mention two of these.

Extant drafts for the Symphony show that at one time or another all parts of the planned work were subtitled in the manner of metaphorically 'vocal' movements: what this or that 'tells me' [erzählt]. The evolution of the episodic (that is, suite-like) overall structure that had taken place in the two preceding works attained an intermediate peak in this symphony: again, the subtitles stand musico-poetic witness, while the considerable differences in size and setting from movement to movement reinforce that impression on the technical level.

The Fourth Symphony is a curious case in that it too appears to be an interruptive presence in the evolution of Mahler's new 'vocal' symphony. While its overall make-up is sufficiently suite-like (knowledge of an early set of programmatic titles supports such a view[25]), discrepancies in the various parameters do not differentiate the movements nearly as dramatically as was the case in the preceding work. Yet this – from our point of view, negative – quality is effectively balanced by the fact that only one of the four movements is 'vocal' (using the term once again in its inclusive sense). In the event it is because of the position and musico-poetic weight of this movement that the Fourth Symphony does in fact constitute an appropriate link in the continuity of Mahler's aesthetic and technical development towards that ultimate 'vocal symphony', Das Lied von der Erde.

The Second and Third Symphonies presented two non-identical but complementary models for an 'accelerating' incorporation of 'vocal' sections into the overall symphonic structure. The Fourth represents the culmination of the process for this phase of the composer's creativity. Here the one texted vocal movement is both the fountain-head and the summa summarum of all that is of technical and musico-poetic importance in the work.

But 'culmination' frequently involves a degree of risk: the Fourth Symphony could have become a dead end in Mahler's oeuvre – at least along the particular

---

25 Paul Bekker ([1921] 1969, p. 145) published such a list of titles consisting of six numbered items which include such curiosities as 'Das irdische Leben' (presumably the song of the same title) and 'Morgenglocken' (presumably a reference to the music we know today as the fifth movement of the Third Symphony).

path of symphonic (or even overall musical) development that he had elected to travel up to that time. It is in this sense that we may best understand the stylistic–generic bifurcation seen in Fig. 1.1. In Symphonies Five to Seven Mahler seemed to abandon the pursuit of a symphonic development that corresponded to his own vision. However, as we know from what came later in the Ninth and Tenth Symphonies, the evolution of this particular 'sub-genre' did actually continue in those purely instrumental works. Indeed it does not seem unreasonable to suggest that this apparent 'detour' continued a developmental line that had been suspended by Mahler when he transformed the First into a new type of 'vocal' symphony.

It follows from the foregoing that the development of this uniquely Mahlerian symphony continued in the series of orchestral songs (especially the cyclic ones) he wrote between c. 1900 and 1905. But it is unnecessary to trace that branch of the development here, particularly as there soon appeared a work that was the logical stylistic and musico-poetic heir to the exquisite concentration of vocality in the Fourth Symphony's Finale. The same work also merged the two strands of the Mahlerian vocal symphony's development after the Fourth; this work was of course the Eighth Symphony.

In August 1906 Mahler included this personal aside in a business letter to Willem Mengelberg:

> I have just completed my Eighth. – It is my grandest creation up to now.
> And so unique in content and form that absolutely nothing can be written
> about it. – Imagine that the universe begins to sound and to ring. These are
> no longer human voices, but orbiting planets and suns.
>   (Blaukopf, 1996, p. 335)

Eleven years earlier, having reached a major junction in his creative development, Mahler found powerfully evocative words and images to formulate a symphonic creed that could serve both as a summary of past achievements and as a blueprint for the future. He then went on to form and re-form the building blocks and edifices of his 'universe'. By using 'all means of the available technique' he made certain that no two works in the resulting series were exactly alike. To put it another way, he established – through material asseveration, as it were – the aesthetic legitimacy of a constantly changing (and thus rejuvenescent) form–content relationship. This also allowed him to bring into special prominence one of those 'techniques' by reconceptualizing, and expanding the effective parameters of, vocal music in the symphonic context. This in turn marked out the necessary conditions for the orderly evolution of the Mahlerian vocal symphony.

Viewing the process from such a historical perspective, it now seems inevitable that the apparent culmination that had been the Fourth Symphony should have yielded six years later to yet another high point along the developmental trajectory. This was Mahler's symphonic 'universe' as it was set 'sounding and ringing' through the all-encompassing vocality of the Eighth. Moreover Mahler implies in the above passage that that condition is so absolute and transcendent that the vocal symphony could break free of the human universe's restraints in this work: the voices became 'orbiting planets and suns'. Predictably, we may think, the intermediate peak in the evolution of an episodic structure that was represented by the Third is supplanted by a new peak attained in this symphony. With his chosen texts as well as with the technical–stylistic means he employed to communicate them, Mahler fashioned two manifestly dissimilar 'parts'. We are able (or rather willing) to accept them as symphonically coherent chiefly because of the special aesthetic and musical conditions and expectations which had been created by, and along with, the evolution of the Mahlerian vocal symphony.

Reading his colourful note to Mengelberg (and many other similarly expressive passages) from the vantage point of our cynical age, it is tempting to scoff at Mahler's hyperbole. But we are restrained by two factors. In the first instance such colourful outbursts almost invariably occur in private communications – personal correspondence or diary entries. With regard to the specific passage at hand, the biographical record is unequivocal in indicating that the summer of the Eighth Symphony was, in human terms, as perfect a time for Mahler as he was destined to enjoy. Less than a year after writing these lines to Mengelberg, Fate was to have dealt him the well-known three 'blows'. In retrospect it seems amazing that he had not only the courage to continue but also sufficient motivation and will to embark on new paths both in his personal life and in his music.

For there were new peaks to scale along both creative paths in the symphonic field. As Mahler was not given enough time to travel the one that passed through the Ninth and the incomplete Tenth Symphonies, we can do no more than speculate about the aspirations and accomplishments that may have remained unrealized because of his early death. But we are able to trace the other path – that of the vocal symphony – to its poignant conclusion within the Mahlerian *oeuvre*.

The pervasive vocality that is the hallmark of the Eighth Symphony is generated by its gigantic choral forces and grand-operatic complement of solo singers or (to recall the composer's suggestive word-picture) its 'universe' of 'orbiting planets and suns'. But aesthetically speaking it could not be surpassed safely with the same musico-poetic and technical methods and resources. Mahler thus executed what may well have been the most original and daring change of direction in his creative development: he wrote the song-symphony *Das Lied von der Erde*.[26] Whereas the earlier evolution of the 'vocal' symphony traced an ascending path, a pattern of expansion and intensification, this work reduced,

---

[26] For a survey of the varied nomenclature that this work has attracted over the years, see Roman, 1975, and Danuser, 1986.

simplified, clarified and rarefied – and yet it convinced then and convinces today as the sovereign, crowning achievement of a cogent and coherent development.

Describing the progression from the Eighth Symphony to *Das Lied* as an 'original' and 'daring change of direction', and characterizing the late work as a 'crowning achievement' at the end of a developmental trajectory that had passed through both of these contiguous works, require some explanation. Recalling now the poems by Frost and Eliot that were introduced at the beginning of this article will assist us in this endeavour.

Symphonically speaking, Mahler chose the 'less traveled road' on two occasions when his development had reached a stylistic 'fork': first, when he rethought and recast the 1888 'symphonic poem' into the First Symphony, and then between the Eighth Symphony and *Das Lied von der Erde*. There can be little doubt that, at least developmentally, the first of those decisions was the more momentous one. Yet it seems no less reasonable to argue that it was the second course change that 'made all the difference', to use Frost's words. Without it, the sense of a stylistic and developmental closure (of the end of a particular 'road', which is the special immanence of *Das Lied*) would almost certainly be missing from Mahler's *oeuvre*.

Above all else it was in the area of the episodic (or suite-like) overall form of the Mahlerian vocal symphony that the composer created a unique yet wholly satisfying work in *Das Lied*. Because the Eighth Symphony had achieved a specific type of culmination in this area, no further 'progress' was possible along the same lines. Therefore Mahler redefined this most essential of parameters, in part by simplifying it, as he did with the other parameters, but also by emphasizing certain musico-poetic and technical elements. 'Simplification' was achieved first by drawing the six-part cycle's texts from the same cultural–aesthetic wellspring (ancient China refracted through the prism of *fin de siècle* European sensibilities); then by employing a germinal (not to say elemental) motivic cyclicity; and finally by a relative reduction in the degree to which the instrumental ensemble is differentiated from song to song. On the other hand the episodic character of the overall structure was underlined by the apparently random selection and ordering of topoi and poems in the cycle, as well as by the alternation of the high and low voices from song to song.

Thus we return to our starting point, to T.S. Eliot's enigmatic lines: 'the end of all our exploring/Will be to arrive where we started/And know the place for the first time'. In the context of this study Mahler 'started' with the transformation of *'Titan', eine Tondichtung in Symphonieform* into the First Symphony. Long drawn out and occasionally uncertain as that process may have been, in the end there emerged a work that was episodic and suite-like yet was also musico-poetically unified as a new type of 'vocal' symphony. In comparison with the original, explicitly programmatic, five-movement work, it represented a reduction formally and a simplification aesthetically. It is the whole of this process (including its final outcome) that we find so strikingly replicated in the relationship of the Eighth Symphony and *Das Lied von der Erde*, and it was thus that Mahler, having chosen this particular 'road' to travel, 'arrived' where he had 'started', both creatively and metaphysically.

But in spite of all the technical and imaginative similarities between the two early and late pieces, *Das Lied* is a brilliantly inventive and radically new work, and thus a 'marker', a 'place' of arrival and departure in the development of musical style at the dawn of a new age. Hence unfolds the riddle wrapped in an enigma (and what could be more fitting for an artwork whose *élan vital* flowed from the East?): by returning to his own beginnings at the end of his exploration, Mahler empowered himself – and us – to 'know the place for the first time'.

Chapter Two

Mahler and the Idea of Nature

JULIAN JOHNSON

Mahler's credentials as an early modernist are often located in his pervasive use of irony. The deconstructive twists of his music make an uncomfortable counterpoint with the attempt to speak 'authentically', a tension we hear as specifically modern. By contrast, Mahler's concern with nature might seem to look back to an earlier aesthetic, one that was already becoming anachronistic by the first decade of the twentieth century. But this judgment is possible only if we ignore both the romantic origins of Mahler's irony (in Jean Paul and E.T.A. Hoffmann) and the continuing preoccupation with the idea of nature in early modernism (as Webern's *oeuvre*, for example, amply demonstrates).[1] Nevertheless, it remains significant that, in the aesthetic context in which Mahler was working, the representation of nature was already becoming associated with a vulgarized kind of artistic practice, epitomized by kitsch landscape paintings sold as souvenirs of summer holidays in the Alps. Mahler's Viennese contemporary and acquaintance Gustav Klimt painted landscapes throughout his life, but he did so relatively privately while on holiday on the Attersee, maintaining his public image in Vienna through more obviously modernist portraits and allegorical pictures. To be sure, the idea of nature continued to play a defining cultural role, but the early years of the new century saw a turning away from the representation of nature as outward, phenomenal existence in favour of an inward turn. The concerns of Schiele and Kokoschka, no less than Freud, were with nature experienced as interiority, a subjective direction exemplified in Kandinsky's path to abstraction through his pared-down landscapes of the years leading up to the First World War. Karl Kraus, a key intellectual influence on Schoenberg and his pupils, expressed the disdain of suave modernity for the materialist pleasures of nature-lovers in a series of epigrams: 'Before high mountains', he wrote dismissively, 'there are only small poets' (Kraus, 1959, p. 83).

That Mahler was already acutely aware of this context is underlined by a letter to Richard Batka of 18 November 1896. Batka, editor of the *Prager Neue*

---

[1] See Johnson, 1999a.

musikalische Rundschau, had asked Mahler to supply him with some biographical information for a forthcoming article. Mahler's reply gives precious little biographical information but dwells instead on his recently completed Third Symphony. In turn, this leads to one of his most overt claims that his music was conceived as 'the sound of Nature' [*Naturlaut*], an idea that dominates this letter and which he was clearly keen to have communicated to Batka's readership as the central category of his music. It is a significant text and worth quoting at length. I begin at the point where Mahler expresses his concerns about the second movement of the Third Symphony (the 'Blumenstück') being performed as a free-standing concert piece:

> The fact that this short piece (more an intermezzo), torn as it is out of the context of the larger work, my most important and large-scale so far, is bound to give rise to misunderstanding cannot prevent me from allowing it to be performed separately. I simply have no choice. If I am at long last to get a hearing I must not be finicky, and so this modest little piece needs must often this season 'lie bleeding at Pompey's feet', introducing me to the public as a 'meditative', finespun 'singer of Nature'. Of course no one gets an inkling that for me Nature includes all that is terrifying, great and also lovely (it is precisely this that I wanted to express in the whole work, in a kind of evolutionary development). I always feel it strange that when most people speak of 'Nature' what they mean is flowers, little birds, the scent of the pinewoods, etc. No one knows the god Dionysus, or great Pan. Well: there you have a kind of programme – i.e. a sample of how I compose. Always and everywhere it is the very sound of Nature! ... I recognize no other kind of programme, at least for my works. If I have occasionally given them titles, it was in order to provide pointers to where feeling is meant to change into imagining.
>
> (Martner, 1979, pp. 197–98)

Mahler's fear of misappropriation is not hard to understand: to hear the 'Blumenstück' without knowledge of the 'Dionysian' first movement intended to precede it is certainly to hear a quite different piece. Taken in isolation, the 'Blumenstück' might well suggest the kind of popular construction of nature as bourgeois idyll that the Third Symphony as a whole exceeds. But this incident points to two important and related aspects of Mahler's nature music: first, that it often occurs as relatively self-contained episodes and, secondly, that heard in isolation these episodes risk a degree of complicity with that bourgeois idyll that is never entirely expunged. Mahler's letter to Batka underlines that his music is conceived of as a narrative totality, and that to remove the episode from the larger process is to risk misunderstanding. At the same time, the episodic construction of the nature passages makes them amenable to just such a hearing. Hans Heinrich Eggebrecht, in one of the most extensive explorations of the idea of nature in Mahler, acknowledges this multivalency in his division of *Naturlaute* into three categories: (1) in the strictest sense, as the noise of creatures, particularly bird calls; (2) in a broader sense, as sounds that do not arise primarily from the art music tradition; and (3) in the broadest sense, it is the musical substance as a whole, rather than any specifically programmatic or representational elements, that links Mahler's music as a totality to the idea of nature (Eggebrecht, 1982a, p. 127). Adorno, for whom the idea of programme music is simply 'invalid' for Mahler's music, states early in his monograph on the composer that the music's substance lies in its 'preoccupation with procedure' (Adorno, 1992a, p. 3). From this point of view, the idea of nature in Mahler lies not in those overt moments of nature representation, but rather in the larger symphonic process to which they belong. This is the idea explored in the present chapter: that Mahler's music, rather than being concerned with a *representation of nature*, is better understood as a *discourse on nature*.

That nature music should appear as apparently self-contained episodes, cut off from the more narrative music that surrounds them, is however a significant aspect of this discourse. The category of nature in Mahler constitutes a key element of the fundamental sense of duality that defines his music. Undoubtedly, Mahler's music is oversimplified when read in terms of familiar binary oppositions: in naming them, one reduces the specificity of the music. But in refusing to name them, one risks reinforcing the idea of this music as unrelated to the larger social discourses in which it is made. Eggebrecht's discussion is centred on the idea that Mahler's *Naturlaut* is, above all, an embodiment of what is Other [*das Andere*] to the world of civilization (Eggebrecht, 1982a, p. 18), and Adorno similarly insists that this music is defined by what it opposes: 'Even where Mahler's music arouses associations of nature and landscape, it nowhere presents them as absolutes, but infers them from the contrast to that from which they deviate' (Adorno, 1992a, p. 15). But the 'otherness' of nature is more than a philosophical idea – it was an idea embodied in the social practice of the *fin de siècle* and thus a historical 'fact' of the social construction of nature. Mahler's own biography, with its division between conducting in Vienna and the summer composing retreats, embodies the division of city and countryside that was (and perhaps remains) a definitive category of modern society.[2] Familiar romantic dualities duplicate themselves here – the city is unhealthy, inhuman, hectic and alienating, whereas the peace of the countryside offers a genuine *Heimat* in which one is restored physically and spiritually to a 'true' self. Mahler's music projects a basic opposition between *das irdische Leben* and *das himmlische Leben*, in which musical signs of the natural become symbols of the heavenly. It is no coincidence, for example, that the childlike vision of heaven in the Finale of the Fourth Symphony is given in the style of Austrian folksong.

Mahler's nature passages risk complicity with this social construction because of their explicit use of well-worn musical conventions or topics of nature representation. But as so often, Mahler makes use of the familiar, the conventional, even the outworn and clichéd precisely in order to create a distance

---

[2] For further discussion of the social aspect of this idea see Johnson, 1999b.

from it – to underline music's aspect as artifice and convention. For Adorno, and many after, the *Naturlaut* is defined through its deviation from stylistic norms.[3] Nature music in Mahler thus becomes a critique of 'second nature', an exposing of the artificiality of art and the delusion implicit in its attempts to render nature in immediate form. Adorno suggests, as an example, the opening of the first movement of the First Symphony, whose sustained pedal A played on string harmonics 'presupposes the official ideal of good instrumentation in order to reject it' – quite literally in this example, since Mahler altered the original scoring of this passage to make it less 'substantial' (Adorno, 1992a, p. 15). One might point to other examples of a radically anti-aesthetic tone in Mahler's orchestra – the extended trombone solo in the first movement of the Third Symphony or the oboe's depiction of the night-bird in the fourth movement of the same work. Eggebrecht uses the term 'transplantation' to capture this sense of Mahler's wholesale importing into the music of something that originates outside it and to which it remains alien. As an example he cites Mahler's use of cowbells, arguing that whereas the horn-calls of the first *Nachtmusik* of the Seventh Symphony can be taken up by the subsequent musical discourse and thus brought into relation with the human world, the cowbells remain stubbornly 'other', incapable of being absorbed into musical syntax since they constitute no musical tone as such (see Eggebrecht, 1982a, p. 22). Mahler urges his performers to attempt a realistic imitation of the tinkling bells of distant Alpine herds, while at the same time denying any programmatic intention. What seems like realism is, more accurately, merely deconstructive. By means of its distance from the tones of art music, the cowbell stands for what remains unappropriated; the idea of 'otherness' is thus embodied by a sound from beyond the hitherto autonomous aesthetic universe of instrumental music.[4] By importing 'real nature' into the symphony orchestra, Mahler exposes the artificiality of the conventional pastoral.

Mahler's use of birdsong, the most ubiquitous *Naturlaut* in Western music, reveals a similar tension. Donald Mitchell has discussed how, in *Das Lied von der Erde*, Mahler presents two kinds of birdsong – that of a stylized, metrically bound bird in 'Der Trunkene im Frühling', and the 'realistic', *senza misura* creature in 'Der Abschied'.[5] In the latter, Mitchell suggests, Mahler's realism results in music that stands outside the art music tradition, seeking the same 'unmeasured freedom' as Mahler's musical analogy to the flowing of the brook in the same passage (Figs 7–10). The overlapping, asymmetric rhythms of these passages

---

[3] Danuser (1988, p. 606) also picks out the idea of 'deviations from or partial negations of a general symphonic musical language' ['Abweichung von oder partielle Negation der allgemeinen symphonischen Musiksprache'].

[4] In a less shocking way, Mahler's use of the guitar and mandolin has a similar effect.

[5] Stravinsky's contemporaneous opera *Le Rossignol* (1908–14) is founded on just this distinction.

create a definitive contrast with the steady tread of the funeral march that otherwise dominates 'Der Abschied', their 'unprecedented beatlessness' standing as a symbol of the 'transcendence of death [and] the reconciliation and identification with the perpetual renewal of earth's beauties' (Mitchell, 1995, p. 173). It is a good example of what Hermann Danuser identifies as *Lautmalerei* in Mahler, as opposed to the eighteenth-century doctrine of *Tonmalerei*, based on an idea of the imitation of nature according to highly stylized and conventional topoi (Danuser, 1988, p. 605). Even Mahler's *senza misura* birdsong remains unrealistic, however: it projects itself as extra-aesthetic while at the same time being part of the musical substance and thus capable of engagement with the other materials. The difference is made immediately apparent by a comparison with a rather later work, Respighi's *Pini di Roma* (1924), in which the recording of a real nightingale embodies a literalism that is the opposite of Mahler's music.

What matters here of course is not the realism with which sounds of nature are reproduced in a musical context, but the presentation of something that appears to enter the musical work from outside its subjectively created world, something that confronts the listener 'as if it were' an objective element of nature. Apparently distant from the lyrical concerns of subjective expression, the *Naturlaut* implies a self-sufficient world, 'undisturbed by civilization, culture, art, time and history' ['von Zivilisation, Kultur, Kunst, von Zeit und Geschichte noch unberührte'] (Eggebrecht, 1982a, p. 128). As in the landscapes of Gustav Klimt, a heterogeneous profusion of natural forms coalesces to imply a nature utterly autonomous of human life and thus strangely distant and foreign. In this way, nature in early modern art becomes not simply alienated, but alienating, as its silent presence underscores the inadequacy of aesthetic language for its representation. Mahler's *Naturlaut* is sometimes like a landscape by Klimt or Schiele, or even Klee: it presents a world in which we struggle to find ourselves at home. Klee's fantastical world of creatures and plants is anticipated in this respect by Mahler's reanimation of the fairy-tale world of *Des Knaben Wunderhorn*. The animals and birds that originate in the *Wunderhorn* songs and migrate into the symphonies are by no means 'beautiful' in the manner of pastoral idylls. At times they are grotesque, satirizing human life as do the animals in the Funeral Cortège of the First Symphony (third movement) or the fish in the Scherzo of the Second Symphony (based on Mahler's earlier setting of 'Des Antonius von Padua Fischpredigt'); at other times they are presented through raw, untamed sonorities, such as the night-bird in the Third Symphony.[6] Never are the creatures of Mahler's symphonies domesticated: the 'unmeasured' nature

---

[6] Mahler is supposed to have said of the first movement of the Seventh Symphony, 'Hier röhrt der Natur'. The sound he refers to is the raw, barking call of a deer. Cited by Hans Redlich as something Mahler was 'reported to have said', preface to miniature score of the Seventh Symphony (London: Eulenburg, 1962), p. vi.

that they embody not only questions the dominant positivism of his age, but thereby displaces the centrality of the rational subject on which that positivism was based. Robert Hirschfeld, in his notorious 1906 criticism of the Third Symphony, wrote with more perspicacity than he knew when he focussed on Mahler's use of sounds considered outside conventional orchestral tones:

> Yet how frivolous, childish and without strength our epoch appears in Mahler's symphonies, with their cowbells, their big and little bells, their rattles and their bunches of twigs, their jumble of echoes and distant sounds, their bizarre sonorities – which do not even seem to have come from musical instruments.
>
> (Hirschfeld, quoted in Franklin, 1991, p. 32)[7]

Presented in unmediated form, the opposition of Mahler's *irdisch* and *himmlisch* categories produces the formal disjunctions that so often rend the surface of his music. Without logical connection or the possibility of mediation, the two worlds simply interrupt one another – as happens in the first movement of the Sixth Symphony, where a pastoral interlude cuts across the progress of the development section (Fig. 21) only to be itself interrupted by the equally sudden return of the movement's dominant march music (Fig. 25). The music that characterizes such oppositional episodes exemplifies the idea of 'otherness' discussed by Eggebrecht, Adorno and others. Their quality of self-containment is itself a structural function, achieved by the exaggeration of some familiar pastoral signifiers. One of Adorno's key Mahlerian categories is that of *suspension*, an idea that contains the principal function of Mahler's 'extra-territorial' nature episodes. Passages like that in the first movement of the Sixth Symphony suspend the more-or-less frustrated attempts at temporal progression that have thus far characterized the musical process. They do so by a variety of means. Pedal notes abound, often at one or both registral extremes, so that harmonic progression is either suspended or significantly slowed. What takes place within this defined harmonic space simply elaborates within it rather than alters it: ostinato figures and motivic fragments without linear consequence replace any more substantial melody. A sense of harmonic stasis is often underlined by percussion tuned to a single note (a timpani roll or single low bell) or else the use of untuned percussion such as tam-tam or cowbells.

Linear progression is suspended by other means. A firm sense of metre is often blurred here, not only by long, sustained sounds, but also by the fragmentary nature of musical events. Movements that have been marching for bars and bars (witness the first movement of the Sixth) suddenly find themselves without their metrical feet (Fig. 21). The lack of harmonic or metrical underpinning often produces a certain kind of weightlessness – witness the flute solo shortly before

---

[7] The original is to be found as part of the Feuilleton 'Zwei Mahler-Sinfonien', *Wiener Abendpost*, no. 254 (5 November 1909), 1–3.

the close of the first movement of the Ninth (beginning in bar 419) marked *Schwebend* [floating], a recurrent marking in Mahler. Loss of metre, and concurrent weightlessness and suspension of linear progression, is also achieved by Mahler's characteristic proliferation of heterogeneous elements. While the musical texture may well be contrapuntal, lines overlap in such a way as to obliterate rather than create a sense of forward motion. Passages associated with the profusion of natural forms or animals (birds, beasts, flowers and fishes) often work in this way: witness the return, in the finale of the First Symphony, of the opening dawn fanfares of the first movement, now considerably more dense in its polyphony of distant fanfares and birdsong (Fig. 38).

But if Mahler's music is founded on dualities, it does not end there. The category of nature can certainly be read as one pole of a binary opposition, and often appears as such, but to take a Mahler symphony as a whole is to engage with such ideas in a more complex, discursive manner. The raw 'otherness' of the *Naturlaut*, presenting a thoroughly alien nature in which humankind no longer recognizes itself, is relatively rare in Mahler. More often, his music concerns the subjective mediation of the opposing poles represented by *Weltgetümmel* [the turmoil of the world] and *Natur*. In this sense, Mahler's music is concerned with pastoral rather than natural history – with the idea of man-in-nature. It has its roots in a familiar and powerful cultural legacy through which the idea of nature serves as a symbol of the heavenly (as Edenic unity) but one in tension with earthly actuality (the fallen world). This tension is a definitive one in Mahler's music and marks his distance from the materialism of an age exemplified in the music of Richard Strauss.[8] To be sure, nature imagery serves for the representation of the heavenly, but as reminiscence and vision rather than as an actualized reality. It has the same function in the poetry of Karl Kraus, Mahler's Viennese contemporary, where the idea of *Ursprung* [origin] serves as both reminiscence and anticipation.

Elsewhere, nature is itself suffering and in need of redemption. Mahler's own comment about the opening of the Third Symphony ('It has almost ceased to be music; it is hardly anything but sounds of nature. It's eerie, the way life gradually breaks through, out of soulless, petrified matter') is of course followed by a programme in which 'Life' gradually breaks free from 'Nature' (Franklin, 1980, p. 59). But the confident idealism of the Third, with its progression from brute

---

[8] A diary entry by Strauss in 1911, shortly after Mahler's death, makes an explicit link between a materialist position and Strauss's sketches for the *Alpensinfonie*: 'I intend to call my *Alpensinfonie* the Antichrist, since it involves moral purification through one's own effort, liberation through work and the adoration of eternal, glorious Nature' ['Ich will meine *Alpensinfonie* den Antichrist nennen, als da ist: sittliche Reinigung aus eigener Kraft, Befreiung durch die Arbeit, Anbetung der ewigen herrlichen Natur']. Cited in Stephan Kohler, 'Richard Strauss: Eine Alpensinfonie, Op. 64', *Neue Zeitschrift für Musik*, 11 (1982), 42–46.

nature to pure spirit, is not preserved intact in Mahler's later symphonies, hence their greater tendency for unmediated oppositions, with nature episodes linked to a formal strategy of sudden, unprepared breakthroughs or collapses. But throughout Mahler's *oeuvre* the function of nature music, even where it appears as apparently self-contained episodes, is inevitably a structural one. Nature episodes are never merely picturesque backwaters in the more important business of symphonic narrative: without exception, they exert a structural function that is definitive for the outcome of the narrative blockages on which the Mahlerian symphonic discourse is based. This structural function arises from the 'otherness' of musical materials that we have already discussed. Key to this structural function is the suspension of the work's linear progression, achieved through materials that tend instead towards stasis.

Pedal points, ostinati, loss of metrical definition, the foregrounding of indistinct or non-musical tones – all of these contribute towards a loss of forward energy in the music. This is nothing new; in one sense Mahler merely exaggerates the conventions of a long-standing pastoral tradition. But in doing so, his music exacerbates a tension that is usually hidden below the surface of tonal music: its fear that time might stand still, that all the forward-thrusting progress of tonal discourse might come to a halt. In earlier nineteenth-century music this is present in two, apparently contradictory, ways: in the idea of tonal stasis embodied in the pastoral (*Naturklang* as *Urklang*, as heard in the opening bars of Wagner's *Das Rheingold*), and in the increasing tendency of chromaticism – the instrument of harmonic motion – to turn into its opposite. It is no coincidence that Adorno, discussing the idea of suspension in Mahler's music, cites a list of examples which are almost without exception presented as nature episodes, from:

> the 'Bird of Death' passage before the entry of the chorus in the Second [fifth movement, Figs 29–31], the posthorn episode in the Third, the episodes in the development sections of the first movements of the Sixth [Figs 21–24] and Seventh [Figs 32 and 37], to the measures evoking spring in 'Der Trunkene' in *Das Lied von der Erde* [Fig. 8] and the passage marked *Etwas gehalten* [somewhat restrained] in the burlesque of the Ninth [26 bars after Fig. 36, beginning in bar 354].
>
> (Adorno, 1992a, p. 41)

As the interruption of linear progression in musical works, nature episodes are by the same token an arrest of the narrative unfolding by which the musical subject was customarily articulated. Nature episodes cut across the more familiar temporal patterning of the music that they interrupt, insisting on something slower and more static. They are the means by which the music confronts its own model of time, identity and subjective experience. While their very presence within the larger symphonic whole has this effect, without exception nature episodes exhibit a more complex structural function than that of simple opposition or juxtaposition. Let us dwell on a very particular structural function – what one might call that of the threshold. Mahlerian nature episodes function as more than reminiscence or vision; from outside of the temporal sequence of the main narrative, they present encounters that alter the outcome of that main narrative and frequently present the resolution so far lacking in the more dynamic, linear music that surrounds them.

As thresholds, nature episodes radically alter the direction and character of the music. They literally suspend linear motion, often to the point of stasis, and in doing so create a sense of anticipation for what must inevitably follow: the opening of the finale of the Second Symphony is a prime example. The emphasis on the spatial aspect gives these passages a sense of an achieved plateau (consider the ending of the third movement of the Fourth Symphony, Figs 11 and 13), a flattening out of the principal linear time of the main narrative. A definitive feature of these episodes is the way in which extension in time is suspended in favour of extension in space – a precondition, it seems, for the realization of the work's temporal goal. Mahler's evocation of space is both literal and figurative. His extensive use of off-stage soloists and ensembles is well known, but his creation of distance effects from within the orchestra is equally significant. These are partly achieved through the careful use of dynamics and mutes: in the third movement of the Fifth Symphony, for example, a sense of distance is created simply by having the obbligato horn echoed by another muted instrument. Elsewhere, Mahler achieves on-stage distance effects by a very particular layering of musical elements, differentiated by timbre, rhythm and register: the opening of the second part of the Eighth Symphony and the opening of the Finale to the Second Symphony are obvious examples. In some cases, certain instrumental voices are deliberately unsynchronized with the rest of the orchestra – like the off-stage trumpets in the finale of the Second Symphony that sound as if they are in an entirely different metre and tempo (Fig. 22), or moments in the Third Symphony where instruments are asked to perform their own accelerando 'without attention to the beat' (for example, in the first movement, 5–6 bars after Fig. 20, piccolo).

Mahler's use of spatial distance (literal or figurative) is of course no mere programmatic whim or representational device: what is distant in space is usually projected as distant in time.[9] Sometimes the music heard from afar is an evocation of something distantly past – a remembrance, such as the posthorn interlude in the Third Symphony. More often, music heard in the distance is anticipatory – a fanfare that pre-empts an arrival often still very distant in time. This anticipatory function is central to the structural function of the threshold. Some Mahlerian thresholds make use of explicit anticipatory imagery – angelic and pastoral episodes being the most common and, indeed, frequently elided. In the Second

---

[9] 'In the distance what is distant breaks open, becomes – in timeless moments of time – close and present' ['In das Fernsein bricht die Ferne an, wird sie – in zeitlosen Augenblicken der Zeit–nahe und gegenwärtig'] (Eggebrecht, 1982a, p. 23).

Symphony, the central section of the 'Urlicht' movement – the encounter with an angel (Figs 3–5) – becomes the axial point of the entire symphony, precipitating the soloist's first expression of the lines 'Ich bin von Gott und will wieder zu Gott!'. In much the same way, the static misterioso setting of Nietzsche's 'Midnight Song' (from *Also sprach Zarathustra*) in the Third Symphony acts as a threshold to the angelic chorus of the following movement. One of the most extended examples of this is found in the Fourth Symphony, whose entire third movement acts as a threshold to the heavenly arrival of the finale. Its ending provides a whole series of liminal crossings effected not just by unprepared harmonic shifts, but also by the cultivation of a very particular sonority that defines the closing bars of this movement as a different musical space. The great eruption of E major (Figs 12–13) that precedes it thus serves as a foil for the gradual reduction of sonorous substance, as the orchestral tone becomes more and more de-substantialized towards the end.

Literal and metaphorical distance merge in Mahler's music: musical material and idea are inseparable; as Adorno puts it, Mahler 'fails to acknowledge the choice between technique and imaginative content' (Adorno, 1992a, p. 3). What is heard as spatially distant in Mahler's orchestra not only signals the idea of temporal distance (reminiscence and anticipation), but furthermore signals the idea of difference itself. In this, his music anticipates some key developments within modernism: in their tone of 'otherness', underlined by their spatial projection, Mahler's nature episodes anticipate not only works that followed soon after (such as Schoenberg's *Die Jakobsleiter*, 1917–22), but the later concerns of electronic music. What underlies this link is a shared musical aesthetic based on an idea of the work pointing beyond itself, projecting a resolution beyond its own formal articulation. It represents a key moment in aesthetic modernism: the formal articulation of the work's own failure as discourse.

One crucial aspect of the transformative function of the threshold is its radical change of sonority. Its presentation of new sonorities marks out the point of crossover from one musical area to another. Often prominent here is an ensemble that Mahler cultivated quite self-consciously as a musical cipher for the heavenly or utopian: that is, harp, celesta, glockenspiel, triangle, harmonium, guitar, mandolin, bells and cowbells, all or some of these often forming a timbral backdrop for the lyrical use of a high solo violin.[10] It is of course a Mahlerian hallmark and a device that connects the ending of *Das Lied* with the vision of the Virgin Mary in Part 2 of the Eighth Symphony (Fig. 106). Elsewhere, the sonority of threshold music is deliberately rather ungraspable, itself hard to delimit: consider Mahler's use of *Schattenhaft* [shadowy] as a substantive

---

[10] Webern was later to employ exactly the same group for very similar purposes in his own orchestral music. The third of the *Five Pieces for Orchestra*, Op. 10, provides the best-known example.

category of his music (the marking appears, for example, at the start of the Scherzo of the Seventh Symphony, and as a key term in the first movement of the Ninth, 12 bars after Fig. 13). Nor is this simply a matter of dynamics: consider those marginal passages in Mahler where string tremolandi, often at registral extremes and in close-scoring, cross the boundary between tone and noise, strangely disembodied because lacking any real gestural form.

This quality of ungraspability is heightened by the tendency of threshold passages to fragment their musical materials, a technique that Mahler came to use often at the ending of movements, as in the case of the first and second movements of the Fifth Symphony or the Scherzo of the Sixth. Its use as a threshold device can be seen in the first movement of the Seventh Symphony, where on two occasions the forward energy of the movement drains away into a fragmentary passage whose second appearance acts as a threshold to the sudden affirmatory arrival of B major (five bars after Fig. 39). Perhaps Mahler's most elaborated musical exploration of the spatial is found in the second part of the Eighth Symphony, although in this there are certainly important points of overlap with both 'Der Abschied' and the Ninth Symphony. Goethe's text to the ending of *Faust* employs a spatial metaphor for the expression of spiritual development. Mahler's musical setting not only responds by delineating a rich spatial layering between the different groups of anchorites and angels, but also structures the entire movement around a sense of expanding space rather than progression through time. Much of the music is static, so that the movement unfolds by contrasting plateaux separated by thresholds that effect the transformation from one to the next.[11]

The Eighth Symphony, with the problematic pounding out of E flat major in its closing bars, raises a problem similar to that of the Second Symphony. Elsewhere in Mahler nature episodes function as a cipher for the 'not-yet'; where fulfilment is glimpsed it arrives, like spring in 'Der Trunkene', in the darkness of the night, not as the result of logical, rational progression. Both Adorno and Eggebrecht dwell on Mahler's *Naturlaut* as a technical deviation from syntactical regularity that constitutes a negative projection of nature: it does not name the 'other', merely deconstructs the language of its misappropriation in order to keep its difference as a possibility. Only as the unattainable, Adorno insists, is the idea given form. The *Naturlaut* is above all the embodiment of the idea of 'otherness', something outside high musical language, ungraspable to representation. In this

---

[11] *Die Jakobsleiter* is indebted to the latter part of Mahler's symphony. In Schoenberg's case, this is revealed most obviously in the extravagant spatial deployment of his orchestral and vocal forces (there are four off-stage groups, two at various horizontal distances from the main body, and two at various vertical distances). But Schoenberg, like Webern after him, was also intrigued by the larger question of spatial directionality in music, and *Die Jakobsleiter* makes clear that the fascination with spatialization in 1917 was entwined with Schoenberg's nascent thinking about serialism.

way it anticipates a more radical form of modernism that conceived spiritualization as negativity towards immediacy and 'naturalness', drawing on the category of the sublime and the idea that a utopian content can be grasped only in reflection, not representation. It is in this sense that Adorno was to go on to suggest that the 'objectivity' of the Second Viennese School becomes a 'sound of nature' (see for example Adorno, 1984, p. 115).

But this view does not tell the whole story. In key ways, Mahler anticipates the metaphysics of the modernist generation with whom he overlapped. But Adorno's analysis of a radical negativity in Mahler, which turns him into the essential logical link between the affirmation of 'other' in 'romanticism' and its purely negative imprint in modernism, may perhaps obscure a key Mahlerian moment – that of affirmation; because Mahler's music does more than deconstruct received linguistic devices and does more than imply the possibility of 'otherness'. It affirms 'otherness' as immanent presence. Eggebrecht, for one, is sceptical about this, arguing that Mahler's apotheosis-like endings and triumphant overcomings are not really successful mediations but rather done only 'as if they were' [als ob sie wäre] (Eggebrecht, 1982a, p. 24). Such noisy conclusions, he continues, entirely within the ambit of traditional orchestral tone and syntax, are possible only as a forgetting or as a repression of the musical 'other' – as if it had never been.[12]

Just as Mahler feared, in his letter to Batka of 1896, his particular configuration of the idea of nature cannot escape the ambivalence on which it rests. Contemporary Mahler reception only reinforces the anxieties expressed by the composer more than a century ago: it is quite clear that Mahler's music can be and frequently is used precisely as an affirmation of what it seeks to question. To contemporary ears, the ironic and critical aspects of the music may often be lost underneath the affirmative orchestral tone, a symptom of the broader fate of a musical tradition now heard predominantly in terms of its musical surface, as style rather than discourse. But for all that, what should not be obscured is this central fact of Mahler's music: it remains partially complicit with that which it seeks to critique. It is not hard to see how Mahlerian episodes, or songs like 'Ich bin der Welt abhanden gekommen' – if taken in isolation – might be read as examples of an ideology of resignation and withdrawal. As Das Lied von der Erde exemplifies, not only does the latent theme of withdrawal in Mahler become explicit in his late work, but its link to the musical construction of nature is also definitive.

The category of natural beauty remains ambivalent. In Adorno's terms, on the one hand it serves as a cipher for 'the recollection of a non-repressive condition', but on the other it easily dissolves into the amorphousness of myth and 'archaic

---

12 One might cite the passage beginning at Fig. 53 in the Andante of the Sixth Symphony as counter-evidence to Eggebrecht's assertion, since here the cowbells clang away merrily as part of an affirmatory reprise.

unfreedom' (Adorno, 1984, p. 102). The argument for a critical aspect to Mahler's nature music, made by Adorno, Eggebrecht and many others, centres on its presentation of a state unconditioned by the prevailing rationality of the music that surrounds it. The moment this is presented as a state of achieved reconciliation, however, that critical potential vanishes. For Adorno, both the means that Mahler employs in the nature episodes and the larger structural function that the episodes serve, prevent them from becoming ideological affirmation. 'The stuttering *ewig* at the end [of *Das Lied*] ... is not pantheism, which opens the view on blissful distances', he insists, and 'no one-and-all is conjured up as consolation' (Adorno, 1992a, p. 154). The 'earth' in this work, Adorno suggests, takes on the aspect of the planet seen from space – distant, fragile and ephemeral – the symbol of a lost beauty, not its present affirmation. What differentiates the ending of 'Der Abschied', or the end of the Ninth Symphony, from the kind of affirmatory triumphs that end earlier works, is a resistance to finitude embodied in the musical language itself. The much-discussed pentatonicism of *Das Lied* is of course no mere orientalism any more than was Mahler's choice of Bethge's reworkings of Chinese texts. It is, rather, a realization of the tendency towards spaciousness and a refusal of the linear insistency of tonal music that has more to do with the atonality of Webern than with the musical language of Haydn and Beethoven. Mahler once insisted to Natalie Bauer-Lechner that 'in every work of art, which should be a reflection of Nature, there must be a trace of this infinity' (Franklin, 1980, p. 149) – an element sometimes presented by the unregulated, unmeasured heterogeneity of Mahler's music (with its variety of human and animal life) and elsewhere by resistance to its own closure.

For the same reasons, Mahler's reactivation of the fantastical world of *Des Knaben Wunderhorn* was more than an anachronistic throwback to an early romanticism unfashionable in the closing years of the nineteenth century. It became the vehicle for Mahler's plural voices and the means by which previously peripheral or dispossessed voices re-enter the sphere of art music. His music gives space to what was increasingly expunged in the real world by the unitary and centralizing forces of an instrumental rationality and its material forms within the late Habsburg Empire. One might read this in directly social terms, drawing on Mahler's own biography as a Bohemian Jew, but also from a broader, more philosophical perspective. The central function of nature music in Mahler's *oeuvre* finds a fascinating parallel, and partial explanation, in the chapter of Adorno's posthumous *Aesthetic Theory* devoted entirely to the category of natural beauty. Both seem to fly in the face of certain notions of modernity but, as Adorno insists, it is a category that retains a radical, critical aspect precisely because of its neutralization in Hegel and the aesthetics of rational idealism. In a world dominated by the autonomous, constitutive subject, the notion of 'otherness' represented by the category of natural beauty is all but lost. The return of nature in Mahler may thus be read as a return of this repressed content and as a vehicle for questioning the status of that autonomous, constitutive subjectivity. It is for this reason that the Mahlerian *Naturlaut* is shockingly pre-linguistic, unsyntactical and resistant to being rationalized as orchestral tone or compositional material. For Adorno, Mahler's music never delivers what nature promises – that is to say, a state of reconciliation, a non-repressive coexistence of subject and object that elsewhere he defines simply as 'peace'.[13] Rather, the deviations embodied in the *Naturlaut*, by revealing the artificiality of art, underline that art remains non-identical with that state which natural beauty serves to symbolize. Thus the open-ended, transparent 'emptiness' of the ending of *Das Lied von der Erde* projects not affirmation or immanent realization of such a state, but an image of liberation through deregulation. The unmeasured quality of natural beauty to which the end of 'Der Abschied' aspires stands not as concrete presence but as a cipher for that which remains anticipated.

---

[13] See Adorno, 'Subject and Object', in A. Arato & E. Gebhardt (eds), *The Essential Frankfurt School Reader* (Oxford: Blackwell, 1978), p. 500.

Chapter Three

Mahler the Thinker: The Books of the Alma Mahler-Werfel Collection[1]

JEREMY BARHAM

Knowledge of Mahler's intellectual interests has frequently been invoked in the analytical and critical literature to enhance understanding of the context and even the putative 'meaning' of certain works. The sources of this knowledge – leaving aside the texts that Mahler actually set to music – have been limited to: (a) Mahler's written comments in letters and sketch material; and (b) the reports of his relatives and acquaintances (see, for example, Blaukopf, 1996, pp. 33, 54, 114, 141–42 & 385; Martner, 1979, pp. 57, 60, 78, 135, 153 & 337; Decsey, 1911, p. 353; Stefan, 1912, p. 28; Adler, [1916] 1982, pp. 19 & 37; Ermers, 1932, pp. 96–97 & 236; Eckstein, 1936, p. 112; Walter, 1947, pp. 92–93; Walter, [1958] 1990, pp. 27 & 117–20; Pfohl, 1973, p. 20; La Grange, 1974, p. 17; and La Grange, 1979, pp. 34–35).[2] These sources suggest that Mahler was an inveterate collector and reader of books from an early age and remained so throughout his life, and that his reading principally consisted of literary fiction (novels, plays and poetry), biography, criticism, correspondence, philosophy and science, and ranged chronologically from the writings of the ancient Greeks to the latest findings of experimental physics.

It is therefore regrettable that no contemporary record of the contents of his book collection – which could confirm the secondary evidence and provide a full account of the composer's intellectual pursuits – is known to exist.[3] Nevertheless, through all the vicissitudes of life in wartime Vienna, the flight to America and

[1] The author gratefully acknowledges the generous financial support provided by the Department of Music, University of Surrey, enabling research into the Mahler-Werfel Collection to be undertaken in August 1996.

[2] For a useful summary of Mahler's reading habits, see Blaukopf, 2002.

[3] A fact noted and lamented by both Blaukopf (1988, p. 5), in connection with Mahler's knowledge of contemporary scientific thought, and Reilly (1993, p. 7), in his discussion of: (a) Mahler's possible ownership of a copy of Georg Scherer's *Jungbrunnen: Die schönsten deutschen Volkslieder* (Berlin: Wilhelm Herz, 1875); and (b) the source of his knowledge of a poem by the Persian mystic Jalal ad-Din [Dschelaleddin] Rumi, which the composer copied out in Rückert's translation.

occupancy of various homes in Vienna, Semmering, California and New York, Alma Mahler-Werfel was able to preserve at least some of her first husband's library after his death. In 1968, four years after her death, her entire library of over five thousand books was donated to the University of Pennsylvania by their daughter Anna; part of this library is now contained in the Alma Mahler-Werfel Collection, housed in the Annenberg Rare Book & Manuscript Library (henceforth abbreviated as ARBML).

This study provides the first systematic examination of the contents of the collection, and includes a concordance linking these contents with pertinent references in the Mahler literature. Through this and its illustration of important annotations and inscriptions, as well as discussion of the problematic issues of provenance and ownership, the following account aims to shed new empirical light on the range of Mahler's experience of literary culture.

Towards a history of the Mahler library

The library that Alma Schindler began to assemble from the age of 15, with the encouragement and assistance of the writer and theatre director Max Burckhard, was first housed in the 'castle' at Plankenberg which her father, Emil Schindler, had purchased in 1884 (see Mahler-Werfel, 1959, pp. 15–16, and [1960] 2000, p. 21). It was later transferred to the apartment at Theresianumgasse 6 in the fourth district of Vienna belonging to Carl Moll (Alma's stepfather from 1895), and then to the villa in the Hohe Warte on the outskirts of the city to which Moll moved the family in September 1901.[4] It was here that her book collection was perused by Mahler, resulting in his well-known admonition against the works of Nietzsche (see Mahler-Werfel, 1959, p. 22, and Mahler 1990, pp. 18–19). After marrying in March 1902, and until 1909, Gustav and Alma occupied the apartment at Auenbruggergasse 2 into which Mahler had first moved with his sister Justine in November 1898.[5] Presumably the combined libraries of Gustav and Alma were then housed both here and in the villa in Maiernigg on the Wörthersee, the holiday residence where Mahler spent his summers from 1901 until the property was sold in 1908.[6] At the time of their marriage, Alma described her library as being even larger than Mahler's (Mahler-Werfel, [1960] 2000, p. 21) – a claim given considerable support by the vast range of reading matter cited in her diaries (Mahler-Werfel, 1997 & 1998).

---

[4] Steinfeldgasse 8, Wien XIX.

[5] Justine moved out of the apartment shortly after her marriage to Arnold Rosé on 10 March 1902.

[6] Alma reported that she supervised 'the removal of our possessions, including furniture belonging to Mahler's childhood' from the Maiernigg villa in the autumn of 1908 (Mahler, 1990, p. 140).

In October 1909 the Mahlers gave up their apartment in Auenbruggergasse because they were spending so much of the winters in New York. Alma reported that she 'packed all the books and china' and that 'all our movable possessions were stored' although she did not specify where (Mahler, 1990, p. 153). In a letter from Amsterdam where he was preparing performances of his Seventh Symphony at the time, Mahler referred to Alma's description of '20 packing cases' [20 gepackten Kisten] (La Grange & Weiß, 1995, p. 413). When they were not in America, they would now be dividing their time between their summer retreat in Toblach and the house of Alma's mother and stepfather in the Hohe Warte.[7] It is therefore possible that the possessions referred to above were stored in the latter location, although on 21 and (probably) 23 June 1910, while Mahler was rehearsing for the first performance of his Eighth Symphony in Munich, he wrote twice to Alma specifically requesting that he be able to have immediate access to the books kept in Toblach on his return there at the beginning of July: 'If necessary send me the requisite keys. I want to be able to get the books out of there and eventually the clothes too' (La Grange & Weiß, 1995, p. 432, Mahler, 1990, p. 331, translation amended); 'I can leave everything until you arrive – except the books, which I must have immediately or else I will die of boredom' (La Grange & Weiß, 1995, p. 434).[8] Ernst Decsey, who stayed with Mahler at Toblach in June 1909, also reported that 'Many books were piled up in his living room ... I mainly saw philosophical literature. In the evening he would often settle down and have someone read to him. ... mostly he wanted me to read Goethe's Faust Part II' (Decsey, 1911, p. 353).[9]

Immediately after Mahler's death in May 1911, Alma remained in the Molls' house before moving into a garden flat at Elisabethstrasse 22 with her daughter Anna in December of that year. The precise whereabouts of Mahler's book collection at this point is not clearly known. However, when Mahler died his entire estate was passed over to Alma,[10] and, given that she was an avid reader with whom Mahler had frequently discussed the finer points of his own literary experiences – and in the absence of any conflicting evidence – it is logical to assume that this undoubtedly large library, which may well have been simply amalgamated with her own, remained in her care. Anna Mahler, for instance, later recalled that her father's library had contained 'all Helmholtz's works' (Blaukopf, 1988, p. 5; see also Blaukopf & Blaukopf, 1991, p. 104).[11]

---

7 In 1907 the Molls had moved to a nearby villa at Wollergasse 10.

8 'Falls nöthig, schicke mir die betreffenden Schlüßel. Ich möchte dort die Bücher, und eventuell auch Kleider herausnehmen können.' 'Alles kann ich lassen, bis Du kommst – nur Bücher, die muß ich gleich haben, sonst sterbe ich vor Langeweile.'

9 'In seinem Wohnzimmer waren viele Bücher gestapelt ... hauptsächlich sah ich philosophische Literatur. Am Abend legte er sich öfter hin und ließ sich vorlesen. ... [m]eistens verlangte er ... daß ich Goethe vorlese, Faust zweiten Teil.'

10 The will that Mahler made in 1904 is cited in La Grange & Weiß, 1995, p. 486.

11 However, dispersal of some items to third parties during the remaining fifty-three years of Alma's life cannot be ruled out. See, for instance, Hilmar-Voit's

The house in Breitenstein a.d. Südbahn, Semmering, for which plans had been laid and the land bought by Mahler in 1910, was completed during the spring of 1914. From then until 1931, Alma divided her time principally between this house and her Vienna flat, time which she shared with her companions Oskar Kokoschka, Walter Gropius and Franz Werfel.[12] In March 1931 she and Werfel, who were now married, moved into a 28-room mansion in Wollergasse on the Hohe Warte close to the Molls, which had been purchased as their main Viennese residence to replace the much smaller rented apartment in Elisabethstrasse. The entire top floor was converted into a studio for Werfel, and Alma's music room and library was located beneath. The building also housed Mahler's desk, library of scores, papers and manuscripts (including that of Bruckner's Third Symphony). At least some of these items were contained in built-in cabinets lining the marble-walled entrance hall of the house. Although no specific reference to Mahler's book collection is to be found, the house would certainly have been spacious enough to accommodate it.

Partly owing to costs and because Werfel was unhappy working there, he and Alma decided to leave the Hohe Warte house in 1937 and move to Semmering. Alma noted in March of that year that she had 'ten thousand books, five thousand sheets of music, pianos, pieces of art et cetera to pack up and secure' (Mahler-Werfel, [1960] 2000, p. 261; see also ibid., p. 259, & 1959, pp. 213–14).[13] Exactly how many of these possessions were moved to Semmering, how many remained in their house (which had been let out from August 1937) and how many might have been stored at the Molls' house is open to question.

Political developments during 1938 compelled Alma and Franz to leave Austria. Alma gave her stepfather Carl Moll, with whom she had often been on less than good terms, power of attorney over her property, including the house in Semmering. She had to leave with 'only two small suitcases' [*nur zwei kleine Handkoffer*] and noted that 'I ... could take nothing with me, for I had let

---

reference to Mahler's copy of the first edition of *Des Knaben Wunderhorn* (Heidelberg: Mohr & Zimmer, 1805–8) – given to him in 1895 by Anna von Mildenburg – which is currently held in a private collection in Vienna (Hilmar-Voit, 1998, foreword, p. xiii). Alma also reported that Mahler's sister Justine 'took away a number of books and papers with her' when she married Rosé and moved out of Mahler's Vienna apartment (Mahler, 1990, p. 143). In addition La Grange (1974, p. 853 fn. 58, & 1979, p. 163 fn. 101), reported that a copy of Sterne's *Tristram Shandy* with numerous handwritten translations (possibly Mahler's) existed in Alma's library. Neither this volume nor any works by Helmholtz were found in the ARBML.

[12] Alma married Gropius in August 1915 and they were divorced in 1920. In 1922 she also purchased a canal-side house in Venice, the Casa Mahler at 2542 San Tomà, as a retreat for herself and Werfel. This house was sold in 1935. She married Werfel in July 1929. Werfel died in August 1945.

[13] 'Ich hatte ... die zehntausend Bücher, fünftausend Noten, Klaviere, Kunstgegenstände et cetera zu verpacken und zu sichern.'

out my house and did not want to be seen there'[14] (Mahler-Werfel, [1960] 2000, p. 275; see also 1959, p. 222), implying that some of her possessions were in fact still stored in this house. Eleonore Vondenhoff, who visited Alma shortly before her departure, reported that she had disbanded her household and secured her valuables in metal crates (see Mahler-Werfel, 1997, p. xiv, 1998, p. xiv). Indeed, later evidence referred to below suggests that she stored a considerable amount of material relating to Mahler and Werfel in the top floor of the mansion in Vienna.

The remarkable and chaotic story of Alma's and Franz's flight through Europe to America, where they arrived on 13 October 1940, has been well documented (see Mahler-Werfel, 1959, pp. 223–48, [1960] 2000, pp. 275–321, Monson, 1984, pp. 252–74, and Keegan, 1991, pp. 266–80). This was a journey that took them to Milan, Zürich, London (where in June 1938 Alma lamented the absence of a piano and her books; Mahler-Werfel, 1959, p. 225, & [1960] 2000, pp. 277 & 278), Paris (where in December 1938 Mahler's manuscript of Bruckner's Third Symphony unexpectedly arrived, having been smuggled out of Austria by Alma's trusted maid, 'Sister' Ida Gebauer, via the wife of Paul Stefan), Sanary-sur-Mer, Marseille, Bordeaux (where they were forced to abandon all their luggage, including books, Mahler's manuscripts and the Bruckner score), Pau, Lourdes, Marseille again (where the trunk containing the music manuscripts and the rest of their luggage miraculously caught up with them from Bordeaux, the latter being sent on to New York), Cerbère, Port Bau, Barcelona, Madrid and finally Lisbon where they boarded the *Nea Hellas*.

Alma occupied three residences in America: a rented house in Los Angeles (December 1940–September 1942), a bungalow at 610 North Bedford Drive, Beverly Hills, which she purchased and lived in until 1952, and a building containing three apartments at 120 East 73rd Street, New York, which she bought upon the sale of the house in California and in which she occupied the third-floor apartment from 1952 until her death in 1964. In the early 1940s she began the laborious task of reclaiming her possessions from Austria. In 1945 she learned that, while the Molls' house had survived undamaged, four Allied bombs had destroyed the top floor of her house in the Hohe Warte where she had stored the desks, letters and manuscripts of Mahler and Werfel, thinking that they would be best protected there. During a largely fruitless trip to Vienna in 1947 she found that the house in Semmering had been sold to the Soviet authorities, and that Moll had willed her father's paintings – her rightful inheritance – to a gallery and sold most other things of value that were supposed to have been held in trust for her: 'the rest of the estate had vanished in the pockets of [Moll's] daughter and her high-ranking Nazi husband' (Mahler-Werfel, 1959, p. 274).[15] All she managed

---

[14] 'Ich ... konnte ja nichts mitnehmen, da ich mein Haus vermietet hatte und dort nicht gesehen werden wollte.'

[15] Moll, his daughter Maria and her husband had all committed suicide when the Russians entered Vienna.

to salvage at this time were two of the small 'notebooks' that Mahler had regularly carried around with him.[16] Nevertheless, according to Giroud and Monson, with the help of American lawyers, military personnel and friends, she was eventually successful in reclaiming a significant portion of her estate:

> Alma obtained quite a sizable number of the smaller items she had owned in Vienna and Semmering; they included books, papers, dishes, serving pieces, and other objects that would fit into suitcases. Each time something arrived in Beverly Hills, she rejoiced in reestablishing a tie with the past.
>
> (Monson, 1984, p. 282; see also Giroud, 1991, p. 153)

As descriptions and photographs attest, the walls of the so-called 'Power of Words' room in her New York apartment were lined from floor to ceiling with books:

> the German classics that Max Burckhard gave me as a girl, Werfel's works in all languages, the works of all the friends I have made over the years and of the great spirits I have admired over the centuries, from Plato to Bernard Shaw.
>
> (Mahler-Werfel, 1959, p. 281; see also the plate between pp. 192 & 193)

The fact that those books which Alma inherited from Mahler are not specifically mentioned should not be taken to indicate that none of them survived. The existence in the Alma Mahler-Werfel Collection of some books that unequivocally did belong to Mahler (since they contain markings or inscriptions) in any case refutes this. It seems likely that those books belonging to Mahler which survived had been absorbed into her own growing library and formed part of the 'ten thousand' that Alma had accumulated by the time she left her house on the Hohe Warte in 1937. Additional evidence from the labelling of the remaining books in the collection to be set out below further supports this thesis. The uncertainty over the location of her stored library during the war years makes precise conclusions difficult. Some books may well have been destroyed in her house on the Hohe Warte; some may have been removed from the house or from the Moll house, and dispersed by her stepfather or by third parties. If the library had been moved in its entirety to Semmering, it may be more likely that it survived intact. However, if Alma's account is reasonably accurate, it should be noted that nearly half of the book collection was either dispersed or did not survive. A typed document in Box 46 of the Mahler-Werfel Papers[17] at the ARBML further confuses the issue of the size and whereabouts of the book

---

[16] It is not clear whether these notebooks correspond to Mahler's two surviving pocket musical sketchbooks: that related to the Seventh Symphony (housed in the Anna Bahr-Mildenburg Nachlaß, Österreichisches Theatermuseum), and that related to the Ninth Symphony (housed in the Musiksammlung of the Österreichische Nationalbibliothek).

[17] These papers, consisting of over 5000 letters, manuscripts and other documents and memorabilia, were presented to the library as a separate gift by Anna Mahler in February 1968.

collection. Entitled 'Personal Property in Austria claimed by Mrs. Alma Mahler-Werfel', it lists furniture, fixtures and a 'library of 2,500 volumes' amongst her personal property in the house at Breitenstein. However, even the presence of a Semmering stamp inside a large number of the surviving books may not be a conclusive indication of their exact provenance.[18]

Provenance and preliminary description of the Alma Mahler-Werfel Book Collection

In 1961 Professor Adolf Klarmann of the University of Pennsylvania, an authority on Werfel and the editor of his collected works, was officially appointed by Alma as literary executor of her and Werfel's estate, which would be inherited by her daughter Anna.[19] In her will, dated 1 September, Alma wrote:

> I leave it to the final decision of my daughter Anna Mahler whether the books in my personal library at the above address [120 East 73rd Street] be given – all or part – to the Library of the University of Pennsylvania, Pa.
> (Copy housed in the ARBML)[20]

Shortly after her mother's death, Anna Mahler decided to deposit the book collection at the University of Pennsylvania, and in May 1965 Rudolf Hirsch, the Associate Director of Libraries, reported the safe arrival of 'your mother's library to Dr. Klarmann ... 150 or so boxes are at present in the Rare Book Collection of the University of Pennsylvania ready to be sorted soon'.[21] Later in the year the collection was valued, and 'inventoried' as shown in Fig. 3.1. Three years later Anna announced to Klarmann her formal intent to donate the book collection to the University: 'Herewith I want to declare that the library of my mother, now in

---

[18] The unreliability of evidence offered by stamps is underlined by the presence in the collection of an anthology of Czech poetry by Urchlický, Sova and Březina, *Tschechische Anthologie*, trans. Paul Eisner (Leipzig: Insel Verlag, editor's note dated 1917), which bears three haphazardly arranged stamps 'GUSTAV MAHLER WIEN' on the recto of the leaf following the title page. This stamp is found in no other book of the collection.

[19] Klarmann, together with Gustav Arlt of the University of California at Los Angeles, became close associates of the Werfels, and helped in the negotiations surrounding the film rights to Werfel's novel *Song of Bernadette* in the early 1940s. Arlt was also responsible for securing the deposit of Werfel's papers and manuscripts in the library of the University of California at Los Angeles in 1948. According to Monson, the furniture and books from Werfel's study were also destined for this library (Monson, 1984, p. 309). See also Mahler-Werfel, 1959, p. 273.

[20] After Alma's death, the contents of her estate were stored in a warehouse on Third Avenue from which certain items 'disappeared in mysterious circumstances' (correspondence from Donald Mitchell to Edward Kravitt (May 1987), cited in Kravitt, 1988, p. 202).

[21] Letter from Hirsch to Anna Mahler, 18 May 1965, housed in ARBML.

In Rare Book Collection:	Books	1157	Pamphlets	160	(1317)
In storage:	Books	3698	Pamphlets	473	(4171)
Total:		4855		633	
Grand total:		5488			

Fig. 3.1   1965 outline inventory of the Alma Mahler-Werfel Book Collection

Philadelphia in your custody, is given by me as a present in her and Franz Werfel's memory to the University of Pennsylvania in Philadelphia.'[22]

As can be seen from the inventory, Hirsch selected 1317 items from the collection (approximately 24 per cent of the total) which he considered worthy of preservation in what was then called the Rare Book Collection. No documentation exists explaining the criteria for his selection other than a brief, undated, typewritten description of the contents of the collection referring to first editions of Werfel's and other twentieth-century writers' works, books with dedications to Alma or Franz (or both), or with autograph notes in Werfel's hand, and a conservative estimate of sixteen titles (eighteen volumes) 'which either belonged to, or were associated with the famous composer Gustav Mahler'.[23] Although Hirsch would undoubtedly have been astute enough to recognize items of intrinsic value, it appears that tracing more than the most patent links between Mahler and the collection was not a decisive factor in his evaluation of its contents. It may also be true that prevailing models in the mid-1960s for establishing which material merited inclusion in a rare book collection would have been different from those in force today. This suggests that the remaining 4171 uncatalogued items, whose whereabouts are currently unknown, would deserve serious examination.[24]

According to the current Humanities Bibliographer at the University of Pennsylvania Library, Stephen Lehmann, certain items preserved by Hirsch were moved from the Rare Book Collection onto the main library shelves at some point between 1965 and 1995.[25] No documentation exists outlining either when, why and by whom this transfer was carried out, or which items were involved.[26] Lehmann examined the collection in 1995 and – on the grounds of antiquarian value, presence of inscriptions and the value of the books to the library as texts – further divided up the contents into those items that would be preserved in the ARBML, those that would be catalogued for the main library shelves, and those that would

---

[22]   Letter from Anna Mahler to Klarmann, 22 January 1968, housed in ARBML.

[23]   Copy housed in ARBML.

[24]   Subsequent research by the author has suggested that these further items were probably either put on the main library shelves or, unfortunately, deaccessioned at the time of the initial examination of the collection.

[25]   Personal communication with the author, August 1996.

[26]   On brief inspection the following books relating to Mahler and bearing the label

be deaccessioned. At the time of writing, the status of the items set aside by Hirsch which remained in the ARBML is that they are still housed in the ARBML, the title pages of those books intended for deaccessioning having been photocopied.

The majority of the books are either stamped 'HAUS MAHLER BREITENSTEIN a.d. SÜDBAHN' or carry the bookplate 'EX LIBRIS ALMA SCHINDLER'.[27] As one would expect, the publication of those books with the latter designation dates from 1902 (the year of Alma's marriage to Mahler) or earlier. However, as can be seen in the following catalogue, there are two significant exceptions to this, one of which is a book bearing a dedication to Gustav and Alma Mahler, dated 1909 (Friedrich Hirth, *The Ancient History of China to the End of the Chóu Dynasty* (New York: Columbia University Press, 1908)). Of those with the former designation, in a small number of cases the lettering is inverted, reversed and/or inside the back cover, suggesting that some or all of the stamping might have been carried out in haste and at a later time immediately before the library was relocated to Semmering, to New York or even to Philadelphia. Three of the books bearing the Breitenstein stamp contain handwritten dedications to Gustav Mahler, while a number of books carry both stamp and bookplate. Although it is difficult to confirm Mahler's ownership of particular books – with the obvious exception of those bearing dedications – these irregularities indicate that the designation, either on its own or considered in combination with a particular publication date up to 1911, cannot unequivocally discount his ownership. Other provisos include: (a) the obvious possibility that any book published in or before 1911 could have been acquired at any later date; (b) even if it can be shown that Mahler did own a certain book, the questions of whether he read it or not, what his reaction to it might have been and what precise influence it might have had on his creative constitution must in most cases remain conjectural; (c) conversely, if a particular book belonged to Alma's library during the time they spent together but was not specifically 'owned' by Mahler, he would nevertheless have had access to it; and (d) even a book containing inscriptions or annotations not in Mahler's hand could have originally been his property. The author acknowledges the uncertainty that such variables inevitably lend to the status of the catalogue. With this in mind, the following catalogue itemizes all books published in or before 1911 belonging to that part of the Alma Mahler-Werfel Collection currently held in the ARBML.

'Franz Werfel Memorial Collection' were located by the author on the main library shelves in the music section of the University of Pennsylvania Library: Adler, 1916; Bauer-Lechner, 1923; Engel, 1932 (with undated dedication from Engel to Alma); Mahler, 1924; Matter, 1959 (with dedication from Matter to Alma, July 1959); Mitchell, 1958; Reich, 1958; Specht, 1913 (with unidentified dedication to Alma, June 1919) & 1922 (with dedication from Specht to Werfel, March 1922); Stefan, 1913; Worbs, n.d.

[27] Diary entries for 16 March and 21 June 1900 document respectively Alma's request to the architect Josef Hoffmann to design her a bookplate, and the delivery of the design with which she seems to have been particularly impressed (Mahler-Werfel, 1997, pp. 476 & 518; ibid, 1998, pp. 264 & 296). See Plate 3.14.

Catalogue of the Alma Mahler-Werfel Book Collection[28]

Table 3.1 Literature, including fiction, biography, correspondence and criticism

Author	Title	Publication details	Designation, inscriptions, markings and other comments[29]	Literature concordance[30]
Peter ALTENBERG	*Wie ich es sehe*	Berlin: S. Fischer Verlag, 1896	HMBS. ELAS	MW 1997: 83 [Altenberg wrote for secessionist journal, *Ver Sacrum*]
	Ashantee	Berlin: S. Fischer Verlag, 1897	HMBS. ELAS	
Leonid ANDREJEW	*Es waren einmal. Das Schweigen. Das Lachen. Die Lüge.* Novellen. Deutsch von Stefania Goldenring	Berlin: Verlag von Neufeld und Henius, n.d.	HMBS. ELAS	
ANON.	*Die Erzählungen aus den Tausend und ein Nächten.* Besorgt v. Felix Paul Greve	Leipzig: Insel Verlag		
	3. Bd.	1907		
	4. Bd.	"		
	6. Bd.	"		
	7. Bd.	1908		
	8. Bd.	"		
	9. Bd.	"		
	10. Bd.	"		
	11. Bd.	"		
	12. Bd.	"		
	Tausend und eine Nacht. Arabische Erzählungen, trans. Dr. Gustav Weil 1. & 3. Bd.	Berlin: Verlag von Th. Knaur Nacht, n.d.	HMBS	

Meyers kleines Konversations-Lexicon	Leipzig & Wien: Bibliographisches Institut	
1. Bd. A bis Golther	1898	ELAS
2. Bd. Goltz bis Petschora	1899	"
3. Bd. Pettan bis Zymotisch	1899	"
Die Blümlein des heiligen Franziskus von Assisi	Leipzig: Insel Verlag, 1911	Ink dedication on first leaf: 'Alma Maria Weihnachten F.B.' [Franz Blei? If so, gift probably post-dates 1916, the year in which Blei first joined Alma's circle]
Die Briefe des Michelagniolo Buonarroti	Berlin: Verlag von Julius Bard, 1907	HMBS
Spielmanns Buch. Novellen in Versen aus den zwölften und dreizehnten Jahrhundert.	Stuttgart: Druck und Verlag von Gebrüder Kröner,	

continued overleaf

[28] The author gratefully acknowledges the generous assistance of the following staff of the ARBML in facilitating the examination and cataloguing of the collection: Lynne Farrington, Ken Holston, Stephen Lehmann, Michael Ryan, Nancy Shawcross, Daniel Traister and particularly John Pollack. A square bracket around an entire entry in the catalogue indicates that the item was published after Mahler's death but has been included for its intrinsic interest.

[29] The following abbreviations will be used: HMBS indicates that the book bears the stamp 'HAUS MAHLER BREITENSTEIN a.d. SÜDBAHN' (on recto of its first leaf unless otherwise stated); ELAS indicates that the book bears the book-plate 'EX LIBRIS ALMA SCHINDLER' (on recto of its first leaf unless otherwise stated). 'App.' refers to the Appendix at the end of this volume, and the number in brackets refers to the relevant table in the Appendix.

[30] The following abbreviations will be used: ABL (*And the Bridge is Love*, Mahler-Werfel, 1959), ABM (*Erinnerungen*, Bahr-Mildenburg, 1921), BW (*Gustav Mahler*, Walter, [1958] 1990), EB (*Erinnerungen und Briefe*, Mahler, 1940), EGR ('*Ein Glück ohne Ruh*'', La Grange & Weiß, 1995), GA (*Gustav Mahler*, Adler, [1916] 1982), GMB (*Gustav Mahler Briefe*, Blaukopf, 1996), HB (Blaukopf, 2002), HGE1 (La Grange, 1974), HGE2 (La Grange, 1995), HGE3 (La Grange, 1999), HGF1 (La Grange, 1979), HGF2 (La Grange, 1983), HGF3 (La Grange, 1984), LWW (*Mahler. His Life, Work and World*, Blaukopf & Blaukopf, 1991), MAL (*Memories and Letters*, Mahler, 1990), ML (*Mein Leben*, Mahler-Werfel, [1960] 2000), MUB (*Gustav Mahler. Unbekannte Briefe*, Blaukopf, 1983), MUL (*Mahler's Unknown Letters*, Blaukopf, 1986), MW (Mahler-Werfel), NAMR (*News About Mahler Research*), NBL (*Erinnerungen von Natalie Bauer-Lechner*, Killian, 1984), NBLE (*Recollections of Gustav Mahler by Natalie Bauer-Lechner*, Franklin, 1980), NBLM (Bauer-Lechner, *Mahleriana* manuscript, collection of La Grange, Paris), SLGM (*Selected Letters of Gustav Mahler*, Martner, 1979), TV (*Theme and Variations*, Walter, 1947), UWO (Gustav Mahler–Alfred Rosé Collection, Music Library, University of Western Ontario). Entries in square brackets indicate general references to authors, references to unspecified volumes, or probable links; all other entries refer to specific volumes.

Table **3.1** continued

Author	Title	Publication details	Designation, inscriptions, markings and other comments	Literature concordance
	Übertragen von Wilhelm Hertz	1886		
	Phidias von Hermann Ubell [from the series *Die Kunst*, hrsg. von Richard Muther]	Bard Marquardt, n.d., n.p.	HMBS	
	Joli Tambour! Das französische Volkslied, hrsg. von Hanns Heinz Ewers und Marc Henry	Berlin: Wilhelm Borngräber Verlag Neues Leben, n.d. [Introduction dated 1911]	HMBS	
	Taschenausgabe der Österreichischen Gesetze	Wien: Manz'sche k.k. Hof-Verlags- und Universitäts-Buchhandlung, 1889	Several paragraphs in the section of 'Kirche und Ehe' entitled 'Gesetz vom 9. April 1870, über die Ehen von Personen, welche keiner gesetzlich anerkannten Kirche oder Religionsgesellschaft angehören, und über die Führung der Geburts-, Ehe- und Sterberegister für dieselben' marked l with blue pencil (see App. for key to symbols)	
	26. Bd. *Gesetze und Verordnungen in Cultussachen*. Mit Benützung von theilweise ungedruckten Materialen zusammengestellt von Dr. Burckhard		HMBS. Blue-pencil markings on pp. 31 & 36	
	Griechischer Anfangskursus Übungsbuch. Zur ersten	Leipzig & Berlin: Druck und Verlag		[ML: 34 & 40]

48

Author	Title	Publication	Location/Dedication	Notes
	Einführung Erwachsener ins Griechische besonders für Universitätskurse. Nebst Präparationen zu Xenophon An. I und Homer Od. IX zusammengestellt von Dr. R. Helm	von B.G. Teubner, 1902		
	Aus der Glanzzeit der Weimarer Altenburg. Bilder und Briefe aus dem Leben der Fürstin Carolyne Sayn-Wittgenstein, hrsg. von La Mara	Leipzig: Druck und Verlag von Breitkopf und Härtel, 1906	Handwritten dedication from Oscar v. Hase [?] to Gustav and Alma dated 'Weihnachten 1905'	
M. ARSSIBASCHEW	Am Letzten Punkt. Roman	[2nd edn] München und Leipzig: Georg Müller, 1911	HMBS	
Gertrude ATHERTON	The Gorgeous Isle. A Romance	New York: Doubleday, Page & Co., 1908	Blue-ink dedication: 'Compliments Gertrude Atherton 1910'	
Hermann BAHR	Der Meister. Komödie in drei Akten	Berlin: S. Fischer Verlag, 1904	HMBS	[Decsey, 1911: 353, Bahr's *Tagebuch*. Closely associated with secessionist journal, *Ver Sacrum*. Burckhard introduces Mahler to Bahr; uncomfortable meeting: EB: 83. Bahr's intention to introduce Mahler as a figure in his next novel, Decsey, 1911: 353]
	Der Franzl. Fünf Bilder eines guten Mannes	Wien: Wiener Verlag, 1901	HMBS	
	Grotesken. Der Klub der Erlöser. – Der Faun. – Die tiefe Natur	Wien: Verlags-Buchhandlung Carl Konegen, 1907	HMBS	
	Dialog vom Tragischen	Berlin: S. Fischer	Handwritten dedication from Bahr to Mahler:	

49

continued overleaf

Table 3.1 *continued*

Author	Title	Publication details	Designation, inscriptions, markings and other comments	Literature concordance
		Verlag, 1904	'Lieber Mahler in aufrichtiger Bewunderung Januar 1905 Hermann Bahr' (transcribed by Herta Blaukopf). See Plate 3.1	
Eduard BELLAMY	*Fräulein Ludington's Schwester*. Ein Roman über die Unsterblichkeit	Berlin: Verlag von S. Fischer, 1890	HMBS	
Otto Julius BIERBAUM	*Stilpe. Ein Roman aus der Froschperspektive*	Berlin: Verlag von Schuster und Loeffler, 1900	HMBS. ELAS. Label on last leaf: 'R. Lechner Wilh. Müller Buchhandlung, Wien Graben 31'. The book contains a postcard from Imst Oberstadt in Tirol addressed to Carl Moll, dated '24 Juni 1944', and bearing a Third Reich stamp with Hitler's portrait. This suggests that Moll may have handled at least some of the books from the Mahler library at a much later date.	MW 1997: 541 & 694; 1998: 312–13 & 422. [Reading Bierbaum and setting a text to music, MW 1997: 646 & 650; 1998: 391 & 394; HGF2: 168. Alma set 'Ekstase' and 'Licht in der Nacht'. Bierbaum wrote for secessionist journal, *Ver Sacrum*] [Mahler's negative general comments, EGR: 107]
Theodor BILLROTH	*Briefe*	Hannover und Leipzig; Hahnsche Buchhandlung, 1897	ELAS. Handwritten dedication on title page: 'Für Alma und Gretl Schindler. Neujahr 1898 ', [illegible name]	
Björnstjerne BJÖRNSON	*Magnhild*. Dem Norwegischen nacherzählt von Emil J. Jonas	Berlin: Verlag von Otto Janke, n.d.	HMBS	MW 1997: 291

			ELAS
Wilhelm BODE	*Paul Lange und Cora Parsberg*. Übersetzung von Mathilde Mann	Paris, Leipzig & München: Verlag von Albert Langen, 1899	
	Über den Luxus	Leipzig: Verlag von K.G.Th. Scheffer, 1904	HMBS
Margarete BÖHME	*W.A.G.N.U.S.* Roman	Berlin: F. Fontane, 1911	HMBS. The following passage on p. 177 is highlighted in pencil and with various words underlined: '<u>Sinfonien</u> von ohrbetäubenden Geräuschen durchrissen die Luft. Klingeln und <u>Pfeifen</u>, Rasseln und <u>Knallen</u>, Schreien und <u>Sirren</u>, das Konzert eines gemischten Höllenchors, ein Ineinanderwirbeln von unzähligen, ohrzerreißenden <u>Dissonanzen</u>'.
Ludwig BÖRNE	*Ludwig Börnes gesammelte Schriften*	Leipzig: Druck und Verlag von Philip Reclam, n.d.	
	1. Bd.		ELAS. Label on last leaf: 'R. LECHNER WILH. MÜLLER BUCHHANDLUNG'
	2. Bd.		" " "
	3. Bd.		" " and HMBS
Georg BÜCHNER	*Dantons Tod.* Ein Drama	Leipzig: Insel-Bücherei, Nr. 88, n.d.	HMBS. Architectural pencil drawing inside front cover with inverted word 'film' inside a rectangle
Max BURCKHARD	*Theater. Kritiken. Vorträge und Aufsätze*	Wien: Manzsche k.u.k. Hof-Verlags- und Universitäts-	[Alma's literary mentor and closely associated with secessionist journal, *Ver Sacrum*; Mahler not

continued overleaf

51

Table 3.1 *continued*

Author	Title	Publication details	Designation, inscriptions, markings and other comments	Literature concordance
		Buchhandlung, 1905		favourable towards Burckhard, MAL: 19; Burckhard introduces Mahler to Hermann Bahr and Gerhart Hauptmann, EB: 83, MAL: 65; Mahler and Burckhard temperamentally opposed, MAL: 140–41]
	1. Bd. (1898–1901)		HMBS. Handwritten dedication on title page: 'Frau Alma Mahler in treuer [?] Freundschaft Burckhard'	
	2. Bd. (1902–1904)		HMBS	
	Quer durch Juristerei und Leben. Vorträge und Aufsätze	Wien und Leipzig: Wiener Verlag, 1905	HMBS. Handwritten dedication to Alma from Burckhard on first leaf	
	Im Paradiese. Komödie in 4 Akten	" 1907	HMBS. Black-ink handwritten dedication to Alma from Burckhard on first leaf	
	Die Insel der Seligen. Roman	Berlin: S. Fischer Verlag, 1909	HMBS. Handwritten dedication to Alma from Burckhard on second leaf dated '26.9.08' (*sic*)	
	Rat Schrimpf. Komödie in fünf Akten	Berlin: S. Fischer Verlag, 1905	HMBS on third leaf. Black-ink dedication to Alma from Burckhard on first leaf dated '29.4.05'	
	Gottfried Wunderlich. Roman	Wien und Leipzig: Wiener Verlag, 1906	HMBS. Dedication to Alma from Burckhard on title page	
	Das Lied von Tannhäuser. Ein romantisches Gedicht	Leipzig: Julius Klinkhardt, 1889	HMBS	
	Wahre Geschichten	Wien und Leipzig: Wiener Verlag, 1905	HMBS	

	Anton Friedrich Mitterwurzer	" 1906	HMBS	
	Trinacria. Roman	Berlin: S. Fischer Verlag, 1910	HMBS. 'M' written above stamp in pencil	
	Zur Reform des Irrenrechtes. Vier Zeitungsartikel	Wien: Manzsche k.u.k. Hof-Verlags- und Universitäts-Buchhandlung, 1904	HMBS	
	Quer durch das Leben. Fünfzig Aufsätze	Wien: F. Tempsky/Leipzig: G. Freytag, 1908	HMBS. Handwritten dedication to Alma from Burckhard dated '19.11.09'	
Lord BYRON	*Lord Byron. Eine Autobiographie nach Tagebüchern und Briefen.* Mit Einleitung und Erläuterung von Eduard Engel	Berlin: der Stuhr'schen Buchhandlung, 1876	HMBS	
Pedro CALDERÓN de la BARCA	*Calderons Größte Dramen.* Aus dem Spanischen übersetzt und mit nötigsten Erläuterungen versehen von Dr. F. Lorinser.	Freiburg: Herdersche Verlagshandlung, 1901	Blue-ink inscription on first leaf: 'F.W. Haus Mahler'	[Mahler saw *Richter von Zalamea* in the Vienna Burgtheater in May 1899, HB: 107]
	3. Bändchen: *Die Jungfrau des Heiligtums – Die Morgenröte in Copacabana*			

continued overleaf

53

Table 3.1 *continued*

Author	Title	Publication details	Designation, inscriptions, markings and other comments	Literature concordance
Giacomo CASANOVA	*Erinnerungen.* Übersetzt und eingeleitet von Heinrich Conrad Bd. I, II, III, IV, V, VI, VIII, IX	München & Leipzig: George Müller, 1907	HMBS Vol. 1 contains a newspaper photograph of a portrait of Casanova pasted on first leaf.	
Eduard CASTLE	*Lenau und die Familie Löwenthal. Briefe, Gespräche, Gedichte und Entwürfe.* 1. Buch: *Reisebriefe und Gespräche*	Leipzig: Max Hesses Verlag, 1906	HMBS	
Samuel Taylor COLERIDGE	*The Complete Works of Samuel Taylor Coleridge*, with an introductory essay upon his philosophical and theological opinions, ed. Prof. Shedd in 7 vols. Vol. V	New York: Harper & Brothers, 1856	Name 'John J. Huntingdon' in pencil on leaf following title page (previous owner?)	
Peter CORNELIUS	*Literarische Werke.* Erste Gesamtausgabe im Auftrage seiner Familie hrsg. 1. Bd. *Ausgewählte Briefe (l)* gesammelt und hrsg. von Carl Maria Cornelius	Leipzig: Druck und Verlag von Breitkopf und Härtel 1904	HMBS. Label inside front cover: 'Breitkopf und Härtel Buchbinderei Leipzig'	

	2. Bd. *Ausgewählte Briefe (II)* gesammelt und hrsg. von Carl Maria Cornelius	1905	HMBS	
Charles de COSTER	*Vlämisch Mären.* Übersetzt von Albert Wesselski	Leipzig: Insel Verlag, n.d.	HMBS	
Felix & Therese DAHN	*Walhall. Germanische Götter- und Heldensagen für Alt und Jung am deutschen Herd erzählt*	Kreuznach: Verlag von R. Voigtländer, 1888	ELAS. Calligraphic, black-ink inscription on second leaf: 'Alma und Gretl'	
Gabriel D'ANNUNZIO	*Feuer.* Roman	München: Hyperionsverlag, n.d. [Italian original written in 1900]	Ten-sided stamp with mountain landscape on first leaf. This stamp, with 'Alma Maria Mahler Haus Mahler Breitenstein' written across it in blue ink, also appears in a volume of Schlegel sisters letters published in 1914, indicating that the stamp probably originates from a period post-1911.	
	Das Martyrium des heiligen Sebastian. Ein Mysterium in fünf Handlungen	Berlin: Erich Reiss Verlag, n.d.	Ink and pencil inscription 'F.W.' on first leaf	
Richard DEHMEL	*Erlösungen. Gedichte und Sprüche*	Berlin: Schuster & Loeffler, 1898	HMBS. ELAS. Handwritten inscription on leaf following title page: 'A.___ [illegible but presumably Mahler] Mai 1900'. A passage from the book's introduction highlighted in pencil includes the following: 'solange einer in sein Kunstwerk noch verliebt ist, solange liebt er die Kunst noch nicht'. Some titles of poems have either – – or **x** (see App. for key to symbols). Many texts of poems are highlighted with l, s,) or L, including *Ansturm* (p. 136) and *Lobgesang* (pp. 146–47) which Alma would set to music. At the	MW 1997: 517 & 809 fn. 1; MW 1998: 294. Alma's diary comments, made a month after the dated inscription, refer to a Dehmel text she set to music. This was probably *Lobgesang*, which is specifically mentioned on 25 September 1900 (MW 1997: 560; 1998: 325). Other poems set by Alma: 'Die

continued overleaf

Table 3.1 *continued*

Author	Title	Publication details	Designation, inscriptions, markings and other comments	Literature concordance
			top right of the page containing the poem *Frühlingsglück* (p. 95) a five-note musical motif is notated, perhaps indicating further compositional plans. Above the poems *Eine Lebensmesse. Dichtung für Musik (Dem Componisten Conrad Ansorge)* (pp. 299–308) and *Nach einem Regen* (p. 309) the following is written in pencil: 'VORGETRAGEN VOM DICHTER AM 6 MÄRZ 1904'. App. (1)	Stille Stadt', 'Waldseligkeit', 'Ansturm'

The recitation must have taken place at or after the concert of Dehmel songs at the Ansorge-Verein (see HGF2: 564 fn. 54; HGE3: 97 fn. 57; MAL: 90) |
| *Aber die Liebe. Ein Ehemanns- und Menschenbuch* | | München: Druck und Verlag von Dr. E. Albert, 1893 | Stamp on last leaf: 'Jakob Dirnboeck's Buchhandlung & Antiquariat EDUARD BEYER Wien, I. Bez., Herrengasse Nr. 12 Ecke Strauchgasse'. Similar pencil highlighting and colours to that in previous example. Likewise, the poem *Jesus der Künstler*, pp. 57–60 has the following written above it: 'VORGETRAGEN VOM DICHTER AM 6 MÄRZ 1904'. | [ML: 21; LWW: 135; HGE3: 97] |
| *Lebensblätter. Gedichte und Anderes* | | Berlin: Verlag der Genossenschaft PAN, 1895 | ELAS. Label on last leaf: 'R. Lechner Wilh. Müller Wien Graben 31' | [ML: 21; LWW: 135; HGE3: 97]

[Mahler not favourably disposed towards Dehmel, MAL: 79. Contrasting evidence, LWW: 135; MAL: 90; HGE3: 98, 136–37. Anna Mahler gives her mother the complete works of Dehmel, July 1918 (ML: 96; ABL: 101). Alma reading *Zwei Menschen* to Mahler, |

56

	Sämtliche Romane und Erzählungen. Neueste und vollständige Ausgabe in sorgfältigster Verdeutschung von Paul Heichen.	Naumburg a/S.: Verlag von Albin Schirmer, n.d.		MAL: 120. Dehmel wrote for secessionist journal, *Ver Sacrum*]
Charles DICKENS	*Martin Chuzzlewhit* [*sic*], 1. Bd., 2. Bd., 3. Bd.		HMBS. Third volume has stamp upside down on last leaf	
	Bleak House, 1. Bd., 2. Bd., 3. Bd.		" In normal position on first leaf	
	David Copperfield, 1. Bd., 2. Bd.		"	
	Dombey und Sohn, 1. Bd., 2. Bd.		"	
	Klein [*sic*] *Dorrit*, 1. Bd., 2. Bd., 3. Bd.		"	
	Nicholas Nickleby, 1. Bd., 2. Bd.		"	
	Die Pickwickier, 1. Bd., 2. Bd.	[translator's note dated August 1894]	"	ABM: 22; HGE1: 335; HGF1: 515
	Unser gegenseitiger Freund, 1. Bd., 2. Bd., 3. Bd.		"	
	Der alte Karitätenladen, 1. Bd., 2. Bd.		"	
	Große Erwartungen, 1. Bd.		"	
	Ein Weihnachtslied in Prosa. Die Sylvester-Glocken. Das Heimchen am Herde		" Markings on pp. 139 & 140 of *Die Sylvester-Glocken*: blue-ink **s** (see App. for key to symbols) against opening text, 'Es gibt der Leute nicht viele … einen Gesang	

continued overleaf

Table 3.1 *continued*

Author	Title	Publication details	Designation, inscriptions, markings and other comments	Literature concordance
	Das Geheimnis Edwin Droods		anzustimmen' ['There are not many people … where it seems to chaunt, in its wild way'] HMBS in normal position on first leaf	
	Barnaby Rudge. 1. Bd., 2. Bd.		"	
	Londoner Skizzen. Schilderungen alltäglichen Lebens und alltäglicher Leute		"	
	Harte Zeiten		"	
	Der ungeschäftliche Reisende. Station Mugby (Gebrüder Barbox) und kleine Erzählungen		"	
	Aus zwei Millionstädten, 1. Bd.		"	
	Der Kampf des Lebens ferner: Zu Boden gesetzt – Der Verwunschene. Keine Durchfahrt. Neue Weihnachts-Geschichten		"	
	Oliver Twist	[translator's preface dated December 1892]	HMBS inverted on first leaf	
C. DIEBIG	*Das tägliche Brot*. Roman in zwei Bänden	Berlin: F. Fontane, 1901	HMBS	
	1. Bd.		"	
	2. Bd.			
Johan Peter ECKERMANN	*Gespräche mit Goethe in den letzten Jahren seines Lebens*	Berlin: Deutsche Bibliothek, n.d.		MAL: 52; EGR: 406; BW: 118; GMB: 137 & SLGM:

58

	1. Bd. 2. Bd.		A large number of pencil (and some light-blue and dark-blue ink markings) consisting of underlinings, marginal lines, question marks and occasional words (probably not in Mahler's hand). App. (2)	155 (1876 Frankfurt Brockhaus edn, vol. 2, p. 63); GMB: 370–71 & SLGM: 325–26 (1908 Jena Diederichs edn, vol. 2, pp. 2–5); NBLM (HGF1: 800, HGE1: 524)
Wolfram von ESCHENBACH	*Parzival*, neu bearbeitet von Wilhelm Hertz	Stuttgart: Verlag der J.G. Cotta'schen Buchhandlung Nachfolger, 1898	HMBS	MAL: 120. [Mahler's studies at the University of Vienna, winter semester, 1877–78 (Barham, 1998, vol. 2: 14 & 48)]
Herbert EULENBERG	*Kassandra*. Ein Drama	Berlin: Egon Fleischel, 1903	HMBS	
	Der natürliche Vater. Ein bürgerliches Lustspiel	Leipzig: Ernst Rowohlt Verlag, 1909		
	Ritter Blaubart. Ein Märchenstück in fünf Aufzügen	Berlin: Egon Fleischel, 1905	HMBS	
EURIPIDES	*Euripides' Werke* 11. Bändchen. *Hekabe*. Prüfenden und erklärenden Anmerkungen von J.A. Hartung	Leipzig: Verlag von Wilhelm Engelmann, 1850	Inscription on p. 55, possibly in Mahler's hand (underneath Hekabe's phrase 'Was fang' ich an? o könnt' ich sterben! weh, o weh!'): 'wohin wird es mit meinem Leben komen' (transcribed by Herta Blaukopf). See Plate 3.2	'Was ist mir aber "Hekuba"?' (Mahler in letter to Alma after seeing *Romeo and Juliet* in Mannheim, Jan. 1904, EGR: 180, MAL: 231)

continued overleaf

Table 3.1 *continued*

Author	Title	Publication details	Designation, inscriptions, markings and other comments	Literature concordance
Gustave FLAUBERT	*Salambo*. Ein Roman aus Alt-Karthago	Leipzig: Insel-Verlag, n.d.	HMBS	
Emil FREUND	*Scheckgesetz vom 3. April 1906 RGBl.* Nr. 84. In Versen von Dr. Emil Freund	Wien: Manzsche k.u.k. Hof-Verlags- und Univ.-Buchhandlung, 1907	HMBS. Handwritten dedication to Alma from Freund on title page dated '8 Juli [?], 1907'	
R.L. GARNER	*Die Sprache der Affen.* Übersetzt und hrsg. von Prof. Dr. William Marshall	Leipzig: Hermann Seemann Nachfolger, 1900	HMBS	
Théophile GAUTIER	*Fortunio, der Indier in Paris*, übersetzt von A. Hippolit	Breslau: Verlags Comtoir, 1840	Name 'F.H. Wildmokr' stamped on title page (previous owner?)	
Joseph Arthur, Comte de GOBINEAU	*Die Renaissance. Historische Scenen.* Deutsch von Ludwig Schemann	Straßburg: Verlag von Karl J. Trübner, 1904	HMBS	
Johann Wolfgang GOETHE	*Goethes Werke*, hrsg. im Auftrage der Großherzogin Sophie von Sachsen:	Weimar: Hermann Böhlaus Nachfolger, 1887–1919	No stamp or label unless otherwise marked	[A complete Goethe edition, MAL: 45; ABL: 30. Mahler's reference to a large-format Goethe edition, EGR: 406. Numerous references to *Faust* as Alma's favourite work, ABL: 12, MW 1997 & 1998, see below; unspecified reference, EGR: 325; MAL: 291]

continued overleaf

II/3 Naturwissenschaftliche Schriften. Zur Farbenlehre. Historischer Theil 1	1893	
II/8 Naturwissenschaftliche Schriften. Zur Morphologie (3)	1893	
II/9 Naturwissenschaftliche Schriften. Zur Naturwissenschaft überhaupt Mineralogie und Geologie (1)	1892	
II/10 Naturwissenschaftliche Schriften. Zur Naturwissenschaft überhaupt Mineralogie und Geologie (2)	1894	
II/11 Naturwissenschaftliche Schriften. Zur Naturwissenschaft. Allgemeine Naturlehre (1)	1893	
III/1 Tagebücher 1775–1787	1887	Inverted blue/purple-ink inscription on recto of penultimate leaf: 'Harriet Hayman 1907'
III/2 Tagebücher 1790–1800	1888	
III/3 Tagebücher 1801–1808	1889	
III/4 Tagebücher 1809–1812 [two copies]	1891	
III/5 Tagebücher 1813–1816	1893	
III/6 Tagebücher 1817–1818	1894	Label on recto of last leaf: 'K.U.K. HOF- u. UNIVERSITÄTS-BUCHHANDLUNG R. LECHNER WILH. MÜLLER WIEN, GRABEN 31'
III/7 Tagebücher 1819–1820	1895	
III/8 Tagebücher 1821–1822	1896	
III/10 Tagebücher 1825–1826	1899	
III/11 Tagebücher 1827–1828	1900	
III/12 Tagebücher 1829–1830	1901	

Table 3.1 *continued*

Author	Title	Publication details	Designation, inscriptions, markings and other comments	Literature concordance
	III/13 *Tagebücher 1831–1832*	1903		
	III/15 (1) *Tagebücher. Register M–S*	1919		
	III/15 (2) *Tagebücher. Register T–Z. Goethes Schriften. Nachträge und Berichtigungen*	1919		[Unspecified vols of letters, GMB: 368; SLGM: 324; Roller, 1922: 19; Kaplan, 1995: 22; correspondence with Schiller, HGE1: 524, HGF1: 800]
	IV/1 *Briefe. Frankfurt Leipzig Straßburg 1764–1771* [two copies]	1887		
	IV/2 *Briefe. Frankfurt Meßlar Schweiz 1771–1775* [two copies]	1887		
	IV/3 *Briefe. Weimar 1775–1778*	1888	Label on verso of first leaf: 'B. KARTMANN BUCHHANDLUNG ELBERFELD'	
	IV/4 *Briefe. Weimar Schweiz Weimar 1. Januar 1779– 7. November 1780* [two copies]	1889	Slip of paper inserted in first copy containing list of numbered letters, and words inserted next to numbers. Many pencil crosses, e.g. on p. 291 against: 'In meinem Kopf ists wie in einer Mühle mit viel Sängen wo zugleich geschroten, gemahlen, gewalckt und Oel gestoffen wird'. Label inside back cover of second copy: 'Max Lüttich Hofbuchbinder Weimar'	
	IV/5 *Briefe. Weimar 7. November 1780–30. Juni 1782* [two copies]	1889	Label inside back cover: 'Buchbinderei Max Lüttich Weimar'. Some pencil crosses in second copy	
	IV/6 *Briefe. Weimar 1. Juli 1782–31. December 1784* [two copies]	1890	Label inside front cover: 'Max Lüttich Hofbuchbinder Weimar'. Some pencil crosses in second copy	
	IV/7 *Briefe. 1. Januar 1785– 24. Juli 1786* [two copies,	1891	Label inside back cover: 'Max Lüttich Hofbuchbinder Weimar'	

second without binder's label]			
IV/8 Briefe. Italienische Reise August 1786 – Juni 1788 [two copies, second with binder's label]	1890	Label inside back cover: 'Max Lüttich Hofbuchbinder Weimar'. Some pencil crosses in first copy	MW 1997: 101, 102 & 105–6; 1998: 52 & 53; [HGF1: 79, earlier edn]
IV/9 Briefe. Weimar Oberitalien Schlesien Weimar 18. Juni 1788–8. August 1792	1891		
IV/10 Briefe. 9. August 1792–31. December 1795	1892		
IV/11 Briefe. 1796 [two copies]	1892		
IV/12 Briefe. 1797 [two copies, second without binder's label]	1893	Label inside back cover: 'Max Lüttich Hofbuchbinder Weimar'. Some pencil crosses and vertical lines in second copy	
IV/13 Briefe. 1798 [two copies, second with binder's label]	1893	Label inside back cover: 'Max Lüttich Hofbuchbinder Weimar'	
IV/14 Briefe. 1799	1893		
IV/15 Briefe. 1800. 1801	1894	Slip of paper inserted containing pencilled list of numbered letters, and words entered next to numbers	
IV/16 Briefe. 1802. 1803 [two copies]	1894	Some pencil crosses in first copy	
IV/17 Briefe. Anfang 1804–9. Mai 1805 [two copies]	1895		
IV/18 Briefe. Nachträge und undatirtes Register zu Bd. 9–18 [two copies, second with binder's label]	1895	Label inside back cover: 'MAX LÜTTICH HOFBUCHBINDER WEIMAR'	
IV/19 Briefe. 9. Mai 1805–Ende 1807	1895	Label inside back cover: 'Max Lüttich Hofbuchbinder Weimar'	

continued overleaf

Table 3.1 *continued*

Author	Title	Publication details	Designation, inscriptions, markings and other comments	Literature concordance
	IV/19 *Briefe. 9. Mai 1805– Ende 1807* [second copy]	1895	Text from letter no. 5098 to Cotta highlighted with I (see App. for key to symbols): 'Nach meiner Überzeugung soll die Kunst, wenn sie sich mit dem Schmerz verbindet, denselben nur aufregen, um ihn zu mildern und in höhere tröstliche Gefühle aufzulösen; und ich werde in diesem Sinne weniger das, was wir verloren haben, als das, was uns übrig bleibt, darzustellen suchen'	
	IV/20 *Briefe. Januar 1808– Juni 1809* [two copies, first with binder's label]	1896	Label inside back cover: 'Max Lüttich Hofbuchbinder Weimar'. Second copy: slip of paper inserted containing pencilled list of numbered letters, and words entered next to the numbers; date on reverse '16/XI/08'. Many pencil crosses, and a bracket against discussion of *Des Knaben Wunderhorn*. App. (3)	
	IV/22 *Briefe. Januar 1811– April 1812*	1901		
	IV/23 *Briefe. Mai 1812– August 1813*	1900		
	IV/25 *Briefe. 28. Juli 1814– 21. Mai 1815* [two copies]	1901		
	IV/26 *Briefe. 24. Mai 1815– 3. April 1816*	1902		
	IV/27 *Briefe. Mai 1816– Februar 1817* [two copies]	1903		
	IV/28 *Briefe. März– December 1817*	1903		
	IV/29 *Briefe. Januar– October 1818*	1904		
	IV/30 *Briefe. Nachträge und*	1905		

undatirtes Register zu Bd. 19–30	1905
IV/31 Briefe. 2. November 1818–25. August 1819	1906
IV/32 Briefe. 30. August 1819–22. April 1820	1905
IV/33 Briefe. 25. April–31. October 1820	1905
IV/34 Briefe. November 1820–Juni 1821	1906
IV/35 Briefe. Juli 1821–März 1822	1907
IV/36 Briefe. April 1822–März 1823	1906
IV/37 Briefe. April–December 1823	1906
IV/38 Briefe. Januar–October 1824	1907
IV/39 Briefe. November 1824–Juli 1825	1907
IV/40 Briefe. August 1825–März 1826	1907
IV/41 Briefe. April–December 1826	1907
IV/42 Briefe. Januar–Juli 1827 [two copies]	1908
IV/43 Briefe. August 1827–Februar 1828	1909
IV/44 Briefe. März–September 1828 [two copies]	1908
IV/45 Briefe. October 1828–Juni 1829 [two copies]	1908
IV/46 Briefe. Juli 1829–März 1830 [two copies]	

continued overleaf

Table 3.1 *continued*

Author	Title	Publication details	Designation, inscriptions, markings and other comments	Literature concordance
	IV/47 *Briefe. April–October 1830* [two copies]	1909	Slip of paper inserted containing pencilled list of numbered letters, and words entered next to the numbers	
	IV/48 *Briefe. November 1830–Juni 1831* [two copies]	1909	Slip of paper inserted containing pencilled list of numbered letters, and words entered next to numbers corresponding to pencil crosses in the text	
	IV/49 *Briefe. Juli 1831–März 1832* [two copies]	1909	Slip of paper inserted containing pencilled list of words corresponding to pencil crosses on pp. 62, 64, 65 & 95 and elsewhere in text	
	IV/50 *Briefe. Nachträge und undatirtes Register zu Bd. 31–50*	1912		
	2 *Gedichte (II)*	1888	Label inside back cover: 'Max Lüttich Hofbuchbinder Weimar'	Mahler's reference to 'Rastlose Liebe', EGR: 460; MAL: 338. 'Trilogie der Leidenschaft', MUB: 126; MUL: 122; 'Am jüngsten Tag', HGE2: 717. 'Wandrers Nachtlied', MW 1997: 9; 1998: 4.
	3 *Gedichte (III)*	1890		
	5 (1) *Gedichte*	1893		
	12 [various contents]	1892		
	13 (1) *Palaophron und Neoterpe; Vorspiel zur Eröffnung des Weimarischen Theaters am 19. September 1807; Was wir bringen; Prolog zu Eröffnung des Berliners Theaters am Mai 1821; Finale zu Johann von*	1894		MW 1997: 311 *(Götz von Berlichingen)*

Paris; Zu Wallensteins Lager; Nachspiel zu Ifflands Hagestolzen; Theaterreden; Götz von Berlichingen			
13 (2) Der Schutzgeist. Ein Schauspiel in fünf Aufzügen von A. von Kotzebue bearbeitet von Goethe	1901		
15 (2) Lesarten zu Faust	1888	Label inside back cover: 'Max Lüttich Hofbuchbinder Weimar'	
16 [large selection including:] Satyros oder der vergötterte Waldteufel	1894	Label inside back cover: 'Max Lüttich Hofbuchbinder Weimar'	
17 Der Triumph der Empfindsamkeit; Der Vögel; Der Groß-Coptha; Der Bürgergeneral	1894		
18 Die Aufgeregten; Das Mädchen von Oberlich; Unterhaltungen deutscher Ausgewanderten; Die guten Weiber; Novelle; Der Hausball; Reise der Söhne Megaprazons	1895	Label inside back cover: 'Max Lüttich Hofbuchbinder Weimar'	
20 Die Wahlverwandtschaften. Ein Roman	1892		MW 1997: 75; 1998: 40; NBLM (HGE1: 524; HGF1: 800)
21 Wilhelm Meisters Lehrjahre (I, II & III)	1898	Label inside back cover: 'Max Lüttich Hofbuchbinder Weimar'	MW 1997: 17; 1998: 10; NBL: 17; NBLE: 24 (earlier edn)
23 Wilhelm Meisters Lehrjahre (VII & VIII)	1901		

continued overleaf

67

Table 3.1 *continued*

Author	Title	Publication details	Designation, inscriptions, markings and other comments	Literature concordance
	42 *Literatur aus dem Nachlass*	1907		
	43 *Benvenuto Cellini (I)*	1890	Label inside back cover: 'Max Lüttich Hofbuchbinder Weimar'	
	46 *Winckelmann; Philipp Hackert*	1891		
	47 *Schriften zur Kunst 1788–1800*	1897		[Unspecified vol. NBLM (HGE1: 524; HGF1: 800)]
	48 *Schriften zur Kunst 1800–1816. Mit 8 Abbildungen*	1897		
	49 (1) *Schriften zur Kunst 1816–1832*	1898	Label inside back cover: 'Max Lüttich Hofbuchbinder Weimar'	
	49 (2) *Schriften zur Kunst 1816–1832*	1900		
	52 [untitled]	1911		
	[53 *Nachträge zu den Gedichten*	1914]		
	Goethes sämtliche Werke. Jubiläums-Ausgabe in 40 Bänden, hrsg. Eduard von der Hellen: (M.E.u.A.v. = mit Einleitung und Anmerkungen von)	Stuttgart & Berlin: J.G. Cotta'sche Buchhandlung Nachfolger, 1902–12 [Introduction dated 'Herbst 1902']	All HMBS unless otherwise indicated	Mahler's reference to a small-format Goethe edition, EGR: 406; same, as gift from Berliner, GMB: 392; SLGM: 321
	1 *Gedichte (I)*		Several markings in vols 1–4. App. (4, 5, 6, 7)	[Werfel reads and discusses Goethe's poetry March 1919, ML: 128. Mahler's reference to 'Rastlose Liebe', EGR: 460; MAL: 338. 'Trilogie der Leidenschaft', MUB: 126; MUL: 122, 'Am jüngsten Tag', HGE2: 717
	2 *Gedichte (II)*. M.E.u.A.v. Eduard von der Hellen			

3 *Gedichte (III)*. M.E.u.A.v. Eduard von der Hellen [includes Goethe's translation of *Veni Creator Spiritus*]		[Mahler's interest in *Veni Creator Spiritus*, MAL: 102]
4 *Gedichte (IV)*. M.E.u.A.v. Eduard von der Hellen		
5 *West-östlicher Divan*. M.E.u.A.v. Konrad Burdach	Some poems marked. App. (8)	EGR: 90, 492 (must refer to earlier edn) & 216
6 *Reineke Fuchs; Hermann und Dorothea; Achilleis.* M.E.u.A.v. Hermann Schreyer		
7 *Jugenddramen; Farcen und Satiren.* M.E.u.A.v. Albert Köster		
8 *Singspiele.* M.E.u.A.v. Otto Pinower		
9 *Zeitdramen; Gelegenheitsdichtungen.* M.E.u.A.v. Otto Pinower	‖ in pencil, p. vi of introduction (see App. for key to symbols)	MW 1997: 311
10 *Götz von Berlichingen.* M.E.u.A.v. Eduard von der Hellen		
11 *Dramen in Prosa.* M.E.u.A.v. Franz Muncker		
12 *Iphigenie auf Tauris; Torquato Tasso; Die natürliche Tochter.* M.E.u.A.v. Albert Köster	Horizontal pencil line, p. 240 in 5th Auftritt of *Die natürliche Tochter*	GMB: 272; SLGM: 244 (*Die natürliche Tochter*)
13 *Faust (I)*. M.E.u.A.v. Erich Schmidt		
14 *Faust (II)*. M.E.u.A.v. Erich Schmidt	Many varied pencil markings on pp. 256–84 of end of *Faust* Part II. App. (9)	[Mahler's increased and continued interest in *Faust*, MAL: 102–3. ML: 214. Decsey, 1911: 353; Walter,

continued overleaf

Table 3.1 *continued*

Author	Title	Publication details	Designation, inscriptions, markings and other comments	Literature concordance
				1912: 170; HGF2: 908 & 910 fn. 157; HGE3: 443 & fn. 188; Korngold, *Lebenserinnerungen* (Lebrecht, 1990b: 178). His many references to or quotes from *Faust*, e.g. EGR: 107, 493 (must be earlier edn), 180, 221, 388–90, 430; MAL: 82, 231, 243, 319–21, 332; GMB: 375; SLGM: 329. NBL: 34, 59, 168 & 198, NBLE: 62 & 178 (must be earlier edn); HGF2: 565 & 899–900 fn. 112; HGE3: 100 & 430 fn. 132. Alma and *Faust*, ABL: 12; MW 1997: 23, 40, 83, 159, 164, 265, 273, 276, 278, 279, 281, 306, 320, 328, 385, 461; 1998: 12–13, 82, 144, 146, 164, 171, 201, 252]
	15 *Dramatische Fragmente und Übersetzungen.* M.E.u.A.v. Otto Pinower			
	16 *Die Leiden des jungen Werthers; kleinere Erzählungen.* M.E.u.A.v. Max Herrmann			
	17 *Wilhelm Meisters Lehrjahre (I).* M.E.u.A.v. Wilhelm Greizenach		No stamp	MW 1997: 17; 1998: 10; NBL: 17; NBLE: 24 (earlier edn)
	18 *Wilhelm Meisters*		No stamp	

Item	Notes	References
Lehrjahre (II). M.E.u.A.v. Wilhelm Greizenach	No stamp. l against whole of p. xxx of introduction (see App. for key to symbols)	EGR: 406
19 Wilhelm Meisters Wanderjahre (I). M.E.u.A.v. Wilhelm Greizenach		
20 Wilhelm Meisters Wanderjahre (II). M.E.u.A.v. Wilhelm Greizenach	No stamp. Horizontal, dark-blue ink line, p. 25	NBL: 62 (Wanderjahre II, chapter 8)
21 Die Wahlverwandtschaften. M.E.u.A.v. Franz Muncker	No stamp	MW 1997: 75; 1998: 40; NBLM (HGE1: 524; HGF1: 800) (must be earlier edn)
22 Dichtung und Wahrheit (I). M.E.u.A.v. Richard M. Meyer		Mahler read this at least as early as 1884 (GMB: 54; SLGM: 78) and Alma by August 1898 (MW 1997: 101; 1998: 52)
23 Aus meinem Leben. Dichtung und Wahrheit (II). Was man in der Jugend wünscht, hat man im Alter die Fülle		
24 Dichtung und Wahrheit (III). M.E.u.A.v. Richard M. Meyer	Some vertical pencil lines, pp. 61–62	
25 Dichtung und Wahrheit (IV) und Anhang. M.E.u.A.v. Richard M. Meyer		
26 Italienische Reise (I). M.E.u.A.v. Ludwig Geiger	Pencil inscription on verso of first leaf: 'Alex H Jones 460 West 149 st Ap 61 NYC'. Several markings. App. (10)	ML: 214; MW 1997: 101, 102 & 105–6; 1998: 52 & 53; [HGF1: 79, earlier edn]
27 Italienische Reise (II). M.E.u.A.v. Ludwig Geiger	Several markings. App. (11)	
28 Kampagne in Frankreich;		

continued overleaf

Table 3.1 *continued*

Author	Title	Publication details	Designation, inscriptions, markings and other comments	Literature concordance
	Belagerung von Mainz. M.E.u.A.v. Alfred Dove			
	29 *Aus einer Reise in die Schweiz 1797; Am Rhein, Main und Necker 1814 und 1815.* M.E.u.A.v. Otto Heuer			
	30 *Annalen.* M.E.u.A.v. Oskar Walzel			
	31 *Benvenuto Cellini (I).* M.E.u.A.v. Wolfgang von Dettingen			
	32 *Benvenuto Cellini (II) und Anhang.* M.E.u.A.v. Wolfgang von Dettingen			
	33 *Schriften zur Kunst (I).* M.E.u.A.v. Wolfgang von Dettingen		Bookmark inserted: 'EX LIBRIS ALMA SCHINDLER'	[Unspecified vol., NBLM (HGE1: 524; HGF1: 800)]
	34 *Schriften zur Kunst (II).* M.E.u.A.v. Wolfgang von Dettingen			
	35 *Schriften zur Kunst (III).* M.E.u.A.v. Wolfgang von Dettingen			
	36 *Schriften zur Literatur (I).* M.E. u.A.v. Oskar Walzel			
	37 *Schriften zur Literatur (II).* M.E.u.A.v. Oskar Walzel			
	38 *Schriften zur Literatur (III).* M.E.u.A.v. Oskar Walzel			

39 *Schriften zur Naturwissenschaft (I)*. M.E.u.A.v. Max Morris			[Unspecified vols, BW: 117]
40 *Schriften zur Naturwissenschaft (II)*. M.E.u.A.v. Max Morris			
Goethes sämtliche Werke in 36 Bände. Mit Einleitung von Karl Goedeke	Stuttgart: Verlag der J.G. Cotta'sche Buchhandlung Nachfolger	No stamp	[Unspecified vols, BW: 117]
33 *Mineralogie und Geologie – Meteorologie – Zur Naturwissenschaft im allgemeinen – Naturwissenschaftliche Einzelheiten – Beiträge zur Optik*	1895	No stamp	
34 *Zur Farbenlehre (I)*. (Didaktischer und polemischer Teil)	1895	No stamp	
35 *Zur Farbenlehre (II)*. (Materialen zur Geschichte der Farbenlehre) – *Nachträge*	1895	No stamp	
36 *Anhang*	1896	No stamp	
Aus Goethes Tagebüchern. Ausgewählt und eingeleitet von Hans Gerhard Gräf	Leipzig: Insel Verlag, 1908	HMBS. –| against entry '1808 März. 15, Weimar – 171. Augusts Besorgnis wegen des Bandwurms glücklich gehoben. Mittags allein: Deutsche gehen nicht zu Grunde, wie die Juden, weil es lauter Individuen sind', p. 49 (see App. for key to symbols)	

continued overleaf

73

Table 3.1 *continued*

Author	Title	Publication details	Designation, inscriptions, markings and other comments	Literature concordance
	Goethes Unterhaltungen mit Friedrich Soret. Nach dem französischen Texte als eine bedeutend, vermehrte und verbesserte Ausgabe des dritten Teils der Eckermannschen Gespräche. Hrsg. von C.A.E. Burkhardt	Weimar: Hermann Böhlaus Nachfolger, 1905	HMBS	
	Pandora. Ein Festspiel	Leipzig: Insel-Bücherei Nr. 30, n.d.	HMBS. Pencil drawing of profile on first leaf; elaborate pencil drawing of lamp on last leaf, both typical of Alma	
	Faust II	Hammersmith: The Doves Press, June 1910 [from Weimar edn of 1899]	HMBS	
Iwan GONTSCHAROW	*Oblomov*. Roman in vier Teilen	Berlin: Verlag von Bruno Cassirer, 1910	HMBS	
Maxim GORJKI [GORKY]	*Die alte Isergil*. Gesammelte Erzählungen aus dem Russischen von Michael Feofanoff	Leipzig: Eugen Diederichs, 1902	HMBS	[EGR: 44; HGF2: 162, HGE2: 425]
	Im Gram	"	"	
	Gewesene Menschen	"	"	

Title	Place / Date	Notes	References
In der Steppe. Ausgewählte Erzählungen, übersetzt von Michael Feofanoff	„ 1904	„	
Einst im Herbst, übersetzt von Michael Feofanoff	„ 1901	HMBS inverted, inside back cover	
Frühlingsstimmen. Gesammelte Erzählungen aus dem Russischen von Michael Feofanoff	„ 1902	HMBS	
Nachtafyl. Scenen aus der Tiefe in vier Akten. Deutsch von August Scholz	München: Dr. J. Marchlewski & Co. Verlag nordischer und slavischer Litteratur, 1903	HMBS	
Christian Dietrich GRABBE *Sämtliche Werke in vier Bänden.* Hrsg. von Eduard Grisebach	Berlin: B. Behr's Verlag		[EGR: 153; MAL: 228]
1. Bd. *Dramatische Dichtungen: Herzog Theodor von Gothland – Nannette und Maria – Scherz, Satire, Ironie und tiefere Bedeutung – Marius und Sulla – Ueber die Shakspearo-Manie*	1902	ELAS. Label on last leaf: 'MANZSCHE k.u.k. HOF-VERLAGS & UNIVERS. BUCHHANDLUNG IN WIEN I. KOHLMARKT 20'	
2. Bd. *Don Juan und Faust – Die Hohenstausen I: Kaiser Friedrich*	1902	„	

continued overleaf

Table 3.1 *continued*

Author	Title	Publication details	Designation, inscriptions, markings and other comments	Literature concordance
	Barbarossa – II: Kaiser Heinrich der sechste – Aschenbrödel			
	3. Bd. *Napoleon – Barbarossa im Kyffhäuser – Rosciuszlo – Hannibal – Der Cid – Die Hermannsschlacht – Fragmente: Alexander der Große – Christus*	1902	" "	
	4. Bd. *Das Theater zu Düsseldorf – Recensionen einzelner Aufführungen – Vermischte kleinere Schriften – Briefe – Biographie*	1902	" " The name 'Werfel' in a letter of 1821 on p. 154 underlined and asterisked in pencil	
Eduard GRISEBACH (ed.)	*Chinesische Novellen. Die seltsame Geliebte. Das Juwelenkästchen. Deutsch, mit einer bibliographischen Notiz von Eduard Grisebach*	Stuttgart: J.G. Cotta'sche Buchhandlung Nachfolger, n.d. [A second title page has: Berlin: Verlag von E. & P. Lehmann, 1886. The penultimate leaf has: Gedruckt bei W. Drugulin in	HMBS	

76

continued overleaf

Robert HAMERLING	*Hamerlings Werke.* Volksausgabe in vier Bänden. Ausgewählt und hrsg. von Dr. Michael Maria Rabenlechner	[Leipzig und vollendet am 2. September 1883. indicating that the volume has been rebound]		
		Hamburg: Verlagsanstalt und Druckerei A.-G. (vorm. J.F. Richter), n.d. [foreword to vol. 1 dated 1900]		
	1. Bd.		ELAS	
	2. Bd.		"	
	3. Bd.		"	
	4. Bd.		"	
Knut HAMSUN	*Unter Herbststernen. Die Erzählung eines Wanderes.* Einzige berechtigte Übersetzung aus dem Norwegischen von Pauline Klaiber	Munich: Albert Langen Verlag für Litteratur und Kunst, 1908	HMBS	
	Neue Erde. Roman, übersetzt von Maria von Borch	Köln & Paris: Verlag von Albert Langen, 1894	ELAS	*[Neue Erde, Pan. Aus Lieutenant Thomas Glahns Papieren, or Redakteur Lynge, MW 1997: 605; 1998: 359]*
	Pan. Aus Lieutenant Thomas Glahns Papieren, übersetzt	Paris, Leipzig & München: Verlag	ELAS	

77

Table 3.1 *continued*

Author	Title	Publication details	Designation, inscriptions, markings and other comments	Literature concordance
	von Maria von Borch	von Albert Langen, 1899		
	Victoria	München: Albert Langen, Verlag für Litteratur und Kunst, 1911	HMBS	Alma had first read *Victoria* in April 1900 (MW 1997: 488; 1998: 273)
	Redakteur Lynge. Roman. Übersetzt aus dem Norwegischen von Maria von Borch	München, Leipzig & Paris: Verlag Albert Langen, 1898	ELAS	
	Hunger. Roman. Übersetzt aus dem Norwegischen von Maria von Borch	München: Verlag Albert Langen, 1901	ELAS	
Otto HARNACK	*Goethe in der Epoche seiner Vollendung. 1805–1832. Versuch einer Darstellung seiner Denkweise und Weltbetrachtung*	Leipzig: J.C. Hinrichs'sche Buchhandlung, 1901	HMBS	
Carl HAUPTMANN	*Einhart, der Lächler*. Roman 1. Bd.	Berlin: Marquardt, 1907	HMBS. Handwritten dedication: 'Gustav Mahler und Frau mit herzlichsten Abschiedsgrüßen Carl Hauptmann' (transcribed by Herta Blaukopf). Label inside back cover: 'Brentano's Booksellers & Stationers, NEW YORK'	[HGF3: 434]
Gerhart HAUPTMANN	*Die Jungfern vom Bischofsberg*. Lustspiel	Berlin: S. Fischer Verlag, 1907	HMBS	

Work	Publication	Provenance	Notes / references
Gesammelte Werke in sechs Bänden 1. Bd. Soziale Dramen 2. Bd. Soziale Dramen und Prosa 3. Bd. Familiendramen 4. Bd. Märchendramen	Berlin: S. Fischer Verlag, 1906	HMBS " " "	[Gustav and Alma saw *Der arme Heinrich* at the Vienna Burgtheater in 1904. Mahler saw *Rose Bernd* at the Burgtheater in 1904 and at the Deutsches Volkstheater in 1905, MAL: 67–68 & 83; HGF2: 444, 447, 566 & fns 67 & 68; HGE2: 701 & 705; HGE3: 102 & fns 78 & 79. Mahler meets Hauptmann; discussion of *Der versunkene Glocke*, MAL: 65–66; HGF2: 443–44; HGE2: 700–701]
5. Bd. *Florian Geyer* 6. Bd. *Märchendramen und Fragmentarisches*	Berlin: S. Fischer Verlag, 1894	" "	HGF2: 565; HGE3: 100
Das Friedensfest. Eine Familienkatastrophe	Berlin: S. Fischer Verlag, 1894		Mahler saw *Das Friedensfest* in January 1907, Berlin, and commented against its realism (EGR: 308 & 309–10; MAL: 285–86)
Griechische Frühling	Berlin: S. Fischer Verlag, 1908	Label inside front cover: 'EX LIBRIS Milton and Estelle Getz'	
Kaiser Karls Geisel. Ein Legendenspiel	Berlin: S. Fischer, 1908	HMBS	
Sketches for the play *Elga*, published in *Die neue*		HMBS. Handwritten dedication: 'Gustav Mahler in Freundschaft. Gerhart Hauptmann	

continued overleaf

Table **3.1** *continued*

Author	Title	Publication details	Designation, inscriptions, markings and other comments	Literature concordance
	Rundschau, XIVter Jg., Bd. 1, 1905 (see below under VARIOUS)		Weihnachten 1904'. Inscription in Hauptmann's hand (below the opening sentences of Der Ritter, 'Ich dachte schon, wir würden heute im Freien nächtigen müssen. So haben wir es ja noch gut genug getroffen', and next to the reply of Der Diener, 'Ja, Herr'): 'Ihr lieben, verehrten Kenner [?], wann kommt Ihr den[n] einmal zu uns herauf?' (transcribed by Herta Blaukopf). See Plate 3.3	
Lafcadio HEARN	*Kokoro. Mit Vorwort von Hugo von Hofmannsthal. Übersetzt von Berta Franzos*	Frankfurt a. M.: Literarische Anstalt, Rütten & Loenig, 1905	HMBS. The volume, a study of Japanese culture and history, contains the following chapters: 'Die Macht des Karma'; 'Götterdämmerung'; 'Die Idee der Präexistenz' (at the beginning of which the book string has been inserted); 'Der Geist der Japanischen Zivilisation'	
	IZUMO. Blicke in das unbekannte Japan. Übersetzt von Berta Franzos	" 1907	ELAS	
	Kyūshū. Träume und Studien aus dem neuen Japan	" 1908	HMBS	
	[Contents include: *Der Traum eines Sommertags Vom Ewig-Weiblichen Fragmente vom Leben und vom Tode*] Übersetzt aus dem Englischen von Berta Franzos. Buchschmuck von Emil Orlik [as in previous vols]			

Friedrich HEBBEL	*Sämtliche Werke.* Historisch-kritische Ausgabe besorgt von Richard Maria Werner	Berlin: B. Behr's Verlag. 1901–5		
	I. Abteilung:			
	1. Bd. *Dramen I (1841–1847) Judith. – Genoveva. – Der Diamant*	1901	HMBS. Label inside back cover: 'MANZSCHE k.u.k. HOF-VERLAGS & UNIVERS. BUCHHANDLUNG IN WIEN I. KOHLMARKT 20'	
	2. Bd. *Dramen II (1844–1851) Maria Magdalene. – Ein Trauerspiel in Sicilien. – Julia. – Herodes und Mariamne*	1901	" "	
	3. Bd. *Dramen III (1851–1858) Der Rubin. – Michel Angelo. – Agnes Bernauer. – Gyges und sein Ring. – Ein Steinwurf. – Verkleidungen*	1901	"	
	4. Bd. *Dramen IV (1862) Die Nibelungen*	1901	"	Alma first read *Die Nibelungen* in July 1898 (MW 1997: 82; 1998: 41), suggesting that this later published series may have been Mahler's
	5. Bd. *Dramen V (1830–1863) Fragments, Pläne*	1902	"	
	6. Bd. *Dramen VI. Demetrius (1864) – Gedichte I Gesamtausgabe. 1857. –*	1902	"	

continued overleaf

Table 3.1 continued

Author	Title	Publication details	Designation, inscriptions, markings and other comments	Literature concordance
	Gedichte II. Aus dem Nachlaß 1857–1863			
	7. Bd. Gedichte III. Nachlese 1828–1859	1903	"	"
	8. Bd. Novellen und Erzählungen. – Mutter und Kind. – Pläne und Stoffe (1835–1863)	1902	"	"
	9. Bd. Vermischte Schriften I (1830–1840). Jugendarbeiten. – Historische Schriften. – Reiseeindrücke I	1902	"	"
	10. Bd. Vermischte Schriften II (1835–1841). Jugendarbeiten II. – Reiseeindrücke II. – Kritische Arbeiten I (1839–1841)	1903	"	"
	11. Bd. Vermischte Schriften III (1843–1851). Kritischen Arbeiten II	1903	"	"
	12. Bd. Vermischte Schriften IV (1852–1863). Kritische Arbeiten III	1903	"	"
	II. Abteilung: 1. Bd. Tagebücher 1835–1839. Hamburg – Heidelberg – München – Hamburg. Nr. 1–1865	1905	HMBS	
	2. Bd. Tagebücher 1840–1844. Hamburg –	"	"	

82

	Kopenhagen – Hamburg – Paris – Rom. Nr. 1866–3277 3. Bd. *Tagebücher 1845–1854. Rom – Neapel – Rom – Wien. Nr. 3278–5265* 4. Bd. *Tagebücher 1854–1863. Marienbad – Wien. Kollektaneen, Gedanken und Erinnerungen. Nr. 5266–6347. Register*	" "		
	Ausgewählte Werke in sechs Bänden. Hrsg. und mit Einleitungen versehen von Richard Specht 1. Bd. *Biographische Einleitung – Gedichte – Mutter und Kind* 3. Bd. & 4. Bd. [in one volume] *Herodes und Mariamne – Michel Angelo – Agnes Bernauer – Gyges und sein Ring*	Stuttgart & Berlin: Verlag der J.G. Cotta'schen Buchhandlung Nachfolger, n.d.	HMBS. Handwritten dedication on second page: 'An Frau Alma Mahler … Wien, März, 1905 Richard Specht' HMBS	
Alfred von HEDENSTJERNA	*Allerlei Leute.* Bilder aus dem schwedischen Volksleben von Deutsch bearbeitet von Alexis von Krusenstjerna	Leipzig: Verlag von H. Haessel, 1892	ELAS. Illegible name 'A. ___ ' (not Mahler) possibly dated 1898, on first leaf	
Heinrich HEINE	*Sämtliche Werke in zwölf Bänden.* Mit einer	Stuttgart: Verlag der J.G.		MW 1997: 556; 1998: 323 [Mahler's early unfinished

continued overleaf

83

Table 3.1 *continued*

Author	Title	Publication details	Designation, inscriptions, markings and other comments	Literature concordance
	biographisch-litterarhistorischen Einleitung von Stephan Born	Cotta'schen Buchhandlung Nachfolger, n.d.		song settings of 'Es fiel ein Reif in der Frühlingsnacht' and 'Im wunderschönen Monat Mai'; Mahler's reported use of a Heine quote, HGF2: 371; HGE2: 629]
	1. Bd. *Buch der Lieder. – Poetische Nachlese*	[introduction to vol. 1 dated 'Juli, 1886']	ELAS	Heine's poetry is mentioned frequently as texts set to music by Alma (MW 1997 & 1998). Surviving setting: 'Ich wandle unter Blumen'
	3. Bd. *Romanzero. Poetische Nachlese*		"	
	Heine und die Frau. Ausgewählte Bekenntnisse und Betrachtungen des Dichters zusammengefügt von Karl Blanck	München: Eugen Rentsch Verlag, 1911	Blue-ink inscription on title page: 'F.W. Haus Mahler'	
Ernst Theodor Amadeus HOFFMANN	*Die Serapions-Brüder. Gesammelte Erzählungen und Märchen* [8. Bd., 9. Bd. & 10. Bd. of *Sämtliche Werke in fünfzehn Bänden*, hrsg. Eduard Grisebach in single volume. Includes *Lebensansichten des Katers Murr*]	Leipzig: Max Hesse's Verlag, 1900	ELAS	EGR: 44 (*Die Bergwerke von Falun* from *Die Serapions-Brüder*) & 71–72; MAL: 206 (*Rat Krespel* from *Die Serapions-Brüder*)
	Sämtliche Werke in fünfzehn Bänden, hrsg. Eduard Grisebach			[Mahler's general interest in Hoffmann, GA: 37; BW: 119; Stefan, 1912: 28; HGE1: 849

84

continued overleaf

Author	Title	Publication	Label / Markings	Notes
	1. Bd. *Biographische Einleitung. – Fantasiestücke in Callot's Manier*	"	ELAS. Label on inside cover: 'A. SCHÖNFELD BUCHHANDLUNG ANTIQUARIAT WIEN IX. UNIVERSITÄTSSTR. 8'	fn. 51; HGF1: 116 fn. 75; NBLM (HGE1: 580 & HGF1: 892); HGF2: 931–32; HGE3: 463]
	4. Bd. *Seltsame Leiden eines Theater-Direktors*	"	No label	
	11. Bd. *Prinzessin Brambilla.* Mit acht Abbildungen nach Callot	"	ELAS	
Hugo von HOFMANNSTHAL	*Die Gedichte und kleinen Dramen*	Leipzig: Insel-Verlag, 1911		[Wrote for secessionist journal, *Ver Sacrum*]
Friedrich HÖLDERLIN	*Hölderlins gesammelte Dichtungen in zwei Bänden mit biographischer Einleitung.* Hrsg. von Berthold Litzmann	Stuttgart: J.G. Cotta'sche Buchhandlung Nachfolger, n.d. [Litzmann's foreword is dated '30. September, 1895']		[Mahler's general interest in Hölderlin, EGR: 95 & 325; MAL: 215; GA: 37; Stefan, 1912: 28; request to be sent the 'complete works' (poems?) HGE1: 303; HGF1: 465. Must be earlier edn]
	1. Bd. *Gedichte*	"	ELAS. Several markings. App. (12)	NBL: 33 & 56; NBLE: 38 & 234 ('Der Rhein'). BW: 119 ('Patmos', 'Der Rhein', and later works]
	2. Bd. *Hyperion. Empedocles*	"	HMBS	
Korfiz HOLM	*Thomas Kerkhoven.* Roman	München: Albert Langen, 1906	HMBS	

85

Table 3.1 *continued*

Author	Title	Publication details	Designation, inscriptions, markings and other comments	Literature concordance
Arno HOLZ & Oskar JERSCHTE	*Traumulus*. Tragische Komödie	München: R. Piper, 1905		
Henrik IBSEN	*Sämtliche Werke*	Berlin: S. Fischer		
	1 Bd. *Gedichte*. Deutsch von Christian Morgenstern, Emma Klingenfeld, Max Bamberger. *Nachtrag zu den Gedichten*. Deutsch von Ludwig Fulda, Emma Klingenfeld, Max Bamberger. *Prosaschriften. Reden. Catilina*. Deutsch von Christian Morgenstern	1903	HMBS. Label on last leaf: 'MANZSCHE k.u.k. HOF-VERLAGS & UNIVERS. BUCHHANDLUNG IN WIEN I. KOHLMARKT 20'	[Alma was already reading Ibsen's poetry by October 1899 (MW 1997: 382 & 383; 1998: 201). Unspecified vol., MW 1997: 729; 1998: 447. General Mahler reference, EGR: 249; MAL: 236; GMB: 272; SLGM: 244. Mahler's reference to Löhr's article on *Catilina*, GMB: 198 & 444 fn. 85; SLGM: 193 & 422. This reference pre-dates publication of this edition]
	2. Bd. *Das Hünengrab. Die Herrin von Destrot*. Deutsch von Emma Klingenfeld. *Das Fest auf Solhang*. Deutsch von Christian Morgenstern. *Olaf Liljerans*. Deutsch von Emma Klingenfeld	1898	ELAS	
	3. Bd. *Die Helden auf Helgeland (Nordische Heerfahrt)*. Deutsch von Emma Klingenfeld. *Komödie der Liebe*.	n.d.	"	

86

Deutsch von Christian Morgenstern. *Die Kronprätendenten.* Deutsch von Adolf Strodtmann			
4. Bd. *Brand. Peer Gynt.* Deutsch von Christian Morgenstern	n.d.	"	EGR: 209; MAL: 239; GMB: 48 & 432; SLGM: 74 & 390–91 (*Peer Gynt*)
5. Bd. *Kaiser und Galiläer.* Deutsch von Paul Hermann	n.d.	"	
6. Bd. *Der Bund der Jugend.* Deutsch von Adolf Strodtmann. *Die Stützen der Gesellschaft.* Deutsch von Emma Klingenfeld. *Ein Puppenheim.* Deutsch von Marie von Borch	n.d.	"	
7. Bd. *Gespenster. Ein Volksfeind. Die Wildente.* Durchgesehen und eingeleitet von Georg Brandes, Julius Elias, Paul Schleuther	n.d.	"	
8. Bd. *Rosmersholm. Die Frau vom Meere. Hedda Gabler. Baumeister Solneß*	n.d.	HMBS	
9. Bd. *Klein Eyolf. John Gabriel Borkman. Wenn wir Toten erwachen*	n.d.	ELAS	Alma saw Ibsen's play *John Gabriel Borkman* at the Vienna Volkstheater in May 1900 (MW 1997: 508; 1998: 287)
10. Bd. *Briefe*, hrsg. mit Einleitung und Anmerkungen von Julius Elias und Halvdan Roht	n.d.	HMBS	

continued overleaf

Table 3.1 *continued*

Author	Title	Publication details	Designation, inscriptions, markings and other comments	Literature concordance
Karl Leberecht IMMERMANN	*Deutsche National-Literatur.* Historisch kritisch Ausgabe, hrsg. von Joseph Kürschner	Berlin und Stuttgart: Verlag von W. Spemann, n.d.		[MW 1997: 132]
	159. Bd. (II) Immermans [*sic*] Werke I (2). *Merlin. Tristan und Isolde. Goethe und die fallschen Wanderjahre*, hrsg. Prof. Dr. Max Koch		HMBS	
Jens Peter JACOBSEN	*Marie Grubbe.* Aus dem Dänischen übersetzt von J.D. Ziegeler-Glücksburg	Halle: Druck und Verlag von Otto Hendel, n.d.	ELAS	
	Frau Marie Grubbe. Bilder aus dem 17. Jahrhundert	Leipzig: Verlag von Otto Janke, n.d.		
JEAN PAUL (RICHTER)	*Jean Paul in einer Auswahl von Herbert Eulenberg*	Berlin: Deutsche Bibliothek, n.d.	Blue-ink inscription on first leaf: 'F.W. Haus Mahler'	[Mahler's enthusiasm for, knowledge of, and references to Jean Paul, HGF1: 79; HGF2: 931; HGE3: 463; EGR: 208; MAL: 110, 238; GMB: 58, 286 & 434 fn. 18; SLGM: 82 & 254; NBL: 32; NBLE: 37; TV: 114; GA: 37; Stefan, 1912: 28. Unspecified vol., GMB: 39 & 144; SLGM: 64 & 159. *Titan*, Karbusicky, 1978: 93–94; *Titan* and *Siebenkäs*, BW: 119; *Flegeljahre*, BW:
	Levana oder Erzielehre	Leipzig: Druck und Verlag von Phillip Reclam jun., n.d.	HMBS	
	Jean Pauls sämtliche Werke	Berlin: G. Reimer, 1841	Blue-ink inscription on first leaf: 'F.W.'	
	9. Bd.			
	Jean Pauls Werke, hrsg. Rudolf Wultmann	Leipzig und Wien:		

		Bibliographisches Institut, n.d.	HMBS		[119–20; UWO[31]]
	4. Bd. [includes *Vorschule der Ästhetik*]	Bibliographisches Institut, n.d.	HMBS		[119–20; UWO[31]]
Johannes B. JENSEN	*Das Rad.* Roman	Berlin: S. Fischer Verlag, 1908	HMBS		
Georg KAISER	*Die jüdische Witwe.* Biblische Komödie	Berlin: S. Fischer Verlag, 1911			
Gottfried KELLER	*Das Sinngedicht*, Novellen. – *Sieben Legenden*	Berlin: Verlag von Wilhelm Hertz, 1900	ELAS.	*Das Sinngedicht* is a cyclic frame story.	MW 1997: 716. Mahler, the 4th Symphony and *Sieben Legenden*, Korngold, *Lebenserinnerungen* (Lebrecht, 1990b: 175) [unspecified vol., MW 1997: 605; 1998: 359; probably *Das Sinngedicht*; Alma reading Keller with Zemlinsky, c. March 1901, HGF2: 168]
	Der grüne Heinrich I & II, Roman	" 1899			
	Gesammelte Gedichte I, 7th edn [Gesammelte Werke, 9. Bd.]	" 1891	No label. Several markings App. (13)		
	Gesammelte Gedichte I, 13th edn [Gesammelte Werke, 9. Bd.]	" 1900	ELAS		
	Gesammelte Gedichte II	" 1889	No label		

31 Mahler wrote to his sister Justine at the end of August 1891: 'I congratulate you on your reading of Jean Paul – it is a hard crust, and happy is he who can digest it' ['Zu Deiner Jean-Paul Lektüre gratuliere ich – es ist harte Krust, und wol dem, der es verdauen kann']. The author is grateful to Stephen McClatchie for providing this information.

Table 3.1 *continued*

Author	Title	Publication details	Designation, inscriptions, markings and other comments	Literature concordance
	[Gesammelte Werke, 9. Bd.]	" 1900	ELAS	
	Gesammelte Gedichte II, 13th edn [Gesammelte Werke, 9. Bd.]	" 1899	"	
	Martin Salander, Roman [Gesammelte Werke, 8. Bd.]	" 1900	"	
	Züricher Novellen, 24th edn [Gesammelte Werke, 6. Bd.]	" 1900	"	
	Der grüne Heinrich III [Gesammelte Werke, 2. Bd.]	" 1900	"	
	Die Leute von Seldwyla. Erzählungen. I [Gesammelte Werke, 4. Bd.]	" 1900	"	
	Gesammelte Werke 2. Bd.	" 1900	No label	
	Gesammelte Werke 3. Bd.	" 1900	ELAS	
	Gesammelte Werke 4. Bd.	" 1900	No label	
	Gesammelte Werke 5. Bd.	" 1900		
Rudyard KIPLING	*Im Dschungel*, übersetzt von Curt Abel-Musgrave [vol. 6 of series *Die Welt der Fahren und Abenteuer*]	Freiburg: Friedrich Ernst Fehlenfeld, 1898	HMBS. Handwritten name on first leaf: 'Dr. Theobald Pollak'	
Heinrich von KLEIST	*Werke*, im Verein mit Georg Minde-Pouet und Reinhold Steig, hrsg. von Erich Schmidt. Kritisch	Leipzig und Wien: Bibliographisches Institut, n.d.		[UWO: Mahler refers to the study of Kleist by Otto Brahm (1884)[32]]

durchgesehene und erläuterte Gesamtausgabe [from the series *Meyers Klassiker-Ausgaben* hrsg. von Prof. Dr. Ernst Elster]		HMBS		
2. Bd. *Penthesilea*. Ein Trauerspiel, bearbeitet von Erich Schmidt		"		
3. Bd. *Prinz Friedrich von Homburg*, bearbeitet von Erich Schmidt		"		
4. Bd. *Kleinere Gedichte*, hrsg. von E. Schmidt. *Kleinere Schriften*, hrsg. von R. Steig		"		
5. Bd. *Briefe*, bearbeitet von Georg Minde-Pouet				
Erzählungen	Berlin: Deutsche Bibliothek, n.d.			
Friedrich Gottlob KLOPSTOCK				
Oden und Epigramme	Leipzig: Phillip Reclam jun., n.d.			
Klopstocks Werke. Der Göttinger Dichterbund. [from the series *Bibliothek deutscher Klassiker für Schule und Haus.* Begründet von Dr. Wilhelm Lindemann.	Freiburg i. B.: Herdersche Verlagshandlung, 1907		The entire text of Mahler's 'Aufersteh'n' as used in the final movement of the Second Symphony is written in purple ink by two different hands (possibly Alma's and Franz Werfel's) over the printed version of Klopstock's original on pp. 336–37. See Plate 3.4	[GMB: 137; SLGM: 155]

continued overleaf

32 Mahler wrote to his sister Justine on 31 August 1893: 'I have already bought and read *Kleist* by Brahm. A wonderful book, like his *Schiller*!' ['*Kleist* von Brahm habe ich bereits gekauft und gelesen. Ein prachtvolles Buch, wie sein Schiller!']. The author is grateful to Stephen McClatchie for providing this information.

Table 3.1 *continued*

Author	Title	Publication details	Designation, inscriptions, markings and other comments	Literature concordance
	Zweite Auflage hrsg. von Prof. Dr. Otto Hellinghaus. 1. Bd.]			
A. KUTSCHBACH	*Lassalles Tod.* Im Anschluß an die Memoiren der Helene von Racowitza: Meine Beziehungen zu Ferdinand Lassalle	Chemnitz: Verlag von Ernst Schmeitzner, 1880	HMBS	
Jules LAFORGUE	*Sagenhafte Sinnspiele.* Mit einer Vorrede von Maurice Maeterlinck. Mit unbekannten Briefen an Max Klinger, Théophile Ysaye und Klary. Verdeutscht und eingeleitet von Paul Wiegler	Stuttgart: Axel Juncker Verlag, 1905	Blue-ink inscription on first leaf: 'F.W. Haus Mahler'	
Else LASKER-SCHÜLER	*Der siebente Tag.* Gedichte	Berlin: Verlag des Vereins für Kunst, 1905	Some pages uncut	
Ninon von LENCLOS	*Der Ninon von Lenclos Leben und Briefe nebst den Briefen der Babet aus dem Französischen übersetzt*	Leipzig: in der Weidmannischen Buchhandlung, 1755	Black-ink inscription on title page: 'Felix Neumann 10 Februar 1877' [previous owner?]. Some pencil and ink underlinings, unknown source	
Christian und Friedrich LEOPOLD Grafen zu Stolberg	*Gesammelte Werke* 13. Bd.	Hamburg: Perthes und Besser, 1823		

Richard LIBIGER	*Gedichte*	Photocopy on rice paper dated 'Dezember 1906'		
Detlev von LILIENCRON	*Poggfred.* Kunterbuntes Epos in 12 Cantussen	Berlin: Verlag von Schuster & Loeffler, 1896	ELAS	ML: 21 [Liliencron wrote for secessionist journal, *Ver Sacrum*]
Hermann LINGG	*Gedichte*	Stuttgart: Verlag der J.G. Cotta'schen Buchhandlung, 1866	Blue-ink inscription on first leaf: 'F.W.'	
Siegfried LIPINER	*Adam. Vorspiel zur Trilogie Christus*	Handwritten bound copy	Located in Box 12 of Alma Mahler-Werfel Collection, separate from book collection. Title in purple ink; 'von Siegfried Lipiner' written below in pencil; name 'Siegfried Lipiner' on recto of first leaf in pencil. Pencil handwriting is different from that in ink.	GMB: 263–5, 272 & 273; SLGM: 236–7, 243 & 244; NBLM (Barham, 1998: 235 fn. 31, HGF1: 524, HGF1: 800). [Wider implications of Mahler's relationship with Lipiner, Barham, 1992 & 1998]
J.C. LOBE	*Consonanzen und Dissonanzen. Gesammelte Schriften aus älterer und neuerer Zeit*	Leipzig: Baumgärtner's Buchhandlung, 1869	HMBS. ELAS	
Rudolph LOTHAR	*Salbnaturen.* Ein Wiener Roman	Leipzig: Georg Heinrich Meyer, 1899		[Mahler interviewed by Lothar in 1903, EGR: 174]
Otto LUDWIG	*Ausgewählte Studien und kritische Schriften*	Leipzig: Max Hesse's Verlag, n.d.	ELAS. Some pencil lines against text	

continued overleaf

93

Table 3.1 *continued*

Author	Title	Publication details	Designation, inscriptions, markings and other comments	Literature concordance
Maurice MAETERLINCK	*Der Blaue Vogel*. Ein Märchenspiel in fünf Aufzügen und zwölf Bildern	Berlin: Erich Reiss Verlag, 1910 [4th edn]	HMBS	[EGR: 66. Mahler's negative comments, EGR: 107 & 146; MAL: 225]
	Aglavaine und Selysette. Drama in fünf Akten	Leipzig: Eugen Diederichs, 1900	"	
	Théâtre II. Pelléas et Mélisande. Alladine et Palomides. Intérieur. La Mort de Tintagiles	Bruxelles/Paris: P. Lacomblez/Per Lamm, 1902	HMBS. ELAS	MW 1997: 568; 1998: 331 (*La Mort de Tintagiles*). Comments made in October 1900. Therefore the text must have been that which appeared in *Ver Sacrum* II, 1899 Heft 6, trans. Oppeln-Bronikowski. See MW 1997: 812 fn. 21; 1998: 329 fn. 13
	Das Leben der Bienen	Leipzig: Eugen Diederichs, 1901	HMBS	
	Das Wunder des Heiligen Antonius. Satirische Legende in zwei Aufzügen	Jena und Leipzig: Eugen Diederichs, 1904	HMBS	
	Les Aveugles (L'Intruse – Les Aveugles)	[8th edn] Bruxelles: Paul Lacomblez, 1898	HMBS. Black-ink inscription on top right of title page: 'J. Perrin'	Reference to Perrin and Maeterlinck, EGR: 146, 147 & 496
Heinrich MANN	*Zwischen den Rassen*. Roman	München: Albert Langen, Verlag für Litteratur und Kunst, 1907	HMBS. Some light-blue ink (possibly ballpoint) underlining pp. 145–51	

Author	Title	Publisher	Marks	Notes
Thomas MANN	*Tristan.* Sechs Novellen von sechste Auflage	Berlin: S. Fischer Verlag, 1906	HMBS	[Not the book given to Mahler by Mann in 1910, MAL: 342]
Josef MAUTHNER	*Gedichte*	Berlin: Concordia Deutsche Verlags-Anstalt, 1896	ELAS. Label on second leaf: 'BUCHBINDEREI HÜBEL & DENCK LEIPZIG'	
Conrad Ferdinand MEYER	*Hüttens letzte Tage* [Dichtung]	Leipzig: Verlag von H. Haessel, 1901		[Mahler knew very little of Meyer's poetry (NAMR, 11 (March 1983): 7]
	Angela Borgia [Novelle]	" 1900	ELAS	
	Die Versuchung das Pescara [Novelle]	" 1900	ELAS [a frame story]	
	Der Heilige [Novelle]	" 1901	"	
	Jürg Jenatsch [Bündnergeschichte]	" 1900	"	
	Gedichte	" 1900	"	Mahler given vol. of Meyer's poetry by Josefine von Winter, October 1910 (NAMR, 11 (March 1983): 7)
	Engelberg [Eine Dichtung]	" 1900	"	
Günther MÜRR	*Der Entrückte*	Hamburg: Kugel-Verlag, n.d.	Blue-ink inscription 'F.W. Haus Mahler' on first leaf	
Edgar Allan POE	*Werke in zehn Bänden*, hrsg. von Hedda & Arthur Moeller-Bruck	Minden: I.W. & J.C.C. Bruns' Verlag, n.d.		[Alma reading Poe with Zemlinsky, c. March 1901, HGF2: 168]
	1. Bd. *Leben und Schaffen* 3. Bd. *Heureka und Anderes* & 4. Bd. *William Wilson* [in single vol.]		HMBS "	

95

continued overleaf

Table 3.1 *continued*

Author	Title	Publication details	Designation, inscriptions, markings and other comments	Literature concordance
	5. Bd. *Der Geist der Bösen. Der Novellen zweite Reihe* 7. Bd. *Hans Pfaalls Mondfahrt. Der Novellen vierte Reihe* 9. Bd. *Der Teufel im Glockenstuhl. Der Humoresken erste Reihe*		" " "	
L. PRELLER	*Griechische Mythologie* 1. Bd. *Theogonie und Goetter*	Leipzig: Weidmannsche Buchhandlung, 1854	Slip of paper inserted in front of book has 'Mahler' written in pencil	
Helene von RACOWITZA [Frau von SCHEWITSCH]	*Von Anderen und mir. Erinnerungen aller Art*	Berlin: Verlag von Gebrüder Paetel, 1909	HMBS. 'M' written on title page	
Hans REINHART	*Der Tag*. Mit vier holzschnitten und Buchumschlag von Karl Hofer. 1899-1903	Ostern: Gedruckt im Auftrage des Verfassers, 1903	Black-ink dedication: 'Herrn Gustav Mahler zum Schöpfer der Symphonie Nr. 2 in C-moll (die ich am 15. Juni 1903 in Basel zum e. male hörte) in grosser und herzlicher Verehrung zugeignet Zürich, den 17. Juni 1903 Hans Reinhart'.	
Gustav RENKER	*Der See*. Roman	Klagenfurt: Eduard-Kaiser-Verlag, n.d.	Blue-ink dedication on title page: 'Frau Alma Mahler mit ehr____ [?] Weihnachtswunschen Gustav Renker'	
Fritz REUTER	*Fritz Reuters Meisterwerke*	Stuttgart: Verlag von Robert Lutz, n.d. [Translator's		

96

		introduction dated Jan. 1905]	HMBS	Alma was first read this by her mother in August 1898 (MW 1997: 98-9 & 104), suggesting this later published series may have been Mahler's
	I *Aus der Franzosenzeit. Wie ich zu'ner Frau kam.* Übertragen von Heinrich Conrad		"	
	II *Aus meiner Festungszeit*		"	
	III *Aus meiner Stromzeit (1)*		"	
	IV *Aus meiner Stromzeit (2)*		"	
	V *Aus meiner Stromzeit (3)*		"	
	VI *Dörchläuchting*			
Gabriele REUTER	*Aus guter Familie. Leidensgeschichte eines Mädchens.* In zwei Theilen	Berlin: S. Fischer Verlag, 1898	ELAS	MW 1997: 363
	Wunderliche Liebe	" 1905	HMBS 'inside out' and correct way superimposed	
William RITTER	*Leurs Lys et Leurs Roses.* Roman	Paris: Société du Mercure de France, 1903	HMBS. Undated, handwritten, black-ink dedication from Ritter to Gustave Mahler: 'A Monsieur Gustave Mahler dont la quatrième symphonie décrite aux premières pages d'un de mes prochains romans est devenue la hautise du cerveau passionnement épris de son admiration William Ritter Biedersteinerstrasse 10a München-Schwabing'. See Plate 3.5	

continued overleaf

97

Table 3.1 *continued*

Author	Title	Publication details	Designation, inscriptions, markings and other comments	Literature concordance
Hermann ROLLETT	*Die Goethe-Bildnisse*	Wien: Wilhelm Braumüller, 1883	ELAS	
Richard SCHAUKAL	*Kapellmeister Kreisler. Dreizehn Vigilien aus einem Künstlerdasein. Ein imaginäres Porträt*	München und Leipzig: Georg Müller, 1906	HMBS. Handwritten dedication: 'Gustav Mahler im Zeichen Kreislers Richard Schaukal Wien 1. Mai 6'. See Plate 3.6	
	Tage und Träume. Gedichte	Leipzig: Verlag von C.F. Tiefenbach, 1899	Handwritten dedication: 'An Director Mahler Richard Schaukal'.	
Johannes SCHLAF	*Der Prinz.* Roman in zwei Bänden	München & Leipzig: Georg Müller, 1908		
	1. Bd. & 2. Bd.		Both HMBS	
	Die Nonne. Novellen	Wien & Leipzig: Wiener Verlag, 1905		
Adele SCHOPENHAUER	*Tagebücher*	Leipzig: Insel-Verlag, 1909		
	1. Bd.		HMBS	
	2. Bd.		"	
Madame de SÉVIGNÉ	*Correspondances.* Précédées d'observations littéraires d'après M. Sainte-Beuve	Paris: les belles Éditions, n.d.	Some words in pencil in margin next to corresponding underlined French words in text, not in Mahler's hand	
Heinrich SIENKIEWICZ	*Ohne Dogma.* 1. Bd.	Stuttgart, Leipzig, Berlin & Wien:	ELAS	MW 1997: 144; 1998: 71

98

continued overleaf

[Heinrich SPIERO]	Gerhard Hauptmann	Deutsche Verlags-Anstalt, 1892 Bielefeld & Leipzig: Verlag von Velhagen & Klasing, n.d.	Stamped: 'GUCKI MAHLER WIEN 1., Elisabethstrasse 22'.']	
Carl SPITTELER	Olympischer Frühling. Epos	Leipzig: Eugen Diederichs, 1900	ELAS	
Franz STELZHAMER	Characterbilder aus Oberoesterreich. Mit einem Geleitspruch von Gerhart Hauptmann	Wien und Leipzig: Wiener Verlag, 1906	HMBS. Handwritten dedication: 'Frau Director Mahler herzlichst 26.10.05 M Burckhard [?]' (transcribed by Herta Blaukopf)	
STENDHAL	Ausgewählte Werke			[EGR: 44; HGF2: 162, HGE2: 425]
	1. Bd. Rot und Schwarz, übertragen von Friedrich von Oppeln-Bronikowski	Leipzig: Eugen Diederichs, 1901	ELAS	
	2. Bd. Rot und Schwarz, übertragen von Friedrich von Oppeln-Bronikowski	"	"	
	3. Bd. Über die Liebe, übertragen von Arthur Schurig	Jena: Eugen Diederichs, 1907	HMBS. Many pencil and ink marginal markings: I and II (see App. for key to symbols)	
	6. Bd. Die Kartause von Parma (I), übertragen von Arthur Schurig	Jena: Eugen Diederichs, 1906	HMBS	
	7. Bd. Die Kartause von Parma (II), übertragen von Arthur Schurig	"	HMBS. Blue/black-ink dedication on second leaf: 'Auch ein Roman zum 31.8.10 Walter' [Gropius]	
Adalbert STIFTER	Sämtliche Werke.	Prag: J.G.	HMBS	

99

Table 3.1 *continued*

Author	Title	Publication details	Designation, inscriptions, markings and other comments	Literature concordance
	1. Bd. *Studien*, hrsg. August Sauer [from the series *Bibliothek deutscher Schriftsteller aus Böhmen*. Hrsg. im Auftrage der Gesellschaft zur Förderung deutscher Wissenschaft, Kunst und Literatur in Böhmen. Bd. XI]	Calve'sche k.u.k. Hof- und Universitäts-Buchhandlung, 1904		
Gottfried von STRASSBURG	*Tristan und Isolde*, neu bearbeitet von Wilhelm Hertz	Stuggart & Berlin: J.G. Cotta'sche Buchhandlung Nachfolger, 1901	ELAS. Inscription on verso of first leaf: 'Meiner Alma zum 31. August 190[2?] Mie' (= 'Tante Mie', Marie Henneberg, wife of the graphic artist and photographer Hugo Henneberg, who, together with her husband, developed a close friendship with Alma's family). Bookmark with 'EX LIBRIS ALMA SCHINDLER' inserted.	MAL: 120
August STRINDBERG	*Totentanz*	Berlin und Leipzig: Verlag von Hermann Seemann Nachfolger, n.d. [4th edn] [first published in original language, 1901]	HMBS	[Farewell student gathering led by Schoenberg and Zemlinsky rates Strindberg above Mahler's preferred Dostoyevsky, 1907, MAL 126]
Henry D. THOREAU	*Walden. Oder Leben in den Wäldern*	Jena und Leipzig: Verlegt bei Eugen Diederichs, 1905		

continued overleaf

Author	Title	Publisher	Code	Notes
Ludwig TIECK	_Ludwig Tieck's Schriften._ 5. Bd. _Phantasus (II)_	Berlin: G. Reimer, 1828		Faded blue-ink inscription on first leaf: 'F.W. Haus Mahler'
Claude TILLIER	_Mein Onkel Benjamin._ Deutsch von Paul Heichen	Berlin: Verlag von Neufeld & Lenius, n.d.		
	Mein Onkel Benjamin	Leipzig: Insel-Verlag, n.d.	HMBS	
Leo TOLSTOY	_Briefe 1848-1910_, hrsg. P.A. Sergejenko	Berlin: J. Ladyschnikow Verlag, 1911		[Mahler's references to _The Kreutzer Sonata_, ML: 39; HGF2: 636; HGE3: 165; _A Confession_, MAL: 238; _Resurrection_, NBL: 153; unspecified vol. and general comment, EGR: 206; MAL: 236]
Julius von der TRAUN (pseudonym of Alexander Schindler, Alma's great-uncle)	_Excursionen eines Österreichers 1840-1879_ 1. Bd.	Leipzig: Verlag von Duncker & Humblot, 1881	ELAS	
Iwan TURGÉNJEW	_Ausgewählte Werke_ 1. Bd. _Väter und Söhne_	Mitau: E. Behre's Verlag, 1902	HMBS	
	2. Bd. _Eine Unglückliche. Das Abenteuer des Lieutenants Tergunow. Ein Briefwechsel. Assia._ Vier Novellen	" 1881	"	

101

Table 3.1 *continued*

Author	Title	Publication details	Designation, inscriptions, markings and other comments	Literature concordance
	3. Bd. *Rudin. Drei Begegnungen. Mumu. Drei Novellen*	Hamburg & Mitau: E. Behre's Verlag, 1884	"	
	4. Bd. *Das adelige Nest. Drei Portaits. Zwei Novellen*	" 1884	"	
	5. Bd. *Visionen. Helene. Zwei Novellen*	" 1884	"	
	6. Bd. *Ein König Lear des Dorfes. Frühlingsfluthen. Zwei Novellen*	Mitau: E. Behre's Verlag, 1901	"	
	8. Bd. *Skizzen aus dem Tagebuch eines Jägers (I)*	" 1902	"	
	9. Bd. " " (II)	" 1902	"	
	10. Bd. *Neu-Land. Ein Roman*	" 1877	"	
	11. Bd. *Stilleben. Faust. Die erste Liebe. Drei Novellen*	Hamburg & Mitau: E. Behre's Verlag, 1881	"	
	12. Bd. *Zwei Freunde. Eine seltsame Geschichte. Yakow Pasinkoff. Tagebuch eines Ueberflüssigen. Hamlet und Don Quichotte*	" 1884	"	
Johann Ludwig UHLAND	*Uhlands gesammelte Werke in sechs Bänden.* Mit einer biographisch-litterarhistorischen Einleitung von Hermann Filcher	Stuttgart: Verlag der J.G. Cotta'schen Buchhandlung Nachfolger, n.d.		[MW 1997: 605; 1998: 359. Poem 'Weihefrühling' provided title for secessionist journal, *Ver Sacrum*]
	1. Bd. *Gedichte*		ELAS	

102

continued overleaf

	3. Bd. *Sagenforschungen* 5. Bd. *Zur deutschen Poesie und Sage*		" "	
[URCHLICKÝ, SOVA & BŘEZINA]	*Tschechische Anthologie.* Übertragen von Paul Eisner. Österreichische Bibliothek Nr. 21	Leipzig; Insel Verlag, n.d. [editor's note is dated 1917]		Several haphazard stamps 'GUSTAV MAHLER WIEN' and pencil drawings of buildings and a church on first leaf. Geometrical pencil drawings on inside back cover and previous leaf. Some blue-ink and pencil markings on pp. 63–66 of the same type seen in other books published in or before 1911. This stamp is not found in any other book of the collection.]
Henry VAN de VELDE	*Amo*	Leipzig; Insel-Bücherei, Nr. 3, n.d.		Pencil inscription on second leaf: 'Genauso, wie Sie ihn gestern schilderten!! [Karl] Wiener'. Label inside cover: 'k.k. Univers. Buch. Georg Szelinski Wien I Kärntnerstr. 59'
VARIOUS	*Deutsche Classiker des Mittelalters.* Mit Wort- und Sacherklärungen. Begründet von Franz Pfeiffer	Leipzig: F.A. Brockhaus		MW 1997: 706; 1998: 430
	1. Bd. Walther von der Vogelweide [various poetry], hrsg. Karl Bartsch.	1880	ELAS	
	2. Bd. [Anon.], *Kudrun*, hrsg. Karl Bartsch	1880	"	
	3. Bd. *Das Nibelungenlied*, hrsg. Karl Bartsch	1886	"	
	4. Bd. Hartmann von Aue (I), *Êrec der Wunderaere* (I), hrsg. Fedor Bech	1893	"	
	5. Bd. Hartmann von Aue (II), *Lieder. Die klage Büchlein.*	1891	"	

103

Table 3.1 *continued*

Author	Title	Publication details	Designation, inscriptions, markings and other comments	Literature concordance
	Grêgorjus. Der arme Heinrich, hrsg. Fedor Bech	1888	"	Mahler's studies at the University of Vienna, summer semester, 1878 (Barham, 1998 vol. 2: 14 & 49)
	6. Bd. Hartmann von Aue (III), *Iwein, oder der Ritter mit dem Löwen*, hrsg. Fedor Bech			
	7. Bd. Gottfried von Strassburg, *Tristan* (I), hrsg. Reinhold Bechstein	1890	"	MAL: 120
	8. Bd. Gottfried von Strassburg, *Tristan* (II), hrsg. Reinhold Bechstein	1873	"	
	9. Bd. Wolfram von Eschenbach, *Parzival und Titurel* (I), hrsg. Karl Bartsch	1875	"	MAL: 120; Mahler's studies at the University of Vienna, winter semester, 1877–78 (Barham, 1998 vol. 2: 14 & 48)
	10. Bd. Wolfram von Eschenbach, *Parzival und Titurel* (II), hrsg. Karl Bartsch	1876	"	
	11. Bd. Wolfram von Eschenbach, *Parzival und Titurel* (III), hrsg. Karl Bartsch	1877	"	
	12. Bd. *Erzählungen und Schwänke*, hrsg. Hans Lambel	1883	"	
	ENGLAND UND AMERIKA. Fünf Bücher englischer und	Minden i. W.: J.C.C. Bruns'	Inscription on title page: 'F.W.'	

amerikanischer Gedichte von den Anfängen bis auf die Gegenwart. Hrsg. von Julius Hart	Verlag, 1885		
Die Ernte aus acht Jahrhunderten deutscher Lyrik. Gesammelte von Will Vesper. Geschmückt von Käte Waentig	Düsseldorf und Leipzig: W. Langewiesche-Brandt, 1906	HMBS on front cover. Black-ink dedication on first leaf: 'En souvenir amical et très reconnaissant Vienne Oct. 1906 F. Galsworthy [?]'	
Die Insel. Monatsschrift mit Buchschmuck und Illustrationen, hrsg. von Otto Julius Bierbaum, Alfred Walter Heymel, Rudolf Alexander Schröder.	Berlin: Schuster & Loeffler	ELAS	
1. Jahrg. 1. Quartal Oktober bis Dezember 1899			
1. Jahrg. 2. Quartal Januar bis März 1900		"	
1. Jahrg. 3. Quartal April bis Juni 1900		"	
1. Jahrg. 4. Quartal Juli bis September 1900		"	
2. Jahrg. 1. Quartal Oktober bis Dezember 1900		"	
2. Jahrg. 2. Quartal Januar bis März 1901		"	MW 1997: 706; 1998: 430 (1901–2 subscription)
2. Jahrg. 3. Quartal April bis Juni 1901		"	
2. Jahrg. 4. Quartal Juli bis September 1901		"	MW 1997: 714; 1998: 437 (September issue)
Freie Bühne für modernes Leben	Berlin: S. Fischer		

continued overleaf

Table 3.1 *continued*

Author	Title	Publication details	Designation, inscriptions, markings and other comments	Literature concordance
	I. Jahrg. Heft 1–26	29. Januar, 1890	HMBS. Pencil inscription on first leaf: 'Dostoyewsky für ____ [two illegible words] Seite [?] 600'. This makes reference to Dostoyevsky's 'Eine heikle Geschichte' on pp. 600–608.	
	II. Jahrg. Heft 1–26	1891	HMBS	
	Neue deutsche Rundschau (Freie Bühne)	Berlin: S. Fischer		
	XIV. Jahrg. 3. und 4. Quartal	1903	HMBS	
	XIV. Jahrg. 3. und 4. Quartal. 2. Bd.	1903	"	
	Die neue Rundschau	Berlin: S. Fischer		
	XVIter Jahrg. der Freien Bühne			
	1. Bd.	1905	HMBS	
	2. Bd.	1905	"	
	XVIIter Jahrg. der Freien Bühne			
	1. Bd.	1906	HMBS	
	2. Bd.	1906	"	
	XVIIIter Jahrg. der Freien Bühne			
	1. Bd.	1907	HMBS	
	2. Bd.	1907	" This volume contains Nietzsche's letters of 1888 including one about his essay *Nietzsche contra Wagner* (pp. 1387–88) in which he writes: 'die Schrift (drei Bogen etwa) ist extrem antideutsch'.	
	Schwarz und Weiss. Wiener Autoren den Wiener	Das Festcomité der Kunst-		

	Kunstgewerbeschülern zu ihrem Feste am 6. Februar 1902	gewerbeschüler. Für das Redactionscomité Otto M. Miethke [presumably 1902]		[Wrote for secessionist journal, *Ver Sacrum*]
Emile VERHAEREN	*Drei Dramen*. Nachdichtung von Stefan Zweig	Leipzig: Insel Verlag, 1910	HMBS	
	Gedichte, übersetzt von Erna Rehwoldt	Berlin, Stuttgart & Leipzig: Axel Juncker Verlag, n.d.	ELAS	
Francis VIELÉ-GRIFFIN	*Sappho* [large-format book of poetry]	Paris: Bibliothèque de l'Occident, 1911		
Friedrich Theodor VISCHER	*Briefe aus Italien*	München: Süddeutsche Monatshefte, 1908	HMBS	UWO: Mahler acknowledges receipt of the book from Justine and Arnold Rosé[33]
	Auch Einer. Eine Reisebekanntschaft	Stuttgart, Leipzig, Berlin & Wien: Deutsche Verlags-Anstalt, 1893		
	1. Bd.		Handwritten dedication: 'Seinem lieben G.M. Weihnachten 93 Z.[ur] E.[rinnerung] an A.[rnold] B[erliner]' [?] (transcribed by Herta Blaukopf). See Plate 3.7	

33   Mahler wrote to Justine and Arnold Rosé in mid-February 1908: 'I have received the book by Vischer and I send you my deepest thanks' ['Das Buch von Vischer habe ich erhalten, und laße ihr schönsten danken']. The author is grateful to Stephen McClatchie for providing this information.

continued overleaf

Table 3.1 *continued*

Author	Title	Publication details	Designation, inscriptions, markings and other comments	Literature concordance
	2. Bd.		Label on last leaf: 'C. BOYSEN Buchhandlung 9. Heuberg 9. HAMBURG'	
Max VOIGT-ALY	*Der Lawiring. Eine Tetralogie des Menschentums* 1. Teil: *Jtisu*	Dresden: Hans Schultze Verlags-Buchhandlung, 1904	Handwriten dedication: 'Dem Componisten und Künstler G. Mahler in Ergebenheit der Verfasser Dresden 1905' (transcribed by Herta Blaukopf). Two pages of instructions with musical examples on graph paper pasted into front of book, perhaps suggesting a musical setting of the contents of the book; not in Mahler's hand	
Jacob WASSERMANN	*Die Schwestern*	Berlin: S. Fischer Verlag, 1906		
Frank WEDEKIND	*Frühlings Erwachen*. Eine Kindertragödie	München: Albert Langen, Verlag für Litteratur und Kunst, 1908	HMBS	Mahler saw *Frühlings Erwachen* in January 1907, Berlin (EGR: 305 & 307; MAL: 283 & 284); negative reference to Wedekind's later works (EGR: 307; MAL: 284)
	Hidalla. Schauspiel in fünf Akten	München: Verlag von Etzold, n.d. [written 1904]	HMBS. Some I and II (blue/purple-ink) pp. *22–25* & 29 against the following: (p. 24, II) Berta: 'Das Leben der Tiere wird von den Menschen überwacht, um die Entwicklung ihrer Kräfte möglichst zu fordern; und unser Leben wird von der [x inserted here] Gesellschaft überwacht, um	

			unsere geistige und körperliche Entwicklung möglichst zu hindern. Darin stehen wir unter dem Haustier.' [x and 'unsere [?] Familie' is written in the margin against this passage.] (p. 29,1) Hetmann: 'Der Durst nach Schönheit ist ein nicht minder göttliches Gesetz in uns als der Trieb zur Bekämpfung der Erdenqual!' Berta: 'Schade nur, daß in der ganzen Welt die Erdenqual noch so übergewaltig ist, daß das Vergnügen an der Schönheit ihr gegenüber kaum als Sonnenstäubschen in die Wagschale fällt!' (see App. for key to symbols)	
H.G. WELLS	Die Zukunft in Amerika	Jena: Eugen Diederichs, 1911	HMBS. Several pencil underlinings and vertical marginal lines against passages dealing with economics and politics	
Walt WHITMAN	Hymnen für die Erde	Leipzig: Insel-Bücherei Nr. 123, n.d.	Black-ink inscription on first leaf: 'F.W. Haus Mahler'. Label inside cover; 'K. Andrésche Buchhandlung Max Berwald Prag-I, 969 Graben (Pulverturm)'	
Oscar WILDE	Dorian Grays Bildnis. Deutsch von Felix Paul Greve	2. Auflage Minden in Westf.: J.C.C. Bruns' Verlag, n.d. [first German edn dated from 1902]	HMBS	EGR: 206 & 209; MAL: 239 [Mahler saw The Importance of Being Earnest in Munich, November 1906, EGR: 298; MAL: 278. Reference to Salome, HGF2: 671; HGE3: 200–201]
Ernst von WILDENBRUCH	König Laurin. Tragödie in fünf Akten	Berlin: G. Grote'sche Verlagsbuchhand-lung, 1902		[Mahler visits Wildenbruch in Berlin, 1888, HGE1: 177; HGF1: 271]

109

continued overleaf

Table 3.1 *concluded*

Author	Title	Publication details	Designation, inscriptions, markings and other comments	Literature concordance
Thornton WILDER	*Die Alkestiade*. Schauspiel in drei Akten. Mit einem Satyrspiel: *Die beschwipsten Schwestern*. Deutsch von Herberth E. Herlitschka	Frankfurt: S. Fischer Verlag, n.d. [typescript]		

Table 3.2 Philosophy, science, aesthetics and religion

Author	Title	Publication details	Designation, inscriptions, markings and other comments	Literature concordance
Rt. Hon. Lord AVEBURY [Sir John LUBBOCK]	Ants, Bees and Wasps. A Record of Observations on the Habits of the Social Hymenoptera. The International Scientific Series, volume XLII	New York: D. Appleton & Co., 1908	HMBS. Label on inside back cover: 'Brentano's. Booksellers & Stationers, NEW YORK'	
Henri BERGSON	Zeit und Freiheit. Eine Abhandlung über die unmittelbaren Bewusstseins-Tatsachen	Jena: Eugen Diederichs, 1911	HMBS	[Wessling, 1974: 293. NB the accuracy of some of the findings in this book is open to question]
Arnold BERLINER	Lehrbuch der Experimentalphysik in elementarer Darstellung	Jena: Verlag von Gustav Fischer, 1903	Handwritten dedication to Gustav and Alma Mahler from Berliner on title page: 'mein Kopf ist dein/du hast ihn erkies't/entfräg'st du mir nicht/was dir frommt/lös' ich's mit Lehren nicht ein. J.C. [?] Gustav, Alma Mahler in alter Freundschaft der Verf. Berlin, d. 18.v.03'. See Plate 3.8	GMB: 300; SLGM: 267 [Mahler's close relation with unspecified 'physicist friend'/'eminent physicist' (probably Berliner), BW: 117; TV: 93. Mahler receives gift of large quantity of books from Berliner, June 1908, GMB: 364; SLGM: 321]
Wilhelm BÖLSCHE	Die Abstammung des Menschen	Stuttgart: Kosmos, Gesellschaft der Naturfreunde Geschäftsstelle: Franckh'sche Verlagshandlung [author's	HMBS	

111

continued overleaf

Table 3.2 *continued*

Author	Title	Publication details	Designation, inscriptions, markings and other comments	Literature concordance
		introduction dated 'Neujahr 1904']		
Giordano BRUNO	*Gesammelte Werke* 3. Bd. *Zwiegespräche vom unendlichen All und den Welten*, hrsg. von Ludwig Kuhlenbeck	Jena: Eugen Diederichs, 1904	HMBS. Old slip of paper inserted in front of book on which is written 'Mahler'; **?** against text on p. III of Kuhlenbeck's introduction: 'so beginnen die ernstlichen Versuche, sich ein wissenschaftliches Bild von dem Bau und der Größe des Universums zu machen, erst mit dem Erwachen eines vom Priestertum befreiten philosophischen und wissenschaftlichen Denkens im hellenischen Altertum'	Foerster, 1955: 705 (Bruno's *Gesammelte Werke* vol. 1). [MAL: 120]
Houston Stewart CHAMBERLAIN	*Immanuel Kant* [also includes chapters on Goethe, Leonardo, Descartes, Bruno and Plato]	No details [probably published in 1905]	Black-ink inscription on first leaf: 'Alma Mahler'. Above this, a list of reading in unknown hand: 'Jackman Borowski' (blue ink), 'Wasianski – Kant, Kant-Reflexionen (Erdman ed.), Kants Briefe (Berliner Akademie ed.), Paul Natorp Platos Ideenlehre 1903' (pencil)	
Charles DARWIN	*Das Variiren der Thiere und Pflanzen im Zustande der Domestication.* Übersetzt von J. Victor Carus	Stuttgart: E. Schweizerbart'sche Verlagshandlung (E. Nägele), 1899		[Mahler's general relation to Darwinian thought, Olsen, 1992: 226–38]
	1. Bd. 2. Bd.		HMBS "	
	Über die Entstehung der Arten durch natürliche	"	"	MW 1997: 580 & 585 [663]; 1998: 341 [401]

Zuchtwahl oder die Erhaltung der begünstigten Rassen im Kampfe um's Dasein. Hrsg. von J. Victor Carus	" 1901	"	
Der Ausdruck der Gemüthsbewegungen bei dem Menschen und den Thieren. Übersetzt von J. Victor Carus	" 1901	"	
Die Abstammung des Menschen und die geschlechtliche Zuchtwahl. Übersetzt von J. Victor Carus	" 1902	"	
Reise eines Naturforschers um die Welt. Übersetzt von J. Victor Carus	" 1899	"	
Gustav FECHNER [Dr. MISES] [Dr. Mises] *Stapelia Mixta* [includes *Vier Paradoxa*]	Leipzig: Leopold Voß, 1824	HMBS	
Ueber die Seelenfrage. Ein Gang durch die sichtbare Welt, um die unsichtbare zu finden [An anti-materialist tract. Chapters include: 'Begriffliches über Seele, Geist, Körper, Leib, Natur' 'Allgemeine Gegengründe gegen die Ausdehnung des Seelenreiches über die Menschen- und Thierwelt hinaus'	Leipzig: C.J. Amelangs Verlag, 1861	HMBS. ELAS	[Unspecified vols, ML: 182; EGR: 173; Pfohl, 1973: 20; Stefan, 1912: 28; *Vorschule der Aesthetik*, EGR: 257, MAL: 263; *Vergleichende Anatomie der Engel. Eine Skizze*, Pfohl, 1973: 20, TV: 93]

continued overleaf

113

Table 3.2 *continued*

Author	Title	Publication details	Designation, inscriptions, markings and other comments	Literature concordance
	'Die Pflanzenseele. Gegengründe' 'Die Pflanzenseele. Positive Gründe dafür' 'Die Seele der Gestirne und der Welt']			
	Zend-Avesta. Dritte Auflage. Besorgt von Kurd Lasswitz. 1. Bd. & 2. Bd. [in one volume]	Hamburg und Leipzig: Verlag von Leopold Voß, 1906	HMBS. Some markings: pp. 114–15, in chapter 'Die Seelenfrage' (vol. 1), illegible pencil inscriptions, possibly in Greek; p. 140, in chapter 'Die Erde, unsre Mutter' (vol. 1), pencil inscription 'Homunculus', against text 'In der Tat, wo wäre ein Grund, ein Schluß, eine Erfahrung, die uns wirklich glauben oder den Glauben rechtfertigen lassen könnte, daß je Beseeltes anders als wieder von Beseeltem geboren werden könne; ein Leib, der Seele einschließt, von einem Leibe, der keine einschließt?', in unidentified hand. Handwritten, black-ink dedication from Gustav Mahler to Theobald Pollak on title page: 'Meinem lieben Freunde Theobald Pollak diesen treuen Begleiter auf seinem Wege zur Genesung Wien, Mai 1910 Gustav Mahler'. Transcribed by Antony Beaumont. See Plate 3.9. Small slip of paper inserted in book with 'Mahler' written at top in pencil	EGR: 148; MAL: 226; TV: 93 (but must have been earlier edn); BW: 117
	Nanna oder über das Seelenleben der Pflanzen. Dritte Auflage mit einer Einleitung von Kurd Laßwitz	Hamburg und Leipzig: Verlag von Leopold Voß, 1903	HMBS. Slip of paper inserted in book with 'Mahler' written at top in pencil	TV: 93 (earlier edn); BW: 117
				[Wider implications of

114

			Mahler's interest in Fechner: Barham, 1998]
August FOREL	*Die sexuelle Frage. Eine naturwissenschaftliche, psychologische, hygienische und soziologische Studie für Gebildete*	München: Ernst Reinhardt Verlags-Buchhandlung, 1905	HMBS
Ernst HAECKEL	*Die Welträthsel. Gemeinverständliche Studien über monistische Philosophie.* Volks-Ausgabe mit einem Nachworte Das Glaubensbekenntnis der reinen Vernunft	Bonn: Verlag von Emil Strauß, 1903	HMBS	[Decsey, 1911: 353]
William JAMES	*Der Pragmatismus. Ein neuer Name für alte Denkmethoden. Volkstümliche philosophische Vorlesungen.* Übersetzt von Wilhelm Jerusalem	Leipzig: Verlag von Dr. Werner Klinkhardt, 1908	HMBS	[Wessling, 1974, 293]
Paul KAMMERER	*Experimentelle Veränderung der Fortpflanzungstätigkeit bei Geburtshelferkröte (Alytes obstetricans) und Laubfrosch (Hyla arboren)*	Wien: aus der Biologischen Versuchsanstalt, Eingegangen am 24. Mai 1905	HMBS	[Mahler visited by Kammerer in 1908, ML: 53–54. Alma's subsequent contact with Kammerer, ML: 54–55 & 86; ABL: 70–71 & 73–74]
	Das Terrarium und Insektarium [part of the series *Der Naturforscher*]	Leipzig: Theod. Thomas Verlag, n.d. Geschäftsstelle der Deutschen Naturwissen-	HMBS	

continued overleaf

Table 3.2 *continued*

Author	Title	Publication details	Designation, inscriptions, markings and other comments	Literature concordance
		schaftlichen Gesellschaft		
Graf Hermann von KEYSERLING	*Unsterblichkeit. Eine Kritik der Beziehung zwischen Naturgeschehen und menschlicher Vorstellungswelt*	München: J.F. Lehmanns Verlag, 1911	HMBS. Many markings, and inscriptions in two hands, neither Mahler's. App. (14)	
Rudolf Hermann LOTZE	*Kleine Schriften*	Leipzig: Verlag von S. Hirzel		[Unspecified vols, ML: 182; Stefan, 1912: 28. *Microcosmos*, BW: 117]
	1. Bd. [Contains 'Ueber den Begriff der Schönheit']	1885		
	2. Bd. [Contains 'Über Bedingungen der Kunstschönheit', 'Recension von G.T. Fechner, über das höchste Gut']	1886		
	3. Bd. (I)	1891		
	3. Bd. (II)	[presumably 1891]		
Ernst MACH	*Populär-wissenschaftliche Vorlesungen*	[2nd edn] Leipzig: Johann Ambrosius Barth, 1897	ELAS on second leaf	
	Erkenntnis und Irrtum. Skizzen zur Psychologie der Forschung	Leipzig: Verlag von Johann Ambrosius Barth, 1905		

	Die Analyse der Empfindungen und das Verhältnis des Physischen zum Psychischen. Dritte vermehrte Auflage. [First chapter entitled 'Antimetaphysische Vorbemerkungen']	Jena: Verlag von Gustav Fischer, 1902	ELAS. Calligraphic inscription on verso of first leaf: 'Alma Mahler'
Th. NEWEST	*Einige Weltprobleme. Die Gravitationslehre … ein Irrtum! 2. Theil: Gegen die Wahrvorstellung vom heissen Erdinnern* [in one volume]	Wien: Verlag von Carl Konegen, 1905 [second part 1906]	HMBS. Some pencil annotations
Friedrich NIETZSCHE	*Nietzsches Werke*	Leipzig: Druck und Verlag von C.G. Naumann	[Complete edition, MAL: 18–19; ABL: 22. Alma's immersion in Nietzsche, MAL: 20; HGF2: 162. 2 unspecified vols, MW 1997: 606; 1998: 360. ML: 28 & 182; ABL: 28. Unspecified vols, GMB: 119 & 441; SLGM: 140 & 407–8; Stefan, 1912: 28. Mahler's negative comments in general and on Nietzsche's 'Herrenunmoral', EGR: 107 & 146; MAL: 225. Positive description of the 'Mitternachtslied' from *Also sprach Zarathustra*, NBL: 35; NBLE: 40. Mahler's general interest in Nietzsche: NBL: 73; NBLE: 73; Scharlitt,

continued overleaf

Table 3.2 *continued*

Author	Title	Publication details	Designation, inscriptions, markings and other comments	Literature concordance
	1. Abtheilung 1. Bd. *Die Geburt der Tragödie. Unzeitgemässe Betrachtungen, erstes bis viertes Stück*	1899	ELAS. Label on last leaf: 'BUCHBINDEREI ALBERT GÜNTHER WIEN'. Several purple-ink marginal lines in the second of the *Unzeitgemässe Betrachtungen, Vom Nutzen und Nachteil der Historie*, e.g. section 1, concerning happiness and forgetting the past; section 2, fleeing from resignation and the demand for a *monumental* history; inartistic natures v. strong artistic spirits and evolving art; section 4, cultivated and uncultivated inwardness; section 5, the subjectless personality and the hollowed-out cultivated man; the fourth *Meditation, Richard Wagner in Bayreuth*, section 8, the description of Wagner's *Tristan* as the 'opus metaphysicum of all art' (see literature concordance). App. (15)	1920: 310; GA: 37; GMB: 202–3; SLGM: 197–98; Ritter, 1906: 249 (HGF2: 141); HGE1: 654–55; HGE2: 403. Wider implications of Mahler's relation with Nietzsche's thought, Barham, 1992 & 1998] MW 1997: 539, 541–42 & 571 (direct reference to section 8 of *Richard Wagner in Bayreuth*, no. 4 of *Unzeitgemässe Betrachtungen*); 1998: 310, 313 & 334. Mahler's allusion to *Unzeitgemässe Betrachtungen*, Scharlitt, 1920: 310. Pernerstorferkreis studying *Unzeitgemässe Betrachtungen*, LWW: 30
	2. Bd. *Menschliches, Allzumenschliches. Ein Buch für freie Geister I*	1900	HMBS. ELAS. Same label as vol. 1. Several markings. App. (16)	MW 1997: 581
	3. Bd. *Menschliches, Allzumenschliches. Ein Buch für freie Geister II*	1900	HMBS. ELAS. Same label as vol. 1. Several markings. App. (17)	

5. Bd. *Die fröhliche Wissenschaft*	1900	HMBS. ELAS. Same label as vol. 1. Several markings in two hands, neither Mahler's. App. (18)	[3rd Symphony title. GMB: 149, 150, 151 & 152; SLGM: 163, 164, 165 & 166. NBL: 36; NBLE: 41. All these references pre-date the publication of this edition]
7. *Jenseits von Gut und Böse. Zur Genealogie der Moral*	1899	HMBS. ELAS. Same label as vol. 1. Several markings. App. (19)	MW 1997: 411–12; 1998: 220 (Alma copies out Part Two, section 41 of *Jenseits von Gut und Böse* in capital letters); MW 1997: 415–16 & 418; 1998: 222 (Alma copies out sections 67 (in capitals), 68, 70, 100, 120, 123, 143 & 153 from the fourth main section of *Jenseits von Gut und Böse*, 'Sprüche und Zwischenspiele')
8. Bd. *Der Fall Wagner. Götzen-Dämmerung. Nietzsche contra Wagner. Der Wille zur Macht I* (I. Buch: *Der Antichrist*). *Dichtungen* 2. Abtheilung	1899	HMBS. ELAS. Same label as vol. 1. Several markings, some inscriptions in two hands, neither Mahler's. App. (20)	[NB Alma first read *Also sprach Zarathustra* (1883–92) in May 1898 (MW 1997: 58; 1998: 33) suggesting her copy may have belonged to an earlier published series or was an earlier edition in the same series. She was reading the book again in June and September 1900 (MW 1997: 520, 551; 1998: 320). Mahler reading *Zarathustra* in mid-1890s, NBL: 215, TV: 93. Undated reference, BW: 118. Reference to 'Übermensch', MUB: 127; MUL: 123]
7. Bd. *Nachgelassene Werke* von Friedrich Nietzsche. *Ecce Homo. Der Wille zur Macht*, erstes und zweites Buch. Zweite, völlig neugestaltete und vermehrte Ausgabe des *Willens zur Macht*	Leipzig: Alfred Kröner Verlag, 1911	HMBS. Several markings and inscriptions in two hands (one Alma's). App. (21). In *Ecce Homo* against passages referring to Nietzsche's grandmother; Buddha and 'pitiable' Christianity; indigestible German cuisine; German climate and metabolism; journeying from Turin to Milan; no books or outside stimuli when in a state of spiritual 'pregnancy'; poet unable to endure his own work, e.g. *Zarathustra*; Berlioz, Wagner,	

continued overleaf

119

Table 3.2 *continued*

Author	Title	Publication details	Designation, inscriptions, markings and other comments	Literature concordance
	Friedrich Nietzsches Gesammelte Briefe, hrsg. von Peter Gast und Dr. Arthur Seidl	Berlin und Leipzig: Schuster & Loeffler, 1900	Delacroix, Baudelaire; *Tristan* as Wagner's '*non plus ultra*'; imagining Turin to be a German town or city; Darwinism.	
	1. Bd		ELAS	
	Morgenröthe. Gedanken über die moralischen Vorurtheile	Leipzig: Verlag von E.W. Fritzsch, 1887 [handwritten facsimile]	HMBS. ELAS. Label on last leaf: 'BUCHBINDEREI ALBERT GÜNTHER WIEN'. Several markings. App. (22)	
	Aldus Sprak Zarathustra. Een Boek voor Allen en Niemand	Amsterdam: S.L. Van Looy, 1905	Handwritten dedication on first leaf: 'An Gustav Mahler, dem Meister, in enthusiastischer Bewunderung seiner göttlichen dritten Symphonie L.S.A.M. von Römer med. doct. Amsterdam Leidschegracht 113. 29[4?] November '05'	
Friedrich PAULSEN	*Einleitung in die Philosophie.* Zweite Auflage	Berlin: Verlag von Wilhelm Hertz, 1893	HMBS. ELAS. Label on last leaf: 'C. BOYSEN Buchhandlung 9. Heuberg 9. Hamburg'. Pencilled date at top right of last leaf: '20/6/94'. Date of publication and place of purchase suggest this was Mahler's book	[EGR: 148]
Arthur SCHOPENHAUER	*Arthur Schopenhauers sämtliche Werke in zwölf Bänden.* Mit Einleitung von	Stuttgart: Verlag der J.G. Cotta'schen		[Unspecified vols, MW 1997: 595, 605 & 613; 1998: 359; ML: 28 & 182; ABL: 28; GA:

Dr. Rudolf Steiner	Buchhandlung, Nachfolger, n.d.		
1. Bd. *Ueber die vierfache Wurzel des Satzes vom zureichenden Grunde*		On leaf facing inside front cover and on inside back cover in listing of other publications, the following are underlined in pencil: 'Byrons poetische Werke', 'Calderons Ausgewählte Werke', 'Cervantes Ausgewählte Werke', 'Goethes Gespräche mit Eckermann', 'Hölderlins Gesammelte Dichtungen', 'Horaz' Sämtliche Dichtungen', 'Jean Pauls Ausgewählte Werke', 'Immermans Ausgewählte Werke', 'Rousseaus Ausgewählte Werke', 'Sophocles' Sämtliche Werke'. Final leaf contains geometrical pencil diagrams linked to Schopenhauer's text	37; BW: 112 & 118; Stefan, 1912: 28. Unspecified reference. GMB: 224; SLGM: 213; HGF2: 838 & 931; HGE3: 372 & 463. Influence of Schopenhauer on Alma. MAL: 20. Mahler gives complete edn to Walter, 1894, TV: 93. Mahler's negative comments on Schopenhauer's 'chapter on women', EGR: 107. This refers to 'Über die Weiber' ('On Women') in *Parerga und Paralipomena II*, in which Schopenhauer denigrates women on physical and intellectual grounds]
2. Bd. *Die Welt als Wille und Vorstellung I & II* 3. Bd. *Die Welt als Wille und Vorstellung III & IV*		ELAS several markings. App. (23)	MAL: 47; GMB: 124; SLGM: 412. [NBL: 68; NBLE: 67, 'Ixion-wheel' reference]
4. Bd. *Kritik der kantischen Philosophie. – Ergänzungen zum I. Buch der 'Welt als Wille und Vorstellung'*		ELAS	
5. Bd. *Ergänzung zum II. Und III. Buch der 'Welt als Wille und Vorstellung'*		ELAS	
6. Bd. *Ergänzungen zum IV. Buch der 'Welt als Wille und Vorstellung'. Ueber den Willen in der Natur*		ELAS. Pencil inscription on final leaf: 'Bhagawad – Gitä über ____ [?] von Dr. F. Hartmann Kabbala, von Papus Verlag, M. Altmann'	

continued overleaf

Table 3.2 *concluded*

Author	Title	Publication details	Designation, inscriptions, markings and other comments	Literature concordance
	7. Bd. *Die beiden Grundprobleme der Ethik* 12. Bd. *Farbenlehre. Aus dem Nachlaß*		ELAS ELAS	
Emanuel SWEDENBORG	*Immanuel Swedenborg theologische Schriften,* übersetzt und eingeleitet von Lothar Briegel-Wasservogel	Jena und Leipzig: Eugen Diederichs, 1904	ELAS Pencil inscription on second leaf: 'Werfel 1917'	[ABL: 121]
[VARIOUS]	*Die Wunder der Natur. Schilderungen der interessantesten Natur-Schöpfungen und -Erscheinungen in Einzeldarstellungen.* 1. Bd.	Berlin & Leipzig: Deutsches Verlagshaus Bong, 1912	Stamped: 'GUCKI MAHLER WIEN 1., Elisabethstrasse 22'. Title page contains many childish pencil scrawlings and animal pictures.]	
Richard WAHLE	*Über den Mechanismus des geistigen Lebens*	Wien und Leipzig: Wilhelm Braumüller k.u.k. Hof- und Universitätsbuch-handler, 1906	HMBS. Handwritten dedication to 'Frau Director Alma Mahler' possibly from author [name is illegible], dated '1. Januar 1907'.	

122

Table 3.3 Music and visual art

Author	Title	Publication details	Designation, inscriptions, markings and other comments	Literature concordance
ANON.	Programme booklet for *Muziekfeest Arnhem*, 17/18 October 1903, where the 4th and 5th movements of Mahler's Third Symphony had been performed on 16 October 1903. The complete Symphony was performed on 17 October. Contains programme notes and a list of 23 musical motifs. In the list of movements, 'Was mir die Blumen auf der Wiese erzählen' is given with the second movement; the text of 'Ablösung im Sommer' is given with the third movement; and only the sung texts and tempo markings are given for the other movements.	Arnhem: Boekdrukkerij Karel F. Misset		HGF2: 383, 385–86 (fn. 119) & 386; HGE2: 638–39 (fn. 149) & 642
	Tonkünstlerfest (43. Jahresversammlung) 29. Juni bis 2. Juli 1907 in Dresden. Programmbuch	Allgemeiner deutscher Musikverein	Notable for the performance on 'Sonntag, 30. Juni, vormittags 11 Uhr im Vereinhause, Zinzendorfstrasse 17' of 'Arnold Schönberg: Streichquartett (in einem Satze) op. 7' played by Arnold Rosé, Paul Fischer, Anton Ruzitska and Friedrich Buxbaum	
	Goya [an introductory text by Carl Moll]	Wien: Galerie Miethke, März –	Pencil inscription on title page: 'herzliche Grüsse Carl (Moll)'. The last name is written in different	[HGF2: 661–63; HGE3: 189–90; HGF3: 311–12]

continued overleaf

123

Table 3.3 *continued*

Author	Title	Publication details	Designation, inscriptions, markings and other comments	Literature concordance
	Hohe Warte [a picture-book about houses, buildings and interiors]	April, 1908	pencil and handwriting.	
		No details	Pencil inscription on top right of first leaf: 'Mahler'	
Ludwig van BEETHOVEN	*Sämtliche Briefe und Aufzeichnungen*, hrsg. von Fritz Prelinger	Wien und Leipzig: C.W. Stern, 1907		EGR: 325; MAL: 291
	1. Bd. 1783–1814 2. Bd. 1815–1822		HMBS "	
[Alban BERG]	*Arnold Schönberg Kammersymphonie Op. 9. Thematische Analyse von Alban Berg*	Wien & Leipzig: Universal Edition, Nr. 6140, n.d. [published 1913]	Blue-ink dedication on title page: 'Meiner lieben Alma in inniger Verehrung Alban']	
Eugène DELACROIX	*Mein Tagebuch*	Berlin: Verlag Bruno Cassirer, 1909	HMBS. Many pencil, some blue and blue-purple ink markings. App. (24)	
Sigmund FREUD	*Eine Kindheitserinnerung des Leonardo da Vinci* [vol. 7 of Schriften zur angewandten Seelenkunde, hrsg. von S. Freud]	Leipzig und Wien: Franz Deuticke, 1910		
Eduard HANSLICK	*Am Ende des Jahrhunderts [1895–1899]. Der 'Modernen Oper' VIII. Teil. Musikalische Kritiken und Schilderungen*	Berlin: Allgemeiner Verein für deutsche Litteratur, 1899	Handwritten dedication to Gustav Mahler: 'Herrn Director Gustav Mahler freundschaftlichst zugeeignet von EdH[anslick] Wien, 10 April 899' (transcribed with assistance from Herta Blaukopf). See Plate 3.10	

			HMBS. ELAS	
W.M. HUNT	*Kurze Gespraeche ueber Kunst.* Übersetzung von A.D.J. Schubart	Straßburg: J.H. Ed. Heitz (Heitz und Mündel), 1897		
Ernst JENTSCH	*Musik und Nerven II. Das musikalische Gefühl*	Wiesbaden: Verlag von J.F. Bergmann, 1911	Black-ink inscription on title page: 'Mahler'. Many pencil and purple-pencil markings in more than one hand (not Mahler's; two of them are probably Alma's and Werfel's), including one purple-pencil reference to Mahler. App. (25)	
[S. KATO]	*Recollection of Japan. Life of a Musician. Klaus Pringsheim* [in Japanese]	Tokyo: Kengenshe, n.d.	Photographs at end of book include one of Mahler. Book purchased in Ginza, Tokyo, according to label on inside cover]	
Heinrich KOCH	*Musikalisches Lexicon.* Zweite Auflage hrsg. von Arrey von Dommer	Heidelberg: Akademische Verlagsbuch-handlung von J.C.B. Mohr, 1865	Faint pencilled name on second leaf, possibly 'Mahler'. Concert ticket inserted in book: 'Saal Bösendorfer. Fünf Quartett-Productionen. A. Rosé (1. Violine) A. Loh (2. Violine) S. Bachrich (Viola) R. Hummer (Violoncell) an Dienstagen 17. November, 1. und 15. Dezember 1885, und 26. Jänner 1886, Abends halb 8 Uhr. Abonnement Parterre Rechts 10. Reihe Sitz 1'. A letter with pressed flowers is also inserted in the book.	
Lilli LEHMANN	*Studie zu Fidelio*	Leipzig: Druck und Verlag von Breitkopf und Härtel, 1905	Handwritten dedication: 'In treuer Freundschaft, treuem Gedenken und herzlicher Verehrung Lilli. 1904'. See Plate 3.11. Some pages of the book remain uncut.	[Lehmann sang in *Fidelio* at the Vienna Hofoper on 4 & 13 May 1904]
	Studie zu Tristan und Isolde	No details	Handwritten dedication: 'Meinem lieben alten Freunde Gustav Mahler in Liebe und Verehrung Lilli. 1906' (transcribed by Herta Blaukopf). See Plate 3.12	[Lehmann sang Isolde at the Vienna Hofoper on 22 May 1898 and a truncated last act in May 1907, replacing the indisposed Mildenburg at very short notice]

continued overleaf

125

Table 3.3 *continued*

Author	Title	Publication details	Designation, inscriptions, markings and other comments	Literature concordance
Rudolf von der LEYEN	*Johannes Brahms. Als Mensch und Freund*	Düsseldorf und Leipzig: Verlag von Karl Robert Langewiesche, 1905	HMBS	
Berthold LITZMANN	*Clara Schumann. Ein Künstlerleben nach Tagebüchern und Briefen* 1. Bd. 1819–1840	Leipzig: Druck und Verlag von Breitkopf und Härtel, 1902	HMBS	
Rudolph LOTHAR	*Das Wiener Burgtheater*	Leipzig, Berlin und Wien: Verlag von E.A. Seemann und der Gesellschaft für graph. Industrie, 1899		[Mahler interviewed by Lothar in 1903, EGR: 174]
Felix MENDELSSOHN	*Felix Mendelssohn-Bartholdys Briefwechsel mit Legationsrat Karl Klingemann in London*, hrsg. Karl Klingemann	Essen: G.D. Baedeker Verlagshandlung, 1909	HMBS	
J.E. SCHINDLER	*J. E. Schindler's Künstlerischer Nachlass.* Auction 5. December 1892 und folgende Tage, Künstlerhaus, Wien	Wien: Verlag H.O. Miethke [presumably] 1892		

Richard SPECHT	*Die Musik. Sammlung illustrierter Einzeldarstellungen*, hrsg. Richard Strauss	Berlin: Marquardt		
	30. Bd. *Johann Strauss* von Richard Specht	1909	HMBS. Handwritten dedication to Alma from Specht dated 'Wien, Mai 1909'	
	Gustav Mahler [from the series *Moderne Essays*, hrsg. Dr. Hans Landsberg]	Berlin: Gose & Cetzlaff, n.d. [1905]	Handwritten dedication to Alma from Specht dated 'Wien, Juni 1905'	
Paul STEFAN	*Gustav Mahler. Eine Studie über Persönlichkeit und Werk*	München: R. Piper, 1910		Mahler receives a copy of Stefan's book before the première of the Eighth Symphony in September 1910 (HGF3: 747)
Josef STRZYGOWSKI	*Der Dom zu Aachen und seine Entstellung. Ein kunstwissenschaftlicher Protest*	Leipzig: J.C. Hinrichs'sche Buchhandlung, 1904	Illegible black-ink message from author on title page	[Mahler visits Strzygowski, 1905 (HGF2: 557; HGE3: 91–92)]
Hermann UBELL	*Praxiteles* [from the series *Die Kunst*, hrsg. Richard Muther]	Berlin: Julius Bard, 1902 [date taken from printed dedication]	Large stamp on inside cover: 'EX LIBRIS' with no name.	
VARIOUS	*Ver Sacrum. Organ der Vereinigung bildender Kuenstler Österreichs*	No details	Label on last leaf: 'Buchhandlung & Antiquariat Alfred Bermann Wien I. Johannesgasse 17'	MW 1997: 8, 763 (Bahr article in vol. 1); ibid.: 18, 766 fn. 58, MW 1998: 11 &
	I. Jahrg. Heft 1.–12. [in 1 volume] Januar 1898			

continued overleaf

Table 3.3 *continued*

Author	Title	Publication details	Designation, inscriptions, markings and other comments	Literature concordance
				fn. 27 (articles by Zuckerhandl & Kurzweil in vol. 2); MW 1997: 27, 1998: 14 (vol. 3); 1997: 132, 1998: 64 (vol. 10); 1997: 159, 1998: 81 (vol. 11)
	Ver Sacrum. Mitteilung der Vereinigung bildender Künstler Österreichs	No details		
	VI. Jahrg. Kalender 1903			
	Monographien moderner Musiker. Kleine Essays über Leben und Schaffen zeitgenössischer Tonsetzer, mit Portraits	Leipzig: Verlag von C.F. Kahnt Nachfolger	HMBS	
	1. Bd.	1906		
Richard WAGNER	*Mein Leben*	München: F. Bruckmann, 1911		
	1. Bd. 2. Bd.		HMBS. 'M' written through stamp in pencil HMBS. 'M' written below stamp in pencil	
	Briefwechsel zwischen Wagner und Liszt	Leipzig: Druck und Verlag von Breitkopf und Härtel, 1887	Handwritten dedication: 'Seinem lieben Freunde Gustav Mahler Zu Weihnachten 1887 Albert'	[GMB: 316 & 317; SLGM: 279–80]
	1. Bd. Vom Jahre 1841 bis 1853			

	Title	Publication	Notes	References
	2. Bd. Vom Jahre 1854 bis 1861		[Spiegler]. See Plate 3.13	
	Richard Wagner an Mathilde Wesendonck. Tagebuchblätter und Briefe 1853–1871. Dritte Auflage	Berlin: Verlag von Alexander Duncker, 1904	HMBS. Label on inside back cover: 'F. A. Unrasch BUCHBINDEREI & PAPIERHANDLUNG Dresden – Mosczinskystr. 5'. Some pencil marginal lines, e.g. p. 239, I against the following passage: 'Ich fühle mich rein: ich weiss in meinem tiefsten Innern, dass ich stets nur für Andre, nie für mich wirkte; und meine steten Leiden sind mir das Zeugen' (see Appendix for key to symbols)	EGR: 201, 209–10 & 214; MAL: 237–38, 239 & 240; Alma recommends the letters to Zemlinsky (HGF2: 437 fn. 144; HGE2: 694 fn. 170)
Hugo WOLF	*Hugo Wolfs Briefe an Hugo Faißt*, hrsg. Michael Haberlandt	Stuttgart & Leipzig: Deutsche Verlags-Anstalt, 1904	HMBS. Pencil inscription on top right of title page: 'Mahler'. To the left of this in pencil: 'A. [?] M.'.	
Bertha ZUCKERKANDL	*Zeitkunst. Wien 1901–1907*	Wien und Leipzig: Hugo Heller und Cie., 1908	HMBS. Unsigned handwritten dedication to Alma	

Table 3.4 History, politics and miscellaneous items

Author	Title	Publication details	Designation, inscriptions, markings and other comments	Literature concordance
ANON.	*Vom Studium und vom Studenten. Ein Almanach*, hrsg. vom Akademischen Verband für Literatur und Musik in Wien	Berlin: Verlag von Bruno Cassirer, 1910	HMBS (inverted). Black-ink inscription on first leaf, possibly in Paul Kammerer's hand: 'Alma Maria Mahler wird gebeten, den Aufsätze Seite 219–231 zu lesen. Er enthält in nuce Kamm's gesamte naturwissenschaftliche und ethische Weltanschauung, ist gleichsam das Monogramm derselben'. The chapter in question is P. Kammerer (Wien), 'Erbliche Entlastung und gegenseitige Hilfe', whose title is underlined in same ink.	[On Kammerer: ABL: 70–71 & 73–74; ML: 53–55, 86]
Houston Stewart CHAMBERLAIN	*Die Grundlagen des Neunzehnten Jahrhunderts*	München Verlgsanstalt F. Bruckmann A.-G., 1899		MW 1997: 380
	Das XIX. Jahrhundert (1)		HMBS. ELAS. Several pencil inscriptions and markings, not in Mahler's hand; probably in Werfel's hand. For example, p. 217: 'der ganze subalterne Materialismus der Rassenlehre'	
Heinrich FRIEDJUNG	*Österreich von 1848 bis 1860* – in zwei Bänden. 1. Bd. *Die Jahre der Revolution und der Reform, 1848 bis 1851*	Stuttgart & Berlin: J.G. Cotta'sche Buchhandlung Nachfolger, 1908		
Curtius von HARTEL	*Griechische Schulgrammatik* bearbeitet von Dr. Florian Weigel	Wien: Verlag von F. Tempsky, 1903	Many pencil and blue- and red/brown-pencil underlinings and encirclings. Some words written in pencil	[ML: 34 & 40; ABL: 34]

Author	Title	Publication	Notes	References
Friedrich HIRTH	*The Ancient History of China to the End of the Chóu Dynasty*	New York: The Columbia University Press, 1908	ELAS on second leaf. Handwritten dedication: 'To my friends Mr. and Mrs. Gustav Mahler With kind regards and bon voyage New York, April 7th 1909 Friedrich Hirth'.	[Mahler's relationship with Hirth and possible discussions on Far Eastern subjects, HGF3: 301 & fn. 145; MAL: 146]
Hieronymus LORM	*Der Naturgenuss. Ein Beitrag zur Glückseligkeitslehre*	Wien & Leipzig: Salon-Bibliothek k.u.k. Hofbuchhandlung K. Prochaska, n.d.	HMBS	
Grete MEISEL-HESS	*Weiberhaß und Weiberverachtung. Eine Erwiderung auf die in Dr. Otto Weiningers Buche 'Geschlecht und Charakter' geäußerten Anschauungen über 'Die Frau und ihre Frage'*	Wien: Verlag 'Die Wage', 1904	HMBS	
[J. OVERBECK]	*Pompeji in seinen Gebäuden, Alterthümern und Kunstwerken für Kunst- und Alterthumsfreunde*	Leipzig: Verlag von Wilhelm Engelmann, 1866	Blue-ink inscription on first leaf: 'Haus Werfel [?] Mahler Febr. 19'. Several pencil underlinings]	
Josef POPPER	*Fundament eines neuen Staatrechts*	Dresden: Verlag Carl Reissner, 1905	Inscription on title page: 'F.W.'	
Artur RÖSSLER	*Kunst und Natur in Bildern. Dalmatien*	Wien & Leipzig: Verlag Brüder Rosenbaum, n.d.	Many pencil-drawn portraits on inside of front and back covers and on first leaf	
Karl SCHENKL	*Griechisches Elementarbuch*	Wien und Prag: Verlag von F. Tempsky, 1902	Many pencil underlinings, crosses and words.	[ML: 34 & 40; ABL: 34]

131

continued overleaf

Table 3.4 *concluded*

Author	Title	Publication details	Designation, inscriptions, markings and other comments	Literature concordance
Reinhold SCHOENER	*Rom* [picture-book with accompanying text]	Wien & Leipzig: Verlag Emil M. Engel, n.d.	HMBS. Label on last leaf: 'k.u.k. Hof- & Universitäts-Buchhandlung R. Lechner Wilh. Müller Wien, Graben 31'	
[Wilhelm WAGNER	*Rom* [history and picture-book]	Leipzig: Verlag von Otto Spamer, 1912	Stamped: 'GUCKI MAHLER WIEN 1., Elisabethstrasse 22'.]	
Theobald ZIEGLER	*Die geistigen und socialen Strömungen des neunzehnten Jahrhunderts*	Berlin: Georg Bondi, 1899	HMBS. ELAS	

A note on significant absences, inscriptions and markings

It can be seen from the catalogue above that certain important works of literature and philosophy known to have been read by Mahler, and to have been of significant interest to him, have not survived in the remains of his library. In terms of literature, the collection lacks any works by Dostoyevsky (Mahler's deep involvement with *The Brothers Karamazov* is described by Walter (Walter, 1947, p. 92));[34] Schiller, whom Mahler defended in his early conversations with Alma (Mahler, 1990, p. 20);[35] Rückert (see La Grange & Weiß, 1995, pp. 148 & 325, and Mahler, 1990, pp. 226 & 291); Lenau, whose poems 'Der Postillon' and 'Das Posthorn' are strongly associated with the third movement of the Third Symphony (see Decsey, 1911, p. 356); Angelus Silesius, from whose mysticism he derived much comfort, according to Walter (Walter, [1958] 1990, p. 119); Sterne, whose *Tristram Shandy* is described, again by Walter, as one of Mahler's favourites (ibid.), or Tolstoy (see La Grange & Weiß, 1995, p. 206, and Mahler, 1990, p. 236, and the reference to *A Confession* [*Meine Beichte*], La Grange & Weiß, 1995, p. 201, and Mahler, 1990, p. 238). The following are also missing: Grillparzer's *Die Argonauten* (the second part of the trilogy *Das goldene Vließ* (1818–20), on which Mahler based his early, unfinished and now lost operatic project; see also Blaukopf, 1996, pp. 271–72), Clemens Brentano's comedy *Ponce de Leon* (1801) mentioned in a letter of 1884 (Blaukopf, 1996, pp. 54, 55 & 434), Cotta's 1862 two-volume Stuttgart edition of Sulpiz Boisserée's autobiography and correspondence with Goethe, Dorothea Schlegel and Friedrich Schlegel mentioned in the same letter (ibid.), Bielschowsky's biography of Goethe (see Mahler, 1990, p. 103), Euripides' *Bacchae* (see Blaukopf, 1996, p. 264, Martner, 1979, p. 236, La Grange, 1974, p. 524, & La Grange, 1979, p. 800), Paul Sabatier's *François d'Assise* (see La Grange, 1974, p. 524, & La Grange, 1979, p. 800), Cervantes's *Don Quixote* (one of Mahler's favourite works of comic literature; see Bahr-Mildenburg, 1921, p. 22, Walter, [1958] 1990, p. 35, and Killian, 1984, p. 215), *Max Havelaar* by Multatuli (pseudonym of Eduard Douwes Dekker), read to Mahler by Alma in 1903 (see La Grange & Weiß, 1995, pp. 168–69 & 499, Mahler, 1990, p. 247, and

---

[34] For further references to Dostoyevsky see Pfohl, 1973, p. 20, Adler, [1916] 1982, p. 37, Stefan, 1912, p. 28, Specht, 1913, pp. 35–36, Pringsheim, 1960, p. 7, Mahler, 1990, pp. 20 & 184, La Grange & Weiß, 1995, p. 468, Walter, [1958] 1990, p. 120, Blaukopf, 1996, p. 17, Martner, 1979, p. 28, and La Grange, 1984, pp. 645–46.

[35] Mahler's familiarity with Otto Brahm's biography of Schiller (Berlin, 1888–92) is also apparent from a letter he wrote in mid-May 1892 to his sister Justine: 'The book I am sending you is a *Schiller Biography* that has just appeared and may be counted among the *best* biographies in existence – truly a rare commodity' ['Das Buch, das ich Dir schicken werde ist eine eben erschienen[e] *Schiller-Biografie*, und gehört zu den *besten* Biografien, die existiren – wahrlich eine seltene Ware']. The author is grateful to Stephen McClatchie for providing this information.

Blaukopf, 2002, pp. 110–11), an unnamed volume by Dmitri Merezhkovski (see La Grange & Weiß, 1995, pp. 322–23), Theodor Mommsen's *Römische Geschichte* (see Mahler, 1990, p. 51, and a probable reference to the same book in ibid., p. 291, and La Grange & Weiß, 1995, p. 325), an unspecified Shakespeare volume (see La Grange & Weiß, 1995, p. 325, and Mahler, 1990, p. 291), the works of the contemporary poet Peter Rosegger (see Decsey, 1911, p. 355), Bahr's *Tagebuch* (ibid., p. 353), Mann's novel *Königliche Hoheit* (given to him by the author in 1910), Bethge's *Die chinesische Flöte*, Mahler's probable first copy of *Des Knaben Wunderhorn* (Berlin: Hempel, 1883), and a number of works by Jean Paul (e.g. *Siebenkäs*).[36] In philosophy and science there is no complete set of Kant which, according to Alma, had lined the shelves of Mahler's composing hut in Maiernigg (Mahler, 1990, p. 45); there are no works of Helmholtz, many volumes of which, as referred to above, were contained in Mahler's library according to his daughter Anna; there are no volumes of Nietzsche (particularly *Also sprach Zarathustra*) dating from the period during which he composed the Third Symphony, or earlier; there is no natural philosophy of Johannes Reinke, described by Stefan as a particular interest of Mahler's in his early years (Stefan, 1912, p. 28); there are no volumes of *Brehms Tierleben* which Decsey reported to have been piled up on Mahler's living-room table in Toblach (Decsey, 1911, p. 353); there is no *Geschichte des Materialismus* of Lange, *Mikrokosmos* of Lotze, *Vergleichende Anatomie der Engel* of Fechner, philosophy of Hartmann, or further works of Bruno – all known to have been of fundamental importance to Mahler's intellectual constitution (see Mahler, 1990, p. 120, Walter, [1958] 1990, pp. 117 & 118, Walter, 1947, p. 93, Pfohl, 1973, p. 20, Stefan, 1912, p. 28, and Foerster, 1955, p. 705).

As far as the books that do exist are concerned, there is considerable difficulty in ascribing definitive authorship to the large number of inscriptions and markings they contain. While the catalogue records isolated or infrequent markings in certain books, the Appendix lists – according to type and colour of ink/pencil – the vast majority of those markings found in the more copiously annotated items of the collection. The first thing to note from this survey is that, with three possible exceptions (Euripides' *Hekabe*, Goethe's *Gedichte* and

---

36 Furthermore Mahler was evidently familiar with a biography of Goethe that is not located in the ARBML, writing to his sister Justine on c. 26 November 1891: 'Now something else to have close at hand! Something biographical for example! – If possible get *Lewes's "Göthe"* or something similar!' ['Nun mal was Anderes zur Hand! Biografisches zum B[eispiel]! – Verschaffe Dir wenn möglich *Lewes "Göthe"* oder Ähnliches!']. The author is grateful to Stephen McClatchie for providing this information. According to Renate Stark-Voit, Mahler must also have owned a copy of Brentano's *Das Märchen von Gockel und Hinkel* (1838) – the source of a text that he first inserted in, and then deleted from, 'Urlicht' – since Anna Mahler recalled being read the fairy tale by her father when she was a small child (personal communication, 22 April 2002). This book is not to be found in the ARBML.

Delacroix's *Mein Tagebuch*), no verbal inscriptions can be definitively attributed to Mahler, while inscriptions in other hands are plentiful. Although in themselves disappointing, these findings should not necessarily be taken to imply that few books in the collection either belonged to, or were read by, the composer. It may simply be that Mahler was not in the habit of writing in books, a hypothesis which is supported by the absence of markings either in the copy of *Des Knaben Wunderhorn* given to him by Anna von Mildenburg mentioned in footnote 11,[37] or in any of the books listed in the catalogue which bear personal dedications to the composer. It is also known that Mahler preferred to copy out texts of poems onto separate sheets of paper for use during summer composing periods rather than to annotate the original volumes and carry them around with him.

The only known example of a printed text purportedly annotated by Mahler – a review in the *Leipziger Zeitung* of his performance of Weber's *Der Freischütz* in 1886 (plate 16 in La Grange, 1979, between pp. 566 & 567) – contains not only written comments in the right-hand margin, one curved marginal line and frequent underlinings of short phrases (one in duplicate, another in triplicate, and some with wavy lines), typical of many books in the ARBML, but also three examples of the type of curled bracket } found only once among the books in the ARBML, all in black ink.[38] In addition, two long, intertwining curved lines in pencil of an unspecified colour can be seen in the background, running down the length of the page, also in the right margin. Although it would be wrong to draw wide-ranging conclusions based on such limited evidence, it would be equally wrong to ignore it. In writing his musical manuscripts, and in making additions and corrections to these and other scores, Mahler is known to have used pencil, red pencil, orange-red pencil, blue pencil, black indelible pencil, black ink, brown or light-brown ink, and red ink writing implements. The Appendix shows that the books of the collection contain markings mostly in pencil and purple ink, with occasional use of other pencil colours (red, red/brown, blue, blue/purple, and thick black (possibly indelible)), and other ink colours (dark, medium and light blue, red, as well as various shades of purple, whose differentiation is possibly attributable to the ageing process, to the use of the same ink with varied writing implements, or to Alma Mahler's habit of diluting ink with brandy: see Mahler-Werfel, 1997, pp. xi & 104). Alma's preferred medium of writing seems to have been violet or purple ink (see La Grange & Weiß, 1995, p. 17, and Mahler-Werfel, 1997, p. x, & 1998, p. xii), and her diaries are mostly notated in varied tints of this kind – from purple and violet to aquamarine and turquoise – although she also occasionally used black ink, and pencil while travelling.[39]

---

[37] The author is grateful to Renate Stark-Voit for supplying this information.

[38] The author is grateful to Henry-Louis de La Grange for confirming the ink colour used in the original copy.

[39] The author is grateful to Antony Beaumont for supplying additional information on the ink colouration of Alma's diaries.

To this should be added the observations that: (a) a volume in the collection dating from 1940 and inscribed 'A.M.W.' contains several examples of the type of upright but curved pencil lines and question marks in the margin found in books of the collection dating from 1911 or earlier; (b) a volume in the collection given to Alma in 1958 contains examples of straight and curved upright lines, as well as small crosses, in pencil and ink in the margin, also to be found in earlier books; (c) in a volume of Werfel's poetry bound by Alma and dating from 1917, there are several pencil markings consisting of long V-shapes and crossing curved lines similar to those found in some earlier books; (d) it can be assumed with reasonable certainty that any book bearing the blue-ink inscription 'F.W. Haus Mahler' or 'F.W.', regardless of its date of publication, was indeed the property of Werfel, since identical inscriptions can be found in both pre- and post-1911 books (for example, *Calderons Größte Dramen* (Freiburg: Herdersche Verlagshandlung, 1901) and Bergson's *Einführung in die Metaphysik* (Jena: Eugen Diederichs, 1912)), and it would be difficult – though not impossible – to accept that Werfel 'appropriated' books that were not originally his;[40] (e) the book *Die Bildnisse von Gustav Mahler* (Vienna: E.P. Tal & Co., 1922) contains a handwritten dedication from Alma to Walter Gropius in a distinctive purple ink which matches the colouration of earlier markings; (f) the use of blue pencil was not exclusive to Mahler, since the book *Le rôle des Arméniens dans la civilisation mondiale* (Belgrade, 1938) bears the inscription 'Bitte dem Herr Franz Werfel zu übersenden' in blue pencil on its front cover; (g) comparison with autograph Werfel material in the Department of Special Collections at the library of the University of California at Los Angeles strongly suggests that the numerous pencil inscriptions in the copy of Houston Stewart Chamberlain's *Die Grundlagen des neunzehnten Jahrhunderts* (Munich: F. Bruckmann, 1899) are in Werfel's hand.[41] The markings accompanying these inscriptions – also in pencil – include exclamation marks, question marks and some underlining but, significantly, no other kind of marking such as the straight or curved, single and double, upright lines found with such regularity in many of the Mahler-Werfel books in the ARBML; and (h) while the markings in the one book which Mahler is known to have read perhaps in more depth and with greater frequency than any other – Eckermann's *Gespräche mit Goethe* – might at first be considered to offer paradigms of Mahlerian annotation methods, it should be noted that (i) none of the accompanying verbal inscriptions appear to be in Mahler's hand; and (ii) the publication details of the book (Berlin: Deutsche Bibliothek, n.d.) correspond with neither of the two editions referred to by Mahler in letters (Frankfurt: Brockhaus, 1876, and Jena: Diederichs, 1908).

---

[40] It should also be noted that copies of Werfel's works held in the Mahler-Werfel collection (presumably given to him by his publishers) contain no stamps, bookplates or inscriptions on their title pages or first leaves.

[41] The author is grateful to Lilace Hatayama and Carol A. Turley for providing this material.

As these observations suggest, undertaking a completely reliable, scientific examination of the origins of the markings and inscriptions in these books and thereby forming any coherent interpretation of their significance may be problematic at best. Such an analysis, whether or not it may be considered to lie within the bounds of worthwhile scholarly activity, falls beyond the scope of the present study. Nevertheless it cannot be ruled out that, through the application of appropriate investigative methodologies, its prospective findings will eventually complement the valuable insights into previously unknown areas of Mahler's literary experience offered by the contents of the library outlined in the foregoing catalogue, and likewise contribute to an increased awareness of the distinctive shape and dimensions of the wider intellectual environment within which he lived and worked.

Plate 3.1 Hermann Bahr, *Dialog vom Tragischen* (Berlin: S. Fischer, 1904): inscription by Bahr on second leaf. This plate and those that follow are reproduced by kind permission of the Annenberg Rare Book & Manuscript Library, University of Pennsylvania.

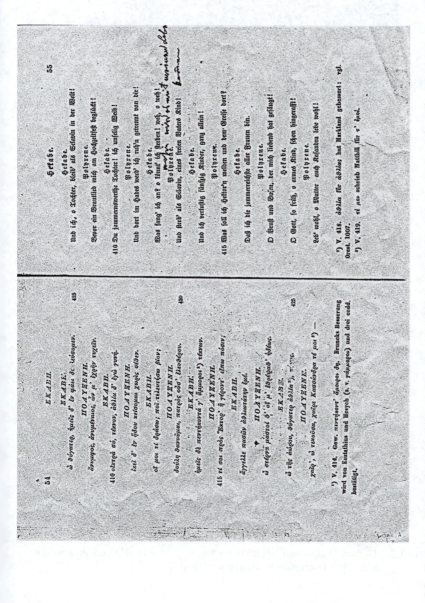

Plate 3.2 Euripides, *Hekabe* (Leipzig: Wilhelm Engelmann, 1850): inscription in an unknown hand (possibly Mahler's) on p. 55

Plate 3.3   Gerhart Hauptmann, sketches for the play *Elga* in *Die neue Rundschau*, 14 (1), 1905: inscription by Hauptmann on p. 1

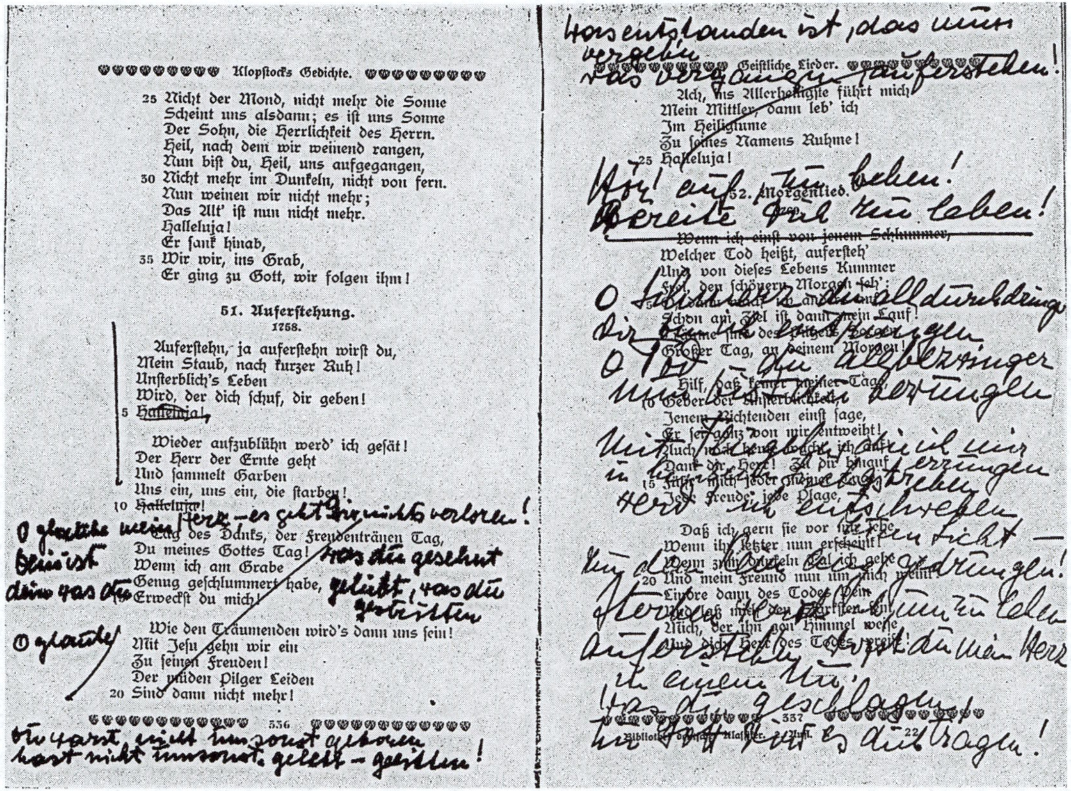

Plate 3.4 *Klopstocks Werke* (Freiburg: Herdersche Verlagshandlung, 1907): inscriptions in unknown hands (possibly Alma's and Werfel's) on pp. 336–37

141

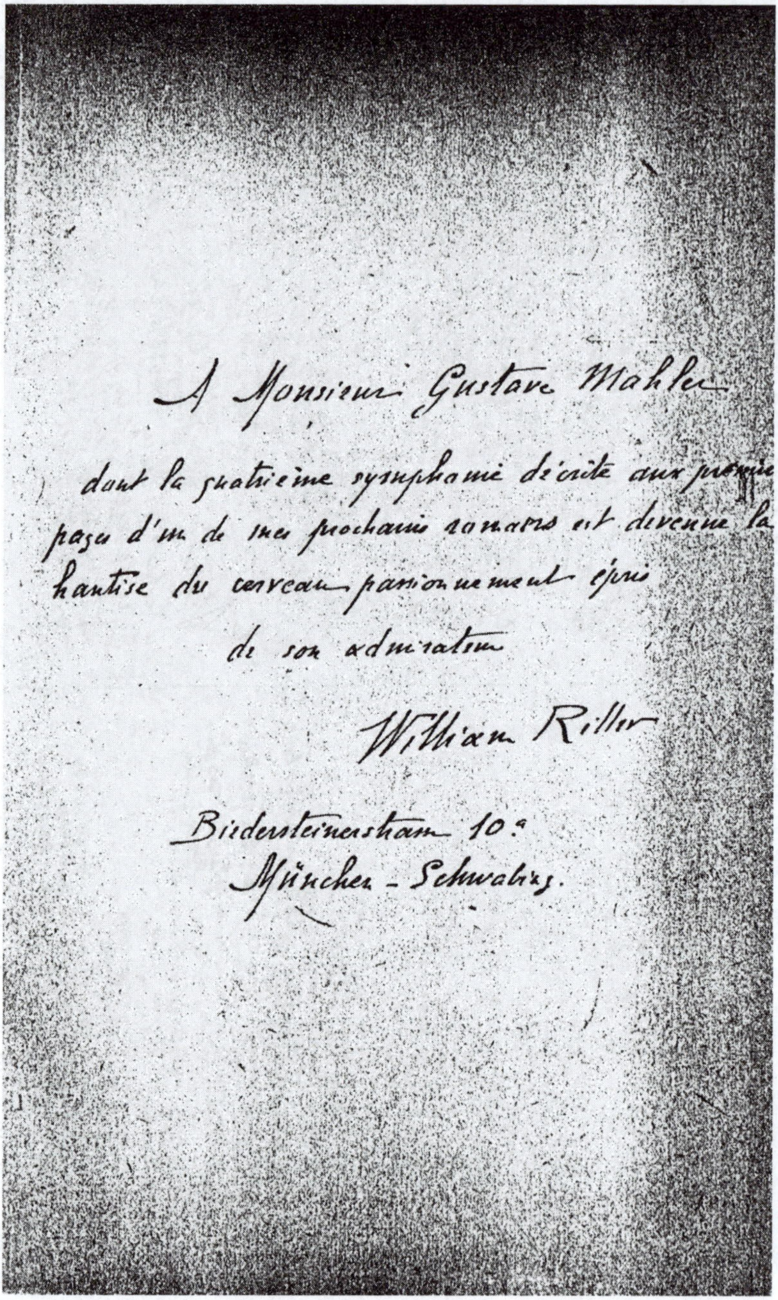
A Monsieur Gustave Mahler

dont la quatrième symphonie décrite aux premières pages d'un de mes prochains romans est devenue la hantise du cerveau passionnément épris de son admirateur

William Ritter

Biedersteinerstrasse 10a
München - Schwabing.

Plate 3.5 William Ritter, *Leurs Lys et leurs Roses* (Paris: Société de Mercure de France, 1903): inscription by Ritter on second leaf

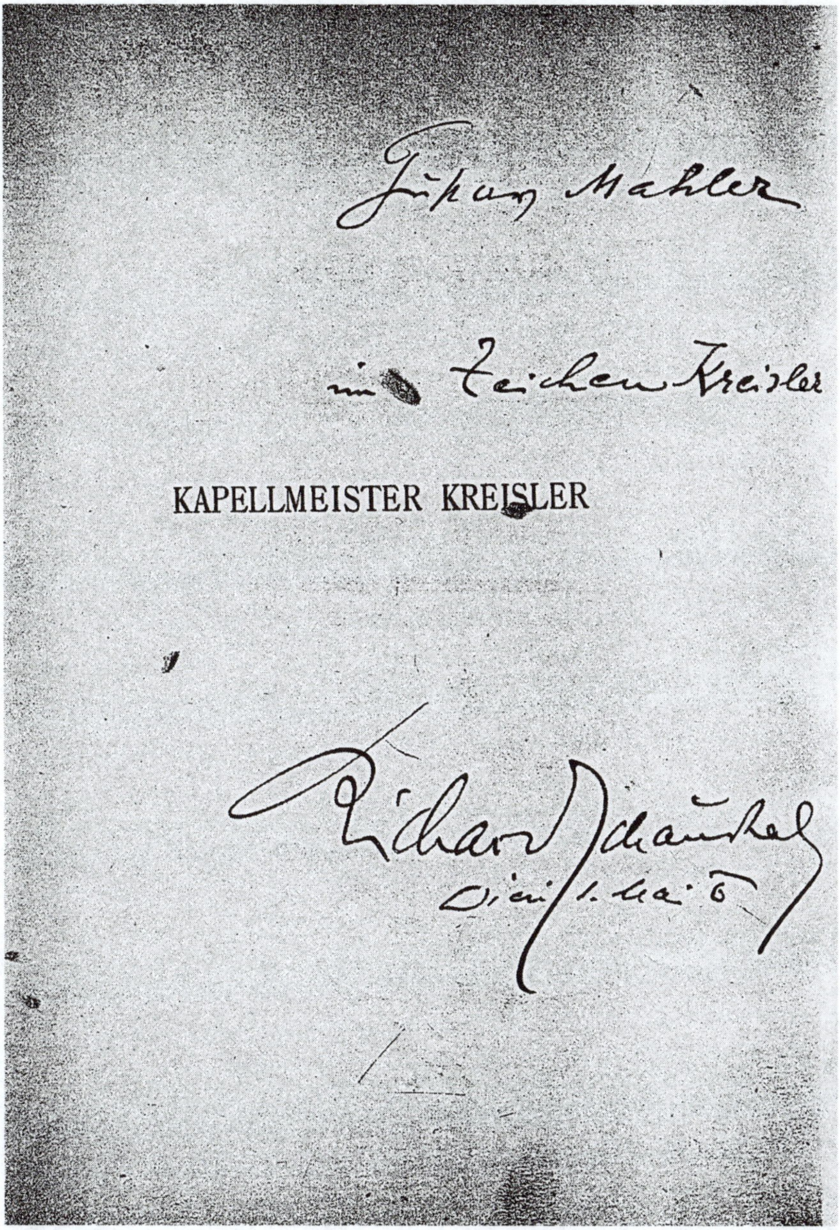

Plate 3.6 Richard Schaukal, *Kapellmeister Kreisler* (Munich & Leipzig: Georg Mueller, 1906): inscription by Schaukal on second title page

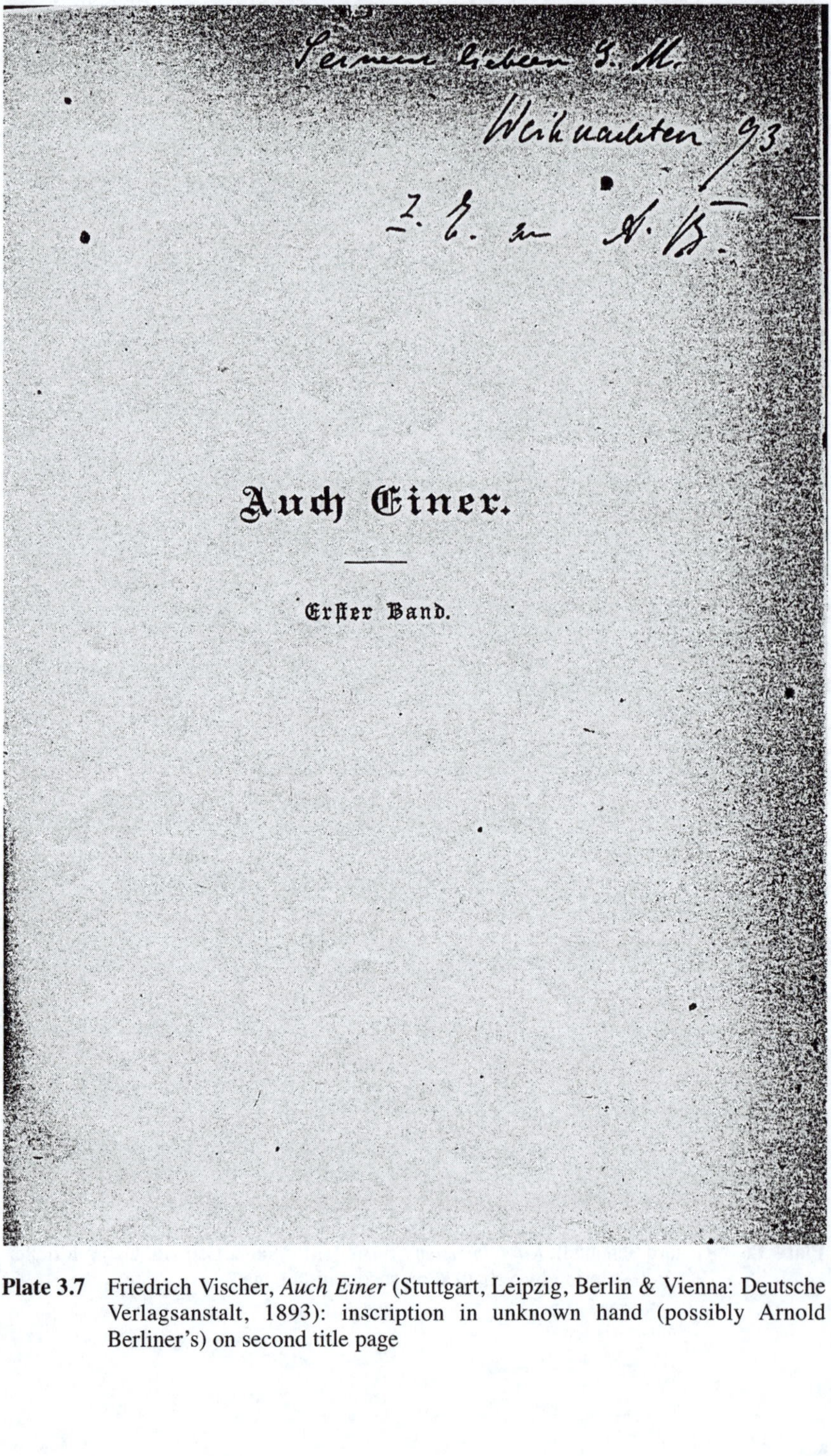

Plate 3.7 Friedrich Vischer, *Auch Einer* (Stuttgart, Leipzig, Berlin & Vienna: Deutsche Verlagsanstalt, 1893): inscription in unknown hand (possibly Arnold Berliner's) on second title page

mein Kopf ist dein
du hast ihn erkiest,
entfrägst du mir nicht
was dir frommt,
lös' ich's mit Lehren nicht ein.   *J. c.*   Gustav
                                              Alma } Mahler
LEHRBUCH   *in alter Freundschaft*
DER
                                    der Verf.
                                    Berlin, d. 18.v. 03

EXPERIMENTALPHYSIK
IN ELEMENTARER DARSTELLUNG.

VON

D^R. ARNOLD BERLINER.

MIT 3 LITHOGRAPHISCHEN TAFELN
UND 695 ZUM TEIL FARBIGEN ABBILDUNGEN IM TEXTE.

VERLAG VON GUSTAV FISCHER IN JENA.
1903.

Plate 3.8   Arnold Berliner, *Lehrbuch der Experimentalphysik* (Jena: Gustav Fischer, 1903): inscription by Berliner on title page

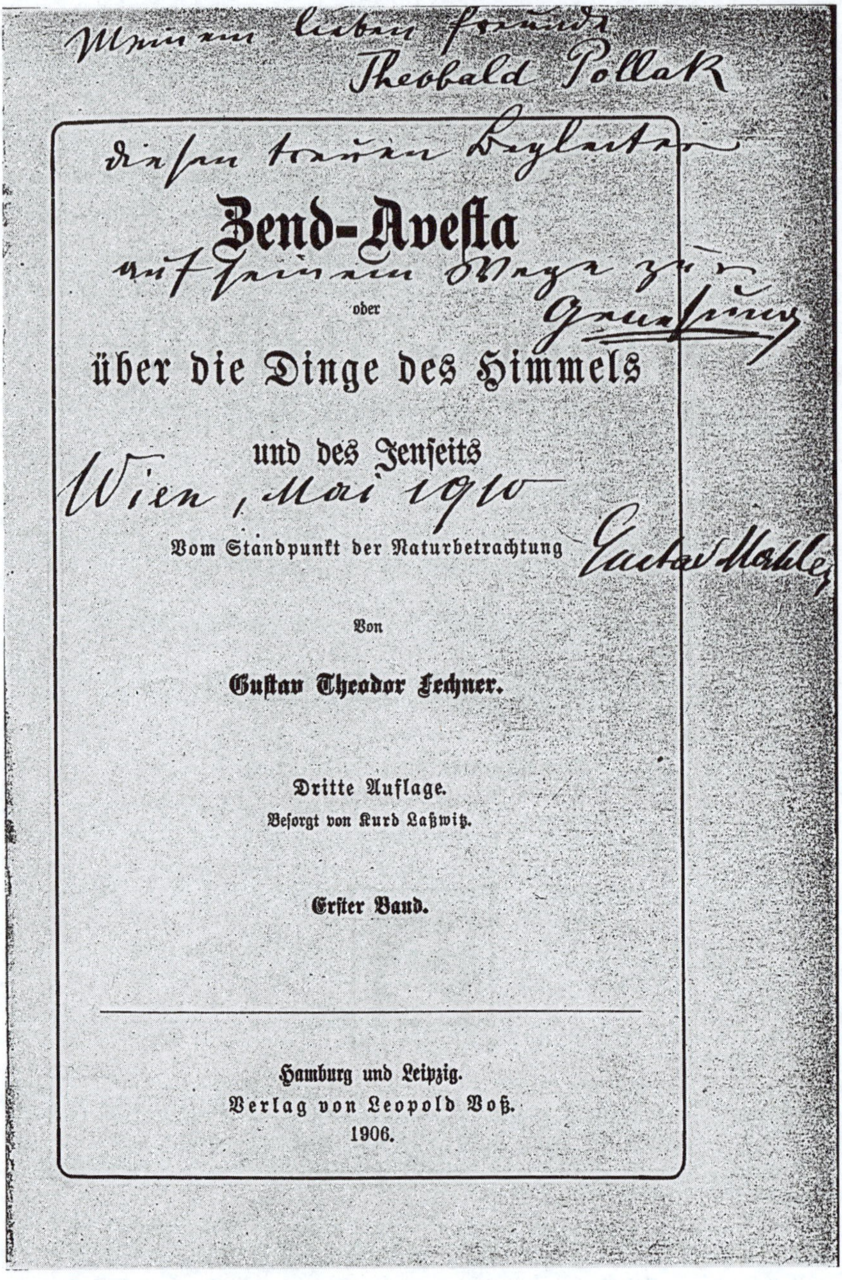

Meinem lieben Freunde
Theobald Pollak
diesen treuen Begleiter
auf seinem Wege zur
Genesung

Zend-Avesta

oder

über die Dinge des Himmels

und des Jenseits

Wien, Mai 1910
Gustav Mahler

Vom Standpunkt der Naturbetrachtung

Von

Gustav Theodor Fechner.

Dritte Auflage.

Besorgt von Kurd Laßwitz.

Erster Band.

Hamburg und Leipzig.
Verlag von Leopold Voß.
1906.

Plate 3.9 Gustav Fechner, *Zend-Avesta* (Hamburg & Leipzig: Leopold Voss, 1906): inscription by Mahler on title page

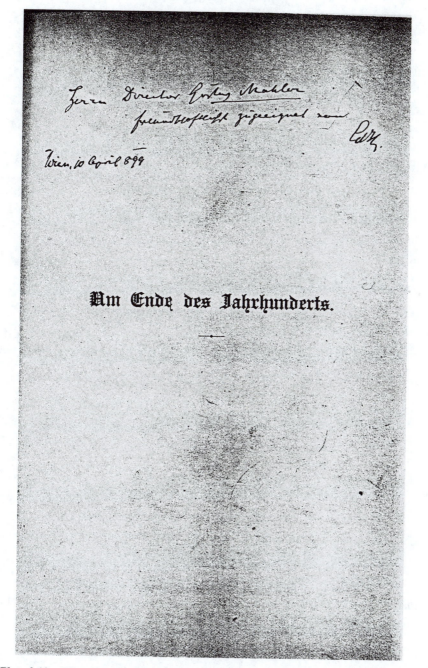

Plate 3.10 Eduard Hanslick, *Am Ende des Jahrhunderts* (Berlin: Allgemeiner Verein für Deutsche Litteratur, 1899): inscription by Hanslick on second title page

Goethe sagt:

Die Kunst stellt eigentlich nicht Begriffe dar, aber die Art wie sie darstellt, ist ein Begreifen, ein Zusammenfassen des Gemein= samen und Charakteristischen d. h. der Stil.

Studie zu Fidelio

von

Lilli Lehmann.

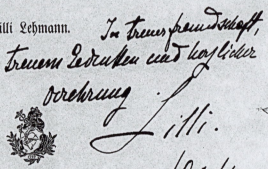

Leipzig, Druck und Verlag von Breitkopf und Härtel 1904.

Plate 3.11 Lilli Lehmann, *Studie zu Fidelio* (Leipzig: Breitkopf und Härtel, 1904): inscription by Lehmann on title page

Plate 3.12   Lilli Lehmann, *Studie zu Tristan und Isolde* (no details): inscription by
Lehmann on title page

Plate 3.13 *Briefwechsel zwischen Wagner und Liszt* (Leipzig: Breitkopf und Härtel, 1887): inscription by Albert Spiegler on second leaf

Plate 3.14   *Hamerlings Werke* (Hamburg: Verlagsanstalt und Druckerei A.-G. (vorm. J.F. Richter), n.d. [foreword in vol. 1. dated 1900]), vol. 3: inner leaf with the bookplate designed for Alma in 1900 by Josef Hoffmann

Chapter Four

Mahler's Untimely Modernism

MORTEN SOLVIK

One of the many ironies of Mahler's artistic persona lies in his troubled relationship with modernism. For all the innovations of his music and the profound changes he brought to operatic performance practice, Mahler's outlook on life in many respects set itself apart from the attitudes espoused by his avant-garde colleagues. In the philosophical traditions he embraced, the artistic works he admired and the intellectual ground he defended Mahler was largely a cultural conservative. How do we make sense of a composer and conductor at the vanguard of his art who, as an intellectual, clung to ideals that many of his time considered *passé*? Why, in light of this background, did Mahler's works nevertheless come to represent such a significant achievement? Unravelling the contradictions inherent in this complex of traits sheds light not only on the artist who embodied such divergent tendencies but also on the issues that have come to bear on the ninety years that have passed since Mahler's death.

One need not look any further than Mahler's *oeuvre* to begin to gain an impression of a world-view virtually divorced from the influences of contemporary art. Here, among the quotations and references to the likes of Klopstock, Goethe, *Des Knaben Wunderhorn*, Rückert, Jean Paul, Dante, E.T.A. Hoffmann, Hölderlin, Lenau and Schopenhauer, there lurks a searching spirit combing through the literary and philosophical past to give expression to the ideas that most moved him. No trace of Dehmel, Hofmannsthal or others making a name for themselves among the literary elite at the time. Though the works of these and other contemporary writers are linked to numerous musical compositions of the turn of the century, not one of them played even a minor role in Mahler's songs and symphonies.[1] Instead, Mahler's works reference a

---

[1] The only near-contemporary writer who appears in Mahler's works is Friedrich Nietzsche. Mahler's attitude towards the philosopher was, however, quite complex and ultimately dismissive; for more on Nietzsche's influence on Mahler's conception of art and religion, see the author's dissertation (Olsen, 1992, pp. 61–66 & 109–13). Hans Bethge, a true contemporary, was not the original author but rather the writer of the *Nachdichtungen* (re-worked from German, English and French prose versions of Chinese poems) rendered in *Das Lied von der Erde*.

heterogeneous mix of ideas largely borrowed from Christianity, folk poetry and the German Romantic movement – directions of thought hardly viewed as progressive in avant-garde circles of late nineteenth-century Austria.[2]

In large part this characteristic of Mahler's output can be understood as a deeply personal response to a philosophical problem that profoundly influenced his creative thinking. Mahler felt driven to seek answers to the ultimate existential dilemma with almost obsessive fervour. As he put it in a letter to Alma of 14 December 1901 regarding the Second Symphony:

> What now? What is this life of ours – and what is death?
> Is there for us a life in the beyond?
> Is everything just a deranged dream, or do life and death have a meaning?
> We must answer this question if we are to go on living.
>   (La Grange & Weiß, 1995, p. 87; see Mahler, 1990, p. 213)[3]

True to his own pronouncement Mahler tackled this question with almost every work he wrote. His response betrays the workings of a complex mind whose contradictions became the very subject of his art. On the one hand he crafted a remarkably consistent approach to the resolution of the problem. The texted and openly programmatic symphonies, for instance, clearly portray a universe in which struggle gives way to redemption. Whether in the hero's triumph (Symphony No. 1), the victory of life after death (No. 2), the crowning of existence in love (No. 3), the child's innocent vision of heaven (No. 4) or the otherworldly power of the eternal feminine (No. 8), Mahler evokes the promise of an ideal realm lurking beyond the appearances of daily existence.[4] In his letter to Alma cited above Mahler continues with his description of the final movement of the Second:

> Gently there sounds the choir of saints and heavenly beings:
> 'Rise up, yes you shall rise up.' God's magnificence appears before us! A wonderful, gentle light passes through us into our hearts – all is still and blessed! ... An overwhelming feeling of love shines through us with blessed certainty and being.
>   (La Grange & Weiß, 1995, p. 89; see Mahler, 1990, p. 214)

But the transcendental vision that Mahler seems to offer in so many of his symphonic works was highly problematic. Reaching so consistently for the metaphor of overcoming forced him to part company intellectually with many of

---

2   This is not to say that Mahler isolated himself as an intellectual. Indeed, he revealed strongly eclectic characteristics, read widely and was certainly aware of the artistic trends among his contemporaries.

3   Translations are the author's own unless otherwise noted.

4   *Pace* Adorno ('Mahler was a poor yea-sayer' ['Mahler war ein schlechter Jasager'] (Adorno, 1992a, p. 137, 1960, pp. 180–81)) I also hear Mahler reaching for this vision in the Fifth and Seventh Symphonies. The Sixth and the Ninth present anti-heroic conclusions that are fascinating, but nevertheless exceptional in his symphonic output.

his contemporaries, to seek assurances in a world-view whose legitimacy was fading, and ultimately to question the foundations of his own artistic project. It was not that Mahler was content with pat solutions to world-philosophic questions. Despite the religious overtones of this and other programmatic descriptions it was not enough for him, for instance, simply to embrace the tenets of Christianity. As Oskar Fried noted in his recollection of the composer:

> He was a God-seeker. With incredible fanaticism, with unparalleled dedication and with unshakeable love he pursued a constant search for the divine, both in the individual and in man as a whole. … But from time to time he would doubt this heavenly mission and worry momentarily whether he had the ability to carry it through, even though he was convinced of nothing so firmly as his faith in himself. In such moments of inner conflict, he needed, so as not to perish in the moral wilderness, some earthly support to cling on to … .
>
> (Cited in Lebrecht, 1987, pp. 174–75)[5]

In part as a consequence of his mistrust of dogma Mahler sought out philosophers who could construct an argument for the transcendental as an intellectually viable approach to bridging the gap between body and spirit, between life and what may lie beyond it. Foremost among these thinkers stands Arthur Schopenhauer, whose *Die Welt als Wille und Vorstellung* left a lasting impression on the composer and many intellectuals in the mid to late nineteenth century. Schopenhauer argued that, for all the epistemological mystery that shrouds existence, life in its truest form could nevertheless reveal itself to the fortunate few, including artists endowed with divine inspiration. Given the make-up of his personality and the artistic culture that inspired him, Mahler took this revelation as a mandate in his own work as a creative artist to pursue the profound questions of life in his musical compositions. This sense of mission was further compounded by the urgings of Richard Wagner, particularly in his essays

---

[5] 'Er war ein Gottsucher. Mit einem unerhörten Fanatismus, mit einer beispiellosen Hingabe, mit einer unerschütterlichen Liebe war er, stets auf der Suche im Menschen, in einem jeden, nach dem Göttlichen. … Aber von Zeit zu Zeit hatte er Augenblicke, da er diese himmlische Mission anzweifelte, und es würgte ihn dann beständig die Angst, ob er auch tatsächlich die Erfüllung in sich trage, obwohl er in nichts so unerschütterlich verankert war als in dem Glauben an sich selbst. In solchen Momenten des inneren Zwiespaltes bedurfte er, um in einer irdischen Ernüchterung nicht zu erlahmen, stets eines irdischen Stützpunktes … .' Oskar Fried, 'Erinnerungen an Mahler', *Musikblätter des Anbruch*, 1 (1919), cited in Lebrecht, 1990b & 1993, p. 172. Mahler's mistrust of dogma emerges in a telling account by Alfred Roller: 'I once asked him why he did not write a mass, and he seemed taken aback. "Do you think I could take that upon myself? Well, why not? But no, there's the credo in it." And he began to recite the credo in Latin. "No, I couldn't do it."' ['Ich fragte ihn einst, warum er eigentlich keine Messe schreibe. Er schien betroffen. "Glauben Sie, daß ich das vermöchte? Nun, warum nicht? Doch nein. Da kommst das Credo vor." Und er begann das Credo lateinisch herzusagen. "Nein, das vermag ich doch nicht."'] Cited in Lebrecht, 1987, 1990b, p. 164.

on art, and Friedrich Nietzsche, particularly in *Die Geburt der Tragödie*, both of whom on this count can be seen as epigones of Schopenhauer. It is important to point out that in his revision of the Kantian critique of metaphysics, Schopenhauer, and even Kant himself, posit a world beyond the accidents of daily life: that is, a domain not accessible by means of sensory perception but nevertheless at the fundament of existence. It was in the philosophical demonstrability of this transcendental realm and its mystical rendering through music that Mahler sought his spiritual reassurance.

Other philosophers whom Mahler consulted include Gustav Theodor Fechner (1801–87) and Eduard Hartmann (1842–1906), thinkers generally forgotten today whose writings nevertheless afford a revealing glimpse of Mahler's idealist world-view. Fechner's approach to life affirmed the notion of a universal soul, a form of consciousness that adhered to all forms of life where nature itself represented merely the surface of a mystical essence.[6] In taking an inductive approach to the natural sciences, Hartmann was equally engaged in defending a vitalistic view of life from the inroads of mechanistic materialism. His philosophical position, self-described as 'transcendental realism', has led one commentator to sum up his stance in terms of a 'cosmic drama of redemption'.[7]

For all of the seriousness of these philosophical inquiries, the ideas espoused by Mahler's favourite thinkers would have struck many of the avant-garde of his time as outdated. By the end of the nineteenth century, many of the leading lights in science, philosophy, politics and the arts had come to question seriously the intellectual terrain Mahler so firmly defended. Do we need to look beyond appearances to an ideal realm when empirical science can explain, indeed predict, the world so well? How is grasping the infinite even possible when the mind and human experience are so beset by inherent limitations? For many the time had come to break free from old beliefs and habits of thought, to approach life from a new perspective, in short, to embrace the 'modern'. As Herman Bahr, an Austrian contemporary of Mahler, put it in an article entitled 'Die Moderne':

> There is a wild suffering running through our time and the pain is no longer bearable. ... The modern ... is out there everywhere, outside us. It is not in our spiritual being. Rather, it is the suffering and the feverish sickness of the century that the spirit has run out of life. Life has changed to its very core and changes constantly anew, every day, restless and unstable. But the spirit

---

6   There have been numerous publications on Fechner; see, for instance, Heinrich Adolph, *Die Weltanschauung Gustav Theodor Fechners* (Stuttgart: Strecker und Schröder, 1923); for a detailed background and a discussion of Mahler's reception of Fechner, see Barham, 1998, especially Chapters 1 and 2.

7   See Robert Audi (ed.), *The Cambridge Dictionary of Philosophy* (Cambridge: Cambridge University Press, 1995), p. 310. Though a prolific writer, today Hartmann is usually associated with a single work, his *Philosophie des Unbewußten* (1869).

remained old and petrified and did not budge and did not move and now
suffers helplessly because it is lonesome and abandoned by life.
(Bahr, 1890, cited in Wunberg, 1981, p. 189)[8]

The challenges posed by modern philosophy and science at the turn of the
century awakened the suspicion among many intellectuals that something
essential was missing from the equation, that there was a yawning gap between
what we are taught to be true and what we sense to be true about the world around
us. Bahr's essay can be read as an indictment of a world-view no longer capable
of sustaining its arguments, as an attempt to come to grips with a sense of
alienation between the conceptual framework designed to describe life and life
itself.

An impulse of many intellectuals in this climate of uncertainty was to seek
new answers to old questions in radically novel ways: to abandon idealism or
even the notion of God, to reduce existence to the fullness of the moment, to see
life as a series of discrete events, or to analyse the human condition as a response
to impulses beyond our control. Nearly all of these attempts to forge a new
definition of reality had one trait in common: the conscious effort to avoid
imposing a rationale on the ways of the world. The sense took hold that a
universal explanation capable of plumbing the depths of existence was beyond
the ken of human thought. An even more sobering suspicion was growing that
such an overarching reason did not even exist – that if the veil of appearances
could be lifted it would reveal but a hollow shell. Gone was the all-embracing
ambition to explain the world; what was left for the modern spirit was, according
to Hofmannsthal, two extremes: science, the cold examination of the material
world, and self-indulgence, basking in the individual's sensory perceptions.
Hofmannsthal writes:

> Today there are two things that appear to be modern: the analysis of
> life and the escape from life. There is little interest in active doing,
> in the interaction between the outer and inner forces of life, in the
> lessons of life à la *Wilhelm Meister* and in the grand scheme of
> things in the Shakespearean sense. One engages in the anatomy of
> one's own soul, or one dreams. Reflections or fantasy, mirror or
> imagination. Modern are old furniture and young nervousness.
> Modern is psychologically listening to the grass grow and babbling
> in the purely imaginary world of wonder. Modern is ... the
> dissection of atoms and playing ball with the universe; modern is

---

8 'Es geht eine wilde Pein durch diese Zeit und der Schmerz ist nicht mehr
erträglich. ... Die Moderne ... ist draußen überall, außer uns. Sie ist nicht in unserem
Geiste. Sondern das ist die Qual und die Krankheit des Jahrhunderts, die fieberische und
schnaubende, daß das Leben dem Geiste entronnen ist. Das Leben hat sich gewandelt, bis
in letzten Grund, und wandelt sich immer noch aufs Neue, alle Tage, rastlos und unstät.
Aber der Geist blieb alt und starr und regte sich nicht und bewegte sich nicht und nun
leidet er hilflos, weil er einsam ist und verlassen vom Leben.'

the dismemberment of a mood, a sigh, a scruple; and modern is the instinctual, almost somnambulistic surrender to every revelation of the beautiful, of a colourful chord, a shimmering metaphor, a wonderful allegory. ... two urges: the urge to experiment and the urge to beauty, the urge to understand and that to forget.

(Hofmannsthal, 1893, cited in Wunberg, 1981, pp. 342–43)[9]

This mindset left telling traces on the accomplishments of intellectuals active in this period. Whether in the social criticism in the plays of Ibsen or in the self-centred reflections in the poems of Maeterlinck, whether in naturalist drama or *l'art pour l'art*, many artists seem to have perceived their role in terms very similar to the bipolar opposition laid out in Hofmannsthal's essay.

It is precisely here, in the opposition between the inner and outer realms which had become so problematized in the 1890s, that Mahler parted company with most of his contemporaries. Rather than plunge headlong into the experiments and new perspectives of the self-proclaimed modernists, Mahler refused to abandon the project of German idealism, a tradition to which he saw himself a rightful heir. Examining the ties between spiritual and material existence, seeking out a higher logic in the seeming chaos that surrounds us, grappling with an explanation for the ways of the world – for all the hopelessness attached to these ambitions by those around him, Mahler steadfastly maintained his ground.[10] It comes as no surprise, then, to learn that Goethe and Shakespeare, those authors

---

[9]   'Heute scheinen zwei Dinge modern zu sein: die Analyse des Lebens und die Flucht aus dem Leben. Gering ist die Freude an Handlung, am Zusammenspiel der äußeren und inneren Lebensmächte, am Wilhelm-Meisterlichen Lebenlernen und am Shakespearischen Weltlauf. Man treibt Anatomie des eigenen Seelenlebens, oder man träumt. Reflexion oder Phantasie, Spiegelbild oder Traumbild. Modern sind alte Möbel und junge Nervositäten. Modern ist das psychologische Graswachsenhören und das Plätschern in der reinphantastischen Wunderwelt. Modern ist ... das Zerschneiden von Atomen und das Ballspielen mit dem All; modern ist die Zergliederung einer Laune, eines Seufzers, eines Skrupels; und modern ist die instinktmäßige, fast somnambule Hingabe an jede Offenbarung des Schönen, an einen Farbenakkord, eine funkelnde Metapher, eine wundervolle Allegorie. ... dem Experimentiertrieb und dem Schönheitstrieb, dem Trieb nach Verstehen und dem nach Vergessen.'

[10]   The untimely quality of Mahler's intellectual project was not lost on some of his contemporaries. Georg Göhler published the following observations in 1910 in honour of Mahler's fiftieth birthday: 'Mahler struck out on his own beyond [his contemporaries]. For the last twenty years, a time adverse to idealistic tendencies, he continued to tread a lonely track in the wake of the greatest artists of all time and, on his own terms, sought to approach the eternal problem of all great art, the problem of bringing together the human and the divine, the earthly and the unearthly in their inner essence and to tackle the meaning of life. ... He has been immune to all temptations, because he had a goal, a life's purpose, because his uncompromising idealism drove him ever higher. He did not take up any of the fashionable topics, not even the ever-popular topic of sex with which artists have earned so much money in the last decades. He saw everything in the light of a more pure world, one that is permeated by a superhuman, godly force, by a sacred,

singled out by Hofmannsthal as unmodern, counted among those individuals in human history, along with Beethoven and Wagner, whom Mahler most revered (see, for example, Killian, 1984, pp. 26 & 33, and Franklin, 1980, pp. 30 & 38).

It would be wrong, of course, to suggest that the artists of Mahler's generation were singularly opposed to the composer's world-view. Most maintained a transcendental streak in their thinking, all the while flirting with such 'modern' concerns as sexuality, neurosis and social malaise. Nevertheless, Mahler stood out for his hard-line rejection of such fashionable topics, an attitude that also informed many of his personal relationships with his famous contemporaries. A case in point is Gerhart Hauptmann (1868–1946). Hauptmann emerged as one of the leading playwrights at the turn of the century, a long-lived writer with an uncanny sense of the tastes of his time. He first met Mahler on a visit to Vienna in 1904; in his diary entry on 5 February he writes: 'Made the acquaintance of Gustav Mahler yesterday. Outstanding mind. Demonic force of nature. Stamp of great genius unmistakable' (Machatzke, 1987, p. 386; see also La Grange, 1995, p. 701).[11] It was the beginning of a lasting acquaintance, though Mahler's personal affections in no way clouded his artistic judgment. Not even being dragged off to a performance of Hauptmann's *Friedensfest* by the dramatist himself prevented him from giving his honest opinion. Mahler related the episode as follows in a letter to Alma dated 14 January 1907:

> Then it was off to the German Theater to 'Friedensfest'. (Hauptmann was very anxious that I should see it, otherwise I would have preferred to stay at home.) A dreadful, realistic affair. If you can work up an enthusiasm for this kind of art, you certainly get your due. I totally adopted the author's point of

---

all-pervasive life-giving spirit' ['Mahler ist abseits von ihnen seinen eigenen Weg gegangen. In einer Zeit, die wie die letzten zwanzig Jahre idealistischen Richtungen abhold war, ging er einsam weiter auf den Spuren der größten Künstler aller Zeiten und suchte dem ewigen Problem aller großen Kunst, dem Problem, Menschliches und Göttliches, Irdisches und Überirdisches in inneren Zusammenhang zu bringen und den Sinn des Lebens zu ergründen, auf seine Weise beizukommen. ... An allen Versuchungen ist er vorbeigekommen, weil er ein Ziel, eine Lebensaufgabe hatte, weil sein rücksichtsloser Idealismus ihn immer weiter aufwärts führte. Keines der Modethemen griff er auf, nicht einmal das so beliebte Sexuelle, mit dem in den letzten Jahrzehnten die Künstler so viel Geld verdient haben. Alles sah er im Lichte einer reineren Welt, die durchlebt ist von einer übermenschlichen, göttlichen Kraft, von einem heiligen, alles belebenden Geiste'] (Göhler, 'Gustav Mahler', *Der Kunstwart*, July, 1910, 2nd vol., repr. in La Grange & Weiß, 1995, pp. 480–84, citation on p. 483). Mahler held Göhler's essay in high esteem, calling it 'the most beautiful and best [writing] about me that I have ever read' ['Der Aufsatz von Göhler ist das Schönste und Beste, was ich über mich noch gelesen habe'] (see Mahler's letter to Alma on 8 July 1910 in La Grange and Weiß, 1995, p. 439; the editors identify this reference on p. 428. Göhler published another similarly flattering and revealing review in 1910: 'Über die Stellung zu Mahlers Kunst', *Die Musik*, 9 (23), 272–75.

[11] 'Gestern Gustav Mahler kennengelernt. Hervorragender Kopf. Dämonische Naturkraft. Stempel des großen Genies unverkennbar.'

view so as to do him justice. (Hauptmann asked if I could come up to him
the next morning to talk about it.[)] ... Early this morning, straight after
breakfast, Hauptmann walked in. 'Well, I've come to get my critique.' So I
presented my criticism and we chatted quite pleasantly.
(La Grange & Weiß, 1995, pp. 309–10; see Mahler, 1990, pp. 285–86)

The play, which centres on the conflicts and complexes that rise to the surface
within a bourgeois family as it meets to celebrate Christmas, clearly left Mahler
cold. The 'dreadful realism' of an artistic work that presents such mundane
matters as aesthetically worthy content could hardly have impressed him.[12] That
the incident seems not to have impinged on their relationship in the slightest
speaks well for both of them.

The same cannot be said for Mahler's acquaintance with Hermann Bahr
(1863–1934), a respected writer and cultural commentator with a large following
in Vienna, and the author of the essay on modernity cited above. It is clear that
the two men had contact with one another,[13] and it is equally clear that Mahler
preferred to see as little of the writer as possible. Writing to Alma in Salzburg in
June 1909, he commented: 'If you are good and can wait then I am thinking about
coming there to pick you up. But only if [Hermann] Bahr and [Anna von]
Mildenburg aren't there, since I couldn't very well ignore them' ['Wenn Du brav
ausharrst, so gedenke ich, Dich dort abzuholen. Aber nur, wenn nicht [Hermann]
Bahr u. die [Anna von] Mildenburg dort sind, an denen ich nicht leicht
vorübergehen könnte'] (La Grange & Weiß, 1995, p. 385). Anna von Mildenburg,
a well-known soprano in her day, had been Mahler's mistress in the mid-1890s
while they were both at the Hamburg Opera. The relationship had cooled rapidly,
and by the time both were working at the same opera house again Mahler had
asserted a polite distance between them. Bahr's marriage to Mildenburg in 1909
certainly coloured any relationship Mahler may have had with him, but from
Mahler's perspective this did not represent much of a loss. An article by Bahr in
1910 inspired considerable disdain on the part of the composer, whose reaction
betrayed anything but professional respect: 'But that Bahr can explain something
to me – that I find comical. It really reminds me of Pythia, a stupid woman who,
numbed by fumes, babbles nonsense which the sages then interpret into golden
doctrines' ['Aber daß Bahr mir etwas erklären kann, finde ich drollig. Das
erinnert schon wirklich an die Pythia – ein dummes Weib, welches von
Dämpfen betäubt, Unsinn schwatzt, den die Weisen zu goldenen Lehren
umdeuten'] (ibid., p. 454).

Mahler's analogy reveals as much about its author as about its supposed
victim. Pythia was the legendary figure at Delphi who, after questions were posed

---

[12]   Despite these differences one finds convincing points of intersection in some of
their works. For a comparison of Hauptmann's *Hanneles Himmelfahrt* with Mahler's
Third and Fourth Symphonies, see Olsen, 1992, pp. 309–14.
[13]   See, for instance, La Grange, 1995, pp. 699–700 for an account of a meeting of
the two men that Max Burckhard arranged in 1904.

to the oracle, spoke as a medium at Apollo's temple. Bahr was likewise a medium of sorts, a spokesman and prophet for a group of literary intellectuals in Vienna called 'Junges Wien' that included the likes of Arthur Schnitzler, Richard Beer-Hofmann, and Hugo von Hofmannsthal. If this quote serves as any indication we can well imagine what Mahler thought of Bahr and his colleagues and those who were impressed by what they had to say. Writers such as Bourget, Barrès, Jacobsen, Swinburne, Maeterlinck and Huysmans favoured by this circle (see Wunberg, 1981, p. 281) did not exactly elicit Mahler's enthusiasm either. Mahler described Maeterlinck's work to Alma as 'dreary, tipsy thoughts inspired by cheap liquor' ['der fuselhaft trübe Gedankendusel Maeterlincks'] (La Grange & Weiß, 1995, p. 107; see also pp. 146–47). The self-absorbed, experiential perspective of these and other writers did not rest easily with Mahler's vision of art as a mandate from a higher realm. Indulging in feeling merely for the sake of describing the interplay between sensation and thought must have struck Mahler, as the epithet indicates, as a waste – even an abuse – of artistic talent.

In all, Mahler's contact with the intellectual and artistic elite of his time demonstrates an almost universal detachment, a desire to keep his contemporaries at a distance for lack of mutual empathy and comprehension.[14] Mahler's bearing and relentless dedication to art struck many of those who knew him as the prickly exterior of an ascetic soul, an individual unwilling to compromise his lofty and somewhat old-fashioned ideals. For his part, Mahler could not bring himself to adopt the attitudes called for by the heralds of modernism. In setting himself apart in this way, Mahler came face to face with an undeniable sense of isolation, something he admitted to Alma early in their relationship:

> But I have always struggled to be understood, appreciated by my equals, even if I don't end up finding them in my lifetime (and in fact they can only be sought outside of time and space); and from now on this should be the highest goal of my life! You must stand by me in this, my beloved! And you know, to win this reward, this wreath of honour, one has to renounce the applause of the masses, yes even that of the good, the noble (who also sometimes simply cannot keep up). ... Yes I am all too aware that the little respect that I have won for myself could possibly be merely attributed to a misunderstanding, in any case only the vague inkling of something higher yet unattainable.
>
> (La Grange & Weiß, 1995, p. 84; see Mahler, 1990, pp. 209–10)

Mahler's lament goes beyond the complaints of a misunderstood artist longing for recognition. Instead, he resigns himself stoically to the prospect of hollow acclaim, of finding adherents who nevertheless cannot divine the true, 'higher' nature of his works. This prophetic insight would haunt Mahler to the end of his

---

[14] A few of the exceptions among Mahler's acquaintances include Siegfried Lipiner, Arnold Berliner and Richard Horn.

life. Even by the time he had become truly famous as a composer, he could not escape the suspicion that only a few could comprehend his music. Astonishingly, suffering this fate did not dampen Mahler's self-confidence as an artist. Indeed, the very resistance he detected seems to have increased his resolve to carry on.

Nothing more aptly demonstrates both this determination and the intellectual gulf that divided Mahler from his own time than a passage from a letter he wrote to Alma during a brief stay in Salzburg to conduct *The Marriage of Figaro* in the summer of 1906. Considerably annoyed at the pomp and empty gestures of the vain and powerful with whom he was forced to spend time in his position as head of the Court Opera, Mahler lashed out at his surroundings:

> The devil take the whole damned lot of them. Strauss has already composed a few scenes from *Electra* (Hofmannsthal). He won't give it up for less than 10 percent per evening and 100,000 Marks. (Granted, this is only an assumption of mine[)]. Since I wasn't asked I also told him nothing of my antiquated existence this summer. I think it would impress him very little to learn with what old-fashioned rubbish I am keeping myself busy this summer. O blessed, o blessed to be modern! [O selig, o selig modern zu sein!]
>
> (La Grange & Weiß, 1995, p. 282; see Mahler, 1990, p. 276)

The passage is rich in allusions to what Mahler considered typical of the pseudo-sophistication of modern society: crass materialism (demanding exorbitant royalties), competing for artistic recognition (with Richard Strauss, a rivalry that would long plague him), and a fondness for modish works of art (Hofmannsthal's *Elektra*, which had been published in 1903). Mahler contrasts this fashionably avant-garde world with his own, outdated existence, a comparison that struck him with particular clarity at the time. That very summer he was at work on his Eighth Symphony, a vast tableau that incorporated texts by Goethe, an icon of the early nineteenth century, and Hrabanus Maurus, a medieval cleric. As this sideward glance at his contemporaries makes clear, Mahler was entirely aware of how far removed he was from the tastes of his time.

Yet this did not seem to discourage him. For all the pressure he might have felt at not embracing the fashion of the day, Mahler ends with a biting comment that ridicules the short-sightedness of his contemporaries ('O selig, o selig modern zu sein!'). The quip is a paraphrase of a line from 'Sonst spielt' ich mit Zepter', a song in Albert Lortzing's *Zar und Zimmermann*, one of Mahler's favourite operas.[15] Looking more closely at this source reveals how the reference served Mahler's commentary on his fellow artists in a particularly apt manner. The Singspiel centres on Peter the Great of Russia who, disguised as a shipbuilder,

---

[15] *Zar und Zimmermann* was premièred in Leipzig in 1837. For Mahler's high regard of Lortzing, see Killian, 1984, p. 200, and Franklin, 1980, p. 181. The quotation is identified in Mahler, 1990, p. 243.

has come to Holland incognito in order to learn more about the ways of Western culture. While abroad he learns of the unrest that has befallen his homeland in his absence and now must make a hasty return to save his country from chaos. The burden of his duties weighs heavily on his shoulders in the third act as he sings of his sacrifice for the unappreciative masses:

Zar allein:	*Tsar alone* [speaks]:
Glückliche, beneidenswerte	Happy, enviable people! The future
Menschen! Euch lächelt froh die	shines on you as in the golden days
Zukunft, wie in der Kindheit	of childhood when not a care
goldnen Tagen, wo noch kein	troubled the soul.
Kummer die Seele drückt.	
	[sings]
Sonst spielt' ich mit Zepter, mit	I once played with sceptre, with
Krone und Stern;	crown and star;
Das Schwert schon als Kind, ach,	Even as a child how happy I was to
ich schwang es so gern!	swing the sword!
Gespielen und Diener bedrohte	My glance threatened playmates
mein Blick;	and servants;
Froh kehrt' ich zum Schoße des	I cheerfully returned to my father's
Vaters zurück.	lap.
Und liebkosend sprach er: Liebe	And tenderly he spoke to me: Dear
Knabe, bist mein!	boy, you are mine!
O selig, o selig, ein Kind noch zu	O blessed, how blessed still to be a
sein!	child!
Nun schmückt mich die Krone, nun	Now the crown adorns me, now I
trag ich den Stern,	carry the star,
Das Volk, meine Russen, beglückt'	The people, my Russians, how I
ich so gern.	long to make them happy.
Ich führ sie zur Größe, ich führ sie	I lead them to greatness, I lead
zum Licht,	them to the light,
Mein väterlich Streben erkennen	My fatherly efforts they do not
sie nicht.	recognize.
Umhüllet von Purpur nun steh ich	Wrapped in purple robe I now
allein –	stand alone –
O selig, o selig, ein Kind noch zu	O blessed, how blessed still to be a
sein!	child!
Und endet dies Streben und endet	And once the striving is over and
die Pein,	the pain has passed
So setzt man dem Kaiser ein	Then they will raise a monument of
Denkmal von Stein.	stone to the emperor.
Ein Denkmal im Herzen erwirbt er	A monument in their hearts he will
sich kaum,	hardly achieve,
Denn irdische Größe erlischt wie	For earthly greatness dissolves as if
im Traum.	in a dream.
Doch rufst du, Allgüt'ger: 'In	But you, the All-Beneficent, call
Frieden geh ein!'	out: 'Enter in peace!'

So werd ich beseligt dein Kind   Thus blissful, I will be your child
wieder sein.   again.

(Wilhelm Zentner, ed., *Albert Lortzing. Zar und Zimmermann* (Stuttgart:
Philipp Reclam Jun., 1981), pp. 70–71)

In the context of his letter to Alma, Mahler co-opts the message of this aria to assume the role of the composer sovereign looking down on the uncomprehending masses, wistfully reflecting on the bliss of ignorance while all the while keenly aware of his higher duties. Being 'modern' is rendered simply a product of the crowd mentality whose significance will fade. Despite the traces of haughtiness, Mahler's attitude is not merely dismissive. The mixture of emotions reveals a person dedicated to a thankless mission who cannot deny a slight yearning, even jealousy of those who take a simpler view of life. Seen from this perspective, the image of the monarch whose greatness is not yet truly appreciated emerges as a curious blend of stoic resignation and artistic conceit.

The tsar's song served Mahler on a number of occasions as a metaphor for his plight as a composer. In fact, references to the Lortzing aria appear in letters to Alma with regard to every symphony that was premièred after their relationship began in earnest at the end of 1901. After rehearsals for each of these premières (Symphony No. 5, Cologne, 1904; No. 6, Essen, 1906; No. 7, Prague, 1908) and in the letter cited above (with reference to the Eighth) Mahler sends off a missive to his wife with a direct allusion to the song of Peter the Great (La Grange & Weiß, 1995, pp. 220, 277, 363 & 282 respectively; see Mahler, 1990, pp. 243, 304 & 276). This type of consistency in depicting his lofty and lonely role as an artistic outsider accentuates an undeniable disregard for his contemporaries and an extraordinary self-confidence in the lasting value of his artistic achievement.

The most revealing of these letters demonstrates Mahler's scepticism regarding the approaching première of the Fifth Symphony, particularly the third movement:

> The Scherzo is an accursed movement! It is going to have a long tale of suffering to tell! Conductors are going to take it too fast for the next 50 years and make a mess of it, the public – oh heavens – what faces will it make at this chaos that continually brings forth a new world only to collapse again moments later, at these primitive earthly sounds, at this howling, roaring, raging ocean, at these dancing stars, at these breathless, shimmering, flashing waves? What else can a herd of sheep say to a 'tournament of fraternal spheres' [*Brudersphären-Wettgesang*] other than to bleat!? ... Oh, if only I could première my works 50 years after my death!
> (La Grange & Weiß, 1995, pp. 220–21; see Mahler, 1990, p. 243)[16]

---

16   The première of the Fifth Symphony occasioned the critic Emil Krause to label Mahler among the 'extreme avant-garde of contemporary artistic creation' (La Grange, 1999, p. 140). The contradiction inherent in Mahler's progressive musical language and the decidedly 'unmodern' mindset from which this grew adds to the richness of the

Here, too, a poetic allusion opens a deeper perspective on Mahler's assessment of the incompetent conductors and ignorant public who are confronted with his works. The quotation ('Brudersphären-Wettgesang') can be traced to the words of the archangel Raphael at the outset of the 'Prologue in Heaven' from Goethe's *Faust*:

Die Sonne tönt, nach alter Weise,	The sun intones, in ancient tourney
In Brudersphären Wettgesang,	With brother spheres, a rival air;
Und ihr vorgeschriebne Reise	And his predestinated journey,
Vollendet sie mit Donnergang.	He closes with a thunderous blare.
Ihr Anblick gibt den Engeln Stärke,	His sight, as none can comprehend it,
Wenn keiner sie ergründen mag;	Gives strength to angels; the array
Die unbegreiflich hohen Werke	Of works, unfathomably splendid,
sind herrlich wie am ersten Tag.	Is glorious as on the first day.[17]

(trans. from Walter Kaufmann,
Goethe's Faust (New York:
Doubleday, 1961), p. 83)

Again we find Mahler setting himself on a higher plane, his music like the intoning of the celestial spheres. Even the original act of creation is called into play ('as on the first day'), shoring up, as it were, Mahler's conviction in his godly mission. Odd as it might seem at first, Mahler's intellectual isolation no doubt gave him strength in this regard. Distanced from the currents of thought considered avant-garde, he came to see himself as an artist of another time, removed from his own generation and thus not caught up in trying to win their acclaim. By not connecting intellectually he was free to go out on his own and hope for a time beyond his death when his message could be heard.

Perhaps more astounding than the aplomb of Mahler's *post mortem* prophecy is its ultimate veracity. Though the composer's popularity '50 years after [his] death' might seem to vindicate the composer's independent aesthetic stance, it does not sufficiently address the paradox of the intellectual heritage that it perpetuates. On first consideration the German romantic spirit that speaks to us from these scores rests uneasily with the often brutal realities and very different mindset that have descended upon us in the interim. That Mahler's music nevertheless negotiates this distance speaks to a crucial aspect of his intellectual profile and one of the central factors in his popularity today. More than projecting a fervent belief in an ideal realm beyond mortal existence or a naive conviction in the mystical nature of being, Mahler's transcendental vision is rife with conflict and unsettling questions. Thus, his idealism is an idealism hard won; just beyond the hope in a better world looms a formidable shadow of doubt. To take

---

composer's artistic personality, an intriguing and lengthy topic that will be discussed elsewhere.

17   Source identified in La Grange & Weiß, 1995, p. 221.

but one example, the triumphant conclusion of the First Symphony arrives only after a bitter battle; with the biting sarcasm in the Funeral March followed by the cry of terror at the outset of the Finale the threat of collapse is never far away, even as the promise of overcoming seems fulfilled. Indeed, Mahler's redemptive closing gesture takes on something of a manic character, as if enacting – in symphony after symphony – the reassurance he so desperately sought in order to allay his own misgivings.

The complexity and contradiction of the composer's world-philosophical ambitions find remarkable parallels in a reconsideration of the readings that most preoccupied him. Rather than flee the dilemma, Mahler sought out literature, philosophy and even science that confronted head on the potential weaknesses of the world-view he did his best to espouse. To take an example: Jean Paul's *Siebenkäs*, one of Mahler's favourite literary works, is riddled with sarcasm and philosophical reflection. Particularly revealing in this respect is a chapter entitled 'Blumenstück, Rede des toten Christus vom Weltgebäude herab, dass kein Gott sei' ['Flower-Piece, Speech of Christ, after Death, from the Universe, that there is no God'], which describes the dream of a godless world. All begins rather innocuously: 'Once on a summer evening I lay upon a mountain in the sunshine, and fell asleep. Then I dreamt that I awoke in a cemetery' ['Ich lag einmal an einem Sommerabende vor der Sonne auf einem Berge und entschlief. Da träumte mir, ich erwachte auf dem Gottesacker'].[18] Soon graves creak open, ghosts and spirits fly about, and the dead return to the church for a holy sermon delivered by Christ:

> A lofty, noble form, having the expression of a never-ending sorrow, now sank down from above upon the altar, and all the dead exclaimed, – 'Christ! Is there no God?' And he answered, – 'There is none!'[19]

Christ then describes his search for God in the highest realms and the empty, pitiless reply from chaos. All is without hope. As souls shatter upon hearing the news, Christ delivers his bitter reflections:

> he lifted up his eyes to the Nothingness, and to the empty Immensity, and said: 'Frozen, dumb Nothingness! Cold, eternal Necessity! Insane Chance! Know ye what is beneath you? ... Is that a man near me? Thou poor one! Thy little life is the sigh of Nature, or only its echo. A concave mirror throws its beams upon the dust-clouds composed of the ashes of the dead upon your earth, and thus ye exist, cloudy, tottering images! Look down into the abyss over which clouds of ashes are floating by. Fogs full of worlds arise out of

---

18 All quotations from Jean Paul, *Siebenkäs* (Frankfurt am Main: Insel Verlag, 1987), pp. 274–85; English translation: *Flower, Fruit, and Thorn Pieces*, trans. Edward Henry Noel, 2 vols (Boston: Ticknor and Fields, 1863), vol. 1, pp. 347–61.

19 'Jetzo sank eine hohe edle Gestalt mit einem unvergänglichen Schmerz aus der Höhe auf den Altar hernieder, und alle Toten riefen: "Christus! ist kein Gott?" Er antwortete: "Es ist keiner."'

the sea of death. The future is a rising vapor, the present a falling one. Knowest thou thy earth?'[20]

The apocalyptic vision rises to a deafening climax. Then, the infinity that had been opened up suddenly collapses and the dreamer awakens: 'My soul wept for joy, that it could again worship God; and the joy, and the tears, and the belief in him, were the prayer' ['Meine Seele weinte vor Freude, daß sie wieder Gott anbeten konnte – und die Freude und das Weinen und der Glaube an ihn waren das Gebet'].[21] In Mahler as in Jean Paul, a vision of faith is accentuated, even challenged by the horrors of mortal suffering and the potential revelation that all is but a dreadful farce.

Mahler's forays into philosophy demonstrate an equally persistent tendency to ask difficult questions of his own beliefs. Here we find a surprisingly pragmatic streak in many of the thinkers he most admired. Fechner, for instance, was a highly respected figure in the field of psychophysics, an innovator in investigations into the connection between physical stimulus and sensory perception.[22] Tellingly, his scientific work addressed the problem of bridging the gap between spirit and substance and ultimately pondering the relationship between sentient and corporeal being. As with Mahler, the mystical bent of Fechner's natural philosophy was coupled with a need to investigate the world around him. Seeking to provide, if possible, a rigorous substantiation of idealist philosophy, Fechner exhibited a compelling urge to tackle the mystery that distinguished mere matter from the essence of the soul. Here, in the ineffable divide that separated materiality from life itself, lay the wondrously imponderable proof of the necessity of a realm beyond purely physical being.

In examining Fechner and other thinkers Mahler emerges as a searcher whose world-philosophical bent and obsessive curiosity drove him to pursue all manner of evidence regarding the true nature of existence. In fact, the composer also took

---

[20] 'so hob er groß wie der höchste Endliche die Augen empor gegen das Nichts and gegen die leere Unermeßlichkeit und sagte: "Starres, stummes Nichts! Kalte, ewige Notwendigkeit! Wahnsinniger Zufall! Kennt ihr das unter euch? ... Ist das neben mir noch ein Mensch? Du Armer! Euer kleines Leben ist der Seufzer der Natur oder nur sein Echo – ein Hohlspiegel wirft seine Strahlen in die Staubwolken aus Totenasche auf euere Erde hinab, und dann entsteht ihr bewölkten, wankenden Bilder. – Schaue hinunter in den Abgrund, über welchen Aschenwolken ziehen – Nebel voll Welten steigen aus dem Totenmeer, die Zukunft ist ein steigender Nebel, und die Gegenwart ist der fallende. – Erkennst du deine Erde?"'

[21] The tone of this passage from Jean Paul also appears in a poem that Mahler wrote in his youth entitled 'Nach Tages Wechsel saß ich stumm verloren'. Here, too, we find an apocalyptic vision that dissolves as the character awakens: 'Then I awoke, with laughter and tears, and an overwhelming longing seized me.' For the original text, see La Grange, 1973, pp. 829–31.

[22] For an introduction to Fechner's pioneering work in psychophysics, see Robert I. Watson, *Basic Writings in the History of Psychology* (New York: Oxford University Press, 1979), pp. 105–13.

a keen interest in scientific discoveries.[23] One of his closest friends in the 1890s and early 1900s was the German physicist Arnold Berliner (1862–1942). Berliner achieved some fame in his day as the author of a standard physics textbook, the *Lehrbuch der Physik in elementaren Darstellungen* (Jena: Gustav Fischer, 1903), and as the editor of *Die Naturwissenschaften*, a scholarly periodical in science during the first half of the century. Berliner was a friend of Albert Einstein and, as his publications demonstrate, was thoroughly versed in turn-of-the-century scientific thinking. He was well qualified to inform Mahler of the latest findings of the day. Mahler made good use of his friend's expertise, as Bruno Walter recalled in his autobiographical reflections on the composer:

> Friends of his, professionally occupied with natural science, were hard pressed by his deeply penetrating questions. An eminent physicist whom he met frequently could not tell me enough about Mahler's intuitive understanding of the ultimate theories of physics and about the logical keenness of his conclusions or counter-arguments.
>
> (Walter, 1947, p. 93)

Mahler was not simply a passive listener in these conversations. He queried Berliner and others extensively and even suggested scientific thoughts of his own. Bruno Walter relates:

> Mahler was pleased also by my interest in natural science. In his conversations with me he gave free rein to his imaginative ideas concerning physical theories. For instance, he would replace the attractive power of the earth by a repelling power of the sun and insist that his idea was more effective than Newton's law of gravitation. Or he would animate atomism by explaining atomic energy by a theory of inclination and disinclination.
>
> (Ibid.)

Walter's discussion of Mahler's scientific bent leaves little doubt of the composer's genuine interest in such matters. Of particular importance, perhaps, is that Walter's account reveals two areas which held a particular fascination for Mahler: gravity and atomism.

Existing documents allow us to explore the composer's approach to these two topics in some detail and to observe the characteristic turn of mind with which Mahler tackled scientific theories. While science supposedly dealt with objective reality, Mahler saw no contradiction in framing the theories of the hard sciences in terms of an idealistic understanding of existence. Essentially, since the human view of the world underwent constant changes, science itself was variable. In Mahler's mind, such perspectivism could even apply to the laws of nature, as

---

[23]   Herta Blaukopf has written on this topic on a number of occasions. See, for instance, 'Metaphysik und Physik bei Mahler', in Nikkels & Becqué, 1992, pp. 37–41 and 'Musik als Wissenschaft und umgekehrt', in Stadler, 1997, pp. 119–32.

revealed in this fascinating letter from December 1903 written to a lawyer by the name of Richard Horn:

> Dear Herr Dr. Horn,
>
> Further to our discussion a few evenings ago I am sending you the enclosed article (*Kölnische Zeitung*) on 'Matter, Ether and Electricity', which I have just read. What do you think now of the immutability of scientifically based views? – What will 'description' be like once our experience in this obscure field is as well ordered as, for instance, our views on astronomy are today? – And even my dictum (approximately) 'the laws of nature will remain the same, but our views about them will change', I must further add that even that does not strike me as certain. It is conceivable that in the course of aeons (perhaps as a result of a natural law of evolution) even the laws of nature may change; that for instance the law of gravity may no longer hold – does not Helmholtz even now assume that the law of gravity does not apply to infinitely small distances? Perhaps (I myself add) not to *infinitely great* distances either – for instance very distant solar systems. Just think that through to its logical conclusion.
>
> Yours in haste,
Mahler
>
> (Martner, 1979, p. 300; see also Blaukopf, 1996, p. 342)

In this pronouncement on gravity, Mahler demonstrated both a noteworthy awareness of recent scientific thinking (such as Helmholtz's questioning of gravitational theory) and a strong tendency to fit such findings into a world-view that had not yet abandoned the notion of metaphysics.

This tendency also characterized Mahler's understanding of the second topic mentioned by Bruno Walter: namely, particulate matter. Atomic theory made enormous strides at the turn of the century and provided strong evidence for the notion that the world consisted of minute particles that interacted in predictable ways.[24] Such advances in scientific thinking suggested that reality was entirely grounded in the physical realm. This offered a serious challenge to thinkers such as Mahler who insisted on believing in a transcendental existence. As quoted above, Mahler 'would animate atomism by explaining atomic energy by a theory of inclination and disinclination'. Rather than deny the existence of atoms, Mahler infused them with an inner nature that related, ultimately, to a realm beyond matter.

The impetus for Mahler's thinking came from a revival of the Leibnizian notion of monads at the end of the nineteenth century. In its simplest outline, this theory proposed that the world consisted of basic particles (atoms) each of which possessed a soul. A leading proponent of this mystical scientism was Rudolf Hermann Lotze (1817–81),[25] whose *Mikrokosmos* (1856–64) was one of

---

[24] Einstein and others were, of course, also taking physics to vistas beyond Newtonian mechanics at this time.

[25] For a discussion of Lotze's life and works, see *Neue deutsche Biographie*, vol.

Mahler's favourite books.[26] Lotze's theory of sentient particles called for a twofold perspective on the behaviour of atoms. From the outside, monads moved according to patterns that could be explained by laws of mechanics. Internally, however, each monad acted in realization of a willing consciousness. All of these individual expressions of will in turn were joined together in a harmonious whole that fulfilled the divine intent of God.[27] Thus Lotze formulated a philosophy that could satisfy both the spiritual and rational tendencies of the time – a quasi-scientific formulation of animistic philosophy that had many adherents in the late nineteenth century.

Mahler recommended yet another book to Bruno Walter that reflects the composer's deep interest in science: *Geschichte des Materialismus* (1866) by Friedrich Albert Lange (1828–75).[28] Lange, like Lotze, presented a massive amount of scientific information on the world amended by a thoroughgoing treatment of the philosophical implications of knowledge. The manner in which we view scientific findings is not merely an epistemological issue, argued Lange, but also an ontological one. While a description of existence that confines itself to material substances may succeed in defining the reality accessible to our cognitive faculties, it cannot reach to the thing-in-itself. According to Lange even a mechanical explanation of the world that proved consistent with the laws of nature as we perceive them would fail to provide a true measure of reality. The critical shortcoming stems from the ephemeral nature of perception itself:

> What is the body? What is matter? What is the physical? And physiology today, as well as philosophy, must answer to these questions that everything is only our representation [of things] – necessary representations, representations that follow the laws of nature, but, nevertheless, not the things themselves.

---

15 (Berlin: Duncker & Humblot, 1987), pp. 255–56; for a contemporary account of the philosopher from Mahler's time, see Richard Falckenberg, *Hermann Lotze* (Stuttgart: Fr. Fromanns Verlag, 1901). See also Max Wentscher, *Fechner und Lotze* (Munich: Ernst Reinhardt, 1925).

26 'Lotze's *Microcosm* occupied him for quite a long time, and especially his atomic theory, which progressed to the immaterial, grew to be a most stimulating subject of thought' (Walter, 1937, p. 138, trans. amended) ['Lotzes *Mikrokosmos* beschäftigte ihn lange Zeit hindurch, und besonders dessen ins Immaterielle entwickelte Atomtheorie wurde ihm zum anregendsten Gegenstand des Denkens'] (Walter, 1936, p. 94).

27 For a close description of Lotze's book, see the entry by Jean Faurot and Keith E. Yandell in Frank N. Magill (ed.), *World Philosophy. Essay-Reviews of 225 Major Works*, vol. 3, 1726–1896 (Englewood Cliffs, NJ: Salem Press, 1982), pp. 1343–52.

28 For a discussion of Lange's life and works, see *Neue deutsche Biographie*, vol. 13 (Berlin: Duncker & Humblot, 1982), pp. 555–57; for a contemporary account of the philosopher from Mahler's time, see O.A. Ellissen, *Friedrich Albert Lange* (Leipzig: Julius Baedeker, 1891). See also Hans Vaihinger, *Hartmann, Dühring und Lange* (Iserlohn: Verlag von J. Baedeker, 1876).

... The eye, with which we believe we see, is itself only a product of our representation ... so we should never forget that the eye, along with its parts, the optic nerve as well as the brain and all its structures – things like this that we would like to reveal as the cause of all thought – are all only representations; they form a self-consistent world, but it is a world that points beyond itself.

... Therefore, one can surely no longer espouse any form of materialism, for even if our researches based on sensory perception must unavoidably assume that for every mental function there must exist a material cause, then this material and all that comes from it is only an abstraction of our images of representation.

(Lange, 1873–75, vol. 2, pp. 427 & 430)[29]

Such reasoning appealed to Mahler. Like Lange, Lotze and others, he acknowledged the advances of modern science, but could not accept a world devoid of spirit.

Trapped between believing in a higher existence and calling his entire world-view into question, Mahler harboured a tortured soul that maintained a tenuous balance between idealism and nihilism. It is the brutal honesty of that inner conflict that leads us to the core of the paradox of Mahler's conservative world-view. If there was a naivety at the turn of the century, it lay in the assumption of the avant-garde that self-indulgence and indifferent analysis of the human condition would suffice to sustain the needs of the coming generations, that the much-heralded death of God would find widespread acceptance. Mahler challenged these assumptions while not denying the quandary in which he was left, seeking to instil hope while hiding none of his insecurity. The simultaneity of these contrary perspectives – coming to grips with a material world that somehow nevertheless retains a spiritual essence – constitutes one of the prime aspects of Mahler's modernity, for it rests on a dilemma that continues to haunt us today.

---

29 'Was ist der Körper? Was ist der Stoff? Was ist das Physische? Und die heutige Physiologie muss uns, so gut wie die Philosophie, auf diese Fragen antworten, dass dies Alles nur unsre Vorstellungen sind; nothwendige Vorstellungen, nach Naturgesetzen erfolgende Vorstellungen, aber immerhin nicht die Dinge selbst.

... Das Auge, mit dem wir zu sehen glauben, ist selbst nur ein Product unsrer Vorstellung ... so dürfen wir nie vergessen, dass auch das Auge sammt seinen Einrichtungen, der Sehnerv sammt dem Hirn und all den Structuren, die wir dort noch etwa als Ursachen des Denkens entdecken möchten, nur Vorstellungen sind, die zwar eine in sich selbst zusammenhängende Welt bilden, jedoch eine Welt, die über sich selbst hinausweist.

... Damit ist nun freilich kein Materialismus irgend welcher Art mehr zu behaupten; denn wenn auch unsre auf sinnliche Anschauungen angewiesene Forschung mit unvermeidlicher Consequenz darauf ausgehen muss, für jede geistige Regung entsprechende Vorgänge im Stoff nachzuweisen, so ist doch dieser Stoff selbst mit Allem, was aus ihm gebildet ist, nur eine Abstraction von unsern Vorstellungsbildern'.

PART TWO

Reception: The Jewish and Eastern European Questions

Chapter Five

Jewish Identity and Anti-Semitic Critique in the Austro-German Reception of Mahler, 1900–1945[1]

KAREN PAINTER

Introduction

Mahler was the most important composer in the Austro-German anti-Semitic literature not only during his lifetime but also in the decades after his death. It was hard to establish any 'Jewish' character in Mendelssohn's music, and Schoenberg's modernism was more likely to be rejected than to seem threatening. Mahler's music, however, provoked contradictory responses. The so-called modern elements were met with anti-Jewish tropes,[2] especially in the years before 1908, both a symbolic turning point in Schoenberg's break from tonality and a shift in Mahler's positioning of himself with respect to tradition and modernism, with the première of the Seventh Symphony that autumn. Yet precisely the 'German' symphonic character also made his music problematic for later writers.

It is appropriate to ask: what is the purpose of analysing literature that is at once morally repugnant and intellectually vacuous? The anti-Semitism that Mahler himself faced, whether from members of the Vienna Philharmonic or from the press, had a continuing presence in his life and, one can suppose, in his creative work, even if only strengthening his own assimilationist aspirations. Moreover, understanding the nature of the arguments, undoubtedly some of the

[1] Some of the sources for this essay are located in: (a) the Vondenhoff collection at the Musiksammlung, Österreichische Nationalbibliothek, Vienna; and (b) the Steininger collection at the Geheimes Staatsarchiv, Preußischer Kulturbesitz, Berlin. I am grateful to Jeremy Barham and Charles S. Maier for their comments on earlier versions.
[2] I invoke here the useful distinction, made by Sigurd Paul Scheichl (1987), between anti-Semitic attitudes that had political implications and subtle forms of anti-Jewish language. These categories overlap, admittedly, in the indirect consequences that can follow from any kind of racial hierarchy or critique.

darkest and ultimately most dangerous moments in the history of musical thought, also sheds light on the position of Mahler's advocates. Within the wider history of German anti-Semitism, the reception of Mahler is a revealing example of the change from anti-Jewish cultural criticism to outright anti-Semitism.

Historians have often focussed on the alleged transition from religious to racial hostility to account for the ultimate radicalization of German attitudes and policy. This celebrated contrast may indeed have provided an intellectual rationale for a far more rigorous exclusion of Jews from any possibility of national assimilation. It meant that conversion and even cultural assimilation could not overcome an 'organic' and genetic legacy. But in the discourse of exclusion that characterized debate over art and thought, allegedly incompatible cultural traits had to be discussed on their own terms, and here music provides one of the most influential examples, beginning with the impact of Wagner's *Judaism in Music* in 1850 and its revision in 1869. While historians like Jens Malte Fischer (1997) have been tempted to trace a teleological course from Wagner's *Judaism in Music* to the inauguration of brutal and exclusionary National-Socialist policies, this essay will emphasize the fundamental changes in the nature and role of anti-Semitic discourse in musical thought.

Anti-Semitism before the First World War

What has been called the transfer of anti-Semitism from politics into 'a more academic, quiescent, and respectable forum' in the early twentieth century (Mosse 1964, p. 134) was by no means complete and clear-cut. Music was no longer a quiet respite from politics and the bustle of the world. Increasingly, neither the production of the art work nor its reception seemed free of cultural and political meaning. The abstract communication offered by music was still cherished, and all the more by Jewish critics for whom assimilation seemed a desirable social goal. It was therefore the failure of a composition that provoked cultural criticism, and with it anti-Semitic tropes. Such tropes were one among various ways to suggest a failure in symphonic power; 'feminine' tropes were another.

The personification of music, including its personification as 'Jewish', had a practical function of explaining aesthetic qualities (and the lack thereof). Cultural interpretation was useful for describing novel compositional practices and musical style that defied technical explanation. This metaphorical discourse was also helpful for concert-goers who needed guidance as a result of the general lowering in standards of musical training and because of their more diverse social make-up. Whatever the perhaps benign intentions of music critics, including some assimilated Jews, the 'anti-Jewishness' of some feuilleton writers took on new meaning against the backdrop of rising anti-Semitism in everyday politics. Anti-Semitism gained a political platform during the very years in which Vienna was admired as the world centre for Jewish liturgical music, and as an intellectual centre with such figures as Freud, Karl Kraus and Franz Werfel, as Schoenberg recalled, with bitter nostalgia, in 1935 (Schoenberg, 1935, p. 504). The anti-Semitic Christian Socialists established a permanent and rowdy caucus in Vienna. Karl Lueger acceded to the mayoralty as their leader in 1897; the Christian Socialists secured fifty-one seats in the lower house of the Austrian diet by 1902, and sixty-seven by 1907 (Pulzer, 1988).

Mahler's adaptation of Christian themes evoked an intensified anti-Semitism. The Second and Eighth Symphonies, with their religious themes and texts, challenged some critics to address the unsuitability of Mahler's intention and his ability – in the veiled rhetoric of the day, his 'will' and his 'nature'. In the years around 1900 there was rarely, however, any explicit discussion of Jewish characteristics of the music itself. Maximilian Muntz, who wrote for the right-wing *Deutsche Zeitung*, railed against the Mahlerian clumsiness [*Mahlerisches Machwerk*] and decadence, but the only explicit reference to Jews was in his attack on the enthusiasts in the audience whom he compared to 'Young Israelis' [*Jung-Israelis*]. Muntz speculated that even an 'almost entirely Jewish public' [*ein fast durchwegs jüdisches Publicum*] would not have enjoyed the music in so demeaning a manner (Muntz, 1899).

Soon after 1906 (the year that saw the première of Mahler's Sixth Symphony) the composer's music was no longer viewed as modern in any threatening way: one reason for this was Mahler's turn to specific traditions in the Seventh and Eighth Symphonies and the sense of distance in his 'late' style. Another is the presence of Schoenberg as a target for attacks on modernism. The main criticism of Mahler before about 1908 was that motifs and themes were evocative of those of other composers and were not of his own invention. But the success of the Seventh at its première in Prague in September 1908 and at its German première in Munich a month later invalidated any such criticism. With its allusions and self-conscious invocation of symphonic tradition, the Seventh was seen as an essay in music about music.

By 1910–12, when Mahler's Eighth Symphony received its first performances in Germany and in Vienna, this hesitation to address Jewish traits had disappeared. More than any other of his works, the Eighth Symphony provoked discussion of Mahler's ethnicity. The multiple exchanges between the Munich critic Paul Ehlers and university professor Robert Holtzmann, summarized by various scholars (for example, Namenwirth, 1985, and Wildhagen, 2000) were only the starting point. Mahler's ambitions in this work, along with the use of a Catholic text in its first part, failed to sweep away some sceptics – all the more so because audiences responded so enthusiastically. 'Take whatever position you will on Gustav Mahler', Josef Stolzing (1912) wrote in one review:

> you cannot dispute that this nervous artistic soul, consumed by raw ambition, honestly aspired to grandeur. The German Jew, born in Bohemia, was undoubtedly an idealist who paid no heed to the mere success of the day, for

with his abundant talent that path had certainly come easily to him. Moreover he passionately sought to achieve a German essence.[3]

Nevertheless Stolzing could express admiration for Mahler's conducting, although here too he felt compelled to invoke Jewish stereotypes by quoting Wagner on Meyerbeer and substituting Mahler's name for that of the Jewish composer.

Even for critics who were neither detractors nor anti-Semites, Mahler's Jewish heritage had a supposed explanatory power. In a review of the Eighth Symphony, *Die Zeit*, one of Vienna's most established newspapers and by no means an anti-Semitic organ, spoke of 'a fanatical will, the like of which perhaps no musician before Gustav Mahler possessed'. 'In the control and development of such masses no one has achieved anything similar to Gustav Mahler. … The spectacle of this strength of will is truly unusual and incomparable.' The critic went on to summarize at length a book by William Ritter, the self-professed anti-Semitic Mahler enthusiast: 'To his Jewish roots [Mahler] owes the often epileptic nervousness of his musical expression and his unrestrained drive to achieve the desired extravagance and beauty at any price' (Anon., 1913a).[4] It is no coincidence that, in both cases, Stolzing and the anonymous reviewer of *Die Zeit* rely on other sources to address Mahler's Jewish heritage. Faced with a new area of inquiry, and in a desperate attempt to seek authority, individual reviewers drew on other authors to an extent never seen in other aspects of music criticism. Extended quotations added a scholarly gloss and even a pseudo-scientific character to arguments that otherwise rested on prejudice and stereotyping.

It is useful to distinguish between pure anti-Semitism, where the denigration of Jews had no artistic or cultural function, and cases where anti-Jewish views came as part of a critique of assimilation or artistic modernism. Pure anti-Semitism attributed the flaws in a work to the indelible characteristics brought by the Jewish artist, while the critique of efforts at assimilation entailed a less direct denigration of the work in its own right. While many critics attacked the modernist and – in code words – Jewish character of Mahler's difficult Sixth Symphony, the Seventh Symphony met strong and nearly unanimous approval

---

[3] 'Man mag sich zu Gustav Mahler stellen, wie man will, so wird man doch dieser nervösen, von einem glühenden Ehrgeiz verzehrten Künstlerseele nicht ein ehrliches Streben ins Große absprechen können. Der in Böhmen geborene deutsche Jude war ohne Zweifel ein Idealist, der seine Sache nicht auf den bloßen Tageserfolg gestellt hatte, denn bei seiner reichen Begabung hätten sich ihm wahrlich jene Wege leicht geboten. Inbrünstig suchte er auch in deutschem Wesen aufzugehen.'

[4] 'eines fanatischen Willens, wie sie vor Gustav Mahler vielleicht kein Musiker besessen hat. ... solcher Massen hat niemand Aehnliches geleistet wie Gustav Mahler. ... Das Schauspiel dieser Willenskraft ist wirklich ungewöhnlich und unvergleichlich. ... Seiner jüdische Abstammung verdanke er jene oft epileptiforme Nervosität seines musikalischen Ausdruckes und seinen unbezähmbaren Trieb, um jeden Preis gewollte Extravaganz und gewollte Schönheit durchzusetzen.'

from audiences and reviewers alike. The fact that Paul Ehlers (1908) responded so negatively to this work is a clear indication of pure anti-Semitism. (Indeed he would later become active in the Third Reich's reorganization of the musical profession. See Kater, 1997, p. 16.) Mahler's music had an 'inner eclecticism' [*innerer Eklektizismus*]; its only distinguishing traits were a 'harsh "brown" timbre' [*herbe 'braune' Klangfarbe*], a 'ghetto rhythm' [*Ghettorhythmus*] and a 'sharp, hard-hitting design' [*scharfe, hartstrichige Zeichnung*]. While the Seventh Symphony does indeed embrace a range of styles and moods, Ehlers's modernist critique seems implausible. The wealth of quotations and symphonic archetypes (the struggling Allegro, lyrical inner movement and rejoicing Finale) suggests a play with convention but is rarely modernist in tone. If there was any provocation for this Munich critic it perhaps arose from the aggressive advertising for the symphony: it was billed as part of a series performed by 'Masters of Conducting', and, as William Ritter had observed the previous year when the Sixth was performed in Munich, the name 'Mahler' appeared in capital letters plastered all over the city – a publicity effort that Ehlers lamented as the 'industrialization of Munich musical life' [*Industrialisierung des Münchener Musiklebens*] (Ehlers, 1908).[5] Moreover, by that point Mahler had moved to New York and with few exceptions did not remain a force in European musical life. Anti-Semitic critique of the person – the controversial and powerful conductor and, by his own opinion, partly assimilated Jew – was a very different matter from attacks on the music.

'Pure' anti-Semitism further entailed an effort to marginalize the Jewish composer. It was only to cast Mahler as a derivative and inferior composer that Rudolf Louis drew him into the discussion of a book on Bruckner. Louis compared two of Bruckner's 'students', Mahler and the anti-Semite Friedrich Klose. Klose, who wrote mainly operas, is seen to have grasped the inner qualities of his teacher (namely, one might speculate, consistency in thematic writing and scoring that cohered into a unified whole). Mahler was influenced by Bruckner in the choice of genre, formal construction, and the broad thematic working, but the similarity remained superficial 'because his whole nature was in essence ... so absolutely foreign to that of Bruckner' ['Sicherlich ist aber seine ganze Natur der Bruckners ... so absolut wesenfremd'] (Louis, 1905, pp. 135–36). It is certainly true that the few works of Mahler performed by that point in Louis's native Munich – the Second, Third and Fourth Symphonies – had brought major departures from Bruckner's structural emphases. But the political nature of the discussion was clear from Louis's idle speculation that

---

[5] See Meylan, 2000, p. 467. William Ritter's letter to Mahler, from mid-October 1906, is quoted and paraphrased in La Grange, 1999, p. 512. Carbon copies of Ritter's letters to Mahler beginning in 1902 are preserved in his copybook located in the collection of his papers at the Schweizerische Landbibliothek, Berne (see La Grange, 1999, p. 508 n. 166).

without Bruckner as a model, Mahler could not have developed his own symphonic form.

Anti-Semitism and polemic, 1911–1930

As Wistrich has shown (1990, p. 33), anti-Semitic agitation, which many Social Democrats in Germany now dismissed as an old-fashioned utopian dream, decreased for a brief interval before the First World War. The Kaiser dedicated the new Fasanenstrasse synagogue in Berlin, and a politician of Jewish origin took over the Colonial Ministry. These gains, however, seemed precarious. During these same years, Heinrich Class, the leader of the Pan-Germans, proposed double taxation of the Jews. This tension between progress for Jews and radical politics could be played out in cultural discourse, where ambiguity and contradictions sat more comfortably than in the political arena. Social unity and assimilation were no longer the goals in cultural criticism, including music criticism. Instead, the categories of 'Jewish' and 'German' art became more emphatic, characterizing social exclusion rather than attempts at conformity. Wagner's cultural critique of 'Jewishness' did not fit into the new conception of anti-Semitism based on purportedly scientific race theories. The metaphor of music as language and dialect, so prominent in Wagner and adapted in Rudolf Louis's *Die deutsche Musik der Gegenwart*, disappeared.

Mahler's defenders confronted anti-Semitic critique by stressing how German the composer actually was. It was perhaps merely fortuitous that Mahler's new Eighth Symphony with its massive liturgical setting of *Veni Creator* was performed just as debates on German-Jewish identity issues became a continuing fixture of the cultural press from 1911 to 1914. Nonetheless, such a religious offering was bound to intensify debate. In a review of the Eighth Symphony, Paul Stefan argued that Mahler's critics had misunderstood 'race theory' when impugning the composer's '"contrived" naivety', 'restlessness', and 'brooding' quality as 'untrue' and 'un-German'. Race undeniably affected the production of culture, Stefan conceded, but metaphorically: only 'the *idea* of races as such' can be an agent. 'Hardly any artist has lived more according to the German idea and the German ideal' than Mahler, Stefan insisted, citing his Lieder above all. Moreover, Stefan added, 'if since Wagner, being German means to pursue something for its own sake, then certainly no one has been more German' (Stefan, 1910, p. 490).[6]

---

6 '"gemachte" Naivität des Komponisten, das "Unruhige," "Grübelnde" ... als unecht und, in mißverstehender Rassengelehrsamkeit, als undeutsch zu verdächtigen. ... Weit davon, die Bedeutung des Rassenmoments für die Kultur zu leugnen, kann ich solches Agens nur die Rassen*idee* des gelten lassen. ... [K]aum je ein Künstler mehr in der

Other writers argued that Mahler's aesthetic shortcomings did not emanate from his Jewish origins. Walter Niemann's book on 'music since Wagner' was an important step towards the development of a non-ideological view of Jewish identity: Jewish traits could be positive or negative as could German traits. Niemann lamented a 'blind and stupid hatred of Jews' ['den blinden und törichten Judenhaß'] that formed part of the reception of Mahler's music. True, there might be Jewish characteristics, he continued, but they were not necessarily worthy of praise or blame in themselves. The fact that Mahler's music was not always German – 'it is often insufferably sentimental, sweet, untrue, deliberately convulsive, calculatingly cold, and outwardly theatrical' – did not mean that it was therefore 'Jewish', a word he set off in quotation marks. Even Niemann's chapter headings neutralized the discussion of Jewish traits: 'Gustav Mahler as architectonic and eclectic melodist' captures the two extremes associated with, respectively, German and Jewish musical character. Another heading lists 'the Austrian, religious and Jewish elements in his art'. Niemann also warned against any critical judgment of Jewish identity per se: 'To see the Jewish blood in his works, however, and to reject it as Jewish with a contemptuous tone, seems thoroughly premature and malicious – as long as one maintains that this Jewish element is felt or intimated, rather than capable of being analysed conceptually and ascertained beyond any doubt' (Niemann, 1913, pp. xiv & 140).[7] Even when critics made a plea for judging an art work on its own terms rather than based on the ethnicity of its creator, it was difficult to avoid the vocabulary that had emerged in the cultural interpretation of music. For example, in the same year that Niemann's book appeared, Ernest Neufeld made a plea for art above ethnicity in a lecture on 'Gustav Mahler and his Eighth Symphony' reported in a Silesian newspaper. After discussing Mahler's 'Jewish heritage', Neufeld went on to say: 'If Mahler has something to say to us as an interesting and significant person, then we should enjoy his personality and his particular manner' (Neufeld, 1913).[8] Terms like 'personality' and 'particular manner' were code words for Jewish identity.

---

deutschen Idee und im deutschen Ideal gelebt hat, daß kaum einer deutscher gewesen ist als Gustav Mahler. Und wenn deutsch sein nach Wagner heißt, eine Sache um ihrer selbst willen treiben, so ist ganz gewiß keiner deutscher gewesen.'

[7] 'Gustav Mahler als Architectoniker und eklektischer Melodiker' and 'Das Österreichische, Religiöse und Jüdische in seiner Kunst'. 'Sicher, daß Mahlers Musik nicht immer deutsch, daß sie oft unleidlich sentimental, süßlich, unecht, krampfhaft gewollt, kalt berechnend und äußerlich theatralisch ist: "jüdisch" braucht sie deshalb noch lange nicht zu sein.' 'Das jüdische Blut aber in seinem Schaffen zu sehen, es als jüdisch mit dem Unterton des Verächtlichen abzulehnen, erscheint, solange man dies Jüdische mehr fühlt und aufsuggiert erhält, wie begrifflich zergliedern und zweifellos feststellen kann, durchaus verfrüht und gehässig.'

[8] 'Der Redner sprach dann von Mahlers jüdischer Abstammung. Wenn Mahler uns als interessanter und bedeutender Mensch Bedeutendes zu sagen hat, so sollen wir uns seiner Persönlichkeit, seiner besonderen Art freuen.'

One reason for the polemics that emerged during the interwar years is that music history was conceived not as a museum of musical works, but as a process of development or of degeneration. Paul Bekker saw the culminating moment in the history of the symphony since Beethoven as Mahler's gift of the Eighth Symphony to the German nation: 'It took a long time until an artist could make such claims about his work with inner justification. No one before Mahler could do it – though, of course, one cannot forget: everything that was achieved before Mahler was necessary for him to realize his work.' These were not empty claims, but clearly established a lineage in which German and Austrian traditions led to Mahler. Just as Beethoven had been the high point of his era, 'so we experience in Mahler a synthesis of the middle- and North-German group of Mendelssohn–Schumann–Brahms with the Austrian one of Schubert–Bruckner and the New German School, founded on Liszt's instrumental music and culminating in Strauss' (Bekker, 1918, p. 32).[9]

The greater sense of historicity after 1900 only increased the tendency to chart the legacy of composers as a continuing lineage. A composer's contribution to history was described as improving or corrupting the genre. This was true for a composer's *oeuvre* as much as for music history as a whole. More was at stake than a Darwinian narrative of music history. Before recordings became available as household property, the ephemeral nature of music made it hard to formulate a canon of diverse musical styles. Instead, the need for aural memory encouraged – at least in the music-lover's mind – a hierarchy of style, rather than a row of composers in a canon, equalized in stature through the ownership of recordings. In the years before the First World War when Darwinian concepts of struggle and decline became pervasive, an implicit sense of development or decline was widespread. Every composer either advanced or undermined the genre. Aesthetic evaluation thus implied tremendous moral consequences for the progress or decay of art forms. By the 1920s much of the anti-Semitic rhetoric derived from the force of polemic. The debates between Paul Bekker and Hans Pfitzner were only the most famous example.[10] In the right-wing press, extravagant praise from

---

[9] 'Es hat lange gedauert, bis ein Künstler solche Worte mit innerer Berechtigung auf sein Werk anwenden durfte. Keiner vor Mahler hätte es tun können – wobei freilich nicht zu vergessen ist, daß alles, was vor Mahler geleistet wurde, notwendig war, um sein Werk zu ermöglichen. ... [S]o erleben wir in Mahler eine Synthese der mittel- bzw. Norddeutschen Gruppe Mendelssohn–Schumann–Brahms, der österreichischen Schubert–Bruckner und der in der Instrumentalmusik auf Liszt gegründeten, in Strauß gipfelnden neudeutschen Schule.'

[10] The public debate began when Pfitzner responded to the revised and expanded edition of Busoni's *Entwurf einer neuen Ästhetik der Tonkunst* of 1916 with his own *Futuristengefahr. Bei Gelegenheit von Busonis Ästhetik* (1917). Paul Bekker responded with an article in the *Frankfurter Zeitung*, 9 January 1918, 'Futuristengefahr?' as well as 'Erfinder und Gestalter. Eine Antwort auf Herrn Professor Dr. Hans Pfitzner' (1918) and 'Impotenz oder Potenz? Eine Antwort auf Herrn Professor Dr. Hans Pfitzner', *Frankfurter Zeitung*, 6 January 1920. All three were reprinted in Paul Bekker, *Kritische Zeitbilder*

Mahler's supporters was quoted to launch attacks on the composer. Although in the hands of these anti-Semites such material was more a tool than a form of deliberate provocation, some readers were certainly swayed by such devices.

Mahler's most ardent admirers – William Ritter, Ernst Otto Nodnagel and Richard Specht among them – were often highly unconventional, perhaps socially marginalized, individuals whose efforts frequently backfired. This was especially so in the polemical culture that pervaded journalism in the 1910s, which lacked the elegance of the *fin-de-siècle* feuilletonists. In his review of the Eighth, Walter Riezler wrote that after reading Ritter's adulation of Mahler, 'to cool off, one reads in the excellent book of Rudolf Louis ... the section on Mahler: here falsity, "artificiality", is declared to be the basic trait of Mahler's music'. The success of the work was therefore considered superficial in nature. Mahler was 'a great person of unbendable will. With this will he subdued and transfixed the four thousand listeners at the recent première of his Eighth Symphony almost as much as the thousand participants' (Riezler, 1910, pp. 604–5).[11]

The massive changes and devastation of the First World War helped bring about a politicization of writing on music. It was less a change in world-view than the erosion of an earlier resistance to discussing Jewish identity. The less musical and less informed the author, the more political the utterances on 'Jewish' character. In his book on 'musical impotence' [*musikalische Impotenz*] Blessinger (1920) had no tools for critical discussion of Mahler's music and merely spoke of the composer's 'alien' qualities. He nonetheless issued dire pronouncements on 'the Jewish question', and called for the containment of the 'dangerous Jewish influence' [*gefährlicher jüdischer Einfluss*] (p. 79) in music and other areas of life: 'It is impossible to doubt that the Jewish question has now become most acute in all areas of life and that its resolution within a specialized area can only follow in conjunction with its resolution in general' (Blessinger, 1920, p. 74).[12]

The acceptance of Mahler's music into the standard repertoire was one provocation. This had been true with the assimilated Jew Robert Hirschfeld when Mahler's symphonies started to be programmed regularly, rather than merely

---

(Stuttgart and Berlin: Deutsche Verlags-Anstalt, 1921), pp. 265–69 & 300–326. For a good overview, see Weiner, 1993, pp. 50–71, Chapter 1: 'The Polemics of Hans Pfitzner'.

[11] 'Und dann lese man, zur Abkühlung, in dem trefflichen Buche von Rud. Louis ... den Abschnitt über Mahler: hier ist die Unechtheit, das "Gemachte," als der Grundzug der Mahlerschen Musik hingestellt. ... [E]in großer Mensch von unbeugsamen Willen. Mit diesem Willen hat er neulich bei der Uraufführung der Achten Symphonie die viertausend Hörer beinahe ebenso gezwungen und gebannt wie die tausend Mitwirkenden.'

[12] 'Es ist kein Zweifel darüber möglich, daß auf allen Gebieten des Lebens die Judenfrage heute im höchsten Grade akut geworden ist und daß eine Lösung derselben auf einem Spezialgebiete nur im Zusammenhang mit ihrer allgemeinen Lösung erfolgen kann.'

premièred, in Vienna. But in the polemical culture of the 1920s, such responses inevitably became political. The programming of Mahler's First, Second and Fourth Symphonies in rapid succession in Berlin in 1927 (under Bruno Walter, Carl Schuricht and Heinz Unger) led one critic, Erich Urban, to claim the victory of the composer over the 'dark, unwieldy Bruckner, revelling in excessive dimensions' ['das Interesse für den dunklen, ungefügen, in maßlosen Dimensionen schwelgenden Bruckner sichtlich abnimmt'] (Urban, 1927). This article spurred the right-wing critic Paul Zschorlich to turn an aesthetic debate into racial diatribe: 'There is no point in circumventing these issues. The reason why Mahler is favoured over Bruckner is first and foremost the simple fact *that our concert business is primarily in Jewish hands and that Jewish conductors always push their racial colleague Mahler into the foreground*' (Zschorlich, 1927; original italics).[13] This sort of crass charge signalled that any genuine debate over ethnic identity was already over. Zschorlich's accusation merely applied the 'Protocols of the Elders of Zion' to the world of music management. By the 1930s any genuine polemical culture had disappeared. It seemed plausible to criticize the Jewish composer without any aesthetic provocation. Allusions to Mahler's 'supporters' were kept vague in order not to disseminate conflicting opinions. In the meantime, however, the debate had helped to provoke a literature of Jewish self-reflection.

In search of a Jewish identity

Alongside the anti-Semitic attacks on Mahler came attempts to build Jewish pride through the composer. These included defensive moves on the part of music critics as well as Zionist work to claim a unique Jewish identity through art. The most high-profile debates over German-Jewish identity took place in the literary and cultural journal *Die Kunstwart*. A number of articles addressed anti-Semitism from the perspective of the Jew and non-Jew alike. What has not been recognized is the role that music played in these debates. Batka's article on the 'Jewish' qualities of Mahler's music, which appeared in *Die Kunstwart* before these debates filled its pages, may have been a contributing influence (Batka, 1910).[14] The First World War and the division of Central Europe along ethnic lines in 1918 would legitimize discussion of ethnicity in the public realm, just as Zionism and the emerging fields of Jewish studies provided the vocabulary.

---

[13] 'Es hat auch keinen Zweck, um die Dinge herumzureden. Der Grund, warum Mahler vor Bruckner bevorzugt wird, liegt in allererster Linie in der einfachen Tatsache begründet, *daß unser Konzertbetrieb vorwiegend in jüdischen Händen ist und daß die jüdischen Dirigenten ihren Rassegenossen Mahler stets in den Vordergrund schieben.*'

[14] On Batka and his Mahler reception see Painter & Varwig, 2002.

Even by the time discussions of Jewish identity were very much in the air, Mahler's supporters still remained hesitant to probe the issue too explicitly. His friend Richard Specht had initially written in his 1913 biography of the composer: 'I cannot address the Jewishness in Mahler; instead, here I will only hold to the power and truth of Nietzsche's saying: "The font of great cultures is the mixture of races".' Specht hoped to dismiss the enterprise by showing the subjectivity of ethnically based criticism. The 'mystical' sonorities in Mahler's music sounded 'unnaturally Catholic' to some listeners and 'unpleasantly Jewish' to others (Specht, 1913, pp. 37–38).[15] Yet the 1918 edition went on to list his Christian qualities, balanced by the following:

> Mahler (just as much his music, which represents his 'identifying' mode of expression) is a Jew and Jewish in the thrusting power of his intellect, in the feverish restlessness of his search after the meaning and laws of the world, in the dark, impassioned fervour, the frequent lack of proportion and even the captiousness of his nature.
>
> (Specht, 1918, pp. 53–54)[16]

Specht, himself a German Jew, in effect conceded the importance of Jewish identity, but only in so far as it resided in the art work, not the creative process or the person. In contrast, when Mahler's other principal biographer, Paul Stefan, felt compelled to address the subject of Jewish identity in his slender pocketbook on the composer, he did so on biographical terms alone and dismissed any attempts to find '"Jewish" traits' [*'jüdische' Züge*] (as he put it in quotation marks) in the music (Stefan, 1923, p. 23). Neither of these Mahler enthusiasts wanted to concede that Jewish traits could both characterize the artist and permeate the work that he produced.

Adolf Weißmann's book on music and the world crisis was one of the earliest accounts of Mahler as a symbiosis of the German and the Jew (Weißmann, 1922). Weißmann asserted from the start that Judaism was important to the composer's creativity. Acknowledging that Judaism had both positive and destructive traits, Weißmann hoped for a synthesis of German and Jew:

> But it [Jewish blood] has the capacity to grow more refined in such a way that innate Judaism and surrounding Teutonism enter into an indissoluble and nobler union. Then, through combined action of their nerves, the shared birthright of metaphysical thought and the most intense emotion can

---

[15] 'die mystischen Laute seiner Musik bedingt, die die einen als unnatürlich katholisch, die andern als unangenehm jüdisch empfinden. Über das Jüdische bei Mahler kann ich nicht mitreden und halte ich mich nur an die Kraft und Wahrheit der Nietzsche-Notiz: "Wo Rassen gemischt sind, ist der Quell großer Kulturen".'

[16] 'Mahler (und ebenso seine Musik, die seinen "identischen" Ausdruck bedeutet) ist Jude und jüdisch in der Stoßkraft seiner Geistigkeit, in der fieberischen Rastlosigkeit des Suchens nach dem Sinn und Gesetz der Welt, in der leidenschaftlich düsteren Glut, in mancher Ungleichmäßigkeit und auch in mancher Spitzfindigkeit seines Wesens.'

become productive. Furthermore, they advance into limitless regions; they are inclined towards the supra-national.

(Weißmann, 1922, pp. 102–3)[17]

Weißmann saw Mahler as the consummate German Jew. Wagner's definition of a German as someone who 'does a thing for its own sake' becomes, in Mahler's case, someone who 'wears himself out in a cause'. When, a few pages later, Weißmann turned to discuss Mahler's music, his description drew on the anti-Semitic critique that had been so common at the turn of the century. The individual lines were tuneful but were not true polyphony; colour became more prominent than the composer intended; and a 'confusion of styles' [*Stildurcheinander*] revealed Mahler's 'lacerated soul' [*zerrissene Seele*] (Weißmann, 1922, p. 108). It is not surprising that such claims on the part of a Berlin Jewish professor would be exploited by the Nazis: his photograph was included in the exhibition catalogue on 'degenerate music' (Ziegler, 1939). Weißmann himself would later lament the overuse of the term 'race' and hoped that any detectable traces of race in music would soon disappear because of extensive 'racial mixing' throughout Europe (see Weißmann, 1926, p. 86).

To discuss the qualities of Jewish identity, both positively and negatively, in a context that was not anti-Semitic was a normalization of cultural difference so important in the post-assimilationist Germany of the 1920s. In an article on 'The Jewish in Mahler' a Jewish family newspaper reported that Mahler could never deny his Jewishness – certainly not in his music. The author continued: 'It is not easy to speak of such things without eventually running into prejudice and hurting the feelings of excellent people. To discuss the Jewish traits of an art work by a Jew should be as unobjectionable as discussing Wagner as a Saxon.' The traits listed, however, were appropriated from earlier, critical assessments: 'the strongly gesticulating rhythm, the unrest, the preference for biting contrasts, the flickering or fanatical passion of expression all belong to this ...', with ellipses to show just how difficult such commentary was. Finally, however, the author deemed Mahler's music a symbiosis of German and Jewish identity: 'between the stone-masses of the large city we feel a deep, German homesickness for field and meadow' (Anon., 1924).

A younger generation turned to Mahler in an attempt to promote a unique Jewish identity, quite apart from the effort to explain his music. Heinrich Berl (b. 1896) argued that music was necessary for political action and for cohesion as a people, and no less so for Jews. If there had been no secular 'Jewish' music over the past century, Berl speculated in 1923, then a rebirth of Jewry would be

---

17 'Aber es [jüdisches Blut] hat die Fähigkeit, sich so zu verfeinern, daß eingeborenes Judentum und mitgeborenes Deutschtum eine unlösliche veredetere Bindung eingehen. Dann können metaphysisches Denken und höchste Intensität des Gefühls als Erbteil der Geburt durch die Nerven schöpferisch werden. Mehr noch: sie schreiten ins Unbegrenzte; sie haben den Zug zum Übernationalen.'

impossible. Mahler was Berl's prime example: 'The third movement of Mahler's First Symphony is Jewry, the *purest* Jewry. Here one finds everything: march, funeral, irony, folk song, canon, melodic development, harmony, instrumentation: everything here is Jewish; there is hardly more direct evidence' (Berl, 1923, pp. 315–16).[18] Max Brod's essay on Mahler's Jewish melodies was so ideologically driven as to enter into pure speculation. He mused: 'Since hearing Chassidic folks songs, I believe that Mahler quite simply had to make music in this way and no other, from the same unconscious source of his Jewish soul whence sprang these most beautiful Chassidic songs which he never knew.' Brod made a plea for 'intuiting into Mahler's Jewish soul', whereas from 'a German perspective' the First Symphony must seem restless, cynical, and devoid of unity (Brod, 1920, p. 378).[19]

Mahler's 'Jewish' musical identity

The very search for qualities that made up Mahler's Jewish musical identity served to counteract a continuing attempt to deny his status as a composer and to view him merely as one who reproduces the creative works of others in his conducting. Even in the 1920s and 30s, when Mahler's presence as a conductor had long ended, anti-Semitic texts still frequently recognized his conducting at the expense of his composing. In a preview article from the second, revised edition of his *Geist der Utopie*, the philosopher and social critic Ernst Bloch reported how still in 1923 Mahler 'is essentially considered just as an important conductor, and many a pitiable journalist dares to ask, entirely without blushing, whether Mahler had a calling to compose at all' (Bloch, 1923, p. 664).[20] Bruckner's student Klose listed Mahler in the index of his memoirs (1927) solely as a conductor, with no reference to his composing. Karl Blessinger would likewise report unequivocally: 'Whilst Mahler's compositions were at first

---

[18] 'dieser dritte Satz aus Mahlers I. Sinfonie ist Judentum, ist *reinstes* Judentum. Hier ist alles: Marsch, Trauer, Ironie, Volksgesang, Kanon, melodische Entfaltung, Tonart, Instrumentation: hier ist alles Judentum, es gibt kaum eine unmittelbarere Bezeugung.'

[19] 'Seit ich chassidische Volkslieder gehört habe, glaube ich, daß Mahler ganz einfach aus demselben unbewußten Urgrund seiner jüdischen Seele so und nicht anders musizieren mußte, aus dem die schönsten chassidischen Lieder, die er wohl niemals gekannt hat, entsprossen sind. ... Von einem deutschen Blickpunkt aus erscheint dieses Werk daher inkohärent, stillos, unförmlich, ja bizarr, schneidend, zynisch, allzu weich, gemischt mit allzu Hartem. Es ergibt, deutsch betrachtet, keine Einheit. Man ändere die Perspektive, suche sich in Mahlers jüdische Seele einzufühlen.' Excerpts from Brod's article were printed in the *Münchner Nachrichten*, 3 August 1920.

[20] 'Er gilt immer noch wesentlich nur als der bedeutende Dirigent, und mancher elender Zeitungsschreiber wagt durchaus ohne Schamröte zu fragen, ob Mahler überhaupt dazu berufen war, zu komponieren.'

rejected or at least were received with reservation, Mahler quickly gained acceptance as a conductor' (Blessinger, 1944, p. 116).[21]

What ultimately were the allegedly Jewish traits in music and in Mahler's music particularly? Most authors – whether neutral, positive or negative in stance – agreed that 'intensity' was the most common 'Jewish' feature of music. Ernst Bloch argued that by virtue of its 'intensity' Mahler's music failed to achieve the German identity aspired to by its composer, and instead was 'true Jewry' (Bloch, 1923, p. 665).[22] Other qualities included the prominence of polyphony and rhythm. Whether commentators were anti-Semitic or not, approving or critical, they tended to agree on a core group of 'Jewish' qualities in Mahler's music. Heinrich Berl saw Mahler and Schoenberg as 'liberating' music from harmony through polyphony (Berl, 1923, p. 310). In his chapter on Jews and modern music, the pro-Nazi Otto Schumann emphasized what he believed were the negative aspects of Mahler's contrapuntal writing. In transgressing the bounds of the symphonic, Mahler gradually adopted a type of polyphony which 'abandoned the ties with traditional harmony more and more, ultimately arriving at pronounced atonal constructions' (Schumann, 1940, p. 369).[23]

Rhythm for Berl was an essential quality of Jewish music, and Mahler and Schoenberg were his primary examples (Berl, 1923, p. 312). Others felt uncomfortable with such clear-cut, essentialist claims. Arno Nadel, who was deeply involved with Jewish musical and cultural life in Berlin (from 1894 he was a choral director at a Berlin synagogue), arrived at a stylistic definition of Jewish music only through discussion of synagogue chants. He explained the primary traits in this way: 'Recitative corresponds to the free essence of the Jewish soul, the diatonic melodic style to their continuous quiet singing and humming, and the anapaestic to their quest, goals and affirmation; the parallel lines to their philosophizing, questions and answers.' The secondary traits likewise correlated to the Jewish character: 'the meditative to their mysticism – and the changes in key and rhythm to their restless wandering around the world' (Nadel, 1923, p. 235). Turning to the subject of art music, Nadel absorbed into his discussion the very same aesthetic qualities that were upheld in German musical thought in general:

> What Jews have created in Western music is more or less also Western, although the traits which we have described play a large role in their art.

---

21 'Während die Kompositionen Mahlers zunächst abgelehnt oder wenigstens mit Zurückhaltung aufgenommen wurden, hat sich Mahler als Dirigent rasch durchgesetzt.'

22 'Mahler ist deutsch, oder will wenigstens durchaus als deutscher Meister gelten, was ihm freilich nicht gelingt, denn das ist wahrhaftig Judentum in der Musik, jüdisches Weh und jüdische Inbrust.'

23 'aus einer solchen Übersteigerung des Sinfonischen wandelt sich Mahler allmählich zu einer Art von Polyphonie, die immer mehr die Bindung an überkommene Harmonik preisgibt, bis sie schließlich bei ausgesprochen atonalen Aufrissen ankommt'.

They are melodists, they are metaphysicians (meditative creators), they break down the boundaries of tonality but they write in traditional forms and cannot do otherwise. When they innovate they are experimenters, perhaps in the best cases experimenters in the greatest and most valuable manner: like Mahler.

Here too the locus of identity was blurred, defying any potential for stereotyping the Jew as destructive of tradition: 'But Mahler is no experimenter in forms; he is one in spirit, in his soul if you will; Beethoven has a particular world and world-view, Mahler does not. He hovers between Jewry and Christianity; because he has the greatest gifts he is a tragic figure' (ibid., p. 236).[24]

Mahler became the representative musician for scholars of Jewish identity. One such example was Joseph Sachs, who published two books in English during the 1930s celebrating the Jewish contribution to culture and art. In a chapter on Mahler, Sachs challenged simple definitions of Jewish music. He found uncompelling Brod's and Berl's claim that Mahler's march rhythm, in its evocation of Hebrew traditions, evoked 'the masses' or 'the collective'. Sachs instead identified 'the religious intensity of the Jew' in the more expressive qualities of Mahler's music, especially its melodious character (Sachs, 1937, pp. 135–36).

The Third Reich

Right-wing, nationalist publications exploited the Zionist literature which had attempted a positive identification of Jewish qualities in art. Karl Blessinger borrowed from the Jewish discussions of musical identity to sharpen his earlier general critique of Jewish musical qualities. He explained how Mendelssohn and Meyerbeer reputedly failed in their aesthetic ideas, but merely resorted to cataloguing explicit Jewish practices in Mahler and Schoenberg as evaluated by

---

[24] 'Das Rezitativische entspricht dem ungebundenen Wesen der jüdischen Seele, das Melodisch-Diatonische ihrem ewigen stillen Singen und Summen, das Anapästische ihrem Suchen, Zielen und Bejahen, das Parallelistische ihrem Philosophieren, Fragen und Antworten, das Meditative ihrer Mystik – und der Wechsel in den Tonarten und Rhythmen ihrem unruhigen Umherschweifen in allen Welten.'

'Was Juden in der abendländischen Musik geschaffen haben, ist mehr oder weniger auch abendländisch, obgleich die von uns aufgezeigten Merkmale in ihrer Kunst eine große Rolle spielen. Sie sind Melodiker, sie sind Metaphysiker (meditative Schöpfer), sie sprengen die Grenzen der Tonalität, aber sie schreiben in überkommen Formen und können nicht anders. Wo sie Neuerer sind, sind sie Experimentatoren, vielleicht im besten Falle Experimentatoren größten und wertvollsten Stils: wie Mahler.'

'Aber Mahler ist nicht Experimentator in den Formen, er ist es im Geiste, in der Seele, wenn man will; Beethoven hat eine eigene Welt und eine Weltanschauung, Mahler hat sie nicht. Er schwebt zwischen Judentum und Christentum, er ist, weil er höchste Anlagen hat, eine tragische Figur.'

Jewish critics. The anti-Semitic identification of specific traits was derivative, simply manipulating pro-Jewish sources. Blessinger degraded the spiritual quality of 'intensity' as a personal trait, writing that the intensity of Mahler's music resembled the 'fanatical kind of Eastern Jewish Rabbi' [*fanatischen Typus des ostjüdischen Rabbiners*] (Blessinger, 1939, p. 77).

Histories of music and reference books often excluded Jewish musicians except, to quote Hans Joachim Moser, the 'best known, since often only in this way can the reader learn that someone is not Aryan. Such information is indispensable for a cultural-political orientation'. With this, Moser explained that in the 1943 edition of his lexicon of musicians, even more Jews were eliminated than in the 1933 edition (Moser, 1943, foreword).[25] Mahler was among those who could not be so easily excised from the Aryan cultural narrative. His music retained too strong a presence, and embodied the German symphonic ideal too substantially, for it to be simply ignored. Anti-Semitic critics therefore turned to the listener to claim reasons for Mahler's failure according to 'German' standards.

Once the intellectual and spiritual debates over German-Jewish identity and assimilation no longer existed, the claims in anti-Semitic discussion changed. By 1934 Jewish musicians could perform only in the context of the *Kulturbund* of German Jews. The bleak constraints on musical life for Jews remaining in Germany forced a reconsideration of art for art's sake. After Jews had been excluded from public life and expelled from the professions, anti-Semitism took on an eerily moderate tone. Music easily distinguishable from the common practice such as Mahler's and Schoenberg's no longer posed a threat. While journalistic and generalist authors discussed Mahler and 'Jewish' composers in polemical texts, musicologists excised Jews from their histories of German music. Richard Eichenauer followed both tactics in his *Musik und Rasse*, excluding Schoenberg from the index but discussing his music in the text.

The strongest criticism was reserved for a composer like Mendelssohn, whose ethnicity left no traces on his music. Mendelssohn 'seem[s] to us more pernicious than the ruthless self-assertion of the "atonally errant" Arnold Schoenberg who indeed is also Jewish, or than the tragic, compulsive love for the German manner in the fractured music of the Jew Gustav Mahler' wrote Otto Schumann in his history of German music (1940, pp. 281–82).[26]

---

[25] 'so empfahl es sich doch nicht, Artikel über die bekanntesten ganz zu streichen, da der Benutzer oft nur so erfahren kann, daß es sich um Nichtarier handelt. Solches informatorische Material ist zur kulturpolitischen Ausrichtung unentbehrlich.'

[26] 'Aber dieses formsichere Bewegen, diese glatte Problemlosigkeit, dieses schmiegsame Anpassen an Deutsches erscheinen uns verderblicher als die rücksichtslose Selbsbehauptung des "atonalen Mißtöners" Arnold Schönberg, der ja gleichfalls Jude ist, oder als die tragische Zwangliebe zu deutscher Art in der zerrissenen Musik des Juden Gustav Mahler.'

Most troubling was Mahler's use of folk song, for this was the sacred area of National Socialism. The musicologist and critic Richard Litterscheid (b. 1904) tried to persuade readers of the aesthetic failings of Mahler's Lieder stemming from his 'Jewish creative spirit' [*jüdische Schöpferkraft*] and 'Jewish world-feeling' [*jüdisches Weltgefühl*].

> He was unable to grasp the deepest and true emotional value of the German folk song, and therefore, by his own emotional excess and through the greatest expenditure of technical and formal means, he forced it into the realms of sentimentality. The eternal contradictions that arose between the ecstatic, overheated and gigantic dimensions of his symphonies and the humble folk-song themes, forced apart the content and form, which he was unable to bring together creatively in union, despite his most desperate efforts.
>
> (Litterscheid, 1936, pp. 416–17)[27]

Instead, so the essay concluded, Bruckner was the greater Austrian.

Discussion of Mahler became increasingly *ad hominem*, often without sustained consideration of the supposedly 'Jewish' qualities in his music. Karl Blessinger made no attempt to discuss weaknesses of the music itself in his book on Mendelssohn, Mahler and Meyerbeer. He acknowledged the German character attributed to Mahler's music – its 'deep spiritual turmoil' of the Jew [*tiefe seelische Zerrissenheit des Judens*] was often misunderstood as 'a Faustian struggle' [*faustisches Ringen*] (Blessinger, 1939, p. 77).

This passage from Blessinger was quoted in the *Lexikon der Juden in der Musik* (Gerigk & Stengel, 1940, p. 170), which listed all Jewish musicians, past and present, including minor figures identified by only a few words. Blessinger's comments were typical of the later rhetoric about nationalism and ethnicity in the Third Reich: assertions without examination or analysis.

The Jew was excluded from the genre of the symphony. In the chapter 'Neue Musik und Judentum' of his *Geschichte der deutschen Musik*, Otto Schumann criticized Mahler by impugning the aims of the artist: 'It is shocking, but also repulsive [*abstoßend*] when the wish to empathize with the German *Volk*, Jewish hair-splitting and Middle Eastern obsessiveness strive to appear and unite in no less than the true German form: the great symphony' (Schumann, 1940, p. 368).[28]

---

[27] 'Er hat das deutsche Volkslied nicht in seinem tiefsten, echten Gefühlswert erfassen können und hat es darum in eigenen Gefühlsüberschwang mit größtem Aufwand technischer und formaler Mittel in sentimentale Sphären abgedrängt, die volksliedfremd sind. Die unendlichen Widersprüche, die zwischen den ekstatisch überhitzten Riesendimensionen seiner Sinfonien und den schlichten Volksliedthemen bestehen, sprengen darum Gehalt und Form, die er selbst mit krampfhaftester Bemühung nicht schöperisch zur Einheit zusammenzuschweißen vermocht hat.'

[28] 'Erschütternd, aber auch abstoßend, wenn sich Einfühlungswille in deutsches Volkstum, jüdische Spitzfindigkeiten und vorderasiatische Besessenheit gerade in der echt deutschen Form der großen Sinfonie zu verwirklichen und zu verbinden streben.'

The problem lay with the listener: Blessinger spoke of the 'sound masses overwhelming' [*einstürmende Tonmassen*] the listeners, and the demands that Mahler's music placed on them in terms of both length and intensity (Blessinger, 1939, p. 84).

The *a priori* rejection of the Jew as artist prevailed over any criticism of the art work itself. Eichenauer wrote, 'We are not justified in doubting the personal sincerity of Mahler's struggle towards the German spirit, but that should not prevent us from determining that this struggle is nevertheless unsuccessful and must remain so for racial reasons.' The actual discussion of the music remained surprisingly mild: 'Despite the claims of Mahler enthusiasts with their ulterior motives, his symphonies are not in any way the strongest symphonic achievement since Beethoven, but are rather the documents of an inwardly fractured spirit, with their beautiful moments scattered across a mass of mediocrities.' The harshest criticism was in fact aimed at the effect of the music on listeners: 'His fondness for the primitive, deafening effect of incessantly repeated rhythms, arabesque formations, and "endless Nomad marches" ... is precisely what sounds Asiatic. It evokes in Europeans not any awakening will to build, but rather brings about a dreamy desire to be engulfed' (Eichenauer, [1932] 1937, pp. 300–301).[29]

In his book *Beauty and the Jew*, Joseph Sachs established a methodology that was resistant to political anti-Semitism. The 'Jewish' traits in Mahler's music were negative qualities of art but entirely unobjectionable as personal traits: Mahler's music is Jewish in its sentimentality, triviality, and naivety. Any criticism of the music was attributed to personal virtue. The Jew

> is too preoccupied with the ethical and emotional content of life to leave this world and adventure into new worlds, where the moral law yields to the law of art. Thus Mahler may never have completely sublimated his pathos into musical form, just as Chagall has not completely translated his thought and feeling into pure painting. It is just this human content that makes Jewish art so interesting, even though it may never reach the highest forms of pure art.
>
> (Sachs, 1937, pp. 234–35)

---

[29] 'Denn seine Symphonien sind keineswegs, wie zweckbewußte Mahlerschwärmer behaupten, die gewaltigste symphonische Tat seit Beethoven, sondern mit ihren über einen Wust von Durchschnittlichkeiten verstreuten Schönheiten die Urkunden eines innerlich zerborstenen Geistes. ... Wir sind nicht berechtigt, an der persönlichen Lauterkeit von Mahlers Ringen um den deutschen Geist zu zweifeln; aber das darf uns nicht an der Feststellung hindern, daß im ganzen dieses Ringen eben doch erfolglos bleib, aus rassischen Gründen erfolglos bleiben mußte. ... Seine Vorliebe für die betäubend urtümliche Wirkung endlos wiederholter Rhythmen, arabeskenartiger Bildungen, "endloser Nomadenmärsche" (*Moser*, nach Max *Brod*!), die auf den Europäer nicht als Ausdruck eines wachen Bauwillens, sondern eines träumenden Versinkenwollens wirken, mutet geradezu asiatisch an.'

The result of such claims was that Mahler's music was reinscribed with the very meaning that anti-Semitic texts had denied it: 'Spiritual expression is more important than material technique and ... the Jewish genius is essentially lyrical, even when it works in a plastic medium' (ibid., pp. 227–28). Though pervaded by essentialist Jewish categories, Sachs's book shows an attempt to celebrate Jewish art and music without claims that could be exploited by anti-Semites.

Conclusion

Ultimately anti-Semitism in music criticism did not so much serve political ends as reflect the political aims of its audience and author. The tensions and even contradictions inherent in all works of art defied any useful and complete appropriation of cultural stereotype, whether of the German or the Jew. Anti-Semitism (as an ideology, rather than as a political movement) was deeply rooted in the dialectical tradition of German thought. Two influential writers on politics and society show just how variable in content, yet rigid in method and value attribution, such argumentation through oppositions could be. Werner Sombart's study *Die Juden und das Wirtschaftsleben* ([1911] 1982; trans. as *Jews and Modern Capitalism*) contrasted the German 'forest people', who were attuned to the mysterious, immediate, dreamlike and concrete, with the nomadic Jews inclined to abstraction and rationality as a result of the brilliant sunlight and clear nights of the desert. The unpredictability of desert life fostered the notion of limitless acquisition and production, which were antithetical to a stable agrarian community. Richard Nicolaus von Coudenhove-Kalergi's book on culture and technology (*Revolution durch Technik*, 1932) explained through cultural attributes the European orientation towards technology and the Asian tendency to reject technology. Europeans are energetic, active, goal-oriented, romantic, heroic, Dionysian and manly, while Asians are harmonious, rooted and settled, static, classical, idyllic, Apollonian and even effeminate. The European character is oriented towards the domination of nature; the Asian character is oriented towards self-control.[30]

Nor would Mahler's music serve the cause of Zionism – at least not any more, arguably, than had Wagner's operas. Though his accomplishments as creative artist contributed to the pride of German Jews in the 1920s and 30s, the lack of any overt engagement in Jewish culture and religion in Mahler's creative work endangers any attempt to superimpose Jewish identity. To be sure, the dynamics of German–Jewish interaction at this moment in Vienna's rich cultural history and Austro–Hungary's fraught politics affected Mahler's creative thinking. But as with Mahler's conflicted responses to nature and the metropolis, his response

---

[30] This overview of Richard Nicolaus von Coudenhove-Kalergi's *Revolution durch Technik* is drawn from Herf, 1984, p. 210.

to Judaism and Jewish culture should be understood as a historical moment that can be only partly reconstructed and not as a site of essential traits that exist outside place and time.

Chapter Six

Gustav Mahler's Musical Jewishness[1]

VLADIMÍR KARBUSICKÝ
translated by Jeremy Barham

The discovery of sources should go hand in hand with their unbiased interpretation. As the following study documents, this musicological principle is unfortunately seldom respected. The 'inconvenient' is ignored, unpalatable sources disregarded. Interpretation is subject to the arbitrariness of ideological positions.

Portraying an accurate historical image seems to be particularly troublesome as far as Gustav Mahler is concerned. He grew up bilingually in the surroundings of the Hebrew synagogue, as both German and Czech. The language barrier alone cannot explain why the Czech-Bohemian characteristics of his work have escaped precise definition. The Hasidic-Jewish musical sound world has equally been circumvented. Mahler is supposed to be regarded as a German with a Christian soul, a 'Jewish Christian'. Hasidic-Jewish attributes identified by the Jewish composer and musicologist Max Brod are rejected from the start by Constantin Floros, the most prominent representative of the German-national trend in Mahler research. Nor do the opinions of Jewish musicians who are eminently qualified to speak on such topics, for example, Peter Gradenwitz and Leonard Bernstein, count for anything. This has the result of obstructing the analysis and understanding of Mahler's integration within the Jewish community of Iglau. The fact that he was immersed in that environment until the age of 15 is suppressed. He received the confirmation of his *bar mitzvah* in the Iglau synagogue, and these roots in fact had a lasting effect on the development of his creative work.

The prescribed interpretation is conspicuously unmusical. It is based only on verbal statements about Mahler's Jewishness which naturally contradict each other. Of these, the description 'Jewish Christian' seems to be the most

[1] This essay has been adapted by Vladimír Karbusický from his article 'Gustav Mahlers musikalisches Judentum', *Hamburger Jahrbuch für Musikwissenschaft*, 16 (1999), pp. 179–207. Material from this article is reproduced here by kind permission of the journal's editor, Peter Petersen. The following footnotes are editorial. Those marked '(VK)' are based on information provided by Vladimír Karbusický.

convenient. The need for musical analysis is obviated. Even those verbal testimonies which would demand a closer hearing of Mahler's music are suppressed.

The treatment of Mahler's letters of August 1886 to his Jewish friend Fritz Löhr/Löwi is typical of this. Mahler wrote with great enthusiasm from Leipzig about the opera *La Juive* by Jacques Halévy (whose real name was Élias Lévy). This work was first performed in 1835, but nowadays has been almost completely forgotten because the Nazis banished it from the stage and from music literature. Their hatred of everything Jewish created a lacuna in the reception of this work. It is therefore a priority of musicological research to fill this gap for the sake of historical accuracy, and especially since the dramatic conflict of *La Juive* concerns the outward pressure to become baptized – a pressure to which Mahler later submitted in Hamburg.

Mahler wrote in 1886 to his Jewish friend: 'Tonight I am conducting *La Juive* – I am completely taken by this wonderful, sublime work, and rate it as one of the greatest ever written. Do come, for I must play it to you!' (Blaukopf, 1996, p. 75, and Martner, 1979, p. 98; editor's translation). One searches in vain amongst the ideologically prescribed literature for analysis and evaluation of this direct account from Mahler. The letter has been purged from Mahler's life history.

Mahler's enthusiasm is nevertheless of considerable musical importance. He experienced at first hand the deeply affecting lament of the Jew Eléazar (a Hebrew name better known in the form Lazarus). Eléazar calls out, his trembling voice wanting to soar up to the Almighty in heaven. This situation should be understood in Hebraic terms: the Lord of creation is the 'Maker of the Universe', *Riboyno shel oylom*, a universe in which the world of Job rings out, voiced in the long, arching phrases of the Jewish style of lamentation. These waves of lament alternate with the heavy gasps of thrusting rhythmic phrases based on triplet and dotted figures. The A-flat-major tonality (the sepulchral key of death, judgment and eternity according to Schubart's key symbolism[2]) is moulded by the orchestra in urgent, pounding demisemiquavers, expressing extreme exhilaration, and stubbornly returning time and again to the distant, imploring words. At the outburst of yearning for life ('… rises towards you and cries and demands life, life' [' … vers toi se lève et crie et demande la vie, la vie'] – the German version taking 'Lazarus' more as its starting point: 'may God have mercy on the oppressed, the poor' ['Wolle Gott sich erbarmen der Bedrückten, der Armen']) the tremolo is used as a recognizable symbolic expression of fear and anxiety [*Angst*]. One feels 'driven into a corner' (the German term *Angst* comes from the Latin *angustus* meaning 'narrow'): in beseeching the Almighty God the repetition of the despairing call is to some extent a symptom of spiritual anguish. Then there are the 'drums of destiny', the intensified tremoli and the restless

---

2 An example of Schubart's theories is given below.

rhythms which one listens for in the symphonies of Mahler as emblems of his personal style. Halévy's *La Juive* is nevertheless ignored. It does not fit in with the idea of the 'Jewish Christian'.

This attitude towards Halévy is symptomatic. Because Mahler wrote symphonies, comparisons are drawn with the symphonic genre: Mahler and Liszt, Mahler and Bruckner, and so on. Those operas which Mahler studied, directed and discussed in detail with his renowned meticulous care are not examined. In addition, the evidence that Mahler really knew those works being compared is often lacking. For example, on 5 November 1907 he wrote to Alma from St Petersburg about his experience of Tchaikovsky's *Eugene Onegin*: 'Yesterday I went to the local opera. *Onegin*. Very lavish resources but used in a crude and often dilettantish way' (La Grange & Weiß, 1995, p. 349, and Mahler, 1990, p. 298; editor's translation). Can Mahler's stylistic traits be related to the music of Tchaikovsky without consideration of this statement? The Russian folk-music style was quite alien to Mahler. A historical examination of when and how he came to know Tchaikovsky's symphonic music is still lacking.[3]

The Jewish musical environment of Vienna should not be ignored. The Chief Cantor Salomon Sulzer (1804–91) was held in extraordinarily high regard. In 1839 he laid the foundations for the reform of synagogue chant with his *Schir Zion* [*Song of Zion*]. The liturgical compositions of this work became so well known that they inspired admiration even in court circles. Sulzer's voice must have been captivating; indeed he was appointed at the Conservatoire as a teacher of chant. When Schubert asked Sulzer to perform his songs, 'Der Wanderer' had to be repeated three times in succession. Schubert commented: 'Now for the first time I understand my own music and what I felt when I set the words "I wander in silence, with little joy,/And my sighs constantly ask: where?"' ['Jetzt erst verstehe ich meine eigene Musik und was ich gefühlt habe, als ich die Worte: "Ich wandre still, bin wenig froh,/Und immer fragt der Seufzer: wo?" betont habe'] (Friedmann, 1908, p. 125; song text translation taken from Prawer, 1964, p. 37). Liszt describes his visit to the synagogue where Sulzer was the musical director and Cantor: 'Rarely have divine worship and human compassion struck such an overwhelmingly stirring chord in us' ['Selten haben wir eine so überwältigende Erschütterung aller Saiten der Gottesverehrung und des menschlichen Mitgefühls erlebt'] (Friedmann, 1908, p. 124). As a result, Liszt developed historical theories of Christianity's gradual adoption of the music of Israel, theories which he demonstrated to best advantage in his oratorios. In 1876, during the first year of Mahler's studies at the Vienna Conservatoire, the Gesellschaft der Musikfreunde organized a huge celebration of Sulzer's fifty

---

[3] A recent article by Henry A. Lea goes some way towards filling this gap: 'Tchaikovsky and Mahler: A Study in Musical Affinity', *News About Mahler Research*, 44 (spring 2001), 16–27. See also Max Deutsch, 'Tschaikowsky–Mahler', *Mercure de France*, 1104 (August 1955), 619–31 & 1105 (September 1955), 58–75.

years in office. At that time the Conservatoire was housed in the building of the
Gesellschaft der Musikfreunde. It is therefore inconceivable that Mahler would
not have taken part in this celebration, and that Sulzer's fundamental work in
shaping the liturgy of the synagogue was unknown to him. There can be no doubt
that Sulzer's *Schir Zion* was already shaping the worship of the 'Creator of the
Universe' in Iglau where the reformed synagogue was consecrated in 1863 in full
musical splendour. All the sounds of daily life in the community appertained to
this, even the prayer of mourning, the *Kaddish*.

Without the spiritual world of Judaism a number of things in Mahler's
symphonic universe are inexplicable. His Second Symphony is usually called the
'Resurrection Symphony', but only the 'Christian' half of the bipartite final
movement is ever recognized. In terms of the impartial interpretation of sources,
this is inaccurate, for the final movement is an indivisible whole made up of two
elements: apocalypse and resurrection; and this embodies the Jewish world of the
Old Testament.

Apocalyptic images connected with the promise of resurrection can be found
in chapters 6–12 of the Book of Daniel, written in the second century BC.[4] After
the vision of the plagues one reads the following:

> And many of them that sleep in the dust of the earth shall awake, some to
> everlasting life, and some to shame and everlasting contempt. And they that
> be wise shall shine as the brightness of the firmament; and they that turn
> many to righteousness as the stars for ever and ever.
>
> (Daniel 12: 2–3)[5]

This cosmic glance up towards the radiant stars and heavens can be found again
in the first letter of Paul (*Scha-al*) to the Corinthians, in which he quotes from the
Old Testament. In the text it is not the 'trumpets' that sound, as Luther
anachronistically translated it, but the ancient Jewish signalling instrument, the
shofar. This instrument was in use later during the Diaspora and in Iglau
when Mahler was there. The passage from the letter to the Corinthians reads as
follows:

> We shall not all sleep, but we shall all be changed. In a moment, in the
> twinkling of an eye, at the last *shofar*: for the *shofar* shall sound, and the
> dead shall be raised incorruptible, and we shall be changed.
>
> (I Corinthians 15: 51–52, substituting '*shofar*' for 'trumpet')

Belief in resurrection is thus not something purely Christian, and is not a sign
of the division between Christian and Jew. The *Mishnah* Books, edited in the
third century – of which the *Talmud* is the exegesis – excludes from the redeemed
world those who do not believe in resurrection. The vision of resurrection has

---

[4] For a historical and religious examination of the apocalyptic elements of the
Book of Daniel see Rowley, 1965 (VK).

[5] This and subsequent translations are taken from the Authorized King James
Version of the Bible.

been anchored in Judaism since the Middle Ages; for Mahler it was of contemporary relevance.

Friedrich Klopstock's epic poem *Der Messias*, begun during his theological studies in Jena in 1745, naturally takes the Jewish tradition as its starting point. After Klopstock's death in Hamburg on 14 March 1803 an extraordinary funeral ceremony was arranged for him in the Hanseatic city. Ninety years later during the funeral of Hans von Bülow, attended by Mahler, Klopstock's chorale from *Der Messias* was performed: 'Rise up, yes you will rise up,/my dust, after a short rest …!'. As pointed out in the literature, this experience provided Mahler with the spark of inspiration for the final movement of the Second Symphony. However, strangely enough, the movement does not begin with the resurrection. People do not realize that Mahler composed the Second Symphony as a Jew. If it had been composed from the standpoint of a 'Jewish Christian', the final movement ought to have begun straight away with the Klopstock chorale. However, this spark of inspiration for the text immediately reminded him of the familiar world of the Book of Daniel, and he constructed the movement in two parts as apocalypse and resurrection. One recognizes the call of the *shofar* which epitomizes the tone of the Book of Daniel. The sound of this ram's-horn instrument was part of Mahler's experience in Iglau. An explanatory note is in order here: the Jewish Museum in Prague houses about 500 specimens from the synagogues of Bohemia and Moravia which the Nazis had set aside from the furnishings of Jewish places of worship for the planned 'Museum of an Extinct Race' [Museum der ausgestorbenen Rasse]. Some of these bear witness to the vitality of the ancient Jewish experience: a quotation from the third verse of Psalm 81 is engraved on them in Hebrew: 'Tik'u bachodesh shofar bakese lejom chagenu' ['Blow the *shofar* in the new moon, in the time appointed, on our solemn feast day']. The interval of a fifth is characteristic of this instrument's sound; Mahler ended the final bars of his last work, the Tenth Symphony, with such intervals.[6]

The centenary of Mahler's birth in 1960 brought renewed interest in his music. After the neglect caused to a large extent by the Nazis, there was talk of a Mahler renaissance. Recordings of his symphonies came on the market at the same time that the renaissance of Franz Kafka, the Jew from Prague, began. Theodor W. Adorno's monograph, which appeared in 1960, shows how problematic this interest in Mahler was. Adorno was a typical German Hegelian who forced Mahler into his dialectic constructions. When he was attempting to establish himself in Oxford in 1934, he must have been disappointed to realize, as he wrote to Ernst Krenek, that his mode of thought based on the Hegelian system was barely understood at all in England. He nevertheless persisted with his dialectics as the key which would be able to open up and explain all things.

---

[6] See the last three bars of the horns (bars 398–400) in Deryck Cooke's performing version of the Symphony (Cooke, 1989, p. 164).

Adorno had little understanding of the specificity of music outside Germany. He completely derided the Finn Jean Sibelius. Mahler's Czech-Bohemian roots were therefore entirely alien to him. Reference to this *ethnos* appears only once in his extensive book, when he links Mahler and Sigmund Freud: both were 'German-Bohemian Jews' (Adorno, 1960, p. 58, & 1992a, p. 39). Adorno found the sense of reminiscence in the posthorn episode of the Third Symphony – which is coloured with distinctly Czech melodic formulae – merely 'scandalously audacious' (ibid., 1960, p. 54 & 1992a, p. 36). The way in which he forced this captivating Bohemian scene into the Hegelian conceptual system should be quoted:

> If banality is the essence of musical reification, it is both preserved and redeemed by the inspired, improvising voice that animates the concrete. Thus the music incorporates even the fracture without which the whole would disintegrate.
>
> (Ibid., 1960, p. 55 & 1992a, pp. 36–37)

Here, says Adorno – making a leap into sociological dialectics *à la* Marx – Mahler 'inferred the revolt against bourgeois music from that very music' (ibid., 1960, p. 55 & 1992a, p. 37).

Bernd Sponheuer devoted an essay of 1986 specifically to the third movement of Mahler's First Symphony with the Adornoesque title 'Dissonante Stimmigkeit' (in Danuser, 1992, pp. 159–90). Clichés in the style of Adorno are conspicuous here; for example: 'The dialectic of negation and participation in the unified' ['Dialektik von Negation und Partizipation am Vereinten']; 'The unity of the disorganized and the meaningful' ['Einheit des Desorganisierten und des Sinnvollen']; 'The unity of the inconsistent and the dissonant' ['Einheit von Unstimmigem und Dissonantem'], and so on. Sponheuer, who is even prepared to hear 'circus music' in this movement (but just nothing Jewish!), averts his eyes when at one point in his text Adorno traces an element of Jewishness. Astonishingly, Adorno ignores it in the third movement of the First Symphony, where even musical amateurs have noticed the 'Yiddishness' (Leonard Bernstein's term), but detects it in Mahler's Fourth Symphony: 'Synagogal or secular Jewish melodies are rare; a passage in the Scherzo of the Fourth Symphony might most readily point in that direction' (Adorno, 1960, p. 192, & 1992a, p. 149).[7] Adorno is thinking of the passage in the unusually penetrating timbre of the oboes, illustrated in Ex. 6.1. Adorno shows an awareness here of the 'shout for joy' [*Aufjauchzen*] as the most striking characteristic of Hasidic-Yiddish music. It is made particularly clear by Mahler in the second oboe, which pipes out the ascending leap of a sixth. The flutes emphasize this exultation through the liberating effect of their crescendo from *piano* to *forte* in bars 24 and

---

[7] Adorno's footnote at this point refers to the passage beginning at bar 22 in the second movement of the Fourth Symphony.

Ex. 6.1 Oboe parts, bars 22–26 of second movement of Fourth Symphony

26 where they mostly double the oboes. This finding does not fit well with efforts to rid Mahler's music of all that is Jewish. Neither Sponheuer nor the entire ideologically prescribed German Mahler research of recent times heeds this suggestion of Adorno's.

One person who was able to identify the Hasidic idiom beyond doubt was Leonard Bernstein; after all, he did come from a family of Eastern Jews who had emigrated to America. In a BBC broadcast of 1986 he conducted the third movement of the First Symphony with genuine Hasidic accents. The beginning of the B section (according to the formal outline presented below in Fig. 6.1) shown in full score in Plate 6.1 demonstrates that the conductor accurately interpreted Mahler's numerous markings designed to ensure that the Hasidic style was captured. Drawing on his own experience of the tradition, Bernstein achieves this in a highly original way, and refers to some distinctive features in his commentary. Of primary importance is the scale F–G–A–B flat–C sharp–D beginning on the upbeat, and against this the plaintive, descending phrase of the trumpets (*ausdrucksvoll*) in contrary motion, with its chromatic interplay, followed later on by Phrygian elements. The portrayal of 'sobbing' is typically Yiddish and the minor-mode tendency is also characteristic of Yiddish wedding music.

Of the blending of folkloric elements with the motifs of psalmody in Hasidic chant, Peter Gradenwitz, the foremost authority on Jewish music, writes that it is the 'augmented second, regarded as a typical Jewish interval' ['als typisch-jüdisches Intervall angesehene übermäßige Sekunde'] which 'characterizes so many Hasidic songs' ['so viele chassidische Lieder charakterisiert'] (Gradenwitz, 1961, p. 189). One has only to look at the first four bars of the oboe part to see that Mahler immediately uses two unmistakable features of the Hasidic musical style: the augmented second (B flat–C sharp) and the 'shout for joy' in the ascending leap of a sixth. To describe this merely as an 'oboe melody' represents an abdication of the musicologist's responsibility to proceed historically and comparatively in the examination of musical structure, and to identify style with methodological rigour.

Evidence of Mahler's ever-present traumatic preoccupation with death can be found in the plaintive, mournful interjections. It was certainly not, as Floros claims, merely the use of the *marcia funebre* in 'high art' music which influenced him in this regard. The abrupt change from the exuberant joy of the dance to the seriousness of lamentation is typical of the music of the Hasidim. Convincing

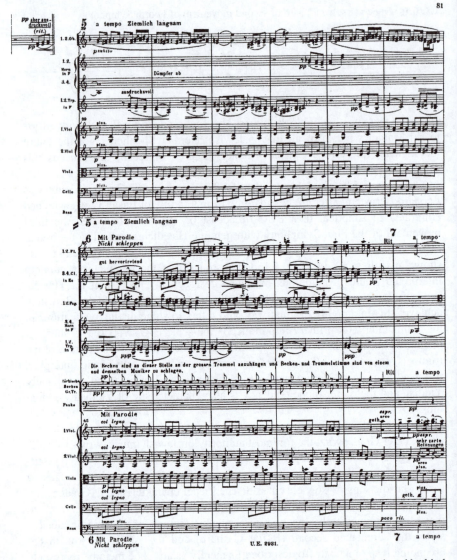

Plate 6.1   Bars 38–50 of the third movement of the First Symphony. Reproduced by kind permission of Universal Edition. © Copyright 1967 by Universal Edition A.G., Wien

examples of this can be found in the extensive documentation of Ruth Rubin (1963).[8] Here one can find not only deeply moving songs of lamentation about the horror of the pogrom, but also ecstatic dance songs from the very same period.

Mahler was familiar with Hasidic music. Within the Habsburg Monarchy at that time, Galicia belonged to a common cultural environment, and Mahler later recalled how as a child he had sung a Czech dancing melody portraying a traveller who wanders through Hungary and dances ecstatically in a tavern.[9] Travelling musicians came to the West and performed Hasidic-Yiddish music at the riotous Purim Festival (in memory of Esther who saved the Jewish people from annihilation), and at weddings and dances. They came to Bohemia mostly from the region of Tarnopol. Their music was not as alien as one might, for ethno-geographical reasons, suppose it to have been. For both textually and musically it absorbed much from the non-Jewish world – preserving specific melodic ideas (the gesture of falling phrases, the jubilant 'shout for joy'), harmonic elements (major/minor ambivalence, minor-mode cadential figures) as well as rhythm:

> Fed by the synagogal modes, the Ukranian and Slavic folk songs of the countryside, Cossakkian dances and military marches, the melodies, created and recreated by the *rebeyim*, their Chassidic [Hasidic] musicians, and their followers, developed a unique style which varied in character and spirit at the various 'courts' … These melodies also served to bind people in gay festivities at the *rebe's table*[10] or among their Chassidim [Hasidim], and to lead the feet in ecstatic dances.
>
> (Rubin, 1963, p. 245)

This integrating quality should be particularly emphasized in the case of march music. The Hasidim were not limited by these melodies in the same way that the military were by 'marching': together with forceful rhythms came joyous, ecstatic dancing. In this respect one could imagine the incursion of 'march music' in bar 45 onwards in the third movement of Mahler's First Symphony in terms of energetic dance movements.

In the German Middle Ages the Hasidim[11] were Jews of deliberate simplicity with a down-to-earth love for honouring the 'Almighty'. After the great

---

[8] Of the many recordings released by Rubin, *Jewish Life in 'The Old Country'* (Folkways Records FS 3801, New York 1958), which has already become of historical value, is particularly important. Texts are given in English, Yiddish and Hebrew. For the most part these are documentary sound recordings produced by East European Jews (VK).

[9] The story is cited from Bauer-Lechner, MS, in La Grange, 1974, p. 15, & 1979, p. 31. For further details of the identity of the song in question and its possible relation to Mahler's reputed first childhood composition – a polka with funeral march – see Rychetský, 1987 & 1989.

[10] The *rebe's table* is the rabbi's community table, at which the poor Jews were fed and his words of wisdom could be heard.

[11] The Hebrew word *hasid* means 'pious' (VK).

plague had struck Western Europe in 1347, Jews were identified as the evil instigators of poverty and hardship, and the papal church stirred up hatred against them. In hordes they escaped from these massacres to those Slav regions that became the centre of new Hasidism in the eighteenth and nineteenth centuries. A new feature of its outlook on life was the rejection of asceticism and a turn towards the more pleasurable side of existence. The founder of this way of life was Rabbi Israel ben Eliezer, named *Baal Schem Tow* [Master of the Good Name], or *Besht* in popular Yiddish (c. 1700–1760). He also became a musical legend: 'Legend has it that the Besht could hear words in the notes of a tune and was able to follow the very thoughts of the singer' (Rubin, 1963, p. 231). According to the tradition that he established, the men would gather at the onset of the Sabbath (Friday evening when the first star began to appear in the sky) in order to sing and dance. At the musical core of this joyous form of divine worship were mystical liturgical melodies of the masters, the *maggid*. The men joined forces in festive dance music which could be subject to abrupt alteration. They were not afraid of absorbing secular influences. Even the *rebe* [rabbi] himself took part enthusiastically in the dancing ('der rebele aleyn – geyt doch tantsn'), and the musical material of the surrounding environment assumed a touch of irony and parody: 'Primitive and secular tunes, rhythmic marches of passing military bands, songs of the non-Jewish countryside were re-fashioned into sacred Chassidic melodies and songs' (Rubin, 1963, p. 233). The resulting musical style, held together by these persistent features, was enhanced by exuberant 'shouts for joy' in wider melodic intervals of rising sixths or sevenths, often accompanied by accents and glissandi. Interjections such as 'aj-aj-aj', 'oj-doj-doj', and 'tam-diri-diri' and so on, were typical. It is well known that the word 'God' was not uttered, but he was familiar to the community as the 'Creator of the Universe'; he was greeted each morning and, as if in one of the songs, was asked the question: 'Reboynoy-shel-oylom, vos hostu fun mir gevelt?' ('Lord of the Universe, what do you want from me?').

This brief examination of the Hasidim's way of life is essential to understanding the 'Yiddishness' of Mahler's music. Even Mahler's anti-Semitic enemies have detected this trait in his music:

> What I find so utterly repellent about Mahler's music is the pronounced Jewishness of its underlying character ... it is abhorrent to me because it speaks Yiddish [*jüdelt*]. In other words it speaks the language of German music but with an accent, with the intonation and above all with the gestures of the Easterner, the all-too-Eastern Jew.
>
> (Louis, 1909, p. 182)[12]

---

[12] 'Das, was so gräßlich abstoßend an der Mahlerschen Musik auf mich wirkt, das ist ihr ausgesprochen jüdischer Grundcharakter ... sie ist mir widerlich, weil sie jüdelt.

The Nazis stirred Mahler's 'blood' into the mix of this sound world – and more besides from their anti-Semitic tirades.

The most conspicuous feature is the 'shout for joy'. This, too, has been interpreted superficially. The structure of the third movement of the First Symphony comprises an apparently bizarre sequence of scenes, for which Mahler used the metaphor of the pictorial world of Jacques Callot (1592–1635). He took this metaphor from E.T.A. Hoffmann's well-known homage to Callot. This led Neville Cardus in his Mahler study of 1965 to a grotesque misunderstanding. He presented the 'shout for joy' as Mahler's portrayal of the animal world, as a musical illustration of Callot's pictures: 'The animals are unmistakably smirking and quirking with glee in this phrase:

Ex. 6.2 E flat clarinet, bars 45–49 of third movement of First Symphony

… Our appreciation of Mahler's bitter-sweet brand of humour is quickened if we make some imaginative allusiveness to the Callot engraving' (Cardus, 1965, pp. 46 & 47). The grotesquerie is heightened because Cardus thinks that Moritz von Schwind's famous picture *Des Jägers Leichenbegängnis* is Callot's work. (Mahler had known Schwind's picture with the 'Bohemian musicians' since childhood.) Viewed psychologically, this is a revealing case of the intentionality of perception. Since the time of Ernst Mach, the forerunner of Gestalt theory, it has been known as the following principle: 'similarity = identity'. (Cardus unwittingly cites the Hasidic shout for joy in the violins' glissando through the interval of a seventh in bars 58–59 of this movement (ibid., p. 47).)

If one does not know anything – or does not wish to know anything – of Hasidic music, one is groping in the dark for interpretations. One way out of the uncertainty is merely to describe the instrumentation. Paul Stefan deals with this in a single sentence (cf. Plate 6.1): 'The oboes tootle a vulgar street musician's tune against the quiet counterpoint of the trumpets; two E flat clarinets, bassoons and flutes play doleful material "with parody", accompanied by an oompah in the percussion' ['Zu einem ruhigen Kontrapunkt der Trompeten dudeln die Oboen eine gemeine Musikantenweise, zwei Es-Klarinetten, Fagotte und Flöten blasen "mit Parodie" klägliches Zeug, begleitet von einem M-ta M-ta des Schlagwerks'] (Stefan, 1912, p. 111). In the centenary year Hans Christoph Worbs (1960, p. 54) also identified the 'melody in the oboes' [*Weise in Oboen*] and went on to describe 'A deliberately vulgar yowling (Louis says speaking Yiddish [*Jüdeln*]).

Das heißt: sie spricht musikalisches Deutsch, aber mit einem Akzent, mit dem Tonfall und vor allem mit der Geste des östlichen, des allzu östlichen Juden.'

Ghostly scraps of melody evoke the ingenious image of a world imbued with "the most unsavoury vulgarity". Mahler was not afraid of developing the trivial and vulgar ideas either' ['Ein bewußt ordinäres Johlen, Louis sagte: Jüdeln, gespenstiche Melodiefetzen rufen ein geniales Spiegelbild von "schalster Gemeinheit" erfüllten Welt hervor. Auch von der Gestaltung des Trivialen und Gemeinen schreckte Mahler nicht zurück']:

Ex. 6.3 E flat clarinet and 1st violins, bars 56–60 of third movement of First Symphony

Not long after this, Max Brod unambiguously defined the movement as drawing on fundamental Eastern-Jewish Hasidic folk music sources: it delights in giving 'striking depictions of joyous as well as deeply painful experiences in the march tempo (naturally in all shades of degree and character)' ['freudige wie tiefschmerzliche Erlebnisse im Marschtempo (natürlich in ganz abgestuften Graden und Charakteren)'] (Brod, 1961, p. 20). Likewise in his portrait of Mahler from 1961, Gradenwitz speaks of a 'melancholic transformation' [*wehmütige Veränderung*] of the march rhythms and melodies so that they are 'frequently suggestive of Jewish songs of the Eastern Slavs, and are reminiscent of Hasidic chants' ['oft an jüdische Lieder des slawischen Ostens anklingen und an chassidische Gesänge erinnern'] (Gradenwitz, 1961, p. 126). If one searches through the subsequent literature in Germany, one comes to the conclusion that neither Brod nor Gradenwitz can have been right: it is as if they, Jews and musicians, understood nothing of the Hasidic style.

Mahler is cleansed of all that is Jewish at the expense of an alarming contravention of scholarly principles. Without historical verification Sponheuer calls the march-like section – whose style Mahler characterized by the instruction 'Mit Parodie' – simply 'circus music' [*Zirkusmusik*]. (Circuses with bands were established only towards the end of the nineteenth century in large cities such as London or Munich, and certainly not in Iglau.) Dieter Krebs argues from the point of view of 'Mahler's assimilation' [*Assimilation Mahlers*], and is unwilling to acknowledge the Hasidic element because he holds Floros's opinion to be authoritative (Krebs, 1997, vol. 2, pp. 35 & 63). Floros rules out Brod's stylistic determinations from the outset (Floros, 1987b, p. 136), and consequently finds a way out in simple description:

> In the first part of the funeral march the dark, eerie canon (bars 1–38) and the 'jovial tune' marked 'Mit Parodie' (bars 45–49) form an extremely strong contrast. Mahler bridges this with the section in which the oboes play a

rocking melody running in thirds and sixths, and the trumpets have an expressive melody against this (bars 39–44).[13]

(Floros, 1985, p. 38, editor's translation; see also Floros, 1994, p. 41)

He concludes with a quotation from Adorno, who also refers to the 'oboe melody' without defining its style (Adorno, 1960, p. 150, & 1992a, p. 113). From bar 138, where the music finds its way back from E flat minor to D minor, Floros hears a 'Czardas-like' melody (Floros, 1985, p. 39). The Magyar or Hungarian (with contrived references to Liszt's *Hungaria*[14]) is more acceptable than the Yiddish. Ad hoc guesswork replaces ethno-cultural and historical comparative study.

It is symptomatic of the writings on the First Symphony that they lack an overview of the third movement's structure. One never encounters a tabular description of it. There are also confusions in attempts to explain its structure. The minor-mode melody 'Bruder Martin' is simply identified with the major-mode melody 'Frère Jacques' (Kennedy, 1974, p. 92, & 1990, p. 118), although Monika Tibbe has made a distinction between the two versions on the basis of the sources (Tibbe, 1971, p. 75). The 'Bruder Martin' section (A in the scheme presented in Fig. 6.1) should be explained in terms of its overall structure and subsequent transformation. The melancholy of D minor changes to the ambivalence of the B section, with its somewhat ironized Hasidic musical material, but the A section returns with 'Bruder Martin' in bar 113. This is by no means simply a 'reprise', as it is often described. The key at this point tells us otherwise: the entire tonal setting suddenly sinks into the sombre region of E flat minor. Like other composers of the romantic period, Mahler was familiar with the key symbolism proposed by Christian Schubart in 1806. His characterization of E flat minor reads as follows:

> Anxious feelings of the most profound spiritual distress; brooding despair; blackest melancholy; the darkest spiritual state. That anguish, that fear of the trembling heart emanates from the dread E flat minor. If ghosts could speak they would do so in something like this key.
>
> (Schubart, [1806] 1969, p. 378)[15]

The third movement as a whole comprises the following sequence of situations and spiritual states shaped by life experiences:

A section ('Bruder Martin') = the melancholy of the dull, miserable funeral band in the Hasidic minor-mode colouration.

B section = the stumbling entry of the Hasidic-Yiddish music idiom where the

---

[13] Bars 39–44 correspond to b¹ in the scheme presented in Fig. 6.1.

[14] See Floros, 1987b, pp. 138–40, 240, 248, 271–72, 314, 399 & 411.

[15] 'Empfindungen der Bangigkeit des aller tiefsten Seelendrangs; der hinbrütenden Verzweiflung; der schwarzesten Schwermuth; der düstersten Seelenverfassung. Jede Angst, jedes Zagen des schaudernden Herzens, athmet aus dem gräßlichen Es moll. Wenn Gespenster sprechen könnten, so sprächen sie ungefähr aus diesem Tone.'

march-like second element (b^2 in Fig. 6.1) is parodied in the voicing style of the A section.

The 'bright spot' of section C follows, the quotation from the fourth of the *Lieder eines fahrenden Gesellen* – 'Die zwei Augen von meinem Schatz' – for which Mahler himself wrote the text: a recollection of his stay in the Czech villages of Moravany and Ronov where 'a blue-eyed girl' unforgettably smiled at him.

Then comes the plunge of the A section into the E-flat minor tonality, expressing pain and anguish. Even the passages of reminiscence from the B section will sound darker in this 'dread E flat minor'. Only in bar 138 do the reminiscences of the B and A sections become calm and fade away into the conciliatory D minor.

If the formal scheme in La Grange (1973, p. 756) is broken down further, the structural outline shown in Fig. 6.1 emerges. The description 'march melody with parody' used here follows the convention but should be understood in the sense of integration referred to above. The funeral music that Mahler encountered is mixed into his distinct layout of the material. The interpretation 'Hasidic dirge' is based on Mahler's painful experience – when only just emerging from his own

A bars 1–38 $a + a^1$	'Bruder Martin' = essentially a dirge in Hasidic minor-mode colouration
B bars 39–44, 45–82 $b^1 \qquad b^2 + d^1 + a''$	Hasidic dance melody (= b^1) and Hasidic 'march melody with parody' (= b^2); d^1 = a new theme in the polyphony
C bars 83–112 $c + a''$	'Die zwei Augen von meinem Schatz' (*Lieder eines fahrenden Gesellen*), 'like a folk tune'
A' bars 113–37 $a'' + a'''$	Plunge of the A section into the dark region of E flat minor; intensified, heart-rending dirge
B' bars 138–68 $b''' + d^2 + a''$	Reminiscences, resigning, conciliatory fading away; $d^2 = a$ new theme in the polyphony

Fig. 6.1 Structural outline of the third movement of the First Symphony

childhood years – of looking after his beloved brother Ernst by telling him stories on his deathbed. Ernst died before his very eyes at the age of 13. In 1893 Mahler spoke to Natalie Bauer-Lechner about his First and Second Symphonies: 'My two symphonies draw exhaustively on the content of my entire life; I have recorded my experiences and sufferings in them' (Killian, 1984, p. 26, & Franklin, 1980, p. 30; editor's translation[16]). Mahler repeatedly emphasized the link with his childhood in Iglau and the tradition of funeral bands striking up cheerful dance and march music while returning from the cemetery after a burial. This is clearly the basis for characterizing the B section 'with parody'. Furthermore, Mahler reportedly said:

> One had to imagine the 'Bruder Martin' funeral march carelessly played through by an extremely bad music band of the type which used to follow funeral processions. Amidst all this, the whole crudeness, joviality and banality of the world, and at the same time the Hero's dreadfully painful lament, can be heard in the strains of any one of these motley 'Bohemian street-bands'.
>
> (Ibid., 1984, p. 174)

One comes to the inescapable conclusion that the Czech-Bohemian element in this movement of the First Symphony blends musically with the Hasidic-Yiddish. The one cannot be separated from the other.

At first glance, one would scarcely look for anything Hasidic-Yiddish in the Eighth Symphony, where the mystery of the 'Creator of the Universe' reverberates so impressively through the ancient Christian sequence *Veni Creator Spiritus*. Indeed the connection with Judaism is only superficially obvious: Mahler asked his Jewish friend Fritz Löhr/Löwi for advice because he wanted to give the correct accents to the Latin text. There is, however, a further piece of evidence unknown to the German literature. An article by Ludwig Landau (b. 1888), the choirmaster of the Jewish community in Frankfurt an der Oder, appeared in *Der Morgen: Monatschrift der deutschen Juden* – a journal whose publication was still permitted by the Nazis – with the title 'The Jewish Element in Gustav Mahler. On the 25th anniversary of his death – 18 May 1936'.[17] Landau found that 'heightened religious feeling' [*religiöse Gefühlsintenstität*] indicative of 'Hasidic intensity' [*chassidische Steigerung*] to be typical of the Eighth Symphony. He also considered the 'declamation of many melodic shapes' [*Deklamation mancher melodischer Wendungen*] in particular to be 'fervently Hasidic' [*chassidisch-inbrünstig*]. Symbolically, the word *ewig*, which Mahler saw as especially distinctive in Part II of Goethe's *Faust*, is repeated seven times in the 'Abschied' of *Das Lied von der Erde*, 'like a Hasidim bidding farewell to

---

16 Extracts from Bauer-Lechner's text published anonymously in 1913 in *Der Merker*, 3 (5), 184–88, contain the additional phrase 'with my own blood' ['mit meinem Herzblut'] in the second part of this sentence (see Franklin, 1980, p. 231).

17 'Das jüdische Element bei Gustav Mahler. Zum 25. Todestage – 18. Mai 1936', *Der Morgen*, 12 (1936), 67–73 (VK).

the earth with the long-echoing word of the Jewish profession of faith, "echad"' ['als nehme ein Chassid mit dem langaushallenden Worte des jüdischen Glaubensbekenntnisses "echad" Abschied von der Erde']. In the Eighth, Landau considered that 'words like "creator", "gratia" ("grace"), "caritas" ("compassionate love"), "infude amorem cordibus" ("pour love into our hearts")' are sung with the 'ecstatic fervour' [*ekstatische Inbrunst*] of Hasidicism (Landau, 1936, p. 69). A longing for compassion and brotherly love thus reverberates in this text of 1936, even across the abyss of the Nazis' lurking 'final solution' which would also snatch away the musically expert Cantor Landau himself. As regards the current tendency to characterize Mahler as a German, Landau wrote at considerable risk under the Nazi regime: 'he never attempted to "overcome" his Jewishness by "seeking" Germanness. There was nothing inwardly Jewish for him to overcome' ['Niemals hat er sein Judentum dadurch zu "überwinden" versucht, daß er Deutschtum "gesucht" hätte. Es gab für ihn innerlich nichts Jüdisches zu überwinden'] (ibid., p. 71).

Further complications arise with reference to the Jewish factor when examining the Eighth Symphony. In his extensive book of 1921 on Mahler's symphonies, Paul Bekker discussed the fact that the work was originally planned in four movements, consistent with a cyclic sonata-form scheme. According to Bekker, who clearly did not have the original concept immediately to hand, it was supposed to contain the following movements: I Hymn 'Veni Creator'; II Scherzo; III Adagio 'Caritas'; IV Hymn: 'The birth of Eros' [*die Geburt des Eros*] (Bekker, [1921] 1969, p. 273). Interpretative confusion has arisen from this, for 'The birth of Eros' is a mythological image which seems implausible in the ideal world of the Eighth. Only in the year of the Nazis' seizure of power did Alma Mahler-Werfel place the original copy of the 'initial idea' of the Eighth at the disposal of the Jewish Mahler biographer Alfred Rosenzweig. He published the autograph sketch together with its dedication to Alma in *Der Wiener Tag* on 4 June 1933. La Grange (1984, pp. 1079–80) and Donald Mitchell (1985, pp. 529–30, 598 & 635–37) have already drawn attention to this publication – the latter in an English translation – but the ideologically prescribed German Mahler literature of recent times has simply ignored it.[18] This literature has become absorbed in speculation about the imprecise concept in Bekker's book. Its invented claim that Mahler had no interest in visual arts is also of some consequence for the present discussion. Albrecht Dürer's mysterious picture *Melancolia* with its cosmic symbolism hung in Mahler's office next to the picture of *St Anthony of Padua Preaching to the Fish*, and he viewed Giorgione's *Monk Playing the Keyboard*[19] with fascination: 'I could continually compose this

---

[18] It should be noted that the sketch is given due attention in a recent extensive study of the Symphony (Wildhagen, 2000).

[19] More familiarly known as *Concert*, the picture was subsequently attributed to Titian.

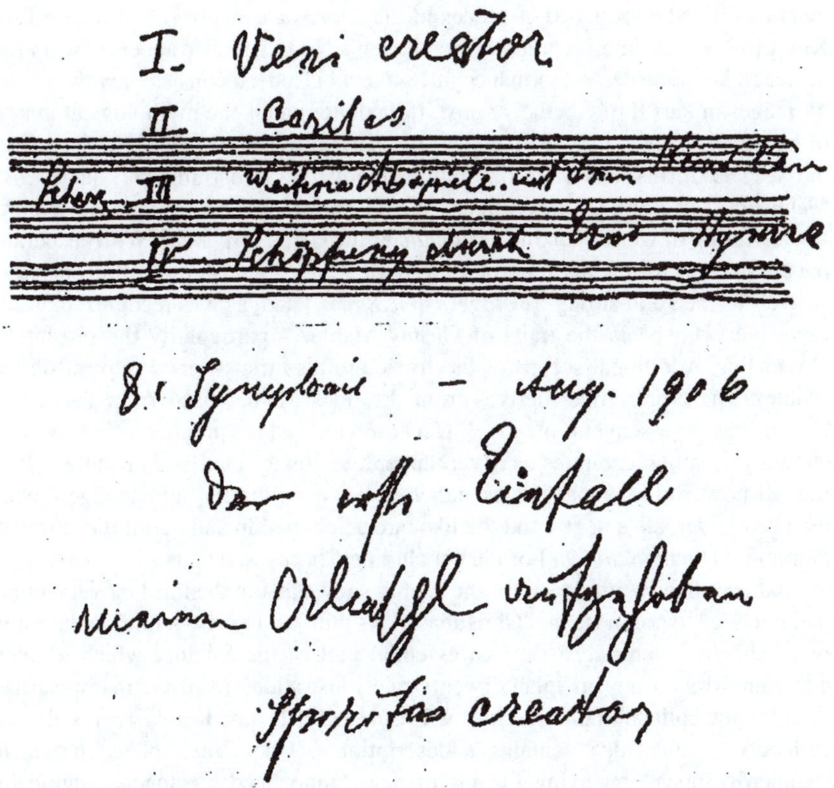

Plate 6.2   Mahler's original conception of the Eighth Symphony with a dedication to his wife. Reprinted from Rosenzweig, 1933, p. 28

picture', he said to his friend J.B. Foerster (1922, 9 April, also cited in Blaukopf & Blaukopf, 1991, p. 103). The thesis that Mahler had no interest in the visual arts has furthermore hindered the evaluation of the original concept published by Rosenzweig (illustrated above in Plate 6.2). Here Mahler clearly writes 'Creation through Eros' rather than 'Birth of Eros'. This explains why the second part of the final version of the Eighth takes Part II of Goethe's *Faust* as its mythological model. The connection with the visual arts now becomes clear, particularly the art of the Viennese circle of Secessionists.[20]

On 15 April 1902 Mahler took part in the unveiling of the Beethoven frieze in the Secession building. For this occasion he conducted his own wind arrangement of the passage from the final chorus of Beethoven's Ninth Symphony with the words 'Brothers! Above the starry canopy/A loving Father

---

[20] See the detailed discussion of Mahler and Klimt's frieze after Part II of *Faust* in Karbusicky, 1998 (VK).

must dwell'. The sequence of scenes in the frieze as conceived and realized by Klimt follows the interpretation of Beethoven's Ninth which Wagner drew up for his legendary Dresden performance in 1846, and is indeed consistent with the use of images in Part II of Goethe's *Faust*. If the latter paints the mythological image of heavenly forms thus: 'Women pass by there, hovering on high', so for Klimt the female forms hovering on high symbolize a 'yearning for happiness' [*Sehnsucht nach dem Glück*]. A line of them is interrupted by figures representing 'the suffering of weak mankind' [*leidende schwache Menschheit*]. With desperate outstretched arms, the highly erotic image of a naked pair implores the one who is 'well formed and strong' [*wohlgerüstete Starke*] and, as was recognized at the time, one who bears the traits of Gustav Mahler – particularly the resolutely closed lips. Additional scenes of the frieze are also transformed into music by Mahler. The erotic effect derives from the lines Mahler used from Part II of *Faust*: the 'messengers of love' [*Liebesboten*] who 'proclaim that which, eternally creating, encircles us' ['verkünden, was ewig schaffend uns umwallt'], the 'all-powerful love that shapes and cherishes everything' ['allmächtige Liebe, die alles bildet, alles hegt'] and the like, are celebrated in song until the 'Eternal Feminine' [*Ewig-Weibliche*] of the concluding Chorus Mysticus.

Mahler's handwritten plan for the Eighth shows that in the third movement he had intended to compose the 'Christmas plays with the (Christ-)child' in the form of a scherzo. Such plays were an essential part of the folklore which Mahler experienced as a boy in Iglau. Twenty-one illustrations from Germany can be found in the collection of Hruschka & Toischer (1891), and Karel Erben's classic collection (1864) also contains a description of the Czech plays in which shepherds appear, receiving the joyful news announced by angels singing in heaven. These plays were the preserve of boys (even the angel in the documented illustration from c. 1900 shown in Plate 6.3 is a boy with curly hair). The motif of music-making on the way to Bethlehem is staged here in theatrical style. Erben describes it thus:

> In the evenings, from Christmas Eve until New Year, the boys go from house to house with the crib, that is to say an illustration of the birth of Christ in the stable in which the little baby Jesus can be seen lying in the manger, and next to him in the foreground Joseph with Mary, and ox and ass in the background. The stable and the figures are made out of either paper or wood and fixed to a small board. There are usually four boys, one dressed as the angel and the others as shepherds, and on entering the house they start singing, right in the doorway.
>
> (Erben, 1864, pp. 43–44)[21]

---

[21] 'Vom Heiligen Abend bis zum Neuen Jahr gehen die Knaben abends von Haus zu Haus mit der Krippe, nämlich mit einer Abbildung der Geburt Christi im Stall, wo das geborene Jesulein in der Krippe liegend zu sehen ist, und bei ihm im Vordergrund Josef mit Maria, im Hintergrund dann Ochs und Esel. Der Stall und die Figuren sind entweder aus Papier oder aus Holz angefertigt und auf einem Brettchen befestigt. Es sind

Plate 6.3   Angel and shepherds in the Christmas plays with the (Christ-)child (drawing taken from Mádl, 1906, p. 37)

They enact the scene in which the shepherds 'play on shawms'; one shepherd calls out 'Gloria in excelsis Deo' in recitative, while the boy as the angel asks in song for the shepherds to make their way to Bethlehem, and so on. The whole thing is a folkloric relic of medieval mystery plays which would have been sung by mendicant schoolboys, with the scene of the angel ('Nunc angelorum Gloria …') and the shepherds ('Pastoribus magnalia nuncciantur gaudia …'; 'Pastores palam dicite in Betleem, quem genuit Maria …'). If Mahler intended to adapt this genre in the scherzo movement it would have been consistent with the medieval hymn *Veni Creator Spiritus*, and the mysticism of Part II of *Faust* – the 'Creation

gewöhnlich vier Knaben, einer als Engel, die anderen als Hirten bekleidet, und beim Betreten des Hauses beginnen sie schon in der Tür zu singen.'

through Eros' – would also have complemented this well. The dramaturgy of the four-movement sonata form had its own inner logic. In Mahler's 'initial idea' of August 1906 everything accords with the medieval world of miracle plays.

This recollection of the 'Christmas plays with the (Christ-)child' left audible traces in the final, bipartite, version of the work. However, the boys' choir has a greater significance than merely filling out the mass of sound. In the original concept these 'plays' were supposed to form an intermediary scherzo movement, but they certainly fitted well with *Veni Creator* and with the scenes from Part II of *Faust*: the brightly shining heavens, the women's choirs of angels, and the boys' voices. Motifs of 'shawm-playing shepherds' appear in different variations in the final version of the Symphony. On several occasions they alter the tonality, and in one exposed passage (Ex. 6.4) the boys' choir sings its 'Gloria' imitating the style of shawms in a 'magical D flat major' [*magisches Des*], as Bekker called this key (Bekker, [1921] 1969, pp. 280 & 288):

Ex. 6.4   Boys' choir, bars 508–11 of first movement of Eighth Symphony

Glo - ri a, glo - ri - a Pa - tri Do - mi - no.

The sketch of the 'initial idea' preserved by Alma is therefore of fundamental importance in understanding the creative process at work in the genesis of the Eighth Symphony.

'Pay attention to the initial idea, it comes from God' ['Achtet auf den ersten Einfall, der kommt von Gott'], so J.B. Foerster, Mahler's friend from Hamburg and Vienna, used to say to his composition students (cited in Tarabová, 1937, p. 6). A brief portrait of Foerster should be given at this point. Josef Bohuslav Foerster, born in 1859, outlived Mahler by some forty years: he died in 1951. Mahler had engaged his wife, Bertha Foerster-Lauterer, as an outstanding singer in Hamburg, and Foerster followed her to the Hanseatic city. His opera *Deborah* (1890–92) had already been premièred in Prague, and Foerster took the score with him. Mahler examined the work thoroughly and with great interest: it appealed to his Jewish nature. Foerster had adapted Salomon Mosenthal's drama *Deborah* with considerable ethical commitment. Deborah had guided a whole host of Jews in their flight from a pogrom, and Foerster became deeply involved in her fate. The lament he composed for the old Jewish woman at the cemetery wall was intensely moving: its harmonic context is A flat major, the sepulchral key according to Schubart. She recalls her devout and peaceful life in her Eastern homeland: 'It is a holy day, the Feast of the Passover … What has happened to those times when we would stand in white vestments over the bread of fasting!' ['Es ist Feiertag, das Passah-Fest … Wo sind jene Zeiten, als wir im weißen Gewand über dem Fastenbrot standen!'] At this point the tonal fabric moves from

Schubart's 'dread E flat minor' to a glowing G flat major, the same key chosen by Mahler for the powerful entry of the resurrection chorus in his Second Symphony (fifth movement, Fig. 31, bar 472). The lament returns to the gloom of E flat minor as Deborah expresses her despair in an overwhelming solo song without orchestral accompaniment: 'And if You, O God, do not come to help us soon, at least destroy our life in one blow!' ['Und wenn du schon, Gott, nicht zu Hilfe kommst, so vernichte wenigstens unsere Leben alle auf einmal!'].[22] This terrifying vision was articulated half a century before Auschwitz.

Mahler and the Foersters enjoyed a close friendship. He visited the couple frequently, and a large number of the visiting cards he used on these occasions survives in Foerster's estate. Mahler of course took up residence at the centre of the Hamburg Jewish quarter around the Grindelallee, in the now quite built-up Fröbelstraße. From there he would go along part of Grindelallee past the main synagogue (which no longer exists, having been destroyed by the Nazis) to the nearby house at no. 3 Bornstraße where the Foersters lived. As *Kapellmeister* at the Hamburg Opera House Mahler gave the first performance of Foerster's Third Symphony on 13 April 1896. When he engaged Frau Foerster-Lauterer at the Vienna *Hofoper*, Foerster followed her there as well. At the end of 1918 the Foersters returned again to Prague, completely impoverished owing to the collapse of the currency. In 1922 Foerster published his recollections, 'Gustav Mahler in Hamburg', in the Jewish-run *Prager Presse*. During the time of the occupation of Prague by the Nazis, 1939–45, his *Deborah* was banned and he was denounced as a dangerous 'friend of Jews'.

In brief conclusion, this historical information has important connections with Alfred Rosenzweig, who was born in Vienna on 21 August 1897. At his enrolment in 1918 at the University of Vienna 'after many years of military service' [*nach mehrjähriger Kriegsdienstleistung*],[23] his religion was registered as 'mosaisch'. In 1924 Guido Adler granted him his doctorate for the dissertation 'On the Historical Development of Richard Strauss's Music Dramas' ['Zur Entwicklungsgeschichte des Richard Strauss'schen Musikdramas']. Adler approved the award against the ill-natured, negative report of Robert Lach, who reproached Rosenzweig for a 'blind idolization of fashionable phenomena', because 'virtually everything that does not travel along the path of the "atonalists" already appears "archaic" [to him]' ['blinde Vergötterung von Modeerscheinungen ... [ihm ... erscheint] fast alles schon "archaistisch", was nicht in dem Geleise der "Atonalisten" sich bewegt'].[24]

---

[22] These citations and further discussion of Foerster's *Deborah* can be found in Karbusicky, 1996a, pp. 88–101 (VK).

[23] From Rosenzweig's curriculum vitae included in his doctoral *Rigorosenakt*, submitted to the philosophical faculty of the University of Vienna on 27 October 1923, and housed in the Archive of the University of Vienna.

[24] From Lach's dissertation report, dated 18 November 1923, in Rosenzweig's *Rigorosenakt*.

The publication of the plan of the Eighth Symphony in *Der Wiener Tag* on 4 June 1933 marked the beginning of Rosenzweig's work on a large-scale biography of Mahler. As a result of his flight from the Nazis, progress on this work encountered many obstacles. In a letter to Foerster from London dated 6 July 1948 he discussed his work in relation to his emigration. After the annexation of Austria he managed to find refuge in the wilds of East Moravia, from where the opera director and Janáček researcher Jaroslav Vogel saved him at the last moment before the Nazis gained a new hold, by facilitating his departure to London. In that letter of July 1948 to Foerster, he asked Mahler's surviving friend for answers to a total of eleven questions posed in his 'questionnaire no. 1'. He regretted that so much had been lost during the Nazi period: the 'estate of the Lipiner family, Siegler, Natalie Bauer-Lechner, Dr Berliner who died completely alone in Berlin at the beginning of the war[25] – everything has disappeared' ['Nachlaß der Familien Lipiner, Siegler, Natalie Bauer-Lechner, Dr. Berliners, der zu Beginn des Krieges völlig vereinsamt in Berlin gestorben ist – Alles verschollen']. Foerster complied with his requests in a letter whose receipt Rosenzweig gratefully acknowledged on 22 August 1948: 'In due course I hope to be able to show you the care and affection with which I will illuminate your wonderful friendship with Mahler, by sending the relevant part of my manuscript' ['Wie sehr und mit welcher Liebe ich Ihre wunderbare Freundschaft zu Mahler beleuchten werde, hoffe ich Ihnen seinerzeit durch Einsendung der betreffenden Teile meines Manuskripts beweisen zu können'].[26]

The manuscript has disappeared and fate did not grant Rosenzweig the opportunity to address a 'questionnaire no. 2' to Foerster.[27] According to the prolonged investigations of Donald Mitchell and the late Kurt Blaukopf, Alfred Rosenzweig died of heart failure in St Charles Hospital, Kensington, on 11 December 1948.

---

[25] Mahler's friend Dr Berliner belonged to Albert Einstein's circle and was driven to his death by the Nazis. In 1942 he committed suicide at the age of 80 (VK).

[26] These letters are contained in Foerster's currently inaccessible estate housed in the Museum of Czech Music.

[27] Rosenzweig's unfinished manuscript has in fact recently come to light and is currently housed in the library of the Guildhall School of Music and Drama in London as part of the Rosenzweig Collection. A translation and critical edition is currently being prepared for publication by the editor.

PART THREE

Analytical Approaches

Chapter Seven

Multi-Stage Exposition in Mahler's Symphonies

RICHARD KAPLAN

Introduction

The symphonies of Gustav Mahler present a number of special analytical challenges, not the least of which is that of discerning his large-scale formal strategies. He developed elaborate extra-musical programmes for several – perhaps most – of his symphonies, yet he invariably withdrew or renounced these programmes as misleading or gratuitous. He adopted conventions associated with classical forms, yet his treatment of these conventions displays such freedom and originality that analysts often find reference to these forms to be of questionable value; and, of course, the scale and proportions of his symphonic structures themselves raise questions concerning Mahler's use of musical time: for example, does he use an unusually large number of themes, are his themes unusually long, or does he repeat them an unusually large number of times?

The issue of programmes, first of all, turns out to be something of a red herring. In a study of Liszt's programme music (Kaplan, 1984) the present author argued that, while a poetic or dramatic association might serve as an impetus in the process of creation of the work, and while this association might be projected in some way by the *nature* of the musical materials, the ordering of these materials and the overall tonal structures must be (and are) coherent on a purely musical basis.[1] Even where the argument for an extra-musical programme is most compellingly adduced, as in Stephen Hefling's penetrating study of Mahler's

---

[1] It is provocative in this light that the tonal structure of the exposition of Mahler's Symphony No. 2, first movement (q.v.) – C minor to E major – is identical with that of two works of Liszt: *Tasso* and the first movement of the *Faust Symphony*. This tonal relation is found in a striking number of C minor pieces throughout the nineteenth century, from Beethoven (Op. 37) to Brahms (Opp. 60 and 68) to Grieg (Op. 45) to Rachmaninov (Op. 18), but invariably in the choice of E major as the key of a slow movement. Its use within a single movement is, I believe, peculiar to Liszt and Mahler.

Todtenfeier (Hefling, 1988), a convincing piece of 'programme music' is first of all a convincing piece of music. In this connection, the distinguished cultural historian Jacques Barzun has written as follows:

> It may be objected that a determined programmer will distort proper musical form so as to fit some part of his program. The rejoinder is that, if so, the attempt is self-defeating: the listener and critic would detect the flaw and declare the work a bad piece of music – incoherent or ill-balanced.
>
> (Barzun, 1990, p. 220)

Indeed, despite their inventiveness, some of the most frankly pictorial pieces of 'programme music' – for example, Elgar's *Falstaff* and the late symphonic poems of Dvořák – do seem to 'work' fully only when the listener is 'in on' the story. On the other hand, the most successful composers of 'programme music' who followed Liszt – Tchaikovsky, Strauss, and Mahler himself – strongly discouraged audience over-reliance on the programme, insisting rather that the public hear and understand their music purely *as music*. In any event, with respect to both Liszt and Mahler, the consistent use of certain formal procedures in works with disparate programmatic implications belies the primacy of programme as a generator of form.

The situation with regard to traditional formal paradigms is more problematic. On this issue, analysts have generally staked out one or the other of two contrasting ideological positions. Some, especially early authors, were content to work more or less entirely within these paradigms, ignoring any attendant procrustean implications (La Grange, 1973, and Murphy, 1975 & 1986); when this music was still unfamiliar, any demonstration of coherent formal strategy was met with general relief. More recent scholars, perhaps partially as a reaction to the unsatisfactory results of these conventional studies, have on the other hand tended to downplay the traditional paradigms, or to abandon them altogether in favour of models drawn from other spheres of intellectual or artistic endeavour (Micznik, 1994, Scherzinger, 1995).

But this becomes an issue of babies and bath water, for we disregard elements of conventional form-types only at the risk of overlooking several important aspects of Mahler's artistic persona. Not the least of these is his relation to the nineteenth-century symphonic tradition, and the power that this tradition continued to exert on his work. Another is the tension between his inclination to embrace this tradition and his status as a symphonic innovator. As his career developed, however, his posture in many ways reflected an increasing recognition that he was in fact heir to this symphonic tradition, and along with this showed an increasing allegiance to at least the outward aspects of traditional forms and genres. Consider, for example, his addition of an exposition repeat to the first movement of the First Symphony sometime after 1893. Although this movement certainly remains an idiosyncratic specimen of sonata form, it is arguably no more so than, say, the first movement of Berlioz's *Symphonie fantastique*.[2] Consider likewise the change of title of this work from the original *Tondichtung* to Symphony, and the change from a five-movement to a more traditional four-movement format. Consider too the 1888 *Todtenfeier*, which in its final form is shorn of its programmatic title and becomes the first movement of the Second Symphony. Finally, consider Mahler's later use of the title 'Symphony' for such generically unique works as the Eighth and *Das Lied von der Erde*, and his designation of no fewer than three symphonic movements as 'Rondo'.[3]

The position of the present author, as it will be developed in the course of this essay, is that both the traditionalist and the innovative aspects of Mahler's creative personality are expressed in his exploitation of the sonata paradigm. The sonata principle (as opposed to more prescriptive textbook models) informs many of Mahler's symphonic structures. I borrow the term from Edward T. Cone, but define it perhaps even more broadly. For Cone, whose frame of reference was the classical style, the sonata principle is embodied in the statement of material outside the tonic key, and the later restatement of that material in – or at least nearer – the tonic (Cone, 1968, pp. 76–77). But it can be argued that by the end of the nineteenth century the sonata principle had broadened to encompass certain other basic formal gestures as well: first, the distinct contrast between thematic entities;[4] second, a development section characterized by tonal instability and motivic fragmentation, and often incorporating the climax of the movement; and third, the 'double return' that constitutes the arrival of the recapitulation, as described in James Webster's *New Grove* account (Webster, 1980, p. 497). A few of Mahler's symphonic movements represent relatively traditional sonata forms (the first movement of the Fourth Symphony, for example); in two movements he goes so far as to indicate exposition repeats – the first movements of the First, as mentioned above, and of the Sixth. In less clear-cut cases, Mahler draws from that repertoire of gestures that characterize the late nineteenth-century sonata, integrating these with other, unique formal strategies. In such movements, the sonata paradigm is a necessary but not sufficient analytical tool; that is, certain movements display some fundamental

---

[2] The two movements in fact form an intriguing comparison: each begins with an extensive introduction that incorporates several tempo changes and that segues directly into the (repeated) exposition; each exposition is disproportionately brief in relation to the scale of the movement as a whole; the Berlioz exposition stays in the tonic until its last few measures, where the modulation to the dominant occurs, while the Mahler conversely moves almost immediately to the dominant, where it remains; and, finally, each movement features a long, episodic development that builds to the movement's climax, a transformed statement of the principal theme that marks the arrival of the recapitulation.

[3] These are the final movements of the Fifth and Seventh Symphonies, each titled Rondo-Finale, and the third movement of the Ninth, Rondo-Burleske.

[4] In Cone's own words, 'The tendency of the nineteenth century is increasingly to emphasize the forces of contrast over those of unification' (Cone, 1968, p. 78).

characteristics of the sonata principle, but cannot be wholly subsumed under any standardized sonata paradigm. We may wish to say that these movements refer to sonata functions, or, in James Buhler's term, 'critique' them (Buhler, 1996). In the author's own analysis of the First Symphony Finale (Kaplan, 1992), the sonata principle is treated as one of several organizational strands that interweave throughout the movement.

The purpose here, then, will be not so much to demonstrate that a particular movement does or does not conform to the sonata paradigm as to consider some of Mahler's responses to one particular challenge of sonata form: the exposition of his thematic materials. In the process, we will find the vantage point of sonata form useful for making certain types of observations regarding Mahler's compositional practice. This essay will examine portions of four of Mahler's symphonic movements – none of them a textbook example of sonata form (anyone's!) – from the perspective of a particular adaptation of sonata form: to wit, his practice of introducing his materials in a fragmentary fashion, followed in a new section by a more fully realized statement of those materials.

The basis of this procedure can indeed be recognized in many of Mahler's works, not just those organized according to the sonata principle. One of the clearest, yet most ingenious, instances of this 'incremental' presentation of a movement's musical materials is the opening of the third movement (Scherzo) of the Second Symphony (Ex. 7.1).

In the first thirteen bars of the movement, the methodical addition of ostinato motifs in lower woodwinds and percussion builds an accompanimental complex that ultimately consists of no fewer than four distinct elements or layers. Comparison of this opening to that of the song on which the movement is based, 'Des Antonius von Padua Fischpredigt',[5] shows two important revisions – one subtle, the other dramatic. The latter consists of the addition of two statements of the G–C timpani strokes at the opening;[6] the former involves a rhythmic sleight of hand in which the second layer (bassoon 1) enters a bar earlier than in the song, the result being that the full complex is reached in the sixth bar of the ostinato (that is, bar 11 of the Symphony movement) rather than the seventh. The entry of the melody in the violins in bar 13, then, is actually elided with the last measure of the cumulative eight-bar ostinato, giving the opening of the Symphony

    [5] Mitchell (1975, pp. 136–38 & 174–76) gives a detailed chronology of the development of the Symphony movement from the song. The Symphony movement pre-dates the orchestral version of the song, yet the latter remains essentially faithful to the original version for voice and piano.

    [6] This revision not only announces in the clearest manner possible the basis of the ostinato complex, and provides a startling shift of mood from that of the dreamy Andante second movement, but also becomes an important element in the movement's climax in bars 465–88. See Kaplan, 1996, pp. 218–23. It is clear that Mahler took a great deal of trouble with the composition of this 'drum prelude'. Its evolution is traced in Mitchell, 1975, pp. 283–84 & 427–28.

Ex. 7.1   Second Symphony, third movement, bars 1–14

movement a less symmetric, more unsettled (and unsettling) quality.[7]

This passage alone is sufficient to illustrate the subtlety with which Mahler introduces his materials in this movement, particularly when its opening is compared with that of the song. It does not become clear until bar 68, however, when the main vocal line from bar 9 of the song first appears, that the entire opening section of the symphonic movement to this point has in fact been a paraphrase of the song *without the tune*. Only here, at the second statement of the

---

[7] All references to bar numbers assume that the anacrusis of the bar is part of the theme or passage in question. Accordingly, if a passage is indicated as beginning at bar 13, that means the passage begins either on the downbeat of bar 13 or with any number of anacruses to bar 13.

violin 'melody', does the real theme of the Scherzo appear, demoting the violin
line to the status of a counter-melody, as in the opening of the song.

Symphony No. 1, fourth movement

The Finale of the First Symphony illustrates most transparently Mahler's practice
in sonata movements of stating his materials piecemeal in a brief opening section,
then shaping them into full thematic statements in a second, more extensive
section. The movement opens with a 54-bar passage that introduces the most
important motivic materials of the movement, but can hardly be called an
exposition: the motifs fail to coalesce into themes, and a dominant pedal subsists
throughout. The first system of Ex. 7.2 shows two central motifs in this opening,
separated at their initial statements by thirteen bars. At bar 55, the pedal resolves
with an emphatic timpani stroke, and the motifs are recast into periodic
structures; it is here that the real exposition begins (compare the second system
of Ex. 7.2). But if this opening passage is not the exposition, then neither is it an
introduction, as La Grange calls it (La Grange, 1973, p. 756): it is in tempo, and
is gesturally and affectively too much of a piece with what follows. Perhaps the
best way to characterize this opening is as an exposition *in nuce*: an embryonic
form of exposition, or, as referred to in the present author's analysis, a preamble
(Kaplan, 1992).

Ex. 7.2   First Symphony, fourth movement, opening theme

Symphony No. 3, first movement

We can recognize the same type of procedure, but now far more fully developed,
in the first movement of the Third Symphony. This is Mahler's largest purely
instrumental symphonic movement, yet it clearly displays many of the sonata
functions identified above. Moreover, sections and thematic areas or groups in
this movement are articulated with particular clarity by means of the kinds of
textural, dynamic, rhythmic and motivic dissolution so thoroughly documented
in Robert Hopkins's study of 'secondary parameters' and closure in Mahler's
music (Hopkins, 1990).

Table 7.1 shows the overall formal structure of this movement. Again the function of the opening measures is problematic: on the one hand, this passage is a sort of introductory pronouncement ('summer marches in', in the original programme), equivocal in its tonal implications and quickly dissolved; on the other hand, it is recapitulated (see bar 643), and it does take on thematic significance in various parts of the movement. The true function of this passage would again seem to be part-way between that of introduction and that of exposition; for practical purposes the chart places it within the exposition.

The opening passage notwithstanding, the most unorthodox feature of this analysis is the identification of two expositions.[8] The two thematic groups, which David Greene characterizes respectively as 'inert material resisting vital impulses' and 'march' (Greene, 1984, p. 144), are each in turn stated in two discrete sections: bars 27–163 and bars 164–368. In the first of these, the opening group – the famous trombone solo stated over an elaborate motivic infrastructure

Table 7.1   Formal structure of the Third Symphony, first movement

---

EXPOSITION I (bb. 1–163)

1–26	Opening announcement
27–131	Group I (minus 'theme') – d
132–63	Group II ('March') – (D–D♭)

EXPOSITION II (bb. 164–368)

164–224	Group I – d
225–350	Group II – d–F–D
351–61	Closing – D
362–68	Codetta/transition

DEVELOPMENT (bb. 369–642)

RECAPITULATION (bb. 643–875)

643–70	Opening announcement
671–736	Group I – d–(D)
737–845	Group II – F
846–56	Closing – F
857–75	Coda – F

---

[8]   La Grange also identifies a double exposition in this movement, but with the second exposition beginning only in bar 369, a reading that among other things places the closing in G flat, and ignores the important parallel between bars 351 and 846 (La Grange, 1973, p. 802).

– remarkably is represented by this infrastructure only (its components are shown in Ex. 7.3); the actual tune enters only in the second exposition.[9] The horn passage that represents the first true 'thematic' element in the first exposition (bar 58) is thus in essence the consequent to a not-yet-stated antecedent.

Ex. 7.3   Motivic infrastructure of the first group, Third Symphony, first movement

The second group – the 'march' – is introduced only briefly and fragmentarily in the initial exposition, and is vastly expanded in the second; correspondingly, in the first exposition this group fails to establish a second tonal area, oscillating between D major and D flat major, whereas in the second exposition it eventually establishes an extensive tonicization of F. Finally, it is in bars 273 and 315 of the second exposition that the opening horn announcement is first stated in harmonized form and thus given an unambiguous tonal interpretation. In these ways the second exposition provides the realization of multiple unfulfilled implications of the first.

Symphony No. 10, first movement

The parallel between these early works and the first movement (Adagio) of the

---

9   This passage is also discussed in Morgan, 1996.

Tenth Symphony is striking, given the many factors that separate these works in Mahler's career. However, since there is no clear consensus regarding sonata organization in the Tenth, this parallel has hitherto gone unrecognized. Kofi Agawu cites several analysts' attempts to describe the movement using such formal categories as 'theme and variations', 'sonata form', 'a subtle combination of sonata and rondo' and 'an overlay of sonata design on a five-part organization' (Agawu, 1986, p. 223); the last of these descriptions is from the present author's own analysis (Kaplan, 1981, p. 36). It is clear that no matter what traditional formal scheme one invokes for this movement, far too much that is of musical importance is left 'hanging over the edges'. On the basis of this perception, Agawu chooses to abandon traditional form-types altogether in favour of a model borrowed from literary theory. But I believe a close inspection of Agawu's analysis and my own shows more commonalities than differences, and suggests that what differences there are may be more a matter of semantics than of musical substance.

Table 7.2 gives the large outlines of Agawu's analysis of the form of this movement, together with that of the present author and Steven Bruns (Bruns, 1989, pp. 266–70).[10] It will be seen that Bruns follows Agawu closely in most respects, the major exceptions being the terminology for the section Agawu labels 'Elaboration' and Bruns labels 'Development and Fragmentation', and the location of the beginning of this section.[11]

Consideration of the present author's chart shows several important features: first, the recurrences of the monodic introduction clearly articulate a five-part arch that displays a near-perfect geometric symmetry in the lengths of its sections; second, the *sectionalization* coincides in part but not invariably with the expression of *formal function*, and in fact suggests a formal linkage between Sections I and II and between Sections IV and V; and third, sonata functions can be ascribed to some sections but not others. In the matter of sectionalization versus formal function, note that Sections I and II are expository, while Section III encompasses both development and recapitulation. This plan is strikingly reminiscent of that of the standard Classical sonata, wherein the principal sectional division follows the repeated exposition, and the development and recapitulation together form the second large section. These observations lead to the author's view that both aspects of formal articulation are important to the logic of the movement: that the first three sections can with little difficulty be associated with conventional sonata functions, but that Sections IV and V concern themselves with issues that are incompletely worked out in the sonata

---

[10] While I have taken the liberty of simplifying Agawu's and Bruns's charts for the sake of clarity, I believe I have fairly represented their essential content.

[11] It is unclear from Bruns's chart whether or not he includes the introduction in the 'Statement', but for present purposes this is of no great moment.

Table 7.2   Three structural outlines of the Tenth Symphony, first movement

bar no.	Kaplan	Agawu	Bruns
1	*Introduction*	Statement (X)	Introduction (X)
16	I (Expo. I) [24 bars]		Statement
	Theme I – F♯	A	A
32	Theme II – f♯	B	B
40	*Introduction*	X	X'
49	II (Expo. II) [56 bars]		
	Theme I – F♯	A	A
81	Theme II – f♯–b♭	B	Development & Fragmentation
105	*Introduction*	X	X
112	III [72 bars]		
	Development	Elaboration	
141	Recapitulation	Restatement	Restatement
	Theme I – F♯	A	A
153	Theme II – f♯–b♭	B	B
178	Theme I – F♯	A	A
184	*Introduction*	X	X
194	IV [52 bars]		
	Climax	Climax	Climax
213	Peroration	Closure	Closing
246	*Introduction*		
253	V [23 bars]		
	Peroration & Coda		

schema represented by Sections I–III.[12]

Agawu rejects the sonata designation on two principal grounds: the lack of a characteristic exploration of key relations, and an absence of thematic conflict. Regarding the second of these, the present author finds in the movement's two main themes a fundamental contrast in character despite the motivic interpenetrations noted in Agawu's analysis as well as the author's own; in any event, this type of conflict has never been regarded as a *sine qua non* in sonata

---

[12]   This latter premise forms the basis of much of the author's analysis in Kaplan, 1984.

form, as numerous 'monothematic' sonata movements illustrate. The matter of key relations is more problematic. The fact that the secondary tonal centre of B flat minor persists in the recapitulation is admittedly irregular, but hardly without precedent in Mahler's work: in the first movement of the Second Symphony, for example, the second tonal area of E major is likewise retained in the recapitulation, and in the first movement of the Third, the exposition closes in D while it is the recapitulation that ends in F. In the Tenth, the lack of tonal resolution in the recapitulation is one bit of 'unfinished business' that precipitates the climax of Section IV, but this hardly negates the sonata functions of Sections I–III.

In any event, the gulf between Agawu's 'statement–elaboration–restatement' and my 'exposition–development–recapitulation' is largely one of terminology. Examination of the first two sections shows Mahler's procedure to be very similar to that of the Third Symphony. In both works, for example, the two sections unfold in parallel but differ in scale, the second being in many ways more fully realized: in the Tenth, Exposition I (bars 16–39) presents two periods of the principal theme; Exposition II (bars 49–104) presents three, with phrase extensions of ever-increasing length and complexity.[13] Exposition I features only a fragmentary second theme and no modulation, merely a modal shift; Exposition II greatly expands this second group, and effects the modulation to the second tonal area of B flat minor. Finally, there are striking correspondences between the phrases beginning in bars 16 and 58, and those beginning in bars 24 and 69; and, in fact, the sketch materials indicate that in the orchestral draft (the final version of the music as Mahler left it) two passages occurring in the respective expositions have exchanged places relative to their original positions in the short score that represents the movement's penultimate form.[14]

Symphony No. 2, first movement

The first movement of the Second Symphony illustrates an expository plan more complex than that of any of the movements discussed so far. Here, first of all, as in the Scherzo (see above), the procedure of fragmentary introduction of materials, followed by their more fully realized presentation, occurs on multiple levels, beginning practically with the movement's opening gesture: as shown in Ex. 7.4, the cellos' and basses' octave scale and dotted-rhythm descent in bars 4–5, which at first seem to be a response to the two opening semiquaver outbursts of bars 2 and 4, in fact initiate a covert but large-scale basso ostinato whose

---

[13] Interestingly, in the expositions, the consequent of each period presents the theme in inversion; in the recapitulation, the original and inverted forms are stated simultaneously.

[14] These are, respectively, bars 18–23 & 51–57.

Ex. 7.4 Second Symphony, opening of first movement: bars 1–6 and 18–21 compared

repetition (a total of 13^1/$_2$ bars, beginning in bar 19) underlies the first theme and yet does not synchronize with it, the theme having begun a measure and a half earlier. Thus, what seemed in bar 6 to be an important thematic statement turns out to be rather the precursor – and eventually the accompaniment – of that statement. The restatement of the ostinato, marked in the example with brackets, thus aligns neither with the perceived beginning of bar 6 nor with the actual entry of the theme in bar 18 – for, as the brackets and arrows in Ex. 7.4 show, the actual ostinato begins with the upbeats to bar 5, with what at that moment sounds like a conclusive gesture rather than one of initiation; and its recurrence begins with the upbeats to bar 20, a bar and a half into the thematic statement that has already begun in bar 18 in the oboe and cor anglais. In a dual musical sleight of hand, Mahler has already initiated the ostinato by the time the listener realizes matters are under way, and then veils its repeat by 'locking in' the recurrence 'out of phase' a full six beats after the theme has started.

That the process of exposition in this movement spans more than one section is widely acknowledged. Hefling, for example, calls the section beginning at bar 64 a 'disruptive, modified repeat' (Hefling, 1988, p. 33). The end of the first exposition is clearly marked by the cadence at bars 59–62, together with the resumption of the opening G tremolo and the varied restatement of the opening theme in C minor at bar 64. But this exposition is highly irregular: while its second tonal area appears to be E major, this E major lasts scarcely nine measures (bars 48–56), and the section actually cadences in E flat minor. Moreover, as shown graphically in Ex. 7.5, the E major is incompletely realized. It subsists entirely over a dominant pedal, producing in effect an expanded cadential six-four. The resulting B major harmony in turn resolves enharmonically as VI of E flat minor. This is the first of many juxtapositions of E and E flat in this movement, culminating in the major-to-minor shift of mode within the C tonic triad seven measures from the end of the movement, a mode shift easily as dramatic – if not as theatrical – as the similar and now universally familiar gesture from the opening of Strauss's *Also sprach Zarathustra*, written some eight years later. Exposition II scarcely clarifies matters; it modulates to G minor (bar 80), the G in turn preparing a return to C in bar 117. This leaves the E major implication unrealized until its arrival in bar 127, which most analysts identify as part of the development.

This reading, however, presents several difficulties. To begin with, it is here that E first asserts itself as a stable tonal area, its structural importance confirmed by its recurrence in the recapitulation, as also mentioned above in the context of the Tenth Symphony. E not only remains the tonal centre for some 44 bars (127–70), but is actually present as a pedal point for the first 30 of these. Secondly, this section presents two important new thematic ideas: the passage at bar 135 for clarinets in parallel thirds and sixths, and the chant-like passage at bar 151 for cor anglais and bass clarinet, the latter repeated almost in its entirety later in the movement (bars 262–70). Finally, the character of this passage is notably

Ex. 7.5   Second Symphony, graph of first movement: bars 43–64

serene, especially in juxtaposition with the passage that immediately follows, beginning in bar 167, which is far more dynamic from both a thematic and a tonal standpoint. Ex. 7.6 summarizes the tonal structure of bars 64–254, encompassing the second exposition, the equivocal section from bars 117 to 166, and the clearly developmental passage from bars 167 to 253. There is a deceptive resemblance between the two portions of the bass-line sketch, each of which describes a large-scale, elaborated stepwise descent; but, whereas the first illustrates motion connecting three large areas of tonal stability – C minor, G minor, and E major-to-minor – the second traces the large-scale motion from E to the dominant of E flat through a series of unstable degrees. The developmental section is thus framed by a large-scale expression of the E/E flat relation which parallels that of the first exposition, further underscoring the fundamental importance of this relation on multiple levels throughout the movement.

Finally, as in the Tenth, the articulation of sections is not necessarily congruent with the identification of formal function: the dotted bar line at bar 117 in Ex. 7.6 shows the clear sectional division here, as articulated by the process of liquidation, the change of key, and the entry of the second-group theme from bar 48 in the strings, and yet the tonal and thematic process is in a sense continuous. By contrast, despite the segue, the formal roles of bars 117–66 and bars 167–253 are quite different. While the prospect of suggesting a triple exposition is not very

Ex. 7.6   Second Symphony, first movement, bars 64–254

appealing, these observations do suggest that a more flexible accounting of the relationship between sectionalization – as articulated by cadences and 'secondary parameters' – and formal functions may provide some useful new perspectives on Mahler's formal strategies. In the movement at hand, the interpretation suggested by Ex. 7.6 is that the G minor tonicization of bars 80–117 represents not so much a structural goal as an intermediate step in the overall motion from C to E, a motion that has already been implied in the first exposition, and that is retained in the recapitulation.

Conclusion

The purpose of this essay has been not so much to demonstrate that the movements from Mahler's symphonies discussed above can be described in terms of sonata functions as to illustrate some of the ways in which Mahler could integrate those functions into novel, dynamic formal and tonal structures. The analyses suggest that a multi-layered approach to form may enable us to avoid the formulaic application of paradigms while not losing the benefit of their analytic power.

Chapter Eight

Form in the First Movement of Mahler's Fifth Symphony

ROBERT G. HOPKINS

Introduction

Analysts who study formal structures in Mahler's symphonic movements quickly learn that the movements often do not obviously and easily conform to standard models. Thus it is not surprising, for instance, that the first movement (that is, the first half of Part I) of the Fifth Symphony, composed in 1901–2, has been variously described as a march with two trios, as a five-part ABABA structure, and as a sonata form. Each of these descriptions has some validity and can account for many aspects of the movement's formal structure. Ultimately, however, the descriptions are incompatible and raise questions both about the assumptions and approaches of the analysts and about the inherent difficulties of formal analysis in the first movement.

In an oft-quoted letter to Georg Göhler on 8 February 1911, Mahler wrote:

> I have finished my Fifth – it had to be almost completely re-orchestrated. I simply can't understand why I still had to make such mistakes, like the merest beginner. (It is clear that all the experience I had gained in writing the first four symphonies completely let me down in this one – for a completely new style demanded a new technique.)
>
> (Martner, 1979, p. 372)

Egon Gartenberg (1978, p. 299) notes that this new style had as its basis a contrapuntal texture. He believes that Mahler's polyphony as well as his use of timbre and texture had a significant impact on twentieth-century music.

It is not only the contrapuntal textures of the Fifth Symphony that provide a challenge to the analyst, but also Mahler's penchant for the continuing development of thematic ideas throughout a movement. Mahler's advice to Max Marschalk, in a letter of 12 April 1896, is illuminating:

> Believe me: we must for the time being keep to the good old principles. *Themes* – these must be clear and *plastic*, so that they can be clearly recognized at any stage of modification or development – and then *varied*

> presentation, holding the attention above all through the logical *development* of the inner idea, but also by the *genuine opposition* of contrasting motives.
>
> (Martner, 1979, p. 182)

Indeed, Mahler's Fifth Symphony demonstrates his adherence to the principle of 'eternal development':

> In my writing, from the very first, you won't find any more repetition from strophe to strophe; for music is governed by the law of eternal evolution, eternal development – just as the world, even in one and the same spot, is always changing, eternally fresh and new. But of course this development must be progressive, or I don't give a damn for it!
>
> (Franklin, 1980, p. 130)

As a result, it is possible to view a main theme, such as the Funeral March of the first movement, as constantly in the process of 'becoming' rather than identifying any particular statement of the theme as the 'original' and others as 'variations'. That is, all statements of the theme may be considered more or less equal – they are simply different perspectives on the same idea.

Coupled with the constant thematic development in Mahler's contrapuntal textures is a decline in the importance of traditional tonal harmonic syntax, often the result of increased chromaticism within a lean polyphonic texture, and the relative absence of traditional, authentic cadences. Donald Mitchell (1980, p. 518) writes: 'In this period [up to 1900] Mahler was an unambiguously tonal composer, though he often used tonality in a very fresh way ... . Only later did his tonality diminish in stability, with a pervasive chromaticism of his harmonic style.'

In Mahler's later works that feature chromatic and contrapuntal textures, constant thematic development, and weak tonal harmonic syntax, it may not often be possible to find a clear-cut, harmonically stable section that concludes unambiguously with a traditional tonal cadence. How, then, does Mahler indicate closure while maintaining the contrapuntal fabric? Other than traditional tonal means, what can provide the analyst with a reliable guide not only to points of closure and distinctly articulated beginnings but also to the relative strengths of the formal articulations? Mahler's use of what can be called secondary parametric processes – in particular to create abating closure and dissolution – are important clues to formal divisions (see Hopkins, 1983 & 1990). Indeed, Mahler's later symphonies, and in particular the first movement of the Fifth Symphony, suggest that a careful examination of secondary parameters – parameters such as register, concordance, dynamics and timbre, as differentiated from tonal melody, tonal harmony and rhythm[1] – is crucial to understanding the formal structure.

---

[1] For a detailed discussion of secondary parameters and the roles they play in articulating form in tonal music, see Hopkins, 1990, pp. 29–63. Secondary parameters are also discussed in a later section of this chapter.

Before examining the role of secondary parameters in articulating the form of the first movement, it will be instructive to consider various analyses of its form.

Analyses of the form of the first movement

All analysts recognize the importance of the opening trumpet fanfare in articulating the form. The fanfare returns in whole or in part at bars 61, 153, 233, 317 and 377,[2] though never exactly the same, of course, as in the opening statement.[3] The fanfares at bars 153 and 317 are quite brief and lead into what some analysts have called two 'trios'.[4] At first glance, such an analysis seems apt: there is a C sharp minor march at bar 35 and at bar 89 that recurs at bar 263, following a contrasting section in B flat minor beginning in bar 155, and preceding another contrasting section in A minor at bar 323. However, referring to the form of the movement as 'a march with two trios' (Banks & Mitchell, 1980, p. 520) is misleading in significant respects. The march to which Mitchell refers is the funeral march first played by the strings, clarinet and bassoon at bar 35; the 'trios' begin at bars 155 and 323. One would presume that an experienced listener's schema for a march and two trios presupposes one main march, with fairly full orchestration, and two different trios characterized by more relaxed music and more thinly orchestrated texture. Neither supposition applies in this case. Moreover, a listener might rightfully assume that 'a march with two trios' both begins and ends with the march. That, too, is not the case here, at least with respect to what Mitchell has defined as the march.

The movement opens 'In gemessenem Schritt   Streng   Wie ein Kondukt' with a fanfare that begins what may appropriately be called a fanfare march in bars 1–27,[5] a passage that is far more than an introduction to the movement. The

---

[2] All references to bar numbers assume that the downbeat of the bar is part of the theme or passage in question. Accordingly, if a passage is indicated as beginning at bar 61, that means the passage begins either on the downbeat of bar 61 or with any number of anacruses to bar 61.

[3] The fanfare idea returns in the trumpet at bar 181 as well, but it is different from other statements in important respects. The fanfare essentially prolongs C for eight bars rather than initiates an ascending triadic pattern. The fanfare appears as a counterpoint to the melodies in the first violins and the upper woodwinds, as opposed to the single foreground element in the texture. The only other statement of the fanfare idea that does not begin on C sharp or D flat is the statement at bar 377, which nevertheless is the foreground textural element at that point and is connected to a statement of the fanfare beginning on C sharp at bar 397.

[4] See, for instance, Kennedy (1974, p. 114), Mitchell (1980, p. 520), Cooke (1980, p. 82), La Grange (1995, p. 809) and Floros (1994, p. 144).

[5] Murphy (1986, p. 102) identifies bars 1–20 as the first march, with bars 21–34 providing a close to the section. While it is true that bars 21–27 are closing in function, it is also clear that the trumpet fanfare's opening four-note motif is reiterated in bars 21–23

solo trumpet fanfare in bars 1–12 might initially be considered only an introduction; but the heavily orchestrated continuation of the fanfare march in bars 13–27 – notably including a harmonized variation of the opening trumpet solo at bars 21–23 – and the varied repetition of the march at bars 61, 232 and 377 convince us that the opening passage is not merely introductory. It is, rather, an essential – indeed, defining – element of an opening and recurring A section (bars 1–60).[6] The fanfare march is not only longer, but also far more fully orchestrated in its second half than the 'main' funeral march in C sharp minor (bars 35–53). Furthermore, the two marches that begin at bars 1 and 35 are linked by a common closing passage first heard in bars 27–34 and repeated at bars 53–60. Thus the first funeral march at bar 1 and the second funeral march at bar 35 together could be said to form the opening A section of the work; bars 61–152 constitute an extended, varied repeat of the opening A section.

If any section of the movement fits the traditional mode of a trio, it would be the funeral march at bar 35,[7] which is relatively subdued and lightly orchestrated compared to the last half of the opening fanfare march. In contrast, the section beginning at bar 155 does not evoke any traditional view of a trio: it is marked 'Plötzlich schneller   Leidenschaftlich   Wild'. As for the section at bar 323, it begins calmly but soon leads to more agitated music that culminates in the 'Klagend' climax of the entire movement at bar 369.

Moreover, we might presume two essentially or entirely different trios in a form described as a 'march and two trios', yet the sections at bars 155 and 323 are actually two versions of the same 'trio'.[8] Ex. 8.1 provides a comparison of the opening bars from the two sections. At first, the two passages differ greatly in dynamics, mood and orchestration, though the motivic resemblance in the melodies is clear. Mahler has rearranged various parts, however: bars 337–44 (emphasizing D minor) correspond to bars 157–64 (in B flat minor) and bars 328–35 correspond to bars 164–71. Both sections make important use of the figure first heard in the trumpet at bars 165–72 (see, for instance, the horn in bars 337–43).

---

and 31–33, and consequently bars 21–34 will be heard as an extension of the march rather than as added, new closing material.

    6 The harmonized second statement of the fanfare march at bar 61 lays to rest any doubts the listener might have that its function might be solely introductory.

    7 This view is shared by Murphy (1986, p. 101).

    8 Floros (1994, p. 144) surely overstates the differences when he says: 'Although the second trio is for the most part based on the thematic substance of the first, Mahler creates something completely different from the material.' Subsequently (p. 145) he allows that 'Common to both trios are indeed several surges of intensification that lead to climaxes (bars 221 and 229 or 369ff.)' and are followed by abating passages that effect a smooth transition to the opening funeral march. Moreover, in his outline of the structure of the piece (pp. 142–43) he identifies the first contrasting section as 'Part B' and the second as 'Part B¹', not 'Part C'.

Ex. 8.1   Fifth Symphony, first movement

(a) Bars 155–71

(b) Bars 323–44

Strong thematic relationships are not the only means by which Mahler establishes important similarities. The first B section, introduced by the trumpet fanfare at bar 153, builds to a triple-fortissimo climax at bar 221, which is followed by a passage that subsides in bars 221–25,[9] then intensifies again in bars 225–31 before subsiding at last in bars 229–34, thereby creating a clear overall

---

[9] Here I use the word 'subside' to mean either: (1) 'to sink or fall to the bottom; to settle' or (2) 'to become quiet; to cease to rage; to be calmed; to become tranquil' (J. McKechnie et al. (eds) (1979), *Webster's New Twentieth Century Dictionary Unabridged*, 2nd edn). This subsiding passage will be discussed in detail in the next section of the chapter.

impression that the section is ending. At bar 233 the opening trumpet fanfare, signalling a return to the opening A section, overlaps the ending of this first B section. In a similar fashion, the second B section is introduced by the opening trumpet fanfare as played by the timpani beginning at bar 317; the section then builds to the full-orchestra, triple-fortissimo climax of the movement at bar 369, whereupon another subsiding passage eventually becomes the background for an overlapping return of the opening trumpet fanfare.

Mitchell himself acknowledges (1999, p. 248) 'how profoundly Mahler has transformed the idea of the trio' in this movement: 'In place of relaxation or relatively simple contrast we have two eruptions of protest *against* the implications of the march ... .' Rather than imbue the word 'trio' with substantially different meaning, would it not make more sense to avoid calling the contrasting sections by that name? They are, simply, contrasting B sections.[10]

Constantin Floros (1994, pp. 142–43) discerns a five-part structure with sections A and B and variations of them:

1–154	Main section (Part A)
155–232	Trio I (Part B)
233–322	Main section (Part A^1)
323–76	Trio II (Part B^1)
377–415	Coda (Part A^2)

Edward Murphy (1986, p. 102) shares an almost identical view of the form, except that he rejects the 'trio' designation and simply identifies the sections as ABABA.[11] Both analysts recognize, however, that what they refer to as the first A section actually includes two statements of both marches: bars 1–60 and 61–152. Given that fact, a formal description of AABABA would seem more apt, and will be adopted here. Both analysts treat the brief fanfares at bars 153 and 317 as transitions to the B sections starting at bars 155 and 323, respectively. Other statements of the fanfare, however, are treated as the beginnings of A sections – even when, as in bars 233 and 377, the fanfare appears to overlap the end of the B sections.[12] One may presume that the listener will hear those overlaps and, at least on first hearing, will consider the fanfare that begins at bar 153 as the beginning of another section. That this new section abruptly takes a very different character at bar 155 does not alter the fact that the fanfare is heard as a beginning gesture, as it was in bars 1 and 61. Murphy breaks down the A

---

[10] They could be designated B and B' or simply referred to as B, given that in Mahler's music the repeat of a section is inevitably varied.

[11] This designation assumes, as is safe to do for Mahler's works, that any repetition of a section is varied and, consequently, indicating a variation by calling succeeding repetitions A' and A", and so forth, is unnecessary.

[12] Mitchell (1999, pp. 247–48) speaks convincingly to this overlapping.

section into March I (bars 1–34) and March II (bars 35–60) and notes that only March I returns in the final A section; Floros identifies these same subsections as two parts of the main section. The second A section in the AABABA form is varied, of course, and is extended by the inclusion of a new march idea in A flat major at bars 121–32.[13]

Nadine Sine, who ultimately argues for a 'fusion of strophic construction (based on funeral-march rhythms) with sonata-form principles', has suggested that the movement may be seen as a strophic funeral march, with five strophes separated by statements of the refrain first heard at bars 1–34 (Sine, 1983, p. 68). This view at least treats all the fanfares consistently as the beginnings of sections. However, the analysis is unsatisfactory given that the fanfares at bars 61–88, 233–62 and 377–415 are so unlike the quickly interrupted renditions in bars 153–55 and 317–22.[14] Further, two of the fanfares – those at bars 233 and 377 – occur in the midst, not following the end, of a closing gesture. In addition, the strophes vary greatly in length, from as short as 26 bars to as long as 78 bars.

Sine also finds sonata-form gestures in the movement, including the fact that the A flat major march at bar 121 is recapitulated in D flat major at bar 295, thereby 'functioning as a kind of second theme' (1983, p. 68). She suggests that bar 153 can be viewed as the beginning of a development section and bar 233 as the beginning of a recapitulation. Barbara R. Barry (1993, p. 54) identifies a clear sonata-form structure: exposition at bar 1, a second exposition at bar 61, the development at bar 153, and the recapitulation at bar 255, where she finds a return of C sharp minor. Barry's analysis has the advantage of recognizing the extended repeat of the exposition at bar 61, though there is no explanation for why the brief A flat major march at bar 121 is omitted from the first exposition if it is the second theme. Further, it seems unusual that the second exposition would end in D flat minor, enharmonically the tonic. Moreover, it is difficult to hear the B section from bar 153 as a typical kind of development section. One important reason for that is its relative harmonic stability, with a clear assertion of B flat minor and then a brief shift to E flat minor (prolonged by a few bars emphasizing C flat major) before returning to B flat minor with a cadence at bars 194–95. Then there is a brief shift to G flat major before a passage emphasizing F minor. Furthermore, the section seems a clear exposition of the trumpet's theme first expressed at bar 155 and reiterated in abbreviated form at bar 195 and again, in even briefer form, at bars 229–33 in the two muted trumpets, the oboes and clarinets. Finally, if the development begins at bar 153, what does one call the similar section beginning at bar 323?

---

[13] This section, interestingly enough, has the same basic shape as the opening fanfare march: the first few bars (here, bars 121–24) are repeated in slightly varied form at the end of the melody (bars 129–32), just as the opening four-bar fanfare idea returns at bar 21 to conclude the first march.

[14] In addition, this explanation does not account for the abridged statement of the refrain at bars 181–88.

If it is difficult to hear the B section beginning at bar 155 as the development, it is a far greater challenge to hear the section beginning at bar 255 as the recapitulation in C sharp minor. Barry acknowledges that the trumpet fanfare at bar 233 anticipates the recapitulation, but one wonders why the listener would now hear the recapitulation as beginning with the *closing* gesture at bar 254. That passage is first heard at bars 21–27 and is later repeated in bars 81–88 as a means of concluding the fanfare march. Further, the passage at bar 254 emphasizes and prolongs G sharp minor, not C sharp minor. If return to C sharp minor is the defining event for identifying a recapitulation – and it is not clear why that must be so – then any recapitulation would have to start at bar 263, where C sharp minor is re-established.

Even Sine's suggestion of a recapitulation at bar 233 is difficult to reconcile with other aspects of the form. The fanfare at bar 233 overlaps the end of the B section that began at bar 155; furthermore, the passage is harmonically unstable. Thus, bar 233 is weakened as a point of arrival. Moreover, if this recapitulation corresponds to the second A section beginning at bar 61, the recapitulation ends with the perfect authentic cadence in D flat major in bars 314–16. Yet Sine (1983, p. 249) proposes that bars 233–415 constitute the recapitulation. To do so is to overlook not only the correspondence between bars 233–316 and bars 61–152, but also the strong connection between bars 155–232 and 323–77.[15]

All the analyses we have considered offer perspectives that shed some light on the form of the movement, but none convincingly demonstrates a consistent approach that addresses the significant articulations and interconnections in the work. The analysts all take as a point of departure the many statements of the opening fanfare, which is used throughout the work both as a means of articulating the beginning of a section and as a means of effecting a transition to a new section. Less attention is paid to the hierarchy of closure that Mahler creates in the music, often with resources other than traditional cadential closure. Given the weakening role of traditional tonal syntactic parameters in Mahler's music, it is fruitful to consider his formal structures from a broader perspective – not only of the primary parameters but also of the secondary parameters.

Secondary parameters and the articulation of form

The theoretical basis for considering secondary parametric processes and patterns

---

[15] The close relationship between these two contrasting B sections undermines Vodnoy's analysis of the movement (1993, p. 8) as an ABA form with extended coda (bars 317–415). Moreover, after the strong cadential closure in bar 316, the passage beginning in the next bar sounds very much like a new contrasting section rather than some kind of extension of the closing passage directly preceding.

for articulating form in music, and in particular in Mahler's music, takes as a point of departure the weakening of traditional tonal harmony as an organizing force (see Hopkins, 1983 & 1990). The relative scarcity of strong traditional cadences in the first movement of the Fifth Symphony invites the possibility that other parameters, such as dynamics, came to play a more defining role in shaping musical form in order to compensate for the gradual breakdown of traditional tonal functions.

Tonal pitch is a term that may be used to define linear pitch patterns with regard to tonal function and significance. If tonal pitch, tonal harmony and rhythm are primary parameters in tonal music,[16] then parameters that have to do with register, concordance, dynamics, timbre and textural density may be considered secondary parameters.[17]

In monophonic music we can identify four secondary parameters: registral pitch (a parameter that defines linear pitch patterns without regard to tonal function or significance), dynamics, duration and timbre. These four secondary parameters may be called *simple* parameters in order to distinguish them from *compound* parameters – those that define a linear succession of composite elements in music with more than one voice. The parameters that define differentiated concurrent durations, dynamics and timbres may be called *compound durations*, *compound dynamics* and *compound timbre*, respectively. *Concordance* is used here to refer to the secondary parameter that defines combinations of pitches without regard to tonal function or significance.[18] The only other secondary parameter is *components*, the number of identifiable and differentiated voices in the musical texture.

Changes in any of the secondary parameters can create directed motion, which may lead to closure. We may identify directed motion as being *intensifying* or *abating*; often such motion is not consistently intensifying or abating, but rather reflects an overall intensifying or abating trend. If 'closure is the result of directed motion toward repose following tension or activity' (Hopkins, 1990, p. 8), then there are two basic processes by which closure is established: one that leads from a point of tension or activity gradually to a point of repose – an abatement – or one that builds in tension to a point of reversal, where rest is achieved – characteristically through cadential closure.

---

[16] Rhythm in the sense it is used here is a summarizing parameter or emergent property dependent on all parameters. Thus, rhythm is a result of the interaction of grouping and metrical structures; see Fred Lerdahl and Ray Jackendoff (1983), *A Generative Theory of Tonal Music*, Cambridge, Mass.: MIT Press, pp. 12–104.

[17] This discussion of secondary parameters and closure is based upon Hopkins, 1983, pp. 1–104, & 1990, pp. 1–63.

[18] Concordance is a secondary parameter whose elements are harmonies that may be ordered with respect to processes of increasing or decreasing concordance (or discordance) rather than with respect to tonality. See Hopkins, 1990, pp. 40–44.

Secondary parameters typically contribute to an abatement.[19] Thus, for instance, an abatement in registral pitch would be a generally descending melodic line, especially if it is conjunct. A point of closure for such an abating process might be the implied return to a specific pitch or the implied arrival at the octave of a specific pitch – in Mahler's music often a pedal note. An abatement in concordance leads to increasingly concordant sonorities, with the unison or octave as an implied point of closure. Dynamic closure may result from a general trend of diminishing dynamics that leads to an extremely soft dynamic level or silence. Durational patterns of increasing length – cumulative patterns – reduce activity and are thus abating. The longest duration of such a pattern is a point of closure. A process of decreasing components is abating and leads to closure when the process reaches a single component.

Component closure in Mahler's music is often supported by diminishing dynamics and increasing concordance. Indeed, such simultaneous abating processes in more than one secondary parameter can have a strong effect in shaping form and creating closure, especially if the terminations of the processes are synchronized. In Mahler's music many passages exemplify what may be called a *dissolution*, a process whereby a musical passage dissolves in some sense – either falling or fading away, or both – typically after a dynamic climax. The effect may be one of a collapse or a more gradual subsidence, or even a fragmentation of musical ideas. The closing gesture beginning at bar 369 (marked 'Klagend') of the Fifth Symphony's first movement is representative of a common kind of dissolution[20] – one of subsidence – whereby a dynamic climax (here triple fortissimo in many parts, fortissimo in others) is followed by clear trends of diminishing dynamics, descending registral pitch, and decreasing components that indicate the section is coming to a close; see Ex. 8.3 and the discussion in the final section.

This passage is remarkable for the overlapping trumpet fanfare statements, but it is exemplary of the kind of multi-functional passage that Mahler often uses to effect both a conclusion and a transition. A significant result of using secondary parametric processes in this way is that Mahler is able to compose continuous music that clearly articulates formal structures without employing traditional tonal cadences that interrupt the flow of the music. Even if a dissolution or other abating passage does not reach closure, the listener both understands that the

---

[19] Simple and compound timbre are generally exceptions because timbre is a multi-dimensional parameter and it is not clear what an abating process would be. It seems that we perceive differences in timbre but not – at least not readily – processes and patterns in timbres in the way that we perceive processes and patterns in pitches, durations and dynamics.

[20] This passage, in light of the form of the movement, will be considered in the discussion to follow. Mahler often uses a passage of subsidence following a fortissimo climax near the end of a movement; see also bars 544ff. in the second movement of the Fifth Symphony.

section is ending and anticipates the start of a new section. Moreover, the last part of the abatement is a relative point of repose.[21] Thus, given Mahler's interest in music that is constantly evolving, it makes sense that in maintaining a contrapuntal texture Mahler often relies on secondary parameters to play an important role in articulating sections, in particular because several concomitant abatements in secondary parameters can effectively shape the end of a section, and suggest imminent closure. Such use of abating processes and patterns in secondary parameters is found frequently in the first movement of the Fifth Symphony.

The form of the first movement reconsidered[22]

As noted above, the first A section of the movement comprises bars 1–60, which incorporate two funeral marches: bars 1–34 and 35–60.[23] The movement's opening trumpet solo is part of a fanfare march that can be subdivided into bars 1–14, 15–20, 21–27 and 27–34. The opening 14-bar unit is mostly a trumpet solo, the first four bars of which constitute a phrase – what I will call the fanfare phrase – that is frequently repeated throughout the movement. The phrase comprises three statements of a four-note motif that I will refer to as the fanfare motif; see Ex. 8.2.

Ex. 8.2   Fifth Symphony, first movement, opening fanfare motif

The fanfare phrase is reiterated and harmonized in the horns at bars 15–17, together with a variation of the trumpet solo from bars 9–10, and again, this time in most of the orchestra, at bars 21–24. There the repeated iv–i progressions and reiterated G sharps serve to extend the tonal closure created by a perfect authentic

---

[21] The listener may retroactively assign closure to the end of an abatement even if the abatement ends before reaching significant closure, that is, a significant sense of satisfactory conclusion that comes with the arrival at an anticipated state of comparative repose.

[22] Much of this discussion is based upon Hopkins, 1983, pp. 167–75.

[23] Both feature abundant examples of short bar forms (aab). For instance, the opening fourteen bars comprise two *Stollen* (bars 1–4 & 5–8) and an *Abgesang* (bars 9–14), and the initial *Stollen* itself is a miniature bar form, consisting of the opening four-

cadence in G sharp minor at bars 18–20. Then in bars 23–27 descending chromatic pitch patterns in the low woodwinds and strings lead from G sharp 3 and G sharp 2 to closure on G sharp 2 and G sharp 1, respectively, in bar 27. That closure is enhanced by the predictable conclusion of the horns' reiterated descending three-note motif beginning at the end of bar 24 and ending on the downbeat of bar 27, where there is an elision with yet one more closing, subsiding gesture. The Neapolitan[6]–i progressions in G sharp minor at bars 28–31 help to prolong the key. The fanfare motif returns in the low strings and woodwinds at bars 32–33, and the final note of the second fanfare motif coincides with the anticipated conclusion on G sharp 2 of a generally descending pitch pattern in the horns at bars 31–33. Registral pitch closure on that G sharp is supported by increased concordance, diminished components, fading dynamics and durational closure. Only the bass drum, which reiterates the rhythm of the trombones in bars 27–31, provides ongoing motion connecting the end of this march to the beginning of the next one, with the anacruses in the strings and woodwinds in bar 34 overlapping the extended G sharp 2 in the timpani in that bar.

The string march of bars 35–60 begins in C sharp minor and can be divided into bars 35–53 and 53–60. The prolongation of G sharp minor in bars 53–60 closely matches bars 27–34, though this time the fanfare motif, first augmented, is heard practically throughout, with the rhythm of the fanfare phrase essentially repeated in bars 57–59, thereby strengthening the sense of closure. Closure in bars 59–60 is stronger than at bars 33–34 for several reasons. A dynamic abatement is terminally synchronized with registral pitch closure on G sharp 2 in bar 59. Further, there is no ongoing motion in the bass drum or any other part, and two crotchet rests separate the end of the march from the return of the fanfare march. Moreover, closure is stronger because bars 53–60 are a return of a passage whose close is predictable. Unlike bars 27–34, the closing passage in bars 53–60 does not follow strong tonal harmonic closure. Despite that, secondary parametric processes and patterns, and the passage's conformance to a previous closing statement, create substantial closure.

The fanfare march repeats in bars 61–88 ('Wie zu Anfang'), but this time the trumpet solo is harmonized and the final closing passage from bars 27–34 is mostly omitted. All that remains are its final two bars, which here serve to complete the reiterated closing gesture from bars 21–27 that concludes the section following a Phrygian cadence in bars 78–80. Abatements in registral pitch, concordance and simple duration conclude in bar 87, and diminishing dynamics in bars 86–87 contribute to the sense of repose. As in bars 33–34, the bass drum in bars 87–88 connects the end of the march to the beginning of the

---

note motif, that motif repeated, and then the motif varied and somewhat extended. The second march, starting at bar 35, begins with another miniature bar form with the initial pattern of bars 35–36 inverted in bars 37–38 before ending with an *Abgesang* in bars 39–42.

second funeral march, the first two notes of which overlap the extended G sharp 2 in the timpani. The absence of the passage from bars 27–32 weakens the sense of conclusion here since the listener would presumably expect the fanfare march to end as it – and the second march – had previously. Had Mahler repeated the passage from bars 27–32 and 53–60, however, the sense of closure would have been too strong, undermining the connection of the fanfare march and the string march as two parts of a single A section.

This time the second march, bars 89–152, is extended not only by the inclusion of a brief A flat major (enharmonically V) passage primarily in the woodwinds at bar 121, but also by extension of the second march itself both before and after the woodwind passage. Thinning texture, a descending melodic pattern and fading dynamics in bars 117–20 shape the end of the subsection that leads to the woodwind theme.[24] After this passage, Mahler returns to the ♩ 𝄽 ♩ 𝄾 ♪|♩ 𝄽 motif in the trombones from bars 27–28 (here doubled by the side drum and prefigured by the tuba and horns in bars 129–32), while the strings play a variation of the second march that emphasizes, at bars 135–36, D major, the Neapolitan of C sharp minor. Note, too, the emphasis melodically of C sharp–D–C sharp in the violins in the same bars. The emphasis on the approach to the tonic through the Neapolitan is a recurring element in the movement. Essentially descending pitch patterns in the violins' melody in bars 137–45, supported in the final few bars by greatly diminishing dynamics, lead to a quick cadence in D flat major (enharmonically the tonic major) at bars 144–45.[25] Mahler elides the resolution with yet another reiteration, in bars 145–52, of the closing passage from bars 27–34 and 53–60. This time the passage is transposed to the tonic and features repeated Neapolitan⁶–I progressions to prolong the tonic. The Neapolitan⁶ over a dominant pedal in bar 150 resolves to a whisperingly soft minor tonic chord at bar 151, extended to bar 152. Again, as in bars 53–60, abatements in dynamics, registral pitch and – to a lesser extent – components contribute to closure. Closure is strengthened because bars 145–52 reiterate a closing passage with a predictable conclusion. Once more, as in bars 27–34, the passage follows an authentic cadence, though this time in the tonic major. Consequently, registral pitch closure at bar 151 and durational closure in bar 152

---

[24] Significantly, the ♩ 𝄽 ♩ 𝄾 ♪|♩ 𝄽 motif in the trombones at bars 27–28 returns in the trombones followed by horns in bars 105–10, and is then shared between tuba and trombones in bars 113–16; since this motif is identified with the closing passage of both the first and second marches in the initial A section, its presence here may help to suggest that a subsection is coming to a conclusion. Mahler paves the way for the re-emergence of this trombone motif by using all but the first note of the motif in the horns' accompaniment to the extended second march at bars 97–98, 99–100 & 103–4.

[25] The authentic cadence is not strong because the altered dominant seventh chord (with flattened fifth) arrives only on the last beat of bar 144 before resolving immediately to the tonic on the downbeat of bar 145.

on a minor tonic chord help create closure that is substantially stronger than at any earlier point in the movement.

Thus the hierarchy of closure that Mahler produces in the first 152 bars of the movement clearly identifies an initial A section in bars 1–60 (subdivided into two marches, bars 1–34 and 35–60) and a varied repeat of that section in bars 61–152 (subdivided into bars 61–88 and 89–152), with the closure at bar 152 being the strongest yet heard in the movement.

The listener would probably interpret any return of the opening trumpet fanfare as the beginning of a section in the movement,[26] and so the entrance of the trumpet at the end of bar 152 signals the beginning of the first B section, bars 153–234,[27] with its end overlapped by the restatement of the opening fanfare in the trumpet at bar 233. As noted above, this B section reaches a triple-fortissimo climax at bar 221, whereupon descending lines in the piccolo, trumpet and violins, and a thinner texture in bars 221–25, suggest the passage is coming to an end. There is a temporary reversal in bars 225–31, where an intensification is created by ascending pitch patterns in the horns and an increase in compound dynamics that lead to a secondary climax on the downbeat of bar 229 and a triple-fortissimo G flat in the trumpet, clarinet and oboe at bar 231. The subsequent subsiding passage in bars 231–34 is characterized by decreasing components (first the violins drop out, then the clarinet and the horns), diminishing dynamics, and descending pitch patterns in the oboes, trumpet, violins and violas. The subsiding gesture does not reach a convincing conclusion; the only closure is compound durational closure at bar 233. Instead, activity in those instruments involved in the closing of the B section ceases temporarily at bar 233 and the listener's attention is diverted to the trumpet fanfare that interrupts the closing of the B section and signals the beginning of another varied A section.

Note, however, that another abating process in dynamics begins at bar 233: the trumpet and violins are marked fortissimo (other instruments play piano), but the trumpet fades to piano and the violins to pianissimo by bar 239. Gradually lengthening durations as a result of the 'Allmählich sich beruhigend' indication at bar 233 support the subsiding gesture in dynamics. Thus Mahler ingeniously involves the solo trumpet in the subsidence that follows the climax at bar 221, even while the trumpet begins a new section. The rest of the orchestra appears to continue the dissolution of the B section for several bars after the trumpet's entrance before gradually (in bars 241ff.) building in intensity to become an integral part of the restatement of the fanfare march. Consequently Mahler uses

---

[26] The listener may re-evaluate this upon hearing the sudden change of texture at bar 155, but the trumpet fanfare continues in bars 152ff. rather than being interrupted. On that basis and the fact that the fanfare has begun previous passages, it makes sense to consider the return of the fanfare as the articulation of the beginning of section B.

[27] One might also choose bar 240 as the end of the B section, given that dynamics continue to abate to that point.

secondary parameters to shape the end of the B section and prepare the listener for the start of a new section, but section B is not closed convincingly – rather, it is seamlessly woven together with the returning trumpet fanfare.

The A section in bars 233–316 again subdivides into the fanfare march (bars 233–62) and the second funeral march (bars 263–316), once more extended as it was in bars 89–152 with a statement, here transposed to the tonic major (written as D flat major), of the A flat major march in bars 295–306. As in the second A section (bars 61–152), the fanfare march closes with a varied return of the gesture from bars 81–88 (itself a variation of bars 21–26 and 33–34), this time following a Neapolitan⁶–i cadence in G sharp minor at bars 252–53.²⁸ In bars 261–62 the bass drum and timpani provide ongoing motion to the beginning of the second march, in which the side drum and brass often repeat the same rhythm.

The movement's first strong traditional tonal closure in the tonic (tonic major, in this case) at bar 315 is also the last. Abatements in registral pitch, concordance, dynamics and duration support a perfect authentic cadence which, as Mitchell (1975, pp. 36–37) has astutely observed, is a quote from *Nun will die Sonn' so hell aufgeh'n*, the first song of the *Kindertotenlieder*. The closure is extremely strong, made all the more so by the fact that, except for duration, the abating processes in the secondary parameters are terminally synchronized with the arrival at the tonic harmony.²⁹ The closure is further enhanced by two beats of rest in bar 316. Though the conclusion is somewhat weakened by the delayed resolution to the tonic halfway through bar 315, this closure is nevertheless as strong as any previous point of closure in the movement. Because of its strength, and the lack of convincing closure at the end of section B, the third section of the movement is a dependent combination of B and A (B–A) such as one might find in the second half of a rounded binary form.

In all previous instances the trumpet had initiated a new section with a repetition of the opening fanfare. At bar 317, however, Mahler chose the timpani to play the fanfare idea to introduce an initially subdued variation of the B section. This B section leads to *the* climax of the movement: a triple-fortissimo, full-orchestra dissonant chord at bar 369, marked 'Klagend'. From there, the section subsides as a result of abating processes in various secondary parameters; see Ex. 8.3. Initially, descending conjunct lines, diminishing dynamics and

---

²⁸ It is significant that Mahler emphasizes D major, enharmonically the Neapolitan, in bars 307–12, just before the cadence in D flat, bars 314–15. This is consistent with Mahler's tendency throughout the movement to emphasize, both melodically and harmonically, the approach to the tonic through the lowered second scale degree.

²⁹ Moreover, the reiteration of the ♩ ♪ ♩ ♪ ♩♩ ♪ rhythm (first heard in bars 27–28) in the tuba and trombones in bars 315–16 seems particularly fitting, given that the rhythm will be associated with closure in the mind of the listener. It is true that the same rhythm is used as an accompaniment figure in certain sections of the movement, but its initial appearance is in the concluding passage of the opening fanfare march.

Ex. 8.3   Fifth Symphony, first movement, bars 369–401

increasing durations (as a result of a slowing tempo; bar 372 is marked 'Zurückhaltend') create the subsiding gesture. This dissolution is interrupted by the forte return of the trumpet fanfare at bar 377, which articulates the beginning of a coda based on the fanfare march of section A. Nevertheless the dissolution continues well beyond bar 377, so the coda overlaps the end of the B section for which – just as before – there is no convincing closure. Instead we again witness an inventive blending of the subsiding gesture shaping the end of the B section and the trumpet fanfare, this time on A, announcing the beginning of the coda. Ex. 8.3 illustrates, in fact, a remarkable instance of a passage that combines a closing function with the function of making a transition to the movement's final closing gesture (bars 401–15).

In addition to substantially decreasing dynamics, the descending conjunct lines from A5 to A3 in the violins at bars 370–90 and from E1 to C sharp 1 in the basses in bars 380–90 contribute to the growing calm. Once the solo trumpet enters with the fanfare, it plays a central role in the continuing dissolution. The number of components decreases from eleven at bar 369 to the solo trumpet at bars 391–92, and the trumpet fades from its forte entrance to pianissimo at bar 389 before fading further at bar 391, where the part is marked 'verlöschend'. Whereas diminishing dynamics effectively create a sense of growing calm in bars 370–92, descending pitch patterns in bars 389–401 are most influential in easing tension: a conjunct line descends from F sharp 5 to C sharp 2 in the trumpet and cellos (the latter doubled an octave lower by the basses). Significantly, the trumpet fanfare motif that began the movement returns on C sharp 4 at bar 397, thereby creating a symmetry that suggests final closure is imminent and also introducing the prospect that the continuing registral pitch descent will end on C sharp, as it does at bar 401. Moreover, the reiteration of the fanfare motif on C sharp constitutes a second entrance of the fanfare that overlaps the dissolution of the final B section. This time, however, what may be considered the final bars of the dissolution ending the B section (bars 393–401) are part of a varied, concluding statement of the fanfare march. Note that the final harmonic resolution in bars 400–401 is another kind of Neapolitan-to-tonic progression, in this case Neapolitan^7–i (or I; there is no third).

The solo trumpet reiterates the movement's opening gesture in bars 401–3 with an important change: the anticipated E is replaced by D sharp and is not extended into a fourth bar. The echo of bars 402–3 in the next two bars confirms that this fanfare will not be introducing another A or B section. The movement closes with a final miniature bar form, this time based on the opening fanfare phrase now expanded to ten bars (406–15). Diminishing dynamics (from piano to pianissimo to triple pianissimo), both in the bass drum and in the fanfare figures played by the trumpet and flute, contribute to the sense of closing, as does the augmented final note of each fanfare motif. Furthermore, the timbre changes from the comparatively rich compound timbre in bars 402–5, where the strings play *col legno* along with horns and low woodwinds, to the nearly pure flute tone in bars 410–12. The stepped dynamic changes in these final bars imply eventual silence, but the final pizzicato Cs in the low strings articulate a specific point of final closure and a return to a more restful register.

The final B section and coda, therefore, combine to form the final section of the movement; there is no clear closure to B, the end of which is overlapped by the beginning of the coda. Mahler uses both primary and especially secondary parameters to create a hierarchy of closures within the movement that defines a kind of composed-out rounded binary form:

A (1–60)   A (61–152)   B–A (153–316)   B–A (317–415)

where the final A section is a coda based on one of the two marches that make up previous A sections.

The first movement of Mahler's Fifth Symphony exemplifies a style that involves constant development of thematic ideas in contrapuntal textures that frequently do not feature traditional tonal cadences. Consequently it is crucial that the analyst consider how processes in secondary parameters help to articulate formal divisions. The many ways in which such processes can contribute to closure – or, conversely, to continuation – provide a rich resource for fashioning formal articulations of various strengths. Mahler's use of secondary parametric processes opened up new possibilities for more continuous, yet clearly articulated, music – as is evidenced, for instance, by the overlapping entrances of the fanfare march that define the beginnings of the final two A sections. The use of secondary parameters to effect a dissolution that indicates the end of one section while simultaneously providing a transition to the next section is an important part of Mahler's 'new' style, and a particularly effective way of creating music that, like the world, 'is always changing, eternally fresh and new' (Franklin, 1980, p. 130).

Chapter Nine

The First Movement of Mahler's
Das Lied von der Erde: Genre,
Form and Musical Expression

ELISABETH SCHMIERER
translated by Jeremy Barham

Mahler's full awareness of the aesthetic and formal implications of genre is the defining feature of his Lieder.[1] Their formal disposition, the technical process of their composition, and their connection with the symphony demonstrate that he must have grappled intensively with the aesthetics of genre. For, unlike other contemporary composers of orchestral Lieder, Mahler did not create that freer type of song based entirely on the details of the text, but rather followed the principles of the Lied and referred back to an aesthetic which had originated a century earlier and seemed long outdated. His ability to raise the music to an extremely high level of expression despite such a backward glance and its all-important implications for the use of formal schemes, is attributable to his particular kind of dialectical interaction with conventional forms which were brought into play to intensify both music and text. The example of the first movement of *Das Lied von der Erde* will demonstrate how this is put into practice in the details of compositional technique.[2]

In view of their related texts, it seems clear that the *Rückert Lieder* of 1901 involve these very same characteristics of the Lied aesthetic such as unity of mood and intimacy, as well as their compositional and technical correlates such as sparseness of setting and strophic form. The first of the *Kindertotenlieder* in particular shows how subtly Mahler treats traditional forms: the dialectic of light and darkness, presented in a different textual formulation in each of the two-line

---

[1] See the chapter 'Gattungsästhetische Voraussetzungen' in Schmierer, 1991, pp. 2–27, repr. as Schmierer, 2001.

[2] The motivically differentiated form of the instrumental sections stretching across the whole cycle, as analysed particularly in Danuser, 1986 and Hefling, 1992 & 2000, will be dealt with only partially here.

verses, is realized in an extremely sophisticated musical manner on the basis of this strophic form.[3] Mahler does not 'compose' the details of the text here, but highlights the contrast through two disparately formed halves of the verse which themselves are very subtly altered from verse to verse. The third verse, which appears to diverge to a greater extent, forms the high point with a text that deviates from the first verse but underlies essentially the same form of instrumental texture, so that despite further distancing from the strophic model, this element of the musical structure is nevertheless retained.

The generic debate seems decidedly pronounced in *Das Lied von der Erde*, since the question has been repeatedly raised, even in contemporary reviews, as to whether the work is a song cycle or a symphony.[4] Compared with earlier song cycles such as *Lieder eines fahrenden Gesellen* or *Kindertotenlieder*, which were already characterized by a great variety of symphonic features, *Das Lied von der Erde* constituted an intensification of the symphonic element, given its dimensions, its instrumentation, and its use of motivic techniques which resemble those of the symphonic genre far more closely than was the case in previous Lieder.[5] Nevertheless the form of the individual movements, apart from that of the extremely prolonged Finale, adheres to earlier principles of the Lied. This is true above all of the first movement, though even here a cross-over between song-like and symphonic formal processes can be seen.[6] Despite the greater deviation of its third verse, which might be understood as a development, the strophic scheme is so clear that the sonata-form model recedes into the background. No symphonic first movement has such a strophic construction, and even the third verse is less a development than simply a more markedly diverging variant of the first and second verses, as in the first of the *Kindertotenlieder*.

However, in contrast to the first of the *Kindertotenlieder*,[7] it is noticeable that the verses of the text seem to be unsuited to strophic form in terms of both structure (different numbers of lines, irregular metre) and content. The text of the second verse, for instance, in no way suggests the possibility of a varied repeat of the first verse. Furthermore the music of the first verse is composed so exceptionally closely 'to the text' that it seems scarcely possible to repeat it to a different text.

The beginning of the vocal part – 'Now beckons the wine' [*Schon winkt der Wein*] – with its rising fourth, derives from a straightforward initial model: any banal drinking song might begin in this way. The simple opening line of this song forms nothing less than a reference to a *Brindisi* (an operatic drinking song),

---

3 See the analysis in Schmierer, 1991, pp. 210–25.
4 See Danuser, 1986, pp. 28–36 & 111–19.
5 See Revers, 2000, pp. 112–13.
6 See especially Danuser, 1986, pp. 37–49.
7 Parallels with the first of the *Kindertotenlieder* have previously been pointed out in Hefling, 1999, p. 447. See also Hefling, 2000, p. 83.

although its harmony immediately calls to mind the additional clause of the song's title, 'of Earth's Sorrow' [*vom Jammer der Erde*]: from the C major (with added sixth, bar 16) of the 'upbeat' it moves unexpectedly to the double subdominant B flat major and through this into the lower regions of the circle of fifths. This harmonic change is especially conspicuous after the previous introduction, which shifts between A minor, pentatonicism and C major. Moreover, it is strongly emphasized by the isolated deployment of the full wind section. The sense of 'upsurge' [*Aufschwung*], evoked by the motifs of the instrumental introduction and by the ascending triads (plus leading note) in the woodwind, bars 20–22, is countered by a descending, chromatic melodic line in first violins and a chromatically infused horn figure falling through a tenth (bars 25–29) – a 'katabasis' *par excellence*.[8] The second, varied entry of the voice (bar 28) leads back to the tonic A minor, its highest note once again in the subdominant region of D major, thereby suggesting A major as the immediate goal. As with the rising fourth at the beginning, here the voice also reflects the influence of the model through the embellishment of the word 'sing' (bar 31). Although this is reminiscent of Mahler's famous turn figure which characterizes the beginning of the final movement, by now even this passage seems ambivalent.

The melodic character of the next two lines of the song (bars 37–48) stresses the contrasting words 'sorrow' [*Kummer*] and 'bursting with laughter' [*auflachend*] through musical figures: on the one hand by the leap of an augmented interval with subsequent Phrygian second (bars 38–39), and on the other hand through an *exclamatio* – a rising triadic figure stretching over a tenth (bars 41–42). The word 'resound' [*klingen*] is, by contrast, characterized onomatopoeically through sweeping – though harmonically overcast – harp arpeggios (B flat minor, G flat major, inverted seventh chord (B flat–D–G–E), and the subdominant region of B flat major (bars 45–52)). Mahler altered the text of these two lines so that *Kummer* and *auflachend* were placed in direct conflict; through the accentuation of this contrast he harked back to an essential structuring process of the *Wunderhorn* years – Jean Paul's idea of 'humour' as the contrast between the tragic and the light-hearted.[9]

If the first two lines of the song convey a certain sense of 'upsurge' (the striking up of a drinking song) – albeit in an ambivalent way – and if the following two lines present a contrast to this, then the penultimate two lines ('When sorrow approaches, the gardens of the soul lie desolate' ['Wenn der Kummer naht, Liegen wüst die Gärten der Seele']) are composed in a manner expressive of 'sorrow': the instrumental motif from the beginning of the introduction (bars 2–3 in the horns) is transformed into a figure containing a

---

[8] *Katabasis* is a back-formation from *katabatic*, a meteorological term referring to the effects of the downward flow of air (from the Greek *katabatikos* meaning 'go down').

[9] See Schadendorff, 1995, pp. 39–59, and Schmierer, 1988.

minor third and minor second (first violin, bar 54, subsequently varied leading into the vocal phrase beginning at bar 56), and G minor becomes the prevailing key, ultimately defining the character of the refrain as well ('Dark is life, and so is death' ['Dunkel ist das Leben, ist der Tod'] (bars 81–89)). The phrase 'Joy and song fade away and die' ['Welkt hin und stirbt die Freude, der Gesang'] (bars 67–74) – a rhythmically augmented variant of the opening vocal motif now leading into yet deeper regions of the circle of fifths (A flat major) – demonstrates a dialectical combination typical of Mahler: the striking up of the drinking song is seen to be at one with its silencing. Here the ambivalence that is latent right from the beginning is, as it were, reinforced.

The conflicts of the first verse – the presentation of a sphere that is 'symbolic of life' and one which is 'symbolic of death'[10] – do not define the second verse, which is characterized instead by the 'sphere of life' (until the refrain). The distinctly word-oriented setting of the first verse scarcely leads one to expect a strophic resumption of its compositional design in the second verse. Nevertheless, the melodic lines of the first verse are taken up in the second verse and altered only to a limited extent – not because of the content of the text, but primarily owing to its structure. The first alteration concerns the beginning (bar 112): the melodic ascent occurs a tone lower since the interlude (or rather introduction) does not modulate back to the tonic but remains in G minor, the key in which the first verse had ended. Because of the brevity of the first line of text, the motif is also shorter. The following line leads melodically back to the tonic through the lengthening of the chromatic motif by three additional notes (bars 117–19).

The readjustment to the altered content is exceedingly subtle, as – above all in the instrumental writing – features of the symbolic 'sphere of life' are introduced and those 'symbolic of death' are eliminated. At the high point of the first line (here at the note F) a 'safer' harmonic variant appears, not a double subdominant but simply a dominant seventh chord (bar 113), which is also given less instrumental emphasis: the upper strings instead play a somewhat more pronounced *exclamatio* appropriate to the cry 'Master of this house!' [*Herr dieses Haus!*] with its exclamation mark, which is then taken up by the lower strings, bassoons and bass clarinet, and combined with the varied opening motif in horns (bar 114) that had symbolized the 'upsurge' at the beginning of the movement. In what follows, the horns do not have the chromatic '*katabasis*', and at the end of the second line (bar 124) the emphatic upbeat (likewise an *exclamatio*) of the introduction, which was not present in the first verse, recurs. However, it is interesting that one of the less obvious elements of the first verse – the harp accompaniment, which at most had accentuated the melodic high points – now

---

[10] Danuser, 1986, pp. 35–37, speaks of a dialectical relationship between 'prevailing moods symbolic of life' and 'symbolic of death' [*lebenssymbolische* and *todessymbolische Grundtöne*].

takes on an interpretative role at the word 'fullness' [*Fülle*] (bars 121–22); in other words, it is conceivable that it was included in the first verse with a clear view to its use in the second.

During the next section (which had formed a contrast in the corresponding part of the first verse) the 'sphere of life' is suggested musically by the opening motif, which initially remains the same as before. Because of the longer text, additional melodic lines are necessary, the last of which, 'These are the things' [*das sind die Dinge*] (bars 145–50) now anticipates the final section of the second verse. The harp accompaniment – previously at the word 'resound' [*klingen*] – now fits well with the reference to the strumming of the lute, and is doubled in length accordingly (bars 137–52), though B flat major initially replaces B flat minor. The fact that the final section – which in the first verse had seemed to point most clearly towards the negative sphere – is here varied only very little indicates the ambivalence of Mahler's compositional method, which at this point lies somewhere between responding to the demands of the text and responding to those of the constructive musical process. That which had previously expressed a 'sorrow' [*Kummer*] (bars 56–74), bringing an end to joy, is now used to express something contradictory: the 'wine' [*Wein*] that is 'worth more' [*mehr wert*] than 'all the kingdoms of this earth!' [*alle Reiche dieser Erde!*] (bars 156–74). The fair copy of the score shows that Mahler clearly did not want to vary this section to match the text but rather to repeat it exactly: the section was at first shorter, because Mahler had not noticed that the text was shorter than that of the first verse. In order to preserve the design, the four missing bars were added later and words of the text repeated.[11]

Just as in the first of the *Kindertotenlieder*, the third verse displays the greatest degree of deviation from the model. In contrast to the previous verses, its individual sections are not preserved in their original sequence. The motifs of the verse are instead freely combined, which is why in terms of sonata-form categories this section has also been described as a development. An additional motif appears, and this is likewise typical of a development section. However, if one thinks in terms of traditional Lied categories one would be more likely – particularly in view of the form of the vocal part – to speak in terms of a contrast, and to take an AABA form with unchanging interludes as one's point of departure. But since Mahler's vocal and instrumental writing are always closely connected to each other, the verses of the song are constructed not just from the vocal part but from the whole vocal–instrumental complex; in other words they encompass introductions, interludes and postludes.[12] In this respect, through its varied development of the material from the introduction, the third verse is not in conflict with the strophic model but rather is integrated into it. The greatest

---

[11]   This passage in the fair copy of the score is referred to in Danuser, 1986, p. 44.

[12]   See the observations made in Schmierer, 1991, pp. 212–20, in relation to 'Nun will die Sonn' so hell aufgeh'n'.

divergence from the strophic model – the beginning of the vocal part in the third verse 'The firmament is eternally blue' [*Das Firmament blaut ewig*] (bars 263–67) – clearly functions as a signal in that it points forward to a central passage in the final movement, anticipating its 'farewell melody' (compare bar 460 of 'Der Abschied').[13] When the allusion becomes melodically less obvious, it is established through the text (first movement: 'and the earth will long stand firm and blossom in spring' ['und die Erde wird lange fest steh'n und aufblüh'n im Lenz'] (bars 268–81); sixth movement: 'The dear earth everywhere blossoms in spring and grows green again!' ['Die liebe Erde allüberall blüht auf im Lenz und grünt aufs neu!'] (bars 459–76)). Nevertheless it is only against the background of the strophic model that the new melody seems so conspicuous and significant. The deviation is thus something exceptional, emphasized even more by the relatively sparse accompaniment which allows the voice to come completely to the fore.

After the initial contrast, though, a reattachment to the strophic model takes place in the voice: the phrases 'is eternally blue' [*blaut ewig*] and 'and the earth' [*und die Erde*] refer back to the frequently repeated motif of the second half of the second verse ('is worth more' [*ist mehr wert*] (bars 162–65)), which in turn originated from the corresponding passage of the first verse 'the gardens of the soul' [*die Gärten der Seele*] (bars 62–65)). With this motif, then, the second section of the third verse begins, continuing as in the second verse with the ascending motif on 'for how long do you live?' [*wie lang lebst denn du?*] (bars 298–302), a variant of the opening vocal motif of the movement which is also made clear by the unusual harmony (here the progression from B flat minor to C flat minor at the high point of the phrase). After this the slightly varied second line of the strophic model follows with its attendant instrumental parts at 'Not for a hundred years may you take delight' ['Nicht hundert Jahre darfst du dich ergötzen'] (bars 307–14).

The process of varying the strophic model in the fourth verse resembles that of the third verse in the first of the *Kindertotenlieder*: the voice is inserted into the instrumental texture of the introduction, not with its strophic melody but – at least at the beginning – with a different melody which takes up instrumental motifs from the introductory material (in the first of the *Kindertotenlieder* it is the interlude that has a text sung to it). It is notable that the '*katabasis*' presented in the first verse is strengthened here as the voice joins in the downward plunge at 'crouches a mad, spectral figure' [*hockt eine wild-gespenstische Gestalt*] (bars 340–44). In view of this, the fourth verse appears to be not so much a reprise as a continuation of the development (the concluding refrain was also missing from verse three), the effect of a true reprise occurring only with the beginning of the 'vocal verse' at the words 'Now take the wine!' [*Jetzt nehmt den Wein!*] (bars 367–70), where the gesture of the drinking song is adopted once more. The

---

13 This connection was pointed out for the first time in Vill, 1979, p. 167.

'actual' verse is now greatly abbreviated, containing only two vocal lines and the refrain. The considerable subtlety of Mahler's strophic method is evident in this fourth verse: the most conflicting levels of expression are integrated within the strophic model, as a result of which the symbolic 'sphere of life', which is clearly expressed at the beginning, appears ambivalent; the 'upsurge' is revoked both through recourse to the sphere symbolizing death and through accentuation of the '*katabasis*'.

The application of the strophic model in the first movement of *Das Lied von der Erde* therefore has multiple functions. In the first place, it forms a kind of semantic model for the 'framework' of the song: a drinking song starts up, and drinking songs are mostly strophic. In the second place, repetition is pre-programmed by the strophic model, and the effect of this on the intensification of expression should in one respect not be underestimated: despite all its complexity the music is extraordinarily memorable, and this is why the very last exhortation 'Now take the wine!' appears as an intensified reprise, summarizing the foregoing progress of the music since it has already been heard several times embedded within different contexts. The unfolding of the movement consists precisely in this specific kind of varied treatment of the strophic model. In the third place, the strophic model provided the best means for Mahler to implement his unique kind of variation. Within the structure of the vocal–instrumental verse, particular elements of the musical texture – depending on the content of the text – are emphasized or taken up by the voice. Actual deviations from the model, such as the vocal part at the beginning of the third verse, seem especially prominent and fulfil a kind of signalling function for the overall cyclic form of the work. In the fourth place, the strophic model offered the possibility of framing the textual ambivalence in subtly differing ways. Prerequisites for this were both a multi-layered texture in the first verse, which allowed the various components to be reinforced or reduced without, in principle, infringing the model, and the self-evident fact that the model exists not just in the vocal part but in the whole vocal–instrumental complex. Mahler's compositional interaction with the model and all its intricacies in the first movement of his last vocal work not only demonstrated an extremely idiosyncratic and deeply reflective approach to handed-down models at a point in history when they were already collapsing, but also intensified that very expressivity which, among other things, was generated by the model itself.

Chapter Ten

Theme, Thematic Process and Variant Form in the Andante Moderato of Mahler's Sixth Symphony[1]

JAMES BUHLER

In an oft-cited story Alma Mahler describes the Sixth Symphony in terms that suggest an autobiographical basis for the work:

> After he had drafted the first movement, Mahler came down from the woods and said, 'I have tried to capture you in a theme – whether I have succeeded, I don't know. You will have to put up with it'.
>
> It is the long, spirited [*schwungvoll*] theme of the first movement of the Sixth Symphony. In the third movement he depicts the arhythmic playing of both small children, tottering through the sand. Horrible – these children's voices become more and more tragic, and at the close a dying little voice whimpers. In the last movement he describes himself and his downfall or, as he said later, the downfall of his hero. 'The hero who receives three blows from fate, the third of which fells him like a tree.' These are Mahler's words.
>
> (Mahler, 1940, p. 90; see Mahler, 1990, p. 70)[2]

Alma's tale paints the Symphony as 'a sort of terrifying *Sinfonia domestica*', to use Warren Darcy's *bon mot* (2001, p. 49), and most analyses of the Sixth, even of individual movements, have been driven, explicitly or not, by the basic autobiographical narrative that she sketches. Her story, however, contains an important lacuna. She tells us that the first movement paints her musical portrait; she implies that the third movement (by which she apparently means the Scherzo) contains a sketch of their children; and the Finale is a prophetic self-portrait of Mahler himself. What is missing in this account is any indication of the significance of the Andante moderato itself. This movement escapes the portrait gallery.

---

[1] I would like to thank K.M. Knittel for extremely helpful comments on various aspects of this project as well as her willingness to share her extensive collection of Mahler reviews.
[2] The published English translation of Mahler, 1940, is not always reliable. The above translation is based on that given in Floros, 1994, p. 163.

Strikingly, her lacuna is mirrored for the most part in the critical literature on the Symphony, which opts to read the Andante as a dream world, a place apart from the tragedy that unfolds in the rest of the Symphony. Early critics, according to Hans-Peter Jülg, read this contrast in terms of the 'conceptual field of "longing, quiet and beauty"' ['Begriffsfeldes "Sehnsucht, Ruhe und Schönheit"'] (1986, p. 98). Thus for Richard Specht the opening violin line is sung 'quietly, mildly and filled with joy' ['Ruhig, mild und friedenvoll singen die Geigen'] (1906, p. 23, cited in Jülg, 1986, p. 97), and the movement as a whole is 'a song of solitude' (cited in La Grange, 1999, p. 827) that enacts 'a flight from the world to a dream island of longing' ['Weltflucht auf eine geträumte Insel der Sehnsucht'] (Specht, 1913, p. 282, cited in Jülg, 1986, pp. 97–98); for Karl Weigl, the movement is 'a piece of deepest quiet' ['Ein Stück von tiefster Ruhe'], where 'nature's voice of rural seclusion' resounds 'with its undisturbed joy' ['die Naturstimmung einer ländlichen Zurückgezogenheit mit ihrem ungestörten Glück'] (Weigl, 1910, p. 120, cited in Jülg, 1986, p. 97). Similarly, Albert Kauders (1907) says that 'the whole movement breathes happy peace, inner bliss' ['Der ganze Satz atmet glücklichen Frieden, innerliche Beseligung']. Julius Korngold (1907) writes that

> In the Andante (E flat major), mild, pastoral tones are struck. The hero flees to the bosom of nature, and this escape was of much benefit to the composer too, who always listened happily to the sounds of nature. A gentle lyricism holds sway, no rough accent breaks through the mood.[3]

For these critics, the Andante offers a beautiful oasis of enchanted happiness. Yet the dialectics of beauty are such that it can end in longing only to the extent that it remains a dream, external to the world. Jülg (1986, p. 98) explains the relationship thus:

> The 'beauty' is distant from reality, contrary to the real world and to what drives the world. Yet longing after 'beauty', after the 'other' can end only painfully since the 'other' cannot be permanent.[4]

More recent criticism has likewise emphasized the remoteness of the movement from the rest of the Symphony, though it tends to frame these issues in terms of formal contrast. Robert Samuels, for instance, writes that

> the Andante ... appears isolated from the rest of the work. Its tonality, melodic profile and mood ... all oppose the content of the other three

---

[3] 'Im Andante (Es-dur) sind milde, pastorale Töne angeschlagen. Der Held flüchtet sich an den Busen der Natur, und dieser Ausflug bekommt auch dem Komponisten wohl, der immer mit Glück den Naturlauten gelauscht hat. Eine zarte Lyrik behauptet den Platz, kein schroffer Akzent durchbricht die Stimmung.'

[4] 'Das "Schöne" ist fern der Wirklichkeit, konträr zur Realwelt und zum Weltgetriebe. Doch kann die Sehnsucht nach dem "Schönen", dem "Anderen", nur schmerzlich enden, da das "Andere" nicht von Dauer sein kann.'

movements, and in addition exhibit a closure of gesture which encourages
the view of the movement as almost a separate *Characterstück*.

(1995, p. 18)

Indeed for Constantin Floros its opening segment specifically suggests a song
without words, 'like the Adagietto of the Fifth and the Andante amoroso of the
Seventh' (1994, p. 176). David Matthews (1999, p. 373) links the isolation
directly to the way in which the movement displaces the struggle between A
major and A minor that otherwise controls the Symphony: 'The Andante's E♭
major, and the whole idyllic character of the movement, "lost to the world", like
Mahler's Rückert song, has once again caused us to forget the fundamental tonal
conflict between A major and A minor.' Darcy too sees tonal issues as central to
the movement's isolation, but for him the issue is as much tone as tonality, its
displacement of tonal turmoil: 'Only the E♭-major slow movement, Andante
moderato, seems isolated from the tonal strife of the rest of the symphony,
whether it is performed before or after the scherzo' (2001, p. 50). Darcy here
echoes many critics who see Mahler's indecision on the placement of the
movement as a sign of its profound otherness within the space of the Symphony.
Hans Redlich, for instance, writes:

> The variable position of the Andante as part of the whole symphonic
> structure derives from the fact that it alone is conceived as an 'Intermezzo'
> with only tenuous thematic interrelations to the rest of the symphony.

(1963, p. 253)

Henry-Louis de La Grange concurs with Redlich:

> This movement brings to the symphony's dark and bleak world its only
> moment of true calm. It is also the only one which does not share motifs with
> the others, the cowbells being one of the few common features.

(1999, p. 827)

The conceptual field has shifted from longing, quietude and beauty to formal
contrast, isolation and character piece – a shift that only barely conceals an
anxiety over the apparent lack of integration of the Andante into the Symphony.
This anxiety finds a concrete discursive outlet in the theme. As Samuels notes:

> the theme has attracted a fair amount of comment, and indeed disquiet, from
> analysts. The feature at which most writers have balked is the simple and
> clear-cut cadence in b. 10, which gives the theme its *volksliedhaft* character,
> but stands at odds with its use as a symphonic subject.

(1995, p. 59)

More precisely most critics balk at its sentimentality, which is seemingly too
dainty and light for the *gravitas* of a twentieth-century symphony. The central
issue has revolved around the extent to which the theme is sentimental, whether
this sentimental quality makes it banal, what sentimentality or triviality might
signify, and how exactly Mahler's irony intersects with all of the above, in itself

and in the movement as a whole. Hans Redlich, for instance, takes the sentimental quality of the theme for granted: 'The Andante's chief melody with the disarming sentimentality of its initial up-beat derives much from the tradition of lesser Romantics like Flotow, Kirchner and Lassen' (1968, p. xii). Undoubtedly the melody, shown in Ex. 10.1, opens with a gesture of calculated simplicity reminiscent of a nocturne – or at least a serenade: tonic pedal and wide-spaced, piano-like figurations. The only complication in these opening bars is the lowered $\hat{2}$ which is quickly absorbed as a piquant element of colour. The overall sense of this basic idea is one of stasis and contentment. Indeed Robert Hirschfeld, that remarkably astute but wholly ambivalent contemporary critic of Mahler, hears the entire theme as being saved from the drawing room only by its accumulation of unexpected chromatic inflections:

> One would be inclined to ascribe the theme to a salon piece or perhaps a sonatina by Fritz Spindler, Op. 389 (or some such number found only in the realm of [musical] mass production), were it not for the fact that in the key of E flat major there are small downward shifts of pitch from F to F flat and from G to G flat. Suddenly inflected in this manner, triviality assumes an interesting appearance and we are drawn towards something individual. The truly creative element of Mahler's nature, leaving aside the percussion, lies in that F flat or G flat. What then follows loses itself in unconnected empty formalities. Every material element of sound in this movement is technically perfect and remains at the highest level of modern *Kapellmeister* culture.
>
> (1907)[5]

Hirschfeld's idea, though stated somewhat sarcastically and no doubt intended as an indictment, is that the music is a staging of domestic tranquillity as seen from outside. We hear Spindler's lovely *Abendslied*, Op. 389 from an external perspective, through the filter of the chromatic impositions, which subjectivize the hearing and place the drawing room beyond reach. Put this way, the perspective embodied in the thematic process is similar to the opening of the Wayfarer songs, if not as clearly marked. An empathetic effect is achieved through irony: music indifferent to the situation is inflected, subjectively altered to take account of the situation. The alteration serves to mark a loss, a region of inaccessibility, which the music laments with a release of pathos. However, Hirschfeld considers that this pathos remains only a deviation for effect, the mark of a mere technician rather than an artist.

---

5 'Das Thema möchte man einem Salonstück oder einer Sonatine von Fritz Spindler op. 389 (oder sonst einer Nummer in der Region der Massenproduktion) zuschreiben, wenn in dem Es-dur ein Nötlein nicht von f aus fes und eines von g auf ges herabgerutscht wäre. So aber macht die Trivialität, plötzlich zuckend, eine interessante Miene, und wir werden auf eine Individualität gewiesen. Das eigentlich Schöpferische in der Mahlerschen Natur, wenn wir vom Schlagwerk absehen wollen, beruht in jenem fes oder ges. Was dann folgt, verliert sich in zusammenhanglosem Formelkram. Alles materielle Klangwesen in diesem Satze ist technisch vollkommen und hält sich auf der Höhe der modernen Kapellmeisterkultur.'

Sixth Symphony, Andante Moderato, main theme, bars 1–10. Analysis of period form after Jülg, 1986, pp. 100–103, and Darcy, 2001, p. 58

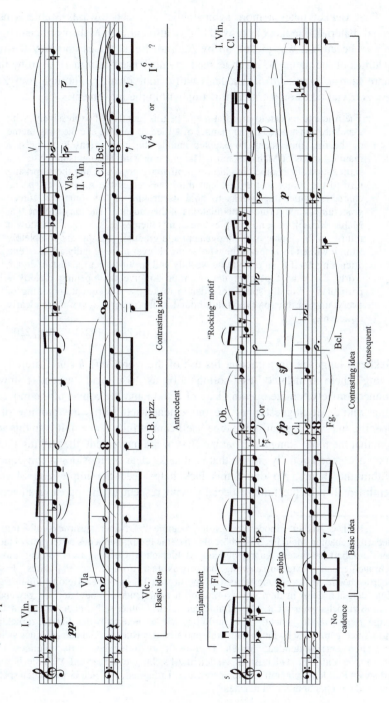

Paul Bekker takes a more sympathetic approach towards Mahler's use of trivial material, one that has proved highly influential in Mahler criticism at least in part because it was picked up by Adorno. Bekker does not deny the trivial qualities of the theme so much as read triviality itself as a mark of irony that is more than a mere sign of Mahler's wilful individuality. Through irony, what seems trivial takes on a critical function within the movement:

> The Andante moderato in E flat major begins 'gently but expressively' with a melody constructed in the manner of a Lied. It cannot, like the song theme of the first movement, be counted among the most intensely propulsive manifestations of Mahler's spirit. The opening with its languishing rise of a sixth sounds like something almost ironizingly popular. Only the surprising turn to the minor in the first and third bars gives the melody its special character, which then seeks to hold its ground in the somewhat forced gracefulness and tortuous modulations of the cadence. One may assume that Mahler himself took no real pleasure in this theme. It is conspicuous how it returns in the course of the movement and gradually disappears completely from it while the image of the whole unfolds ever more grandly as an ascent, alienating itself from everything worldly and striving after the distant dream world. Or was it perhaps the intention to give the opening melody a particularly worldly sound in order to make the subsequent forgetting of everything earthly, of everything bound to the material, even more clearly noticeable?
>
> (Bekker, [1921] 1969, p. 220)[6]

Bekker's language, in particular his use of the word *Aufschwung* (literally 'up-swing', here translated less colloquially as 'rise' and 'ascent'), draws a connection between the opening leap of a sixth and the course of the movement as a whole. He suggests that the movement itself fulfils the promise of that opening interval, a promise the tune itself cannot fully redeem. It is in this sense, too, that the motif 'languishes' at the start of the movement: the striking rise of a sixth is compositionally empty; that is, it lacks clear compositional consequences within the theme. No doubt this lack helps feed the impression of reified sentimentality in the tune, especially with respect to the opening antecedent,

---

6 'Das Andante moderato, Es-dur, beginnt "zart aber ausdrucksvoll" mit einer liedartig gebauten Melodie. Sie gehört gleich dem Gesangthema des ersten Satzes nicht zu den treibhaft stärksten Kundgebungen Mahlerschen Geistes. Der Anfang mit dem schmachtenden Sextenaufschwung hat etwas fast ironisierend Populäres. Erst die überraschende Mollwendung im ersten und dritten Takt gibt der Melodie einen eigenen Zug, der sich dann in dem etwas erzwungen anmutenden, modulatorisch gewundenen Schluß zu behaupten sucht. Man könnte vermuten, Mahler selbst habe an diesem Thema keine reine Freude gehabt. Es is auffällig, wie er innerhalb des Satzes zurücktreten, allmählich ganz verschwinden läßt, während sich das Bild des Ganzen als eines sich dem Irdischen entfremdenden, fernen Traumwelt zustrebenden Aufschwunges immer großartiger entfaltet. Oder ist es vielleicht Absicht, die der ersten Melodie besonders irdischen Beiklang gibt, um das Vergessen alles Erdhaften, stofflich Gebundenen späterhin um so deutlicher spürbar zu machen?'

which never reaches back up above B flat; the high E flat remains quite isolated until the consequent, which likewise leaves its high G unintegrated into the rest of the phrase. For Bekker the theme exists not only to mark an unsettling lack in the world, as it were, but also to testify to a real longing to fill the empty gesture with meaning. He thus reads the trivial quality of the theme as necessary for expressing the Andante's idea of lack and displacement. The theme is an image of the world, its triviality a reflection of the world's hollow demands, its ultimate indifference to meaning. As with Hirschfeld, only the chromatic alterations in bars 1 and 3 reveal Mahler's individuality and his subjective intervention, and bear witness to any resistance to this indifference. Though starting from the theme, the movement is not for Bekker really about the theme, which 'gradually disappears' and is forgotten; rather the movement is about the fulfilment offered by the 'distant dream world', which nevertheless gets its impetus from the longing, languishing quality of the opening leap. In other words this idea cannot be articulated without the theme, indeed without its trivial, worldly emptiness. Bekker breaks off his line of thinking here and takes refuge in a presentation of the opening theme, but in fact this offers only apparent sanctuary: 'So sing the violins', he continues, giving an example of the violin part for bars 1–7, which leaves the high D hanging tantalizingly in mid-air. Bekker's commentary hardly seems able to continue, his discourse profoundly marked by the dark cloud that passes over bar 7 where the strings essentially just give up, song gives way to painful chromaticism, the string sound turns to winds and a new rocking motif is introduced:

> Here the violin tune falters, as if it could no longer find its way through the painfully searching chromaticism. The winds lead back to E flat major with a rocking quaver motif that will emerge later on as something significant.
>
> (Ibid.)[7]

Many critics have nevertheless remained ambivalent about Bekker's approach, which presumes a basic element of triviality and reified sentimentality in the theme itself. Arnold Schoenberg, for instance, works to redeem the theme by emphasizing the logic of the deviations that disturb the otherwise placid surface. Schoenberg focusses on the unusual quality of the expansion of its antecedent into a four-and-a-half-bar phrase and the answering consequent that brings a strong cadential articulation on the downbeat of bar 10. Schoenberg explicates the logic of these expansions to illustrate the structural function of Mahler's deviations. He rewrites the theme into 'normal' four-bar phrases which, whether banal in themselves or not, show how the expansions interact with each other across the period structure:

---

[7] 'So singen die Geigen: [Example of the first violin part of bars 1–7] Hier stockt der Violingesang, als fände er sich in der etwas verquält suchenden Chromatik nicht mehr zurecht. Die Bläser führen mit einem weiterhin bedeutsam hervortretenden wiegenden Achtelmotiv zurück nach Es-dur.'

It is wondrous how these deviations from the conventional balance each other, even postulate each other. This demonstrates a most highly developed feeling for form, such as one finds only in the great masterworks. This is not the trick [*Kunststück*] of a 'technician' – a master would not succeed were he to aim at it. These are inspirations [*Einfälle*] that are beyond the control of consciousness, inspirations that come only to the genius, who feels them unconsciously and formulates solutions without noticing that a problem has been posed.

(Schoenberg, 1912/1948, cited in Jülg, 1986, p. 101)[8]

Schoenberg emphasizes Mahler's compositional intuition, the *Einfälle* or inspired ideas that intrude in or 'fall into' the music as if from outside. Schoenberg explicitly distances an *Einfall* from the conscious compositional intellect which, if untouched by inspired imagination, can produce only *Kunststücke* – effective but ultimately derivative tricks of the trade that are innately reified to the extent that they rest on subjective intention, on a predictable calculus of effect that determines a priori what a particular trick will impart to the music. From this perspective the problem with interpreting the melody as Hirschfeld and to a lesser extent Bekker do is that it reads the ironizing marks of the chromatic inflections too subjectively, too much as *Kunststücke* that simply serve to stamp the music with the composer's wilful individuality. The theme becomes more 'interesting' perhaps, and less immediately banal, but at the cost of intellectualizing it, of reducing it to a mere technical feat of compositional engineering – recall Hirschfeld's charge of *Kapellmeister* music above – that can only mask the underlying banality but never transform it (see Newlin, 1950, p. 14). By contrast Schoenberg proceeds by showing an underlying logic to the deviations in the theme. This logic, Schoenberg asserts, ensures that the theme is not in fact banal, that its deviations are compositionally integrated and coherent. The logic nevertheless unfolds as a product of genius, more intuitive than intellectual; that is, it is not fully calculable though it is rational. In this way the deviations become *Einfälle*: they inspire Mahler's music, Schoenberg implicitly claims, with the breath of *Geist*.

Adorno seems to presuppose much of Schoenberg's analysis but he may have been concerned that the way Schoenberg sets the deviations off against one another to balance the compositional ledger covertly infiltrates a strictly calculable element into the analysis. In any event Adorno gives Schoenberg's

---

8 'Es ist wundervoll, wie sich diese Abweichungen vom Konventionellen gegenseitig das Gleichgewicht halten, ja einander bedingen. Das beweist ein höchstentwickeltes Formgefühl, wie man es nur in den großen Meisterwerken findet. Das ist nicht etwa das Kunststück eines "Technikers" – einem Meister würde es nicht gelingen, wenn er es sich vornähme. Das sind Einfälle, die sich der Kontrolle des Bewußtseins entziehen, Einfälle, die nur dem Genie zukommen, das sie unbewußt empfängt und Lösungen produziert ohne zu bemerken, daß ein Problem vorgelegen hat.' For somewhat differing translations of this passage see Newlin, 1950, p. 23, and Stein, 1975, p. 462.

analysis a characteristic critical twist, reading ambivalence in the logic of the theme's expansions rather than the simple balance that Schoenberg does. The resulting interpretation merges elements of Bekker and Schoenberg:

> Paul Bekker – perhaps over sensitive to the fervent, grieving tone of its melody, reminiscent of the *Kindertotenlieder* – has criticized the triviality of the main theme of the Andante of the Sixth Symphony, which later soars magnificently towards fulfilment. Yet its powerful cantabile quality may not have satisfied Mahler himself. He therefore so arranged the ten-bar theme metrically as to produce ambivalences between the ends and beginnings of the phrases. The repetition of the opening idea falls on the third beat instead of the first, and so on a relatively weak part of the bar; metrical irregularity is the dowry which folksong-like melodies bring with them to symphonic prose.
>
> (Adorno, 1992a, p. 107)[9]

Adorno hears the tune as more *Volkslied* than salon music per se. That is, Adorno claims that Mahler has not corrected the deviations, that he has not remade the tune into a fully proper and upstanding melody in order to make it suitable for the salon. Mahler's compositional retouchings have been directed instead at increasing the ambivalent quality of the deviations, not eliminating them. Adorno draws particular attention to the subtle oddness of bar 5, in particular the way the cadential enjambment of the opening antecedent forces the restatement of the basic idea to enter in the middle of the bar. Interestingly, this particular deviation is 'corrected' in the third and last full statement of the theme (from bar 100) by elongating the cadential enjambment (bar 104) to a full bar so that it is no longer really an enjambment at all.

Ex. 10.2 compares the theme with its second variant, especially with respect to the handling of the joint between the phrases. With the tonic pedal preceding it, the expansion in bar 104 is almost superfluous in this context, and it is really the violin line rather than the remnant of the enjambment motif in the horn that controls the bar. The answering consequent (bar 105) – on the surface perhaps the most regular phrase of the movement – absorbs this expansion by taking over the gesture of enjambment; it sounds strangely curtailed partly because the leap to the D flat that initiates the contrasting idea enjambs the basic idea, encroaching on the end of the basic idea and not allowing it space to breathe. Despite its expansion and, as it were, normalization, the fifth bar of the theme

---

9 'Paul Bekker hat die Trivialität des Hauptthemas des später großartig sich aufschwingenden und erfüllenden Andantes aus der Sechsten Symphonie bemängelt; vielleicht allzu spröde gegen den trübselig innigen Ton der Kindertotenlieder in jener Melodie. Doch mochte ihre ohrenfällige Gesanglichkeit Mahler selbst nicht befriedigen. Er hat darum das zehntaktige Thema metrisch so disponiert, daß sich Ambivalenzen zwischen Phrasenenden und -anfängen ergaben. Die Wiederholung des Anfangsgedankens fällt anstatt auf eins auf drei, also einen relativ schwachen Taktteil; metrische Irregularität ist die Mitgift, welche die volksliedhaften Melodien der symphonischen Prosa einbringen' (Adorno, 1960, p. 142, & 1970–86, vol. 12, p. 252).

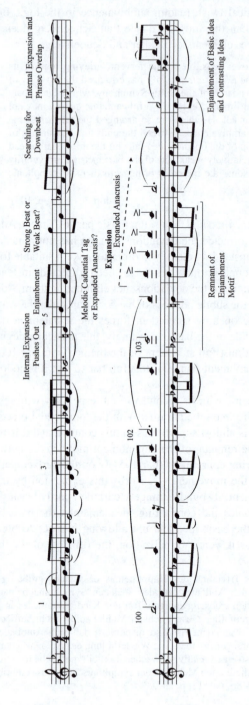

Ex. 10.2 Sixth Symphony, Andante Moderato: theme (bars 1–10) and second variant (bars 100–108) compared

(bar 104), too, seems even more ambivalent here, curiously detached from the antecedent because the descending crotchets in the violin, rather than the horn line which is the remnant of the old cadential descent, control the bar. Structurally the violin line serves to bridge the antecedent and consequent. If this bar, analogous with the function of the first half of bar 5, serves to bring the antecedent to some sort of cadence point, then the violin line itself also sounds like an expanded anacrusis to the downbeat of bar 105. The regularization of the phrase structure with respect to the bar lines has led to increased ambivalence, a point we will return to below.

Jülg adopts Adorno's idea of ambivalence and generalizes it. He offers a lengthy analysis of the theme divided into four two-bar phrases which are organized at a higher level as a period. The theme of the Andante, he writes:

> begins with an ascending, upbeat scalic motif that serves as preparation for the leap of a sixth. This sixth leap constitutes an ascent and becomes the dominant figure of the first phrase, which finds its motivic endpoint in a descending line. The melodic shape thus describes a rising and falling linear motion.
>
> (1986, p. 100)[10]

Jülg draws attention to the apparent symmetry of the basic idea. The rising up-beat is answered by the descending, albeit chromatically inflected, line in bar 1, and this symmetry nicely frames the leap to and away from the high E flat, placing it on a kind of pedestal. Surprisingly, in view of his close attention to the theme as a whole, Jülg does not mention the F flat which is the only element that at all disturbs the placid diatonic premise. However, the contrasting idea (labelled in Ex. 10.1) begins to call this premise into question. Jülg, like Schoenberg, concentrates on the internal phrase expansion in bar 4:

> The first expansion [of the phrase structure] is found in the second phrase of the antecedent (bars 2^4–5^2). It lengthens the phrase by half a bar to two and a half bars. The caesura that, in a four-square rhythm, appears in the fourth bar is stretched out into the next bar through the dotted minim in bar 4. The crescendo of the first violins, continued by the remaining strings and two B flat clarinets, clarifies the phrase extension, as does the absence of a bass note on the downbeat of bar 5. The expansion of the antecedent is felt as a disturbance of the classical tonal idiom.
>
> (Ibid., p. 101)[11]

---

[10] 'Es beginnt mit einem auftaktigen, skalenartig aufwärtsschreitenden Motiv, das als Vorbereitung des Sextsprungs dient. Dieser einem Aufschwung gleichkommende Sextsprung wird zur dominierenden Figur der ersten Phrase, die in einer abwärtssteigenden Linie ihren motivischen Endpunkt findet. Der melodische Duktus beschreibt damit eine auf- und absteigende Linienführung.'

[11] 'In der zweiten Phrase des Vordersatzes (T. 2,4–5,2) findet sich die erste Dehnung. Sie verlängert die Phrase um einen halben Takt auf zweieinhalb Takte. Die Zäsur, die in der rhythmischen Quadratur nach vier Takten auftritt, wird somit durch die Punktierung der halben in T. 4 in den nächsten Takt hinausgezögert. Das Crescendo der 1. Violinen, das von den übrigen Streichern und zwei B-Klarinetten aufgegriffen wird,

Jülg is sensitive to the peculiarities of the expansion. The lack of strong bass articulation in bars 4–5, the disappearance of the cello figurations at the beginning of bar 5, and the continuity across the bar line provided by the low sustained fourth in the clarinets as well as the general crescendo all help link the expanded G flat–G appoggiatura figure with the descending motif in the first half of bar 5. The harmony in bar 4, he suggests, is also ambivalent. The diminished seventh A–G flat on the downbeat is enharmonically part of the dominant complex of G minor, the key of the second theme (from bar 22), and it is only the sustained B flat–E flat fourth in the low register that keeps us centred in E flat; the upper strings which resolve the diminished seventh upward as though the notes were A–F sharp are strongly suggestive, he thinks, of G minor: 'Consequently, the harmony of the bar has the most extreme double meaning' ['Die Harmonik des Taktes ist somit höchst doppeldeutig'] (ibid., p. 103). Jülg may overstate the extent to which this latent G minor progression in the strings poses a threat to the intelligibility of E flat major, but he nevertheless productively draws our attention to something unsettling within the harmony here. The pizzicato of the bass, which might have clarified the harmonic function, is conspicuously absent on the downbeat of bar 4. It is replaced by the bass clarinet, which sustains a B flat but in the register of the cello figure rather than the lower octave that has controlled the bass function. The result is a profound harmonic ambivalence: does the chord on the downbeat represent a secondary diminished seventh of B flat, as the spelling of the chord indicates, or a pivot-note-embellishing diminished chord of E flat (reading F sharp for G flat)? Moreover, even after it becomes clear that this bar is prolonging a second-inversion tonic triad, there remains an ambivalence of mode:

> After the resolution of the suspended A to B flat (bar 4³) there is a turn to the tonic minor (E flat minor) within the main tonality. On the fourth beat of the same bar the second suspension then resolves itself, the minor third becomes a major third, and the chord changes to E flat major. The ambivalent construction is able to veil the end of the phrase and push it out into the next bar.
>
> (Ibid., p. 101)[12]

The ambivalence runs still deeper, however: it remains uncertain whether the harmony in bar 4 is functionally a tonic or dominant. Since the E flat never descends as would be expected in a cadential six-four, and the rising line in the

---

verdeutlicht die Phrasenverlängerung ebenso wie die Aussparung des Baßtons in T. 5,1. Die Ausdehnung des Vordersatzes wird als Störung des klassisch-tonalen Idioms empfunden.'

[12] 'Nach der Auflösung des Vorhaltstons a nach b (T. 4,3) entsteht in der dritten Taktzeit die gleichnamige Mollwendung (es-Moll) der Haupttonart. In der vierten Zählzeit des gleichen Taktes löst sich dann der zweite Vorhaltston auf, die Mollterz wird zur Durterz, und der Akkord wandelt sich nach Es-Dur. Der ambivalente Aufbau vermag das Phrasenende zu verschleiern und in den nächsten Takt hinauszuschieben.'

second violins and violas moves to the sixth scale degree (readable as either the ninth of the dominant or a move into the subdominant region), even bar 5 does not really decide the harmony, which remains wonderfully suspended and lacking in any sense of a harmonic cadence right into the beginning of the next phrase which starts as though a harmonic elision has occurred. The enjambment in the phrase structure of bar 5 is likewise ambivalent, as Jülg explains:

> Even the beginning of the phrase repetition in bar 5^3 deviates, as it were, from the schema since it cannot start on the first beat of a bar owing to the extension of the phrase. It must make do with the relatively weak part of the bar, beat 3. The opening motif of the phrase repetition is related ambivalently to the previous phrase ending. The four-note descending scale segment (bar 5) not only represents the closing motif of the previous phrase, but also takes on the function of the 'full upbeat' of the phrase repetition. The adoption of the same bowing and once again the omission of the quaver figure in the cello can be regarded as further evidence of the ambivalent relations.
>
> (Ibid., pp. 101–2)[13]

Here Jülg hits on an important difference between the presentation of the basic idea in the antecedent and the consequent: the latter lacks the upbeat. Curiously this asymmetry has mostly been ignored by those discussing the theme, even though Hans Redlich, as mentioned above, has drawn attention precisely to the upbeat as a strong mark of sentimentality (1968, p. xii). Jülg's idea is that the suppression of the upbeat creates a further ambivalence in bar 5 since it means that the enjambment in the first half of the bar must serve not only as the close of the antecedent but also as an extended anacrusis of the consequent. To the extent that the enjambed motif does not function as an upbeat, the beginning of the consequent catches us by surprise. Jülg continues:

> Only the dynamic reduction to *pp subito* (bar 5^3) and the resumption of the quaver figure with its accompanying E flat bass note defines the rise of a sixth as a phrase repetition. The ambivalent relations of the fifth bar lead to metrical irregularities [i.e. irregularities in the phrase structure]. The arsis of the phrase repetition falls on the third beat; the 'upbeat' scale segment, by contrast, falls on beat 1. The inner musical definitions run counter to the metrical framework of the opening phrase and the 4/4 time signature.
>
> (1986, p. 102)[14]

---

[13] 'Auch der Beginn der Phrasenwiederholung in T. 5,3 weicht gleichsam vom Schema ab, da er aufgrund der Phrasenverlängerung nicht auf der Taktzeit 1 einsetzen kann. Ihm bleibt der relativ schwache Taktteil 3 vorbehalten. Das Anfangsmotive der Phrasenwiederholung verhält sich ambivalent zum vorangegangenen Phrasenende. Der viertönige, abwärtsgerichtete Skalenauschnitt (T. 5,1–2) stellt nicht nur das abschließende Motive der Gegenphrase dar, er übernimmt auch die Funktion des "volltaktigen Auftakts" der Phrasenwiederholung. Die Übernahme der gleichen Stricharten und das erneute Aussparung der Achtelfigur in den Violoncello können als weitere Indizien der ambivalenten Verhältnisse gewertet werden.'

[14] 'Erst die dynamische Reduction auf *pp subito* (T. 5,3) und die Wiederaufnahme

Like Adorno, Jülg notes how the enjambment in bar 5 reverses the metrical accents in the consequent phrase. What fell in the strong part of the bar in the antecedent now falls on the weak part of the bar. This disjunction between the immanent phrase structure and the external metrical structure is corrected, Jülg says, with the phrase expansion in bar 7, which Jülg also understands as an overlap between the end of the basic idea and the beginning of the contrasting idea:

> Even the consequent of the ten-bar period allows itself to be chopped up into two phrases: the first, from bar 5^3 to bar 7^2, carried in the melodic shape of the first violins, reveals itself as a variant of the opening phrase. Its end coincides with the second expansion, which, for its part, is designed as a phrase overlap.
>
> (Ibid.)[15]

Given his general attentiveness to such details it is surprising that Jülg does not mention the curious effect in the second half of bar 6: the melodic line here sounds extended and a little flaccid, as if the violins have suddenly become conscious of the fact that their phrase is out of alignment with the metrical structure. In any event, unlike the beginning of the consequent, which gives the impression of being a strong beat despite its metrical placement, the second half of bar 6 seems already metrically weak, especially compared with the downbeat of bar 2, the analogous place in the basic idea of the antecedent. The violins stir from their listless hesitancy only to leap recklessly for the downbeat after which they quit the tune for good. Jülg's response to bar 7 is curious:

> The surrender of the melodic line to the first oboe marks the element linking the phrases and at the same time the start of the closing phrase. The many disturbances within the idiomatic structure show that even the main theme of the slow movement follows no stereotypical formula. Although the principle of the rhythmic four-bar phrase is abandoned, the musical syntax still defines a period.
>
> (Ibid.)[16]

---

der Achtelfigur mit dem dazugehörigen Baßton Es definieren den Sextaufschwung als Phrasenwiederholung. Die ambivalenten Verhältnisse des fünften Taktes führen zu metrischen Irregularitäten. Die Arsis der Phrasenwiederholung fällt auf die Zählzeit 3, der "auftaktige" Skalenausschnitt dagegen auf 1. Die binnenmusikalischen Definitionen verlaufen konträr zur Metrik der Anfangsphrase und des Viervierteltaktes.'

15 'Auch der Nachsatz der zehntaktigen Periode läßt sich in zwei Phrasen zergliedern: die erste, von T. 5,3–7,2 und im melodischen Duktus von den 1. Violinen getragen, gibt sich als Variante der Anfangsphrase zu erkennen. Ihr Ende fällt mit der zweiten Dehnung zusammen, die ihrerseits phrasenüberlappend angelegt ist.'

16 'Die Übergabe der melodischen Linienführung an die 1. Oboe kennzeichnet gleichzeitig das phrasenverkettende Element und den Beginn der abschließenden Phrase. Die Vielzahl der Störungen innerhalb des idiomatischen Gefüges zeigt, daß auch das Hauptthema des langsamen Satzes keine stereotypen Formeln ausprägt. Obgleich das Prinzip der rhythmischen Quadratur aufgegeben wird, definiert die musikalische Syntax dennoch eine Periode.'

Much like Bekker, Jülg essentially gives up on trying to explain what happens at bar 7. It is almost as if the only fitting response to the intrusive strangeness of this moment is for the discourse to avert its eyes so as not to embarrass the music. Certainly Jülg's analytical priorities change radically. The detailed syntactical analysis suddenly gives way to vague generalities celebrating the theme's deviations from the stereotype. For whatever reason this moment exposes the raw nerve of banality, which Jülg feels he must address now so as to excise it as a foreign body. The ambivalences, he thinks, ensure that the theme is neither trivial nor banal. He then approaches bar 7 again, but from a different angle:

> The ambivalent relations within the phrases and the linking together of the same also become clear in the broken-up instrumentation. First of all the musical structure begins as a pure string statement into which individual winds are also integrated from the contrasting phrase onwards. Indeed the winds have already achieved dominance of the sonority by the concluding phrase so that the end of the period becomes a pure wind statement. The change in instrumentation and the overlaps within the phrases draw a true picture of the syntactic course.
>
> (Ibid.)[17]

Jülg draws attention to the slow instrumental dissolve from the strings to the winds in the course of the theme, a dissolve that quickly accelerates in bar 7 where the quick change of colour to a double-reed-dominated sonority is reminiscent of the dissolve from the trumpets to the oboes on the major–minor motto in the first movement (bars 59–60). The opening of the movement begins as though it might be a movement for strings like the Adagietto of the Fifth, and Jülg nicely captures this ambiguity in his language, using the phrase 'reiner Streichersatz' which might have been rendered as 'a movement purely for strings'. The string orchestration is also part of its initial sentimental tone, giving it the feeling of an intermezzo or, as many critics like to say (more than a bit defensively), 'a song without words', with its all too ambivalent allusion to Mendelssohn and everything that that implies. The string tone seems to set up the deflating expectation that we are dealing with a pretty, if unambitious, piece of genre painting. The winds begin to complicate this picture beginning with the first expansion in bar 4 where, as discussed above, the low clarinets enter as if to compensate for – or perhaps distract us from – the missing pizzicato bass on the downbeat, adding to the harmonic ambiguity of the sonority. The flute adds pastoral colouring to the opening of the consequent phrase but in a way that

---

[17] 'Die ambivalenten Verhältnisse innerhalb der Phrasen und die Verkettung derselben werden auch in der durchbrochenen Instrumentation deutlich. Zunächst beginnt das musikalische Gefüge als reiner Streichersatz, in welchen ab der Gegenphrase auch einzelne Bläser integriert werden. Doch schon in der abschließenden Phrase haben diese die klangliche Dominanz gewonnen, so daß das Periodenende zum reinen Bläsersatz wird. Der Wandel in der instrumentalen Besetzung und die Überlappungen innerhalb der Phrasen zeichnen ein getreues Abbild des syntaktischen Verlaufs.'

serves to underscore the isolation of the high G since it sustains the B flat across the violin leap in bar 5. The flute as it were highlights the structure of the melody, reinforcing the sense, already hinted at in Bekker's discussion, that the rising-sixth motif is merely ornamental, a striking effect that has been arbitrarily added for its piquant colouring rather than being integrated into the tune as an essential part of the compositional structure. While the repetition of the motif here is necessary for defining the parallel period, this only lays bare the character of empty formalism: any other striking effect might have filled out the period just as well. In this respect the flute in bar 5 represents a self-critical moment of orchestration: it bears witness here to the truth of the empty formalism of the period. Moreover, contrary to that of the opening motif the orchestration is compositionally integrated and carries explicit consequences for the theme. As Jülg points out, the flute prepares the shift to wind registration in bar 7. Ex. 10.3 suggests that it might even anticipate the basic gesture of the oboe line in bars 7–9: a held note followed by a line that drifts downwards.

Ex. 10.3 Sixth Symphony, Andante Moderato: the flute line (bars 6–7) as gestural anticipation of the oboe line (bars 7–9)

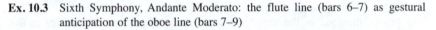

The overall idea may be one of using orchestration to compose out a process of disenchantment: the violins at the opening sing a sweet, sentimental song of arcadian bliss that they find impossible to complete on their own. In the course of the song the winds gently insinuate themselves into the edenic illusion; when the violins falter on the high D and the pastoral illusion nevertheless dissolves, the winds inflate and break through, sounding like an alien presence. If the oboe line, with its characteristic semiquaver rest that stops any sense of lyrical flow, is not wholly an instrumental gesture here, it does represent a break in the singing voice – more sob than song – until the actual cadential descent in bar 9. In this sense it is already a step towards disenchantment, a place where music ceases to sing. Interestingly the intrusion never seems threatening; indeed it almost sounds altruistic, since the winds lead the music safely through the harmonic thicket and back to familiar tonal ground where the strings can again strike a pastoral tone.

The harmonic process mirrors that of the instrumentation. Darcy explains the chord in bar 7 as a sort of cry of anguish, which bursts out when the theme can no longer bear the weight of chromatic alterations intruding from the minor mode:

> Although in E♭ major, the theme is shot through with minor-mode implications – the Neapolitan ♭2̂ in m. 1, the g♭¹ in m. 3, the c♮² in m. 6, and so on. The theme peaks with a sense of anguish in m. 7 on a drawn-out leading tone suspended over a Neapolitan sixth chord. The ensuing cadential descent unfolds a new two-note motive that suggests the old topos of a musical sigh (or gasp).
>
> (2001, pp. 58–59)

Like Hirschfeld and Bekker, Darcy is sensitive to the modal borrowings in the tune. For him these do not simply serve to prepare the harmonic tangle of bar 7 but also form ambivalent harmonies whose latent implications are realized in the course of the movement. Thus, according to Darcy, the F flat in bar 1 forms an implied dominant seventh with flat 5 which 'may resolve to the tonic of either E♭ or A major' (ibid., p. 59). Likewise the chord of bar 7 is enharmonic with the dominant seventh of A. Both A major and E major (as well as their minor complements), he notes, play important structural roles in the movement. He might have added the latent implication of the harmony in bar 4 which, as mentioned above, Jülg argues carries a suggestion of G minor, the key area of the second theme. One can, of course, multiply such relationships almost endlessly: as Ex. 10.4 shows, the C diminished chord above the pedal B flat in bar 8 is also the enharmonic leading-note diminished chord of C sharp minor, the final key of the second theme; similarly the strange inverted augmented sixth chord on the fourth beat of bar 8 is enharmonic with the dominant of B major, the key of the final statement of the theme in the movement; in this sense bars 7–9 might be taken as an anticipatory sketching out, in compressed form, of the harmonic trajectory of bars 124–60, which likewise makes its way from A to E flat via the keys of C sharp and B. With sufficient ingenuity and time one could no doubt show how the key plan of the entire movement grows secretly out of the harmonic quirks in the theme. However far-fetched such hidden organic relations might seem – and this one is certainly dubious on many counts – it does at least have the advantage of mirroring, in the analytical discourse, the fantastic quality of the passage itself. Darcy, on the contrary, proceeds in the opposite direction: his analysis offers harmonic clarity at the expense of effacing the disorienting tonal particularity of the passage: the quality of tonal intrusion. The intelligibility of the key takes analytical precedence over everything else. His analysis of the harmony in bar 7 as an intensified variant of the Neapolitan, while perhaps cogent on its own grounds, ignores entirely the marked change of texture, orchestration and gesture that also enters here and underscores a sense of

Ex. 10.4   Sixth Symphony, Andante Moderato: ambivalent harmonies in bars 7–10

disjuncture. Even in purely harmonic terms the chord in bar 7 remains functionally ambivalent despite Darcy's anxiously dismissive comment that 'the chord is clearly functioning as a tense predominant, not a dominant' (ibid, p. 59, n. 18). There is nothing especially clear about the chord, above all with respect to its functionality which has much the same sense of ambivalence as that of the Tristan chord. The analysis purchases its harmonic cogency by neutralizing the strangeness of the moment. The textual supplement of anguish is the only thing that alerts us that the shadow of something new and fantastic has fallen across the music here. In Darcy's linear analysis of the melody (given here as Ex. 10.5) the particularity of the rocking passage is if anything neutralized even further. He reads bars 7–9 as a prolongation of the 'anguished predominant' (ibid., p. 59). The whole passage oddly enough becomes nothing more than a somewhat elaborated cadential descent. The clarity offered by the graph, however, is false to the extent that it demands, as a Schenkerian graph must, that the music conform to the normative tonal syntax of the cadence. In fact the music is tonally

Ex. 10.5   Sixth Symphony, Andante Moderato, bars 1–10: linear analysis after Warren Darcy, 2001, p. 59; reprinted from *19th-Century Music*, 25 (1), winter 2001, by permission. © 2001 by the Regents of the University of California.

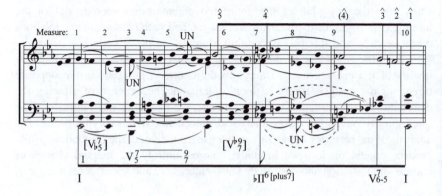

less clear and less focussed on the idea of cadential descent than the graph suggests, or to be more precise, the harmonic direction of the passage is not decisively committed to E flat until the rocking motif disappears, the cloud lifts and the oboe settles into the melodic cadential formula in bar 9. The graph therefore runs counter to the searching quality of the tonal expression here, which resists just the type of clear definition that the graph portrays. The musical process gives itself over, assimilates itself, to the alien sound of radical otherness as it exists in itself, and demands nothing of it, whereas for the sake of drawing out its coherent long line the graph does just the opposite, assimilating what is other by excising what it can and domesticating the rest through beams and slurs to the tonally rational world of all too clear auxiliary and passing motions. What Darcy himself makes of this difficulty is uncertain but he seems to realize that something is amiss, for a most remarkable paragraph lies sandwiched between his discussion of the chord in bar 7 as a Neapolitan with an added leading note and his surprisingly brief discussion of the graph. The bulk of it runs as follows:

> The expressive impact of this theme lies not so much in its phrase expansions or its modal mixture but in its pronounced sense of musical *strain* as it labors to uphold its major-mode premise, labors to avoid collapsing into minor. As a generalized structure, the parallel period, it might be argued, was an Enlightenment product, an expression of balance and symmetry. In other words, it had been essentially a strategy of *containment*, and Mahler may have imposed it here as an artificial constraint, forcing into an ironically positive mold music that is otherwise saturated with negative connotations. Behind such contradictory impulses, of course, lies the larger question of how facile Enlightenment symmetries – part of the long tradition of art music – could possibly be still appropriate or even casually available to the vigorously modernizing society of the early twentieth century. Could anyone in 1904, that is, still believe in good faith in the unforced simplicity and solace of the parallel period?
>
> (Ibid.)

Darcy's comments are directed at Mahler's critical use of the period. The period form itself, he suggests, has been put on display as an empty convention. Darcy mentions the 'strain' of the music and draws our attention to the sound of compositional labour that works to bridge the disjuncture between, on the one hand, the musical form of the period and, on the other, a musical content that chafes against the arbitrary imposition of that form. Like Hirschfeld and Bekker, Darcy hears the intervention of the composing hand especially prominently in the chromatic deviations, but interestingly he situates this intervention less on the side of the deviations, as do Hirschfeld and Bekker, than on the side of the period, which, he suggests, forces the music to honour obligations external – even contrary – to the demands of the material in itself. The mark of the composing hand is consequently also the sound of authoritarian control: the arbitrary imposition of the period form from above deforms the material so as to contain its energies within the socially acceptable boundaries that the form prescribes. The irony emerges, then, from our sense that the music nevertheless means something other than what it is permitted to say; in particular, irony takes shape in the way the music pushes against and resists its containment in the period form. Darcy addresses this point in the final sentence of the paragraph just cited:

> The most telling connection of this theme with the first *Kindertotenlieder* song lies not in a mere similarity of cadence figure, but in a common attempt to mitigate grief by focusing on a familiar pattern – a stock phrase of comfort – that is implicitly arraigned as false (a child died in the night, but the sun will still rise in the morning).
>
> (Ibid.)

The convention no longer fits the expression, if it ever did; yet, when handled ironically, the very hollowness of the convention carries its own profound expressive potential. Darcy's admirable commitment to the otherness of the material is undermined to the extent that his point of identification remains the major mode, which he does not treat with the same ironic distance that he so effectively musters for the period. Perhaps the idea of thoroughly ironizing tonality would present too great a threat to any musical ontology based on Schenkerian presuppositions. In any case where the period is resisted, the major mode is 'upheld'. The chromatic alterations are not understood by Darcy as sites of resistance to major, places where the tonal lip quivers under the forced smile of major; rather the alterations are understood as sites of resistance to minor, places where the tonal process often fends off a catastrophic collapse of the self into the other. Instead of openness there is fear of the other and a demand that the minor-mode implications – signifiers here of the other – be assimilated, that the deviations from the diatonic syntax be domesticated and contained as expressive effects that are permitted only to the extent that they do not threaten the basic diatonic essence, the foundation for the definition of the musical self. The relationship between norm and deviation effectively reflects the social dialectic between self and other, where the other is necessary for self-definition but also extraneous to it. If bar 7 is indeed a cry of anguish, as Darcy supposes, this cry gives voice to the despair of one who knows this dialectic to be irreconcilable and understands the impossible and terrifying demands that it places on those who have not been fully accepted into society. In bar 7 a break in the dialectic is staged before our ears, without, however, turning it into a crisis; there is less a sense of anguish than the sort of melancholic heartbreak felt when one thinks one might be unwelcome. Not just the wind sonority and harmony of bar 7 but the plaintive rocking motif, too, sounds foreign, as though it had intruded from outside, and it seems hardly coincidental that, as many critics have suggested, it is also the motivic element in the Andante with the most explicit thematic links to other movements.[18] Here the cloud of the first movement passes

---

[18] Many critics have made a connection to bars 11–12 of the first movement. While a link between these passages is easy enough to see, I find it less easy to hear through the swirling woodwind line. I hear a strong connection to the gesture, obviously

as a shadow over the music. What is so fascinating about the passage, however, is the response of the musical process to this shadow: its humane openness to otherness, even to what it might not understand. The music here makes no effort to expel the intrusive foreign element for the sake of the pure, unbroken line; and indeed the movement as a whole seems to assimilate itself to the rocking motif, the chromatic intrusions, the ambivalent harmony and the wind sound, all of which play increasingly significant roles over the course of the movement. As Bekker noted ([1921] 1969, p. 220), the rocking motif in many respects carries more musical significance for the shape of the whole movement than does the theme itself, which the movement almost seems to want to forget. Indeed one of the most conspicuous things about the movement, and one of the most difficult things to describe in formal terms, is the way the rhythmic gesture of the rocking motif proliferates throughout the movement, and especially in the areas of the movement that lie outside the jurisdiction of the thematic complexes proper.[19] The motif reappears soon after the cadence that closes out the main theme. The rhythmic motif is hinted at in bar 12, merges with the rising sixth from the opening of the theme in bar 14 and devolves into the accompaniment figure to the modal cor anglais theme in bar 22. It also forms the principal motif of the *Abgesang* beginning in bar 42, which later provides the material for sustaining the breakthroughs in E major (from bar 86) and A major (from bar 124). Given its ubiquity in the movement, it is interesting that the motif almost disappears from the two returns of the theme in the tonic, only to overrun the theme and help dissolve it in the final, non-tonic statement. In the first restatement of the theme the motif appears only in bar 29 and in the newly emerging woodwind line in bar 33; but in both cases it appears in the truncated, non-symmetrical cadential form borrowed from bar 12. The third statement of the theme at bar 100 likewise uses this same cadential version of the motif, but twice: once in bar 101 and again in the answering consequent in bar 106.

Indeed one of the striking things about these medial tonic returns is the way the theme grows progressively more 'normal' – especially with respect to the phrase structure of the consequent – largely through the removal of the rocking motif. Darcy suggests that the thematic process driving the returns is one of progressive disintegration where the theme 'must be opened up, its cadences

---

related to bars 11–12, that occurs at the end of the second theme group of the first movement, though here it lacks the distinctive semiquaver rests (bars 111–12 & 366–67). I find the affinity to the first movement extremely striking when the passage returns, slightly modified and in the high strings, near the end of the Andante movement (bars 180–81).

[19]   One can get a good idea of the extent of the proliferation of this motif by looking at Tables 2.1 and 2.2 in Robert Samuels's important semiotic analysis of the Andante, where he catalogues most of the occurrences of the motif in bars 1–55; but since his concern is interval content rather than rhythmic gesture, his discussion bears only incidentally on the issues at hand. See Samuels, 1995, pp. 22–23 & 30–31.

undermined, and its periodic structure dissolved, so that its motivic material may flow into and merge with the material of the second theme' (2001, p. 60). But this idea seems too influenced by the final, non-tonic return of the theme, which does indeed largely liquidate the thematic structure in order to allow the music to flow into the high point at bar 173. If the earlier statements of the theme participate in this process of dissolution at all, they do so by wearing away the distinctive but potentially disruptive characters such as the original rocking motif, and replacing them with graceful but conventional figures such as turns, which are tonally and gesturally more 'acceptable'. Hirschfeld is especially sensitive to the idiosyncratic quality of the rocking motif, drawing particular attention to the distinctive – if for him disagreeable – break on the semiquaver rest which throws an unrefined hitch into an otherwise undistinguished motif. Hirschfeld reads it as a musical analogue to social awkwardness:

> Thus the small motif of the sixth, which later becomes a fourth and is thoroughly dispersed throughout the Andante, is like a wholly ordinary, insignificant particle of speech that has been heard a thousand times. In a speech this motif would correspond to something like the word: 'Hochverehrte!' ['highly esteemed']. Split up by a semiquaver rest, however, the motif immediately becomes interesting, as if in his speech someone kept wanting to say 'Hochver – ehrte!' Here, then, Mahler's creative idea similarly lies in a mere semiquaver rest.
>
> (1907)[20]

If, as Hirschfeld intimates, the rocking motif leaves its characteristic mark as a trite platitude deformed by halting, broken speech, the subsequent variants at bars 28 and 100 polish it, as a cadential melodic figure, into a charming accent. Graceful turns, on the other hand, are allowed to proliferate, giving the tune an air of dashing, if not flamboyant, sophistication; even this is tempered in the consequent of the second variant where only the cadential turn in bar 107 remains. The musical process of these variants traces, as it were, a path of assimilation where the theme seeks to pass into good society by remaking itself, as best it can, into a proper parallel period.

The theme and its first two variants are compared in Ex. 10.6. In the first return the antecedent plays out as a simple melodic variation of the theme which has been transferred from the violins to the horn. The distinctive opening motif of the rising sixth disappears, masking somewhat the identity of the theme – an effect heightened in the original version of the movement where the turn that introduces bar 31 is conspicuously absent.[21] The F flat, which originally serves

---

20 'So ist das kleine, in das Andante fleißig eingestreute Sexten- und später Quartenmotiv eine ganz gewöhnliche, unbedeutende Redefloskel, die tausendmal gehört wurde. In einer Rede würde jenes Motiv etwa dem Worte "Hochverehrte!" entsprechen. Durch eine Sechzehntelpause aber gespalten, wird das Motiv sofort interessant als ob einer in seiner Rede beständig "Hochver – ehrte!" sagen wollte. Diesmal also liegt die schöpferische Idee Mahlers wieder nur in einer Sechzehntelpause.'

21 See Del Mar, 1980, p. 94. Del Mar seems not to notice that the absence of the

Ex. 10.6 Sixth Symphony, Andante Moderato: the theme (bars 1–10), first variant (bars 28–36) and second variant (bars 100–108) aligned for comparison

283

only as a mark of colour, remains and becomes here a central point of focus, appearing as an upper auxiliary to E flat in bar 29 and a lower auxiliary to F in bar 30. The latter is especially effective at establishing an affinity between the F flat of the theme and the E natural of the codetta phrase that follows the full close of the theme (bars 10, 36 and 108; a variant appears as a secondary idea that opens the coda in bar 185). The preoccupation with F flat in the first three bars of this variant helps integrate it into the thematic process, making it more than the colouristic presence it was in the original presentation. The overall effect of these changes, however, is to make the G flat–G figure in bar 31 into a strong point of emphasis, since the identity of the theme in this iteration comes to rest on its presence: only here do we become certain that we are dealing with a variant of the main theme. As in the opening statement of the theme, this figure is again marked by a change in orchestration: the wind sonority with horns, double reeds and clarinets is reminiscent of bar 7, though the fact that the horn has been playing the melody and the continued presence of the strings temper any sense of intrusion. The harmony of the contrasting idea has also been given a somewhat clearer focus through the continual presence of the harp figuration, which pauses only in bar 32, and the addition of the sustained low B flat in the bass, which gives these bars a much stronger sense of prolonging a dominant harmony. The consequent returns the theme to the violins, which reject the idea of elaborating the theme like the horn and instead opt to play a variant: a partially inverted form of the motif that is perhaps influenced by the proximity to the secondary theme (bar 22) which it resembles. Though the horn drops out of the consequent, the other woodwinds continue, adding a new line above the melody. This line complements the melody in important ways, above all in its use of the cadential form of the rocking motif in bar 33, the imitation of the turn in bar 34, and the taking over of the cadential descent in bar 35, where the melody, migrating from the violins to the violas, prematurely runs out of steam. Here the consequent therefore plays out somewhat similarly to the consequent of the opening theme, though without the shadow passing over the music. Once again the winds intrude, really controlling the music from the 2/4 bar (bar 34) onwards, to bring the music to cadential closure. But here the intrusion sounds much less forced: the harmonic ambiguity of bars 7–8, for instance, gives way to a clear cadential progression in bars 34–35. The phrase still starts in the middle of the bar but the musical reaction this time is one of curtailment rather than expansion: the phrase is six beats shorter than the first time, which means that, with re-barring, it is now

---

turn in the first edition of the movement is an alteration of the theme from the beginning of the movement; that is, the turn in bar 30 is not an anticipation of the added turn in the third statement of the theme at bar 101, but a restoration of the turn to the theme, making it into one of the few invariant elements of the theme. Del Mar may have been thinking of the rhythmic figure in which the turn plays out, which is indeed introduced in the revision of bar 30 and taken up in bar 101, if not the figure of the turn itself.

possible to lay out the theme as a relatively normal four-bar phrase. – This is indeed what happens in the second variant. The consequent now finally begins on the downbeat (bar 105). For the first time it also starts in the woodwinds so that the period is now defined as a pure wind theme. Interestingly the orchestration at the end of the theme to some extent reverses that of the second statement. The violins now play the cadential figure along with the flute (bar 107), while the oboe and clarinet follow the path sketched out by the cellos in bars 34–35. The resulting mix in the orchestration blurs the distinction between the lines, and, since up to this point the woodwinds had been carrying the primary theme, the impression the passage gives to the ear is that the violins have joined the woodwinds for the cadence whereas careful analysis shows just the opposite: that, genetically at least, the cadential figure belongs to the violin line (the violin line in bar 107 is identical with the woodwind line in bar 35). One reason for the confusion here is that, despite its genetic connections to the violin line, the cadential figure clearly fits the shape of the woodwind line better, as the difference between the flute part and the violin part clearly shows. Moreover, the consequent has been assembled from fragments of different lines in the second statement, which makes tracking the genetic relationships of the motifs difficult. The rising-sixth motif is stated in bar 105, for the first time exactly repeating the basic idea of the antecedent and marking the period form as fully parallel. But the woodwind line in bars 32–33 is clearly a sketch of this idea *in nuce*. As mentioned above, the second half of bar 106 and the first half of bar 107 are taken from the cello line in bars 34–35, while the cadential figure is once again derived from the woodwind line in bar 35. Besides the relatively strict adherence to the parallel period, there are three further notable features of this variant. First, on the model of the woodwind line in bar 32, a new ethereal countermelody is heard in the violins and flute (a scoring that recalls bars 5–6 of the original theme). Unlike the woodwind line which emerged only in the consequent and was clearly derivative of the main theme, the countermelody here pushes in radically new directions, casting a great long arch across the period without dissolving it, indeed helping to uphold it and give it definition. Interestingly, as Ex. 10.7 shows, this arch bears an uncanny, if vague, resemblance to the shape of the second theme. Moreover, it is almost mysteriously distant; only the F flat just before the 'close' of this arch on the E flat in bar 107 reflects to any degree the chromatic inflections of the theme itself. At the same time the countermelody, despite its properly diatonic cast, is not indifferent to the theme itself; for instance the descent by the violins to the cadential figure can be read as an exceedingly generous gesture that extends a friendly hand to the flute, with which it had shared the opening of the countermelody. Though the main theme nevertheless remains dominant here, there is a sense of necessity and reciprocity between it and the countermelody. The change in orchestration from oboe and clarinet to bassoon and horn, underscored by the resumption of the normal accompaniment to the theme, is disruptive to the overall flow and means that the arch melody is

Ex. 10.7 Sixth Symphony, Andante Moderato: new countermelody (bars 100–107) compared with the secondary theme (bars 22–23)

the strongest element of continuity into bar 101. Secondly, once the normal accompaniment returns in bar 101, the entire antecedent is supported by a tonic pedal point. The change this makes in bar 103 is especially pronounced because the low E flat in the harp and cello should clarify that the harmony here is now a tonic. This should have allowed us to interpret the sonority on the downbeat as a clear embellishing diminished chord in E flat major, except that when the G flat resolves to G, the second violins and violas continue their chromatic ascent, so that the E flat major triad never actually manages to sound in the bar. The harmony therefore remains ambivalent; in some respects indeed the ambivalence has been increased. Thirdly, the descending line in the violins (bar 104) marks the point of symmetry in the period. As mentioned above in the discussion of Adorno's interpretation of the theme, it was the expansion of this joint between the phrases that allowed the consequent to start on the downbeat. In addition we noted how the enjambment originally occurring at this point in the theme caused a certain ambivalence in the phrase structure – heightened in this bar, which seems on the one hand to be almost superfluous but on the other hand to point both back towards the antecedent as a closing figure and forward towards the consequent as an expanded anacrusis. As illustrated in Ex. 10.8, it is precisely this ambivalence which in fact allows the nine-bar phrase to balance around this empty midpoint, since four bars precede it and four bars follow it. The phrase overlap in bar 108 which launches the codetta phrase is likewise balanced to some extent by the change in scoring in bar 101, which almost has the effect of lopping off bar 100 and turning it into an extended anacrusis. Yet the most striking thing about this statement of the theme is the very thing that is likely to escape immediate detection: just how normal it has become. The anomalies of the original theme have been worn away or contained as charming quirks, and the theme no longer seems especially troubled even when it tips towards minor, as in

Ex. 10.8 Sixth Symphony, Andante Moderato: the second variant, bars 100–108: balance around the expanded phrase joint

the approach to the final cadence (bars 106–7). In many respects, all that prevents the theme from slipping into utter banality here is the new countermelody, which not only gives it an air of refinement but also opens the joint between the phrases, creating a formally empty and superfluous space that is filled with pure blessedness. The overall impression that this statement of the theme leaves, then, is one of successful assimilation: with the help of the countermelody the theme will be allowed to pass as a parallel period. – On the surface at least, the final statement of the theme, shown in Ex. 10.9, calls this success into question. One obvious difference is key: this is the only statement of the theme not in the tonic.

Ex. 10.9 Sixth Symphony, Andante Moderato: the third variant, bars 158–67 (some of the inner voices have been omitted) and its derivation (material from first and second variant has been transposed to B major for ease of comparison)

Another is the way the period structure, which had seemed such a preoccupation of the thematic process, simply disappears. In bar 158 the antecedent begins in the bass register with a new, rather abstract variant of the opening motif. The theme then passes to the tenor register at precisely the point where the orchestration had shifted in the second variant (bar 101). Likewise the accompaniment pattern (which has been omitted from Ex. 10.9 for reasons of space) enters in bar 160, though now with the horns and bassoons rather than the cellos doubling the harp, a shift of colour that gives the music a new sense of estrangement from the material. The new countermelody, however, returns identically to begin with, although the scoring is heavier with the flute and oboe joining the violins. In bar 162 the countermelody takes over at the same time that its line is driven forward through rhythmic diminution – a sort of motivic foreshortening that begins unshackling the theme from the strictures of period form. Underneath, the theme disintegrates into the accompaniment, the G flat–G appoggiatura figure (which in B major would be D–D sharp) losing motivic definition. In bar 164 remnants of the consequent begin to appear in the violin line, which suggests that the phrase joint has again been expanded in bar 163. The repeated turn-leap figures in bars 164–65, though based on the violin line in bars 33–34, leave the actual periodic structure far behind. Even the countermelody is absorbed into the process of dissolution: in what is left of the consequent, the separation between melody and countermelody also melts away, though Ex. 10.10 shows that it remains possible to trace an ascending line from the countermelody's opening F sharp up to the high G that marks the return of the tonic in bar 173. What is striking about this variant is not just the remarkably quick dissolution of the theme, but the way the theme is overrun, as it were, by the rhythmic gesture of the rocking motif beginning in bar 163. The music expands as if making an attempt to absorb the intrusion, and, as Adorno notes, it acquires 'such verve that it seems to burst its confines', the limits of the period (1992b, p. 102).[22] But for this 'verve', it would be tempting to speak of a return of something repressed here, as the elements that had been worn away to remake the theme into a proper period suddenly reappear unbidden to undo it and bring the music down in a collapse, thus showing that the assimilation process demanded by the period was doomed to fail. The verve, however, ensures that the motifs are greeted with open arms, welcomed like old friends; there is in fact no sense of crisis over the loss of the period form here, and the music rises quickly and rather sunnily from this point to the return of the tonic – the magnificent high point at bar 173.

---

[22] The full passage reads: 'Die Erhebung aber, zu der die Durchführung, oder, wenn man will, der letzte "Gang" des Satzes geleitet, verleiht dieser Partie einen solchen Schwung, daß sie aus sich heraus auslaufen, allmählich abebben will' (Adorno, 1970–86, vol. 16, p. 343).

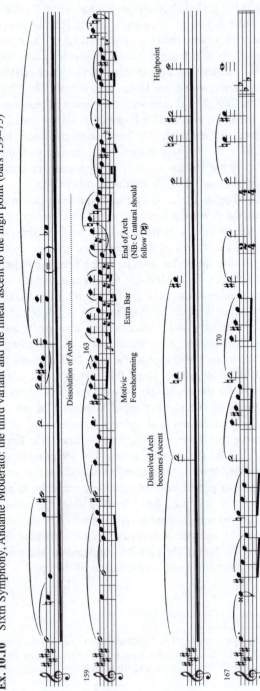

Ex. 10.10 Sixth Symphony, Andante Moderato: the third variant and the linear ascent to the high point (bars 159–73)

Writing about the Andante, Adorno notes how the succession of variants calls into question the form of the movement:

> The Mahlerian principle of the variant, the deviation, becomes the turning aside of the disposition of large forms; the whole movement arrives in its concrete determination somewhere other than the composer, or rather the structural formal plan, wanted.
>
> (Ibid., translation modified)[23]

Adorno's point here is that though the movement plays out formally as a slow rondo with alternations of the theme, the secondary theme and episodes, the actual course of the movement seems not really to be about the rondo at all. The basic principle of the rondo, namely the intermittent return of stable thematic (and generally tonal) identity after forays into various and variable contrasting fields, seems almost beside the point, and it is undermined in the movement precisely by the thematic variant. Consequently, to adapt Adorno's words, the theme 'protrudes strangely from the actual musical process as if the latter were not its own story' (see 1992a, p. 88).[24] Why might this be the case? For one thing, we have already noted that the thematic process of the first two variants seems to be directed towards emptying the theme of content rather than fulfilling it, underscoring the mere formality of the thematic returns and the emptiness of the rondo idea. The identity that the thematic returns offer is consequently somewhat uncomfortable and destabilizing. Furthermore, the spaces outside the theme itself, especially the codetta-like sections that follow the main theme, are typically places that gather in what the period form and tonal conventions demand that the variant must exclude. Adorno calls such spaces *Abgesänge* after the concluding section of bar form. The *Abgesang* answers the repeating *Stollen* with fundamentally new material that leads to a final cadence. It thus stands outside the usual idea of musical economy that 'like interest, derives everything from a basic stock' (ibid., p. 42).[25] Conceptually, *Abgesang* is often applied

---

[23] 'Das Mahlersche Prinzip der Variante, der Abweichung wird zur Ablenkung der Disposition der großen Formen; der gesamte Satz gelangt in seiner konkreten Bestimmtheit woanders hin, als der Komponist, oder vielmehr der tektonische Formplan wollte.' (Adorno, 1970–86, vol. 16, p. 343).

[24] The full passage reads: 'In manchen Sätzen, die Hauptthemen üblicher Prägung benutzen, ragen sie aus dem tatsächlichen musikalischen Verlauf eigentümlich heraus, so als wäre dieser nicht ihre eigene Geschichte; dem Andantethema der Sechsten Symphonie, einer recht geschlossenen Melodie, hat bereits Paul Bekker attestiert, daß sie während des Stückes gleichsam vergessen zu werden trachte' (Adorno, 1960, pp. 119–20, & 1970–86, vol. 12, p. 236).

[25] The full sentence reads: 'Daß, bis zu ihrer Renaissance in Wagner, Abgesänge die gesamte Generalbaßära hindurch kaum geschrieben wurden, erklärt sich wohl damit, daß sie, als Erfüllung eines musikalischen Zusammenhangs durch ein ihm gegenüber wesentlich Neues, mit der Idee der immanenten Geschlossenheit der neueren Musik kollidierten, deren Ökonomieprinzip alles wie Zinsen vom Grundstock hecken ließ' (Adorno, 1960, p. 61, & 1970–86, vol. 12, p. 190).

outside strict bar form, where it can refer to any codetta-like section of music that responds to a theme with a new idea. Such passages give the impression of throwing off the shackles of strict form and opening up vistas where the normal constraints of form and symphonic integration can momentarily be set aside.

> What in Mahler's symphonic writing is not immanent in the form, not calculable, becomes itself, as *Abgesang*, a formal category, other and identical at once. The inauthentic gropes for its In-itself, for what the individual themes have omitted, out of asceticism against the subjective demand to create the whole out of itself from the inside out.
>
> (Ibid., translation modified)[26]

Darcy seems to be getting at this idea of the *Abgesang* when he notes that such passages as bars 10–20 offer 'a space of formally unnecessary, surplus blessedness' (2001, p. 60).[27] The very fact that the space is, strictly speaking, formally extraterritorial – in this case outside the jurisdiction of period form – allows it to escape the normally strict accounting of compositional economy; the *Abgesang* can therefore gather in what must otherwise be excluded, and reap fulfilment – what Darcy fittingly describes as 'surplus blessedness'. The movement in fact pushes its most distinctive elements into the *Abgesang*-like passages. In this sense it is appropriate to speak of the movement as an anti-rondo because the course of the movement is concerned less with the theme than with the codetta-like passages appended to it. For instance the rhythmic rocking motif, as mentioned above, spreads itself throughout the movement, becoming the point of focus especially in the two breakthroughs. The secondary theme is also remarkably short and invariant, especially by Mahler's standards, differing only in tonality and orchestral colour in each appearance. But its little coda, the sequential woodwind counterpoint that grows out of it (bars 24–27), has extremely important ramifications, providing the basic contrapuntal syntax for the high point. Likewise the motif that gives definition to this high point first emerges in recognizable form from the *Abgesang* of the first variant in bar 39. As has often been recognized, the high point itself thus merges a motif from the *Abgesang* of the first theme with a basic syntax derived from the tail of the second theme. Moreover the first, somewhat tentative, appearance of the high point (bar 73 but emerging fully only at bar 76) also falls a little like an *Abgesang*, or at least a 'fulfilment field' to the second theme; whereas the second and final statement follows the dissolved form of the main theme like an

---

26 'Als Abgesang wird in Mahlers Symphonik, was nicht formimmanent, nicht kalkulabel ist, selbst zur Formkategorie, Anderes und Identisches zugleich. Das Uneigentliche tastet nach seinem An sich; nach dem, was die einzelnen Themen aus Askese gegen den subjektiven Anspruch, das Ganze aus sich heraus zu schaffen, ausgespart haben' (Adorno, 1960, p. 61, & 1970–86, vol. 12, pp. 190–91).

27 Darcy curiously calls such passages *Nachsätze*, a term generally reserved in musical analytical discussions for the consequent phrase.

Abgesang (bar 173), except that it also serves to re-establish the tonic and so completely overrides the theme. It is here that the movement turns definitively from rondo to anti-rondo, as the period gladly cedes the course of the movement to the *Abgesang*, opening itself up and transforming itself from the main idea – the thing itself and mark of musical identity – into, as it were, an Auf*gesang* that prepares for, and indeed lifts the music up to, a high point. – Equally interesting in this respect is the history of the rocking woodwind passage from the main theme (bars 7–8). While it is immediately excised from the theme, the passage as a whole returns in two places, both times associated with the appearance of the high point. In bars 79–81 it dissipates the energy of the first high point, turning the music towards the revelatory breakthrough in E major. Here, as in bars 7–8, it is played by the oboe but with intermittent doubling by the violins and flutes alleviating somewhat its gentle melancholic tone. It returns in bars 179–80, once more closing out the high point, but this time, transferred to the violins, it initiates and prolongs the final cadential dominant. Far from being expelled from the music, this passage, which had formerly sounded so intrusive and melancholic, no longer casts a shadow but glows luminously like a cloud at sunset. Its presence is now embraced as something beautiful, before growing, as Bekker says of the end of the movement, 'gently indistinct, like the fading red of evening' ['zart schwimmend, wie ein erblassendes Abendrot'] ([1921] 1969, p. 222). – What is forgotten along with the theme, then, is precisely what is at stake in the theme: identity. The anti-rondo, with its rhetorical emphasis on the *Abgesang* rather than the theme, cherishes non-identity. Savouring the beauty of the fleeting sunset it does not seek to assimilate the other, to capture it and hold it securely in place for the sake of identity, so much as assimilate itself to the other, leaving itself open and vulnerable for the sake of non-identity. Through this openness to what it cannot possess comes the sound of its profound humaneness.

Hans Redlich writes that in the slow movement of the Sixth it is as though 'the sweet landscape of the Adagio wants to pass as an Intermezzo' ['Die süße Landschaft des Adagios will als Intermezzo gelten'] (1920, p. 268). Redlich was surely questioning the symphonic appropriateness of the enchanted, sentimental tone of the movement, which on the surface seems to seek nothing but escape from the world. Unlike an adagio, which risks everything to extend its long line to infinity, an andante eschews the sublime, preferring to dream of simple beauty rather than face down the inevitable existential crises of the infinite.[28] Mahler's Andante constructs a dream world; its idyll dreams of happiness, the acceptance and even cherishing of non-identity. But it also knows the danger of sentimental enchantment. Disavowing identity, his dream turns self-critical and breaches the sentimental subject idealistically built on it, but without crisis and without disowning the world. It reaches for a star so that it might become a beacon to a

---

[28] On the generic difference between Andante and Adagio, see Notley, 1999.

disenchanted earth. The Andante of Mahler's Sixth dreams enchantedly of a world where the spell of identity has been broken; the Finale is a rude awakening that extinguishes the light.

Chapter Eleven

'Ways of Telling' in Mahler's Music: The Third Symphony as Narrative Text[1]

VERA MICZNIK

Meaning and programmes

It has always been a difficult task to pin down what, and how, music means. Because musical meanings are so elusive, any attempt to articulate them in words amounts to a 'construction of meaning' based on acknowledged or subliminal choices to privilege one or more sites from which sources of meaning might arise: the music itself, the composer's life events and emotions, documentary evidence, social context, and so on. Methods of constructing musical meaning have taken various forms, such as composers' prescriptive meanings attached to instrumental works in the form of written programmes;[2] the fictive stories read in the music (such as A.B. Marx's for Beethoven's Eroica Symphony: see Burnham, 1995, pp. 4–20); philosophical readings of music as exemplifying the essence of existence (such as Schopenhauer's or Wagner's); projections of the composer's biographies and feelings onto the unfolding of the music (such as Specht's for Mahler); the recognition of expressive, but impenetrable and unattainable meanings (such as E.T.A. Hoffmann's), and even the structural formalist illusion that the only musical meanings decipherable and available to us are the 'objective, purely musical' ones: all these are manifestations of the same desire to assign meanings to music.

Music historians typically embrace the belief that the key to locating the meaning of a musical work lies in achieving the best possible understanding of

[1] I would like to thank my student Sherry Lee and my colleague Michael Tenzer for having read and commented on the early draft of this chapter, and Jeremy Barham for his thoughtful and constructive editorial help. I am grateful to Oxford University Press and the Royal Musical Association for permission to reproduce extracts from my article 'Music and Narrative Revisited: Degrees of Narrativity in Beethoven and Mahler', *Journal of the Royal Musical Association*, 126 (2) (2001), 193–249.

[2] For example, see Micznik, 1999, for an evaluation of the relationship between programmme and music in Liszt.

the composer's thoughts and intentions, and therefore that the closer we can get to the original context and sources of a work, the better we can grasp its hidden messages. Biographical and genetic information (sketches, words in letters, confessions and so on) – considered theoretically much more 'palpable', 'real', 'factual', 'hard' and therefore more dependable, more unequivocal, more 'objective' data than the 'softer' information provided by critical, allegedly subjective, perceptions or hermeneutic interpretations of the music – tends to be privileged as a producer of meanings. Despite the important historical knowledge provided by 'positivistic musicology' (source studies, documentation of historical surroundings and so forth), our confidence has been reduced that meanings of works can be known from the works themselves, that music can ultimately tell us more truth about its meanings than any outside information we may gather. As Burnham remarks, according to 'the positivist impulse', in order to gain 'legitimacy' for interpretative readings of music one needs to 'break the code' of the 'other order experiences' encoded in music (Burnham, 2001, p. 197). The clash between the occasional wealth of information uncovered about the genesis or production of a work, and the lack of a musicological methodology that can comfortably integrate the history of origins with analytical interpretation, automatically privileges the contribution to musical meaning of the external information, and blinds us to the truths that the music can best tell us. A case in point is Mahler's Third Symphony.

Obsessed as musicology is with providing evidence for any assessments of a work's meanings, there has been hardly any analytical interpretative discussion of Mahler's Third Symphony in the last fifty years or so that has not discussed the music in light of the numerous sources that scholars have been able to uncover for the documentation of the work's origins: Mahler's programmatic pronouncements about the Symphony as a whole, sketches, autographs, confidences, letters, markings on the autograph scores, and other known primary materials. Mahler's various written programmatic associations of the Symphony with 'a musical vision of Nature', with Nietzsche's *Die fröhliche Wissenschaft*, the titles of the various movements, and, in particular, the inscriptions in the first movement – the awakening of Pan and the summer marching in a 'Bacchic procession', which survived into the score as late as the fair copy of the Symphony, and were abandoned only at the publication stage – have served as guides for analysis in the endeavour to elucidate the 'meaning' of this difficult piece (see for example Franklin, 1991, pp. 53–90, and Floros, 1994, pp. 93–107).[3]

---

[3] Thomas Sipe (1993) proposes a new analytical approach to the symphony through the Bakhtinian concept of the novel, yet he still takes some of the titles as a basis for his interpretation. Adorno, on the other hand, hardly involves the titles in his analysis, explaining the musical processes on their own merit (see esp. 1992a, pp. 78–80). While problematizing the relationship of the verbal information with the musical content, Danuser ultimately recognizes that 'in the case of the first movement of the Third

Such a wealth of first-hand resources, combined with the positivistic prejudice that the work's meaning was best known to the composer and to his contemporaries, has been sufficient to induce commentators to impose the story of the evidence upon the music, and to understate (or sometimes even ignore) 'what the music tells us'. Moreover, the privileging of genetic information inherent in this evidence has blinded us to the numerous inconsistencies, contradictions or discrepancies within the evidence itself, and especially to the discrepancies between the programmes or Mahler's statements and what we hear in the music. One need not necessarily deny the relevance of the history of origins to the final aesthetic perception of the work (see, for example, Dahlhaus, 1982, p. 60): knowing all this information is bound to colour our perception of the 'music itself'. But for the sake of understanding how musical meaning is constructed, we need to examine the premises and mechanisms of privileging and exclusion that we operate in the formation of the stories we devise, and to recognize their contradictions and inconsistencies.

Even if historical accuracy is judged according to the reception of the works in Mahler's time (which need not necessarily be the case), it is surprising to find that his contemporaries, much more frequently than later critics, in fact took the music as the site where meaning is produced. Early biographers' notions of 'truth' for their reading of musical works were different from ours. Not having the same knowledge and inclinations to give precedence to the documentary information over the music as we tend to do, they were much less concerned with genesis, programmes or stories about the music; rather, their prejudices lay with the conception of the time that musical works were mirrors of the composer's soul and life.[4] Either because they were catering to Mahler's prevailing official anti-programmatic position, or because the programmes and inscriptions in the score were not yet as widely known and publicized, they actually played down the programmatic aspects, and related their stories of meaning much more closely to thematic analysis. Paradoxically, their observations are often more attuned to the music than those of critics who have been 'spoiled' by their knowledge of the sources.

One of the earliest Mahler monographs by Ludwig Schiedermair of 1901 elucidates the first four symphonies mostly in terms of the thematic analysis and expressive content of the music. Schiedermair characterizes the opening horn

---

Symphony, the information from the general headings and titles of the movements coincides, albeit partially, with the musical content' ['doch läßt sich am Beispiel der Ersten Abteilung der *Dritten Symphonie* skizzieren, daß die Information von Gesamtüberschrift und Satztitel mit dem musikalischen Gehalt, obzwar nur partiell, zusammentreffen kann'] (1991, p. 144. See also pp. 143–46 & 152–68). Reilly provides particularly lucid warnings against overemphasizing the authority of the manuscript findings over the final work (1986; see esp. p. 65).

[4] For a detailed discussion of the 'autobiographical' issue see, for example, Micznik, 1987.

theme of the Third Symphony as 'deep, heavy waves of sound' [*dumpfe, schwere Tonwellen*] and he then reproduces the 'energetic motif' [*energische Motiv*] of the trumpets and trombones (bar 31), the 'main theme [which] enters with powerful impetus' ['mit kraftvollem Schwung tritt das Hauptthema auf'] (bar 57), a 'weaker, lighter theme in the oboe' ['ein weicheres, leichteres Thema ueberläßt der Komponist der Oboe zum Vortrag'] (bars 138–39 [incomplete]), and so on. About the movement as a whole he writes:

> In the treatment, connecting, contracting and development of this musical material the composer sets in front of us a picture filled with striking expression. In wrestling and resignation, conflict and suffering, the striving of the soul is purified, achieving victory and the affirmation of existence. From a purely musical point of view, this movement succeeds through the vitality of its language and the significance of its conceptual material. In contrast with some of the movements of the First and Second Symphonies, the musical logic here attains an inexorable clarity and an astonishing intensity. The composer's climaxes are superbly successful, without mutually undermining one another.
>
>   (Schiedermair, 1901, this and the preceding quotations, p. 26)[5]

The comments on the other five movements continue along similar lines, characterizing the music without even mentioning the ideas of 'nature', 'Bacchus' or 'evolution'. This is not to say that Mahler agreed entirely with his account of the work, since in a letter of November 1900 he admonished Schiedermair for having wrongly characterized his Third Symphony as representing 'the struggles of an individual' [*Ringen einer Individualität*], suggesting that 'it would be more accurate to say: it is nature's path of development (from stiff materiality to the greatest articulation! but above all the *life of nature*!)' ['Eher könnte man sagen: es ist der Entwicklungsweg der Natur (von der starren Materie bis zur höchsten Artikulation! aber vor allem Naturleben!)'] (Hansen, 1985, p. 246; trans. from Blaukopf & Blaukopf, 1991, p. 149; see Mahler's further contradictory remarks on programmes and titles in the same letter).

This exchange illustrates perfectly the unreliability of Mahler's whimsical attitude towards his programmatic ideas. Undoubtedly Schiedermair's characterization bears the imprint of the historical situation under which it was written. Even though Mahler had publicized his programmes to the Third

---

5 'In der Verarbeitung, Verbindung, Verengung und Ausgestaltung dieses Tonmaterials stellt uns der Komponist ein Gemälde voll treffenden Ausdrucks hin. Im Ringen und Entsagen, Bekämpfen und Leiden läutert sich das Streben der Seele, den Sieg und die Daseinsbejahung erreichend. Rein musikalisch betrachtet gewinnt diese Abteilung durch die Lebendigkeit der Sprache und die Prägnanz des gedanklichen Materials. Die musikalische Logik gelangt hier gegenüber einzelnen Sätzen der 1. und 2. Symphonie zu einer unerbittlichen Klarheit und einer staunenswerten Höhe. Prächtig sind dem Tondichter die Steigerungen gelungen, ohne sich gegenseitig zu mildern.'

Symphony among friends and critics,[6] this monograph was written after Mahler's famous public rejection of programmes in 1900 (reported in Schiedermair, 1901, pp. 13–14). Having consulted with the composer to obtain approval for what he was going to write, Schiedermair had obviously been instructed to project Mahler's image as an 'absolute music' composer (in contrast to Strauss), for which purpose he even reproduces in the monograph fragments of an often circulated letter to Seidl which suggest that Mahler was an enemy of programme music (Martner, 1979, p. 212).[7] While Mahler's comment to Schiedermair could be interpreted as supporting his programmatic conception, it is also conceivable that he would not have wanted to be inconsistent concerning the metaphysical 'Nature' programme which he had already publicized, and which might still have seemed to him more suitable than the 'biographical' one.

Richard Specht's early short monograph of 1905 is also remarkable for its attention to musical detail, and its recognition of important generic and expressive qualities of the music:

> The military and folk-song romanticism of Mahler, in conjunction with a highly productive combinatory force, unleashed the most elemental driving power in the first movement. It begins in oppressive solemnity with a D minor theme for eight horns moving in march fashion, which is replaced by a strong, piercing motif accompanied by deep, trembling basses in 3/2 time, and then by another in which the oboes, followed by the solo violin, intone a gently rocking melody: they all celebrate their resurrection and transformation in a vastly constructed and intensified march of orgiastic, indeed almost delirious rapture and frenzy, bustled around by drums and pipes, as they stride along with the most brilliant vital energy accompanied by all sorts of coarse and comical, indeed often vulgar melodic symbols.
>
> (Specht, 1905, pp. 38–39)[8]

Unlike Schiedermair, Specht seems perfectly aware of Mahler's programmatic associations, which he nevertheless downplays and replaces with the idea of autobiography:

---

[6] See, for example, Franklin, 1980, pp. 41, 52, 58–67, 75–76; also letters to Arnold Berliner, Fritz Löhr, Anna von Mildenburg, Bruno Walter and Richard Batka in Martner, 1979, pp. 163–64, 164–65, 188–90, 188–89, 197–98. See also Floros, 1994, pp. 84–90.

[7] See the commentary on this letter in Micznik, 1989, p. 52 & 60–61.

[8] 'Die Soldaten- und Volksliedromantik Mahlers im Verein mit produktivster kombinatorischer Kraft hat in dem ersten Satz die urwüchsigsten Triebe geschossen. Er beginnt in wuchtvollem Ernst, mit einem marschartig bewegten D-moll-Thema der acht Hörner, das von einem schweren, von dumpf erzitternden Bässen im 3/2 Takt begleiteten aufgellenden Motiv und dann von einem anderen abgelöst wird, in dem die Oboen und dann die Solovioline einen zärtlich-schaukelnden Gesang anstimmen: sie alle feiern in einem groß angelegten und gesteigerten Marsch von orgiastischem, ja fast irrem Schwung und Taumel ihre Auferstehung und Verwandlung, in dem sie, von Trommeln und Pfeifen umschwirrt, in hellster Lebenskraft einherziehen, begleitet von allerlei derben, possenhaften, ja oft ordinären melodische Symbolen.'

thus this is a piece of musical autobiography, a diary in notes: the representation in sound of a typical artistic existence, the artist's Bacchus procession through life, in all his proud Dionysian confidence and overflowing joy; with all his demons, his eagerness, his disappointments, and all the low, banal and vulgar things that daily life brings, and whose master he becomes in the triumphant disdain and enrapture of creation.

(Ibid., p. 39)[9]

Paradoxically, however, Specht is not satisfied just with a biographical account of the music, but wants to give his readers even more insight into the composer's mind. Bemoaning Mahler's opposition to programmes, he argues that giving general titles to a musical work does not necessarily amount to imposing a programme:

One almost regrets the fact that, in his dread of programmes and commentaries, the composer suppressed the title which he once gave to his work – for 'Summer Morning Dream' does not even signify any programme, but only the suggestion of a mood that is to be grasped purely musically – similar to Schumann's titles which also touch on just the basic tone of the piece, and do not lead to the somewhat simplistic imitation of real things.

(Ibid., p. 40)[10]

He goes on, discreetly integrating some of Mahler's comments into his own observations about the music: 'as if he had found the syrinx of Pan in some old sacred grove' for the third movement; the 'childish love of God' [*kindliche Gottesliebe*] for the fifth movement; and for the last, 'purely instrumental' movement, 'an Adagio of indescribably beautiful sound, laden with the noblest melody – full of that thoroughly male, quite unfeminine, power of love' (ibid., p. 41).[11] Thus, instead of explaining the music in terms of the external evidence he possesses, Specht fashions his explanatory story of the Symphony in terms of the musical features, only borrowing metaphors from the programmes where he finds them suited to complement what the music tells him.

---

[9] 'so ist dieser ein Stück musikalischer Autobiographie, ein Tagebuch in Tönen: die klanggewordene Darstellung eines typischen Künstlerdaseins, des Künstlers Bacchus-Zug durchs Leben, in all seiner dionisischen stolzen Zuversicht und schenkenden Freude, mit all seinen Dämonen, seiner Gier, seinen Enttäuschungen und allem Niedrigen, Banalen und Pöbelhaften, das der Alltag bringt und dessen er in der sieghaften Verachtung und der Entrücktheit des Schaffens Herr wird'.

[10] 'Man möchte es fast bedauern, daß der Komponist in seiner Scheu vor Programmen und Kommentaren, den Titel den er einmal seinem Werke gab, unterdrückte, – schon deshalb, weil "Ein Sommermorgentraum" eben kein Programm, sondern nur das Andeuten einer rein musikalisch zu bewältigenden Stimmung bedeutet, – ähnlich wie Schumanns Titelüberschriften, die ja auch nur den Grundton des Stückes anschlagen, und nicht etwa zur bloßen Imitation realer Dinge führen.'

[11] 'als hätte er in irgend einem alten Götterhain die Syrinx Pans gefunden. [Die ... Töne ... werden in dem letzten, wieder] rein instrumentalen Satz, [weitergesponnen und zu einem Gebilde von verklärter Weihe und ruhevollster Größe gestaltet:] einen unbeschreiblich klangschönen, von edelster Melodik getragenen Adagio – voll jener durchaus männlichen, durchaus unfemininen Liebesmacht'.

Paul Stefan, in his Mahler monograph of 1910, outlines even more explicitly the marginal role which the programmatic genesis should play in understanding both the creation and the reception of the work: 'The titles are certainly not necessary for the "understanding" [of the Third Symphony]. ... Naturally, they must be taken only as images for the recipient, not as programmes of the creator, who always longed to present sheer music and only music' (Stefan, 1912, pp. 108–9; translation from Stefan, 1913, pp. 94–95 amended).[12] Encouraging a reading of the meanings from what the music itself tells us, he writes that when the 'even worse' notion of a '"suppressed programme"' is cleared away, 'the pure musical form remains behind, which is derivable solely from the development of the music, from the unity of the work, and from the character of the great confession' (ibid., p. 109).[13]

Naturally in producing their construction of meaning, and with their new penchant for pinning down 'objective truths' and their possession of revealing documents conceivably bearing witness to the programmatic origins of Mahler's creative process, many later twentieth-century critics chose from the abundance of details those which offered the best evidence that Mahler needed an extra-musical impulse for his composition.[14] This in turn led to an assumption that the programmatic underpinning contributed greatly to Mahler's creative process, or in other words that the musical decisions were at least partly modelled on, or illustrated, the story line of the programmes. As a result of such an approach, Constantin Floros, for example, assigns the following narrative to the Symphony: 'The idiomatic diversity of the Third as well as its entire compositional form is determined by the basic programmatic idea. Mahler planned to design a musical cosmology ... The six movements ... resemble the six chapters of the highly poetic story of the creation he had in mind' (Floros, 1994, p. 92). Yet the selections of documentary evidence used to argue that Mahler conceived the musical work as a mirror of the programmes omit a wealth of other information which may well lead to the opposite conclusion. There is no need to rehearse all of Mahler's well-known denials of titles and programmes.[15] It suffices to mention

---

[12] 'Zum "Verständnis" sind diese Titel gewiß nicht notwendig. ... Natürlich dürfen auch sie nur als Gleichnisse für den Aufnehmenden, nicht als "Programme" des Schaffenden angesehen werden, der immer schroffer Musik und nur Musik zu geben verlangte.'

[13] 'Wenn nun der Wahn von der Programmusik Mahlers und der noch schlimmere Irrtum der "verschwiegenen Programme" zerstreut ist, so bleibt die rein musikalische Form zurück, die einzig aus dem Werden der Musik, aus der Einheit des Werkes und aus dem Charakter der großen Konfession herzuleiten ist.'

[14] This is no criticism, but rather an observation of ways in which fruitful uses of new epistemological paradigms can advance knowledge through new interpretations. See, for example, interpretative readings by Floros, Mitchell and Hefling.

[15] See, for example, Martner, 1979, p. 179 (letter of 26 March 1896 to Marschalk): 'Just as I find it banal to compose programme-music, I regard it as unsatisfactory and

two of the more revealing examples which show both Mahler's denials of, and ambivalence towards, programmes. In a letter to Josef Krug-Waldsee, who conducted Mahler's Third Symphony on 22 October 1902 in Magdeburg, Mahler writes:

> Those titles were an attempt I made at the time to provide non-musicians with a clue and a guide to the thought, or rather mood, of the individual movements and to the relationship between the movements and their place in the whole. Only too soon, alas, did it become clear to me that the attempt had failed ... leading merely to misinterpretations of the direst sort. ... These titles ... will certainly convey a good deal to you *after* you have got to know the score. They will also give you some hint of how I imagined the constantly increasing articulation of feeling, from the muted, rigid, merely elemental form of existence (the forces of Nature) to the delicate structure of the human heart, which in turn reaches further still, pointing beyond (to God). – Please do express this in your own language, *without citing the utterly inadequate titles*, and you will then have acted in my sense.
>
> (Martner, 1979, p. 266; second set of italics added)

Similarly, in a letter to the critic Richard Batka, Mahler talks about the compromise he had to make by allowing the performance of 'the Flower piece' alone, which, 'torn as it is out of the context of the larger work ... is bound to give rise to misunderstanding'. But he is willing to let this piece 'lie bleeding at Pompey's feet', introducing him to the public as a 'meditative', finespun 'singer of nature':

> Of course no one gets an inkling that for me nature includes all that is terrifying, great and also lovely (it is precisely this that I wanted to express in the whole work, in a kind of evolutionary development). I always feel it strange that when most people speak of 'Nature' what they mean is flowers, little birds, the scent of pinewoods etc. No one knows the god Dionysus, or great Pan. Well: there you have a kind of programme – i.e. a sample of how I compose. Always and everywhere it is the very sound of Nature!
>
> (Ibid., pp. 197–8)

Given such dissonant testimonies from the composer himself, the 'face value' of accounts of his own work must at least be questioned. Such statements make clear that even when Mahler did refer to 'Nature' he used the term as meaning 'The World' with all its components, material, human, ironic, or tragic. Mahler's titles and various pronouncements may well have been meant at least in part to offer the critics a convenient overarching narrative that held together a very

---

unfruitful to try to make programme notes for a piece of music'; p. 172 (letter of 17 December 1895 to Marschalk): 'I should regard my work as a complete failure if I felt it necessary to give men like yourself even the slightest indication of the emotional trend of the work. ... I gladly leave the interpretation of details to each listener's imagination'; see also letters of 1897 and 1902 against programmes to Seidl (ibid., p. 213) and Kalbeck (ibid., p. 262).

unusual six-movement symphony which seemed incomprehensible, even incoherent, if interpreted according to the usual symphonic parameters.

Even more relevantly, at closer observation it appears that the programmes had often been conceived after the fact. Edward Reilly suggests the following:

> These lists, however, were not programs for a finished work. They were rather starting points, often quite vague and tentative, designed ... to help stimulate Mahler's imagination. ... stimulating ... but ... very different from the finished compositions. ... The lists of movements that actually correspond to the music, and the conception of the successive movements as embodiments of an ascending order of different stages of existence, appear *after* the compositional work of the summer of 1895. The great majority of those programs were written within the very short period between 15 July and 2 September ... . And the remaining changes coincide exactly with the remaining compositional work, mainly on the first movement, in the summer of 1896. Thus the music was not written to embody a pre-existent program; rather, the program developed as a means of describing and explaining the character of the music.
>
> (Reilly, 1986, p. 65)

Reilly's point that Mahler also changed the titles of the movements several times, and that therefore one should be doubtful about their fixed associations with his musical ideas, becomes even clearer in light of Natalie Bauer-Lechner's comment from October 1896: 'Trying, as he does, to interpret his creations *after the event*', and having completed the first movement, Mahler came up with a new programmatic explanation: 'It is Zeus destroying Kronos, the higher form overcoming the lower' (Franklin, 1980, p. 76).

Texts

Aside from these observations, the main purpose of this essay is to show that giving exclusive attention to the documentation surrounding the work has discouraged a critical consideration of: (a) the wealth of information, both verbal and musical, that lies within the final work itself; and (b) questions resulting from a confrontation of the readings of the evidence and those of the musical text.

To begin with, the texts involved in one way or another in Mahler's Third give numerous clues as to what the general spirit behind this work might have been. The three *Wunderhorn* poems which participated in various ways in the conception of the Symphony – 'Das Himmlische Leben' (originally a Bavarian folk song called 'Der Himmel hängt voll Geigen'), 'Ablösung im Sommer' and 'Es sungen drei Engel' (originally called 'Armer Kinder Bettlerlied') – all share a pretence of childlike naivety under which folk poetry and fairy tales often hide more disturbing and irreverent truths. Beneath the light-heartedness of the texts one reads a pessimistic ironic tone, an implicit enticement to distrust the ideal of heaven, where, as on earth, there are sins and betrayals, and not everybody is equal. The Cuckoo story in 'Ablösung' can similarly be interpreted as a warning about the indifference of the world which will easily replace an old beloved trustworthy companion with a carefree vociferous boaster without even mourning. In all three cases, Mahler's music clearly shows that he caught these nuances of parody and despair, and that it is a conscious, subtly unifying act that brought these texts together through his 'conception which might link scurrilous humour with tragedy' (Franklin, 1991, p. 61).[16] Whether used with or without the texts, these characteristics survived in the music and their spirit cannot escape the attentive listener. The 'Nature' programmes, while hinting to a small extent at this tragicomic characteristic, certainly do not encourage us to hear the music this way.

The very presence of the text from Nietzsche's *Also sprach Zarathustra* signalled Mahler's interest in the philosopher's work, which might then have been confirmed by the surrounding evidence from his letters and programmes, and especially by Mahler's (eventually withdrawn) title of the symphony after Nietzsche's *The Gay Science* [*Die fröhliche Wissenschaft*].[17] Yet the complexity of the relationship between Nietzsche's thought and Mahler's music is, as Jeremy Barham has shown, only beginning to be unveiled.[18] The misunderstanding of this connection, due in part to a lack of interest in 'what the music tells us', has led

---

[16] Franklin's close discussion of 'Ablösung im Sommer' is very enlightening about how music captures this character of the poem.

[17] The general importance of Nietzsche's ideas for Mahler surfaces several times in his correspondence. See, for example, Martner, 1979, p. 140 (letter of late autumn 1891 to Emil Freund): 'Besides, in the last few weeks I have been reading something so remarkable and strange that it may very well have an *epoch-making* influence on my life.' (Though it remains uncorroborated, the footnote in the original edition, retained by Martner, indicates that Mahler is referring to an unspecified work by Nietzsche); ibid., pp. 407–8 (letter of January 1891 to Bertha Löhr, Fritz's sister): 'And this very day, too, a volume of Nietzsche goes into the post for you. You will then, I hope, cease to pelt me with mean filth'; ibid., p. 236 (letter of June 1899 to Lipiner comparing his poetry with the intoxicating Dionysian power of music): 'No visual representation has ever yet succeeded in capturing what flowers spontaneously from every note of music. ... instead of telling of wine or describing its effects, [your poetry] *is* wine, it is Dionysus! It seems to me, incidentally, that what Dionysus personified to the ancients was simply *instinct*, in the grandiose mystical sense in which you have interpreted it. In your music, as in the myth, those in ecstasy are driven forth to become one with the animals.' See also ibid., p. 163 (letter of 17 August 1895 to Berliner in which the title 'Die fröhliche Wissenschaft' is used in a programmatic outline of the Third Symphony).

[18] For a very lucid evaluation of the complexity of Nietzsche's ideas and, therefore, of the danger of a too facile understanding of the relationship between Mahler and Nietzsche's thought, see Barham, 1992, chapter 'Mahler and Nietzsche', pp. 105–58, and Barham, 1998, chapters 'Aesthetic Nominalism, Narrative Strategies and Formal Totality in the First Movement [of Mahler's Third Symphony]', pp. 257–331 (esp. pp. 318–26), and 'Nietzsche's *Zarathustra* and Fechner's *Tagesansicht*: Movements Four, Five and Six as Musical Metaphors for the Philosophy of Fechnerian *Spätidealismus*', pp. 361–488.

to conflicting statements as to the Nietzschean character of Mahler's music. Floros, for example, writes: 'It may therefore be concluded that the intellectual content of the Third Symphony is diametrically opposed to Nietzsche's philosophy' (Floros, 1994, p. 92); while Henry-Louis de La Grange suggests that 'The tragic undertones of the "nature" episodes in the first movement are thoroughly in keeping with Nietzsche's conception of a tragedy that is inherent in the cosmic principle ... . In Nietzsche's work, as in Mahler's, humor is a consequence, an offspring of this tragic feeling' (La Grange, 1973, p. 801).[19] Moreover, through the recognition of, and reliance on, the work's verbal and resulting musical meanings, one may realize the interesting connection Mahler made in this symphony between the pessimistic humour of the *Wunderhorn* poetry and that of Nietzsche's works: just as the *Wunderhorn* poems scorn an over-serious attitude toward religion, Nietzsche's irreverence and 'light-hearted defiance of convention' in *The Gay Science* suggest that through this title he wanted 'to convey ... that serious thinking does not have to be stodgy, heavy, dusty' (Kaufmann, 1974, p. 5). Similarly, Mahler would not have been insensitive to Nietzsche's statements in the preface of this book, which resonate very much with ideas that can be sensed in a more general vein directly from Mahler's music:

> How the theatrical scream of passion now hurts our ears, how strange to our taste the whole romantic uproar and tumult of senses have become, which the educated mob loves, and all its aspirations after the elevated, inflated and exaggerated! No, if we convalescents still need art, it is another kind of art – a mocking, light, fleeting, divinely untroubled, divinely artificial art that, like a pure flame, licks into unclouded skies. ... what above all is needed for this: [is] cheerfulness.

> (Nietzsche, [1887] 1974, p. 37)

This interpenetration of Nietzschean and *Wunderhorn* aesthetics can be perceived very clearly in Mahler's music, and it provides a more convincing proof of the 'coherence' of the Symphony than the 'nature' programme Mahler provided.

It is not only the contribution of the verbal texts surviving in one way or another in the final work that should be made a fuller participant in the work's meaning, but also – and especially – the wealth of information that Mahler's music itself conveys. Through its reliance on 'known signs', on generic and other connotations of the thematic and gestural materials, Mahler's music, more than most other composers', allows the listeners/analysts to identify and interpret those signs according to their various levels of competence. Moreover, these signs never act on one level alone: they are so contradictory and multi-levelled that, instead of a monological, univalent, straightforward interpretation, they

---

[19] La Grange, 1979, pp. 102–12 and McGrath, 1974, esp. pp. 89–99 present strong arguments in support of the influence of Nietzschean ideas on Mahler through his affiliation with the Pernerstorfer circle in 1878 and his friendship with Lipiner.

suggest polyvalent meanings which on the surface sometimes seem incomprehensible and irreconcilable.

Contexts and narratives

In an attempt to redress the balance among the contributions of the various sources of meaning in Mahler's Third Symphony, the remainder of this chapter will reconstruct some of the musical meanings by giving a voice to the story the music tells us, and placing this in dialogue with the various other kinds of meanings – a process which will lead not to a closed, finite 'solution' or 'key' to the work's meaning, but, rather, to an openness towards the infinite meanings that Barthes's notion of 'plural text' implies (see Barthes, 1977, p. 159). For, as Scott Burnham proposes, 'As soon as a privileged version of a piece's meaning is determined … [led by the 'positivist' rather than by the 'hermeneutic' impulse], the piece is stopped dead in its tracks … [and] rendered a museum of its own meaning' (Burnham, 2001, p. 198). In other words the work should remain open.

Recognizing music as part of 'cultural practice' (Kramer, 1990, p. xii) has proved fruitful for understanding musical meaning alongside other discursive practices, that is, for viewing music in a broader semiotic field related to other disciplines in terms of its ability to present patterns of reality, society or human mental constructions. The notion of plural text as a 'methodological field', introduced by Roland Barthes (1977, p. 157), which views the work as a network of intertextual relations cutting across various cultural languages, answers the need for a reintegration of the musical text within some kind of context. One possibility of hermeneutic assessments of musical meaning has emerged through methodologies from other, especially literary, fields such as narrative theory. For if, as Barthes has observed, 'narrative is international, transhistorical, transcultural: it is simply there like life itself' (ibid., p. 79) and if music is one of the cultural expressions of life, it makes sense to assume that it too might share with other cultural manifestations some basic characteristics in which experiences are fashioned. Hayden White's broad definition – 'narrative might well be considered a solution to a problem of general human concern, namely, the problem of how to translate *knowing* into *telling*' (White, 1981, p. 1) – certainly allows a place for music among cultural artefacts that in some way internalize various kinds of narrative pattern.

Despite their variety, most narrative theories agree on some basic principles, and these can also be applied to music. Both musical and narrative discourse unfold in time; they present 'at least two events … neither of which logically presupposes or entails the other' (Prince, 1982, p. 4) in a specific temporal (that is, discursive) sequence, during which there is 'at least one modification of a state of affairs … into another state' (Prince, 1987, pp. 58–59). In both musical and narrative discourse there is a tension between the temporal sequence in which the events might be presented according to some virtual scheme (what narratologists call 'story time'), and the actual idiosyncratic unfolding and working out of those events in the respective piece (called 'discourse time'). In so far as they 'do not merely recount changes of state' but rather 'constitute[s] and interpret[s] them as signifying parts of signifying wholes' (ibid., p. 60), both literary and musical discourse also represent a particular way of translating some kind of 'knowing' into some kind of 'telling' (White, 1981, p. 1) and thus present narrative features.

Aside from these basic principles, narrative theories differ from one another, and the approaches to, and definitions of, music as narrative – drawn by musicologists from a variety of narratological models – are just as diverse. For example, to define the 'narrative quality' in Mahler's Ninth Symphony, Anthony Newcomb devised a conception that combines Ricoeur's notion of 'narrative activity', the Russian Formalists' idea of 'plot archetype', and the musical features which Adorno found responsible for the novel-like quality of Mahler's music (specifically the composer's loosening of formal schemata and the behaviour of his themes as 'characters'). For Newcomb, 'the narrative quality of Mahler's music comes most powerfully from the intersection of formal paradigm, thematic recurrence and transformation, and ... plot archetype' (1992, p. 119), which together reproduce a 'quest paradigm' characteristic of the romantic *Bildungsroman*. Fred Maus, on the other hand, sees the narrative quality of music from a perceiver's point of view, likening the succession of 'musical events as a series of fictional actions' to the activity of following actions in a play or a novel (Maus, 1991, p. 14).[20] Robert Samuels regards musical narration as a semiotic enterprise most effective in hermeneutically enhancing the 'analytical project' when it is constructed at the 'intersection of different levels of reference and different sorts of codes' (Samuels, 1995, p. 155). His view of musical discourse in the context of a general textuality enables him to state that 'a musical text ... is not a mere sequence of sounds any more than a literary work is a sequence of words' (Samuels, 1994, p. 154), and thus it can be included among all other discourses.

In her book *Unsung Voices*, which was of great influence in the questioning of the validity of narratological approaches to music, Carolyn Abbate rejects the idea of musical narrative as inhering in heard plot paradigms, event-sequence or reordering (Abbate, 1991, pp. 48–49). More specifically, in her criticism that music lacks the ability to narrate because it 'seems not to "have a past tense"' (ibid., p. 52), she agrees with Jean-Jacques Nattiez that narrative features, rather than residing in the musical work, emerge from our own 'narrative impulse' and therefore, '*in itself* ... music is not a narrative and ... any description of its formal structures in terms of narrativity is nothing but superfluous metaphor' (Nattiez,

---

[20] He also provides a convincing discussion of the problems surrounding the notions of 'story' and 'discourse' as applied to music. See Maus, 1991, esp. pp. 21–24.

1990, p. 257).[21] Instead, Abbate narrows down the 'signs of narrative in music' to 'a voice with a characteristic way of speaking' (1991, p. 48), and thus limits music's ability to narrate to rare 'moments that can be identified by their bizarre and disruptive effect' (ibid., p. 29). Lawrence Kramer shares her view that narrative in music consists of unusual, 'disruptive' processes rather than 'normative' ones, and can be found only in musical works that 'explicitly call attention to their own contingent, historical, rhetorical character' (Kramer, 1990, p. 189).

Leaving aside the fundamental question addressed by Abbate and Nattiez of whether one can truly speak of narrative in music, the point made by these analyses is that by decoding musical meanings by analogy with literary or other discourses, they neither betray the *intrinsic musical features* (or what Cone (1982, p. 234) and Agawu (1991, p. 23, borrowing from Jakobson) would respectively call 'congeneric' meaning and 'introversive semiosis') nor claim for music the exact, propositional semantic meanings resulting from subject and predicate linguistic constructions in literary narratives. Rather, they find equivalences between the abstract principles of unfolding which can be shown to be shared by music and narrative. This is what Adorno meant when he wrote of Mahler's music: 'It is not the music wanting to recount something, but, rather, the composer wanting to make music as if someone were narrating' ['Nicht Musik zwar will etwas erzählen, aber der Komponist will Musik machen, wie sonst einer erzählt'] (Adorno, 1992a, p. 62 and 1960, p. 86). Yet at the same time the narrative readings provide a theoretical framework for understanding how these musical features may be translated or mediated intertextually into broader concepts beyond the work itself (in other words into 'extrageneric' meaning or 'extroversive semiosis'): in short, how they produce textual meaning. Ultimately these narrative constructions of meaning belong within the realm of Barthes's concept of 'producing the text' (see Barthes, 1977, p. 157) with its potential plurality of meanings implicitly allowing for an integration between intrinsic and extrinsic information, or between text and context.

One of the many ways of reading the plural meanings of Mahler's Third Symphony would therefore be to evaluate the narratives that the 'music itself' presents, and which could, in turn, be bounced against the surrounding documentary narratives in an attempt to establish possible correlations or

---

[21] Samuels offers the example of Mahler's Fourth Symphony, whose first movement Adorno hears 'in the past tense' (see Adorno, 1960, p. 130, & 1992a, p. 96), as counter-argument to Abbate's claim (Samuels, 1994, p. 154). The status of the past tense as a prerequisite of narrative has also been questioned by certain literary critics. Prince observes, citing A.A. Mendilow (*Time and the Novel*, London: P. Nevill, 1952, p. 94), that 'the preterit in a fictional narrative is not primarily an indicator of time', since the 'past tense in which the events are narrated is transposed by the reader into a fictive present' (Prince, 1982, pp. 28–29).

tensions.[22] The following section of this chapter attempts to do this by using the notions of 'story' and 'discourse' from narrative theory and three further concepts: (1) connotation, which, to summarize Barthes, constitutes a second-level semiotic system in which entire signs from the first, denotative, level of signification become the signifiers of another system, and by being attached to various other signifieds engender an infinite chain of referential signs which thus allow music to project intersubjectively created meanings shared with the world outside itself (see Barthes, 1967, pp. 90–92, & 1974, pp. 6–9); (2) intertextuality, which can be defined as the property of 'texts' (in any field) to refer to, or interact with, other 'texts' (see Barthes, 1977), or which, as Jonathan Culler puts it, 'leads us to consider prior texts as contributions to a code which makes possible the various effects of signification' and becomes 'a designation of [a work's] participation in the discursive space of a culture' (1981, p. 103); and (3) musical topics, which can be considered as units of musical discourse, that is, musical formations which convey a number of associated connotations through their conventional usage within certain social, generic, affective, functional or other situations. Thus the 'recollection' connotation of a chorale topos, the dance character of some folk music, the 'call to arms' implied by trumpet-call-like signals, constitute recognizable (though changeable) signs (see Ratner, 1980, and Agawu, 1991).

The first movement of the Third Symphony

When listening to the opening phrases of the first movement of Mahler's Third Symphony one cannot help but be struck by the bold and multivalent meanings they convey. Their capacity for 'telling us' things – their 'narrative' power – comes from both the nature of the musical materials and the way in which they unfold. These two parameters may be considered analogous to the dichotomy, most commonly posited as the basis of any literary narrative, between 'story' (variously called 'fabula', 'histoire' or 'the narrated') and 'discourse' (variously called 'sujet', 'récit' or 'the narrating').[23] According to most narratologists,

---

[22] In an approach which somewhat overlaps with that of the present author, Raymond Monelle considers Mahler's Third Symphony as a 'musical text', by evaluating the relationship between the 'outside' and the 'inside' of the text, where the musical text is placed at the 'centre of a network of texts', as the 'epistemic nexus, the product of its significations' (Monelle, 2000, pp. 151 & 154–55). Similarly concerned with music as a 'textual field', Robert Samuels discusses Mahler's Fourth Symphony in terms of the 'several codes of listening' that participate in its intertextuality (Samuels, 1994, pp. 156 & 157). See also Lea, 1985, pp. 98–99 & 71–75.

[23] This dichotomy originated in the work of the Russian formalists. For various definitions see Erlich, 1965, Chatman, 1978, Genette, 1980, Prince, 1987 & 1982, Culler, 1981 (esp. chapter 9), Rimmon-Kenan, 1983, and Bal, 1997.

'story' designates the content (the signified) of the narrative, or the narrated events abstracted from their disposition in the text and reconstructed in their chronological order. To abstract the 'story' from a narrative means to isolate the events from the discourse in which they actually occur and to understand them as 'nondiscursive, nontextual given[s], something which exists prior to and independently of narrative presentation, and which the narrative then reports' (Culler, 1981, p. 171).[24] The 'discourse' consists of the means (the signifier) by which the content is communicated in the actual text, in other words the mode of unfolding of the events, or 'the representation of these events in the process of "telling"' (Rimmon-Kenan, 1983, p. 3).[25] Some critics view the narrative signification of a text as dependent on the tension created between the temporal aspects of its 'story' (the events of which it is made) and those of the 'discourse' (or unfolding) in which the events are embedded in that particular text. Thus the global narrative effect of a text emerges from the tension created between two different time orders: the causal and chronological order and time span of the events in the 'story' considered independently of the actual text, and the temporal order and actual reading time in which these events are 'told' or 'presented' in the 'discourse', that is, the ways in which the events actually unfold in the text.[26] The analogy with narrative constructions in literary theory is particularly strong in Mahler's music: the easily identifiable connotative layers of the thematic materials (the 'topical' content resulting from their generic, affective, social associations[27]) render them similar in function to 'events' in the 'story', while their idiosyncratic ways of unfolding – the order of events, their duration and timing, and the processes they undergo – analogically reproduce features of the narrative 'discourse'.

---

[24] An example of events in the 'story' would be: mother kills father; mother is arrested, son commits suicide. It could be argued that composers themselves conceive the thematic materials as the basic events from which they build a narrative since they often sketch those materials and then work out how to present them in sequence.

[25] An example of discursive emplotting of previous events would be: 'just before the son committed suicide, his uncle told him that his mother was in prison because she had killed his father'.

[26] See, for example, Chatman, 1981, p. 118: 'A salient property of narrative is double time structuring. That is, all narratives, in whatever medium, combine the time sequence of plot events, the time of the *histoire* ("story-time") with the time of the presentation of those events in the text, which we call "discourse-time". ... these two time orders are independent'; Rimmon-Kenan, 1983, p. 44: 'time in narrative fiction can be defined as the relations of chronology between story and text [i.e. discourse]'; Genette, 1980, p. 33, quoting Christian Metz, *Film Language: A Semiotics of Cinema*, trans. M. Taylor (New York: Oxford University Press, 1974), p. 18: 'one of the functions of narrative is to invent one time scheme in terms of another time scheme'.

[27] See Ratner, 1980, Agawu, 1991, Hatten, 1994 (esp. pp. 67–90), and the definition above.

We can thus consider the thematic materials of the opening bars of Mahler's Third Symphony as 'events' by treating them as topics and unveiling all their semantic layers of meaning. The eight-horn unison march of the first thirteen bars connotes sternness and ceremoniousness, and even has militaristic connotations; yet it has an enigmatic, provocative quality since several aspects seem to encourage us not to take its seriousness at face value. The harmonic underpinning, filled with fluctuating tonal allusions, brings yet another layer to the topics: the V–I in D minor suggested by the opening A–D fourth is strongly denied by the B flat major suggestion of the descending D–B flat–F arpeggio, but soon flavoured by the Lydian raised-fourth E natural, and a possible implication of G minor in the descent from A to A in bars 9–10. The 'sternness' does not last long, however: it soon relaxes and by bar 14 is neutralized by the oscillating Debussy-like parallel chords of bars 14–20 in the low registers of horns, bassoons and contrabassoons. By revolving long enough around the pitch A these undulations gradually establish it as the dominant of what finally comes to sound like a tonic key of D minor, giving way, by bar 25, to yet another change of topic: the incisive rhythm and short, scattered formulae openly announce a funeral march beginning at bar 27 (see materials labelled 'a' in Section A of Table 11.1 at the end of this chapter).

There is something crooked about this statement. Through the sheer force of the blaring horns, and through its symmetrical phrasing for the first eight bars, the march pretends to advance forwards convincingly yet it makes a *faux pas* straight after the first two notes by pretending to start with V–I as if it were following a generic march formula in D minor but then transposing the clichéd formula by reinterpreting the D as the third of B flat major, the key in which the march continues. This slipping of the march formula down a third makes it seem in retrospect as if the first interval had been distorted from a major sixth to a perfect fourth, as if the 'normal' first two notes had been mistakenly intoned A–D (in D) instead of F–D (in B flat major). In conjunction with the mercurial slipping of the harmony, this intimates that the decisive march was defective, presaging its short-lived nature, until its actual entanglement in the dwindling chords at bar 14.

Many scholars have identified a strong resemblance between this clichéd march formula and the theme of a German song, which, having had links with several different texts, became part of every Austro-German's musical heritage. As Henry A. Lea has asserted, the theme, which originated in 'a Thuringian folk tune', was not only commonly used as a 'well-known German patriotic song' ('Ich hab mich ergeben mit Herz und Hand' ['I've given myself with heart and with hand']), but also adopted for the student song 'Wir hatten gebauet ein stattliches Haus' ['We had built a stately home']. It also bore similarities to another patriotic German song called 'Ich hatt einen Kameraden' ['Once I had a comrade'] (see Lea, 1985, pp. 71–75). During his youthful association with the socialist Pernerstorfer circle (see, for example, McGrath, 1981, pp. 89–99, and

La Grange, 1974, pp. 102–6), and later with other socialist rallies (see Mitchell, 1975, p. 436), Mahler would have been familiar with these tunes which 'served as patriotic rallying and marching songs' (Lea, 1985, p. 72); this is all the more likely given his role as pianist accompanying such nationalistic German marches at some of the socialist meetings of the Pernerstorfer circle (see McGrath, 1981, p. 89). At least one other German critic has identified the theme with a children's marching song (Krenek, 1941, p. 193). But aside from the need for historical accuracy, the exact source of the reference is not ultimately important, because even with slight variations the original tune would contain enough characteristic clichés for it to be associated both by Mahler's contemporaries and in our time with an 'urban march' musical type or topic. As the semantic characteristics of this 'type' are incorporated – yet at the same time distorted – in Mahler's theme, this 'event of the story' embodies an intertextual dialogue between some kind of 'original' version and Mahler's, which 'distorts' the original, and which introduces a sense of irony (as Lea also notices (1985, p. 74)),[28] and of the grotesque. This is subsequently reinforced by the unexpected turn taken by the 'way of unfolding' or the 'discourse' of these events – the quiet abdication of the opening stentorian march in the wavering ambiguity of the chords at bars 14–20 – which is inconsistent with the implications suggested by the events at the beginning. Ernst Krenek perhaps best captured the process through which this opening tells so much:

> The result is obtained by choosing first an obviously outworn, obsolete symbol, so that it appears as a quotation from another age and style, and by then placing it in a surprising context of grandeur and monumentality ... The opening motive of the Third Symphony is literally identical with the first phrase of a marching song which all Austrian school children used to sing. Produced by eight French horns playing at full blast in unison and placed in an empty space, without any accompaniment, at the beginning of a symphonic movement of unheard-of dimensions, this motive takes on a very special significance precisely because of its being associated with that innocent little tune; a significance, however, that it would be difficult to analyse.
>
> (Krenek, 1941, pp. 193–94)

With all these generic and intertextual connotations, it is not difficult to hear in this opening a strong sense of social urban environment gone slightly awry. While Mahler's contemporaries noticed some of these associations, Mahler himself was compelled to integrate this opening programmatically into the

---

[28] Lea writes: 'Whether the opening horn call summons nature to wake from its sleep ... or whether it introduces a vast martial phantasmagoria, its allusions to patriotic songs and a Brahms theme seem to me ironic, but only in the sense of incongruous.' A similarly articulated observation follows on p. 75: 'By transforming the patriotic songs and using them to introduce this unmartial march, Mahler has stripped them of their original meaning, not by parodying them, but by elevating them to a symphonic statement.'

narrative of nature he had offered for the Symphony in the summer of 1895. As he was working on the first movement (the last to be composed) during July 1896, he had to find new ideas that would capture 'programmatically' at least some of the musical character of the introduction without compromising the previous programme. It was then, in conjunction with the first movement, that he brought the mythical Greek characters Pan and Bacchus into the account – associations carried over into the inscriptions on the fair copy of the movement finished on 17 October 1896, whose title page is labelled 'Einleitung: Pan erwacht [;] Nro I: Der Sommer marschirt ein ("Bachuszug")' – thus allowing such ideas as distortion, the grotesque and even terror to characterize this opening, as opposed to the lighter, pastoral character of other parts of the movement.[29] This late programmatic addition is certainly better suited to account for the musical meaning of the introduction than the previous ones connected with nature.

A further topic of musical discourse (or 'event') that is entirely missing from Mahler's verbal programmatic explanations first appears in bars 27–57, and strongly affects the movement's overall meaning (it is labelled 'b1' in section B of Table 11.1). The rhythm ♩ ♪♩ , heard first in the bass drum and then intoned as a full D minor chord in the trombones, gives clear generic markers of a 'funeral march' topic at the beginning of this section. At first we hear only this accompaniment formula, punctuated every other bar by the motif X (Ex. 11.1) in the lower woodwind (first heard at bar 28), and interrupted occasionally by the D minor plus major seventh arpeggio (D–F–A–C sharp) in the trumpet.

Ex. 11.1   Third Symphony, first movement, lower woodwind, bar 28

---

[29] Several things are worth noting here. First, the fact that the idea of differentiating Pan from Dionysus came to Mahler late in the process of composition – most likely *after* he had already finished composing the Introduction – is an indication of his decision to lend the Introduction, and implicitly the rest of the movement, a more lugubrious character as opposed to the lighter, pastoral tone of the original materials for the movement which he had first entitled 'Summer marching in'. (That title possibly corresponded to the 'pastoral' section at bars 132–63 of the finished score, a section which nevertheless is titled 'Pan schläft' in the fair copy of the movement completed on 17 October 1896). Secondly, this turn towards a more gruesome irony through distortion is further attested by the fact that in the Stanford Library sketch (Stanford 630, p. 1) the version of the opening horn melody that appears on the same page with the 'Summer march' material still bears the opening sixth interval from the original quoted march. The change to the ambiguous fourth, and its consequences, are not accounted for in programmes before the 'Pan' association mentioned during June–July 1896. For information on both programmes and titles see, for example, Filler, 1977, pp. 78–82, Franklin, 1980, p. 59, and Olsen, 1992, pp. 354–93; for copies or transcriptions of the sketch see Franklin, 1991, p. 44, & 1977, p. 443, Krummacher, 1990, p. 358, and Olsen, 1992, p. 590.

The bass line is brought to the dominant of D minor three times through a sweeping, ascending scalic gesture in the cellos and double basses (bars 39–41, 45–48 and 52–56) initially marked *wild* in the score (bar 39). While on the first two occasions the harmony remains in the ostinato tonic, the third time, at bar 56, a full shift to the dominant occurs, signalling the end of the funeral march accompaniment, and the beginning of a fortissimo rhapsodic arioso section intoned by the eight horns in octaves (labelled 'b2' in section B of Table 11.1). As the dominant harmony is prolonged for the next eight bars (56–64), this melodic phrase sounds very much like a consequent phrase to the first one, but also like the much-awaited 'melody' that had been missing from the accompanimental formulae of the funeral march.[30] The voice of the horns, passing temporarily into the trumpet (bars 83–98) and back, springs out of the first notes of the funereal motivic formula X, and develops them into a long, undulating, imploring lament, accompanied mostly by tremolos, further theatrical, 'wild' sweeping scales prompting every new harmonic arrival, and the occasional D minor plus major seventh trumpet call, always 'stuck' at the same pitch level, and sounding even more agonized than it had during the funeral march. This lament topic prevails until bar 115, where a short transition in the same vein leads to the next section at bar 132.

If the bombastic, pompous, distorted march of the introduction could be taken as an ironic, even grotesque commentary on mob demonstrations, there is nothing in this funeral march/lament section that brings relief. On the contrary it has a heart-rending quality, heightened especially by a feature of the 'discourse' – the disembodied funeral march accompaniment lacking a melody. The missing melody's arrival at bar 58 in the recitative arioso style confirms the implications of the empty accompaniment: it is a serious plaint, conveying a sense of tragedy and alienation.[31] There is no programmatic indication that conveys the forceful pain of this music. Given the likelihood that Mahler composed the material long after the 'carefree', evolutionary, nature conception of the Symphony had been devised, there was no place for it in the programme.

The arrival of the next section at bar 132 (beginning in the new key of B flat major but slipping miraculously after a few bars into D flat major), with its shimmering, fairy-tale chorale and buoyant, pastoral march characterized by polka-like rhythmic formulae, provides an even more striking contrast (see section C in Table 11.1). A third topic or event is now introduced, whose idyllic

---

[30] See Richard Kaplan's chapter in this book (Chapter 7) for further discussion of this part of the movement.

[31] The music here belongs to a topic similar to that of the so-called 'Grief' motif in the last movement of the Second Symphony, especially where the latter is developed instrumentally in the cello as a 'waltz' version accompanied by distant military signals (Second Symphony, fifth movement, bars 325–c. 379) after which the same motif is gradually transformed into a march topic.

atmosphere and steady rhythm correspond most closely to some of Mahler's programmatic indications. As shown by Mahler's sketches (and also by a study of the score), this light march is not unrelated thematically to the opening urban march, but it none the less shows a counterpart, a totally different face of it. Rhythm, instrumentation and melody all contribute to the rustic nature of this section, whose playful harmonic disjunctions (for example, V of B minor 'resolving' to D flat major in bars 135–36), slightly vulgar clarinet trills, and an exaggeratedly tender, tongue-in-cheek and sentimental rendition of the theme in the violin (marked *zart* in the score), suggest some kind of comic procession. Even though different in topic, like its more serious predecessors, this section does not last long, ending with a comic presentation of the march/polka melody in the double basses (bars 155–56), and with the sounds of a 'magic' percussion march in the triangle, cymbals, tambourine and bass drum fading in the distance to bar 163. Unexpectedly the atmosphere turns instantly dark again at bar 164, with the return of the funeral march and the tragic rhapsodizing lament, now in the similarly plaintive trombone. As at its first appearance, the section ends (at bar 224) with a dissolution. While the musical topic lasts, communicating the presence of grief, the discursive unfolding accentuates the distress by conveying additional semantic ideas: the unfolding of the rhapsodic trombone melody in long, often repetitively circling, notes is very fragmented, proceeding as if the statements attempt to articulate themselves, but then have trouble advancing (especially in bars 185–93). Moreover, by bar 204, the rhapsodic plaint subsides into desperate trumpet calls, leading into the final dissolution at bar 224. With the return of the pastoral march at bar 225, the 'carefree' world takes hold again, and, appropriately, the 'discourse' supports the meaning conveyed by the events of the story. New melodic fragments appear as variations of the initial ones (see, for example, the clarinet melody in bars 254–55), incongruous themes are assigned to lower strings, making their movement awkward (see bars 245–46, where they attempt to play fast arpeggios imitating bird-call fragments), semitone chromatic sliding replaces prepared tonal moves (for example, bars 236–37), contrapuntal lines made out of fragments of different signals and motifs go in different directions, and a sense of neoclassical stasis contributes to the increased chaotic frivolity of the otherwise disembodied comic march which has been reduced to superimposed fragments.

Throughout the movement the craziness increases, as more and more incongruous variations and combinations of these marches occur, culminating with a janissary march or dervish dance-like section at bar 608, leading to what could be perceived as a recapitulation of the opening materials at bar 643 (refer to the sections marked in Table 11.1). Here the funeral march and arioso lament ideas are heard for the last time, and the 'pastoral' and 'urban' marches take over until the end with several superimposed variations (four-part counterpoint at bar 762, three-part counterpoint at bar 832). After achieving a six-bar catastrophic climax and collapse (a failed breakthrough in Adornian terms) at bar 857, the movement ends twelve bars later in a victorious fanfare. If the topics of funeral march, pastoral, and urban march represent 'events', the breakthrough dissolutions point, at the level of the 'discourse', to the notions of impossibility and futility, which could be further connected with similar moments from other movements (for example, the sentimentality of bars 424–40 corresponds to the posthorn episode in the third movement, and some of the dissolutions anticipate the one which occurs before the end of the same movement, bars 541–c. 560).

In terms of musical discourse, the main procedures through which this movement unfolds consist of varied juxtapositions and superimpositions of the three main topics: the 'urban march', the 'funeral march plus the rhapsodizing arioso lament' and the 'pastoral, nature-like march' (see Table 11.1). Not only is this type of unfolding alien to a conventional first-movement sonata form, but also – because of the strongly individualized topics and this additive unfolding – there is a contradiction between the semantic presence of the themes and their traditional functions in a first-movement allegro. The 'progressive tonality' of the movement (beginning in an ambiguous D minor/B flat major key, and ending in F major, the key areas of the main thematic materials being D minor, B flat major and D flat/D major) does not help to clarify which theme is more stable than another. It is thus not surprising that it has been difficult for the Symphony's various critics to arrive at similar partitionings of the movement as a sonata form.[32] For instance, which is the first theme of the exposition: the opening urban march because of its stentorian force, the funeral march because it is stable and tonally anchored in D minor, or the pastoral march even though it appears only at bar 132, in the 'wrong' and unstable key? How can the funeral march be the first theme when it is never developed, and when in any case its rhapsodic nature renders the material unsuitable for development? If the pastoral march is the subordinate theme, why does it occupy the greater part of the movement?

Obviously, the strong semantic connotations of the materials and the irregularities of their unfolding trigger the need to explicate the meaning of the movement in alternative ways, and the concept of 'narrative impulse' might be of help in this. In terms of presence in the movement, the dominant topic is the pastoral march with its variations, churning out each time a plethora of new melodies and clichéd march formulae. The 'urban march' topic (labelled 'a' in Table 11.1) appears by itself only in its distorted version, once at the opening of the movement and once at bar 643 where a quasi-recapitulation occurs. During the rest of the movement the 'urban march', with its multiple variations, is used only in superimposition with the 'pastoral march' (labelled 'c' in Table 11.1), sometimes sharing so many formulae that their genres become confused. The

---

[32] For example, bar 369 is considered to be the start of a second exposition by La Grange (1973, p. 802), the beginning of the development by Floros (1994, p. 94), and 'the first section of the development [which] at first resembles a recapitulation' by Adorno (1992a, p. 80).

third set of materials, the funeral march and the rhapsodic arioso lament (labelled 'b1' and 'b2' in section B of Table 11.1), take proportionally the least duration: they occur only as distinct episodes, at bars 27, 164, 369 (only the arioso lament, not the march), and for the last time at bar 671 in the recapitulation. So the question of which is the 'main theme' and which the 'secondary theme' of the sonata form is impossible to answer through traditional means, since each of the thematic materials here serves a relatively consistent structural/semantic function, and they are all equally important in outlining the 'plot' of the movement: the annunciatory power of the 'urban march' sets in motion both the 'march theme' of the movement and the tragic irony of its distortion; the funeral march and lament articulate the reality of the tragedy (death) and the human reaction to it (lament); and the 'pastoral march' with its variations, distortions and grotesque turns identifies the paradoxical illusion of carefree, unthreatened life. As seen in Table 11.1, the movement is more accurately described as four sets of combinations of these topics, whose logic of ordering in the 'discourse', while not causally determined, results in part from the same principle as that by which events are narrativized in literary discourse: the 'post hoc, ergo propter hoc' principle of narrative formation, that is, the fictitious illusion of 'consecutiveness and consequence' created by discourse (see Prince, 1982, p. 40, Prince, 1987, p. 76, and Barthes, 1977, pp. 98–100). In Barthes's words, 'the mainspring of narrative is precisely the confusion of consecution and consequence, what comes *after* being read in narrative as what is *caused by*' (Barthes, 1977, p. 94). Through the narrative lens, the story of the movement could be called a 'saturnalia of march' with interludes of tragic reality, a formulation to which we have arrived through the music, yet which is strikingly similar to Nietzsche's definition of 'Gay Science' as signifying the 'saturnalia of a spirit who has patiently resisted a terrible, long pressure, without submitting but also without hope, and who now is attacked by hope for health, and the *intoxication* of convalescence' (Nietzsche, [1887] 1974, p. 32). It is through the music that we have now come closer to an understanding of why Mahler would have named the movement after Nietzsche's work.

Demonstrating the rich and quite articulate meanings that it is possible to draw from the musical text itself, and uncovering a possible narrative for the musical text – not by starting from the documentary sources but rather the other way around – might have helped us regain confidence in the music's 'ways of telling'. Yet this does not address the problem of how the information 'extragenerically' surrounding the music narrative can be reconciled with what is internal ('intrageneric'). For in light of the musical 'story' it is difficult, for example, to fathom why Mahler described this movement in June 1896 to Bauer-Lechner as 'lifeless, rigid nature', when the music obviously proclaims human intoxication with life and tragedy. Were we to privilege the documentary sources over the music's narrative potential by distrusting the music's power to signify, we would inauspiciously close the text based on the illusion that we are doing justice to the composer's 'authorial intentions'. Gérard Genette's notion of 'paratext' might provide a way out of this impasse.

Genette codifies the 'accompanying productions' of a text (titles, prefaces, dedications, letters, confessions, and so on; in other words, 'practices and discourses of all kinds dating from all periods' of the text's existence) under the name of 'paratext'. This is a 'threshold', an 'undefined zone' between the outside and the inside of the text, a 'place of pragmatics' which may influence the reception of the text (Genette, 1997, pp. 1–2). In Genette's classification all such materials (private confidences, letters, annotations on the score), which he would call 'the private epitext', are alike in that they are not 'publicly' but, rather, 'privately' addressed. These are further divided into the 'confidential epitext' (addressed to other people) and the 'intimate epitext' (in which the author addresses himself) (ibid., pp. 371–72). While Genette recognizes the contribution of the epitext to meaning (even though it is found by 'peeking behind the author's shoulder') and the necessity of confronting the 'text' with it (as we are attempting to do here), he warns of the dangers of taking its 'documentary value' as 'absolute veridicity' (ibid., pp. 395–96). Furthermore, while a 'threshold exists to be crossed', he advises, 'the paratext is only an assistant, only an accessory of the text' and should not be allowed to 'play its own game to the detriment of the text' (ibid., p. 410).

Heeding Genette's advice, we may now confront the Mahlerian 'text' with the 'paratext' and perhaps learn from the exercise to appreciate the complexity of this threshold. While some kind of connection with nature is conceivable in the 'pastoral march' sections of Mahler's movement, many inscriptions in the score seem either out of place or redundant, in comparison with the richness of the musical story. One might attempt to explain why Mahler himself labelled the introductory 'urban march' *Pan erwacht* in the summer of 1896, by using the argument that his inscription *Der Weckruf!* at the top of the first page of the opening march in the fair copy invokes the calling, reveille-like qualities of the original rallying march tune, and could just as well be applied to the idea of Pan awakening. But Mahler's calling the 'pastoral march' *Pan schläft* (written in the autograph fair copy above bar 132[33]), is one of the private, possibly self-addressed, 'epitexts' which requires a more complex interpretation if it is to be seen as at all meaningful in the narrative of the musical text. In terms of conventional musical language, there is little in this section that directly suggests 'sleep': if anything, the gracious movement of the lively pastoral march connotes 'awakening', and Mahler's other purported association of this passage with the idea of 'Summer marching in' would fit better. Moreover, while the musical materials of this and the previous section could be perceived as presenting two

---

[33] For all these inscriptions the author has consulted the autograph fair copy of the symphony housed in the Pierpont Morgan Library, New York, Robert Owen Lehman Collection, Albrecht 1147 B.

different faces of the idea of 'march' which even have some thematic relationships in common (as confirmed by Mahler's superimposition of the two themes in the sketches), the opposition between the loud opening (awakening) march and this lighter, pastoral and slightly comic march cannot readily be construed as equivalent to the opposition awakening/sleeping (except on an entirely metaphorical level which would be of little help in elucidating musical content). On the other hand the initially shimmering quality of the music and the subsequent unfolding of the march could feasibly be interpreted in the light of the inscription and the mythological qualities of the figure of Pan, who traditionally slept at noon, disliked having his sleep disturbed, and had the ability to project dreams and visions and to make men stampede like cattle in 'panic' terror.[34] In this case, the epitext would step temporarily inside the text and would inspire a multi-layered reading of this and other passages in light of the mythical character. This might be an example in which the private epitexts seem to clarify the text. However, at the same time, as Genette alerts us, the very fact that the author has left them behind should make us suspicious of their innocent authenticity; for despite the 'degree of intention', there is 'no guarantee of comprehensiveness' (Genette, 1997, p. 396), and they can easily turn into an 'impediment' (ibid., p. 410). Perhaps Adorno, with customary brilliance, managed to overcome this threshold most successfully. Allowing a dialogue between the musical text and the epitext, he embraced both the essence of the music and its discrepancy with the external information: 'The literary idea of the great god Pan has invaded the sense of form; form itself becomes something both fearful and monstrous, the objectification of chaos; nothing else is the truth of the concept of nature, especially misused in relation to this movement (Adorno, 1992a, p. 78, & 1960, p. 109).

If in leaving these inscriptions behind Mahler had intended more than a self-reflective act, and wanted them to have an explanatory effect, then he could have made his paratext public; yet, as he rightly intuited, even this would not have guaranteed a better understanding of the music, for once the paratext starts 'playing its own game [it is] to the detriment of its text's game' (Genette, 1997, p. 410). For example, labelling the imitations of bird calls at bar 148 as *Das Herold* seems redundant, because the mimetic bird call is captured anyway in the motif underneath the inscription. Moreover, in general terms the evolutionary 'nature' story that Mahler presented for the entire symphony can hardly be sustained by the content of the musical 'story'. Coming after the stormy first movement, the minuet second movement does not feel at all like an 'evolution' but rather provides respite – a delicate, restful moment whose title 'What the flowers tell me' is not inappropriate, but does not add much to the movement's atmosphere. In one way the third movement's title 'What the animals in the forest

---

[34] I am grateful to Jeremy Barham for offering this idea (personal communication, April 2002).

tell me' is redundant, because the musical materials incorporating the cuckoo fable are expressive enough on their own to suggest a naive, childish fairy-tale 'game'; in another way, the title is misleading, because it does not reflect the nostalgia and melancholic romantic symbolism of the posthorn episode – specifically human sentiments with which Mahler juxtaposes the naive 'fable' music. The *Zarathustra* text of the fourth movement is so philosophically dense that again the title 'What man tells me' tends to trivialize its meaning, while 'Es sungen drei Engel' is, as we have seen, both textually and musically self-explanatory. Finally, the chorale connotations of the last movement's main theme convey the idea of elevated recollection and meditation, which might be more closely reflected in the idea of 'God' (rather than 'Love') which Mahler occasionally associated with the movement.[35]

Conclusion

In this study the author joins the small but important group of musicologists who have started to look critically at the relationship between the meaning of works and associated documentary evidence. First we have to learn not to take the composer's words as the complete or ultimate truth. Walter Benjamin discovered that long ago when he said about Goethe: 'To wish to gain an understanding of *Elective Affinities* from the author's own words on the subject is a wasted effort. For it is precisely their aim to forbid access to critique' (Benjamin, 1996, p. 313). Goethe himself, like Mahler occasionally, acknowledged the cryptic nature of his work: 'I have put many things in it, and hidden much in it. May this open secret give pleasure to you too' (letter of Goethe to Zelter, cited in ibid.).[36] Secondly, we have to re-learn to trust the ability of music to convey meanings beyond the so-called 'musical' ones, and allow ourselves to tease those meanings out without fearing their potential for telling us about the world. These meanings will be different from those we can obtain from other media: they will still be general, elusive and secretive, but they will nevertheless provide as much truth as the documentary 'evidence' will. As Scott Burnham has so elegantly put it recently, this involves

> allowing the poetic and the analytic to mingle freely as mutually enhancing perspectives ... In short, precisely because music is musical, it can speak to us of things that are not strictly musical. This is how we hear music speak:

---

[35] Mahler's comment about this movement in a letter to Annie Mincieux of early November 1896 remains puzzling: while mentioning the motto of the movement 'Father behold my wounds, let no being be lost', he says: 'It is the highest level of structure: *God!* Or if you like, The Superman' (Blaukopf, 1983, p. 127, & 1986, p. 123). See Barham, 1998, for further discussion of this question.

[36] I would like to thank Kristina Muxfeldt for mentioning the Benjamin source to me.

not by reducing it to some other set of circumstances – music is simply not reducible to any other circumstances, whether cultural, historical, biographical, or sexual, and any attempt to make it so has only a cartoonish reality – but by allowing it the opacity of its own voice, and then engaging that voice in ways that reflect both its presence and our own, much as we allow others a voice when we converse with them.

(Burnham, 2001, pp. 199 & 215)

Yet as Douglas Johnson acknowledges, we 'should not have to abandon the rules of evidence. ... All that is necessary is to readmit the evidence of the score' (Johnson, 1998, p. 235). We should remember to 'bring sketch [source evidence] and work alternately into focus' and freely acknowledge that 'one reading of the text may contradict another' (ibid., p. 234). Yet we could have perhaps done this by revisiting what the brilliant critic E.D. Hirsch said many years ago: 'The text is the safest source of clues to the author's outlook ... it is unsound to insist on deriving all inferences from the "text itself" ... the extrinsic information should be brought in with a "verificative function"' (Hirsch, 1967, p. 241). Just like documentary evidence, music is a reliable historical artefact whose own voice should rightfully be allowed to bounce against that of the 'documentary evidence', in the hope that a new flexible, malleable and plural kind of 'historical truth' will result from their intertextual encounter.

Table 11.1 Third Symphony, first movement: form, motivic content and narrative process

Bar numbers	1	27	57	132	164	225	369
'Sonata form'	Exposition				'Devel.'		
Large sections							
Smaller sections	A	B		C	B	C	B
Subsection bars	1 13	27	57 83 99			225 273	
Subsections/ motifs	A chords a	b1 [X]	b2 (3 phrases)	c	b1 + b2	c1, c2 etc., + a mixed snippets of march clichés	b2
Keys	d/B♭	d	d	(B♭) D♭	d	(B♭) D♭ F	d
Instrumentation (predominant)	8 horns	Low strings, ww.	8 horns, trp., low strings	Ww., strings	Melody in trb.	Begins like B at b. 27, but adds brass	Horn
Topics (story/events)	Urban march	Funeral march	Lament, *Klage* recit/arioso	Light, pastoral march	Funeral march + lament	Pastoral march variations	Arioso lament (only)
Discursive features (discourse)	'Urban march', aggressive, militaristic dissolves into chords	Bass rhythm. No melody, but melodic fragments springing from X	Recitative-like, rhapsodic melody, tragic character. Phrases serve antecedent–consequent functions	March rhythm, with comic overtones of a polka rhythm. Begins as if in B♭, but over 4 bars slides chromatically into D♭. Ends with a shimmering percussion march distancing itself	At b. 204 tragic rhapsodizing becomes trumpet calls. Section ends by sliding down	Urban march in an 'original' non-distorted version appears incorporated within the pastoral march and borrows lighter character from it, but then martial character invades pastoral. 3-part counterpoint ends with collapse of march music into curtain of sound (*durchbruch*) leading to the desperate plaint in horns in the next section	Similar to b. 57 but fuller

	411	449	530	643	671	737	857	863–75
Bar numbers	411	449	530	643	671	737	857	863–75
'Sonata form'				Recap.				Coda
Large sections		←——————————→		←—————————→		——————→		
Smaller sections	Interlude	C	C	A	B	C		
Subsection bars		449 478	530 583		671	737 762 800	857	
Subsections/ motifs	c gradually appears variations + a		c, gradually 'a' c + a	a	b1 b2	'c' varied + 'a'		All
Keys	G♭	D F–G♭	b♭ C	d	d	c–B♭– F		F
Instrumentation (predominant)	Trb., cor angl.	Str., ww.	Various orchestral groups	8 horns	Trb.	Groups combined		All
Topics (story/events)	Transformation scene	Pastoral march	Pastoral march 'humorous', then grotesque	Urban march	Funeral march + lament	Mixed march Catastrophic climax (857)		Victorious march
Discursive features (discourse)	Horn calls, rhapsodic pastoral; mollified, legato	Mollified, light	c march with more and more variations, a becomes janissary march. Much superimposition of newly emerging melodic fragments. Sense of chaotic movement	Similar to A	Shorter than the first time	New variations of a and c, culminating with 4- and 3-part counterpoint at bb. 762 and 832. Ends in failed *durchbruch*		Non-thematic

PART FOUR

Mahler in Performance

Mahler's First Season as Director at the k.k. Hofoperntheater: The Composer Waits in the Wings

HERTA BLAUKOPF
translated by Jeremy Barham

In his first season in Vienna, 1897–98, Mahler already set the course for his later operatic reforms. He began by giving uncut performances of Wagner's music dramas; he expanded the repertoire with new works or new productions of neglected ones; he prevented latecomers from entering the auditorium; he prohibited the claque; he himself stood on the rostrum more than a hundred times; he irritated many popular singers of the old school and constantly looked for new artists who were willing and able to travel with him along the difficult path of profuse rehearsals, the path from opera to modern music theatre. For Mahler was not only a conductor but also a stage director, an exacting teacher of singers, orchestra and the public alike. Despite his respect for Weber and Lortzing, he left no doubt during his first season that two composers would be central to his activities: Mozart and Wagner.

The public and critics greeted him well-nigh enthusiastically at his debut as *Kapellmeister* in May 1897. There were already rumours that the new man had been called to even higher things than conducting repertory performances of *Lohengrin* or *Die Zauberflöte*. But why the need for an additional conductor? Vienna had the great Hans Richter who also conducted the Philharmonic concerts, and besides him two other conductors and a further one for the ballet. What was this Gustav Mahler – until recently employed in Hamburg – supposed to do? To be sure, the fact that he had previously directed the Royal Opera in Budapest for two and a half years gave food for thought. No other position engaged the Viennese imagination and passion for gossip more intensively than that of the Director of its Opera and Burgtheater. It is still the case today, and was even more so in the days of the Habsburg Monarchy when the Hofoper was directly under the control of the Imperial and Royal Court represented by the Lord Chamberlain [*Obersthofmeister*]. It made no difference whether or not those who encouraged and spread rumours had ever set foot inside the institution they were speaking about.

Amidst the 'eclectic conglomeration of styles' [*eklektizistisches Stilkonglomerat*] in the late nineteenth century, the eminent Austrian novelist and essayist Hermann Broch discovered a unique area where stylistic tradition still persisted: the dramatic arts (2001, p. 14). In the intellectual life of Vienna, and particularly in the theatre, argues Broch, the patterns of courtly life remained intact: 'the opera continued to have its gala performances where the presence of the Emperor granted the audience a small share in the reflected glory of the Monarchy by the grace of God' ['die Oper hatte auch weiterhin ihre Galaaufführungen, in denen die Anwesenheit des Kaisers dem Zuschauer ein Stück Partizipation am Glanz des Gottesgnadentums vermittelte'] (ibid., p. 52). In northerly Hamburg, Mahler had jokingly referred to 'the god of the southern climes' when dreaming of a call to the Directorship of the Vienna Opera (Killian, 1984, p. 74, and Franklin, 1980, p. 74). He was quite right: the Director of the Vienna Opera was a kind of god, especially compared with directors of court – or indeed municipal – theatres in Germany. Did he not negotiate in the name of His Apostolic Majesty, Emperor Franz Josef I, who covered the deficit out of his 'private purse'?

The rumour mongers who had predicted Mahler's speedy replacement of the virtually blind incumbent Wilhelm Jahn were proved right. By the end of July he had already been appointed Deputy Director. He opened the new season on 1 August with a performance of *Lohengrin*. The house was almost sold out and the takings amounted to a sensational 3686 Gulden.[1] From then until 15 August Mahler stood on the rostrum seven times. He was accustomed to such unremitting activity, for during many of his Hamburg seasons he had conducted over 120 performances. To summarize: in his first Vienna season of 1897–98 he conducted 23 different works in 111 performances (see Willnauer, 1993, p. 39). Through this he got to know the strengths and weaknesses of the repertoire and the ensemble inside out. He quickly learned which performances merely had to be dusted down a little, which ones had to be studied musically afresh with a new cast, and those which had to be produced from scratch. On top of all this, the programme had to be expanded with new works. Since he could not improve everything at once, from time to time he put up with certain compromises: the old stage sets were essentially retained and only some scenes were given new décor.

For the second half of August, however, Mahler planned something even more momentous: a complete performance of Wagner's *Der Ring des Nibelungen* cycle without the many nonsensical cuts which had become customary in Vienna. In August 1896 Mahler had travelled to Bayreuth to experience the so-called 'authentic' *Ring*. He had already visited Bayreuth several times without ever having seen Wagner's *magnum opus*. In fact the *Ring*, which had inaugurated the Bayreuth Festival so magnificently in 1876, was not to be performed again for

---

[1] Information taken from the '*Cassa-Rapporte*, 1 August–31 December 1897', in the Haus-, Hof- und Staatsarchiv, Vienna.

twenty years. While Wagner himself had died in the intervening years, Hans Richter, the conductor of the first performance, was still living. The overall artistic direction lay in the hands of the master's widow, Cosima Wagner. She was always favourably disposed towards Mahler, the devoted Wagner conductor, although he presumably knew only too well that as an anti-Semite she would never allow him to conduct in Bayreuth. He may even have been aware that she intrigued in high-ranking circles against his appointment at the Vienna Opera (see Mahler, 1971, p. 37, & 1990, p. 12). It was therefore very opportune for Mahler that the current Director Jahn had programmed the *Ring* for August: he could now create his own Bayreuth. Strangely enough the revival of the *Ring* began in April of that year shortly before Mahler's arrival in Vienna not with *Das Rheingold* but with the second and third 'days', as Wagner called them. Having brushed up *Siegfried* and *Götterdämmerung* in several stage and orchestra rehearsals, Richter performed them on 26 and 29 April.[2] It is probable that Mahler, having just arrived in Vienna, saw Richter's *Götterdämmerung*.

Immediately after his Viennese debut on 11 May Mahler became immersed in solo and ensemble rehearsals for *Die Walküre*. The preparation of this work seemed particularly important because it would be its hundredth performance at the Hofoper. This jubilee performance was planned for 28 May but did not take place. It had to be postponed until August, a more favourable month for a presentation of the whole cycle because then there were no subscription performances. Mahler began rehearsals of *Das Rheingold* and *Die Walküre* on 9 August at the latest, spending a particularly long time on the ensembles of the three Rhinemaidens and the eight Valkyries. He also arranged several stage rehearsals with piano and with orchestra. The rehearsals for the remaining parts of the *Ring* seem to have been scant by comparison. The Rhinemaidens of *Götterdämmerung* were rehearsed along with several selected scenes which had hitherto been performed only in mutilated form, such as the duet between Siegfried and Brünnhilde in the last act of *Siegfried*. Nevertheless, the performances bore Mahler's personal signature.

The *Ring* project had been accomplished – but not quite. Mahler was not able to perform the four parts of the work on successive evenings as in Bayreuth, but had to insert an evening of ballet between *Die Walküre* and *Siegfried*. He was also unable to cast roles with the same singers throughout. Wotan in *Die Walküre* was different from Wotan in *Das Rheingold*, and the Siegfried of *Götterdämmerung* was not the same youthful hero who had appeared on the previous day. The role of Brünnhilde, on the other hand, was played to great advantage on the three evenings by the same singer, the great Sophie Sedlmair. After the performance of *Die Walküre* she came up to kiss Mahler's hands because he had been mouthing every note and every syllable for her throughout (see Killian, 1984, p. 98, and

---

[2]   All rehearsal information is taken from the 1897 rehearsal book [*Probenbuch*] of the k.u.k. Hofoperntheater housed in the Haus-, Hof- und Staatsarchiv, Vienna.

Franklin, 1980, p. 99). Owing to a lack of suitable singers he did not manage to stage the customarily deleted Norns' scene: not until autumn 1898 was he able to include the three Norns. Nevertheless the composer Hugo Wolf, who was in the audience on all four evenings, seems to have been profoundly impressed: 'We managed to hear what nobody had heard before and what we had already given up hope of hearing, except through looking in the score' (Killian, 1984, pp. 98–99, and Franklin, 1980, p. 100; editor's translation).

The newspapers took little notice of this venture. After all, it was only a matter of repertoire performances, and Mahler's restoration of the previously deleted parts seemed unimportant, if not superfluous, to many a critic. The *Neue Freie Presse*, the leading liberal paper in Austria, contented itself with a brief notice that on the previous day the hundredth performance of *Die Walküre* had taken place: 'None of the artists who took part in the first performance is active any longer, and not even Hans Richter stood at the rostrum as usual, but rather Herr Mahler, whose profound seriousness and great enthusiasm showed that he was the equal of the greatest masters of his art' ['Von den ausübenden Künstlern der 1. Aufführung ist jetzt keiner mehr am Werke und sogar am Pulte saß nicht wie sonst Hans Richter, sondern Herr Mahler, der mit seinem tiefen Ernst und seinem hohen Enthusiasmus es den ersten Meistern seiner Kunst gleich tut'].[3] The anti-Semitically oriented *Deutsche Zeitung*, which despite its name was an Austrian paper, reported on all four evenings. Mahler was praised because he performed *Das Rheingold* without a break, but the reviewer decided after the jubilee performance of *Die Walküre* that Mahler had failed, particularly in the case of the 'magic fire': 'He only revealed to us what we value in Hans Richter' ['Er hat uns erst schätzen gelehrt, was wir an Hans Richter besitzen'].[4] The relationship between Mahler and Richter became a political issue. Notably the same critic found words of appreciation for the barely rehearsed *Siegfried*, while *Götterdämmerung* fared worse despite praise for the reinstatement of cut passages.[5]

Although Mahler and Richter always treated each other with respect and courtesy, they were rivals. The 54-year-old Richter certainly took little pleasure in the day-to-day running of an opera theatre, but he cannot have been indifferent to the appointment of a 37-year-old over his head. Furthermore, although he had no desire to let himself be ousted, he had turned his back somewhat on Vienna and built up a second career as conductor in London and Manchester. The generational conflict was understandably intensified because Richter had many keen supporters in Vienna, and, of course, within the orchestra as well. Anti-Semitic commentators gladly seized the opportunity to play the 'Teutonic' Richter off against the 'Jewish' Mahler. Behind all these personal and political

---

  3 *Neue Freie Presse*, 27 August 1897.
  4 *Deutsche Zeitung*, 26 & 27 August 1897.
  5 Ibid., 29 & 30 August 1897.

conflicts lay a fundamentally different view of musical interpretation. While Mahler saw in Richter merely an 'honest [*biederer*] Hans' (Blaukopf, 1996, p. 141), Richter, though admittedly viewing Mahler as a competent director, also saw in him an arrogant conductor who dared to interfere with the scores of the great masters.[6] Richter gradually withdrew from Vienna. However, in the 1897–98 season he still conducted thirty-seven performances, including eight of *Die Meistersinger von Nürnberg*. 'He conducted the first act, in which I enjoyed him greatly, like a master; the second like a schoolmaster and the third like a master cobbler' reported Mahler, who had heard one of the performances (Killian, 1984, p. 89, and Franklin, 1980, p. 92; translation slightly amended). Richter also conducted parts of the *Ring* (but not the whole cycle), along with many Italian works including *La traviata* and *Il barbiere di Siviglia*. In March 1900 he officially left Vienna and the Hofoper.

Immediately after finishing his *Ring* cycle in August 1897 Mahler began rehearsals for the new production of Lortzing's opera *Zar und Zimmermann*, which had not been given for ten years. The critics were enthusiastic. Mahler was 'the right man in the right place' ['der richtige Mann am richtigen Platz'], noted one of the reviewers,[7] while another wrote 'the mood intensified from one act to the next. We had clearly been expecting a carpenter and we got a Tsar' ['die Stimmung steigerte sich von Akt zu Akt. Man hatte offenbar einen Zimmermann erwartet und ein Zar war gekommen'].[8]

The Hofoper usually celebrated the Emperor's name day on 4 October with a première. The Deputy Opera Director, about to be appointed full Director, chose Smetana's *Dalibor* for this occasion. When Mahler had been engaged at the German Theatre in Prague for the 1885–86 season he had frequently attended the Czech National Theatre [Narodni Divadlo], and got to know Smetana's operas there. In Hamburg he had programmed no fewer than four of Smetana's operas, including *Dalibor*, but scored a public success only with *Prodaná nevěstá* [*The Bartered Bride*]. Now he wanted to try out *Dalibor* – of which he was especially fond – in Vienna as well. There he cut the final scene in order to make the ending, to his mind, more effective, leaving the opera to conclude with the freeing of Dalibor. He himself supervised the design and preparation of the décor and costumes, and worked musically and interpretatively with the soloists (the famous Wagner tenor Hermann Winkelmann and the dramatic soprano Sophie Sedlmair) and chorus, scheduling more rehearsals than was customary in Vienna even for new productions. An orchestral rehearsal was held as early as 15 September, and rehearsals with piano ran concurrently. The orchestra practised daily from 27 September with the whole ensemble until the dress rehearsal on

---

6 *Neues Wiener Tagblatt*, 28 September 1902.
7 *Neues Wiener Journal*, 12 September 1897.
8 *Neue Freie Presse*, 12 September 1897.

2 October, and the first performance took place on 4 October. The day after the première one critic enthused as follows:

> He [Mahler] has not only the power but also the flexibility characteristic of the most inspired conductors. He blends the orchestra, stage set, and voices into an invigorating whole, the individual parts not only working together as in a well-oiled machine, but also appearing to blossom into life like an organism in full flower.[9]

Only an unworldly musical idealist like Mahler could have hit upon the idea of introducing himself to the Vienna of 1897 with a previously unknown Czech opera. The unfortunate Smetana – accused by his compatriots of Wagnerism and consequently of a kind of treason – was, unsurprisingly, regarded by many Viennese in the explosive situation of that time as ultra-Czech, and was rejected on nationalist grounds. It was bad enough to them that *The Bartered Bride* had gained acceptance in Vienna. The latent civil war between Czech and German speakers in the multi-national Habsburg Monarchy had escalated dangerously in recent months. The Polish Count Badeni had been at the head of the Austrian government for about two years, initially holding his ground very successfully amidst the conflict of nationalities. However, in April 1897, in order to resolve the simmering dispute over the official language in Bohemia and Moravia, he had issued a decree – not quite a law – that the Czech and German languages were to be of equal standing in both interior and exterior official communications. All government officials employed after 1 July 1901 had to demonstrate written and spoken proficiency in both languages. The outrage among the German-speaking population was considerable. Protest rallies and acts of violence were provoked by both sides. A few weeks after the *Dalibor* première there were disturbances in the Parliament in Vienna and large street demonstrations which resulted in the dismissal of Prime Minister Badeni. In the midst of this tense situation, which gave advance notice of the ensuing downfall of the Habsburg Monarchy some twenty years later, Mahler presented a Czech opera – in German of course, because it was still not customary at that time to perform operas in the original language despite Badeni's decree.

Mahler presumably thought nothing of it. He had no time to follow political events. But he would have been able to read in the following day's newspapers just how politically his première was regarded. 'Given the subject matter and the author it is understandable that the Slav element was strongly represented in all parts of the house' ['Daß mit Rücksicht auf Sujet und Autor das slawische Element in allen Teilen des Hauses stark vertreten war, ist selbstverständlich'],

---

9 *Wiener Abendpost*, 5 October 1897. 'Er hat die Kraft, aber auch die Elastizität der genialsten Dirigenten. Orchester, Bühnenbild und Sängerkunst bindet er zu einem belebenden Ganzen, dessen Teile nicht nur wie in einem gesunden Mechanismus in einander greifen, sondern wie in einem blühenden Organismus sich lebendig zu entfalten scheinen.'

wrote one liberal paper favourable towards Mahler, 'and one saw people who were not normally in the habit of attending the first performance of a new opera. For instance, a great many Czech members of Parliament were there' ['und man sah Leute, die sonst eben nicht der Erstaufführung einer neuen Oper beizuwohnen pflegen. So waren zum Beispiel sehr viele tschechische Reichsratsabgeordnete da'].[10] The equally liberal *Neue Freie Presse* complained: 'The applause was particularly thunderous and deafening from the fourth gallery, where Czech students had gathered *en masse*' ['Besonders auf der 4. Galerie, wo tschechische Studenten sich in Massen eingefunden hatten, war der Applaus ein donnernder und betäubender'].[11] Mahler was not deterred by this. 'I *beat* my head against the wall', he used to say in such situations, 'but it is the *wall* that gets a hole!' (Killian, 1984, p. 116, and Franklin, 1980, p. 115; translation slightly amended). He repeated *Dalibor* four more times in October to the continued interest of the public, and kept the work in the repertoire until 1904. The hole in the wall was clearly not so large that Mahler undertook the production of another Czech opera. He declined to perform Smetana's *Dvě vdovy* [*The Two Widows*] and *Hubička* [*The Kiss*] which he had presented in Hamburg, and did not perform *Rusalka* although the negotiations with Dvořák were already far advanced. Unfortunately Janáček and his *Její pastorkyňa* [*Jenůfa*] had no luck at the Hofoper either.

Mahler scarcely got his breath back during that autumn. By Imperial appointment he was made artistic Director of the k.k. Hofoperntheater four days after the *Dalibor* première. It was both incredible and untimely that a Jew from Bohemia, although baptized a Catholic, had attained the highest artistic office in the land: incredible because for a long time anti-Semitism had been not just a personal prejudice but the declared programme of powerful political forces; untimely because the pan-German party had long been propagating a racist anti-Semitism to which baptism meant nothing. The equally anti-Semitic Christian-Socialist party had become extremely powerful in Vienna through the franchise laws which favoured the propertied classes. Its populist leader Dr Karl Lueger was elected mayor four times by a majority of the Viennese Municipal Council. But the Emperor, who had to endorse this election, rejected Lueger and he became only deputy mayor. Not until April 1897, the month when Mahler signed his contract as *Kapellmeister*, did the Emperor and Prime Minister Badeni give way for tactical reasons: Karl Lueger, a master of city government and demagogy, was permitted to take up his office. He became mayor of the Imperial capital city of Vienna and as a result anti-Semitism became an official political stance. On 27 August in the middle of Mahler's *Ring* cycle the *Deutsche Zeitung* warned about this Jew, maintaining that his programme pushed 'German

---

10   *Neues Wiener Tagblatt*, 5 October 1897.
11   *Neue Freie Presse*, 5 October 1897.

musicians to the back of the queue' ['die deutschen Musiker in die letzte Linie'].[12]
A few days later the same paper wrote: 'Regardless of the artistic abilities of this
man, the question remains whether it was absolutely necessary to place a Jew at
the head of our premier musical institution, and the answer to this question is
categorically "no"' ['Unbeschadet der künstlerischen Fähigkeiten dieses Mannes,
bleibt die Frage offen, ob es denn gerade notwendig war, einen Juden an die
Spitze unseres ersten Musikinstitutes zu stellen, und diese Frage ist mit aller
Bestimmtheit zu verneinen'].[13]

When Mahler had applied for a position in Vienna towards the end of 1896
and in the first months of 1897, he had asked all his friends in Vienna and
Budapest to make representations on his behalf to the appropriate authorities.
Through written and personal intercession to the *Intendant* of the Hoftheater,
artists, officials and politicians – including some eminent names – attempted
to convince the relevant people that Mahler was no madman, but rather a single-
minded musician who had achieved financial and musical success during his
leadership of the Budapest opera house. One of Mahler's supporters reputedly
pointed out Mahler's Jewish origins to the Lord Chamberlain [*Obersthofmeister*],
Prince Liechtenstein. The Prince is said to have answered, with reference to the
situation in Vienna, 'Things have not yet become so bad for us in Austria that
anti-Semitism is the crucial factor in matters such as this' (cited in Blaukopf,
1976a, p. 210, and Blaukopf & Blaukopf, 1991, p. 122; translation slightly
amended).[14] If the Prince made such decisive comments – and there is little
reason to doubt that he did – can we infer that Mahler's Jewishness not only did
him no harm but was in some respects actually useful? Perhaps the court wanted
to set an example in Mayor Lueger's Vienna. An anti-Semite reigned in the town
hall and a baptized Jew in the opera house a mere ten minutes' walk away.

Surprisingly the latter was accepted enthusiastically by opera-goers. Night
after night during the *Ring* performances in August a group of conservatoire
students and young musicians gathered outside the stage door to greet Mahler
with cheers (Killian, 1984, p. 100, and Franklin, 1980, p. 101). At the repeat
performance of *Dalibor* immediately following Mahler's appointment as
Director the audience wanted to give him an ovation but he brought the orchestra
in so quickly that they were unable to do so. Similarly he did not appear on the
stage at the end of the opera, despite shouts of 'Mahler!' (Killian, 1984, p. 101,
and Franklin, 1980, p. 103). In light of these reports, it should not be overlooked
that the percentage of Jewish opera-goers was higher than the corresponding
percentage of Jews in the general population of Vienna. Compared even with the
large number of Jewish artists in turn-of-the-century Vienna – on whom a

---

12 *Deutsche Zeitung*, 27 August 1897.
13 Ibid., 3 September 1897.
14 'So weit sind wir in Österreich doch nicht, daß der Antisemitismus hier den
Ausschlag gibt.' Letter from Mahler to Ödön von Mihalovich, 25 January 1897.

wealth of literature has been written – there was of course a far greater number of Jewish citizens who frequented the opera and the theatre, bought books and paintings, and, in short, represented a major part of the cultured classes. The young Egon Wellesz may be considered a typical example of those youthful Mahler devotees who gave the composer an enthusiastic reception. He later became a composer and music scholar (specializing in Byzantine studies) and, after emigrating, taught at Oxford. More than sixty years after the event he described the fascination that Mahler held for young people:

> Everyone wondered: 'Who will be conducting this evening?' For it was not customary at the time to put the name of the conductor in the programme. Suddenly a slender figure with dark, fluttering hair approached the desk with rapid steps, and a gasp went round the whole house. A swift downbeat from Mahler at the rostrum, and the performance began.
>
> (Wellesz, 1960, pp. 256–57)[15]

Immediately after his appointment as Director, Mahler turned his attention to *Die Zauberflöte*, which was in urgent need of revision. It was 'staged in a considerably improved version, and as a result encountered the kind of reception that it had not enjoyed here for years' ['in wesentlich aufgebesserter Fassung in Szene und fand in Folge dessen eine Aufnahme, der sie hier seit Jahren nicht begegnete'].[16] This performance was an example of Mahler's partial reform of a production. The essentials of Joseph Hofmann's old stage set were retained but the three boys now came out of the sky in a chariot of clouds, the temples in the Finale of the first act were marked with inscriptions,[17] the Queen of the Night appeared in new surroundings and the scene of the trials of fire and water was altered.[18] Clearly Mahler himself was not as satisfied with the result as were the critics, for he squeezed in a further three rehearsals before the next performance of *Die Zauberflöte* while already preparing a new work, and still more before subsequent performances.

Although Mahler did not present any more Czech operas during his ten-year period of office, he did venture to perform a Russian work as the second new production of the season: Tchaikovsky's *Eugene Onegin*. He had already conducted the work, along with *Dalibor*, in Hamburg, and had received warm praise from the composer, who was in attendance. Since Tchaikovsky had previously been known in Vienna only as a symphonist the *Wiener Abendpost* was now glad to get to know the operatic composer as well, hailing the reduction

---

[15] 'Man fragte sich: "Wer wird heute abend dirigieren?" Denn damals war es noch nicht Sitte, den Namen des Dirigenten auf das Programm zu setzen. Plötzlich mit schnellen Schritten eine schmale Gestalt mit schwarzem flatternden Haar zum Pult, ein Aufatmen ging durch das ganze Haus. Ein kurzer Schlag Mahlers mit dem Stab auf das Pult, und die Vorstellung fing an.'

[16] *Neue Freie Presse*, 17 October 1897.

[17] *Illustriertes Wiener Extrablatt*, 17 October 1897.

[18] *Fremdenblatt*, 17 October 1897.

of the stage area for the letter scene as a technical innovation.[19] The *Fremdenblatt* praised Director Mahler's thorough preparation of the opera down to the last detail.[20] But even here the bitter nationalistic tone was not far away. Though the *Neues Wiener Journal* admittedly viewed it as 'the bounden duty of a great cultural institution to provide haven to genuine artists regardless of national differences' ['Ehrenpflicht eines großen Kunstinstitutes, echter Künstlerschaft ohne Unterschied der Nation Obdach zu bieten'],[21] it once again immediately qualified this cosmopolitanism: 'What were we supposed to think when straight after the first scene … enthusiastic cheering erupted, forcing the cast to appear four times in front of the curtain? Do we wish to celebrate the triumph of pan-Slavism in the Hofoper?' ['Was soll man dazu sagen, wenn schon nach dem 1. Bild … ein Enthusiasmus losbrach, der die Mitwirkenden 4mal vor den Vorhang zwang? Wollte man einen Triumph des Panslawismus in der Hofoper feiern?']. The poison of nationalism had such a powerful effect that political intentions were presumed to exist behind every performance of a Slavonic opera. The *Deutsche Zeitung* considered that the performance in the Hofoper was 'nevertheless justified' [*immerhin gerechtfertigt*] but that 'the Empress's name day in German Vienna would have been more tactfully celebrated with a German, especially an Austro-German, opera' ['den Namenstag der Kaiserin im deutschen Wien taktvoller mit einer deutschen, besonders deutschösterreichischen Oper gefeiert'].[22]

Straight after this première Mahler prepared a new production of a thoroughly German work: Wagner's *Der fliegende Holländer*. This was performed at the end of a fiendish week: on Saturday 28 November Mahler conducted *Eugene Onegin*, on the following day *Zar und Zimmermann*, on 1 December *Dalibor*, on 2 December *Die Zauberflöte*, on 3 December *Onegin*, and on 4 December the partly revamped *Holländer*, which had required eight rehearsals. Officially it was just a new production of existing repertoire, but one improvement after another occurred to Mahler. He reinstated the remaining cut passages – the performance lasted half an hour longer[23] – and recast all the roles except the Dutchman.[24] The scenery was also partly new. Mahler thus evoked the atmosphere of 'an intimate chamber' [*ein trauliches Gemach*] from a hall in Daland's house, reducing the usual large number of chorus members to 30.[25] Nevertheless years later Hans Richter criticized Mahler for following the original score and not Wagner's revised version.[26] The title role was sung by the highly popular baritone Theodor

19 *Wiener Abendpost*, 20 November 1897.
20 *Fremdenblatt*, 20 November 1897.
21 *Neues Wiener Journal*, 20 November, 1897.
22 *Deutsche Zeitung*, 21 November 1897.
23 Ibid., 5 December 1897.
24 *Illustriertes Wiener Extrablatt*, 5 December 1897.
25 *Neue Freie Presse*, 5 December 1897.
26 *Neues Wiener Tagblatt*, 28 September 1902.

Reichmann, 'a Dutchman of thoroughly demonic power and sublime melancholy' ['vom Wirbel bis zur Zehe ein Holländer an Dämonik und großartiger Melancholie'], although he did not always comply with Mahler's wishes because of his overacting (Killian, 1984, p. 107). In fact Reichmann belonged to that part of the ensemble which persistently opposed the new Director's musical and dramatic ideas. The writer Felix Salten described the relationship between the singers and their Director, drawing on Reichmann's diary:

> Mahler pressurized him, forced him to retrain. Reichmann responded with torrents of indignation lasting for days, page after page – outbursts of anger vented on paper. He noted down his plans one of these days to throttle this impudent little Jewish Director who drilled him, the *Kammersänger*,[27] like a beginner. In the evening, after the performance, however, Hallelujah! The success was blurted out in the diary: thanks be to God and ... Mahler!
>
> (Salten, 1924, p. 69)[28]

These prayers of thanks were not surprising given that after the première he would read that his Dutchman 'had in many respects been even more profoundly accomplished' ['in mancher Hinsicht noch tiefer durchgebildet gewesen sei'][29] and that he had 'immersed himself more deeply in the dark hues of the role's character' ['sich noch tiefer in die dunkle Charakterfarbe der Rolle hineingesenkt [habe]'].[30]

Under the enormous pressure of his work Mahler's moods alternated between euphoria and resignation. At times he wanted to pack up and leave, or at least so he said. He longed for a kind of Bayreuth where he could prepare a limited number of works to an immaculate standard instead of the Vienna Opera where daily performances had to be given (see Killian, 1984, p. 102, and Franklin, 1980, pp. 103–4). He was nonetheless optimistic: 'In five years ... I will have solved my problem: all performances must be alike; the production of *Cavalleria rusticana* will demonstrate the same level of perfection as that of *Die Meistersinger*' ['In 5 Jahren ... werde ich meine Aufgabe gelöst haben, es wird eine Vorstellung wie die andere sein müssen, die Wiedergabe der Cavalleria rusticana wird dieselbe Vollendung aufweisen wie die der Meistersinger'] (Karpath, 1934, p. 88). When his close friend Natalie Bauer-Lechner urged him to do something about performing his symphonies – the First, Second and Third

---

27   A title given to a singer of outstanding merit.
28   'Aber Mahler bedrängt ihn, Mahler zwingt ihn umzulernen. Nun kommen Entrüstungsstürme bei Reichmann, tagelang, seitenlang, Wutausbrüche, verrast auf dem Papier. Vorsätze schreibt er nieder, diesem dreisten, kleinen jüdischen Direktor, der ihn, den Kammersänger, wie einen Anfänger drillt, nächstens an die Gurgel zu springen. Am Abend nach der Vorstellung aber Hallelujah! Den Erfolg ins Tagebuch gestammelt, Dankgebete zu Gott und ... Mahler!'
29   *Neue Freie Presse*, 5 December 1897.
30   *Fremdenblatt*, 5 December 1897.

had already been written – he said: 'At the moment it does not matter to me whether my works are accepted a few years earlier or later; I am such a stranger to myself at the moment, and it often seems that I am not myself at all' (Killian, 1984, p. 102, and Franklin, 1980, p. 104; editor's translation). How fortunate it was that others took care of these symphonies. Towards the end of 1897 Mahler's old friend Guido Adler, a musicologist who taught at the German University in Prague, procured a considerable subsidy to support the printing costs of the score and parts of the First and Third Symphonies as well as the parts of the Second Symphony. The institution that provided the money was known as the Society for the Promotion of German Science, Art and Literature in Bohemia [Gesellschaft zur Förderung deutscher Wissenschaft, Kunst und Literatur in Böhmen]. Mahler was thus regarded as a German composer, at least in Bohemia.

Soon after his appointment as Director he introduced some innovations that caused more of a stir than his artistic endeavours. He prevented latecomers from entering the auditorium – particularly awkward in the case of *Das Rheingold*, which Mahler performed without breaks – and prohibited the singers from making use of the claque. Naturally he met some resistance because of this since the Viennese public saw opera not in terms of a musical drama whose progress was impaired by extraneous noises and even applause between scenes, but as a musical entertainment in which favourite singers showed off their vocal artistry at its best. All the soloists promised their Director as a matter of course that they would dispense with claqueurs but it was not so easy to keep this promise. One could take action against the paid claque but only with difficulty against the unpaid claque. For example there was the case of the tenor Hermann Winkelmann, who had created the role of Parsifal during his time at Bayreuth and now sang the great Wagner roles as well as Dalibor under Mahler. He had sung with Hans Richter in London, given guest performances in America and was so popular in Vienna that a Winkelmann Society had been formed which cheered its hero towards every high note and was not going to let any Director put a stop to it. After the end of the season Winkelmann released a statement in which he tried to justify himself:

> Despite declaring on my honour that I pander neither to the paid nor to the unpaid claque, I am yet again continually held responsible both by the esteemed management and by a part of the press for the incidents arising from the public's current tumultuous displays of appreciation. In order to exonerate myself completely, nothing remains for me to do – since unfortunately I have already tried every other means in vain – except to ignore the curtain calls which do me such honour.[31]

---

31 *Neue Freie Presse*, 3 March 1898. 'Trotz meiner ehrenwörtlichen Erklärung, daß ich weder für bezahlte noch unbezahlte Claque bei meinen Auftritten sorge, werde ich sowohl von der löblichen Direktion wie auch von einem Teil der Presse stets von Neuem für die durch die stürmischen Beifallsbezeugungen des P.T. Publikums entstehenden Vorkommnisse verantwortlich gemacht. Um mich von Verdächtigungen gründlich zu

It was small wonder that Mahler looked around for new singers. Immediately after his appointment as Director he petitioned the *Intendant* of the Hoftheater to engage the soprano Frances Saville and the tenor Franz Naval, who had recently been so outstanding in Puccini's *La Bohème* at the Theater an der Wien. To begin with they both appeared as guest artists at the Hofoper but before long they joined the ensemble. It was with some trepidation that Director Mahler viewed the prospect of a guest performance that had been planned for some time. On 8 December Anna von Mildenburg from the Hamburg Stadttheater made a guest appearance as Brünnhilde in a performance of *Die Walküre* conducted by Richter. Two years before this she had arrived in Hamburg as a complete beginner. Mahler had worked with her on all her roles and created an incomparable artist out of a gauche young lady with a big voice. Like a musical Pygmalion he had fallen in love with his creation and did not realize that the woman who was about twelve years his junior was not yet ready for the mutual affection which he demanded. After he had prepared her for the role of Kundry in *Parsifal* she was engaged by Cosima Wagner at Bayreuth and auditioned with great success in Vienna for the then Director Wilhelm Jahn. Now, however, Director Mahler stood in his place: a man who certainly wanted to obtain this most exceptional singer, but who was disappointed as a lover and above all did not wish to expose himself to gossip. 'I ask you now, dearest Anna', he had written earlier that summer, 'Do you feel you have the strength to work with me in Vienna, and – at least in the first year – to forgo personal contact and any preferential treatment on my part?' (Blaukopf, 1996, p. 251). We do not know what her answer was; nevertheless she appears to have accepted Mahler's conditions. After having sung Ortrud in *Lohengrin* under Mahler and Leonore in *Fidelio* under Richter as guest artist, she joined the ensemble of the Vienna Hofoper in June 1898. Her artistry was described as 'the greatest example of that creative power of dramatic performance truly formed and experienced from the music' ['das höchste Beispiel einer wirklich aus der Musik heraus formenden und erlebenden schöpferischen Kraft der tondramatischen Darstellung'] (Specht, 1919, p. 104).

Two months later a young Danish tenor by the name of Erik Schmedes, who was to become the most frequent of Mildenburg's singing partners, gave guest performances as Siegfried at the Hofoper. Together they sang the title roles in the forward-looking 1903 production of *Tristan und Isolde*. The third important new recruit was the baritone Leopold Demuth, whom Mahler already knew from Hamburg and who initially made guest appearances as René in *Un ballo in maschera* and Wolfram in *Tannhäuser*. Thus the new Director began his first few months by expanding and rejuvenating the ensemble. However, he never considered this quest for new and improved personnel to be finished, and the press continually criticized him for the frequency of guest

---

reinigen, bleibt mir, da ich jedes andere Mittel schon und leider vergeblich versucht habe … nichts anderes übrig, als den mich so ehrenden Hervorrufen nicht Folge zu leisten.'

performances, especially for the large number which did not result in contractual engagements.

The New Year

The *Intendant* of the Hoftheater was not only responsible for engagements but also for the overall accounts. The so-called 'preliminary' [*Präliminare*], fixed on the basis of previous revenue, was the amount that the Hofoper had to earn each day and during each calendar year from subscriptions and ticket sales. Mahler took over on 1 August with a deficit of 7986 Gulden but managed to end 1897 with a surplus of 13367 Gulden. His position was therefore consolidated not just artistically but also commercially. In the first week of the New Year Mahler conducted four performances, but without rehearsal since the first première was a ballet. He did not begin the serious preparation of another new work until 11 January. This was *Djamileh*, a comic opera by Georges Bizet which did not fill a whole evening's programme and was therefore coupled with various ballets. Mahler was extremely pleased: 'I have now delivered three operas: *Dalibor*, *Onegin* and *Djamileh* and turned them into box-office successes, while everywhere else they have failed. This is due even more to my stage production than it is to the musical performance', he reported to Natalie Bauer-Lechner (Killian, 1984, p. 110). This is one of the few statements in which he acknowledges his work as a stage director. He designed scenes based on the stylistic characteristics of the music. Through close observance of every musical nuance he guided singers towards a previously unknown sincerity of gesture, and through such gesture to more effective vocal expression.

In January a new production of Bellini's *Norma* was given under Hans Richter. The famous soprano Lilli Lehmann made a guest appearance in the title role, although no long-term engagement was planned. She was the dramatic prima donna of her day and had known Mahler since 1890 when he was Director in Budapest. In Vienna she sang Donna Anna in *Don Giovanni* and Leonore in *Fidelio* as well as Norma. No sooner had she gone than Mahler wrote to her with an invitation to give another guest performance in May (see Blaukopf, 1983, p. 100, & 1986, p. 96). She came with her pupil Olive Fremstad and they both appeared on 22 May in *Tristan und Isolde* under Mahler, although Fremstad, who sang the part of Brangäne, was not taken under contract. Mahler was to encounter her again ten years later at the Metropolitan Opera in New York where, having transformed herself into a soprano, she sang Isolde under his direction.

However, no guest appearance or première caused such a sensation, even at the rehearsal stage, as Leoncavallo's *La Bohème*. Mahler rated Mascagni very highly but did not like Leoncavallo: 'Shallow, overblown, oppressive, tinged with vulgarity throughout. The orchestration is superficial and noisy' ['Hohl, aufgeblasen, aufdringlich, überall Stich ins Gemeine. Instrumentation äußerlich, lärmend'].[32] He was far from happy therefore when Director Jahn sent him to Venice even before his debut in Vienna as *Kapellmeister*, in order to hear *La Bohème*. His negative report was to no avail. Jahn took on the opera and Mahler had to perform it. The situation was exacerbated by Leoncavallo's attendance at the rehearsals in Vienna. He was disgruntled from the start because Mahler had programmed the première for the end of February and not the autumn of 1897. Moreover he gave an ultimatum that the tenor Ernest Van Dyck must sing the role of Marcello – not an unreasonable demand since Van Dyck excelled in both Wagnerian roles and the French repertoire, had been engaged in Vienna for ten years and was one of the leading singers of his day. On 19 February the tenor announced by letter that he was indisposed and requested that the première be postponed from 23 to 26 February. Mahler, who had prepared the opera with two casts, was not willing to comply with this request since it would have disrupted all his plans for the repertoire and subscription performances. If Van Dyck would not or could not sing, then the tenor Andreas Dippel would do so in the première. As a result of this Leoncavallo wrote a letter to Mahler in which he also expressed support for the postponement because it seemed to him that 'the ensemble was not sufficiently well prepared and polished' ['das Zusammenspiel noch nicht genügend vorbereitet und abgerundet'] and besides he wanted Van Dyck to sing in the première.[33] Things came to a head at the next rehearsal, tempting even the *Neue Freie Presse* out of its usual noble reserve. Before the start Mahler, 'with obvious irritation' [*mit unverkennbarer Erregung*], made a short speech which referred to Leoncavallo's letter and continued:

> It is very good that Herr Leoncavallo is present and that his Italian friend can translate for him everything that is being said. I consider his doubts superfluous. An élite group of artists has assembled here on the stage and in the orchestra which will give the best performance of his work, certainly better than could be given anywhere else. As Director and *Kapellmeister* I can vouch for that. With a double cast I am able to prevent individual singers from causing me difficulties.[34]

Mahler wanted to begin the rehearsal but Leoncavallo then stood up and presented his arguments once more, until Mahler cut short the discussion with the

---

[32] Letter from Mahler to Richard Heuberger, 31 May 1897, published by Robert Hernried along with other letters of Mahler in *Anbruch*, 18 (3), May 1936, 65–69. The citation is from p. 67.

[33] *Neue Freie Presse*, 20 February 1898.

[34] Ibid. 'Es ist ganz gut, daß Herr Leoncavallo anwesend ist und daß ihm sein italienischer Freund gleich alles übersetzt, was hier gesprochen wird. Ich halte seine Bedenken für überflüssig. Hier ist auf der Bühne und im Orchester eine Elite von Künstlern vereinigt, die sein Werk aufs beste aufführen wird, gewiß besser, als es irgendwo anders aufgeführt werden kann. Dafür kann ich als Direktor und Kapellmeister einstehen. Bei einer doppelten Besetzung kann ich mir durch einen einzelnen Sänger keine Schwierigkeiten bereiten lassen.'

words: 'No more will be said here; there will be silence and we will rehearse!'
['Hier wird nicht mehr gesprochen, sondern geschwiegen und Probe gehalten!'],
whereupon Leoncavallo put on his hat and left the opera house.[35] As chance
would have it, two days before the première Leoncavallo attended the
performance of *Der Bajazzo* at the Hofoper and was informed of the successful
dress rehearsal of *La Bohème*. A letter from Mahler did the rest. Leoncavallo
resigned himself to the matter and the première was staged as planned on 23
February with Andreas Dippel as Marcello. It was a great spectacle in the Italian
style. Four archdukes attended in the court box. After the first act passionate
tributes were paid to Leoncavallo amidst the vocal ensemble. All's well that ends
well? Not if we read the opinion of the most famous critic in Vienna, the critic
who has gone down in music history for his opposition to Wagner: Eduard
Hanslick.

It was evident that neither Puccini's nor Leoncavallo's *La Bohème* did
anything for him, although he believed that 'greater musical talent and natural
feeling can be discerned in Puccini's opera' ['in Puccinis Oper mehr
musikalisches Talent und natürliche Empfindung wahrzunehmen'].[36] In a very
detailed review, Hanslick summed up his overall impression of Leoncavallo's
opera as follows: 'Considerable orchestral technique and understanding of the
stage, some *esprit*, but no creative power, no individuality, no sense of beauty'
['Viel Orchestertechnik, viel Bühnenverstand, einiger Esprit – aber keine
schöpferische Kraft, keine Individualität, kein Schönheitssinn']. On the tenor
Dippel who had replaced Van Dyck, he wrote: 'The difficult and demanding role
of Marcello the painter was sung expressively and with vigour by Herr Dippel,
and was well acted too' ['Der Maler Marcell, eine anstrengende und schwere
Partie, wird von Herrn Dippel sehr frisch und ausdrucksvoll gesungen, auch gut
gespielt'].[37]

That was Mahler's final new work of his first season. In the end he performed
Leoncavallo's *La Bohème* only six times. The season continued until 12 June but
Mahler was laid low by a long-standing illness and reduced his activities a little.
There were more new productions but he left *Un ballo in maschera*, *Robert le
Diable*, *Das Heimchen am Herd* and *Das Nachtlager in Granada* to other
conductors. Only the revival of *Aida* on 29 April 1898 did he take on himself.
One critic wrote: 'A new production under Mahler's direction means a complete
redesigning' ['Neu einstudiert unter Direktor Mahlers Leitung bedeutet eine
Neugestaltung von Grund auf'].[38] Mahler stood at the rostrum for the last time
that season on 3 June with *The Marriage of Figaro*.

---

[35] Ibid.
[36] *Neue Freie Presse*, 25 February 1898.
[37] Ibid.
[38] *Wiener Abendpost*, 30 April 1898.

In retrospect we can see that Mahler's first season was perhaps his most successful. He showed the path he wanted to pursue and, with a few exceptions, the public and critics followed him. He presented three new works which sparked the public's interest despite much politically motivated and uncultured opposition, and a fourth – *La Bohème* – which strengthened his position within the opera house. He demonstrated that neither the will of a singer – even if he were a star – nor that of a composer counted, but only the will of the Director who was both *Kapellmeister* and stage producer and who bore the ultimate responsibility. Mahler had gained many admirers and loyal supporters among Vienna's critics, whom he jokingly called the 'superiors' [*Vorgesetzten*], and they provided his performances with the necessary publicity, though not all of them remained his friends in subsequent seasons. In addition he could point to considerable financial success. The takings between 1 January and 12 June 1898 yielded a surplus of more than 12 600 Gulden compared with the 'Preliminary'. Mahler had every reason to be pleased with himself, as indeed he was. But he knew that his dedication to the Vienna Opera prevented him from doing more important things: 'I feel like a tradesman who travels on his own business and has to conduct business for other people on the side – only in my case the other people's business has had to become my main task and there is no longer any time or opportunity left for the work that the good Lord entrusted to me' (Killian, 1984, p. 116, and Franklin, 1980, p. 114; editor's translation).

Chapter Thirteen

Mahler on Record: The Spirit or the Letter?[1]

DAVID PICKETT

Mahler wrote his symphonies for concert performance in large halls. He had no idea that nearly a century after his death more people would listen to studio recordings of them through loudspeakers – and some through headphones while jogging in the park – than in live performance. Yet there is no doubt that the development of recording technology was largely responsible for their acceptance during the last forty years. In identifying factors that contributed to the explosion of interest in Mahler during the 1960s, Kurt Blaukopf wrote that 'perhaps the most decisive of all was the advent of the technically perfected stereo record' (Blaukopf, 1973, p. 248). Optimistically, as we shall see, Blaukopf also wrote: 'Studio-recording the music largely removes the risks of particular concert hall acoustics. ... If the strings threaten to be overpowered by the rampant brass, the balance can be restored by careful placing of microphones and by sensitive sound-editing at the mixer' (ibid., pp. 252–53). But Blaukopf was thinking in ideal terms, with which commercial considerations are often not consonant, and the intervening years have shown modern recording technology to be a mixed blessing. In exploring the demands made by a Mahler symphony on the recording process and examining whether it has lived up to Blaukopf's expectations, this study considers the work of fourteen conductors. Discussion is limited to the first seven symphonies, which Mahler himself conducted, to those conductors with connections to Mahler, and to the conductors central to the stimulation of interest in the composer in the middle of the twentieth century.[2]

---

[1] This chapter is dedicated to the memory of Kurt Blaukopf (1914–99) who, in addition to many other important contributions to musicological research, broadened the whole scope of Mahler studies with his concise biography and documentary study of the composer.

[2] The lack of detailed discussion of Barbirolli here is due both to the confinement of his Mahler conducting largely to Manchester and Berlin, and to EMI neglecting to record him in more than two of the symphonies, facts which unjustly limited his influence as a Mahler interpreter during his lifetime.

Mahler gave more detailed instructions about dynamics, tempi and colours than any composer before him. He told Natalie Bauer-Lechner about the care he took in scoring his works so that the right balance might be achieved without effort on the part of the performers, adding:

> In order that there should not be the slightest inaccuracy in rhythm, I have racked my brains to notate it as precisely as possible. Thus, I avoid indicating the shortness of notes, or the space between them, by dots or other staccato marks. Instead, everything is spelled out in detail by means of the note-values and rests. Of course, I am referring to the things that can be written down. All the most important things – the tempo, the total conception and structuring of a work – are almost impossible to pin down. For here we are concerned with something living and flowing that can never be the same even twice in succession. That is why metronome markings are inadequate and almost worthless; for unless the work is vulgarly ground out in barrel-organ style, the tempo will already have changed by the end of the second bar. Therefore the right inter-relationships of all the sections of the piece are much more important than the initial tempo. Whether the overall tempo is a degree faster or slower often depends on the mood of the conductor; it may well vary slightly without detriment to the work. What matters is that the whole should be alive, and, within the bounds of this freedom, be built up with irrevocable inevitability.
>
> (Franklin, 1980, pp. 45–46)

No less than Stravinsky, Mahler tried to make his scores conductor- and orchestra-proof. Unlike his predecessors who might be said to have described the effect they sought, Mahler wrote recipes for the performance of his works. He was able to do this because of his talents and experience as a conductor. He had heard enough bad performances to know the common mistakes made by conductors and orchestras and he made every effort to forestall them. He revised his scores many times after publication largely for this reason, thereby blurring the distinction between what was written by Mahler the composer and Mahler the conductor.

From players who worked with Mahler in New York, we know several details of his approach to music-making: he changed his mind about exact balance and tempi from day to day, he changed tempi freely from bar to bar as the work proceeded, and he liked to hear an articulation between phrases (Malloch, 1964).[3] The relevance of these characteristics needs to be determined by the interpreter of his works. We also know that Mahler composed with the expectation of first and second violins on either side of the concert platform. Disregarding this seriously diminishes the impact of passages like *II, v, 97–136*,[4] which has two-part writing that alternates abruptly between first and second violins, and which

---

[3] Some of these comments by orchestral players can be heard on the CD recording containing Mahler's piano rolls cited in the discography.

[4] The convention has been adopted of referring to the Mahler symphonies by italicized large roman numerals. Small italicized roman numerals indicate movement

might otherwise have been divided simply between the sections, or scored for one or both of the sections to play together; and yet out of the many hundreds of recordings only a few have respected this crucial Mahlerian sound element.[5]

Perhaps the sheer number of Mahler's instructions is the biggest hurdle for any conscientious conductor to overcome: changes of instrument, intricate dynamics, tempo marks, *Luftpausen* and more of them than in any other composer's scores, even Elgar's; these take time to absorb and memorize. Indeed, many of Mahler's notes for the conductor might well be taken as insulting, as when he specifically instructs: 'Um die Continuität des Tempo's zu befestigen, empfiehlt es sich, in den ersten Takten noch Viertel anzuschlagen' ['In order to establish continuity of tempo, it is advisable still to beat in crotchets in the first bars'] (*II, v, 672*), or 'Achtung auf den Unterschied zwischen *f* und *ff*' ['Pay attention to the difference between *f* and *ff*'] (*III, iii, 382*).

Bauer-Lechner describes how Mahler 'showed me in the score [of the Fourth Symphony] that, when he wants a passage played somewhat more slowly, he does not mark it *ritardando* (which the orchestra would immediately exaggerate) but "do not hurry" ["nicht eilen"]. Conversely when he wants an *accelerando* he writes "do not drag" ["nicht schleppen"]. "That's how you have to treat musicians – with cunning!"' (Franklin, 1980, p. 179). Mahler's cunning is amusingly exposed in *VIII, i, 76*, where simultaneously the choral basses have *nicht schleppen!* and the sopranos *sich Zeit lassen!* The interpreter must therefore determine which of Mahler's directions are to be taken literally and which are part of his cunning plan. When Mahler writes *ohne Hast* or *nicht eilen* does he mean just that, or does he really mean *etwas schleppend*? Is an extreme dynamic indicative of an intention to shock the listener, or merely there to ensure that an instrument at the rear of the orchestra or in a weak register can be heard in balance with the rest of the ensemble? It must also be borne in mind that nearly all the instruments used today by most orchestras are different in tone and carrying power from those known to Mahler.

The skills of the recording team are no less influential on the artistic success of a recording than those of the conductor and players, and since Mahler strove so hard himself to achieve clarity, the correct balance of voices and sections of the orchestra is crucial. Generally, with limited possibilities for spot microphones, recordings made before about 1960 are well balanced sonically, and one is grateful for the natural stereo sound accorded to conductors like Walter and Klemperer by virtue of the small number of microphones used. Many stereo

---

numbers and italicized arabic numerals are used for bars. Thus *II, v, 97* indicates Second Symphony, fifth movement, bar 97.

[5] Among the conductors discussed here, only Klemperer and Kubelik made stereo recordings with second violins on the right, though it should be noted that Wyn Morris and Eliahu Inbal are also among those adhering to this layout, while Simon Rattle and Riccardo Chailly sometimes employ it.

radio broadcasts have also benefited from this approach. The BBC recording of Horenstein's 1959 performance of the Eighth Symphony gives a true impression of the scale of the work. Instead of providing the aural effect of a close wide-angle lens, or a collage of superimposed close sounds, the microphone placing enables one to imagine the ensemble ranged from front to back and left to right. One can hear clearly what else is going on when the soloists sing, whereas most other recordings feature an undignified fight for precedence between the soloists.

While it might be expected to confer great benefits in the case of a composer whose watchword was clarity, the adoption of extra microphones has often resulted in grossly distorted balances. Mahler's post-publication changes to his scores reflect his experience in the concert hall; and in recordings, when microphones are placed close to woodwind, harps and percussion instruments, it is sometimes helpful to know what his first thoughts were. A good case is the one-note entry of the clarinets in *V, iii, 397*. This note (E) is nothing more than the completion of the E minor arpeggio in the first violins marked *piano*. In the original manuscript Mahler instructs the first clarinet to play *mezzo forte*, since the player is at the back of the orchestra. In the first edition the note is assigned to two clarinets and by the second edition we find three clarinets marked *ff*. The ludicrously comic effect that a close-miked clarinet section produces on many recordings with this one note is quite amazing.[6]

That this is not an isolated problem is demonstrated by Horenstein's 1970 recording of the Fourth Symphony, which suffers in many places from excessive highlighting of the harp and wind instruments. The most flagrant examples are the horns in *iv, 48* and *iv, 117–19* and clarinets and bassoons elsewhere. At *ii, 234* the first bassoon is clearly highlighted, and in the passage which begins at *ii, 254* the woodwind microphones inflate Mahler's late revisions of scoring and *ff* dynamic for the clarinets and bassoons to the point of caricature.[7] Even in tuttis like *i, 251–61* the orchestra's internal balance is poor, with booming timpani. This is a great pity, since Horenstein's tempi are exemplary. Did he listen to the final result and approve this misrepresentation of Mahler's intentions?

Mahler also told Bauer-Lechner: 'If a string player has a solo, he thinks it is there only so that he can play as loudly and prominently as possible' (Franklin, 1980, p. 98). This is no less true today: there are few recordings in which the solo violin does not drown out everything else in *IV, i, 103–7*. Other passages which, much to their disadvantage, have been assimilated by players, are the double-bass solo in the First Symphony, which is now much easier for the average player than

---

6 Benjamin Zander's 2000 recording illustrates this to perfection.

7 Mahler's fair-copy manuscript indicates at *IV, ii, 254* two clarinets *mf etwas hervortretend*. The first published score has *ff*, and Mahler's later revision, incorporated in the 1963 Internationale Gustav Mahler Gesellschaft score, adds a third clarinet, with reinforcement by two bassoons in bars 257–59 and 261 and four flutes in bar 260. These changes were a response to Mahler's rehearsal and concert experiences. I am grateful to Reinhold Kubik for making available a copy of these bars in the autograph.

it was in Mahler's day. Yet this and the scordatura violin solo in the Fourth Symphony are designed to sound unusual and eerie. There is also a considerable danger that the trombone solos in the Third Symphony and the many horn solos are perceived merely as opportunities for virtuosic display, and are played without consideration of their context.

Some of Mahler's requests are commonly ignored. An example of this is his instruction in *II, ii, 196*: 'Die Triolenfigur immer gleichschnell, die Pausen breiter ausführen' ['Always play the triplet figure equally fast and make the rests longer']. Thus, while the notes which occupy only the first beat of the bar are played at an equally rapid pace, the silent second and third beats are to become longer. Another is the instruction given in *III, i, 634* for the distant snare drums to enter 'in alten Marschtempo, ohne Rücksicht auf Celli und Bässe' ['in the old March tempo, without regard for the cellos and basses'].

Mahler's few repeats were often not observed by the older generation of conductors. In the First Symphony neither is observed by Walter or Mitropoulos; Scherchen, Barbirolli and Abravanel observe the second movement repeat only; Kubelik omits the latter but gives the repeat in the first movement. The repeat of the Sixth Symphony's exposition was omitted by Barbirolli, Scherchen, Mitropoulos, Abravanel and Flipse.

Mahler's piano rolls

Had Mahler lived in a later age he might, like Elgar and Stravinsky, have had an opportunity to record his own performances. But the audio recordings of his day were not a serious musical tool and we should perhaps be thankful that we do not have to interpret them. Were we able to hear a recording of him conducting in good sound it would be interesting to know whether Mahler himself succeeded in persuading his soloists in the Eighth Symphony to sing with regard for each other; exactly how fast he took the Scherzos of his Second and Fourth Symphonies; and, above all, how the cowbells should sound. We do, though, have 23 minutes of his music on four piano rolls which Mahler himself cut in 1905. We do not know how seriously he took this exercise, since no letters have survived in which he describes the session; but his experience of hearing Oskar Fried conduct the Resurrection Symphony the previous day may have convinced him of the possible value of such a recording.

Though the Welte-Mignon system was more faithful than most, absolute tempi and refinement of dynamics are hard to ascertain from a piano roll. Nevertheless, Mahler's tendency to change tempo from bar to bar is clearly heard, and one is made acutely aware of his rubato throughout the recordings. Some details, like the triplets of the opening movement of the Fifth Symphony, bear out his admonitions in the score, while other subtleties are possible only on the piano. The omission of other details in this piano roll, like the soft timpani rhythm of bar 316 and parts of the trumpet fanfares of bars 236–37, may indicate an inadequacy of the system. Significantly, in bar 23, Mahler demonstrates that he does not expect ritenuto every time he writes *pesante*, and his sforzandi are always in proportion to the prevailing dynamic. The trombone motif which makes its first appearance in bar 27, though marked *schwer* in the score, is often lightened by Mahler. The dotted-crotchet motif in strings and wind (e.g. bars 275–77) is frequently almost double-dotted. The relationship between the two basic tempi of the movement is less extreme than one might expect. Thus bars 153 and 154 are ♩ = c. 60, and the speed of the next six bars (*Plötzlich schneller. Leidenschaftlich. Wild*) is a moderate ♩ = 104, though this is modified when Mahler surges ahead at ♩ = c. 126 for bars 174–77.[8]

Mahler plays the Finale of his Fourth Symphony extremely delicately, particularly the grace notes. Again, there are many changes of tempo from bar to bar which are not indicated in any score, and Mahler's gradual accelerando beginning in bar 87 – marked *allmählich (aber unmerklich) etwas belebend* – is a model for all conductors. Unlike performances by some other conductors, the ritornelli between the verses are not at all hectic, and, without the distractions of the changes of timbre in the orchestral version, Mahler is easily able to play bars 118–21 as a long diminuendo. Perhaps this was also his intention in orchestral performance. The subtle left-hand rubato with which Mahler accompanies bars 25–35 cannot easily be conveyed in words, and one would be astonished, though charmed, to hear it on the orchestra. The same delicate touch is apparent in the other two songs, 'Ging heut' Morgen über's Feld' being particularly freely treated, with an extremely swift accelerando in bars 23–29.

Mahler's disciples

Oskar Fried (1871–1941)

It was at Mahler's own suggestion that Fried conducted a performance of the Second Symphony in Berlin on 8 November 1905. Mahler attended the dress rehearsal and between this and the performance coached Fried in the tempi and style of the work. Otto Klemperer was in charge of the off-stage forces and tells how Mahler instructed him that, though asked to play loud (*II, v, 376*), the instruments were to be heard softly, since he expected them to be placed at a great distance. In 1923 or 1924, Fried recorded the symphony. This was an extremely adventurous undertaking for an acoustic recording, and also a highly successful one which can only have been achieved by careful planning and experimentation.

---

8 The two basic tempi agree with metronome marks which Webern claimed to have received from Mahler for the first three movements of this symphony. (See Swarowsky, 1979, p. 273, n. 41.)

Balance is generally satisfactory, with the exception of one or two places in the first movement, such as the oboe at bar 131, and the flute and solo violin in bars 217–21. As is normal for acoustic recordings, the tuba can sometimes be heard helping out the bass line and the percussion instruments are the most compromised. While the timpani sound good, and are well tuned, the cymbals, when audible, sound more like a slapstick. The Ruthe in the Scherzo clearly had to be brought close to the recording horn, and the triangle was replaced by pitched tubular bells, which today sound startlingly loud in *iii, 429–32* and elsewhere.

Fried must surely have tried to follow Mahler's advice of twenty years earlier. With the exception of his inability to control the 'imperceptible' accelerandi which begin in bars 163 and 262, his tempi in the first movement impress, and the *Luftpausen* that Mahler indicated are judged appropriately for the dry acoustic demanded by the recording process. Fried is the only conductor surveyed here who follows Mahler's instructions to the letter at bar 235 (*Immer noch etwas vorwärts*): other conductors stay in tempo from this point for the next eight bars, whereas Fried rushes headlong into the abyss. One oddity is Fried's interpretation of Mahler's hairpins on the string tremolo in *i, 390–91*. The crescendo reaches almost forte by the end of bar 390, stops, and begins again in the following bar *pianissimo*. This is not countenanced by any of Mahler's scores, and no other conductor does it.

It seems that Fried paces the second and third movements as Mahler intended. In the Andante we may have a model for the performance of the glissandi marked by Mahler, although Fried adds further sighs for extra measure. There is one basic tempo, modified only as indicated, and Fried's rubato underlines the climaxes of the melodies perfectly. The lead back from the first interlude to the main material is especially well judged. Mahler is said to have particularly commended Fried for his performance of the Scherzo (see Blaukopf 1983, p. 47, & 1986, p. 47): it is slower than normal here at ♩ = c. 53, though it is probably fair to assume that the even slower tempo at bar 348 is due to the change of 78 side. An effective detail in this movement is that the *fortissimo* interruptions of bars 524–27 are played slightly faster than the prevailing tempo. Was this something Mahler taught Fried? Mahler marked *v, 194 Maestoso – sehr zurückhaltend*, and Fried has the courage to take this much more slowly than anyone else, holding the fermata very long. It is noticeable that Fried continues to assign *v, 601–11* to the contralto, as Mahler suggested he did for his Berlin concert (see ibid., 1983, p. 53, & 1986, pp. 52–53).

Willem Mengelberg (1871–1951)

Willem Mengelberg heard Mahler conduct the first performance of the Third Symphony in 1902. He immediately invited him to conduct his Concertgebouw Orchestra, and Mahler made four visits to Amsterdam to introduce his first five and Seventh Symphonies. Mengelberg prepared the orchestra beforehand, giving Mahler unrestricted use of podium time, and undoubtedly attended every one of Mahler's rehearsals and concerts in Holland.

Mengelberg's only studio recording of Mahler's music, the Fifth Symphony's Adagietto, is beset with problems – at least on the CD transfer: the pitch of the second side of this 1926 acoustic recording is a quarter-tone sharper than that of the first. There are also problems with the performance, in that the harp is a quaver ahead by the time the first violins enter and also ahead in bar 10. There is more portamento in this recording than in Fried's, and it would be interesting to know whether this was already the style of the Concertgebouw strings when Mahler conducted them. Frequent additional hairpins are also indicated in Mengelberg's score.[9] Mengelberg makes an accelerando in bar 91, as if Mahler had forgotten to add the same indication as in bar 28.

The recording of the Fourth Symphony under Mengelberg derives from a 1939 concert broadcast. It has been studied in detail elsewhere (Kropfinger, 1985) and one important point which emerges is that Mengelberg does not often adhere to the metronome marks which he wrote into his own score. Thus, while *i, 4* is indeed *recht gemächlich*, by bar 7 an allegro ($\downarrow$ = c. 104) has set in, despite Mengelberg's marking of 80 in his score. Perhaps the metronome marks in Mengelberg's score are closer to Mahler's tempi; but the tempi on this recording diverge in so many ways from Mahler's own indications that one must assume that Mengelberg's own interpretative ideas developed radically over the intervening years. However, it is mainly in the question of tempi and agogics that Mengelberg appears arbitrary. Dynamics and instrumental balances follow Mahler's markings though, again, the authenticity of the frequent string portamenti might be questioned. A critical examination of Mengelberg's scores and orchestral parts would usefully extend our knowledge of his place in the Mahler tradition. For instance, a cello part shows that, as on Mahler's piano roll, he notated the quavers of *V, ii, 269–70* as semiquavers.[10]

Bruno Walter (1876–1962)

From the creation of the Second Symphony onwards, Bruno Walter had the privilege of learning Mahler's symphonies as they were composed, both by hearing Mahler play them and by playing them with him on the piano (see Franklin, 1980, p. 43). He was present at Mahler's concerts and rehearsals and also prepared singers for the Eighth Symphony's première. In a recorded interview, Egon Wellesz (1885–1974) said of Walter that he was 'a replica of

---

9 See the reproduction of Mengelberg's score in Stephan, 1979a, pp. 86–87; also the colour reproduction in de Leur, 1997, p. 85.

10 See the reproduction of Mengelberg's cello part in de Leur, 1997, p. 90.

Mahler, only Mahler had more force in his rhythm. Mahler had the rhythm of Toscanini and the heart of Walter.'[11]

There are several Walter recordings of the First Symphony. His 1954 concert with the New York Philharmonic is particularly exciting, with a double-bass solo in the third movement which is suitably on the edge. Mahler marks the middle section of this movement $\downarrow = 72$ but the fact that nobody, Walter included, plays it so fast makes one wonder whether Mahler himself did. Walter's tempo is $\downarrow = c. 54$–56 in all three recordings listened to. What is nowadays thought of as klezmer music in the third movement is not rendered in a particularly Jewish or gypsy style. In his book on Mahler, Walter referred to it as 'that music full of brazen derision and shrill laughter' (Walter, 1937, p. 108), giving cause to wonder how Mahler interpreted it.[12] It is disappointing to discover that Walter is as perplexed as most conductors by Mahler's indication of rubato in *iv, 211*, being content to respond by speeding up. Walter's studio recordings of the First Symphony represent essentially the same interpretation, though they are more studied.

Walter's earliest extant recording of the Second Symphony is of a 1948 concert with the Vienna Philharmonic. The opening movement is more deliberate and four-square than Klemperer's, and Walter is also more inclined to linger over the tender moments, giving the movement a more sombre and less angry quality than either Klemperer or Fried. The Vienna Philharmonic uses portamento more frequently than the Vienna Symphony Orchestra for Klemperer, recorded three years later. Walter's interest in the final statement of the theme of the second movement twice brings it almost to a halt in bars 268 and 274, and the third movement tends to get faster as it proceeds. Consequently Walter inserts a ritenuto in *iii, 268* to prepare the new tempo. Whereas most other conductors ignore Mahler's instruction, Walter, like Fried, lengthens slightly the sixth and eighth notes of the horn fanfares in *v, 78* and *v, 162*.

Walter's studio performance of the Second Symphony is well recorded, despite audible tape joins and the movement of the trombones from left to right in *v, 390*. Regrettably, someone had persuaded Walter of the impossibility of recording in stereo with second violins on the right. The last two movements were recorded after a concert performance in February 1957, but a heart attack delayed recording of the rest until one year later. An air-check of the concert broadcast reveals that Walter recorded a generally less passionate performance than the concert, though the climax of the Finale is enormous. The New York string playing is cleaner than in his Viennese performance.

Walter's commercial recording of the Fourth Symphony is inhibited

---

[11] Quoted from a 1962 BBC interview with Egon Wellesz by Deryck Cooke.

[12] Concerning the failure of the record producer John McClure to persuade Walter to talk about Jewish elements in Mahler's music, see Ryding & Pechefsky, 2001, pp. 406–7.

throughout by an emotional detachment not usually associated with him. Tempi are brisk, reportedly on account of the demands of the 78 side (La Grange, 1995, p. 769, n. 60) and the playing of the New York Philharmonic lacks charm. Luckily two acceptably well-recorded concert performances with the Vienna Philharmonic give a better impression of Walter's sensitive way with this music.[13] The orchestra understands how to balance the different voices and colours, and the scordatura solo violin stands out well. Walter does not respect all Mahler's tempo markings – hardly slowing down, for instance, for the second section of the second movement. In the 1950 recording he successfully emulates Mahler's gradual diminuendo in *iv, 118–21*.

The 1994 CD remastering of Walter's recording of the Fifth Symphony provides significantly richer sound than previous issues. The first movement has the same crispness of rhythm noted in Mahler's piano roll, and the timing of 11:36 is consistent with Mahler's own approach. The second movement exhibits a ferociousness not expected from Walter, particularly in the approach to the Chorale (*ii, 428–63*). The strange thing about this performance is Walter's fast tempo for the Scherzo. Mahler predicted that conductors would take it too fast for fifty years, probably without imagining that Walter would be one of them (Mahler, 1990, p. 243). Walter conducts the Adagietto movement in this and an earlier recording with the Vienna Philharmonic faster than Mahler himself – less than eight, as opposed to nine minutes – without appearing to rush. In the earlier recording Walter accelerates in bar 91, though less than Mengelberg. The hairpins of bar 50 and elsewhere are downplayed. The Finale fully demonstrates one quality of Walter's conducting which he shared with Mahler, and which is apparent in all his recordings: his ability to shade the balance of the orchestra from bar to bar without obscuring the rest of the texture, so that the listener is always able to discern the most important voice at any given time without losing the whole picture.

Otto Klemperer (1885–1973)

Otto Klemperer had particular ties with the Second Symphony, since he played his own piano transcription of its Scherzo from memory to Mahler. In addition to his success with the off-stage band in Fried's concert, he played an off-stage snare drum in the first movement of the Third Symphony when Mahler conducted it in Berlin on 14 January 1907. He also attended Mahler's rehearsals for the premières of the Seventh and Eighth Symphonies.

Klemperer conducted only the Second, Fourth, Seventh and Ninth Symphonies, making recordings of all of them plus *Das Lied von der Erde*.

---

[13] Erik Ryding's listing of Walter recordings at www.geocities.com/ walteriana76/BWrecordsB.htm gives no fewer than ten recorded concert performances of the Fourth Symphony, plus five of the First and three of the Second.

Regrettably, the earliest of these were made in May 1951, by which time Mahler had been dead for forty years and the 66-year-old Klemperer was fighting serious physical problems. It is valuable, therefore, to have no fewer than five recordings of the Second Symphony, as the listener to just one of these would be forced to draw unfair conclusions about Klemperer's interpretation and conducting abilities. The earliest recording, with the Vienna Symphony Orchestra, while powerful and passionate, suffers from inadequate session time and from lack of familiarity with the work on the part of the orchestra. One of the oboes falters in *i, 18* on the assumption that Klemperer is beating two and not four, and the strings' playing of the second movement betrays a lack of sympathy, with only sparing use of portamento. A live recording from the Concertgebouw two months later shows clearly that the tradition was still alive there, with string playing that is a positive delight, particularly in the second movement. A 1963 concert recording with the Vienna Philharmonic also has idiomatic string playing, though not all Mahler's requests for portamento are observed. While the orchestra is recognizably the Vienna Philharmonic, the Klemperer sound is not evident, and the recorded balance is defective in the Finale. The recording that gives the best impression of Klemperer's approach to the work and preserves his characteristic gruff sound was made in concert with the Bavarian Radio Symphony Orchestra. The orchestra plays idiomatically, though with less attempt at glissandi than the Vienna Phiharmonic, and the soloists are balanced too loud.

If we just had Klemperer's stereo EMI recording with the Philharmonia Orchestra, we should have to put up with audible joins, one of which engenders a change of tempo in *i, 43*.[14] The Philharmonia's attitude to Mahler's glissando and portamento markings lies somewhere between that of the Concertgebouw and Bavarian Radio Orchestras. Though both recording and performance are fine, they are complemented by the live recordings. Klemperer habitually made two extra *Luftpausen* before *i, 293* and *i, 295*, marked by Mahler as small commas – unlike the gap before *i, 291* which is marked *Cäsur* – and always conducted *v, 194–95* at the tempo of the following Allegro energico instead of Mahler's *Maestoso sehr zurückhaltend*.

Klemperer's performance of the Fourth Symphony received one of the most natural-sounding Mahler recordings ever, with the clarity and perspective characteristic of Kingsway Hall. In view of Mahler's call for a 'voice with light, childlike expression: entirely without parody' ['Singstimme mit kindlich heiterem Ausdruck: durchaus ohne Parodie!'], Schwarzkopf was not the most suitable of sopranos, though nearly everything else follows Mahler's instructions, despite a few passages where clarinets or trumpets are too loud. For some reason no orchestra seems to use Mahler's bowings in *i, 21–23*, though this is one of the few recordings to observe them in the important motif of *i, 8*, with the dotted

---

[14] The corresponding passage in Klemperer's EMI mono recording, although derived from the same sessions, was not edited in this way.

quaver held for its full value. Klemperer does not rush the second movement, as most conductors do; though he does not slow down much in the Trio either. What, for Klemperer, is an uncharacteristic sudden increase in tempo at *ii, 298* could well be due to a tape join.

Klemperer's controversial recording of the Seventh Symphony was also made in Kingsway Hall, and has an even better sound. The clarity of texture provides a valuable object lesson: even the second violins on the right have no trouble in being audible and the brass, no matter how loud, are unable to overpower the strings. These are the indisputable good points. On the other hand, this is Klemperer at his slowest. Nevertheless this is the only recording by a great conductor who was actually present at Mahler's rehearsals and first performance, and who presumably did his best to remember Mahler's intentions sixty years later. There is no reason to suppose that Mahler's tempi were identical, though the performance has impressively vivid detail and conviction.

The second generation

Hermann Scherchen (1891–1966)

In Hermann Scherchen we encounter a conductor in many respects similar to Mahler himself in his love of experimentation. He played the viola in Fried's 1910 Berlin première of the Seventh Symphony and conducted his first Mahler performance in 1914. A series of all the Mahler symphonies under Scherchen planned for 1938 in Vienna only got as far as the First and Third. Most of his Mahler recordings were also made in Vienna in the early 1950s. Transparent sound and respect for the dynamics are characteristic of this conductor. It often seems as though he was not well served by his recording engineers, though recent reissues of some of the recordings with vastly improved sonics give hope for the future.

The First Symphony with the London Philharmonic Orchestra is not one of the great recordings. The fast music is given full rein with impressive climaxes, though more tender moments are less well realized. The trio of the Scherzo is elegant but not Austrian in feeling and the D flat theme of the Finale appears too contrived to touch the heart. The Second Symphony with the Vienna State Opera Orchestra suffers from scrawny recorded sound and a balance which varies from excellent to a total travesty of Mahler's intentions, as at *II, ii, 149–52* where a close timpani microphone obliterates the violins. There are also several bad tape edits. The performance is nevertheless worth listening to: there is total – if in places wrong-headed – involvement on the part of the conductor, and one senses the influence of Fried. Tempi in the first movement are extreme, with only the timpani able to keep up at bar 196, and it is no exaggeration to describe the section that begins at bar 392 as reminiscent of a battleground the day after. Like Fried, Scherchen paces the middle movements moderately.

Scherchen's studio recording of the Fifth Symphony has a much better sound. The Vienna State Opera Orchestra generally plays well, though it does not always manage to keep up with the conductor. Tempi aside, Scherchen – here as elsewhere – really tries to make sense of Mahler's requests. The dynamics are respected, with sforzandi in proportion to the prevailing level. At a moderate tempo, the Scherzo is extremely successful, as is the Adagietto, and the contrapuntal episodes of the Rondo-Finale are well projected. Scherchen manages to give the impression of a live performance, in which the listener is left in no doubt that the orchestra would follow him over the edge of a cliff. Live recordings of this work show that Scherchen's performances, like Mahler's, were never the same twice. That with the ORTF orchestra in 1965 is lacking 512 bars from the Scherzo, which reduces its duration to five minutes and also possibly explains the ponderous tempo for the only appearance of the Trio.[15] The Adagietto, not helped by Scherchen's refusal to move faster in the middle section of the movement, now takes four minutes longer, lasting 13:07, and the spectacular glissando of bar 72 is no compensation for this. The tempo of the Finale, which also has cuts, is well beyond the orchestra's ability in places.[16]

Scherchen also made swingeing cuts in the Scherzo and Finale of the Sixth Symphony in a performance during the Leipzig Gewandhaus celebrations of the Mahler year.[17] According to the organizer of the concert, Klaus Richter, Scherchen's reason was lack of preparation time,[18] but because of it only one hammer blow and one traversal of the Trio survived. This is a great pity, as otherwise the white-hot performance has much to commend it.

It is not surprising that the Seventh Symphony was a perfect vehicle for Scherchen. A recent transfer of the Vienna State Opera Orchestra recording reveals a much better sound quality than hitherto, and this is usefully supplemented by an earlier live recording with the Vienna Symphony Orchestra which, despite some playing lapses, has better management of tempi in the Finale. Both performances present this often maligned work in a good light and without hysteria. The studio recording is mostly well balanced, and very clear. In both recordings the cowbells at *ii, 126* are too active, the concert performance

---

[15] It should be recalled that in America Mahler himself made directly comparable cuts in the Scherzo of Beethoven's Seventh Symphony.

[16] Scherchen cut bars 174–489 and bars 578–763 from the Scherzo, both times by means of a general pause. In the Finale he omitted bars 329–537 and (quite inexplicably) bars 749–58.

[17] Scherchen cut from Fig. 82 to Fig. 97 in the Scherzo, and in the Finale from Fig. 129 to Fig. 140.

[18] See notes by René Trémine in the booklet accompanying the Tahra recording. Rehearsal time might have been saved by the omission of the Adagio of the Tenth Symphony from the programme.

in particular giving the unfortunate impression of a whole herd of cows trying desperately to attract the attention of a bull in the next field.

Charles Adler (1889–1959)

Charles Adler does not appear in any Mahler biography, though according to Jack Diether he 'was one of a group of young musicians who attended and were allowed to discuss Mahler's rehearsals with him' (Diether, 1960a, pp. 33–34). Gerald S. Fox states that he assisted Mahler in preparations for the première of the Eighth Symphony.[19] Much later, Adler's confident and well-structured performances kept the flame burning at a time when Mahler's reputation was still low. The recordings of the Third and Sixth Symphonies with the Vienna Symphony Orchestra were remarkably well prepared, considering that each was recorded in one day.

The Third Symphony is raw where this is called for: there are no over-refined trombone set pieces here. The performance is not free from wrong notes. Bars 92–98 of the Finale should have been retaken, since the second violins enter and stay two bars late, and it is a pity both that a low timpani was not available and that the posthorn sounds like a trumpet. The Sixth Symphony, with the slow movement in second place, bears no evidence of a real hammer. The cowbells are no more or less convincing than in most other recordings, the low bells in *iv, 254–59* suffer from being in pitches that fit the prevailing harmonies, and one of the timpani goes flat in the last bar. Trumpets and horns are never allowed to dominate in this recording, almost to a fault; but the horn and trombone vibrato in the coda is a most effective response to the battle which has preceded it. Adler's tempi are deliberate and he declines to slow down significantly at bars 183 and 355 of the Scherzo.

Eduard Flipse (1896–1973)

By the time of his 1954 and 1955 Holland Festival Mahler recordings, Eduard Flipse had been conductor of the Rotterdam Philharmonic Orchestra for twenty-five years. This is evident in the performances, and it is surely not fanciful to imagine that he learned from the Concertgebouw Mahler tradition. In the absence of any by Mengelberg, his recordings of the Sixth and Eighth Symphonies thus have an enduring historical significance. The Sixth Symphony was recorded without highlighting any particular section of the orchestra. The balance of brass and strings is ideal and, despite the single channel, it is much easier to focus at will on any section of the texture here than in many stereo recordings. Tempi are good, with a well-controlled flexibility in the slow movement which is in second

---

[19]   See the extensive biographical notes by Gerald S. Fox in the Conifer CD reissue of Adler's Mahler recordings.

place. The recording features narrow-bore trombones and has an amazingly small number of blemishes, with a perfect balance in the short passages with solo violin. The phrasing is very natural, and so generally faithful is Flipse to Mahler's markings that one is surprised when he occasionally ignores them: the horns play staccato rather than the tenuto indicated in bar 174 ff. of the Scherzo; he expunges the first violins' diminuendo in *iv, 524;*[20] and he refuses to press forward as indicated in *iv, 516.* For once the cowbells are discreet – but so is the hammer.

Dimitri Mitropoulos (1896–1960)

Dimitri Mitropoulos championed Mahler in the USA when few cared, conducting more Mahler in New York than Walter. In 1940 he gave the first US performance of the Sixth Symphony and also made the first ever recording of the First Symphony. Although the hall acoustics were extremely dry, and the winds therefore sound closer than expected, this recording is well balanced and detailed. The orchestra follows Mahler's dynamics faithfully. Mitropoulos carries the line well and the D-flat theme of the last movement is seamless. His technique allows for a subtle rubato which he uses to good effect, although the Trio of the Scherzo sounds unidiomatic, and is not helped by the clean playing of the strings, with few portamenti and only meagre glissandi.

All other Mahler recordings by Mitropoulos come from radio broadcasts, most benefiting from clear, well-balanced sound, and revealing that he worked entirely from a study of Mahler's scores, unaided by any tradition. Mitropoulos's legendary insistence on committing all details of a score to memory before he began rehearsals paid dividends in his general respect for Mahler's markings. He was able to read Mahler's *nicht eilen* and *nicht schleppend* as instructions to slow down and move ahead, respectively. Yet he consistently missed the lilt of the frequent Austrian dances, and impeded the flow of the Adagietto of the Fifth Symphony by lingering over too many bar lines. His interpretation of the Sixth Symphony was not encumbered by such problems. The Cologne musicians particularly give the impression of going like lambs to their inevitable slaughter in the Finale. On the other hand, the New York recording of the Third Symphony from 1956 is best forgotten. Mitropoulos allowed himself to make substantial cuts in the first, third and sixth movements, took the 9/8 section of the second movement at a breakneck speed, and also rushed the posthorn solos.[21] It is

---

[20] Of the conductors discussed here only Scherchen observes this diminuendo, though both Mitropoulos and Bernstein (1988) place a diminuendo in bar 529.

[21] The cuts in Mitropoulos's New York recording of the Third Symphony are: first movement, bars 455–81, 530–38, 540–53, 574–82, 703–36; third movement, bars 382–413; Finale, bars 108–23 & 267–74.

disappointing to discover Mitropoulos's qualities as a Mahler interpreter to be so inconsistent in those few recordings that exist.

Complete cycles

Though the development of stereo recording played a part, the centenary of Mahler's birth was the catalyst for the complete recorded cycles of his music. Table 13.1 shows that the first to get under way was Bernstein's with the New York Philharmonic. Excluding the Adagio of the Tenth Symphony, his first Mahler cycle was recorded over a seven-year period. This was necessary since Bernstein did not have all the symphonies in his repertoire in 1960 when the series began. As Music Director of the New York Philharmonic, he took part in their Mahler centenary celebrations, though he conducted only the Second and Fourth Symphonies and some of the songs.[22]

Solti's Decca/London cycle was next to begin, in 1961, although it did not really get under way until five years later following the perhaps unexpected success of the first two instalments. This set is the least unified of the four, having been made with three different orchestras and in four different countries as convenience dictated. In 1962, Haitink recorded the Second Symphony with the Concertgebouw Orchestra, but the gap of nearly four years before recording the Third Symphony indicates that Philips, too, probably did not originally envisage a complete set. The recording dates indicate a similar lack of original intention on the part of the Abravanel cycle for Vanguard; in this case there were good enough commercial reasons to record the Seventh and Eighth Symphonies for the first time in stereo. But by the time Kubelik and the Bavarian Radio Symphony Orchestra started their cycle for Deutsche Grammophon in 1967, Mahler was unquestionably a commercial proposition.

Leonard Bernstein (1912–1990)

Possessed of a technique which enabled him to realize his interpretations fully, Bernstein responded enthusiastically to Mahler's manifold instructions, revelling particularly in the Ivesian spirit which they often invoke. Despite his closeness to Mitropoulos and opportunities of studying Walter's New York performances, he followed no tradition. Unlike Walter he took all the repeats and was not afraid to

---

[22] Symphonies 1, 5, 9 and the Adagio of No. 10 were conducted by Mitropoulos and *Das Lied von der Erde* by Walter. Symphonies 3, 6, 7 and 8 were not performed in this festival. However, none of these three conductors was quite as enterprising as the Hungarian, Erno Rapee (1891–1942), who with his Radio City Music Hall Orchestra broadcast Symphonies 1–5, 8, 9 and *Das Lied von der Erde* during the first four months of 1942. See *Chord and Discord*, 2 (4), 1946, pp. 94 & 107.

Table 13.1   Dates of the earliest recorded cycles of Mahler's symphonies

	Bernstein	Solti	Haitink	Abravanel	Kubelik
Feb 1960	4				
Feb 1961		4			
Apr 1961	3				
Sept 1962			1		
Jan 1963	5				
Sept 1963	2				
Dec 1963				8	
Feb 1964		1			
Dec 1964				7	
Dec 1965	7, 9				
Apr 1966	8				
May 1966		2	3		
Oct 1966	1				
Mar 1967					9
Apr 1967		9		2	
May 1967	6				3
Oct 1967					1
Dec 1967			4		
Jan 1968		3			
Apr 1968				4	4, 10 i
May 1968			2		
Dec 1968					6
Feb 1969			6		2
Apr 1969				3, 9	
June 1969			9		
Dec 1969			7		
Mar 1970		5			
Apr 1970		6			
June 1970					8
Nov 1970					7
Dec 1970			5		
Jan 1971					5
Apr 1971		7			
Aug 1971		8			
Sept 1971			8, 10 i		
May 1974				1, 5, 6, 10 i	
Apr 1975	10 i				

bring out the Jewish elements of the third movement of the First Symphony and elsewhere. Like Mahler himself, he was often controversial: in his second cycle he employed a boy soprano soloist in the Fourth Symphony; but while the theory of innocence sounds fine on paper, the implementation – as with his use of a baritone in *Das Lied von der Erde* – is not convincing.

The recorded quality of Bernstein's first cycle is variable, although it is generally on a high level, and that of the First and Seventh Symphonies compares favourably with modern challengers.[23] A comparison of the 2001 CD reissues with the original LPs shows that, with the exception of the fifth movement of the Third Symphony where the voices have now been reduced in level to give a more natural balance, only stereo tapes were available for the remastering. Unfortunately this movement still suffers from an inadequate balance within the orchestra, with tam-tam and glockenspiel far too loud as elsewhere in the symphony. There is no doubt that the engineers manipulated faders to strengthen string tone in certain passages: the cellos are pushed at the listener in *V, iv, 12–16*, and it sounds as though all the strings have been amplified in *II, i, 331* and *V, iv, 94*.

The original British LP pressings of the Fifth and Sixth Symphonies illustrate one problem of that medium: restricted dynamic range. In *V, ii, 188* the level is raised by about six decibels for the quiet section, remaining so until about bar 267. The CD reissue does not have this problem, although instrumental balances are still defective in places. The beginning of the second movement sounds very confused, with close woodwinds and timpani drowning out the basses in bars 145–55. One is also obliged to tolerate the over-amplified clarinets in *V, iii, 397*, both here and in Bernstein's later recording, where the problem is even worse. Although the loud climaxes of the Sixth Symphony's Finale were reduced in level on the 1968 British LP issue, the CD and LP dynamics match very closely from bar 530 onwards.

The separate microphones used for the off-stage band of *II, v, 343* work entirely against Mahler's intentions: 'muss so schwach erklingen, dass es den Character der Gesangstelle Celli und Fag. in keinerlei Weise tangiert. Der Autor denkt sich hier, ungefähr, vom Wind vereinzelnd herüber getragene Klänge einer kaum vernehmbaren Musik' ['it must sound so faint that it in no way affects the character of the melodic lines in the cellos and bassoons. The composer has in mind roughly the sounds of a barely audible music sporadically carried across by the wind'].

Bernstein's second cycle was made from concert performances, with the use of three different orchestras intended to exploit their perceived strengths. The New York Philharmonic collaborated in the Second, Third and Seventh, the

---

[23] The exceptionally well-recorded and -performed 1994 recording of the Seventh Symphony by Chailly and the Concertgebouw Orchestra evinces great care over Mahler's instructions, even using Mengelberg's specially made drum for the low D flat of *v, 506*.

Concertgebouw in the First and Fourth, and the Vienna Philharmonic in the Fifth and Sixth. This also allowed the recordings to be made closer together in time – the Seventh in 1985, the first five all in 1987, and the Sixth in 1988.[24] Recording in concert presents special challenges, which have, in the main, been met here successfully. Though there is usually more than one live performance, and rehearsals and make-up sessions are often recorded to ensure that the final master is as perfect as possible, it is not always easy to edit convincingly between performances. In order to avoid picking up audience noises, microphones have to be put closer than they might be in the studio, and level compressors are often employed to avoid distortion in the event that the performers get carried away and play louder in the concert. This may be the reason why Bernstein's 1988 recording of the Sixth Symphony actually allows the level of sound to reach within one decibel of the maximum level for a CD on many more occasions in the Finale, whereas only the places with the hammer blows come close to this on the earlier recording.

Bernstein's command of the orchestra allowed him to keep things moving, and he knew where the tempo can be changed without it showing. His understanding of tempo is well illustrated in the second movement of the Fourth Symphony which, though fast by the metronome, fails to sound hasty because of light accentuation. Although slow, the fourth movement of the Seventh Symphony is invested with a forward impulse that minimizes awareness of the bar lines and prevents monotony in the repeated rhythmic cells from which it is built. Bernstein's Mahler interpretations developed over the years, permitting refinements. A good example is the sudden change of tempo in the middle of *VI, iv, 528*, which might be taken for an edit point in the New York recording but which proves to be deliberate when one hears a smaller tempo change in the later performance.

Although there are rare cases when Bernstein decides to change Mahler's dynamics and balances, he generally respects them: the horns never blare as they do with some other conductors, and accents are always related to the prevailing dynamic. Proportion is also evident in his control of climaxes and refusal to over-inflate moments of Mahler's music at the expense of the total picture.

Though not born or brought up in Europe, Bernstein instinctively understood the character of Mahler's many dance movements and episodes. In the First Symphony (1966) he gives the impression of an inebriated dancer in the Trio of the Scherzo, with *Luftpausen* between the first two bars and flowing rubato to follow. The third movement is suitably ghoulish, with a Bohemian gypsy flavour to the passage beginning at bar 39 and a grief-stricken ending. In 1987 the Concertgebouw Orchestra played with an uncanny *beklemmt* feeling to the middle section of this movement and with more controlled grieving at its end. Bernstein's treatment of the D flat theme of the Finale is idiomatic,

---

[24] Recordings of Symphonies 8 and 9 were selected after Bernstein's death.

and quite appropriate given Mahler's un-elaborated request for rubato (bar 211).

Extra *Luftpausen* are a feature of Bernstein's interpretations. In his first recording of the Fourth Symphony, he adds them after *i, 115* and *ii, 71, 77 and 83*. By the time of his later recording there is no *Luftpause* after *i, 115*, but those in the second movement receive more emphasis. Instead of Mahler's swell on the culminating note of the phrase in *III, vi, 16* he inserts a pianissimo, an effect emphasized in the later recording with a small *Luftpause*.[25]

Bernstein was particularly good at using Mahler's articulations, string appoggiaturas and slides to give shape to the melodic line, which is after all their reason for being there. The slow movement of his later recording of the Fourth Symphony gives many examples of this, and also includes one detail where Bernstein's insight into Mahler's intentions was unique. This is in the placement of the first violins' glissando up to the crucial F sharp of bar 332.

Bernstein's early skill in handling the waltzes in the Scherzo of the Fifth Symphony was masterly; but even so his recording with the Vienna Philharmonic outclasses the earlier one, with its notably desolate and tired-sounding opening movement turning to desperation by its end. Crucial details include the Viennese rotary valve trumpet (which produces the right sound to blend with the violas in *i, 278–86*), and the first violins' understanding of Mahler's request of a change of strings and glissando which introduce *iii, 136* and set an ideal tone for the first Trio.

In the Sixth Symphony Bernstein stressed continuity. His urgent tempo for the opening movement in the early recording does not sacrifice weight, and prevents the Scherzo from appearing too similar. Following these with a subdued slow movement throws the emphasis on the long Finale, which is also restrained until about bar 288, thus maximizing the effect of the hammer. While using the 1963 Ratz edition from which it is suppressed, Bernstein retained the third blow, though its effect is upstaged by the climax in bar 733. Extreme dynamics on the earlier recording are reserved for the climactic moments of the first two hammer blows and bar 773, which are much less restricted in their impact on CD than on the original LP issue. The balance of the instruments is not always perfect in the later recording, which also lacks depth. Though the opening movement is even faster than before, tempi elsewhere are slower, as, for instance, at bar 355 of the Scherzo, which Mahler marks *fast langsam*, and which in Bernstein's Vienna recording is in fact *ganz langsam*. Bernstein's interpretation is even more bleak than earlier, with noticeably greater emphasis on the tam-tam at climaxes.

Bernstein's first recording of the Seventh Symphony has been widely recognized as a landmark, and its reissue on CD reveals a more refined sound than was apparent on the LPs, though as with the Third Symphony the first movement is recorded with more depth than the rest of the work. Instrumental

---

[25] The fact that Solti and Barbirolli also add this *subito pp* makes one wonder whether they both studied the Bernstein recording.

balances are excellent in this movement and generally more than satisfactory elsewhere. The cowbells are discreet and sparingly played. Lightly applied accents give the Scherzo the shadowy quality Mahler specified. Bernstein's tempi have an inevitability about them and are well integrated, aiming towards the last page of the score. Unfortunately, the wider dynamic range of the later recording sounds artificial and Bernstein's interpretation has less sweep and energy; but the first recording shows that, at his best, Bernstein gives more bar-to-bar variety of character in his Mahler than previous generations of conductors – without losing sight of the overall conception.

Bernard Haitink (b. 1929)

Haitink directed the Concertgebouw Orchestra for longer than anyone except Mengelberg. His complete cycle of studio recordings is generally faithful to Mahler's instructions but has been judged by many to be too cautious – a victim of the strange theory that music has to be played differently for home listening from in concert. This theory is demolished by recordings of live Eurovision Christmas matinees from the 1970s, which present well-played performances in variable though generally well-balanced concert hall sound. Mahler's dynamics are scrupulously respected in a string-based texture with a solid and noble brass tone, and Haitink's rhythmic flexibility allows the music to breathe. One advantage of a live recording is that the balance does not change between movements, as frequently happens in studio recordings, while a further advantage of recording in the Concertgebouw is the hall's quite exceptional clarity in the low bass. The Fifth Symphony's bass line is particularly well nourished, notably from *ii, 499*, where in other recordings the brass section is allowed to dominate completely.

In addition to his mastery of Mahler's long-scale thought, Haitink occupies himself with details. In the First Symphony these include the truly wintry double-bass solo, and the fact that he follows Mahler's instruction in this first section of the third movement to avoid any crescendo – as much as is physically possible, given that more instruments are added all the time. Haitink allows the D-flat tune of the last movement to breathe, with ideal support given by horns and trombones.

Both the performance and recorded sound of the Second Symphony in this series put many other recordings to shame. When instruments emerge from the texture, they are always to be found justified by Mahler's score, though a Beckmesser would point out that a few things are inexplicably inaudible: the lowest cello part at *ii, 216* and the trombones' solitary chord in *iv, 58*. Haitink observes Mahler's agogic distortion in the horns in *v, 78*, though not in *v, 162* – perhaps on the grounds that the magician should not do the same trick twice. The off-stage band is well balanced, being no louder than when heard live. Though more measured this is no less inspiring than a Bernstein performance.

In the Third and Fourth Symphonies there are a few miscalculations of balance on the part of the engineers, and Haitink ignores some of Mahler's instructions (although by no means as many as Mengelberg does). Contrary to Mahler's wishes, the second movement of the Fourth is 'hasty', and in *iii, 326–31* Haitink reads Mahler's commas as *Luftpausen*, even though the score shows them only as articulations of the accompanying chords. The performance of the Seventh Symphony has many successful features, including a well-balanced mandolin in the fourth movement and strikingly effective interplay between woodwind and strings in *iv, 313–18*, though Haitink ignores Mahler's express tempo relationships in the first movement, and is not as convincing in the Finale as Bernstein, Scherchen or Kubelik are in their different ways.

Georg Solti (1912–1997)

Mahler recordings by Solti were welcomed eagerly in the 1960s, probably because it was expected that the series would turn out as well as his *Ring* recording. But John Culshaw, senior Decca producer and the prime mover behind the Decca *Ring* cycle, could not stand Mahler's music, and handed the project over to a colleague after producing the First Symphony (Culshaw, 1982, pp. 341–42). That recording did indeed show promise. Aside from some obvious spot miking, it had a generally excellent instrumental balance and some sensitive playing. But, as was the case with other candidates from a time when stereo recordings were still new, the technology seduced many into thinking that the musical values of the recording were commensurate. The repeats are there, but this does not compensate for the 'over-civilized' double-bass solo or the uneventful playing of the D-flat theme of the Finale. Nearly twenty years later, a re-recording in Chicago does not show any maturing of Solti's interpretation, though the technical execution is undeniably better. The orchestral playing and balance of his 1961 Concertgebouw recording of the Fourth Symphony are largely impeccable, though Solti often elicits harsh accents from the brass, and the horns and trumpets are sometimes too loud. Glissandi and portamenti are minimal, and Solti presses the music hard. One cannot say that these are bad performances, but by comparison with Walter, Barbirolli, Bernstein or Haitink, Solti is dull and strait-laced.

Solti brings much energy to the Third Symphony, but again fails to respond to Mahler's request for rubato at *i, 65* and elsewhere. When issued, this recording was considered most favourably despite microphones being noticeably faded in and out. But some instruments, like the trumpets at *v, 67*, are just too loud given the dynamic levels indicated by Mahler, destroying any real sense of a well-placed climax; and the boys' choir is inexplicably inaudible in *v, 92*, despite Mahler's *ff* marking.

Solti's 1970 recording of the Fifth Symphony was reissued in a CD series called 'The Solti Collection', with an introduction by the conductor indicating his approval. It is all the more shocking, therefore, to discover that the recording is plagued by problems caused by too many microphones fighting for the listener's ear. Some of Solti's changes of tempo are baffling, such as the sudden slowing for *ii, 131–32*. Either deliberate or an insert from a different take, it certainly arrests the progress of the movement. By *ii, 189* the cellos, who at *ii, 145* were extremely close, appear to have moved about 10 metres further back. Mahler's *klagend* direction is in vain here, as they appear to be communing only with themselves. In *ii, 234* it is the turn of the woodwinds to be elbowed out of the way by the violins, and in *ii, 474* the overall level is abruptly reduced. In sum, the proportions of this movement are ignored by both conductor and recording team, and this style is maintained through the rest of the work. Solti also adds accents where Mahler avoids them, as in *iii, 670–81*. In *iii, 745*, instead of Mahler's *a tempo moderato*, Solti accelerates. The Adagietto is well paced, apart from slowing down at bar 50. Unlike other conductors, Solti does not accelerate in bar 91 and the harp is nicely audible, as are most of the grace notes of the strings; but the movement does not seem to draw the listener in. Dynamics are also compressed in parts of the Rondo-Finale (bars 308–9, 374–414, 531–33 and 581–92), and the horns are also overemphasized by means of faders in bars 670–72 and 707–10.[26]

Given the extremely high quality of the playing, it is sad to note that the Sixth and Seventh Symphonies – though not without many well-conceived and well-recorded individual passages – also suffer from too many crude recorded balances and an overall lack of direction from Solti, whose tendency to maintain a strict tempo and plough ahead misses the music behind the notes, and thereby the essence of Mahler.[27] It is hard to believe from this evidence that Solti really cared for Mahler's music in the way that Barbirolli and Bernstein obviously did, or to resist the conclusion that he merely followed the Mahler bandwagon as a fellow traveller.

Maurice Abravanel (1903–1993)

It is disappointing that the cycle by Maurice Abravanel and his Utah Symphony Orchestra rarely rises above the routine, and never for a whole symphony. Although made in the superb acoustics of the Mormon Tabernacle, the recordings lack depth and warmth. Extra microphones create a balance that sometimes, as in *V, i, 172* ff., places woodwinds closer than strings. Bowing styles are good but the

---

[26] Decca's 1997 recording of the Fifth Symphony with the Concertgebouw Orchestra and Chailly is disfigured by comparable gross lapses in balance.

[27] In *VII, i, 343–52* and elsewhere the strings play clear demisemiquavers which, although not specified by Mahler, are normally played tremolo in the romantic tradition of Weber (cf. *Der Freischütz* Overture, bars 25–35 and 91–108).

string playing is wooden, with a lack of articulation in the melodic phrasing. The performances, while respectful of Mahler's instructions, are bland and often mechanical. At the beginning of the Sixth Symphony the basses play their repeated notes with a nonchalant air, and the cowbells in the same movement sound more like wind chimes during a gale. The Scherzo is also taken fast and with a light tread, and the lack of *gravitas* throughout this performance is most disconcerting. Also disconcerting, both here and elsewhere, is the transformation of dotted rhythms into triplets, most damagingly in the Fifth Symphony where the tendency may be observed right from the opening trumpet call. It is hard to understand why Abravanel hastens though two 'red lights' in the last movement of this symphony (*Nicht eilen* in *v, 511* and *v, 517*) and then brakes hard in *v, 525*.

Abravanel was generally a conscientious interpreter; but in these recordings he seems unable to see the wood for the trees and demonstrates that even following Mahler's recipe in general is not a sufficient guarantee of success.

Rafael Kubelik (1914–1996)

Rafael Kubelik's cycle was begun in the same year that Bernstein completed his first cycle, and was recorded within four years. The orchestral playing is on a consistently high level throughout, but unfortunately this is not always matched by the recorded sound. The second violins are on the right, though the orchestra's positioning in the acoustic varies from symphony to symphony. As in Bernstein's 1963 recording, the use of extra microphones renders the off-stage band in the Second Symphony much more audible than Mahler wanted.

The First Symphony opens with a very wide and deep image yet closes with violins sawing away extremely close to the listener. Individual instruments are sometimes recorded very close in the Third and Fourth Symphonies, but one extra microphone that enhances the effect well is that on the scordatura violin of the second movement of the Fourth. As in Horenstein's recording, the close microphones cannot help but overemphasize the clarinets and bassoon in the passage which begins in *IV, ii, 254*. Possibly because of the large number of microphones and the change of balance from point to point, it is hard to find a single satisfactory setting of the playback volume for this recording, and this undermines any illusion of continuity. The recording of the Sixth Symphony fails to deliver total clarity: the whole ensemble is balanced extremely close with little depth, and the spotlight is often on the first violins at the expense of the seconds, who are frequently swamped by all the brass and timpani on the right. Orchestral balance is extremely variable in the Seventh Symphony: good in the middle movements, but with violins and trumpets frequently close and overbearing in the outer movements.

In the First Symphony Kubelik handles well Mahler's planned long and gradual accelerando which is so important a structural element of the first movement, but then inexplicably pulls back during bars 408–11.[28] The second movement is cleanly played, with overtones of genteelness in the Trio. Technically the third movement is also superb, but the double-bass solo is 'too perfect' and the trumpets at *iii, 39* have a wailing jazz-influenced sound which one would not imagine to be acceptable to a native Czech. The Finale is also disappointing, with little flexibility in the slow sections and a bloodless ending. Many of Mahler's specific requests to hold back or move forward are ignored, while Kubelik himself decides to interrupt the flow at *iv, 85* and *iv, 572*. Kubelik's approach to Mahler's glissandi in this symphony is not consistent, and even when he allows them they sound unnatural and 'over-civilized'. Mahler's *col legno* requests at bars 45–49 and 135–38 are either played very discreetly or ignored: it is hard to tell.[29]

The Second Symphony is played with a refined approach to Mahler's dynamic marks and the tempi are well proportioned. Many of the details, such as the internal balance of the orchestra, fall into place exactly as Mahler planned them, and yet the overall effect is of precision without involvement.

In the Third Symphony Kubelik, like many conductors, takes no notice of Mahler's instruction that the snare drums should enter in *i, 634* at the old march tempo, ignoring the cellos and basses; also specifically forbidden by Mahler is Kubelik's fermata on the last chord of the second movement. The strings do not sound to be playing *col legno* at the end of the third movement. On the positive side, as far as details are concerned the violin solos are played with respect for Mahler's markings and do not dominate the proceedings, for instance in *i, 458–62* and *iii, 229–36*.

The Fourth Symphony is handled very lightly. The tempi of the first movement are more flexible than anything in the first three symphonies. Where used, glissandi are still very clean, though *col legno* is now part of the strings' arsenal. The string playing in the slow movement, while expressive, is also impeccably 'clean': even the solos of *iii, 98–106* are played without the portamenti marked by Mahler.

Both sonically and musically, the Fifth Symphony – the last to be recorded – is in many ways the best of the series. The bass is clearer, the string tone deeper, the acoustic is more transparent and there are no problems with unnatural highlighting of instruments. The separation of violins is even more of an advantage here. Kubelik double-dots rhythms as on Mahler's piano roll, also introducing a snap to the rhythm of one of the important Scherzo motifs (for example, the trumpet in *iii, 84*), and there are more glissandi and portamenti than elsewhere in the cycle. While it cannot in any way be described as 'heart on

---

[28] See Mahler's notes above bars 378 and 416.
[29] String players are often reluctant to play *col legno*, yet Mahler's effect is heard clearly on Walter's recordings.

sleeve' in the Bernstein or Barbirolli style, the performance convinces from beginning to end.

Kubelik's interpretation of the Sixth Symphony hits hard. This is achieved by brisk tempi in the first and Scherzo movements, a full-blooded performance of the Andante movement, and an exciting Finale with particularly chilling vibrato on the horns and trombones (marked *espressivo*) in the epilogue. However, the cowbells and deep bells are too continuous to be convincing, given that Mahler specifies an intermittent sound.

Kubelik's 1970 studio recording of the Seventh Symphony is at the opposite extreme from Bernstein's extrovert 'carnival'. Where Bernstein and Scherchen are content to let Mahler's music ramble, Kubelik seems to want to remind us that this is a purely instrumental symphony and invest it with decorum. Six years later his tempi with the same orchestra in concert are comparable, but a 1981 concert recording with the New York Philharmonic reveals that Kubelik later rethought his interpretation, adding 15 minutes to the total playing time, and allowing more of the extremes of the music to tell.

It is clear that Kubelik's intention was to document the symphonies in sound, and not to duplicate a concert experience. David Hall, the producer of Kubelik's early Mercury recordings, relates Kubelik's observation that 'when conducting for a live audience you may poetize, but when recording for the home, the phrasing must be more taut and pointed' (Hall, 1993, p. 12). It is also noticeable that, at least in his early recordings, he refuses to follow many of Mahler's markings.[30] While one cannot rule out the possibility that this approach may have been a reaction to Bernstein, Kubelik may simply have found himself unable to make all of Mahler's markings convincing. Even more intriguing is the possibility that he was consciously trying to purge the scores of those elements which he considered representative of Mahler the conductor, and not Mahler the composer. For, if these had not been the same person, and markings had been put in the scores by, say, Mengelberg, another conductor would certainly want to distinguish them from the composer's own and might well feel free to ignore them.

The future

Forty years ago, when widespread interest in Mahler was just emerging, Jack

---

[30] However, a recently released CD of a live performance of the Fifth Symphony, from the same Holland Festival as Klemperer's performance of the Second Symphony, not only confirms that the Mahler–Mengelberg tradition was still alive at the Concertgebouw but also reveals a young Kubelik who took great pains to follow all Mahler's instructions. The combination of orchestra and conductor resulted in a transparent texture with excellent instrumental balance, highly prominent glissandi and flexible tempi that avoid any lapse of good taste and sound completely natural.

Diether wrote: 'If the LP enabled us, for the first time, to hear and rehear the great bulk of [Mahler's] music, stereo will simply enable us to hear it better. ... [Stereo] must suggest that the apocalyptic horns and trumpets of Mahler's Second are indeed coming from the distant heavens, the cowbells of his Sixth and Seventh from slopes far below' (Diether, 1960b, pp. 100 & 103). A decade later Ulrich Dibelius called for a collaboration between conductors and engineers, in order to realize Mahler's symphonies in the medium of stereo recording, which, he noted, is governed by different rules from those that apply in the concert hall and which requires a different approach to respond creatively to the demands of the score (see Dibelius, 1971). Sadly, as we have seen, this has not yet happened; there are few instances of a successful planned interaction between engineers and musicians, and the choice is still largely between recordings which reproduce the sound of an orchestra at a distance, as heard from most concert hall seats, or an unbearably close sound which falsifies Mahler's instrumental balances.[31]

Since about two thousand recordings have already been made of Mahler's symphonies, one may perhaps wonder whether any more are needed; yet it is hard to imagine that Mahler would not himself have been excited at the possibilities of multi-channel surround sound. For this new technology to offer a more realistic experience than the best stereo recordings, it will be necessary for the performing musicians to work with a recording team as committed to realizing Mahler's vision through loudspeakers as John Culshaw and his associates were to Wagner's when they recorded the *Ring* – for Mahler's approach to concert music was no less a *Gesamtkunstwerk* than Wagner's in the opera house. But apart from the creation of an acoustic and placing that makes sense of the cowbells and promotes that clarity for which Mahler never ceased to search, what constitutes the spirit of Mahler performance? We have seen that it is not guaranteed by observance of the letter, though this certainly helps to make clear Mahler's larger vision behind the details.

One experiment which Mahler himself made in conducting Beethoven's Ninth Symphony in Hamburg was the replacement of the orchestra by an off-stage band in the B flat march of bars 331–430 of the last movement. Blaukopf summarized Walter's comments:

> Walter adds that Mahler was, of course, 'on the wrong track' in this case. Yet Walter emphasises that this questionable experiment had suggested to him an unquestionable basic idea: in order to achieve an authentic interpretation, one must argue back from the fixed notation of a musical work of art to the flux of its inception.
>
> (Blaukopf, 1973, p. 249)

Mahler the conductor tried to do this, notably with Beethoven's symphonies, changing their instrumentation and dynamics to satisfy his own idea of how

---

[31] Though incomplete at the time of writing, the series conducted by Pierre Boulez presents an intermediate approach.

Beethoven heard them in his head and adapting this to the acoustics of the late nineteenth-century concert hall. A similar approach could be adopted in recording Mahler's own works, though it would be at the opposite end of the spectrum from the philosophy of the Mahler Society Gesamtausgabe: instead of recording the last versions of the works that Mahler prepared for concert hall performance, it calls for a look behind Mahler's 'fixed notation' to discover his intentions. In evaluating the different solutions that Mahler considered for the instrumentation and balance of his textures it may be discovered in many cases that Mahler's first version is more appropriate for recording. A good example of this is the isolated clarinet note of *V, iii, 397*, discussed earlier, to which Mahler continued to add tone until he heard what he wanted in the concert hall. Many recordings would sound truer to his intention had they been made with one clarinet playing mezzo forte as he originally planned.

Any team taking on the Herculean task proposed will surely discover that, even with the option of doing yet another take, perfection is neither possible, nor the real goal. Arnold Schoenberg reported that 'after the first performances of his Seventh Symphony he [Mahler] said to me: "I don't know which you find more important. In the first performance I achieved more precision, in the second I got my tempi across better"' (Stein, 1975, p. 327). Conductors, producers and engineers can perhaps take comfort from this admission by Mahler himself of his inability to realize fully his own carefully laid plans.

Discography

Information not made available with the recordings themselves has been supplied from Fülöp (1995). Most of these recordings have been issued in more than one format. The catalogue numbers given are those of the actual versions used for this survey.[32] Information is given in the following format: *performers; place, date; company and medium, year of issue, catalogue number.*

Abbreviations

BRSO	Bavarian Radio Symphony Orchestra
CA	Concertgebouw, Amsterdam
CH	Carnegie Hall, New York
CO	Concertgebouw Orchestra
CSO	Chicago Symphony Orchestra
HM	Herkulessaal, Munich
KH	Kingsway Hall, London
LC	Lincoln Center, New York
LPO	London Philharmonic Orchestra
LSO	London Symphony Orchestra

---

[32] I should like to thank Julian Azar, Michael H. Gray, Edward R. Reilly and Erik Ryding for their generosity in making recordings and information available to me.

MT   Mormon Tabernacle, Salt Lake City, Utah
MV   Musikvereinssaal, Vienna
NPO   New Philharmonia Orchestra
NYP   New York Philharmonic
PO   Philharmonia Orchestra
USO   Utah Symphony Orchestra
VPO   Vienna Philharmonic Orchestra
VSO   Vienna Symphony Orchestra
VSOO   Vienna State Opera Orchestra

Maurice Abravanel

Symphony 1: USO; MT, May 1974; Vanguard CD, 1997, 08 6163 71
Symphony 2: Beverly Sills, Florence Kopleff, University of Utah Civic Chorus, USO;
    MT, April 1967; Vanguard CD, 1997, 08 6155 71
Symphony 3: Christina Krooskos, University of Utah Civic Chorus, Granite School
    Children's Choir, USO; MT, April 1969; Vanguard CD, 1998, 08 6178 72
Symphony 4: Netania Davrath, USO; MT, April 1968; Vanguard CD, 1997, 08 6164 71
Symphony 5: USO; MT, May 1974; Vanguard CD, 1997, 08 6156 71
Symphony 6: USO; MT, May 1974; Vanguard CD, 1997, 08 6157 71
Symphony 7: USO; MT, December 1964; Vanguard CD, 1997, 08 6158 71

Charles Adler

Symphony 3: Hilde Rössl-Majdan, Vienna Boys' Choir, Vienna State Opera Chorus VSO;
    Vienna, 27 April 1952; Delta LP, 1962, TQD 3056/7[33]
Symphony 6: VSO; Vienna, 7 April 1953; Conifer CD, 1997, 75605-51279 (coupled with
    III and *X, i*)

John Barbirolli

Symphony 1: Hallé Orchestra; Free Trade Hall, Manchester (?), 11–12 June 1957;
    Vanguard LP, 1967, SRV-233 SD
Symphony 3: Kerstin Meyer, Boys of Manchester Grammar School, Hallé Choir and
    Orchestra; Free Trade Hall, Manchester, 23 May 1969; BBC Legends CD, 1998, BBCL
    4004-7
Symphony 6: NPO; KH, 17–18 August 1967; EMI LP, 1968, ASD 2376/7

Leonard Bernstein

Symphony 1: NYP; LC, 4 & 22 October 1966; Sony CD, 2001, SMK 60732 in set SX12K
    89499
Symphony 1: CO; CA, October 1987; DG CD, 1989, 427 303
Symphony 2: Lee Venora, Jennie Tourel, Collegiate Chorale, NYP; LC, 29–30 September
    1963; Sony CD, 2001, SMK 63165/6 in set SX12K 89499
Symphony 3: Martha Lipton, Transfiguration Church Boys' Choir, Schola Cantorum,
    NYP; Manhattan Center, New York, 3 April 1961; CBS LP, 1962, SBRG 72065/6; CBS
    records CD, 1986, M2K 42196; Sony CD, 2001, SMK 61832/3 in set SX12K 89499

---

[33] Some forty bars were omitted from the third movement in this issue: side 2 fades
out during bar 340 and side 3 resumes at bar 382.

Symphony 3: Christa Ludwig, Brooklyn Boys' Chorus, New York Choral Artists, NYP; LC, November 1987; DG CD, 1989, 427 329/30

Symphony 4: Reri Grist, NYP; St George Hotel, Brooklyn, New York, 1 February 1960; Sony CD, 2001, SMK 60733 in set SX12K 89499

Symphony 4: Helmut Wittek, CO; CA, June 1987; DG CD, 1988, 423 607

Symphony 5: NYP; LC, 7 January 1963; CBS LP, 1964, SBRG72182/3; Sony CD, 2001, SMK 63084 in set SX12K 89499

Symphony 5: VPO, Alte Oper, Frankfurt, September 1987; DG CD, 1988, 423 608

Symphony 6: NYP; LC, 2 & 6 May 1967; CBS LP, 1968, S77215; Sony CD, 2001, SMK 60208 in set SX12K 89499

Symphony 6: VPO, MV, September 1988; DG CD, 1989, 427 698/9

Symphony 7: NYP; LC, 14–15 December 1965; Columbia LP, 1972, M31442/3 in set M4X 31441; Sony CD, 2001, SMK 60564 in set SX12K 89499

Symphony 7: NYP; LC, November/December 1985; DG CD, 1986, 419 212/3

Das Lied von der Erde: James King, Dietrich Fischer-Dieskau, VPO; Sofiensaal, Vienna, April 1966; London CD, 1989, 417 783

Riccardo Chailly

Symphony 5: CO; CA, October 1997; London CD, 1998, 289 458 860

Symphony 7: CO; CA, April 1994; London CD, 1995, 444 446

Eduard Flipse

Symphony 6: Rotterdam Philharmonic Orchestra; Rotterdam, 25 June 1955; Epic LP, 1956, SC 6012

Symphony 8: A. Kupper, H. Zadek, C. Bijster, A. Hermes, L. Fischer, A. Woud, L. Fehrenberger, F. Vroons, H. Schey, G. Frick, D. Hollestelle, combined Rotterdam choirs, Rotterdam Philharmonic Orchestra; Ahoy Hall, Rotterdam, 3 July 1954; Epic LP, 1955, SC6004

Oskar Fried

Symphony 2: Gertrud Bindernagel, Emmi Leisner, Berlin Cathedral Chorus, Berlin State Opera Orchestra; Berlin, 1923 or 1924; Naxos CD, 2001, 8.110152/3

Bernard Haitink

Symphony 1: CO; CA, 25 December 1977; Philips CD, 1999, 464 322 in set 464 361

Symphony 2: Roberta Alexander, Jard van Nes, Groot Omroepkoor, CO; CA, 25 December 1984; Philips CD, 1999, 464 323/4 in set 464 361

Symphony 3: Carolyn Watkinson, Groot Omroepkoor, Noord-Hollands Jongenskoor, CO; CA, 25 December 1983; Philips CD, 1999, 464 324/5 in set 464 361

Symphony 4: Maria Ewing, CO; CA 25, December 1982; Philips CD, 1999, 464 326 in set 464 361

Symphony 5: CO; CA, 25 December 1986; Philips CD, 1999, 464 327 in set 464 361

Symphony 7: CO; CA, 25 December 1985; Philips CD, 1999, 464 328 in set 464 361

Jascha Horenstein

Symphony 4: Margaret Price, LPO; Town Hall, Barking, October or November 1970; EMI LP, 1971, CFP 159

Symphony 8: Joyce Barker, Beryl Hatt, Agnes Giebel, Kerstin Meyer, Helen Watts, Kenneth Neate, Alfred Orda, Arnold van Mill, BBC Chorus, BBC Choral Society, Goldsmiths' Choral Union, Hampstead Choral Society, Emanuel School Boys' Choir, Orpington Junior Singers, LSO; Royal Albert Hall, London, 20 March 1959; BBC Legends CD, 1998, BBCL 4001-7

Otto Klemperer

Symphony 2: Ilona Steingruber, Hilde Rössl-Majdan, Wiener Akademie Kammerchor, Singverein der Gesellschaft der Musikfreunde, VSO; Vienna, May 1951; Vox CD, 1996, CDX2 5521

Symphony 2: Jo Vincent, Kathleen Ferrier, Amsterdam Toonkunstkoor, CO; CA, 12 July 1951; London CD, 1982, 425 970

Symphony 2: Elisabeth Schwarzkopf, Hilde Rössl-Majdan, PO and Chorus; KH, 22–24 November 1961, 15 & 24 March 1962; EMI LP, 1963, SAX 2473/4

Symphony 2: Galina Vishnevskaya, Hilde Rössl-Majdan, Wiener Singverein VPO; MV, 13 June 1963; Music & Arts CD, 1995, CD-881

Symphony 2: Heather Harper, Janet Baker, BRSO and Chorus; HM, 29 January 1965; EMI CD, 1998, CDM 7243 5 66867 2 4

Symphony 4: Elisabeth Schwarzkopf, PO; KH, 6, 7, 10 & 25 April 1961; EMI LP, 1962, SAX 2441

Symphony 7: NPO; KH, 19–21 & 24–28 September 1968; EMI CD, 1992, CMS 7 64147 2

Rafael Kubelik

Symphony 1: BRSO; HM, October 1967; DG CD, 1990, 429 043 in set 429 042

Symphony 2: Edith Mathis, Norma Procter, BRSO and Choir; HM, February & March 1969; DG CD, 1990, 429 044 in set 429 042

Symphony 3: Marjorie Thomas, Tölzer Knabenchor, BRSO and Women's Chorus; HM, May 1967; DG CD, 1990, 429 045/6 in set 429 042

Symphony 4: Elsie Morison, BRSO; HM, April 1968; DG CD, 1990, 429 047 in set 429 042

Symphony 5: CO; CA, 21 June 1951; Tahra CD, 2001, TAH 419

Symphony 5: BRSO; HM, January 1971; DG CD, 1990, 429 048 in set 429 042

Symphony 6: BRSO; HM, December 1968; DG CD, 1990, 429 049 in set 429 042

Symphony 7: BRSO; HM, November 1970; DG CD, 1990, 429 050 in set 429 042

Symphony 7: BRSO; HM, 5 February 1976; Audite CD, 2001, 95.476

Symphony 7: NYP; CH, 28 February 1981; NYP The Mahler Broadcasts 1948–1982 CD, 1998, No. 7

Gustav Mahler

Ging heut' morgen über's Feld, *Ich ging mit Lust*, Symphony 4, iv, Symphony 5, i: Welte-Mignon player-piano; rolls made Leipzig, 9 November 1905, audio recording Festeburg-Kirche, Frankfurt, 21–22 June 1992; Kaplan Foundation/Pickwick Group CD, 1993, GLRS 101

Willem Mengelberg

Symphony 4: Jo Vincent, CO; CA, 9 November 1939; Philips CD, 1986, 416 211
Symphony 5, iv: CO; Town Hall (?) Amsterdam, May 1926; Polygram Special Products
    (with New Sounds New Century, taken from EMI CD CDH 769956, c. 1988), 1997,
    441 917

Dimitri Mitropoulos

Symphony 1: Minneapolis Symphony Orchestra; Northrop Auditorium, Minneapolis,
    Minnesota, 4 November 1940; Sony CD, 1996, MHK 62342
Symphony 1: NYP; CH, 9 January 1960; Music & Arts CD, 1998, CD1021-1
Symphony 3: Beatrice Krebs, Westminster Choir, NYP; CH, 15 April 1956; Music & Arts
    CD, 1998, CD1021
Symphony 5: NYP; CH, 2 January 1860; Music & Arts CD, 1998, CD1021-3
Symphony 6: NYP; CH, 7 April 1955; NYP The Mahler Broadcasts 1948–1982 CD, 1998,
    No. 6
Symphony 6: WDR Orchestra; Cologne, 31 August 1959; Music & Arts CD, 1998,
    CD1021-4

Hermann Scherchen

Symphony 1: LPO; London, September 1954; MCA CD, 1991, MCAD2-9833
Symphony 2: Mimi Coertse, Lucretia West, Vienna Academy Choir, VSOO; Vienna,
    1958; MCA CD, 1991, MCAD2-9833
Symphony 5: VSOO; Vienna, July 1953; MCA CD, 1996, MCAD 80081
Symphony 5: Orchestre National de l'ORTF; Théâtre des Champs-Élysées, Paris, 30
    November 1965; Harmonia Mundi CD, 2000, HMA 1955179
Symphony 6: Leipzig Radio Symphony Orchestra; Kongresshalle, Leipzig, 4 October
    1960; Tahra CD, 1994, TAH110
Symphony 7: VSO; MV, 22 June 1950; Orfeo CD, 1992, C 279 921 B
Symphony 7: VSOO; Vienna, 1953; DG CD, 2002, 471 263-2

Georg Solti

Symphony 1: LSO; KH, 17–18 January, 3 & 5 February 1964; Decca LP, 1964, SXL 6113
Symphony 1: CSO; Orchestra Hall, Chicago, October 1983; London CD, 1984, 411 731
Symphony 3: Helen Watts, Wandsworth School Boys' Choir, Ambrosian Chorus, LSO;
    KH, January 1968; London LP, 1985, 414-254
Symphony 4: Sylvia Stahlman, CO; CA, 20–21 February 1961; London LP, 1961, CS
    6217
Symphony 5: CSO; Medinah Temple, Chicago, March 1970; London CD, 1991, 430 443
Symphony 6: CSO; Medinah Temple, Chicago, April 1970; London CD, 1986, 414 674
Symphony 7: CSO; Krannert Center, Urbana, Ill., April 1971; London CD, 1986, 414 675

Bruno Walter

Symphony 1: NYP; CH, 12 February 1950; Urania CD, 2000, URN 22.141
Symphony 1: NYP; CH, 25 January 1954; Sony CD, 1998, MHK 63328
Symphony 1: Columbia Symphony Orchestra; American Legion Hall, Hollywood, Calif.,
    14 & 16 January 1961; CBS Records CD, 1985, MK 42031

Symphony 2: Maria Cebotari, Rosette Anday, Vienna State Opera Chorus, VPO; MV, 15 May 1948; Arlecchino CD, n.d., ARL 177/8

Symphony 2: Emilia Cundari, Maureen Forrester, Westminster Choir, NYP; CH, 18 February 1957, 17 & 21 February 1958; CBS Records CD, 1985, M2K 42031

Symphony 4: Desi Halban, NYP; New York, 10 May 1945; Philips LP, c. 1960, GBL 5608; Sony CD, 1994, SMK 64 450

Symphony 4: Irmgard Seefried, VPO; Festspielhaus, Salzburg, 24 August 1950; Arlecchino CD, n.d., ARL 177

Symphony 4: Hilde Güden, VPO; MV, 6 November 1955; DG (Jubiläums-Edition der Wiener Philharmoniker) CD, 1991, 435 334

Symphony 5, iv: VPO; MV, 15 January 1938; Dutton CD, 1997, CDEA 5014

Symphony 5: NYP; New York, 10 February 1947; Philips LP, 1957, ABL3188/9; Sony CD, 1994, SMK 64 451

Benjamin Zander

Symphony 5: PO; Watford Colosseum, Watford, 7–10 August 2000; Telarc CD, 2001, 2-CD-80569

William Malloch

I Remember Mahler (programme broadcast on KPFK, Los Angeles, 7 July 1964); NYP The Mahler Broadcasts 1942–1882 CD, 1998, Nos 11 & 12

Chapter Fourteen

Adagietto: 'From Mahler with Love'[1]

GILBERT KAPLAN

Just before boarding a train in Vienna on 9 December 1901 to Dresden, where he was to assist at rehearsals of his Second Symphony,[2] Mahler dashed off a short letter to Alma Schindler. He had met the Viennese beauty only a month earlier,[3] and despite their age difference (he was 41, and she, 22) they had immediately fallen in love. Two days before he wrote the letter they had become secretly engaged,[4] and even though he had only just left her, Mahler missed Alma desperately. He urged her to write, as 'even the smallest sign of your existence which is so dear to me will instantly make me forget the pain of separation' (La Grange & Weiß, 1995, p. 76, and Mahler, 1990, p. 207; translation amended).

It was at about this time that Mahler was at work on his Adagietto, the fourth movement of his Fifth Symphony.[5] The Adagietto would become among the best

---

[1] An earlier version of this chapter appeared as an introductory essay for the facsimile edition of the autograph manuscript of the Adagietto movement (New York: The Kaplan Foundation, 1992), pp. 11–29.

[2] The concert was conducted by Ernst von Schuch on 20 December 1901. See Blaukopf, 1983, p. 116, & 1986, p. 112.

[3] In her memoirs (Mahler, 1990, p. 14, & 1940, p. 23) Alma wrote that she and Mahler first met on 9 November 1901. In her diaries she lists the date as 7 November (see Mahler-Werfel, 1997, p. 723, 1998, p. 442, and Mahler, 1990, p. 357), although she also describes a chance encounter with Mahler while cycling between Gosaumühle and Hallstatt on 11 July 1899 (Mahler-Werfel, 1997, pp. 317–18, & 1998, pp. 162–63). Alma's recently published diaries provide revealing insight into her developing emotional attraction to Mahler as man and musician.

[4] See Mahler, 1990, p. 363, although Alma wrote nothing explicit about this in her diaries (see Mahler-Werfel, 1997, pp. 733–37, & 1998, pp. 450–55). Nevertheless, Mahler's letter to Alma on 9 December makes it clear that they had made plans for their future together (see La Grange & Weiß, 1995, p. 77 & Mahler, 1990, p. 208). Their 'official' engagement took place on 23 December in the presence of Alma's mother and stepfather (see Mahler-Werfel, 1997, p. 747, and Mahler-Werfel, 1998, p. 464).

[5] The precise chronology of the composition of the Fifth Symphony is open to question. It is possible that Mahler may not have originally designated the Adagietto as the fourth movement. In the autograph score, the number '4' is written over some scraped-out

known of all Mahler's music. From examination of a chain of compelling evidence detailed in this essay, it is clear that it symbolized his love for Alma. So familiar is its dreamy melody, filled with passion and yearning, that it has been described as Mahler's signature melody, and its haunting opening notes as 'one of Mahler's most readily recognized fingerprints' (Cardus, 1965, p. 181).

Mahler performed the Adagietto ten times, on nine occasions as part of the complete Fifth Symphony and once by itself.[6] In fact, it remains the only orchestral movement from any of Mahler's symphonies that is often performed independently.[7] Moreover, long before the complete symphony was first recorded in 1947 by Bruno Walter,[8] the Adagietto had already been recorded twice – by Walter himself in 1938 and by Willem Mengelberg in 1926.[9]

The Adagietto has provided the musical basis for other art forms. It has inspired more than twenty choreographers around the world and served as the principal musical content of the soundtrack for Luchino Visconti's 1971 film of Thomas Mann's novella *Der Tod in Venedig* [*Death in Venice*], published in 1912.[10] It has even been made the subject of cartoons (see Plate 14.1).

---

writing. See La Grange, 1995, pp. 799–804, and Mitchell, 1999, pp. 241–44, for a general discussion of the background and chronology of the symphony; and La Grange, 1995, p. 817, and Mitchell, 1999, pp. 308–18, for specific reference to the Adagietto.

[6] The first performance of the Adagietto as an independent movement was probably given by Willem Mengelberg on 1 April 1906. Mahler's only performance of the Adagietto alone took place exactly one year later in the Augusteo in Rome.

[7] In earlier years other movements were heard independently of their symphonies, especially the Ländler (second movement) of the Second Symphony, the Minuet (second movement) of the Third Symphony and the two *Nachtmusik* movements of the Seventh Symphony.

[8] New York Philharmonic, recorded 10 February 1947 in New York (78 rpm: Columbia set MM 718; CD: Sony MPK 47683).

[9] Bruno Walter, Vienna Philharmonic, recorded 15 January 1938 (78 rpm: Victor 12319, HMV DB 3406; CD: Pearl GEMM CD9413). Willem Mengelberg, Concertgebouw Orchestra, recorded May 1926 in the Concertgebouw, Amsterdam (78 rpm: Eng-Columbia L 1798, Odeon 0 8591, AmDecca 25011; CD: Angel 69956).

[10] In his film, Visconti changed the novella's main character, a writer, to a composer who bears an unmistakable resemblance to Mahler. As such, it suggested a highly misleading portrayal. The story of the film bore no relation to any events in Mahler's life. A letter of protest was sent to Warner Bros, the film's distributor, by a group of Mahlerians that included Otto Klemperer, Wolfgang Sawallisch and Erwin Ratz. Gerald Fox (now president of the New York Mahler Society) informed Anna Mahler, daughter of the composer, who was so incensed that she asked Donald Mitchell, one of Britain's foremost Mahler authorities, to try to dissuade the Queen from attending a gala performance of the film in London (cited in Schlüter, 1983, p. 141. See also Schlüter, 1989, pp. 116–19, for discussion of further connections between Mahler's music and film). The Adagietto has been used in at least one other film: *1867*, a 14-minute documentary, directed by Ken McMullen and produced by the Program for Art on Film, about the artist Édouard Manet and his series of four paintings depicting the execution of Emperor Maximilian of Mexico. See Chanan, 1971b, for a discussion of the literary, aesthetic and

Plate 14.1 Cartoon by Rudolf Effenberger produced after the first performance of the Fifth Symphony in Vienna (*Fünfundzwanzig Jahre dienstbarer Geist im Reiche der Frau Musika* (Vienna: Gesellschaft der Musikfreunde, 1927))

Yet for all its popular appeal, the Adagietto has had some detractors. Richard Strauss told Mahler that although the symphony as a whole provided great pleasure, it was 'a pleasure only slightly dimmed by the little Adagietto. But as this was what pleased the audience most, you are getting what you deserve' (Blaukopf, 1984, p. 75). Otto Klemperer called the Adagietto 'very nice; but it is near a salon piece. I mean, it is not enormous' (Chesterman, 1976, p. 109). Theodor Adorno was suspicious of what he caustically described as the 'culinary sentimentality' of the Adagietto (Adorno, 1992a, p. 51, & 1960, p. 74).

In many ways, the Adagietto is uncharacteristic of Mahler as a symphonist.[11] The composer is renowned for some of the longest movements in symphonic literature, but the Adagietto is quite short, extending to only 103 bars, and is the shortest movement Mahler ever composed directly for a symphony.[12] Compared with Mahler's typical rhythmic and harmonic complexities, the Adagietto is simple. Whereas his symphonies usually require large orchestras, the Adagietto is scored for only strings and harp. Indeed, as Donald Mitchell has pointed out, Mahler was probably the first composer since the eighteenth century to write a movement for strings in the midst of an otherwise fully instrumented symphony (Mitchell, 1990).

What exactly is an adagietto? How should it be performed? Most musicologists and conductors are uncertain. Adagietto is a term rarely used by composers. It has been applied to the title of very few complete orchestral works and about twelve separate movements. There are only about twelve works for solo instrument with the marking *Adagietto*. According to the preferred definition of leading musical dictionaries, adagietto should be slightly faster, shorter or lighter than adagio, or some combination of the three.[13] David Fallows describes Mahler's Adagietto as a 'relatively brief slow movement with a relatively light texture' (Fallows, 1980, p. 88).

For Mahler, adagietto meant shorter and perhaps lighter, but apparently not faster. Although he titled the movement Adagietto, he also provided a separate opening tempo mark of *sehr langsam*, the equivalent of molto adagio (which he also wrote at bar 3 of the score). But conductors cannot agree on just how slow *sehr langsam* was for Mahler. He used the term for the opening of only one other

---

philosophical issues arising from the artistic encounter between Mann, Mahler and Visconti.

[11] For an extensive analysis of the Adagietto, see Forte, 1984.

[12] At 68 bars, the fourth movement of the Second Symphony, *Urlicht*, is actually shorter. But Mahler initially wrote this work as a song for the *Des Knaben Wunderhorn* cycle, only later incorporating it into the symphony.

[13] See Michael Kennedy, *The Oxford Dictionary of Music* (Oxford: Oxford University Press, 1985), p. 6; Don Michael Randel (ed.), *The New Harvard Dictionary of Music* (Cambridge, Mass.: The Belknap Press of Harvard University Press, 1986), p. 13; and J.A. Westrup & F.Ll. Harrison, *New College Encyclopedia of Music*, rev. Conrad Wilson (New York: W.W. Norton, 1976), p. 22.

purely orchestral movement, the Finale of the Ninth Symphony.[14] However, for a passage in the first movement of the Second Symphony (Fig. 16), he not only wrote *sehr langsam* but also assigned a precise tempo: $\downarrow$ = 69, a surprisingly fast tempo that is more than 50 per cent faster than any known performance of the Adagietto.[15] Of course, the context of *sehr langsam* in the Adagietto is quite different from that in the Second Symphony, where the term appears ten bars after *schnell* as the starting point of a long, unfolding accelerando. Nevertheless, the metronome mark of 69 provides some support for the view that Mahler did not regard *sehr langsam* as indicating an exceptionally slow tempo.

Evidence of how divided conductors are over the pace at which to play Mahler's Adagietto can be found in the wildly differing tempi that have been adopted over the years. Mengelberg's recorded performance lasts just over seven minutes, while Hermann Scherchen once took over 15 minutes.[16] No other movement of a Mahler symphony produces such wide disparity among interpretations. A difference as great as eight minutes is highly unusual even for Mahler movements lasting more than 30 minutes.

The tendency in recent years has been for conductors to choose slower tempi. Perhaps Mahler's music encourages interpretations that exaggerate its already highly emotional content. Some of the most experienced modern conductors of Mahler have led particularly slow performances of the Adagietto: Leonard Bernstein (over 11 minutes), Klaus Tennstedt and Seiji Ozawa (about $11^{1}/_{2}$ minutes), Herbert von Karajan, Claudio Abbado, James Levine and Lorin Maazel (about 12 minutes) and Bernard Haitink (about 14 minutes).[17]

Traditionally, commentators have characterized the Adagietto as meditative and introspective. For interpreters who perform the Adagietto at conspicuously drawn-out tempi, however, the feelings they seem to want the music to convey are melancholy, despair or even death. Visconti's use of the Adagietto for the film

---

[14] *Sehr langsam* is also indicated as the opening tempo for 'O Mensch! Gib Acht!', the fourth movement of the Third Symphony; and *äußerst langsam* for the Rückert song 'Ich bin der Welt abhanden gekommen'.

[15] The metronome mark appears only in the autograph manuscript (Collection Gilbert E. Kaplan, on deposit at the Pierpont Morgan Library, New York). See also Kaplan, 1986a, p. 32.

[16] Hermann Scherchen, Philadelphia Orchestra, *The Centennial Collections* (label of the Philadelphia Orchestra), vol. 4. Recorded 1964.

[17] Bernstein, Vienna Philharmonic (DG 423 608, recorded 1987), Tennstedt, London Philharmonic (Angel CD 49888, 1978), Ozawa, Boston Symphony Orchestra (Philips 432 141, 1990), Karajan, Berlin Philharmonic (DG 415 096, recorded 1973), Abbado, Chicago Symphony Orchestra (DG 427 254, 1980), Levine, Philadelphia Orchestra (RCA RDC1 5453, 1977), Maazel, concert at Carnegie Hall, New York, 28 February 1992, Haitink, Berlin Philharmonic (Philips 422 355, 1988). The author's performance stands in marked contrast to this 'tradition' (*The Kaplan Mahler Edition*, London Symphony Orchestra, Conifer Classics 75605-51277-2, 1991).

Death in Venice certainly contributed to this tendency. Indeed, the music can be made to suggest such moods. This conception of the Adagietto probably reached its peak in the autumn of 1990. Leonard Bernstein had just died, and many orchestras around the world added the Adagietto to their programmes in his memory. It seemed particularly fitting. After all, Bernstein had been so closely identified with Mahler's music. Moreover, the Adagietto had been performed at funerals before. Years earlier Bernstein himself had chosen to conduct the Adagietto to commemorate the death of his mentor, Serge Koussevitzky, and later at the funeral of US Senator Robert F. Kennedy because of the music's 'great solemnity' (Ames, 1990, p. 79).

What would Mahler have thought about all this? Did he really intend to write a work of 'great solemnity'? Would he have approved of sombre interpretations performed at a funereal pace? In short, is there a 'right' way to perform the Adagietto?

These are questions not normally asked about Mahler's symphonies. His music seems capable of accommodating many interpretative styles. The late Jack Diether, for years America's leading Mahlerian, characterized the Adagietto as an 'all-purpose' work – one capable of expressing many different moods (Diether, 1971). He agreed with Michael Chanan's suggestion that what Mahler created was only 'a matrix into which we pour our own molten feelings' (Chanan, 1971a, p. 28). As this study will demonstrate, Mahler had something much more limiting in mind.

To begin with, many Mahlerians and musicologists argue that slow performances of the Adagietto distort the character and function of the music. The Adagietto can be performed as an independent work; however, most agree with Mitchell that, as part of the Fifth Symphony, the Adagietto 'is not an isolated stretch of slow music but a slow introduction to the rondo finale into which it leads without a break' (Banks & Mitchell, 1980, p. 520). Seen in this light, then, the tempo of the Adagietto should not be too slow. As Paul Banks suggests, at a very slow tempo the Adagietto 'is inflated from being a pendant to the finale into an almost static slow movement in its own right. ... [This] creates a problem out of the finale; the joyous good-humour of that movement all too often seems unmotivated and out of place' (Banks, 1989, p. 262).

Some argue, however, that there is no true Mahler 'tradition' to rely upon because the composer's own ideas about how his music ought to be performed were always changing: he reworked his scores almost continuously (see Lebrecht, 1990a). Most of Mahler's changes, however, were concerned with refining his orchestration and correcting practical problems he encountered when performing his symphonies. In any event, the revisions he made to the Adagietto were minimal.[18]

---

[18] According to Sander Wilkens, who helped prepare the revised critical edition of the Fifth Symphony (ed. Karl Heinz Füssl, Vienna: Peters & Internationale Gustav

Another argument often made is that Mahler simply did not believe in tradition. After all, he was the one who had said, 'Tradition is sloppiness' (Mahler, 1990, p. 115, & 1940, p. 141).[19] As a conductor, he was often accused of taking liberties with other composers' music and was criticized for reorchestrating certain works of Beethoven, Schubert, Schumann and others. Thus, according to this argument, Mahler would surely have approved of – or at least understood – other conductors treating his own music in the same manner.

But in fact, Mahler was adamant that conductors should not interpret his music too freely, an attitude that was entirely consistent with his own behaviour. He was indeed a great interpreter, but he believed he was always fulfilling the composer's wishes. When his performances of others' works were criticized for failing to follow 'tradition', he argued that the tradition on which his fellow conductors had relied too long was a false one that bore no relation to how the composer might have interpreted his own work or wished it to be interpreted by others. 'Then', he complained, 'if someone comes along and fans the nearly extinguished spark in the work to a living flame again, he is shouted down as a heretic and an innovator' (Franklin, 1980, p. 112, and Killian, 1984, p. 112). This pattern was the basis of his 'tradition is sloppiness' remark. As we shall see, today's exceptionally slow performances of the Adagietto could well be a modern-day version of the same false-tradition phenomenon deplored by Mahler.

Even in the case of his reorchestrations, where it appeared that Mahler was deliberately disregarding the composer's notation, he emphasized that his aim was always to be faithful to the composer's intentions. In the case of Beethoven, Mahler explained that changes in brass instruments and in the size of orchestras since Beethoven's time required some rebalancing of the orchestra. He nevertheless stressed that, in making any changes, his sole aim was 'to pursue Beethoven's will down to its minutest manifestations, not to sacrifice one iota of the master's intentions' (cited in Blaukopf, 1973, p. 155). This attitude is consistent with Mahler's view that other conductors should fine-tune his own orchestration when necessary. For example, during a rehearsal of his Second Symphony for his 1907 farewell concert in Vienna, Mahler struck out a trombone

---

Mahler Gesellschaft, 1988), the Adagietto 'has undergone only the slightest revisions compared to the other movements' (letter to the author, 20 January 1990). This view is supported by Herta Blaukopf of the Internationale Gustav Mahler Gesellschaft in Vienna: 'The Adagietto seems to have been considered practically faultless and complete from the very beginning' (letter to the author, 16 August 1990). See also Wilkens, 1989.

[19] According to La Grange, however, the origin of the 'tradition is sloppiness' saying was a dispute Mahler had with the chorus master of the Vienna Opera, who insisted that the entire male chorus participate in the prisoner chorus, 'O welche Lust', from Beethoven's *Fidelio* because it was a Viennese 'tradition'. Mahler is supposed to have said: 'What you theatre people call your tradition is nothing but your inertia and your sloppiness' (cited in La Grange, 1999, p. 4).

passage because the instruments were covering the soloists' voices, saying 'I salute conductors who, when the occasion arises, modify my scores to suit the acoustics of the hall' (Wellesz & Wellesz, 1981, p. 46). Otto Klemperer reported that once, when Mahler was changing many details during a rehearsal of his Eighth Symphony, he turned to Klemperer and other young conductors present as observers, and said: 'If, after my death, something doesn't sound right, then change it. You have not only the right but the duty to do so' (Heyworth, 1985, p. 34).

While Mahler approved of conductors making adjustments to his orchestration, his view was very different when it came to interpretation and especially to tempi. According to Alma, 'It was Mahler's wish to hand down his own interpretations as a tradition' (Mahler, 1990, p. 115, & 1940, p. 141), and his 'tradition is sloppiness' comment should not be read as a contradiction. As we have seen, Mahler believed in tradition only when it emanated from a composer.

Consider, for example, what he told a friend after the poor reception of his Fifth Symphony in Berlin and Prague in 1905:

> So I thought to myself: Is it the fault of the symphony or the conductor?[20]...
> We musicians are worse off than writers in that respect. Anyone can read a book, but a musical score is a book with seven seals. Even the conductors who can decipher it present it to the public soaked in their own interpretations. *For that reason there must be a tradition, and no one can create it but I.*
> (Mahler, 1990, pp. 92–93, & Mahler, 1940, p. 117, italics added)

Some years earlier, after hearing a performance of his Second Symphony that 'took the wind out of his sails', Mahler expressed the same sentiment, complaining that the tempi, expression and phrasing were wrong, even though it

> was directed and rehearsed by someone who will imagine and claim that he inherits the 'tradition' straight from me! From this, you may learn the truth about every so-called 'tradition': There is no such thing! Everything is left to the whim of the individual, and unless a genius awakens them to life, works of art are lost. Now I understand perfectly why Brahms let people play his works as they pleased. He knew that anything he told them was in vain. Bitter experience and resignation are expressed in this fact.
> (Franklin, 1980, p. 141, and Killian, 1984, p. 149)

Mahler was especially concerned that conductors get his tempi right. Nowhere is there any evidence to suggest that Mahler considered tempi to be a 'free-for-all'. The opposite was the case: 'Tempo is for me a matter of feeling. ... You know how meticulous I am in my work. I never trust the conductors or their capacities. Yet even if they follow every indication, all is lost if they make a mistake in the first tempo' (cited in La Grange, 1974, p. 314). Mahler could have

---

[20] Arthur Nikisch.

made it easier for conductors by providing metronome marks, and in some of his early works he did so. But he later removed most of them because he felt they put a straitjacket on music that needed room for some flexibility. Mahler called metronome markings 'almost worthless; for unless the work is vulgarly ground out in barrel-organ style, the tempo will already have changed by the end of the second bar' (Franklin, 1980, p. 46, and Killian, 1984, p. 42).

Mahler would have been the last person to argue that there was only one correct tempo for any of his works. Indeed, as we shall see, his own performances differed somewhat from one another. For Mahler, music was 'something living and flowing that can never be the same even twice in succession' (ibid.). But that did not mean he approved of *any* tempo. He said that an overall tempo could be a 'degree' faster or slower depending on the mood of a conductor and that it could vary only 'slightly' without otherwise harming the work (ibid.).

Mahler provided several clues to the limits of what he regarded as acceptable tempo flexibility. One metronome mark he did leave in a published score, for the opening tempo of the first movement of the Second Symphony, is a range: $\bf \downarrow$ = 84–92, about a 10 per cent range.[21] A further clue is Mahler's reaction to the timing of one of his own performances (with which he was apparently satisfied): he expressed 'amazement' that 'he, the composer' had taken a few minutes longer to perform one movement of the Third Symphony (probably the fourth) than he had on another occasion (ibid.). Finally, there is his criticism of his protégé Oskar Fried, whom he visited when Fried was rehearsing the Second Symphony in Berlin in 1905. Mahler told him that his tempi were 'too fast by half' (Mahler, 1990, p. 267, and La Grange & Weiß, 1995, p. 267). The next day Fried told his musicians that 'everything I did during the rehearsals was wrong. This evening I will take entirely different tempi' (Klemperer, 1960, p. 15).

There seems little doubt, then, that Mahler wanted other conductors to follow his tempi, with room for some flexibility. The problem remains, however, of knowing what Mahler's tempi were. There are no recordings of any Mahler performances, and while Mahler made piano rolls of some of his music,[22] the

---

21 *Symphonie Nr. 2, c-moll* (Vienna: Internationale Gustav Mahler Gesellschaft in conjunction with Universal Edition, 1970; rev. edn, Vienna & London: Universal Edition, 1971), p. 3.

22 The four piano rolls that Mahler made of his own music with the firm M. Welte & Söhne in Leipzig on 9 November 1905 include the songs 'Ging heut' Morgen über's Feld' from *Lieder eines fahrenden Gesellen* (piano roll 767) and 'Ich ging mit Lust' from *Lieder und Gesänge [aus der Jugendzeit]* (piano roll 768), the first movement of the Fifth Symphony (piano roll 769), and the last movement of the Fourth Symphony (piano roll 770). Mahler's tempo on this last piano roll may suggest that most performances of this movement today are substantially slower than he might have intended. These piano rolls are available on the CD recording produced by the Kaplan Foundation 'Mahler Plays Mahler: The Welte-Mignon Piano Rolls' (Pickwick Group Ltd, Golden Legacy of Recorded Music, GLRS 101, 1993).

Adagietto was unfortunately not among them.[23] All that most conductors know about Mahler's intention for the opening tempo of the Adagietto is his direction, *sehr langsam.*

However, much more can in fact be revealed about Mahler's own approach. To begin with, there is good evidence of his own tempi. In one of Mahler's personal scores, there is a timing of seven and a half minutes for the Adagietto.[24] This score – probably the one he used for the 1904 première in Cologne – is the small 'study' size, the only type published at the time of the first performance,[25] and it includes autograph revisions. According to Sander Wilkens, two letters from Mahler to his publisher provide further evidence that the score was used at the première (see Wilkens, 1989, pp. 59 & 271, & 1988, p. 11).

The seven-and-a-half-minute timing was apparently written in by Bruno Walter, who was present at the première.[26] Regardless of whether it derived from Mahler's performance that night or from one of Walter's subsequent performances, its appearance in this archival score is especially significant. This timing closely matches Mahler's last performance of the Adagietto in St Petersburg on 9 November 1907.[27] There, one of the players in the second desk of the double basses (probably L. Slovachevsky) wrote timings for most of the movements in his part. The timing for the Adagietto was seven minutes.[28] A timing of nine minutes appears in a set of printer's proofs corrected by Mahler for the first edition of the full-size score. While some of the corrections appear to be autograph, the inscription indicating nine minutes could have been written by

---

[23] For further analysis of Mahler's approach to conducting his own works, see Kaplan, 1986b, and Banks, 1987 & 1989.

[24] First edition of the study score (plate no. 9015) (Leipzig: Peters, 1904). This can be found in the Bruno Walter collection in the Bibliothek der Universität für Musik und darstellende Kunst in Vienna, signature B.W.II.38390. The timings of the other movements are: first, 12 minutes; second, 13^1/2–14 minutes; third, 15–15^1/2 minutes; fifth, 14 minutes. See also Wilkens, 1989, pp. 59 & 271.

[25] This first edition of the study score was published in September 1904, the première took place on 18 October, and the full (conducting) score was published in November.

[26] According to Wilkens, 'there is no possible doubt' that the timing was written in by Walter (letter to the author, November 1991).

[27] A performance of the Fifth Symphony scheduled for Paris in January 1911 was cancelled. It is not clear whether Mahler was to be the conductor (see Mahler, 1990, p. 392).

[28] The set of parts is divided between collections in the Wiener Stadt- und Landesbibliothek (Universal Edition archive) and the Internationale Gustav Mahler Gesellschaft, Vienna. The bass part of the Adagietto is housed in the former collection. Timings for the other movements are: Part I (first and second movements), 27 minutes; Part II (third movement), 17 minutes. No timing is listed for the fifth movement (see Banks, 1989, pp. 261–62).

someone else.[29] Finally, a timing was recorded at the last rehearsal, on 12 March 1905, for Mahler's concert in Hamburg the next day. Mahler's friend Hermann Behn wrote nine minutes for the Adagietto in his personal score.[30]

Mahler's timings are reinforced by recorded performances of his disciples Bruno Walter and Willem Mengelberg.[31] The seven-minute recording by Mengelberg has already been mentioned. He also wrote a timing of nine and a half minutes for the Adagietto in his score.[32] Like Walter, he was present when Mahler conducted his Fifth Symphony.[33] The timing of Walter's first recording of the Adagietto alone in 1938 was 7 minutes 58 seconds, and, in his 1947 recording of the whole symphony, the duration was 7 minutes 37 seconds. The rationale behind seven- to eight-minute recordings on a single disc is sometimes attributed not to conductors' intentions but to the technical limitations of 78 rpm recordings, where, it is asserted, slower performances could not fit on two sides of one record. However, even in 1926, when Mengelberg made his seven-minute recording, it was possible to put more than nine minutes of music on two sides of a single 78 rpm record. For example, in the 1925 Columbia recording of Berlioz's *Symphonie fantastique* with Felix Weingartner and the LSO, a single side (no. 12) takes 4 minutes 35 seconds. Thus a much slower Adagietto was certainly technically possible. A summary of timings is shown in Table 14.1.

What this evidence reveals is that during Mahler's lifetime, performances of the Adagietto by the composer as well as by his close colleagues averaged about eight minutes. Mahler was painfully aware that conductors tended to 'exaggerate and distort' all his indications: 'the *largo* too slow, the *presto* too fast' (Franklin, 1980, p. 175, and Killian, 1984, pp. 195 & 196). However, he could

---

[29] The printer's proofs are in the collection of the Arnold Schoenberg Institute, Vienna; shelf mark SCO W 23, Vol. I and Vol. II. Not all of Mahler's corrections found their way into the printed score. Two Adagietto timings are listed. On the reverse side of the final page of the second movement Mahler listed 35 minutes (most probably for the first and second movements, the '5' having been corrected from what was originally '0'); Scherzo 17 minutes; Adagio [*sic*] 10 minutes; 14 minutes (fifth movement); 76 minutes (the whole work). At the end of the Scherzo Mahler additionally noted down 15 minutes; and at the end of the Adagietto, 9 minutes (corrected from 10).

[30] This score is in the Department of Special Collections of the Stanford University Libraries, Stanford, California. Timings of the other movements are: first movement, 12 minutes; second movement, 15 minutes; third movement, 17 minutes; fifth movement, 15 minutes.

[31] However, timings and interpretations of Mahler's music by different 'disciples' could vary. Klemperer, for his part, did not believe that there was a tradition for Mahler's music (see Chesterman, 1976, p. 108).

[32] Mengelberg's score, owned by the Amsterdam Concertgebouw Orchestra, is housed in the Nederlands Muziek Instituut, Willem Mengelberg Archive Foundation, The Hague.

[33] On 8 March 1906, with the Concertgebouw in Amsterdam.

Table 14.1 Fifth Symphony: Adagietto timings by Mahler and his disciples

	Timings (minutes: seconds)
Mahler's score (probably used for the 1904 première)	7:30
Bass part used for Mahler's St Petersburg concert, 1907	7:00
Hermann Behn's score (final rehearsal for Mahler's 1905 Hamburg concert)	9:00
Printer's proof for the 1904 first edition of the full-size score corrected by Mahler	9:00
Recording by Willem Mengelberg, 1926	7:04
Mengelberg's score	9:30
Recordings by Bruno Walter:	
1938	7:58
1947	7:37

never have anticipated the distortions to which his Adagietto would be subjected in subsequent years. Today, many conductors perform the Adagietto at a pace, as Mahler might have put it, too slow by half. La Grange notes:

> Mahler certainly did not anticipate, nor would he have wished for, the excessive sentimentality which most conductors today indulge in when playing this short piece. The slowed-down tempo at which they take it completely distorts its tender, contemplative character and changes it into a syrupy elegy.
>
> (La Grange, 1995, p. 817)

If Mahler's timings reflected only his own mood at a particular performance, one could understand that some conductors might not feel compelled to follow his tempi. But his timings are critical because they reflect the mood Mahler wanted the music to project, a mood that would be destroyed by an excessively slow tempo. For Mahler, mood was all-important. 'What matters is only the *mood* that has to be expressed', he once said (Martner, 1979, pp. 177–78, and Blaukopf, 1996, p. 170), and 'What is best in music is not to be found in the notes' (Walter, 1937, p. 84). In talking to orchestras he would often focus on the mood of a work: 'You must *feel* with me', he once told some New York musicians.[34] A first-desk

---

[34] Alfred Friese, interviewed by Jerry Bruck, private tape, cited in Lebrecht, 1990a, p. 302.

violinist in the New York Philharmonic summed it up thus: 'He just explained that it was all mood.'[35]

The mood that Mahler apparently wanted the Adagietto to project was one of romantic love, rather than sadness or solemnity. There is evidence to suggest that the Adagietto served as a 'love letter' from the composer to Alma, probably shortly before they were married. This evidence is contained in a note that Mengelberg wrote on the opening page of the Adagietto in his personal copy of the Fifth Symphony (illustrated in Plate 14.2).[36]

In the margin, Mengelberg wrote these words (most probably his own) to accompany the first violin part:

Wie ich dich liebe,	How I love you,
Du meine Sonne	You my sun
Ich kann mit Worten Dir's nicht sagen	I cannot tell you in words
Nur meine Sehnsucht	I can only lament my yearning
Kann ich Dir klagen	And my love for you
Und meine Liebe	My happiness!
Meine Wonne!	

At the top of the page, Mengelberg wrote, 'Heartfelt, love but noble, sweet' and over the opening melody, 'Love, heartfelt, tender yet ardent!!!' Finally, at the bottom of the same page, he added, 'If music is a language, then it is one here – "he" tells her everything in "tones" and "sounds" in: music'. According to Floros, Mengelberg's 'love-letter' revelation helps to explain Mahler's citation of the 'Glance Theme' from Wagner's *Tristan und Isolde* (see bars 45–48 of the Prelude to Act I) in bars 61–71 of the Adagietto (Floros, 1994, p. 155).

Alma often served as Mahler's inspiration. The Fifth Symphony was a special bond that united them in the early years of their marriage. She described how the symphony 'had been my first full participation in his life and work, (Mahler, 1990, p. 72, & 1940, p. 92). It was this symphony that dominated their first summer together, and Alma played a personal role in its creation. While Mahler was scoring the symphony, Alma would copy it out. 'We had a race to see who got through first, he scoring or I copying' (Mahler-Werfel, 1959, p. 30, & [1960] 2000, pp. 32–33). She later made a fair copy of the whole score (see Plates 14.3

---

[35] Comments by Herman Martonne on *I Remember Mahler*, radio programme by William Malloch first broadcast on 7 July 1964, on KPFK Los Angeles (Pacifica Radio), cited in Lebrecht, 1987, p. 294. These comments can also be heard on the CD 'Mahler Plays Mahler: The Welte-Mignon Piano Rolls' cited in fn. 22 and on *The Kaplan Mahler Edition* cited in fn. 17.

[36] The first writer to draw attention to Mengelberg's inscription appears to have been Edna Richolson-Sollitt (n.d. [1934], p. 34), followed by Rudolf Stephan (1979a, p. 88) and Kühn & Quander (1982, p. 24). Subsequent discussion of the musical implications of Mengelberg's inscription has appeared in La Grange, 1983, pp. 277 & 1132, La Grange, 1995, pp. 538 & 816–18, Floros, 1985, pp. 148–49, 1994, pp. 154–55, Mitchell, 1985, p. 131, and Mitchell & Nicholson, 1999, pp. 315–18.

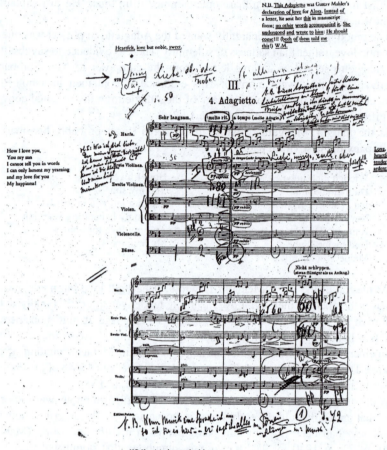

Plate 14.2   Fifth Symphony: the opening page of the Adagietto, from Willem Mengelberg's personal copy of the score. Reproduced by kind permission of the Collection Netherlands Music Institute/Willem Mengelberg Archive Foundation, The Hague.

N.B. Dieses Adagietto war Gustav Mahlers Liebeserklärung an Alma! Statt eines Briefes sandte er ihr dieses im Manuskript; weiter kein Wort dazu. Sie hat es verstanden u. schrieb ihm: Er solle kommen!!! (beide haben mir dies erzählt!) W.M.

N.B. This Adagietto was Gustav Mahler's declaration of love for Alma! Instead of a letter, he sent her this in manuscript form; no other words accompanied it. She understood and wrote to him: He should come!!! (both of them told me this![37]) W.M.

---

[37] Mahler introduced Mengelberg to Alma on 27 May 1906 in Essen when Mahler

Plate 14.3 Fifth Symphony: the first page of the Adagietto in Mahler's hand; excerpt from the autograph manuscript reproduced by kind permission of the Pierpont Morgan Library, Mary Flagler Cary Music Collection, New York (MS Cary 509).

and 14.4). It was also the first new work that Mahler played in its entirety for Alma: on the piano in his small composing hut in the woods above their summer

conducted the première of his Sixth Symphony (see Mahler, 1990, p. 100, & 1940, p. 124). This could well have been the occasion on which Alma told him about the Adagietto 'love-letter' episode. Mengelberg had just performed the Adagietto as an independent work (1 April 1906), and Mahler had recently conducted the Fifth Symphony (8 March 1906) – both with the Concertgebouw, Mengelberg's orchestra.

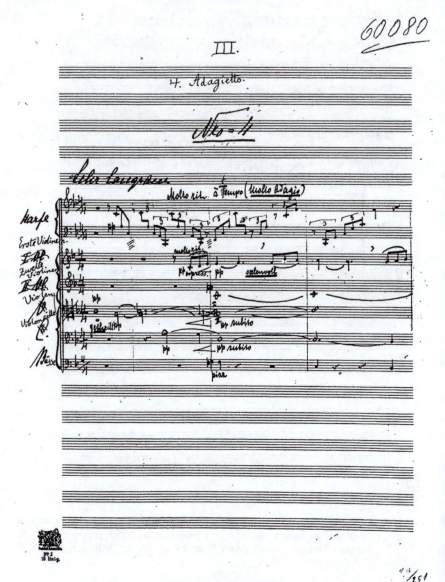

Plate 14.4   Fifth Symphony: the first page of the Adagietto in Alma's hand; excerpt from the *Stichvorlage* reproduced by kind permission of the Music Division, the New York Public Library for the Performing Arts, Astor, Lenox and Tilden Foundations (Job 85–9). By the time Alma made her copy, the seventh note of the first violin melody had been changed from Mahler's original G to the familiar B flat.

villa in Maiernigg. Alma recalled that she and Mahler 'climbed arm in arm up to his hut with all solemnity for the occasion' (Mahler, 1990, p. 47, & 1940, pp. 62–63). Mahler penned a dedication to Alma in his autograph score: 'To my dear Almscherl, the faithful and brave companion on all my journeys'.

The Adagietto continued to touch Alma throughout her life. In 1931, on the twentieth anniversary of Mahler's death, she made a gift of Rodin's bust of Mahler to the Vienna Opera. At her request, the Opera orchestra performed the Adagietto at the presentation ceremony (see Mahler-Werfel, 1959, p. 193, & [1960] 2000, pp. 226–27). Then, in New York in 1948, friends arranged a private performance of the Adagietto for her sixty-ninth birthday (see Mahler-Werfel, 1959, p. 277).

By using the Adagietto as a 'love letter', Mahler clearly pointed to the mood he wanted. It was this that apparently determined his choice of tempi. In order to convey a sense of romantic love, there seem to be limits to how slowly the Adagietto can be played without distorting its essential character. Mitchell suggests that the Adagietto is a 'song without words' for orchestra, and that therefore

> the successful interpretation of the Adagietto will be that which sustains the long melody as if it were written for the voice. No singer could possibly sustain the very slow tempi some conductors have adopted. Mengelberg's and Walter's tempi, on the contrary, are paced by that hypothetical singer.
>   (Mitchell, 1990, cited with slight alterations in Mitchell, 1999, p. 313)

A very slow tempo might be more appropriate if Mahler envisaged the Adagietto as a particularly tragic or painful love song. While there is no denying the bitter-sweet quality of some of its music, it is difficult to imagine that Mahler, in the first blush of his passion for Alma, might have composed a musical 'love letter' of this nature. Moreover, even if Mahler had composed the Adagietto (at least as a sketch) before he met Alma, it seems unlikely that in selecting a work which would deliver, without the support of any accompanying words, his declaration of love, he would have chosen music he intended to be sombre or solemn. Mengelberg surely understood this. His own description of the Adagietto was 'love, a love comes into his life'.[38]

It was certainly in character for Mahler to express his love for Alma in music. In the summer of 1902 he composed the love song 'Liebst du um Schönheit', and planned to surprise her with it at their summer home in Maiernigg by leaving it hidden inside a piano score of a Wagner opera.[39] When Alma failed to use the score for some time, Mahler became impatient, picked it up himself and let the song fall out. That was how Alma discovered it.

---

[38] Mengelberg's score of the Fifth Symphony, p. 2.

[39] In Mahler-Werfel, [1960] 2000, p. 33, the opera is described as *Siegfried*. In Mahler, 1940, p. 78, & 1990, p. 60, it is described as *Die Walküre*.

There is also the well-known 'Alma theme' beginning in the first and second violins at the upbeat to Fig. 8 in the first movement of the Sixth Symphony. Interestingly, this theme is in the same key as the Adagietto (F major), shares the same ascending upbeat and is likewise accompanied by extensive harp arpeggios.[40] It is also worth mentioning a possible link between Mahler's Adagietto and what was probably the only other Adagietto he knew: the third movement from Bizet's *L'Arlésienne: Suite No. 1* (1872), which Mahler conducted three times (in New York in 1911). It is scored for strings only, it is also in F major, the first bars are closely related to Mahler's, and it was composed to accompany a scene between 'lovers ... who have long concealed from each other their affection' (see Ex. 14.1).[41]

Love was often the theme when Mahler wrote an adagio. Only three movements (other than the Adagietto) of his completed nine symphonies are in the spirit of an adagio, and two of them 'expound' this theme: the final movement of the Third Symphony, which was once entitled 'What love tells me' and the last movement of the Ninth, which, while often thought to express a sense of farewell, could also be said to convey Mahler's deep love of life.[42]

For some, it is difficult to accept romantic love as the characterizing mood of the Adagietto because Mahler used similar music to suggest completely different feelings of solitude and withdrawal in the song 'Ich bin der Welt abhanden gekommen'. This song and the Adagietto have strong links.[43] They were composed at about the same time, and their final cadences are melodically and harmonically very similar (compare bars 61–67 of the song with bars 95–103 of the Adagietto). La Grange has described 'Ich bin der Welt abhanden gekommen' as 'perhaps the high point of Mahler's Lieder output as a whole' (La Grange, 1995, p. 792). Mahler's own description was more personal: 'It is my very self!' (Franklin, 1980, p. 174, and Killian, 1984, p. 194), sentiments echoing those of Rückert's poem, written for his fiancée, Louise Wiethaus.

Some conductors believe that because of the musical links with 'Ich bin der Welt abhanden gekommen', the Adagietto should also be characterized by the reflective and introspective mood of Rückert's poetry. Indeed, it might seem puzzling that Mahler would use similar music to suggest feelings of both withdrawal (in the song) and love (in the Adagietto). However, he had previously

---

[40] See also Taylor, 1988, pp. 89–90.

[41] I am indebted to Donald Mitchell for this insight. Citation taken from the synopsis of the play by Daudet for which Bizet wrote his music, in Biancolli, Louis & Mann, William S. (eds), *The Analytical Concert Guide* (London: Cassell, 1957), p. 111.

[42] The third movement of the Fourth Symphony is also in the style of an adagio. In addition, the incomplete Tenth Symphony, whose composition is linked with Mahler's marital crisis and whose manuscript contains poignant messages of devotion to Alma, begins with a movement designated as Adagio.

[43] The Adagietto is also related to the second of the *Kindertotenlieder*, 'Nun seh' ich wohl', given the latter's frequent melodic use of a rising, three-note anacrusis.

Ex. 14.1   Opening bars of Bizet's Adagietto from *L'Arlésienne: Suite No. 1*

used the same music for a song and a symphonic movement, each suggesting a radically different mood. Nearly all of the music of the *Des Knaben Wunderhorn* song 'Des Antonius von Padua Fischpredigt', for example, is included in the Scherzo of his Second Symphony, and yet the 'stories' with which they are associated are very different. The song tells a cynical tale about St Anthony, who, finding his church empty, goes to deliver his sermon to the fish in a lake (they listen but pay no heed). Mahler headed the song with the instruction *mit Humor*, but when he used practically the same music (without words) as the basis for the much expanded symphonic movement, the expression of humour was evidently not at the forefront of his mind.[44] He described the music in this case as portraying the view of a person who sees the world 'distorted and crazy, as if reflected in a concave mirror'; 'Life then becomes meaningless. Disgust of existence in every form'; 'the appalling shriek of this tortured soul' (compiled from Franklin, 1980, p. 44 (Killian, 1984, p. 40), Martner, 1979, p. 180 (Blaukopf, 1996, p. 173), and Mahler, 1990, p. 213 (Mahler, 1940, p. 262)). No doubt Mahler expected the mood of the music in the song and in the symphonic movement to be different, and conductors certainly make this distinction.

Moreover, for the concluding bars of the Adagietto, where the musical similarities to 'Ich bin der Welt abhanden gekommen' are most pronounced, Mahler indicated significantly different tempi and dynamics in some sources. In the song, he maintains the *äußerst langsam* opening tempo and the dynamic mark *pp*, but in the set of printer's proofs of the Adagietto mentioned above he replaced the original marking *sehr zurückhaltend*, present in the autograph manuscript, with *vorw[ärts]*, and in the first edition of the conducting score (November 1904) the tempo marking appears as *drängend* and the dynamic indication as *ff*.[45] At these prescribed tempi and dynamics, the song seems to end in a mood of hushed withdrawal, and the Adagietto in one of passion and commitment. Thus, while it is seemingly paradoxical, the two works may indeed be considered to 'express ... completely different sentiments' (La Grange, 1983, p. 1133).

Because of the weight attached here to Mengelberg's 'love-letter' revelation, it is important to consider the reliability of his inscriptions. Mengelberg often wrote detailed comments in his scores reflecting information, advice or performance requirements given to him by Mahler personally.[46] According to Frits Zwart of the Nederlands Muziek Instituut, an acknowledged authority on the conductor, it would have been completely out of character for Mengelberg to write something in his score about which he had any doubts. Mengelberg was an ardent champion of Mahler, with whom he enjoyed a particularly close friendship. Mahler said of him: 'There's no one else I could entrust a work of mine to with entire confidence' (Mahler, 1990, p. 273, & 1940, p. 354). Mahler said this in 1906, the same year in which he conducted his Fifth Symphony (8 March) and Mengelberg performed the

---

[44] Mahler did retain the indication *mit Humor* in the Scherzo for three brief passages in the E flat clarinet, bars 52–57, 91–96 & 395–400.

[45] See Kubik, 2001, pp. 7–8, for a discussion of the concluding tempi of the Adagietto in the context of preparing the new edition of the Symphony published as part of the Kritische Gesamtausgabe.

[46] These comments appear throughout Mengelberg's scores of Mahler's symphonies. For example, he wrote 'Mahler said here' and 'Mahler himself demanded here' on pp. 3 & 8 of his score of the First Symphony.

Adagietto alone (1 April), both in Amsterdam with the Concertgebouw Orchestra.

There is yet further evidence about the 'love-letter' story. According to Herman Nieman of the Dutch Mahler Society, Mengelberg told the tale to members of both the Concertgebouw and the New York Philharmonic orchestras.[47] Edna Richolson-Sollitt, a writer who visited Mengelberg at his home in Switzerland, reported that after listening to the Adagietto together in the moonlight, Mengelberg recounted the story in full (Richolson-Sollitt, n.d. [1934], p. 34). After hearing a performance of the symphony under Mengelberg in 1906, the conductor Alphons Diepenbrock described the Adagietto as a 'love song' (Reeser, 1980, p. 23).

One possible basis for questioning the accuracy of Mengelberg's account is that the existence of a specific programme for the Adagietto seems to contradict the widely held view that with the Fifth Symphony Mahler abandoned the kind of programme that had been associated with his first four symphonies. In his biography of Mahler, Bruno Walter concurs: 'Nothing in any of my conversations with Mahler and not a single note point to the influence of extra-musical thoughts or emotions upon the composition of the *Fifth*' (Walter, 1937, p. 122). Yet, at the same time Walter was aware of, and believed, the 'love-letter' story, which he told to Georg Solti (whose own performance of the Adagietto lasts about nine and a half minutes).[48]

One way of reconciling Walter's conflicting statements is offered by the possibility that, as mentioned above, Mahler composed the Adagietto (at least as a sketch) before he met Alma and only later assigned it the 'love-letter' role. Whether or not Alma was the inspiration for the Adagietto is less significant than the fact that Mahler clearly believed the music capable of successfully delivering the declaration of love, as it in fact seemed to do.

Furthermore, it would appear that Mahler may have had some kind of programmatic idea in mind for the Fifth. The first movement bears the title 'Funeral March', a programmatic indication as Mitchell has long suggested (see, for example, Mitchell, 1999, pp. 282–85).[49] Even more significant, Mahler's own description of the Scherzo was typical of Mahlerian programmes: 'a human being in the full light of day in the prime of life' (Franklin, 1980, p. 173, and Killian, 1984, p. 193).[50]

---

[47] Letter from Nieman to the author dated 8 August 1990.

[48] This information was communicated by Solti in conversation with the author. Solti's performance of the Symphony with the Chicago Symphony Orchestra was recorded in 1990 (Decca, 433 329-2DH).

[49] See Barry, 1993, for further discussion of the putative programmatic nature of the Fifth Symphony.

[50] This description relates to the title Mahler had given to a scherzo ('Die Welt ohne Schwere' ['The World Without Care']), also in D, that he had intended to write for

A final issue is the absence of any mention of the 'love-letter' episode in Alma's diary or memoirs. Alma kept a highly detailed and intimate account of her daily life and frequently emphasized the role she played in relation to Mahler's music (see Mahler-Werfel, 1997 & 1998). She did recount in full the story about 'Liebst du um Schönheit' (Mahler, 1990, p. 60, & 1940, p. 78). Why Alma never entered the Adagietto incident in her diary is indeed a mystery. But equally, no evidence exists that she ever disavowed the story during the fifty years or more that she lived following Mahler's death: years during which she was in close contact with many of Mahler's friends and biographers.

Although a few Mahlerians do not believe Mengelberg's account, most feel it is to be trusted. As Mitchell puts it:

> There seems no reason to doubt Mengelberg's scribbled reminiscence. I cannot believe for one moment that this was a fabrication, though it may have been written down a while after the event and tidied up a bit in the process.
>
> (Mitchell, 1985, p. 131, & memorandum to the author, 31 January 1991.
> See also Mitchell, 1999, p. 316)

While La Grange, who knew Alma well, broadly accepts Mengelberg's story: 'It seems to us impossible to take lightly such precise testimony ... words which without doubt Mahler himself had communicated to him' (La Grange, 1983, pp. 1132–33; see also La Grange, 1995, p. 817), he none the less expresses some reservations on the grounds of the similarity between the Adagietto and 'Ich bin der Welt abhanden gekommen', and the fact that Alma never mentioned the story in her diary or memoirs during the years that followed Mahler's death (see La Grange, 1983, p. 277, & 1995, pp. 538 & 817).

The evidence presented above clearly supports the case against exceptionally slow tempi for the Adagietto: Mahler's own timings; his determination that other conductors should follow his interpretations; the timings of Mahler's disciples, Mengelberg and Walter; the need for an appropriate tempo relationship between the Adagietto and the Rondo-Finale; the 'romantic' mood indicated by Mahler's use of the Adagietto as a 'love letter'; and finally, the conviction of leading Mahler scholars. All this surely makes it clear that to play this music extremely slowly is to succumb to a false tradition which exceeds the boundaries of interpretative licence.

---

the Fourth Symphony. It could well be that the Scherzo in the Fifth Symphony is the one that he had originally planned for but never included in the Fourth (see Bekker, [1921] 1969, p. 145).

Chapter Fifteen

'Progress' and 'Tradition': Mahler's Revisions and Changing Performance Practice Conventions

REINHOLD KUBIK
translated by Jeremy Barham

The problem of Mahler's versions

It is common knowledge that Mahler revised his works throughout his life. He did this on his own initiative, and not under the influence of other people as was the case, for example, with Bruckner. Nor were his versions a response to altered performance conditions, as pertained, for instance, to baroque opera, Bach's cantatas or Schoenberg's *Gurrelieder*. Mahler very seldom made structural revisions (if one leaves aside *Das klagende Lied*, whose two-movement version is the only exception), directing his attention instead to the texture which he adapted to the level of instrumental aesthetics and technique he had reached at the time. Mahler firmly believed in the progress of his own abilities and repeatedly made comments to the effect that only the latest version of a work was the one that should be performed. To this extent, the decision of the founder of the Complete Critical Edition, Erwin Ratz, to publish exclusively the *Fassungen letzter Hand* was right.

Three further points nevertheless deserve consideration: in the first place it is clear that Mahler never viewed his works as finished. Why else would he have insisted in August 1910 that Universal Edition 'allow those alterations which I have made since the appearance of the aforementioned four symphonies [Symphonies 1–4] to be added to all the plates of the score and orchestral parts at your cost'[1] but in addition agreed that 'future changes are not included in this arrangement' ['Künftige Neu-Änderungen stehen ausserhalb dieser

---

[1] 'jene Änderungen, welche ich seit Erscheinen der erwähnten 4 Symphonien vorgenommen habe, auf Ihre Kosten in sämtliche Platten der Partitur und der Orchesterstimmen eintragen zu lassen'.

Vereinbarung']?[2] Mahler thus reckoned on making further revisions but could not burden the publisher with the costs. In *Der Mann ohne Eigenschaften* Robert Musil quoted an official memorandum of the Austrian War Ministry written shortly before the First World War which aptly characterizes Mahler's stance towards his works and suitably qualifies the concept of *Fassungen letzter Hand* and its validity in his case: 'provisionally definitive' [*Vorläufig definitiv*].[3] The second point is whether, from our current perspective, Mahler's later versions eliminate the authenticity, independence and right to existence of earlier versions. When the present author took over the editorship of the Complete Edition in 1993 the (earlier) piano versions of the *Wunderhorn* songs were in the process of being adapted to match the (later) orchestral versions – something which for obvious reasons was immediately stopped. As a result of this process, the piano versions were effectively being denied their right to independent artistic existence. After the publication of the original three-movement version of *Das klagende Lied*, occasional objections were voiced against its performance among circles of established Mahler scholars. The author none the less believes that early versions are entirely deserving of our interest: they are in fact the unmediated results of the creative process, and in terms of content and sound reflect precisely that stage of development in which Mahler found himself at the time of their conception. The third point is related to the fact – demonstrated below through examples from the revisions of the Fifth Symphony – that while Mahler did indeed aspire to put into practice 'developments' in his own technique of instrumentation, at the same time he took little notice of current 'developments' in orchestral performance practice.

Mahler and historicism

Mahler's work at the frontier between romanticism and modernism has many differing and contradictory dimensions. This perhaps constitutes part of his fascination. Current research for the most part emphasizes the progressive elements: *New Sounds, New Century* is the overtly programmatic title of a recent publication on the Fifth Symphony (Mitchell & Straub, 1997). However, Mahler was not only a 'contemporary of the future' [*Zeitgenosse der Zukunft*] as the title of a standard work on the composer refers to him (Blaukopf, 1969), but also a contemporary of that artistic movement labelled historicism which, in the form of the so-called *Ringstraßenstil*, bequeathed many important examples in Vienna that were brand new when the 15-year-old Mahler went to study in the city. It

---

[2] Contract between Mahler and Universal Edition Vienna, signed 11.8.1910 in Toblach, housed in the Universal Edition archives, Vienna.

[3] Musil, Robert, *Der Mann ohne Eigenschaften*, ed. Adolf Frisé, Hamburg: Rowohlt, 1978, vol. 1, p. 226.

should also be remembered that Mahler registered at the University of Vienna for Middle High German seminars and lectures on the history of Old German literature. This, together with his admiration for Wagner, whose works are all set in the past, left its clearest traces in the early works, for example in the choice of subject matter and in the archaic linguistic style of the poetry in *Das klagende Lied*. Evidence of Mahler's awareness of music history can also be found in this work: in order musically to reconstruct notions of 'the past' and 'memory' within the narrative, the young composer employed period instruments which by then had become obsolete, namely valveless natural horns [*Waldhörner*] (see 'Hochzeitsstück', from bar 159).

There is conclusive evidence that Mahler's basic musical education, like that of Schubert, was extremely conservative (one only has to consider the latter's 'baroque' notation of triplets which is hardly ever present in the considerably older Beethoven). Indeed from today's perspective we would maintain that certain 'performance practice' conventions of older music are preserved by Mahler. There are countless examples of these. One need only look at the solo violin scordatura in the Scherzo of the Fourth Symphony – a baroque practice particularly common in the seventeenth century but long forgotten by Mahler's time. To take another example, the irregular length of dotted rhythms is typical of baroque practice, where the dot can sometimes be worth less than half the value of the note, thus corresponding to a triplet rhythm, and at other times can be worth more than half, as in the so-called 'French' style of the opening section of a baroque operatic overture. Parts of the first movement of the Third Symphony (from Fig. 2) are reminiscent of the latter, where the sharp 'French' dotting is stipulated in a footnote: 'Play these triplets fast, at approximately the same time as the bass drum strokes' ['Diese Triolen schnell, ungefähr mit den Vorschlägen der grossen Trommel zusammen']. In the second movement of this symphony, a footnote to bar 32 in the first violin requires the execution of a dotted figure during the ritardando in a 'baroque' manner which was clearly no longer familiar in Mahler's day: 'The semiquavers should be equally fast at all times; the rit. is to be transferred to the dots' ['Die Sechzehntel immer gleich schnell; das rit. in die Punkte zu verlegen']. This practice of not stretching out a rhythmic formula even during a reduction in overall speed, but retaining its own specific tempo while the intervening rests continually increase in length, had already been used in the piano version of 'Der Schildwache Nachtlied' (bars 29–30: rit. with the instruction 'the triplets equally short each time' ['die Triolen immer gleich flüchtig']). Mengelberg's annotations on page 16 (and at equivalent places) of his conducting score of the Fifth Symphony also correspond closely to this. They evidently reflect Mahler's performance instructions at rehearsals in Amsterdam in March 1906. From bar 120 Mengelberg noted down double-dotted crotchets plus semiquavers instead of dotted crotchets followed by quavers. This is a baroque style of playing supported by, among others, Leopold Mozart: 'It is therefore always better if the note following the dot be played somewhat late' ['Man thut demnach allezeit besser, wenn man die nach dem Puncte folgende Note etwas später ergreift'] (Mozart, [1787] 1968, p. 145; trans. from Mozart, [1787] 1985, p. 130).

It seems that Mahler did not have a very high regard for that kind of continuous legato and vibrato playing almost universally practised today – 'a liquefied pulp without substance or form' as he once remarked to Natalie Bauer-Lechner (Killian, 1984, p. 41, and Franklin, 1980, p. 45; editor's translation) – but favoured instead a short-range, declamatory style of 'baroque' articulation. Evidence of this from the revision of the Fifth Symphony will be provided below. The instruction 'vibrato' in bar 86 of the first violin part in the Adagietto indicates that the strings of the orchestra normally played without vibrato. In fact vibrato was regarded as a kind of ornamentation, exclusive to solo music.[4] The violinist Otto Strasser (b. 1901) gave the following account of his audition with the Vienna Philharmonic in 1922:

> When I went for my audition the panel consisted of the Opera Director Schalk (it was difficult to engage Strauss for this kind of activity), the conductors [*Kapellmeister*] Reichenberger and Alwin, and the orchestral leaders [*Konzertmeister*] headed by Arnold Rosé. ... He [Rosé] was an imposing artist and was so firmly rooted in tradition that he was not very keen at all on the vibrato which had long ago become common practice, employing it only sparingly. Therefore when, after some difficult passages, he put in front of me the violin cantilena from the entry of Lohengrin and Elsa into the cathedral, and I began playing away to my heart's content with vibrato, Schalk, who shared Rosé's views, interrupted me with the words: 'stop bleating like that'.
>
> (Strasser, 1974, p. 20)

Mahler may also have expected declamatory articulation without continuous legato (and perhaps even without continuous vibrato) from his singers:

> The intelligent singer shapes things, brings out the sound from the words and through doing this gives it a content and soul which is communicated to everyone. The unintelligent singer produces the notes without articulation, performs them only from the point of view of the sound, without thinking about the text.
>
> (Killian, 1984, p. 195; editor's translation)

'Baroque' vocal practice also involved reducing the volume of high notes by avoiding the chest register (*di petto*).[5] The *pp* in bars 15 and 16 of 'Blicke mir nicht in die Lieder' is an example of this. More compelling is the instruction 'the lower notes are for singers who do not have a head voice at their disposal' ['Die unteren Noten für Sänger, die über keine Kopfstimme verfügen'] in bar 42 of the song 'Zu Straßburg auf der Schanz'.

---

[4] A useful summary of this topic is given in Moens-Haenen, 1987.

[5] On this subject, see Harris, 1990.

Everywhere we thus come across performance practices which by Mahler's day had evidently disappeared or were falling into disuse. The revisions of the Fifth Symphony, first performed in 1904, reflect precisely this change in patterns of performance practice which began noticeably around the turn of the century. This is why Mahler, in making his revisions, felt compelled among other things to clarify his intentions, for his 'outmoded' notation presupposed a body of knowledge on the part of musicians which had been lost. Mahler knew that older music relied on universally understood conventions and that therefore it had not been necessary to notate every single detail: 'Beethoven counted on artists, not mechanics ... He did not write everything out in such meticulous detail as Richard Wagner was later to do' (Killian, 1984, p. 41, and Franklin, 1980, p. 45; editor's translation).

The revisions of the Fifth Symphony: notation and performance practice

At almost every performance of his Fifth Symphony Mahler carried out improvements in notation and orchestral retouchings. His reference score, in which the alterations up to and including the time of the St Petersburg performance of November 1907 were inserted, seems to have been lost.[6] However, two complete sets of parts exist, the first of which (St1) was in use up to the time of this performance, while the second (St2) was further revised in Mahler's last winter in New York, both for a planned performance there and as the basis for a new edition.[7] The purpose of carrying out some of the alterations was to achieve precisely that kind of accurate notational technique which became an obvious necessity after 1900, when the continuous style of vibrato and legato that still persists today began its triumphant march of progress.

> Those people who, like me, are continually horrified at the misunderstandings and interruptions arising from this [i.e. imprecise notation] will understand how anxiously and carefully I therefore treat my works. ... When, say, the musical sense requires that successive notes be played detached, I do not leave it to the judgment of the players but, for example, divide up the passage between first and second violins rather than

---

[6]   The existence of this score can be traced to the Peters publishing house at the end of 1919. Max Hinrichsen took it with him to London when he emigrated in 1937 (letter to Erwin Ratz, 30 October 1957). During the 1940s in Oxford, Egon Wellesz borrowed the score from Albi Rosenthal. After that it disappeared.

[7]   Most of these two sets of parts are housed in the Internationale Gustav Mahler Gesellschaft in Vienna and in the Universal Edition archive which is preserved in the Vienna Stadt- und Landesbibliothek. In the course of preparing the new edition of the Symphony it was possible to identify St2 definitely as that set of parts which Mahler received in July 1910 from Henri Hinrichsen, took with him to New York and revised there during winter 1910–11. St1 was used for the first time in May 1905 in Strasbourg and for the last time in November 1907 in St Petersburg.

leaving it all to the firsts or seconds. … So that there can be no possibility of the slightest discrepancy in rhythm, I have racked my brains to find a way of notating it as precisely as possible. And so I avoid indicating the shortness of notes or the gaps between them with dots or similar staccato marks. Everything down to the last detail is conveyed by means of note values and rests.

(Killian, 1984, p. 41, and Franklin, 1980, pp. 45–6 (excerpt only); editor's translation)

From experience, Mahler drew the obvious conclusion that the modern musician no longer knew the basic rules of baroque articulation, such as that when two notes are slurred the first is to be accented and played long, and the second is to be unaccented and played short: 'the second [quaver] is slurred on to it quite smoothly and quietly, and somewhat late' ['die darauffolgende Achttheilnote ganz still daran schleifen'], as Leopold Mozart put it (Mozart, [1787] 1968, p. 267; trans. from Mozart, [1787] 1985, p. 220).

Plate 15.1   Fifth Symphony: facsimile reproduction from seventh and eighth staves on p. 22 of second violin part in St1 (fifth movement, bars 668–72 & 678–80). All facsimiles from St1 and St2 are reproduced by kind permission of the Internationale Gustav Mahler Gesellschaft, Vienna, where the originals are housed

The excerpt from p. 22 of the second violin part in St1, illustrated in Plate 15.1, shows in the upper staff (the seventh) a shortening of the final note at the end of the slur, and in the lower staff (the eighth) an accent on the note at the beginning of the slur so that despite the preceding *diminuendo* and *piano* markings the note retains the necessary weight in relation to the 'recessive' second note. The insertions in all the following facsimile illustrations are autograph and always written in blue pencil; some are drawn over existing autograph pencil insertions. Plate 15.2 shows an excerpt from the sixth staff of p. 16 in the first violin part. Mahler reiterates by hand the printed accent over the first note of the second bar, and shortens the second note. There are countless examples of the shortening of the last of a group of slurred notes. Plate 15.3 illustrates just a few of them from St1.

Plate 15.2   Fifth Symphony: facsimile reproduction from sixth staff on p. 16 of first violin part in St1 (third movement, bars 635–37)

(a)

(b)

(c)

(d)

(e)

Plate 15.3   Fifth Symphony: facsimile reproduction from: (a) ninth staff on p. 14 of
second violin part in St1 (third movement, bars 662–76); (b) first staff on
p. 14 of viola part in St1 (third movement, bars 633–41); (c) thirteenth staff
on p. 7 of double-bass part in St1 (second movement, bars 346–47); (d) ninth
and tenth staves on p. 1 of oboe part in St1 (first movement, bars 122–24 &
129–32); (e) fifth staff on p. 3 of oboe part in St1 (first movement, bars
294–98)

The caesura inserted before the staccato note in Plate 15.3e came from the hand of an oboist, but was nevertheless based on an instruction from Mahler because St1 was used exclusively at performances under his direction.

In some cases Mahler replaces simple variants of articulation in the original with those that are 'rhetorical' in a thoroughly baroque, short-range sense. An example of this can be seen in bars 678–81 of the Scherzo. The variant in the autograph score (housed in the Pierpont Morgan Library, New York) was printed in the first editions of the study score (September 1904) and the conducting score (December 1904), both published by Peters in Leipzig. During the course of the Strasbourg performance in May 1905 Mahler switched to the variant reading which appears in the author's new edition (see Plate 15.4).

The cello and double-bass slurs in bars 597–607 of the third movement, likewise added for the first time in the Strasbourg score, are classic examples of baroque markings (see Plate 15.5a). To compare, Plate 15.5b shows an excerpt from Minuet I of Bach's Third Partita for solo violin, BWV 1006, in the composer's hand.

In the performance of baroque music the dot can be replaced by a rest, resulting in a particularly 'eloquent', expressive style. Mahler frequently uses this effect, but because it had fallen into disuse by that time, he had to notate it using rests instead of dots, as in Plate 15.5c, and as in the corresponding passage for cellos and double basses (Plate 15.5d).

The motif from the Scherzo shown in Plate 15.5d occurs frequently, and in other instruments as well. At its initial appearance in the first violins in bar 136 Mahler provides a footnote vividly calling to mind the following passage by Leopold Mozart: 'Further, care must be taken to play ... the short notes, following a dot or short rest, late and rapidly' ['Ferner muß man sich befleissigen ... die nach einem Punkte oder kleinen Sospir folgenden kurzen Noten aber spät und geschwind wegzuspielen'] (Mozart, [1787] 1968, p. 264; trans. from Mozart, [1787] 1985, p. 224). Mahler's footnote reads as in Plate 15.6a.

Instead of 'dots or similar staccato marks', 'the shortness of notes or the gaps between them' are notated 'by means of note values and rests' as Mahler reportedly said to Bauer-Lechner (Killian, 1984, p. 41, and Franklin, 1980, p. 46; see above). As illustrations of this, see Plate 15.6b and c.

As Plate 15.6c shows, Mahler clearly did not believe the instruction 'staccatissimo' to be convincing enough for the player, although in reality it would certainly have been sufficient. One can also see in Plate 15.6b and c that Mahler used staccato strokes in the same way that he used staccato dots elsewhere (these were always standardized as dots by copyists and engravers). Older traditions of notation perhaps continued to have an influence even here. Although the implication of these markings for both Mozarts – dots to indicate shortening, strokes as an indication of a change of bow (see, for example, Seiffert, 1993) – is irrelevant on this occasion, the later use of dots to denote lightly accented staccato, and strokes to denote sharply accented staccato (as, for

(a)

(b)

Plate 15.4   Fifth Symphony: (a) facsimile reproduction of bars 678–81 in the autograph manuscript of the third movement Scherzo, New York, Pierpont Morgan Library, MS Cary 509. Reproduced by kind permission of the Pierpont Morgan Library; (b) the same bars from the most recent edition of the Fifth Symphony, ed. Reinhold Kubik (Frankfurt: Peters, 2002). Reproduced by kind permission of the publishers

Plate 15.5 Fifth Symphony: (a) facsimile reproduction of first–third staves on p. 14 of double-bass part in St1 (third movement, bars 596–619); (b) autograph manuscript of Minuet I of Bach's Third Partita for solo violin, BWV 1006 (Berlin, Staatsbibliothek Preußischer Kulturbesitz, Mus. ms. Bach, P 967), bars 19–26. Reproduced by kind permission of the Staatsbibliothek zu Berlin, Preußischer Kulturbesitz, Musikabteilung mit Mendelssohn-Archiv; (c) facsimile reproduction from fourth staff on p. 8 of oboe part in St1 (third movement, bars 61–66). The dots after the notes were scratched out and quaver rests added; (d) facsimile reproduction from fourth staff on p. 15 of cello part in St1 (third movement, bars 633–35)

(a)

*) Anmerkung für den Dirigenten:

In diesem Motiv ist das Achtel stets etwas flüchtig = nachlässig
auszuführen, in welches Instrument es auch gelegt ist; also ungefähr so:

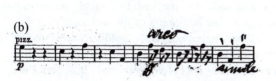

(b)

(c)

(d)

Plate 15.6   Fifth Symphony: (a) Mahler's footnote to bar 136 of the first violin in the
Scherzo, ed. Reinhold Kubik (Frankfurt: Peters, 2002), p. 167. Reproduced
by kind permission of the publishers ['Conductor's note: in this motif the
quaver is always to be played somewhat fleetingly = casually, in whatever
instrument it occurs; that is, approximately thus:']; (b) facsimile reproduction
from fourth staff on p. 11 of double-bass part in St1 (third movement, bars
185–90); (c) facsimile reproduction of tenth staff on p. 19 of double-bass part
in St1 (fifth movement, bars 357–63); (d) facsimile reproduction of
fifth–eighth staves on p. 11 of double-bass part in St1 (third movement, bars
191–225)

example, in Beethoven) remains pertinent. An example of staccato strokes and dots used on the same page is shown in Plate 15.6d.

It should be said however that, without carrying out a corresponding examination of Mahler's entire output, the application of these various markings in the Fifth Symphony is not nearly systematic enough to draw far-reaching conclusions for future editions.

Finally a marking which likewise quickly disappeared after 1900 is found with relative frequency in the Fifth Symphony: the swell [*Schweller*]. It originated in sixteenth-century vocal practice and indicates the so-called *messa di voce*, a swelling up and down of the voice. At the beginning of the nineteenth century this practice – which before 1750 was never notated – gradually went out of fashion so that it became necessary to indicate explicitly when a *messa di voce* was intended. Carl Friedrich Zelter, for instance, frequently does this, and Plate 15.7 illustrates the beginning of his song 'Erster Verlust', composed in 1807 to a text by Goethe.

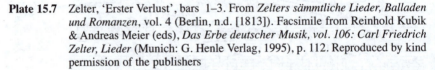

Plate 15.7   Zelter, 'Erster Verlust', bars 1–3. From *Zelters sämmtliche Lieder, Balladen und Romanzen*, vol. 4 (Berlin, n.d. [1813]). Facsimile from Reinhold Kubik & Andreas Meier (eds), *Das Erbe deutscher Musik, vol. 106: Carl Friedrich Zelter, Lieder* (Munich: G. Henle Verlag, 1995), p. 112. Reproduced by kind permission of the publishers

The *messa di voce* marking occurs quite often in the Adagietto, where, even in the autograph manuscript, one can easily distinguish it from the use of successive crescendo and diminuendo brackets, despite the fact that Mahler does not always write the *messa di voce* at the start of a note like an accent mark (even accents, however, are frequently placed on the wrong side of the note). See Plate 15.8a. Not even Alma fully understood Mahler's notation, writing the same passage in her copy – which was used as the printer's model [*Stichvorlage*] and is now housed in the New York Public Library – as illustrated in Plate 15.8b. As a result, this passage was printed in the first edition of the study score as shown in Plate 15.8c. Mahler corrected it in the study score which he used to conduct the first performance,[8] inserting the *messa di voce* markings in red ink over the notes – a correction that was not carried out by the publisher in the subsequent printing of the conducting score (Leipzig: Peters, 1904), perhaps because the music engravers were no longer familiar with the sign. The precise distinctions of the original notation only appear in the new edition of 2002, as illustrated in Plate 15.8d (the crescendo and diminuendo brackets in bar 71 of the second violin stem from the parts, St1 and St2). The *messa di voce* marking, as Mahler used it, might therefore have signified a rapid crescendo and diminuendo, similar to an accent, which takes place at the beginning of a long note, as opposed to the combination of both crescendo and diminuendo brackets which of course denotes a gradual swelling up and down, spread over the whole duration of the note.

In the final examples, shown in Plate 15.9, one can see how Mahler's autograph notation was transferred into the printed parts. The new edition reads all three dynamic markings as the same, in other words as *messa di voce* signs, thereby offering the more musically convincing interpretation of the passage, as shown in Plate 15.9c.

These examples should offer sufficient proof that Mahler tried to adhere to performance styles and notational methods which harked back at least to the time of Viennese classicism. By 1900 some of these had already fallen into disuse and others were on the point of disappearing. Only close study of the performance practices of older music – the kind of study that was to be reserved for a much later period – enables these facts to be identified and interpreted.

---

[8] Study score in the estate of Bruno Walter, housed in the Bibliothek der Universität für Musik und darstellende Kunst, Vienna, signature B.W.II.38390.

(a)

(b)

(c)

(d)

Plate 15.8   *caption opposite*

Plate 15.8 Fifth Symphony: (a) facsimile reproduction of excerpt of bars 67–71 in the autograph score of the fourth movement Adagietto, New York, Pierpont Morgan Library, MS Cary 509. Reproduced by kind permission of the Pierpont Morgan Library; (b) facsimile reproduction of excerpt of bars 67–71 of the *Stichvorlage* of the fourth movement Adagietto (New York Public Library, Job 85-9). Reproduced by kind permission of the Music Division, the New York Public Library for the Performing Arts, Astor, Lenox and Tilden Foundations; (c) facsimile reproduction of excerpt of bars 67–71 of the fourth movement Adagietto in the first edition of the study score (Leipzig: Peters, 1904); (d) facsimile reproduction of excerpt of bars 67–71 of the fourth movement Adagietto from the most recent edition, ed. Reinhold Kubik (Frankfurt: Peters, 2002). Reproduced by kind permission of the publishers.

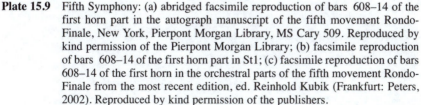

Plate 15.9 Fifth Symphony: (a) abridged facsimile reproduction of bars 608–14 of the first horn part in the autograph manuscript of the fifth movement Rondo-Finale, New York, Pierpont Morgan Library, MS Cary 509. Reproduced by kind permission of the Pierpont Morgan Library; (b) facsimile reproduction of bars 608–14 of the first horn part in St1; (c) facsimile reproduction of bars 608–14 of the first horn in the orchestral parts of the fifth movement Rondo-Finale from the most recent edition, ed. Reinhold Kubik (Frankfurt: Peters, 2002). Reproduced by kind permission of the publishers.

PART FIVE

Sketches, Editions and 'Performing Versions'

Chapter Sixteen

Re-evaluating the Sources of Mahler's Music

JAMES L. ZYCHOWICZ

What can be learned from Mahler's manuscripts? What can they reveal that is not already part of the published works? Is it possible to gain any new insights into Mahler's music through his manuscripts and other autograph sources? Or is such sketch study a musicological 'glass-bead' game that may ultimately be inconsequential? These are difficult but not impossible questions, and anyone who deals with the source materials for any composer, including Mahler, must address the issues raised by them.

Notwithstanding such concerns, deeper knowledge of the important information contained in manuscripts and other primary sources can only augment current understandings of Mahler and his music. At the same time it would seem best to approach Mahler's manuscripts with the scepticism that he himself expressed about the study of Beethoven's sketches. In the context of a discussion of his own sketches, Mahler commented to Natalie Bauer-Lechner in August 1901 on the study of Beethoven's sketches and wondered whether anything of consequence could be gained from such investigation:

> What have they divined from Beethoven's [sketches]! That, for instance, he supposedly worked on compositions that are completely different from each other in the same volume [sketchbook]. That's nothing! All sorts of things merely occurred to him continuously, which he jotted down and preserved for a later time, and which he then used at the right opportunity. Or they say that the completed work signifies such progress beyond the sketched draft; meanwhile they have no notion of what entirely different things could have come from such a first inkling in his hands.
>
> (Bauer-Lechner, MS, cited & trans. in Hefling, 1981, p. 125[1])

---

[1] 'Was haben sie aus Beethovens herausgelesen! daß er z.B. an dem Inhalt und der Zeit nach völlig getrennten Werken zugleich gearbeitet habe, weil Skizzen sich zu beiden in jenen Heften beieinander fanden. Keine Spur! Es fiel ihm nur fortwährend alles mögliche ein, welches er sich notierte, und für spätere Zeit aufhob und das er bei

Despite Mahler's own scepticism about contextuality in sketches, it is the very things to which he himself objects that can lead to a deeper understanding of his own compositional process and the music he created. For example, although one should be cautious about drawing premature conclusions, the various ideas that someone like Beethoven could take up in the same sketchbook or on the same page nevertheless offer clues about the kinds of musical material he was considering. With Mahler, who was a more reticent sketcher, fewer pages of materials exist as evidence of his working method, but the extant sketchbooks[2] and sketchbook pages[3] that have come to light are important documents.

In addition the full scores left by Mahler shed important documentary light on the compositional process. As Mahler took a finished work to performance and, ultimately, publication, he was concerned with the nuances of scoring, phrasing and notation. At times he would leave his rescinded second thoughts in the margins, as for example in the tuba part he added in the fair copy of the Scherzo of the Fourth Symphony.[4] Elsewhere, as in the Seventh Symphony, he inscribed in the margins a fuller scoring than originally planned without looking for music paper of appropriate size to rewrite the passage cleanly.[5] An examination of this and other fair-copy manuscripts shows Mahler's active shaping of the score as he brought each work to completion in this stage of work.

Similarly Mahler also revised his scores after publication. While he never changed the substance of the musical content at that point, his alterations to the

---

Gelegenheit dann verwendete. Oder sie sagen, daß das Vollendete gegenüber dem Skizzenentwurf einen solchen Fortschritt bedeute; indes sie keine Ahnung haben, was aus so einer ersten Andeutung sonst noch alles unter seinen Händen daraus hätte werden können!'

[2] To date, two sketchbooks have come to light. One is inscribed 'Letztes Skizzenbuch' by its erstwhile owner, the singer Anna Bahr-Mildenburg. The contents of the 'Letztes Skizzenbuch' bear a relationship to some of the music Mahler took up in the Seventh Symphony; it is catalogued as V Ba MK 905 in the Theatersammlung of the Österreichische Nationalbibliothek, Vienna. The other sketchbook, which contains ideas related to the Ninth Symphony, is in private hands. This has been transcribed in Matthews, 1989, and discussed in Matthews, 1974. A photocopy of the latter sketchbook is catalogued as Ph 57 among the holdings of the Internationale Gustav Mahler Gesellschaft, Vienna. Further discussion of the Seventh Symphony Sketchbook can be found in Zychowicz, 1988, vol. 1, pp. 188–212. See also the analysis by Stephen Hefling in Hefling, 1997, pp. 169–216.

[3] The extant sketchbook pages are among the holdings of the Bibliothèque Musicale Gustav Mahler, Paris. For a detailed list of these materials see Zychowicz, 1994.

[4] The fair copy is housed in the Gesellschaft der Musikfreunde, Vienna, and is catalogued as 'Gustav Mahler: IV. Symphonie G-Dur Partitur, XIII.35824'. For a discussion of this score see Zychowicz, 2000, p. 145.

[5] See, for example, pp. 61–63 (of the facsimile) in Mahler, 1995. The insertion to the trumpet part on the bottom of p. 61 corresponds to the passage in the first movement, two bars before rehearsal Fig. 58; on pp. 62–64 the longer insertion of the timpani part, again at the bottom of the page, corresponds to the passage two bars before rehearsal Fig. 60 and continues into the first five bars after that rehearsal figure.

details of the scores – those elements that are sometimes described as 'secondary parameters'[6] – are significant. Depending on the work, Mahler made the revisions in the printed score and various kinds of printer's proofs. Some of the changes were incorporated within Mahler's lifetime into published editions while other alterations remained unpublished until long after his death.[7] The provenance of revisions is a matter that demands careful consideration when arriving at suitable editions of Mahler's music.

In Mahler's case, source study is a critical area that requires further exploration, but to date this kind of scholarship seems to be less voluminous than that in other areas of Mahler study, especially biography.[8] Manuscript study is important not least because sketches are useful for understanding the compositional process and, to a degree, can be used to verify some biographical assumptions. With editions, however, the situation is more complex. On one level it is important to review the status of Mahler's music as it exists in published form, starting with the Gesamtausgabe. At another level study of the various editions of Mahler's music is critical for arriving at a better understanding of the reception of his music. Further analysis of the extant materials can yield details about the works that they represent, but the areas of source study as outlined in Fig. 16.1 have yet to be explored sufficiently.

Sketches and composing

Sketches are crucial for understanding a composer's compositional process since they are the documents that show from within how a given work took shape. Yet care must be taken to prevent misunderstandings or falsely placed intentionality. Unlike his eventual audience, a composer like Mahler did not have the benefit of the finished score to judge the progress of individual sketches. Rather the sketch pages offer tantalizing suggestions about the ways in which the composer took his musical inspiration to the written page before he committed himself to the eventual form of the completed composition. Furthermore the contents of sketches may often help to dispel conjecture about the circumstances under which he wrote a piece, although conclusions must be drawn with care. For Mahler, whose extant sketches are a fraction of the volume of Beethoven's, the situation is different: the contents of the sketches suggest the existence of a larger

---

[6] 'Secondary parameters' are discussed in an analytical framework in Hopkins, 1990. For a basic definition, see pp. 29–33. See also Chapter 8 of the present book for a consideration of these parameters in an analysis of the first movement of Mahler's Fifth Symphony.

[7] Among the better-known sets of revisions are those for the Fourth Symphony, which were reported as early as 1929 but did not find their way into any edition until Ratz incorporated them in the Gesamtausgabe in 1964. See Stein, 1929, & 1953, pp. 31–33.

[8] For a summary of sketch studies for Mahler's music, see Reilly, 1995/1996.

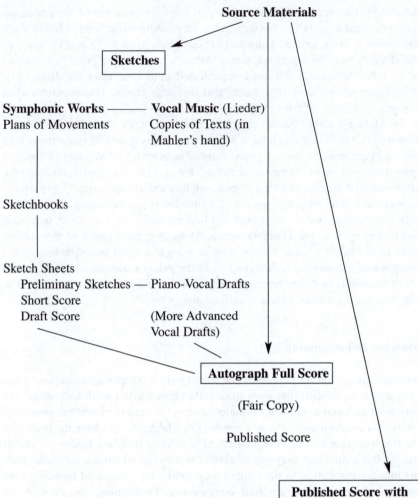

Fig. 16.1   Mahler's manuscripts and autograph materials

amount of materials originally used by Mahler in the process of arriving at the finished work. Although he expressed the wish that his own sketches be destroyed after his death, it may be that he himself carried this out during his lifetime: after all, once he completed one stage of composition and took the materials into another, he would have had no need for the earlier materials. None the less some pages from several stages of work have survived, and they offer clues to his working process.

It is important to distinguish the sketches Mahler composed early in his career – those he used up to the completion of work on the Third Symphony – from the kind of sketches he left for the Fourth Symphony and later works. While comparatively fewer sketches exist for the earlier symphonies, the ones that do survive reveal that he used an upright format (the style of paper referred to as *Hochformat*) and that his process of working through ideas was not necessarily as systematic as it subsequently became. His later practice was to use oblong formatted paper (*Querformat*) for the preliminary sketches through to the short score and the draft score. With the later symphonies Mahler's use of paper in *Hochformat* signalled the completion of work, since that was the style he used for the fair copy. The fair copy is usually inscribed on a higher grade of paper distinguished by a watermark,[9] and not solely by a trademark (*Schützmarke*) at the bottom of formally printed music paper. This distinction is important since it represents a change of style separating the sketches from the finished work. While Mahler may have made further changes once he arrived at the fair copy, the work was essentially finished at this stage, and revisions of the substance of the work were then relatively rare.

In taking his early ideas into the finished work Mahler developed connections between material, and worked towards an increasingly continuous draft. This is particularly evident in the sketches he left for the Scherzo of the Fourth Symphony where all the essential ideas for the movement are found on a set of five sketch pages. The principal themes are notated on these pages, and his explicit verbal indications suggest the places where he would vary or combine ideas at a later phase of composition.[10] While it remained for him to work out individual sections in the next stage of work, Mahler seems to have restricted himself to the use of the themes indicated in the earlier sketch pages rather than pursue entirely new ideas. Only later would he add introductions and transitions, to delineate the primary sections underscoring the structure of the music.

Some would argue that distinguishing between sketch stages may be at best artificial, since everything prior to the finished work is preliminary and can only be regarded as draft work. This argument should not preclude a closer investigation of the earlier and later sketch materials which reflect Mahler's

---

[9] See Zychowicz, 1988, vol. 1, pp. 353–55. A tracing of one watermark occurs on p. 355.

[10] For a discussion of this movement see Zychowicz, 2000, pp. 72–85.

attempts at reworking specific passages that he may have felt required improvement. From the existing sketches it seems that Mahler sometimes returned to the materials to make revisions. Yet some sketches seem to be the result of more spontaneous work rather than formal revision: he may have made adjustments as he went along. Thus the sketch page on which Mahler crossed out material in the same hand may not always represent several stages of effort. Sketches are the written artefact of the compositional process, and though closely tied to the act of composing they are not its exact equivalent.

At the same time it is important to note that Mahler's sketches do not include the kind of continuity draft associated with Beethoven.[11] Instead Mahler's process includes successive efforts at refining his ideas. At times it is possible to view this process of revision within a single page of sketches; yet this same self-critical working out of ideas also occurs between similar kinds of material where certain early pages seem incrementally more refined than others. Moreover it is possible to find different kinds of sketches prior to the draft score that reflect increasingly detailed and continuous work, and which internal evidence suggests may have emerged at different times.

By analysing sketches in detail it is possible to appreciate Mahler's working method as he progressed towards a more continuous and consistent structure. Such investigation reveals certain traits that are peculiar to specific phases of work. For example the preliminary sketches are Mahler's earliest continuous ideas after the sketchbook stage. While it is logical that sketchbooks should precede preliminary sketches, the evidence does not always exist to substantiate this assumption. As early as 1896, at the time Mahler was working on the Third Symphony, Bauer-Lechner reported seeing the composer with sketchbooks (see Killian, 1984, p. 61, and Franklin, 1980, pp. 64–65[12]) but no such materials are known to have survived for that work. At the same time a number of the existing preliminary sketches are comparatively rough manuscripts that may contain some of his earliest ideas for various parts of the work.

This kind of discussion suggests a need to identify more precisely the style of work found in preliminary sketches. The extant preliminary sketches offer only hints of what Mahler did at this stage of work. He may also have left some ideas in the state in which he initially inscribed them, since a sketch could easily serve as an *aide-mémoire* for him to pick up his thoughts later when he would compose the short score or a subsequent draft. For the most part the surviving materials are pages that Mahler preserved in order to create the short score, since they include

---

[11] While a continuity draft is not unique to Beethoven, it is often associated with his sketches. A useful overview of the various styles of sketch is found in Nicholas Marston, s.v. 'Sketch' in Sadie, 2001, vol. 23, pp. 472–74. For a detailed study of Beethoven's compositional process, see Barry Cooper, *Beethoven and the Creative Process* (Oxford: Oxford University Press, 1990).

[12] Note that the English translation follows the text of the earlier German-language edition, Bauer-Lechner, 1923.

most of the musical ideas in the order in which they occur in later stages of work. However, those very pages sometimes differ from each other in style. Some are relatively rough and crude with just a few scrawled ideas on each system, while others appear to be more advanced sketches that must have succeeded less finished pages.

For many of the preliminary sketches, too, the ideas are continuous within a single page without necessarily having continuity from page to page. It is as though Mahler worked through ideas on the single, detached, bifolio sheets of preliminary sketches and at some point reviewed them before proceeding with the short score. Then he probably destroyed the other preliminary sketches, including more primitive versions of the preserved materials. In reviewing the materials, Mahler sometimes marked insertions on individual pages by inscribing a caret at the point of insertion and another caret at the materials to be inserted, which were usually placed at the bottom of a page if space allowed. Sometimes he added an entirely new page to be inserted after a page he had already sketched, and he showed the continuation by labelling the page explicitly as *Einlage* [insertion]. This kind of self-critical work may be found in sets of preliminary sketches as well as in short-score manuscripts. A noteworthy example of Mahler's use of insertion pages occurs in the short score of the third movement of the Fourth Symphony (see Zychowicz, 2000, pp. 98–101). Within this set of sketches it is possible to observe the structure of the movement as Mahler initially conceived it by considering the materials without the pages labelled *Einlage*. This shows both the careful consideration that Mahler gave the movement when he returned to the sketches to revise the structure, and the fact that the ultimate design of the movement was by no means accidental.

While the layers of sketches so far discussed concern symphonic movements, it is important to consider the various drafts of vocal works, which for the most part are continuous from the start. Mahler did not leave a large number of exclusively melodic drafts with text underlay. Rather he seems to have worked through his initial musical ideas in a piano-vocal score that would have some bearing on the eventual orchestral draft. The vocal sketches are usually not as extensive as the symphonic ones, and this may explain the discrepancies that sometimes exist between the piano-vocal and orchestral versions of some songs.

When it comes to discriminating between the preliminary sketches and the short score, what sets the sketches apart from each other often depends on the mechanics of the page. Beyond identifying themes and motifs it is useful to analyse what is happening to them on the page, and to compare that assessment with other, similar pages. The mechanics of a sketch include Mahler's use of scoring, his verbal notes about the content, the non-verbal markings on the page, including circles and arrows that reflect ways in which he wanted to treat material, as well as the numbering and renumbering of pages. By considering these elements along with the analysis of the sketches' contents, it is possible to distinguish between stages of work and, to an extent, between the phases within each stage. Again the findings may be conjectural, but they would at least be based on some consideration of the details of the page.

In analysing sketches it is also important to approach the materials in terms of what they are, not what they will become. The hindsight resulting from knowledge of the completed work can become an obstacle to understanding the workings of the sketch page, which was still evolving when the composer left it. Only through taking the ideas further was Mahler able to move beyond individual sketches by choosing to continue with some ideas or to abandon others. By working through later sketches and drafts Mahler eventually arrived at a finished score reflecting the desired compositional content in terms of ideas, sequence, textures and orchestration. Thus it is possible to find Mahler pursuing various kinds of elements in the sketches: themes and thematic groups often appear in the preliminary sketches, but at times these are discontinuous.

In the short score that usually followed, Mahler found ways to present the ideas more continuously, and the sketches from this stage of work sometimes contain alternative passages that reflect this process. The short score also contains more of the textures he wished to use, with notes about orchestration brought forward from earlier sketches or inscribed as he worked on continuity. Only the draft score contains the composer's first attempt at a full orchestration, and at this stage of work he also introduced tempo markings, expression marks, and other related elements. By examining all of these materials thoroughly it is possible to gain a sense of Mahler's working method and the systematic approach he adopted to bring his ideas into focus. His conversations with Natalie Bauer-Lechner and the reminiscences of Alma Mahler are useful sources about some aspects of his composing, but the sketches themselves contain the history of the work as Mahler himself developed it. They present first-hand, written evidence of the compositional process that should supersede any second-hand accounts of his working method.

Knowledge of Mahler's sketches is also important when it comes to identifying and classifying other sketch material. Internal evidence such as handwriting style, colour and style of ink (or pencil), foliation, and other elements may again be useful in connecting various sketches that may have become separated. Sometimes two pages that once existed in the same stage of work may be held in different collections, and only a thorough knowledge of the sketching process helps to ascertain their conceptual proximity.

This kind of understanding is critical for evaluating unfamiliar sketches or the materials that Mahler left for an unfinished work like the Tenth Symphony. With such unfinished pieces the situation is complex, and no one other than the composer could know how to proceed. Yet a deep knowledge of Mahler's working method would assist in separating various versions of material from more continuous passages of preliminary draft, and discerning what properly belongs in the short score. The orchestral draft (*Partiturentwurf*) – the draft score – is another matter, and anyone wishing to complete it is at a loss except for the few annotations that exist in the surviving materials. With the Tenth Symphony and other unfinished pieces one can approximate Mahler's orchestration, but it is difficult to reproduce with absolute certainty all the nuances he would have wanted to include in the finished work. This is not to dismiss the performing versions of any of the unfinished music but to offer a note of caution about the nature of 'completions'. While the results may be worthy efforts, 'completions' of abandoned ideas are questionable since the composer had reasons for stopping work. The finished score would have been something very different had the composer himself been able to pursue it. These and other issues remain to be addressed in manuscript study, and they may never be entirely resolved.

However much one can gain a sense of the inner history of a composition through analysis of the sketches, it is important that such assessment not become confused with other kinds of analysis. Useful though Allen Forte's *Compositional Matrix* may be,[13] the employment of sketches for structural analysis is at best a difficult proposition. It would seem better both to use the sketches to gain a sense of the composer's priorities and focus at the time the work was taking shape, and to maintain a continuous distinction between the sketches and the finished works rather than blur them. No matter how much Mahler's efforts may have shown an emphasis on various elements *en route* to completion, it is each work as a whole that the composer ultimately left to posterity. Yet even here further work needs to be undertaken to arrive at a suitable way of presenting his music and rendering in print his final thoughts on his works.

Editions, performance and reception

Source study also concerns the use of manuscripts and other source materials to arrive at an appropriate edition of the music. The Internationale Gustav Mahler Gesellschaft in Vienna is the publisher of the Critical Edition of the composer's works, which was inaugurated in 1959 by Erwin Ratz and is still in progress albeit under a different editor.[14] The Gesamtausgabe has included Mahler's symphonies, Lieder, and the two-movement version of the cantata *Das klagende Lied* in its main publications. For the most part these are the works that Mahler published under his name and in the versions he saw into print. However, the

---

[13] Allen Forte, *The Compositional Matrix*, repr. edn (New York: Da Capo Press, 1974). See Joseph Kerman's succinct comments about Forte's approach in *Contemplating Music* (Cambridge, Mass: Harvard University Press, 1985), pp. 136–37.

[14] Gustav Mahler, *Sämtliche Werke. Kritische Gesamtausgabe* (Vienna: Internationale Gustav Mahler Gesellschaft, 1959–). The founding editor, Erwin Ratz, was succeeded by Karl-Heinz Füssl; after Füssl's death, Reinhold Kubik became the chief editor in 1993.

Mahler Gesellschaft has also published *Todtenfeier*, the single-movement tone poem that Mahler revised as the first movement of the Second Symphony, the early – and fragmentary – Piano Quartet, and the original, three-movement version of *Das klagende Lied* as part of the Supplement to the Edition.[15] It should be understood that none of these works was published in the composer's lifetime in the format published in the Supplement, and for this reason they remain outside the main edition of his collected works.

In addition to these versions of his own works there are the revisions Mahler made of other composers' music in the course of his career as a conductor. These include symphonies by Beethoven and Schumann, and various operas by Mozart and Weber. For example Mahler edited the score of Beethoven's Ninth Symphony several times, and the revisions provide evidence of his status as a respected interpreter of Beethoven's music. Likewise the revisions of Weber's *Oberon* were substantial, and exemplified a late nineteenth-century conductor's solution to a sometimes problematic score. With alterations usually referred to as *Retuschen*, these scores were not intended to be part of the Gesamtausgabe as it was originally envisaged. Yet a case could be made for *Die drei Pintos* since Mahler played a stronger role in giving shape to the opera, and without his efforts the music Weber left would not have become a finished opera. As unique an undertaking as *Die drei Pintos* may be, the work is not in the purview of the edition because the content is not exclusive to Mahler himself.

When it comes to the various revisions of his own music, Mahler did not sanction alternative versions but preferred his later revisions. This is generally not a problem except in the case of the first version of the First Symphony, which is a five-movement work. In revising it and publishing the score Mahler dropped the internal movement entitled 'Blumine'. Nevertheless some conductors have performed and recorded the movement by itself and also in the context of the Symphony. Plans exist for the Mahler Gesellschaft to publish this early, five-movement Hamburg version, and this departs from the Gesamtausgabe's usual practice of establishing a single, basic text for a work. Although, in general, the Mahler Gesamtausgabe differs from, for example, the collected-works edition of Anton Bruckner's music by avoiding the side-by-side publication of a work in multiple editions of scores that evolved in the composer's lifetime, the

---

[15] Gustav Mahler, *'Totenfeier'. Symphonische Dichtung für großes Orchester. Frühfassung (1888) des ersten Satzes der Zweiten Symphonie*, ed. Rudolf Stephan, Sämtliche Werke, Kritische Gesamtausgabe, Supplement, vol. 1 (Vienna: Universal Edition, 1988). *Klavierquartett 1. Satz für Violine, Viola, Violoncello und Klavier*, ed. Manfred Wagner-Artzt, Sämtliche Werke, Kritische Gesamtausgabe, Supplement, vol. 3 (Vienna: Universal Edition, 1997). *Das klagende Lied. Erstfassung in drei Sätzen (1880) für Soli, Chor, großes Orchester und Fernorchester*, ed. Reinhold Kubik, Kritische Gesamtausgabe, Supplement, vol. 4 (Vienna: Universal Edition, 1997). Some useful comments about the nature of the last two of these editions are found in reviews by Jeremy Barham in *Music & Letters*, 80 (1), 1999, pp. 163–65, & 83 (1), 2002, pp. 177–80.

Supplement series to the Gesamtausgabe nevertheless began in the 1980s to include different versions of several works, and in so doing prevented them from competing with standard editions of the music. Thus along with *Todtenfeier*, the Supplement includes the alternative, piano-vocal version of *Das Lied von der Erde*,[16] and other works that contain substantial differences. If published in the Supplement to the Gesamtausgabe, the scores of the variant versions have a clear place as an appendix to the standard versions of the works. When published alongside – and given equal weight to – the standard versions, the inclusion of the variant scores would blur the intent behind the Gesamtausgabe to have a single, definitive score for each work as the essential text. To publish variant versions at the same level as the standard scores would result in a hybrid that strives to be a critical edition yet at the same time tends to be more historical in nature.

Although the original intention behind the Gesamtausgabe was more limited in scope, it is encouraging to see the publication of several volumes in the Supplement to the Edition, since they offer a broader and more comprehensive sense of Mahler works. The first volumes to appear in the Gesamtausgabe were editions of the Seventh Symphony (1959) and Fourth Symphony (1964), with other volumes following as they were ready. For the most part these volumes were based on editions published in Mahler's lifetime or shortly after his death. While some of the recent publications, such as the collection of *Verschiedene Lieder* or the piano-vocal versions of settings of *Des Knaben Wunderhorn*,[17] are newly typeset, and there is an ongoing effort to bring specific volumes up to date, the majority of the volumes, including scores of the larger works, replicate the editorial practice and typographical style of early editions.

Even though the Gesamtausgabe represents the standard edition of Mahler's music, it has not been accepted without question. When it was just beginning Hans Redlich (1966) criticized Ratz's efforts since he was of the opinion that the principles upon which the publication was founded did not satisfactorily address the situation pertaining to Mahler's music. His criticism of the Gesamtausgabe concerned the nature of the edition itself, which is built on the principle of the 'Ausgabe letzter Hand'. This philological principle establishes the precedent of an edition in the last known revisions of the author – or composer – as the authority for the final text of a work, and contrasts with the conflation style of

---

[16] Gustav Mahler, *Das Lied von der Erde für eine hohe und eine mittlere Gesangstimme mit Klavier*, ed. Stephen E. Hefling, Sämtliche Werke, Kritische Gesamtausgabe, Supplement, vol. 2 (Vienna: Universal Edition, 1989). See especially the introduction, pp. vii–xii, and Hefling, 1992.

[17] Gustav Mahler, *Verschiedene Lieder für eine Singstimme mit Klavier*, ed. Zoltan Roman, Sämtliche Werke, Kritische Gesamtausgabe, vol. 13/5 (Mainz: Schott, 1990). Gustav Mahler, *Fünfzehn Lieder, Humoresken und Balladen aus Des Knaben Wunderhorn*, ed. Renate Hilmar-Voit and Thomas Hampson, Sämtliche Werke, Kritische Gesamtausgabe, vol. 13 (Vienna: Universal Edition, 1993).

editing used with works transmitted by manuscript, or the kind of historic critical edition associated with some of Bruckner's works. Ratz decided upon this methodological principle as the basis for the Gesamtausgabe since it would then be possible to incorporate in it all the revisions that Mahler left and that were yet to be implemented. This is one strategy to adopt in editing Mahler's music but it is not the only possibility.

In theory an edition based on the principle of the 'Ausgabe letzter Hand' is a goal appropriate to the music, since Mahler's own revisions show him striving towards an improved score. He neither returned to earlier versions of works nor overtly questioned the improvements he made. In fact anecdotal evidence suggests that he approved of an ongoing review of his scores in terms of their effectiveness in performance. For example Otto Klemperer recalled Mahler's comments at the rehearsals for the première of the Eighth Symphony in Munich. At that time Mahler adjusted the scoring in rehearsals when he found ways to make it work better, just as he had done with those earlier works for which various sets of revisions exist. With the Eighth Symphony he explicitly suggested that other conductors make similar changes in order to enhance the performance of his music (see Heyworth, 1985, p. 34). Taken at face value this comment would seem to open the door to any amount of editorial intervention. Yet common sense would put the instruction in perspective and allow conductors to make minor improvements that reflect the context of a specific performance and the skill of the musicians involved in it. At bottom it seems that Mahler attempted to remove infelicities from his scores. Apart from misprints and typographical errors Mahler revised tempo markings and other verbal instructions, articulations, rhythms and doublings. In essence he attempted to make his scores increasingly clear, with fewer arbitrary elements that might be left to interpretation or could potentially distort his intentions.

Yet the nature of Mahler's final intentions is not always clear and may be open to interpretation. For some works Mahler's final written-out revisions suffice, especially when they correct obvious errors in the score. Yet some of the revisions may need to be corroborated in performance and allowed only if they have some practical basis. For example the final revisions of the Fourth Symphony which Ratz allowed into the Gesamtausgabe have their basis in autograph sources but had not been adopted in performance. Whether evidence of performance is crucial to validating the composer's intentions is a debatable issue. In fact the evidence suggests that Mahler's own last performance of the Symphony made use of the version published in 1906 rather than incorporating any revisions he had made after that date (see Zychowicz, 2000, p. 160). It is natural, then, to question the authority of an edition that uses the final version without having established an editorial policy that includes criteria for validating the sources used. A case may be made for arriving at an edition based on the last published version of the music rather than on the final changes that were not seen into print.

Even then difficulties exist if the basis of a critical edition is either tied to performance considerations or connected to publishing history. The latter would disallow works that the composer had left unpublished and unperformed at his death. With Mahler this is an important issue since it would require some rethinking about the status of his last three works, *Das Lied von der Erde*, the Ninth Symphony and the torso of the Tenth Symphony. These works are critical when it comes to Mahler's significance as a composer, and it would be folly to consider excluding them from his *oeuvre* for technical reasons alone. Nevertheless the editorial situation with regard to these three works differs from that of Mahler's earlier ones, since he neither took his last three compositions to performance nor had the opportunity to revise the scores. While he completed two of the works in full score, Mahler left the Tenth Symphony unfinished, and no precedent exists amongst the composer's other music for dealing with such a significant fragment.

Thus it may be difficult to arrive at a critical edition based unequivocally on the principle of the 'Ausgabe letzter Hand' since not all works and the corresponding materials fit comfortably within the framework that must exist for editorial practice. It may be that this kind of distinction lies at the core of Redlich's criticism of the edition. To base an edition on the principle of the 'Ausgabe letzter Hand' is a stance that gives priority to the last known revisions, no matter how tenuous some might be. It is a fairly bold approach, and without some qualification the practice of using the last known materials may cause an unintended dismissal of earlier materials that may still be valid. A collected-works edition like the Mahler Gesamtausgabe should contain the basic texts of the composer's works but the choices made *en route* are not always easy ones.

In arriving at the editorial basis for the Gesamtausgabe it is essential to determine from the outset the kinds of material that should be used, and to establish an approach for prioritizing the sources. One approach to this process is offered in Fig. 16.2. While this outline is by no means the only way to proceed with an edition, it offers a comprehensive approach that can be useful in evaluating and arriving at a set of sources. Although this may be the goal of most editors of Mahler's music and the works of other composers, it is sometimes difficult to achieve an appropriate balance in the resulting publications. Some editorial motion in this direction is already part of several recent editions of the Gesamtausgabe, including the publication of Mahler's *Wunderhorn Lieder*.[18]

A related issue is the overall nature of the existing Gesamtausgabe. For those volumes that are based on earlier printings, the engraving style reflects the

---

[18] See fn. 17 and Gustav Mahler, *Des Knaben Wunderhorn. Gesänge für eine Singstimme mit Orchesterbegleitung*, ed. Renate Hilmar-Voit, Sämtliche Werke, Kritische Gesamtausgabe, vol. 14/2 (Vienna: Universal Edition, 1998). See also the review of this edition by Jeremy Barham, *Music & Letters*, 83 (2), 2002, pp. 330–33.

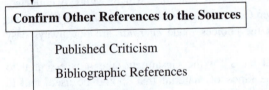

Fig. 16.2 Criteria for evaluating sources

preferences of an earlier age and does not always serve present-day standards of music notation well. Compound slurs are one example, and it is important to consult sources which might have phrase markings that vary from the existing printed ones. Performance parts – provided they can be authenticated – can be used in preparing an edition, and it may be useful to show differences that exist within the parts. With the current practice of using an existing published edition as the basis for an edition, it is not possible to show an alternative phrase marking or slur by rendering it with broken lines; neither is it possible to add editorial dynamics and articulations without disrupting the legibility of the music.

Nevertheless conventions exist in which traditional notation can be modified to reflect editorial practices, such as enclosing newly included elements in brackets and using different fonts to indicate the editor's intervention. It is also possible to use the traditional bold-italic font to indicate the composer's original dynamic marking, and to designate added dynamics editorially in bold (without italics). This kind of editorial practice is followed in the Verdi edition, which employs various notational devices to make the editing apparent on the musical page.[19] It is important that graphic presentation of this sort does not preclude the provision of a thorough critical report and an explanation of the editorial method adopted in preparing an edition. Such a report containing a detailed list of specific editorial changes and, perhaps, relevant passages to corroborate them is essential for any critical edition. With such materials supporting the printed page it is possible to understand the nature of the edition and the level of editorial intervention undertaken in its preparation.

If a score were to be presented in the manner of the Verdi edition, that is with editorial layers represented graphically, it would need to be newly typeset and not simply overlaid onto an existing edition. For various reasons, using the earlier engravings as the basis for a modern edition is often impractical. While scanning can reproduce individual pages, character recognition falls short in recreating specific components on each page, and it would be impossible to edit the scanned image with existing music-typesetting software or even to reformat the scanned images successfully. An edition including editorial markings in the score would therefore need to be newly set, and this is no simple task. Time would need to be devoted to proofreading the edition note by note in order to avoid introducing errors. In the case of the Verdi edition the process of publishing over thirty operas and other volumes of his music is an endeavour lasting decades. With Mahler's music less time would be required, and it would be prudent to work within a shorter time-frame than that of the current Mahler Gesamtausgabe. Certainly some of the inconsistencies that exist within the Gesamtausgabe are the result of a process that has extended over three decades. While efforts have been made to publish revised critical editions of some works, including the First and Fifth Symphonies, these editions are based on scores published during Mahler's lifetime. Slurs, ties and phrase markings are not uniformly executed, and other aspects of the notation have not been regularized for these editions. It is laudable that various editions are being updated, but isolated efforts do not constitute an editorial policy and a publishing plan that arrives at a uniform edition of Mahler's music.

---

[19] For a representative volume of the Verdi edition, see Giuseppe Verdi, *La Traviata: Melodramma in Three Acts*, libretto by Francesco Maria Piave, ed. Fabrizio Della Seta; *The Works of Giuseppe Verdi, Series I: Operas* (WGV-O) (Chicago: University of Chicago Press, 1996). This volume is noteworthy for its inclusion of alternative settings of several numbers, along with transcriptions of sketches in the appendix to the score.

Other considerations for editing Mahler's music involve the orthography and hyphenation of text, the disposal of parts, the relationship of the full score to rehearsal scores (piano reduction), and piano-vocal versions that differ substantially from the orchestrated version. Differences exist, for example, between the orchestral and piano versions of the *Lieder eines fahrenden Gesellen*, *Das Lied von der Erde*, and several other individual songs. Hyphenation and orthography are another matter, and they need to be carefully considered. For example it may be correct to use modern spelling but inauthentic when it is a question of complete fidelity to certain sources. Phrasing also may be technically incorrect when rendered in the style prevalent in Mahler's lifetime, yet that kind of presentation may be sufficiently meaningful to performers in a way that modern, plainer notation may not be. Additive or multiple slurs that connect a single, longer phrase (that is using two slurs to connect three notes, or three slurs to connect four) are no longer in usage. The treatment of these elements, however, is best handled on an individual basis, and depends on an explicit editorial practice being stated at the outset and applied systematically to the entire edition.

It may not be necessary to adopt a different editorial method for Mahler's works. Because of the nature of Mahler's music, the existing Gesamtausgabe could be sufficient. Yet the situation is made more problematic because the Gesamtausgabe has not superseded various competing editions of the works that are easily accessible and correspond to readily available sets of parts. Most of the scores that compete with the critical editions essentially reprint earlier editions that should have become obsolete. This proliferation of editions is indicative of Mahler's continuing popularity. At the beginning of the twenty-first century Mahler's reputation seems remarkably well established, and his music appears regularly in concert programmes and recording catalogues. The situation was different in the 1960s when a revival of interest in Mahler's music began. If nothing else, the abundance of scores and the availability of the music in print are positive signs at a time when the demand for printed music seems to be in decline.

On closer inspection the existing editions seem to be divided between those that are reprints of historical publications and those more recent volumes of the Gesamtausgabe that include Mahler's final revisions. New versions of several later volumes of the Gesamtausgabe have appeared. While some revised editions indeed correct errors in the first editions – as for example in the case of the Fourth Symphony – others, such as that of the First Symphony, include changes based on later research and further revisions in the details of the scores. This effort to establish Mahler's final revisions stands in contrast to the various reprints of earlier editions that are available from the original publishers, Universal Edition (Vienna), and from other reprint publishers such as Dover Publications.

While no publisher has explicitly stated why it issues reprints or keeps reprinted editions in its catalogue, Mahler's popularity is certainly a crucial factor. The economics of music publishing often dictate the nature of new publications, and few publishers would spend money on music that has no market. Given this, one wonders why the music of such a popular composer as Mahler is not more readily available in newly engraved editions. Nevertheless the cost of producing such scores is so great that it is rare to find editions that have been typeset entirely anew. As we have seen, even the Mahler Gesellschaft used the last published scores of many of Mahler's works as the basis for its edition, other new publications being the exception rather than the rule. Among the newly engraved editions are Deryck Cooke's 'performing version' of Mahler's Tenth Symphony published by Faber,[20] and the critical edition of *Die drei Pintos* published in the Recent Researches series of A-R Editions.[21] Under the purview of the Mahler Gesellschaft, the newly typeset volumes often involve collections of Lieder for voice and piano rather than entire symphonies.

The publication of Mahler's music presents a mixed image, and this is not necessarily a negative judgment. Indeed the various editions of the music reflect the popularity of the composer, and the fact that succeeding generations rely on both the Gesamtausgabe and earlier editions suggests that the performance of Mahler's music is part of a living tradition. Many important composers do not enjoy Mahler's continuing popularity, which, itself generating new recordings and performances, keeps the music alive for future generations.

Conclusion

Evaluating the sources of Mahler's music involves consideration of both the sketches that the composer used to finish a work and the completed score as the composer left it. For Mahler, though, composition did not stop with publication but continued in his various subsequent revisions. Throughout his life he continually altered the details of his scores to bring their musical content into sharper focus, and it is the principle of the 'Ausgabe letzter Hand' – the preference for the last known revisions – that has guided the Internationale Gustav Mahler Gesellschaft in its publication of a critical edition of the composer's collected works. This edition offers a single version of Mahler's works, the one that contains the last revisions that he saw into print. Yet these volumes exist side by side with other earlier editions that are readily accessible in various reprint editions. This situation is symptomatic of the composer's

---

[20] Gustav Mahler, *A Performing Version of the Draft for the Tenth Symphony*, prepared by Deryck Cooke in collaboration with Berthold Goldschmidt, Colin Matthews and David Matthews, rev. edn (London: Faber Music, 1989).

[21] *Gustav Mahler: Die drei Pintos. Based on Sketches and Original Music by Carl Maria von Weber*, Recent Researches in the Music of the Nineteenth and Early Twentieth Centuries, vols 30 and 31, ed. James L. Zychowicz (Madison, Wisc.: A-R Editions, 2000).

reception history and his current secure presence in performances and recordings. Nevertheless, the question of a suitable edition of Mahler's music remains to be pursued since the principle of the 'Ausgabe letzter Hand' as it has been applied may not necessarily serve the music as well as it could.

The situation is different with the sketches since relatively few of these manuscripts survive. The sketches are crucial above all for understanding Mahler's working process, which changed between the time he finished the Third Symphony and when he started work on the Fourth. From that point on, the working process documented in the sketches became visibly more systematic in its presentation and execution. At times it is possible to observe conscious choices, and on rare occasions to have confirmation of his plans with explicit words and phrases. While it is difficult to establish with absolute certainty Mahler's intentions during the composition of a work, the extant sketches show the ideas he pursued and the way he dealt with them. They provide evidence of his creativity which eventually found its expression in the finished works, and these in turn serve as evidence of his unique talent and the care he took to present his music as clearly as possible.

Chapter Seventeen

Unfinished Works of Mahler: The Scherzo in C minor, the Presto in F major, the Tenth Symphony and Comparative Arguments for 'Performing Versions'

SUSAN M. FILLER

Gustav Mahler's wife wrote that, in 1907, a physician diagnosed a heart ailment which was, in her words, 'the beginning of the end for Mahler' (Mahler, 1990, p. 122). This account influenced a widespread belief that Mahler was living on borrowed time in the four years from the diagnosis until his death in 1911. At best, this view manifests misjudgment of Mahler's problem; at worst, it is a fallacy based on the notion of a tragic aura around the last works of a 'dying composer'. This essay addresses the effect of this idea on our assessment not only of Mahler's last symphony but also of the two unknown movements, the Scherzo in C minor and the Presto in F major, which he left unfinished a decade earlier, and how connections may be made between the development of the manuscripts and Mahler's medical history.

According to Alma Mahler, Dr Blumenthal identified Mahler's heart problem; but she was vague about the nature of the condition, noting only that the doctor said that Mahler 'had no cause to be proud of a heart like that' (ibid.). She recounted Mahler's subsequent consultation with Professor Kovacs, who confirmed the diagnosis. Mahler himself was much more specific in a letter to Alma late that summer:

> I had myself inoculated yesterday. By Dr. Hamperl, who examined me too at the same time. He found a *slight* valvular defect, which is entirely compensated, and he makes nothing of the whole affair. He tells me I can certainly carry on with my work just as I did before and in general live a normal life, apart from avoiding over-fatigue.

> (Ibid., p. 289)

Modern medical research, notably the groundbreaking work of Nicholas Christy and Stuart Feder, places Mahler's problem in perspective.[1] There are two known causes of a defect in any of the four valves of the human heart. First, it may be a side effect of rheumatic fever, which is usually contracted in childhood or adolescence; second, it may be genetically transmitted from parent to offspring. However Mahler acquired his problem, it had not appeared suddenly but was probably present from his childhood, possibly from birth. That is to say that, although the doctors made the diagnosis when Mahler was 47 years old, the problem had existed for most, if not all, of his life. *Ergo*, we must consider two possibilities. The first is that death hung over Mahler's head all the time. This offers a dramatic view of his entire work as composer, conductor and pianist, since he could have died at any time without even being informed of his problem by the physicians. The second, conversely, is that the problem was not as serious as Alma alleged. While potentially fatal complications of his condition were a possibility, Mahler had not experienced them before the diagnosis, nor for several years after it; we should therefore accord respect to Mahler's own account.

What is more, Mahler had survived at least two medical crises as an adult. The first was an illness in Hamburg in 1893 (which has been linked, although without conclusive proof, to a cholera epidemic which began in 1892).[2] The second was a haemorrhage in Vienna, in 1901, which required urgent surgery; but even that was not Mahler's first such operation. It is this latter crisis which may be linked with the termination of his work on the Scherzo in C minor and the Presto in F major.[3]

---

[1] I am indebted to Nicholas Christy and Stuart Feder, and to David Levy, for sharing their knowledge of the medical aspects of this subject. See also Christy et al., 1970, Feder, 1978, Levy, 1986, and Kravitt, 1978.

[2] According to La Grange, 1979, pp. 394–95, the cholera epidemic in Hamburg had been brought from Russia by sea. It also reached Le Havre, Paris and Antwerp. The worst of the epidemic in Hamburg was in 1892, but Mahler fell ill in 1893. Not perhaps coincidentally, a few weeks later Tchaikovsky died from the same illness in St Petersburg. See also Alexander Poznansky, 'Tchaikovsky's Suicide: Myth and Reality', *19th-Century Music*, 11 (3), spring 1988, 199–220.

[3] In my own work on these two draft symphonic movements, I have reached the conclusion that – while neither manuscript is dated – secondary evidence substantiates that their composition dated from the period around the turn of the twentieth century, i.e. the time of the Fourth and Fifth Symphonies. See Filler, 1984, pp. 69–80. This differs from the opinions written by Alban Berg in the 1920s, when he examined the manuscripts of the two movements and wrote covering pages in which he suggested that both of them were from Mahler's student period. See Hilmar-Voit, 1991, for a facsimile of both manuscripts including the cover pages Berg wrote after studying them, which are filed with the manuscripts in the Wiener Stadtbibliothek (the Scherzo) and the Pierpont Morgan Library (the Presto). The most credible reason for the unfinished state in which Mahler left these scores is that his work was interrupted by the haemorrhage and the surgery, and that he did not return to them after the crisis.

The complication of the mitral valve defect which eventually took Mahler's life was caused by the bacterium *streptococcus viridans*. Levy noted[4] that this organism is actually quite common, and that different people react to it in different ways; it is often harmless. For patients like Mahler, who do experience complications, effective treatment was achieved more than thirty years after his death with the discovery of antibiotics and the initiation of surgery to repair defective heart valves.[5] The physicians who examined Mahler in 1907 offered advice for dealing with his problem in accordance with their knowledge at that time. We have already noted the advice of Dr Hamperl, which Mahler mentioned in his correspondence. Professor Kovacs, according to Alma, 'forbade [Mahler] mountain ascents, bicycling and swimming; indeed he was so blind as to order a course of training to teach him how to walk; first it was to be for five minutes, then ten, and so on until he was used to walking' (Mahler, 1990, p. 122).

It is interesting that conducting – which was surely demanding on Mahler's physical strength – was not prohibited along with walking, mountain climbing, bicycling and swimming. Feder (1978, p. 135) pointed out that such an approach to Mahler's problem would not be considered appropriate today.[6]

Without treatment Mahler could have lived with the infection, bacterial endocarditis, for three to six months, which suggests a genesis in late 1910 or early 1911. Among differing theories about the event that might have triggered the infection, Christy (1970, p. 207) suggested that the frequent throat infections Mahler suffered produced the bacteria which invaded the defective valve; but, according to his correspondence, these throat problems were chronic and had not previously had such an effect. Sue Taylor, a Mahler specialist in St Louis, suggested in conversation with the present author that a routine procedure like a dental cleaning could have caused the infection (which would be forestalled today by administration of antibiotics beforehand); but, again, Mahler had been treated earlier for dental problems without complications.[7] David Levy has essentially been alone in suggesting that there may not have been a single definable incident which triggered the infection.[8]

---

[4] In personal communication with the present author.

[5] I am indebted to James Frederiksen from the Department of Cardiothoracic Surgery at Northwestern Memorial Hospital, Chicago, for his illuminating explanation of treatment for these problems, in which he has extensive professional experience.

[6] Ottorino Respighi died in 1936 from the same problem that Mahler had had; he lived closer to the time when antibiotics and surgery would have been available for his care, but neither treatment had yet been perfected. Much later, Benjamin Britten – who had a similar defect of his aortic valve – did have such treatment available to him. His death in 1976 was apparently from heart failure, another possible complication of this kind of valvular defect.

[7] Alma Mahler mentioned a visit to a dentist for a toothache in 1904, although she did not note whether the tooth was extracted. See Mahler, 1990, p. 69.

[8] Dr Levy mentioned this in conversation with the present author.

Concerning the possibility that Mahler inherited his condition from one or both of his parents, no documentation of any heart problem in the case of his father, Bernhard Mahler, is known to exist. There has been extensive discussion about his mother, Marie Mahler; Alma, for instance, stated that 'all the [Mahler] children, Gustav included, were handicapped by their mother's heart-disease' (Mahler, 1990, p. 9). This is at best dubious, since, according to the research of Henry-Louis de La Grange,[9] some but not all of the Mahler children had documented heart problems; and, among the conditions of those who did – including Gustav, his brothers Ernst and Alois,[10] and apparently their sister Justine – there is such wide disparity that even a medical geneticist could not reasonably argue a connection between them.

Only private observation from eyewitnesses gives us any information about Marie Mahler's alleged heart problem. She has been described as walking with a limp, which was also noted of Gustav Mahler. Nicholas Christy and Stuart Feder have both considered the possibility of a condition called Sydenham's chorea (formerly known as St Vitus' Dance), which is related to hereditary rheumatic heart disease.[11] In Mahler's case, it is one of several theories cited by such eyewitnesses as Alma Mahler, Bruno Walter, Guido Adler and Alfred Roller, among others. Roller's description is especially notable:

> As a child he was supposed to have suffered involuntary movements of the extremities. This not unusual ailment, especially among mentally animated children, can, if it is neglected, degenerate into the so-called 'St Vitus' Dance,' but usually disappears completely with regular bodily and spiritual influences during increasing growth. Unfortunately in Mahler's case the involuntary twitching of his right leg remained for life. He never spoke to me about that, and I therefore suppose that it was conspicuously embarrassing for him. In walking it was manifested in the pattern from one to three short steps dropping out of rhythm; in standing, in a slight stamping of his foot, in a way walking in place. His uniquely strong will generally held this impulse in confinement. But were his will in any way diverted or relaxed, then every time this striking mannerism of the right leg set in. If his will was relaxed by surprise, an annoying or amusing event, the reaction was invariable. It was thus an error when, as it often happened, this stamping was held to be evidence of impatience or increasing anger.   (Roller, 1922, p. 13)[12]

---

9 The discussion of this subject in La Grange, 1979, pp. 24–25, is embodied in his list of the fourteen children of Marie and Bernhard Mahler, of whom Gustav was the second.

10 See Filler, 1997, for an account of Mahler's only brother to survive him, including his medical history. The death certificate cites two medical conditions, one of which was 'chronic myocarditis', an infection of the heart muscle. However, the primary cause of Alois's death was cancer. Dr Frederiksen pointed out to the present author that there is no traceable genetic connection between Alois's problem and Gustav's endocarditis, and that the surgery which Gustav might have undergone if it had been used in his time would have been inappropriate for Alois.

11 See fn. 1, above.

12 'Er soll als Kind an unfreiwilligen Bewegungen der Extremitäten gelitten haben. Dieses, besonders bei geistig regen Kindern, nicht gar seltene Leiden kann, wenn es

In attributing Mahler's irregular walk to Sydenham's chorea, Roller connected it not with a heart problem but rather with what were then considered neurological disorders, without mentioning the possibility of a family connection. Indeed, he may have been influenced instead by a theory widely held in Mahler's time which attributed 'nervous diseases' originally to Jews, in other words a kind of super-heredity among a whole people rather than a single family. Roller is not known to have been anti-Semitic, but he may have been influenced by pseudo-racial theories regarding the human body, which he closely observed in his work as an artist.[13]

Whether Mahler inherited such a condition from his mother is speculative. The only other information we have about Marie Mahler from eyewitnesses is that she was physically delicate. However, this picture is contradicted by the documented fact that she survived fourteen pregnancies and deliveries at a time when the mortality rate in childbirth was appallingly high. Furthermore, she lived to the age of 52, ten years beyond her last pregnancy, which was essentially life expectancy in her time (and longer than most of her children). That is to say that, whatever the nature of her heart problem, it was not significant enough to compromise her health during the pregnancies and deliveries.

However, it is important to note that the myth about Mahler's mother cannot be attributed to Alma, who never knew her mother-in-law. The most likely source of her information would have been Mahler and his surviving siblings, Justine, Emma and Alois, whose memories of their mother may have been subjective. In the society in which they lived, the patriarchal family structure was common; the subordinate position of the wife, especially in the physical function of childbearing, could have been confused with psychological subordination.[14]

---

vernachlässigt wird, zum sogenannten "Veitstanz" ausarten, verschwindet aber bei richtiger körperlicher und geistiger Beeinflussung mit zunehmenden Wachstum des Körpers gewöhnlich restlos. Bei Mahler blieb leider das unfreiwillige Zucken des rechten Beines für Lebenszeiten zurück. Er hat zu mir nie darüber gesprochen und ich nehme deshalb an, daß es ihm als auffällig peinlich war. Beim Gehen äußerts es sich in der Form von ein bis drei kurzen aus dem Rhythmus fallenden Schritten. Beim Stehen in einem leichten Aufstampfen, in einer Art Tretens auf dem Platz. Sein unvergleichlich starker Wille hielt diesen Reiz für gewöhnlich gebannt. Wurde der Wille aber irgendwie abgelenkt oder entspannt, dann stellte sich jedesmal dieses auffällige Gehaben des rechten Beines ein. Ob die Willensentspannung durch Überraschung, durch ein ärgerliches oder ein lustiges Vorkommnis verursacht war, blieb in der Wirkung ganz gleich. Es war also unrichtig, wenn, wie dies oft geschah, dieses Stampfen für ein ausschließliches Zeichen der Ungeduld oder des aufsteigenden Ärgers gehalten wurde.' This citation is from the introduction, as the book in question is primarily devoted to photographs and other visual representations of Mahler.

[13] See Knittel, 1995, for a discussion of the racial theories which supposedly influenced not only the critics who reviewed Mahler's performances but the artists who drew silhouettes and caricatures of Mahler on the podium.

[14] A similar family structure can be found in the early life of Adolf Hitler, who was born twenty-nine years after Mahler, in the late period of the Austrian Empire, when the

Justine and Emma in particular may have resented this 'pecking order', especially comparing the burdens of pregnancy which had been much heavier for their mother than for either of them.[15]

It is interesting to note that, when Mahler had been informed of his heart problem by the physicians, his professional achievements were not those of an ailing man. It appears that he heeded the advice of his physicians during those four years. The present author has not found any references to either gradual or sudden changes for the worse in his physical health during this period. He wrote *Das Lied von der Erde* and the Ninth Symphony before doing significant work on the Tenth, oversaw publication and conducted the premières of the Seventh and Eighth Symphonies, revised the orchestration of the Fourth and Fifth Symphonies, and maintained a busy performing schedule in the United States, France, Italy, Germany, Austria, Russia, Bohemia, Finland and the Netherlands. Such multifarious activity would hardly have been possible with a problem which progressively undermined his health, making death only a matter of time. If he had had to curtail his activities, it would have made sense to limit his conducting rather than his composition, especially since other conductors including Toscanini, Strauss and Mengelberg could – and in Toscanini's case did – commit themselves to positions within Mahler's purview.

In 1908 Mahler wrote to Bruno Walter:

> It is certainly not that hypochondriac fear of death, as you suppose. I had already realized that I shall have to die. – But without trying to explain or describe to you something for which there are perhaps no words at all, I'll just tell you that at a blow I have simply lost all the clarity and quietude I ever achieved, and that I stood *vis-à-vis de rien*, and now at the end of life am again a beginner who must find his feet.
>
> (Martner, 1979, p. 324)

Mahler's troubling reference to 'the end of life' suggests that he expected to die. But his denial of the 'hypochondriac fear of death' belies any preoccupation with death beyond the knowledge that it is the conclusion of every human life. He did not curtail his work while waiting for a date that his physicians could not predict. Also, it is worth noting that in those four years he experimented with a compositional idiom which had only been foreshadowed in the previous works; he may have called himself a 'beginner who must find his feet' in the musical as well as the personal sense.

While Mahler's correspondence included such sobering remarks as those quoted above, these are balanced by others like 'I am in relatively good health'

---

family centred on the overbearing father was quite common; but it would require consideration from a psychiatrist to make any judgment about the very different directions taken by the lives of these two men.

[15] Emma and her husband, Eduard Rosé, had two sons, Ernst and Wolfgang. Justine and her husband, Arnold Rosé (Eduard's brother), had a son Alfred and a daughter Alma.

(ibid., p. 332) to Alfred Roller in 1909, or 'I am pretty well at the moment, with a frantic amount of work which I am coping with very well' (ibid., p. 369) to Emil Freund in 1910. Indeed, he seems to have been more concerned about his wife and their daughter Anna than himself; while Alma was uninformative about her own problems, Mahler wrote to his mother-in-law in 1910, 'I have weathered this year very well, without actually sparing myself; of the three of us, I have actually been the only one who was always fit' (ibid., p. 353).

It is interesting to compare these accounts with the circumstances surrounding the composition of the Scherzo in C minor and Presto in F major a decade earlier. Certainly, during the time when he was apparently drafting the two movements, he suffered a haemorrhage in early 1901 that endangered his life, although the problem was in no way related to his heart and may be considered acute (his correspondence makes reference to 'my subterranean troubles'[16] on multiple occasions over a period of several years). If he had died on that occasion, he would have left an 'unfinished symphony' (in the sense that he had drafted two movements which would have been presumed to be part of a larger whole), and there remains a mystery because the movements do not correspond to any in the ten known symphonies. It is with the benefit of hindsight that we compare these manuscripts with that of the Tenth Symphony a decade later and note that, although in this case Mahler had not reached the stage of orchestration (as he did in parts of the Tenth Symphony), the two movements were sufficiently developed to assume an identity of their own. The manuscript materials for the Scherzo in C minor comprise nine oblong pages, including four covering the 'particell' (short score) of the scherzo and trio sections, followed by a transitional section in which the scherzo and trio themes are combined, leading to a *da capo* initiating the return to the scherzo section (see Exx. 17.1–3).

Ex. 17.1 Scherzo in C minor, main theme of scherzo section

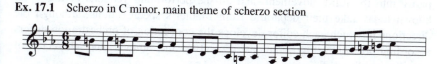

Ex. 17.2 Scherzo in C minor, main theme of trio section

---

[16] See Martner, 1979, pp. 233–34, for two letters to Albert and Nina Spiegler from 1898 in which Mahler referred to this problem more than two years before the haemorrhage.

Ex. 17.3   Scherzo in C minor, transition section from trio to return of scherzo

The remaining five pages are sketches covering sections of the movement; while these often parallel passages in the short score they also provide information that enhances it harmonically. The Presto in F major, which covers only three pages (with additional material on the reverse side of the first), is nevertheless so concentrated that its content is comparable to that of the Scherzo in terms of detail; the pages are primarily in short score with some alternative versions of passages on the same pages. The first two pages cover the main theme and episodes in rondo form; the third page comprises a coda which is harmonically related to the main theme.

Mahler's *modus operandi* in composition compels consideration of the time factor in finished and unfinished works alike. Throughout his compositional career, he usually worked first on sketches before proceeding to a 'short score'; this was the earliest stage at which a symphonic movement assumed formal identity along with the harmonic and contrapuntal texture foreshadowed in the sketches. He left orchestration for development in a subsequent stage of composition, although preliminary planning of scoring (in the form of intermittent verbal notes in the short score) was not unusual. It is a feature of the short score of the Tenth Symphony, which was laid out in orchestral score only partly into the third movement; and all the performing versions of the Tenth known today take their departure from Mahler's specifications, although the directions in which each editor develops the conception of orchestration differs according to contrasting opinions respecting the amount and character of necessary additions.[17]

The case of the two movements differs from the Tenth Symphony only in the stage of development reached. Mahler had essentially gone through the stage of harmonic texture with the basic melodic outline in both of these movements, and had arrived at the short-score stage, establishing the forms of the two movements:

---

[17] Frans Bouwman focusses on such differences between the versions of the Tenth Symphony by Deryck Cooke, Joe Wheeler, Clinton Carpenter, Remo Mazzetti and Rudolf Barshai in Chapter 18 of this book. It would be interesting to relate their ideas to their professional background, since conducting, composition and musicology are all represented in this group.

a scherzo with trio and a rondo[18] with coda. The primary theme of the rondo form was originally written in G major but then Mahler decided to move it a whole tone down to F major (indicated in a verbal note in the upper margin) (see Ex. 17.4).

Ex. 17.4   Main theme of Presto in F major

The coda section on the third page of the Presto materials is in D major, but a close harmonic connection with the main rondo theme in F major suggests that Mahler might have rethought the tonal layout of this movement more than once – a not unusual feature of his compositional *modus operandi* (see Ex. 17.5).

Ex. 17.5   Presto in F major, main theme from coda

There are few clues foreshadowing orchestration in either draft. However, it is worth recalling a remark Deryck Cooke made in the course of his work on the Tenth Symphony which is equally applicable in the case of the two movements:

> I need no telling that to attempt to orchestrate Mahler would be a ludicrous impertinence. But 'orchestrate' is not quite the right word here: Mahler conceived his music orchestrally, and his short scores are blueprints for instrumentation; if studied and auralized persistently enough, they score themselves – in essentials.
>
> (Cooke, 1967, p. 149)

The scoring of music that Mahler had not orchestrated himself is best approached by comparative study of scoring in works that he had completed. In the case of the Tenth Symphony, the orchestral score that Mahler had committed to paper through the first two movements and thirty bars of the third movement is valuably supplemented by assessment of the immediate predecessors of this symphony, *Das Lied von der Erde* and the Ninth Symphony. In the case of the two unknown movements, there is a common factor with the Tenth to be found

---

[18] The designation 'Presto' gives no clue to the form of this movement, and the rondo form is established by assessment of bar-by-bar continuity, which would not have been possible if Mahler had failed to reach the short-score stage. Although the formal continuity of this movement is not easy to read on the page, it can be established with knowledge of Mahler's use of space (especially when he was short of it on a page). It is a matter of debate whether Mahler would have kept the designation 'Presto' in later stages of composition, especially after orchestration.

in the comparison of these movements with the works finished most closely in time to their genesis, namely the Fourth and Fifth Symphonies. In addition, careful consideration of the projected position of the two movements in the finished symphony for which they were probably planned has special merit because it allows comparison with harmonic balance and scoring of movements in similar positions in the finished works. It is most likely that both the Scherzo in C minor and the Presto in F major would have been internal movements in any symphony where they would have been situated; this is borne out not only by comparison with the corresponding movements of the Second, Third and Fourth Symphonies – all of which have scherzos in the same key as this one – but also by comparing the Seventh Symphony, which was yet to come, with the two *Nachtmusik* movements.[19] That is to say that there is sufficient existing ground to assess the two movements not only in terms of possible orchestration (the most plausible possibility being a modest orchestra by Mahler's standards) but also by development of inter-movement balance, even without additional movements which would have supplemented the two we do have, making a four- or five-movement symphony. For a symphony only partially planned (and it was not unusual for Mahler to compose internal movements of a symphony before flanking movements, as part of the developing process of inter-movement balance, which was quite frequently subject to modification), the two movements represent a significant achievement for a composer who appears to have been interrupted in the conceptual process by an acute life-threatening haemorrhage.

Only cryptic references to this incident are found in Mahler's correspondence, and none at all to the composition of either of the two movements. Presumably there was no question of a symphony cut short by Mahler's death, and thus no aura of the 'dying composer' around the two movements. Unlike the heart problem which ultimately resulted in Mahler's death, the haemorrhage in early 1901 has not been romanticized; this may be because we know with hindsight that, close as he was to death on that occasion, he did not die. Or it might also be possible that the nature of the problem did not lend itself to the myth of the dying composer. Even Alma Mahler, who wrote extensively about her husband's last years (with scant regard for medical accuracy concerning the nature of his heart problem), did not speculate about the possible effect of this other problem on his compositional work. Certainly she had not yet met and married Mahler when the haemorrhage occurred, but her knowledge of his life prior to their marriage was widely demonstrated in her biography of him.[20] Obviously, the myth of the dying

---

[19]   The composer Alan Stout noted the fact that the two *Nachtmusik* movements are in the respective keys of C minor (with an A flat major contrast section) and F major, which corresponds to the keys of the Scherzo and Presto. I would develop this comparison further by pointing out that the two movements show similarities in thematic organization to the two *Nachtmusik* movements, being planned with principles of theme-and-variation technique even when the main features of form are scherzo-and-trio and rondo.

[20]   A comparison of her account of the haemorrhage in *Gustav Mahler* (which was

composer and his unfinished last work is subject to laymen's interpretation of medical facts, and the absence of references to the two movements in the sources where we would expect to find them may be related to *a posteriori* views of factors in his medical history which might have influenced his death. If Mahler had died from the haemorrhage rather than heart problems, it is doubtful that his death and the unfinished compositions left in its wake would have been exploited by Alma Mahler, and the unfinished manuscripts themselves might well have been subject to scrutiny and completion in performing versions much earlier than they in fact were.

Mahler has been credited with superstition regarding the number nine because *Das Lied von der Erde*, which followed the Eighth Symphony, is a symphony without a number. There is no overt reference to any such superstition in Mahler's correspondence. However, Alma wrote:

> At first he wrote *Das Lied von der Erde* as the Ninth, but then crossed the number out. When later he was writing his next symphony which he called the Ninth, he said to me: 'Actually, of course, it's the Tenth, because *Das Lied von der Erde* was really the Ninth.' Finally when he was composing the Tenth he said, 'Now the danger is past.' And yet he did not live to see the Ninth performed or to finish the Tenth. Beethoven died after his Ninth Symphony and Bruckner before finishing his Ninth; hence it was a superstition of Mahler's that no great writer of symphonies got beyond his ninth.
>
> (Mahler, 1990, p. 115)

Arnold Schoenberg discussed the 'jinxed' number shortly after Mahler died:

> His Ninth is most strange. In it, the author hardly speaks as an individual any longer. It almost seems as though this work must have a concealed author who used Mahler merely as his spokesman, as his mouthpiece. This symphony is no longer couched in the personal tone. It consists, so to speak, of objective, almost passionless statements of a beauty which becomes perceptible only to one who can dispense with animal warmth and feels at home in spiritual coolness. We shall know as little about what his Tenth ... would have said as we know about Beethoven's or Bruckner's. It seems that the Ninth is a limit. He who wants to go beyond it must pass away. It seems as if something might be imparted to us in the Tenth which we ought not yet to know, for which we are not yet ready. Those who have written a Ninth stood too near to the hereafter. Perhaps the riddles of this world would be solved, if one of those who knew them were to write a Tenth. And that probably is not to take place.
>
> (Stein, 1975, p. 470)

These statements by Alma Mahler and Arnold Schoenberg have been debated by such scholars as Deryck Cooke, Eveline Nikkels, Dika Newlin and Jack Diether,

---

first published in 1940) with her daily entries in her diary (see Mahler-Werfel, 1997 & 1998) shows that, even if she had been made aware of the incident at the time it occurred (through newspapers or the Viennese gossip mill), she took no notice of it. When she did refer to it in *Gustav Mahler*, it was treated as secondary to her account of his heart problem.

among others.[21] A few observations should be added. In the first place an unfinished symphony, by Mahler or anyone else, is not always attributable to the death of the composer. In the case of the two unknown movements, the medical crisis at the time of the haemorrhage should be considered in conjunction with the 'revolution' in his compositional style about the turn of the twentieth century, when he was finishing the Fourth Symphony and planning the Fifth. Since he actually retained many elements of style developed in the first four symphonies during the composition of the Fifth Symphony (1901–2), this process was a continuum rather than a break with the past, and it posed a crisis of creative doubts. The two movements were a part of that crisis, and that may explain their survival. Such creative crises have been suggested in connection with other composers, notably Schubert, whose work influenced Mahler as much as that of Beethoven did.[22]

The numbering of Mahler's symphonies, or those of any other composer, can hardly be considered a major issue since it is subject to the vagaries of interpretation. If Mahler did indeed consider the 'danger' past after the Ninth Symphony was composed – and there do not seem to be any references to such a superstition in Mahler's own correspondence, or any confirmation from other associates of Mahler in the last four years of his life – any superstition about the number nine could have been easily addressed in either of two ways. Mahler could have retrospectively called *Das Lied von der Erde* the Ninth and made the next symphony the Tenth; or, better still, he could have avoided the number entirely by calling *Das Lied* by its non-numerical name and then gone on to the number ten.[23] In either instance, the last work would have been the *de facto* Eleventh Symphony. Indeed, the question of numbering the two unknown movements as an uncompleted symphony, were it to be raised, would confuse the issue even further.

---

[21] See Cooke, 1967 (one of several articles he wrote during work on his performing version of the Tenth Symphony), Nikkels, 1991, Newlin, 1979, and Diether, 1963.

[22] After writing his Sixth Symphony, Schubert left at least three others unfinished; and it was only with the last of them – the one generally known as the 'Unfinished' Symphony – that he seems to have emerged from this stage and later finished the Great C major Symphony. Schubert scholars have long been uneasy about the business of numbering after the Sixth Symphony; Mahler was probably aware of this, since it was during his lifetime that scholars and publishers were trying to come to terms with the problem after the long-belated discovery and publication of the 'Unfinished' Symphony.

[23] The tradition of the titled symphony goes back at least to Haydn, although it often coexists with numeration. It was probably during the nineteenth century that composers like Berlioz and Liszt designated symphonies by title alone. See Frank Kirby, 'The Germanic Program Symphony in the Nineteenth Century (to 1914)', in E. Arias, S. Filler, W. Porter & J. Wasson (eds), *Essays in Honor of John F. Ohl: A Compendium of American Musicology* (Evanston, Ill.: Northwestern University Press, 2001), pp. 195–211, for a discussion of titles applied to programme symphonies.

With respect to Bruckner, who did not live to complete his Ninth Symphony,[24] there is a similar game of numbering. Bruckner had in fact written two symphonies before his First, one without number, the other now known as 'Die Nullte' or 'No. 0'. This suggests that he, too, had creative doubts which resulted in suppression of the two works. The symphony he did not live to complete was the eleventh in order of composition. A similar case may be adduced with Antonín Dvořák, who also wrote nine symphonies, suppressed four of them – again, because of creative doubts – but wrote his last symphony, the 'New World' Symphony, a full decade before his death, and followed it with equally ambitious works including the Cello Concerto, five tone poems and three operas.

Whether the existence of a suppressed work – as Mahler's Tenth Symphony was for half a century after his death, and the Scherzo in C minor and Presto in F major were for almost two further decades – is known by anyone but the composer is hardly worth consideration if we allow that superstition is a personal matter: if any of these composers, including Beethoven, had reservations about the number nine, it was for the composer to find a way around it. Also, numbering means little by itself; the large variation in the numbers of symphonies between Mahler's predecessors, contemporaries and musical descendants compels us to admit that the historical context in which the symphony developed was more important than any number. As well as the composers cited above, we are compelled to consider Mozart (who wrote over fifty symphonies), Haydn (over a hundred), Brahms (four), Sibelius (seven) or Shostakovich (fifteen). It is obvious that the number of symphonies a composer writes is meaningless unless the scope of each symphony and the importance of the form in the composer's total *oeuvre* are accorded equal consideration. Since Mahler was aware of the influence of his predecessors in the symphonic genre, perhaps he too realized the limitations of numbers.

Secondly, there is still misjudgment of the reasons why Mahler did not finish the symphony which did prove to be his last work. We know that he was drafting the Tenth Symphony in the summer of 1910,[25] and ceased work on it in August; but he lived another nine months. Clearly, death was not the immediate reason that the work remained unfinished. The necessity for reconsideration of the factors which halted the work leads us to the disparate accounts of Alma Mahler and Sigmund Freud, both of which were recorded many years after Mahler's death.

In brief, Alma's account comprises the story of her relationship with the young architect Walter Gropius, the discovery of their affair by Mahler, and the choice

---

[24] See Cornelius van Zwol, 'Die Vollendung bei Anton Bruckner. Der Finalsatz seiner IX. Symphonie', in Op de Coul, 1991, pp. 193–205, for a discussion of the problems connected with the fourth movement, which Bruckner did not complete.

[25] This information is documented by secondary means rather than assessment of the manuscript, which is undated.

between the two men that Mahler placed before her. She dutifully chose to stay with her husband, and supposedly broke off communication with Gropius until they met again and were married four years after Mahler's death. But the research of the late Reginald Isaacs revealed that Alma omitted crucial information which was prejudicial to her account. When Mahler went to Munich in September 1910 for the final rehearsals and première of the Eighth Symphony, Alma joined him only to slip away and meet Gropius. They continued to see each other after the première, before she and Mahler departed for New York, and to exchange letters when personal meetings were no longer possible.

Reginald Isaacs, a disciple of Gropius and his successor at Harvard, obtained access to the archives that yielded this information and published it in his biography of Gropius (Isaacs, 1983–84). Alma – who had long been divorced from Gropius – knew that the information from the Gropius archives which Isaacs incorporated into his book would compromise the credibility of her story; and, indeed, it did necessitate a reassessment of the conditions of Mahler's work in the summer and autumn of 1910, most notably by Henry-Louis de La Grange (1991), after Alma's death. Mahler's shock on learning of his wife's liaison with another man was surely reason enough to halt his work on the Tenth Symphony. There is no reason to doubt that he wrote verbal comments into the score of the Tenth *after* the discovery of her infidelity, since such examples as 'Für dich leben! Für dich sterben! Almschi' in the last movement substantiate the change in tone of his letters to her in the course of the summer of 1910. For instance, in June he wrote:

> It worries me today to have no letter from you after your so sad one of yesterday. Are you hiding something? For I feel there must be something to be read between the lines. ... You are always in my thoughts, my Almscherl; write every day, do, if only a p[ost] c[ard].
>
> (Mahler, 1990, p. 330)

In September, however, after the crisis, he wrote:

> Believe me, I am sick with love. Since Saturday at 1 o'clock, I live no longer. Thank God – I've just got your two dear letters. Now I can breathe again. ... I'm a dead man if you stay away for another whole week.
>
> (Ibid., p. 337)

These two drastically different ways of saying 'Why don't I hear from you?' do suggest an anxious husband who suddenly suspects his wife. The change in tone in the three months between these letters is startling and disturbing. It is proof of Mahler's attitude towards his own mortality – an acknowledgment conspicuously at variance with his reaction to the discovery of his heart problem three years previously. In this instance, Mahler himself registered a change in the circumstances of his life which affected his work; but a comparison of his comments to his wife and Bruno Walter three years previously with those that Alma wrote from hindsight show that she was the one who tried to prove that his work was affected years before this marital crisis – and her version of the story is suspect at best.

Besides the crisis, Mahler's conducting schedule in the autumn and winter of 1910–11 surely resulted in postponement of work on the Tenth Symphony. At that point, he had no reason to doubt that he could return to it and finish the orchestration in the summer of 1911. It was also not coincidental that Mahler was involved in the preparations for publication of Alma's first book of songs,[26] and he was working with her on other songs which would be published after his death.[27] Needless professional rivalry between these husband and wife composers, which had brewed since before their marriage, had been thrown into Mahler's face by Alma during the crisis; as a result, Mahler placated her by working with her songs instead of his own symphony.

If we compare these circumstances with those surrounding the time of genesis of the two unknown movements, we note the following points, some of which are comparable, some not:

1. The only reference to the crisis in the spring of 1901 which was contemporaneous with the event was from Natalie Bauer-Lechner, who did not quote any remarks from Mahler about the two movements and how they might have been affected (Killian, 1984, p. 184 (see also p. 228, n. 182)).
2. There are no dates in either of the two manuscripts, and no citations of the two movements in any list of works by Mahler until La Grange cited them in 1984 on the basis of the work of the present author (La Grange, 1984, pp. 1290–91).
3. The assessment of the style of the music, including possible outside influences, must be supplemented by study of the paper, which contradicts the opinion of Alban Berg that both movements are from Mahler's early period as a student.[28]

---

[26] *Fünf Lieder*, 1910.

[27] *Vier Lieder*, 1915. The manuscript of these four songs, two from 1901 and two from 1911 (according to the published score), is in the collection of Henry-Louis de La Grange. A critical edition of these songs, based on comparison of the manuscript with the published score, was published in the anthology *Women Composers: Music Through the Ages* (New York: Gale Group, 2004).

[28] See Filler, 1984, for discussion of these factors. The author has expanded study of this subject in papers presented to the New York Mahlerites in 1992, the Midwest Chapter of the American Musicological Society in 1993, and at the Central Conservatory of Music (Beijing, China) and the Conservatory of Music (Xi'an, China), the last of which is published in *Naturlaut* (Newsletter of the Chicago Mahler Society) 2/1 (June 2003), pp. 2–6, and in Chinese translation by Yu Zhigang in *Journal of the Central Conservatory of Music* [Beijing], 3 (2002), pp. 79–86. Berg wrote separate covering pages for the Scherzo and the Presto when he examined them in the 1920s. They are located with the respective manuscripts in the Wiener Stadtbibliothek and the Pierpont Morgan Library.

4. Mahler himself was uncommunicative about the crisis in his correspondence, and never mentioned the two movements at all, much less the effect of his health problems on their composition.

The physicians whom Mahler consulted for any medical condition were specialists; one of them, Sigmund Freud, garners special interest for his account of Mahler's visit after the crisis with Alma in the summer of 1910. He was quoted many years later on the subject:

> I analyzed Mahler for an afternoon in Leyden. If I may believe reports, I achieved much with him at that time. ... In highly interesting expeditions through his life history, we discovered his personal conditions for love, especially his Holy Mary complex (Oedipal fixation). I had plenty of opportunity to admire the capability for psychological understanding of this man of genius. ... No light fell at the time on the symptomatic facade of his obsessional neurosis. It was as if you would dig a single shaft of light through a mysterious building.
>
> (Jones, 1953–57, vol. 2, pp. 88–89)

Freud's account is at least as important for what it does not say as for what it does say: he did not mention Mahler's medical history. Considering that Freud had been thoroughly educated in medicine before his controversial work in the relatively new field of psychiatry, this is an odd omission. It is unlikely that he would ignore any medical information Mahler might have discussed with him; the question arises as to whether Mahler himself considered that subject significant or relevant enough to introduce it while the two men talked. If Mahler's health problems had been a major factor in the marital crisis, he could have returned to the physicians who had made the diagnosis three years earlier. But there is no evidence that he saw any physician but Freud that summer, and then only reluctantly.

The accounts from Alma Mahler and Sigmund Freud do not cancel each other out; but Freud's, although hobbled by theories which have been called into question by subsequent psychiatric researchers, is reliable, if only because he viewed the situation on which the crisis was based from an independent viewpoint which Alma could never have achieved.

Conflicting accounts of the cause of Mahler's death were offered by physicians and laymen. The most accurate, and the best-documented, was from Mahler's physicians in New York, as a result of consultation between his personal doctor, Josef Fraenkel, and the specialists Emanuel Libman and George Baehr, who reached the diagnosis of bacterial endocarditis on the basis of a blood culture documented in Libman's record.[29] This methodology was cited by Baehr in correspondence with Nicholas Christy and in interview with Stuart Feder;[30] the record is now in the National Library of Medicine in Bethesda, Maryland. In

---

[29] See fn. 1, above, and Filler, 1990.

[30] See fn. 1, above.

contrast, accounts from Mahler's associates and the press over-dramatized and distorted the facts. For instance, Alma said:

> You cannot imagine what Mr. Mahler has suffered. In Vienna my husband was all powerful ... but in New York, to his amazement, he had ten ladies ordering him about like a puppet. He hoped, however, by hard work and success to rid himself of his tormentors. Meanwhile, he lost health and strength. Then, after an excursion to Springfield, he contracted angina. At his last concert in New York, rather than disappoint the public, he conducted when he was in high fever. Now the angina has been complicated by blood poisoning. My husband cannot read or work. Heaven only knows how it all will end.[31]

Quite apart from the dramatic tone of this account and the oversimplification of the information about Mahler's condition, we should be wary of terms like 'angina' and 'blood poisoning' which have either changed in definition since Mahler's death or carry different nuances of meaning in English and German. In contrast, Mahler's own statement was plain: 'Mahler wants the world to know that it is by no means overwork in America that has shattered his health: "I have worked really hard for decades and have borne the exertion wonderfully well. I have never worked as little as I did in America".'[32]

There is no extant medical documentation comparable to the accounts of Libman and Baehr about the near-fatal crisis in 1901. If the records kept by the doctors were destroyed, there are three possible reasons which we might consider:

1. Medical records are not retained for ever. These may have been destroyed as irrelevant after a period of time that cannot be measured today.
2. The nature of the problem which caused the crisis in 1901 may well have been considered sensitive, and – given Mahler's prominent position – privacy may have been a consideration in the destruction of records documenting the haemorrhage and the surgery.
3. Politics after Mahler's death – particularly the suppression of information about his life and work during the Nazi period – may have been a factor.

After Mahler's death, an obituary in the newspaper *Egyetértés* in Budapest alleged:

> Mahler's death, in all likelihood, was caused (or at least hastened) by his sojourn in America. ... So many irritations awaited him in America that it is not surprising that the fatal illness developed and overcame him in short order. First of all, he had to take a *pro forma* oath that in time he will acquire American citizenship; his second trial consisted of having to take ... formal examinations in piano playing and music theory.[33]

---

[31] Quoted in *Musical America*, 5 May 1911, p. 1.

[32] Quoted in *Neue Freie Presse*, 21 April 1911; English translation in Blaukopf, 1976b, p. 272.

[33] The original obituary in Hungarian is on p. 7 of the issue of 19 May 1911, as cited in Roman, 1991. Roman's English translation is on p. 181.

There was no mention of the constant irritations which had made Mahler's life difficult, but had not killed him, in the positions he held before coming to New York – including those in Budapest and Vienna, where anti-Semitism was a far more significant factor than any health problem Mahler had during his life. This sounds more like political propaganda than ethical journalism. Unfortunately, such accounts were only the beginning: Alma Mahler perpetuated the myths in her two books, which were published many years after her husband's death.[34] Alma's early accounts may have been compromised by ignorance, especially in subjects that pre-dated their marriage (including the crisis of 1901); but ultimately she had a vested interest in telling the story her way, since her life after Mahler's death was controversial enough to require reinterpretation when she wished to whitewash her reputation. Mahler was not there to tell his side of the story.

The death of their daughter Maria in 1907 was a tragedy which surely recalled the many deaths among Mahler's siblings. Eight brothers had died during childhood. One sister, Leopoldine, had died in young adulthood (from causes unclear even today), and another brother, Otto, had committed suicide in 1895. Although the suicide is often cited as the most terrible of these experiences, the closest parallels to the death of Mahler's daughter were rather the deaths of three young brothers from scarlet fever or diphtheria, both of which had contributed to Maria's death. With the benefit of hindsight, Alma claimed that Mahler foreshadowed the tragedy in the composition of the *Kindertotenlieder* and in the three hammer blows in the last movement of the Sixth Symphony. These examples, however, belong in the same category as the alleged superstition about a Ninth Symphony: bending the meaning of facts *a posteriori*, unsubstantiated by any known comments from Mahler himself. The question of whether to give a number to the two movements as an 'unfinished symphony' remains unanswered; the present author would suggest that it be considered No. 4a, in order to establish its position chronologically. It is worth speculating whether, in composing *Das Lied von der Erde* (begun shortly after the death of his daughter), Mahler was confronting not so much the possibility of his own death as the reality of the child's death (which perhaps became a latter-day *déjà vu* after he had lived so many years beyond most of his siblings). When he purchased a gravesite in Grinzing Cemetery, Maria was the first to be buried there; he was brought there years later.

The author has suggested elsewhere that Mahler had originally planned the Tenth Symphony as a four-movement work, adding the present Finale only after

---

[34] Her first book, *Gustav Mahler: Memories and Letters*, was originally published in German in 1940, and has been translated into many other languages; the most recent edition in English dates from 1990. Her second book was published in German as *Mein Leben*, in 1960. The English version, *And the Bridge is Love*, had been published in New York in 1958 and in London in 1959. The English and German versions of this autobiography are very differently organized and the content, while related, is not the same.

drafting the pre-orchestral scores of the other movements (Filler, 1977 & 1991). As all five movements were apparently drafted before he began to write the orchestral score, this indicates that what we now hear as the end of the Tenth Symphony was not the last work Mahler did on the Symphony. I suggest that where he did stop was at the thirtieth bar of the orchestral score in the third movement, which trails off in the middle of the first system on the second page. As we know, the manuscript is riddled with comments addressed to Alma, probably as a result of the crisis in the Mahlers' marriage. Knud Martner has raised a question about the title page of the third movement, which carries the words *Purgatorio oder Inferno* on the top half of the page; the bottom half is missing. Martner suggests that the missing part of the page included a quotation from *Il Purgatorio* by Siegfried Lipiner, an old friend whom Alma hated. Her hatred may indeed have influenced her to destroy that segment of the page;[35] we should also consider the possibility that the lost words were in a very different vein from Mahler's passionate declarations in the score or his letters. If he stopped in the middle of the movement, when he discovered her betrayal of their marriage, he may well have written something more bitter than the words she did not hesitate to publish later. There was no way she could alter what he had written on the manuscript when the facsimile of the Tenth Symphony was published in 1924; a year later, when the first collection of Mahler's letters, which she had edited, appeared in print, it was a very different story.[36]

Thus, after Mahler's death, Alma planted the seeds of a myth which not only prevented the symphony that turned out to be his last from getting a fair hearing for half a century; consciously or not, she influenced a distorted view of the circumstances underlying the composition of other works, including not only *Das Lied von der Erde* and the Ninth Symphony – the predecessors of the Tenth – but even the earlier work on the two unfinished movements which pre-dated her marriage to Mahler. Even now, it is difficult to study or hear such works without imagining the shadow of death over them. Half a century after Mahler's death, Alma obstructed the performing versions of the Tenth Symphony (a 'private love letter' to her?) until she was persuaded that those who wished to bring the work to public attention were not damaging her credibility but championing the great work Mahler had done almost to the end of his life. He wrote the works of 1907–10 at the height of his creative powers, and in his usual state of health, and this must strongly influence our consideration; he finished the first two works, and the postponement of completion of the last one, which had begun with the

---

[35] See Martner, 1991, pp. 214–16, for a summary of his argument at the Utrecht symposium of 1986.

[36] Both were published by Paul Zsolnay of Vienna, who had begun issuing the works of Franz Werfel, with whom Alma was living at the time and married in 1929. Later, Alma's daughter Anna Mahler was briefly married to Zsolnay, and they had a daughter, Alma.

discovery of his wife's secret, was compounded by the multiplicity of professional responsibilities which an ailing man could not have undertaken in the following months. The summer of 1911, which would have seen the completion of the orchestration of the Tenth, never came for him. Thus, the Tenth Symphony was left unfinished when he died, but not because of his death; he was not dying when he wrote the work, or its two predecessors, nor is there any reliable proof that he anticipated or feared death, a fact which we would be well advised to consider today.

The final irony is that Alma's position also deprived us of two movements of a totally different symphony which Mahler drafted before he knew or married her, and the delay in bringing these works to public attention has been almost twice as long as that in the case of the Tenth Symphony. This too is an unfinished work, and while we may consider the possibility that it was interrupted by a medical crisis which nearly caused Mahler's death, the compositional process itself was not overshadowed by the spectre of death; nor is there any evidence in the manuscripts of the Scherzo in C minor and the Presto in F major that Mahler was experiencing any emotional upheaval comparable to the events in the summer of 1910. The two movements remained unknown so long because of Alma's carelessness with the manuscripts and Alban Berg's imperfect knowledge of their provenance; and the sole argument against them today is not their unfinished state but rather their status as a 'lesser' work. In closing, let it be noted that even the greatest composers do not always write great works; but it benefits all listeners to hear whatever works Mahler chose to write, finished or unfinished, without ignorance or prejudice.

Chapter Eighteen

Mahler's Tenth Symphony: Rediscovered Manuscript Pages, Chronology, Influences and 'Performing Versions'

FRANS BOUWMAN

Introduction

Important new material has emerged on Mahler's Tenth Symphony which will undoubtedly be of interest not only to scholars but also to all who are drawn to this enigmatic, unfinished masterpiece. This material involves pages of the autograph score, long unavailable to the public, which were buried in the archives of Hans Moldenhauer, the German-born musicologist who fled to the USA in 1938 and died there in 1987. These pages are now housed in the Bayerische Staatsbibliothek (BSB) and include the entire short score (SS) of the first-movement Adagio – that is, some material that was not known to those who have previously studied and worked on the manuscript.

Through the efforts of various editors working over the years from Mahler's incomplete manuscript (and unaware of the 'Moldenhauer pages') there are now six fully fledged editions of the whole symphony: two of them are from the Britons Deryck Cooke (in collaboration with Berthold Goldschmidt, David Matthews and Colin Matthews) and Joe Wheeler; two are from the Americans Clinton Carpenter and Remo Mazzetti; one is from the Russian conductor Rudolf Barshai; and one is from the Italians Giuseppe Mazzuca and Nicola Samale. The German Hans Wollschläger also made a 'performing version' but withdrew it after subsequent doubts about the enterprise. Another American, Barry Guerrero, is currently considering producing another version. It is fascinating to compare the choices made in these 'performing versions' in light of the newly discovered material.[1]

---

[1] The question arises as to what this work should be called when performed. Cooke et al. concede that what we hear is no more than a 'performing version of the draft of

While these 'new' pages clearly add to our knowledge of Mahler's intentions, other material and new analysis shed light on two further problematic issues: the order in which Mahler composed the fragments that survive; and the alleged influence on the Symphony of songs by his wife Alma and a piano piece by Josef Suk. These questions will also be discussed below.

History

Mahler produced his last work during a period of strain that was exceptional even in his tumultuous and often tortured life. While composing in his 'Komponierhäuschen' in the hamlet of Alt Schluderbach near Toblach, he discovered that his wife Alma was having an affair with the young architect Walter Gropius. Years earlier Mahler had insisted that Alma give up any composing of her own if they were to marry – a condition she accepted with great reluctance. Now under the impact of the Gropius connection and in a bid to save his marriage, Mahler suddenly showed intense interest in Alma's songs, which (according to her own reports) he found 'excellent' (Mahler, 1990, p. 176). After Mahler's death in 1911 Alma kept the unfinished manuscript of the Tenth Symphony to herself, although she displayed part of it on the wall of her sitting room as a kind of trophy. Later she also gave away pages to those who did her favours. In 1924 she felt it her duty to disclose to the world the last thoughts of her husband.[2] She published a facsimile edition of almost the entire manuscript. Earlier she had tried in vain to persuade Willem Mengelberg to complete the work. Mengelberg declined because of the huge sum she demanded for its performance. She then 'compelled' Ernst Krenek, her future son-in-law, to complete the work.[3] Krenek consented only to minimal editing of the Adagio and 'Purgatorio'. The rest he regarded as 'guesswork pure and

---

Mahler's Tenth Symphony', and that terms such as 'arrangement', 'Bearbeitung' or 'completion' should therefore be avoided. The word 'realization' may offer solace to some, but what exactly has been realized – the unfinished manuscript (with all the limitations described above) or the finished product that Mahler failed to write down? Cooke's careful wording therefore seems accurate. Clinton Carpenter felt that the music did not sound 'finished' in the Cooke edition. Adherence to the manuscript was not a priority for him, and he wanted to present his edition as a fully fledged 'completion'. Remo Mazzetti and Rudolf Barshai also toyed with the idea of calling their version a 'completion'. Marius Flothuis purposely exaggerated when he said that all versions of Mahler's Tenth should be called 'Symphony by X based on sketches of Gustav Mahler's Tenth Symphony' (1991, p. 25).

   [2] See the preface to Mahler, 1924.

   [3] In personal communication with the author, Herta Blaukopf reported that when Krenek was asked why he had agreed to Alma's request that he edit the manuscript, he had blushed and said 'she forced me'.

simple'.[4] This transcription formed the basis for three performing versions of these two movements, by Franz Schalk, Willem Mengelberg & Cornelis Dopper, and Alexander Zemlinsky. All were performed almost simultaneously at the end of 1924, each with its own additions.[5] The score with additions mostly by Zemlinsky served as the model for the first printed edition, edited by Otto Jokl and published in 1951 by AMP (now Schirmer). This edition was heavily criticized by Erwin Ratz, former president of the Internationale Gustav Mahler Gesellschaft (IGMG), who in 1964 edited a critical edition of the Adagio, purged of all additions, with the help of Hans Wollschläger. Since Mahler's death interest in the work has continued unabated with new surges of attention during 1924, the Mahler Centennial in 1960 and the 'Mahler X Symposium' held in Utrecht in 1986. At the beginning of September 2001 Rudolf Barshai performed four movements of his version in progress in Ljubljana, and the première of the version by Mazzuca and Samale was given in the same month in Perugia, Italy.

New discoveries: eight pages of manuscript and four title pages

The Zsolnay facsimile edition (Mahler, 1924) contains the majority of the manuscript, comprising the orchestral drafts (OD) for the Adagio, Scherzo in F sharp minor and 30 bars of the 'Purgatorio'. All the (draft) SSs are printed, except that of the Scherzo in F sharp minor. The Ricke facsimile edition (Ratz, 1967, henceforth RF) contains all this material plus 45 previously unpublished sketch pages, among which is the draft SS of the Scherzo in F sharp minor. The Cooke edition (1976 & 1989) contains a further three sketch pages relating to the first movement, a page of the SS of the Scherzo in F sharp minor, and a page of the draft SS of the Scherzo in E minor. Most of the autograph manuscripts are held in the Österreichische Nationalbibliothek (ÖNB).[6] The BSB houses a further 15 pages, including the entire SS of the Adagio, six pages of which were hitherto unpublished.[7] One copy of another unpublished page containing bars 49–78 of the Adagio

---

4   See the letter from Krenek to Robert Becqué cited in Op de Coul, 1991, p. 237.

5   Otto Klemperer conducted the Adagio in Berlin on 29 December 1924. He probably used Krenek's transcription – the only score available at that time – rather than the scores of Schalk, Zemlinsky or Mengelberg. The first-movement Adagio and 'Purgatorio' edited by Krenek (with minimal additions by Franz Schalk) were first performed on 12 October 1924 in Vienna.

6   Among them is one hitherto unpublished page of the Adagio, discussed as MS page no. 8 below, as well as two title pages.

7   Three of them are published here and all six are reproduced, together with a large number of other Mahler autographs and a comprehensive catalogue, in *Patrimonia. 157. Gustav Mahler: Briefe und Musikautographen aus den Moldenhauer-Archiven in der Bayerischen Staatsbibliothek* (Munich: Bayerische Staatsbibliothek und Kulturstiftung der Länder, March 2003). Readers should note that although the present chapter pre-dated *Patrimonia. 157*, its publication before that of the latter was prevented by copyright

in portrait format belonged to Gottfried von Einem.[8] In the Pierpont Morgan Library (PML) in New York there are three sketch pages for the Scherzo in E minor, as well as one title page inscribed 'Ada/gio/nte' and another inscribed 'à la Scherzo'. It is possible that more pages are hidden in public or private archives.

The BSB has permitted publication of three of its pages here, and brief descriptions of these and other newly emerged pages are provided below. The BSB's complete SS of the Adagio includes the previously 'missing' pages 6 and 7. The title page of this SS bears the ink inscription 'Adagio' and was printed thus by Zsolnay. At some point after this, the word 'Partitur' was lightly pencilled in, and the word 'Skizzen' written over it in Alma's hand. The BSB holds page VI of the pre-draft SS in portrait format, page I of the draft SS in landscape format, the page that follows RF38 comprising the continuation of the draft SS of the 'Purgatorio', and the very first draft of the beginning of the Scherzo in E minor. Presumably Mahler wrote at least six pages of pre-draft SS of the Adagio in portrait format which preceded both the draft SS in landscape format[9] and obviously the SS proper and OD. At least three of these pre-draft SS pages in portrait format are still missing.

In the coda of the Adagio Mahler at times went through no fewer than eight drafts for a few bars. The BSB pages lend credibility to the view that Mahler completed four cycles of drafts for the Adagio:[10]

1. A pre-draft SS in portrait format with roman numerals, with the first 'new' PML title page 'Ada/gio/nte'.[11]
2. The draft SS in landscape format, again with roman numerals, with a second 'new' ÖNB title page in red pencil labelled 'Adagio'.
3. The SS with arabic numerals and the BSB title page inscribed 'Adagio' in ink. 'Partitur' was later added in a third hand, and 'Skizzen' in Alma's hand.
4. The OD, also with arabic numerals, with the ÖNB title page inscribed 'I' in blue pencil as well as in ink, plus 'Adagio Partitur' in ink.

If the above assumption is correct, the third newly discovered title page – the ÖNB title page '1. Satz' in bold blue pencil – was possibly meant for the draft

---

restrictions on reproducing the manuscript material held in the BSB. The writing of this chapter also pre-dated the publication of Rothkamm, 2003.

8 This page was wrongly thought to exist in the library of the Gesellschaft der Musikfreunde in Vienna. It has yet to be located.

9 These are most of the pages in the Ricke facsimile, with Ratz's numbering 1–53 (labelled with the abbreviation RF).

10 The pages RF1–4 consist of one superseded insert plus three sketch pages. They do not carry page numbers pertaining to a sequence of drafts.

11 This title page is in landscape format and so appears not to belong with the portrait-format pages. However, the title is written slightly towards the left so as to be at the centre of a portrait-format page. Moreover a demarcation line towards the right suggests a fold to accommodate the portrait-format pages.

SS for the Scherzo in E minor. The fourth 'new' title page is labelled 'à la Scherzo' and probably pertains to the draft SS of the Scherzo in F sharp minor.

Previously unknown manuscript pages

1. BSB Music manuscript 22745 [1] (see Plate 18.1)

Plate 18.1 BSB Mus. ms. 22745 [1]. Reproduced by kind permission of the Bayerische Staatsbibliothek Munich, Musikabteilung.

This is page VI (bars 159–77) of the pre-draft score of the Adagio in portrait format. A draft counterpoint can be seen in bars 162–64. Mahler also noted 'Polyphon' but did not duplicate this counterpoint in RF12 or on page 6 of the SS. Cooke, Mazzetti and Barshai guessed correctly that a counterpoint should be included here, although theirs was of course a different one (see Ex. 18.1). It is debatable whether Mahler would have retained this counterpoint, and whether future editors should employ it. After being informed of it Barshai nevertheless decided to give preference to his own counterpoint. Cooke's counterpoint in the bassoon, derived by analogy from bars 81–84, 153–56 and 217–20, works well, despite remaining in the same register in order to connect to the cellos in bar 165. Mazzetti and Barshai guessed correctly that this counterpoint would ascend, as do the first violins. Bars 170–72 show a second voice in F clef that was superseded in RF12 by Mahler's new counterpoint, also in F clef. This remained the same on page 6 of the SS. In the OD Mahler wrote this counterpoint for the second violins in G clef. This BSB page therefore supports Cooke's assumption (1989, p. 168) that Mahler made a copying error here.[12] Marius Flothuis took the same view, and suggested using bassoons for this counterpoint, keeping the string parts intact.[13] This BSB page also reaffirms that the horn should begin on the second beat of bar 172. This is clear in all SSs but ambivalent in the OD. The page ends with the inscription 'Schluss und coda'.

2. BSB Music manuscript 22746 [1]
This is page I of the draft SS of the Adagio in landscape format. It actually precedes RF7 and belongs to the generation of drafts that follows RF6 and 22745 [1] in portrait format. This 'new' page contains the first appearance of the viola solo. The first bar contains erasures suggesting that there was no preceding draft of this solo. Like RF6 it contains the inverted Adagio theme of bar 24 but with the preparatory passage as it occurs in bars 54–57. The assumption that Mahler ultimately wanted the first violins in bars 20–21 to be an octave lower is reaffirmed here.[14]

---

[12] Correspondence between Erwin Ratz and Hans Wollschläger housed in the IGMG shows that the former was exasperated to discover through Cooke et al. that RF12 – the then rediscovered draft SS page – clearly shows the counterpoint in the bass. Wollschläger reassured him that he never thought the counterpoint in second violins sounded wrong. However, Ratz may well have opted to read the counterpoint in the F clef had the Adagio not already been printed. A change of heart in the second edition of 1968 (which remained unaltered) would have meant overt deference to the Cooke team. Nothwithstanding Ratz's pioneering role in the propagation of Mahler's legacy, it is a pity that the search for the truth with regard to the interpretation of the manuscript has been blurred with false arguments and rivalry.

[13] Personal communication with the author.

[14] See Bouwman, 2001, p. 48, where all the drafts (except the BSB page) are given for these bars. Of the six drafts four have the lower register. In the SS (the fifth draft)

Ex. 18.1 Tenth Symphony, Adagio, bars 162–65

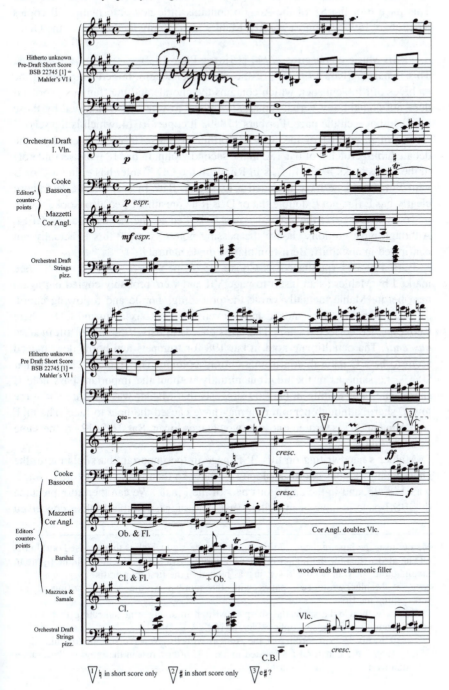

3. BSB Music manuscript 22744 [13]

This page 6 of the SS of the Adagio contains little new information. It copies RF12, bars 159–77, almost exactly. Mahler altered only the last bar in the OD.

4. BSB Music manuscript 22744 [15] (see Plate 18.2)

This is page 7 (bars 178–213) of the SS of the Adagio, buried for years in the archives of Moldenhauer, which contains the chorale and the 'famous chord'. It does not contain any verbal remarks, contrary to what was suggested by those who had not seen the page. For bars 178–93 it copies RF14, which is the second setting of page VIII of the SS.[15] Unfortunately there is no accidental on the debated third crotchet of bar 182 in the second violin. In bar 183, the second note in the horns looks like F flat, as in RF14. In the OD Mahler has either a C or B with flat. Could he have intended a harsher F flat? In bar 183 the last chord clearly has E flat, not E double flat or D as Ratz presumed (see also Cooke, 1989, p. 168). In bar 192, the second voice C is tied to the next bar as in RF14. Although most editions choose the passing note C sharp,[16] this is actually not confirmed in any draft. Bernstein played the C natural.[17]

Bars 199–205 (published as Cooke, 1976, p. xxv, & 1989, p. xxix) were marked by Mahler as an insert to page VII and were probably copied out again here before Mahler actually wrote the preceding chorale and following chord. The key signature does indeed have seven flats, not six as in the OD – here Cooke judged correctly again. The brass chords in bars 195–98 are still *in statu nascendi*. The penultimate note in bar 198 for trumpets and horns does indeed seem to be a C natural, confirming current opinion. The 'famous chord' in bar 204 is the same as in the OD, but initially without the important bass note C sharp. The faint writing in bar 209 suggests that Mahler was not sure about the low C sharp, although perspiration may have caused the note to fade. The high solo A in bar 207 is written one and two octaves lower. Bars 209–12 are the same as in the OD.

Mahler's handwriting on this BSB page in the important bars relating to the chorale and 'famous chord' is sloppy – more so than in the preceding passage, bars 178–93, and in the analogous bars of the Finale. We can therefore presume this BSB page to have been written first. The suggestion that Mahler conceived

---

Mahler uses the high register, adding an '8va bassa' sign which is then crossed out. In the OD he also writes for the higher register but writes '8va bassa' and the melodic figure to facilitate the entry an octave lower, just as he had in the first four drafts.

[15] Mahler wrote two pages with the number 8, the second setting clearly superseding the first.

[16] In the Cooke score the sharp is written in small print indicating that it is an editorial addition. See also Cooke, 1989, p. 168.

[17] In his 1975 recording of the Adagio with the New York Philharmonic (Sony SM3K 47585) the C natural is repeated in bar 192 after a rest in the previous bar, rather than tied over.

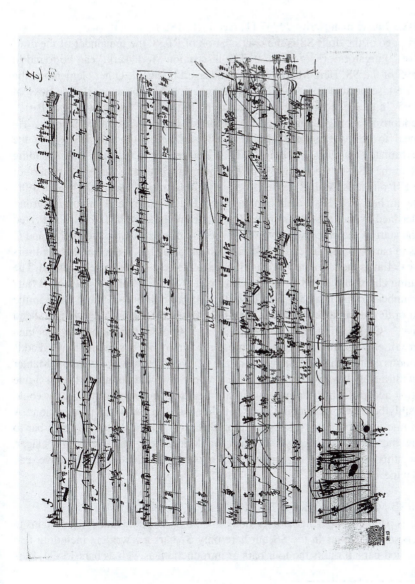

this 'famous chord' while composing the Finale could nevetheless still be valid. The evidence implies that he wrote the climaxes for both movements late in the composition process and more or less simultaneously.

5. BSB Music manuscript 22747 [1] (see Plate 18.3)

This page of the draft SS is the continuation of RF38, the remainder of the draft SS of 'Purgatorio' (bars 82–end). The inscription 'Tod: Verk:' can be found in bar 95 of the SS. Here Mahler wrote 'Todesverkündigen'. Other elements in the SS are also present here: the flat sign for the E, and 'Pos[aunen]' and 'Bass' at bar 95. In the SS it was unclear whether the last note of bar 96 was A or B flat. Theodore Bloomfield suggested to the author that an A sounded insipid.[18] He proved to be correct since Mahler did write B flat. On this BSB page the penultimate semiquaver of bar 120 is an octave higher than the corresponding note in the SS (see Cooke, 1989, p. 73), thus anticipating the arpeggio pattern of bar 121 onwards. Mahler stopped before writing bar 123 and only resumed the coda in bar 159. His vacillation between B flat major and minor is further underlined by the fact that from bar 159 to the end he kept the five flats indicated at the start of the *da capo*. However, it seems unlikely that he intended D and G flats in bars 164 and 165. In the SS the upbeat to bar 168 is unclear. Most editors have G flat as the last note. On this BSB page the note seems to be G natural. The ensuing chord of bar 168 is very unclear: is it D flat–E natural–G natural–B flat? The upbeat to the last bar (170) is written B flat–D [flat?]–B flat.[19] Only in the next draft did Mahler write C–D [flat?]–B flat. Here in 22747 [1] Mahler added 'Bass – C[ontra] F[agott]'. In the SS he first wrote 'F[agott]' which was then overwritten with 'B[ass]'. Cooke scores only for double bass while Barshai adds bassoons, stating that double bassoons are too weak. However, given that Mahler may ultimately have wanted double basses only, it would not really matter if one or two added double bassoons were not heard sufficiently clearly: they could possibly be added to the double basses in line with Mahler's initial indications. A thin line is visible after the last note on this page, thus creating an extra bar to allow the sound to die away.[20] The fact that Mengelberg, and later Wollschläger, added this extra bar in their conducting scores suggests that they might have seen this page.

6. BSB Music manuscript 22748 [1]

This is page I of the Scherzo in E minor and precedes RF40 and 39. It pertains to the first 112 bars as in the SS but here only 57 bars are written, including five encircled bars. It omits the four bars of introduction, as well as bars 15–24. Bars

---

[18] This was later confirmed in Bloomfield, 1991: see the examples on p. 124.

[19] Compare the last three notes of the Scherzo in the Sixth Symphony.

[20] Barshai argued in personal communication with the author that the fermata is sufficient and that the extra bar is superfluous.

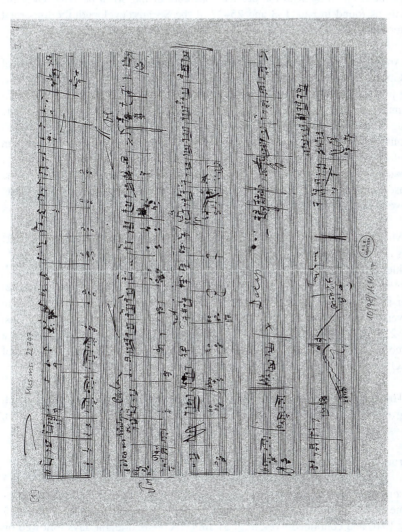

Plate 18.3 BSB Mus. ms. 22747 [1]. Reproduced by kind permission of the Bayerische Staatsbibliothek Munich, Musikabteilung

39–47 are also missing, and the page lacks the 'motto' chords F–A–C–E, F sharp–A sharp–C sharp–E and G–B–E, which are sketched for the first time in RF40.[21] The music after bar 44 again starts with the main motif, only to decay quickly into an encircled passage of four bars. The page then has the same music as in the SS starting with the deleted four bars of the SS in bar 107. Only the motifs as found in bars 1–3 and 25–27 of the SS are developed, the important material in bars 15–24, 39–47 and 57–106 being absent.

7. An as yet unpublished manuscript page formerly in the possession of Gottfried von Einem (G v E)

The present location of the original is unknown. A copy is housed in the IGMG, Vienna. This page is the pre-draft SS in portrait format of bars 49–78 of the Adagio. It contains no page number and has 32 staves, eight more than in manuscript examples 1 and 2 discussed above. This page probably precedes them but follows RF6. It again shows Mahler's vacillation in the use of the higher register in bars 19–21. The conducting scores from 1924 that are based on the transcription by Ernst Krenek ignore the '8va bassa' sign that Mahler wrote above the first violins.

8. Musik. Handschrift 41000/6. An as yet unpublished page housed in the ÖNB

This is a draft SS page in landscape format of bars 1–57 of the Adagio. Curiously Mahler used a red pencil here just as for the second title page labelled 'Adagio'. Above the first bar Mahler wrote 'Adagio', then erased it and wrote 'Andante' over it. It is unclear whether this indecision applies to the tempo of the entire movement or just that of the first fifteen bars. This page comes after BSB Mus. ms. 22746 [1], RF6, G v E. and RF7, but before the SS proper. It provides a welcome piece in the puzzle of the Adagio, confirming the C natural in bar 39 of the OD where the natural sign in the SS had been unclear.

These manuscript discoveries have been incorporated into the graph of all known sources of the Symphony included at the end of this chapter (Table 18.1).

Chronology of composition

According to the detailed discussion by Rothkamm (1999) of the possible time-frame of the composition of the Tenth, Mahler started work between 6 and 17 July 1910 and continued work until 31 July.[22] A break of eight days followed on

---

[21] The implications of the appearance of these chords for the alleged influence of Alma's songs and the order of composition are discussed below.

[22] See also Filler, 1977, pp. 387–410, Jongbloed, 1991, and Matthews, 1996.

account of a letter from Walter Gropius and the subsequent crisis.[23] From 8 to 14 August work resumed apparently at Alma's insistence.[24] On 14 August Alma wrote to Gropius as follows:

> Only now will I really be able to get any music out of Gustav – he wants to read through some difficult works with me … wanting to live *only for* me, *forsaking* the 'paper' life (as he calls his rigorous musician's existence) – although he has just finished a whole symphony – with *all* of the current horrors in it.[25]

On 17 August Mahler wrote a poem describing the flute melody from the Finale (see La Grange & Weiß, 1995, pp. 448–49). This suggests that the Finale was not yet written when Alma wrote the above. On 22 August Mahler suffered an attack of angina, and on 25 August he left for Leiden to consult Sigmund Freud. On 2 September he returned, reassured, to Alt-Schluderbach and possibly carried out what was to be his last work on the Symphony over the next two days. On 4 September he suffered an attack of acute tonsillitis.[26] On 6 September he departed for Munich to rehearse and perform his Eighth Symphony. The manuscript of the Tenth was allegedly put in a safe in Vienna and did not accompany Mahler to New York.

Let us accept Rothkamm's timeframe as a credible one and, for lack of further evidence, reject the possibility that the Adagio and one of the Scherzos were written before July 1910. Nevertheless, the order of composition has often been debated, and two schools of thought have emerged: one which believes the Scherzo in E minor to have been written next in order after the Adagio (Filler, 1977, Jongbloed, 1991, Matthews, 1996 and Coburn, 2002); and one which holds that the order of composition was the same as the order in which the movements are to be performed (Rothkamm, 1999 & 2003). The first school suggests, among other things, the following:

---

[23] Gropius sent a letter to Alma imploring her to leave her husband. But he addressed it to 'Herr Direktor Mahler' in an apparent bid to provoke a marital split. The attempt was unsuccessful.

[24] Mahler wrote to Alma: 'My princess has banished me down there' ['Meine Fürstin hat mich hinunter verbannt'] (La Grange & Weiß, p. 448). Rothkamm (1999, p. 111, fn. 73) considers that 'hinunter' can only refer to Mahler's composing hut situated at ground level a short distance from their summer retreat at the farmhouse in Alt-Schluderbach.

[25] 'Jetzt erst werde ich wirklich etwas von G.[ustav] haben – er will mit mir schwere Werke lesen – musiziren … *nur für* mich leben wollend[,] das "papierne" Leben [(]wie er sein strenges Musikersdasein nennt)[,] *verlassend* – obwohl er gerade jetzt eine ganze Symphonie gemacht hat – mit *allen* Schrecken dieser Zeit drin.' Cited in Rothkamm, 1999, p. 111.

[26] Stuart Feder suggested to the author that a similar case of tonsillitis, possibly contracted through a visit to a New York dentist, may have precipitated Mahler's final illness. See also Chapter 17 in the present book.

1. The confusing erasures on the title page of the Scherzo in E minor indicate that it must have been written next after the Adagio in the composition process.
2. Because Mahler wrote '2. Scherzo-Finale' on the title page of the OD of the Scherzo in F sharp minor, the Scherzo in E minor must have been written before it.
3. Despite Rothkamm's claim, the '1.' in '1. Scherzo' on the title page of the Scherzo in E minor does not necessarily indicate that the other Scherzo (in F sharp minor) had already been written.
4. The musical influences of Alma and Josef Suk, mentioned below in this chapter, are to be dismissed, and consequently also Rothkamm's conclusion that the 'Purgatorio' was written after August 1910.
5. Presupposing a 'manic' phase in Mahler's creative process, provoked by his depressed state of mind at that time,[27] it is possible that the Scherzo in F sharp minor *was* written after the Scherzo in E minor (the 'dance with the devil').

The second school indicates and suggests the following:

1. The Adagio and Scherzo in F sharp minor form a unity whose conclusion marks a clear caesura before the final three movements.
2. Both movements lack any anguished verbal insertions of the type added by Mahler elsewhere in the Symphony.
3. The Adagio theme and that of the trio of the Scherzo in F sharp minor are more alike than Jongbloed's alleged '*Urlinie*' between the Adagio and Scherzo in E minor.
4. The ' 1.' on the title page of the Scherzo in E minor is only understandable if another Scherzo movement had already been written.
5. The more 'positive' Scherzo in F sharp minor, with all its sense of elation in the coda, could not possibly have been written after the 'dance with the devil' Scherzo, and especially not after the marital crisis.

The present author believes that Mahler *could* have composed the movements in the order in which they are to be performed if one accepts the following: that the vacillation on the title page of both Scherzos only occurred after the writing of the ODs of the first three movements and the Particell of the fourth, but before the composition of the Finale. At a certain point Mahler may well have been working simultaneously on all five movements.

Whatever the case, the relationship between the order of composition and the order of performance may ultimately be of minimal significance for the evaluation of the work.

---

[27] Stuart Feder referred to this possibility in personal communication with the author. While both Coburn (2002) and before him Eveline Nikkels (1991, p. 165) considered the Tenth Symphony to be a special case, others such as Jonathan Carr have been wary of connecting Mahler's composing too directly with the realities of his life situation (an opinion expressed in personal communication with the author).

The influence of Alma's songs and a piano work by Josef Suk

Mahler's state of mind in these weeks of great tension varied from one extreme to another – 'zum Himmel hoch jauchzend bis zum Tode betrübt', as Goethe put it in *Egmont*. According to Alma, in desperation he played only her songs: 'He plays nothing else the whole day long and says that they are simply *outstanding*. … Gustav *lives* for these songs – his entire output is inconsequential to him' ['Er spielt den ganzen Tag nichts andres und sagt, dass sie einfach *genial* sind. … Gustav *lebt* für diese Lieder – seine ganze Produktion ist ihm "wurst"'].[28] Afraid of losing Alma, did Mahler inflate the value of her songs to such an extent that he used chords and motifs from them in his symphony which he subsequently 'forgot' to finish? Unfortunately the original manuscripts of Alma's songs are lost or were destroyed, making it impossible to judge how much Mahler (or Zemlinsky) assisted in their composition. The excerpt from Mahler's transcription of Alma's 'Erntelied', cited in Kravitt, 1988, p. 199, suggests the possibility that some of these notes and chords found their way into Alma's songs which were 'edited' by Mahler. Could he have used the sweet tones in these songs, twisted them to express his anguish and reused them in his Tenth Symphony?

Rothkamm (2000a) argues that the pattern of four descending steps in dotted-crotchet-plus-quaver rhythm in the 'Purgatorio', Scherzo in E minor and Finale were inspired by Mahler's involvement with Alma's 'Erntelied'.[29] Kravitt (1988, p. 200) shows the superseded draft of bar 57 of 'Erntelied' in Mahler's hand. In the second draft the F-sharp arpeggiation in the bass has been flattened to F, and the four descending notes of the vocal line outline the tritone B–A–G–F instead of B–A–G sharp–F sharp.[30] It appears that this motif was already playing on

---

[28] Letters from Alma to Gropius of 17 and 19 August 1910, cited in Rothkamm, 2000a, p. 435. There may be some exaggeration here on Alma's part for the benefit of Gropius, since it is difficult to believe that Mahler regarded his own work in this way.

[29] Rothkamm (2000a, p. 442) compares bars 19 and 57 of 'Erntelied', which contain 'Rosenhügeln' and 'Wanderflüge' as texts, with bars 84, 92, 107 and 113 of 'Purgatorio' and bar 397 of the Finale. (Mahler's predilection for upbeats can be seen in the SS of the Scherzo in E minor. He toyed with the idea of prefixing an upbeat E4–E5 to the chord F–A–C–E in the first bar of the SS and affixed an upbeat B in bar 6, which is scored for woodwind in the Cooke version.) See also 'Purgatorio' bars 92–93, 107–8 and 113–14 and the more 'positive' equivalents in bars 66, 74, and (slightly altered) 89–91. The same descending motif can be found in, for example, bars 123–24 and 210–13 of the Scherzo in E minor, and bars 12–14, 22–24, 29, 38, 42 and 44 of the Finale. More 'positive' equivalents appear in bars 90, 96, 106 and 114–15 of the Finale. Direct quotes of this theme as it appears in 'Purgatorio' are found in bars 119–20 and 125–26 of the Finale. The 'triumphant' theme beginning at bars 145–46 is also derived from these four descending notes. The final appearance of the idea occurs in bar 397 of the Finale, at which point Mahler entered the word 'Almschi!' on the manuscript.

[30] See Mahler's use of a tritone outlined melodically in the Finale, bars 125–26. BSB music manuscript 22744 [20] (the verso of Mahler's first setting of page 8 of the SS

Mahler's mind when he was composing the SS for the Adagio. Those who find Rothkamm's argument credible are invited to contemplate the following observations.

The text 'ich küsse dem Liebsten des Kleides Saum, süsser Traum' ['I kiss the hem of my beloved's dress, sweet dream'] and the sequence of chords F sharp–A–C–E, F sharp–A sharp–C sharp–E, G sharp–B–E appear in bars 97–101 of Alma Mahler's song 'In meines Vaters Garten'. At the very start of RF40 Mahler wrote the chords F–A–C–E, F sharp–A sharp–C sharp–E and G–B–E.[31] BSB 22748 page 1 and RF39 of the Scherzo in E minor still lack these motto chords. They are sketched for the first time in RF40.[32] In bar 97 of the same song, bar 15 of 'Waldseligkeit' and at the word 'Seele' in 'Erntelied' (bar 59) a downward octave E5–E4 was written.[33] This same octave figure opens the Scherzo in E minor and plays a crucial role throughout, occurring far more often than the three motto chords.[34]

Although these songs frequently contain a falling octave in this register they are by no means the only possible source. The interval as it appears in Alma's songs may have reminded Mahler of the Finale of his Sixth Symphony where, 15–13 bars before the end of the movement, the trombone has not only a falling octave E4–E3 – a leap that occurs frequently in the movement and indeed in Mahler's *oeuvre* as a whole – but also the ensuing dotted-crotchet–quaver–minim pattern which, with a shortened final note, went on to form the rhythmic backbone of the Scherzo in E minor. (See Exx. 18. 2–5.) Prefixed with a quaver upbeat, this dotted rhythm (shown in the third bars of Ex. 18.3 and Ex. 18.5) strongly resembles both the opening of the Tenth Symphony's Adagio and the alleged Alma quote that occurs for the first time in bars 83–85 of 'Purgatorio', demonstrating Mahler's versatility in using a rhythmic nucleus.

While the four descending notes that occur twice in 'Erntelied', the three motto chords of 'In meines Vaters Garten' and the falling E5–E4 figure found in

---

of the Adagio) – already published by Zsolnay – shows two bars with the very same four descending notes *preceding* bars 28–30 in the second violins. In the SS and OD these four notes appear *after* bars 28–30 with slightly altered rhythm. The previous drafts on RF1 and 6 lack this counterpoint.

[31] In bar 45 of the Scherzo in E minor Mahler has G sharp, making the last two chords identical while the first differs by one note (F instead of Alma's (?) F sharp). It is possible that the chords in bars 41–45 preceded those at the beginning of RF40 since clearly Mahler bothered about the four bars of introduction only after BSB 22748.

[32] This corrects information previously given in Bouwman, 2001, p. 51, fn. 12.

[33] Notably the accompaniment in the following bar of 'Waldseligkeit' (bar 16) contains the chord F–A–C–E.

[34] Note the frequent use of the pitch E in this particular register in the songs by Alma cited above, and its appearance at the opening of the 'triumphant' theme referred to in fn. 29, starting at bars 98 and 145 of the Finale. It is perhaps significant that preference for this pitch is also evident at the beginning of the phrase 'Die liebe Erde' in 'Der Abschied' of *Das Lied von der Erde* (bars 459–61).

Ex. 18.2   Alma Mahler's 'In meines Vaters Garten', bars 97–101

Ex. 18.3   Mahler's Tenth Symphony, Scherzo in E minor, excerpt from bars 1–5 of the short score

Ex. 18.4   Alma Mahler's 'Waldseligkeit', bars 15–17

Ex. 18.5 Mahler's Sixth Symphony, Finale, 15–13 bars before the end

three of Alma's songs may not in isolation constitute conclusive proof that her music influenced Mahler's last work, in combination they offer a stronger body of evidence to support such a claim.

Vladimir Karbusicky (1996b, pp. 88–89) cited the piano work 'Vroztouženi' ['Liebessehnsucht'] by the Czech composer Josef Suk (1874–1935) whose principal melody bears a strong resemblance to the 'triumphant' theme beginning in bar 145 of the Finale of Mahler's Tenth Symphony (see Plate 18.4). These melodies have both intervallic and rhythmic features in common, notably the 'silent' third beat – identified by Reeser (1997) as a distinctive preference throughout Mahler's output – which characterizes bars 2, 4, 6, 7, 9, 11 and 13 of Suk's piece. Furthermore, on the two rejected versions of page 6 of his manuscript (RF52), Mahler drafted this theme in D flat major, the same key used by Suk. The strong possibility of this allusion to Suk adds a further perspective to the discussion of the influences acting on Mahler at this time: it is well known that Mahler was acutely aware of the music around him, particularly that which was imbued with personal connotations.

Tasks for the editor of a 'performing version'

An editor has two tasks: to interpret Mahler's notation as faithfully as possible, and to orchestrate the musical material with due respect to what is contained in the manuscript. Before an editor even considers orchestration, he or she should carefully transcribe Mahler's manuscript and determine the correct notes from the OD, SS and draft SS. If this initial step of accurately determining the notes from the manuscript is not carried out properly the edition cannot be regarded seriously. The editor should ensure that Mahler's voice is predominant at all times. Where Mahler only jotted down the melody line – for example in a recapitulation of earlier sections – the editor has no option but to transplant the texture, harmony and counterpoint of the analogous bars that were written out, despite the claim that Mahler never repeated himself literally.

The choices made between the ambiguities that were left in the manuscript should be clearly justified in appended critical notes.[35] It requires profound knowledge of Mahler's style and orchestration to judge when one edition is superior to another – when an edition seems 'right'. For instance, in a tutti should

---

[35] Only Deryck Cooke et al. provided such notes.

V roztouženi. – Liebessehnsucht.

Allegro non troppo.

Plate 18.4 The first page of 'Vroztouženi' ['Liebessehnsucht'], the fifth piece from Josef Suk's piano work *Jaro* [*Der Frühling*] (1902; published 1903)

the editor double the principal voice in the strings with woodwinds? Should the editor choose a solo flute or all the flutes? Should an entire phrase be duplicated or the upbeat omitted? Should the slurring of string and wind instruments be adjusted or not? Sometimes the editor's aim should be to facilitate performance through adjusted bowing or phrasing. To recognize these subtleties one needs first-hand experience of Mahler's manuscript and the differences between the editions. Only then is it is possible to judge where one edition seems less effective than another or, more importantly, where an editor ignored or overruled indications in Mahler's manuscript. Analysis of every draft of the manuscript has revealed all the more that deducing the notes accurately is a prerequisite for broaching the subject of orchestration. The art of orchestration itself has to be based on sound philological principles. With each new edition the scope for contributing a new sound or instrumental dimension to this unfinished manuscript diminishes, and this should be borne in mind during the following discussion.

Mixing editions

Would it not be tempting to assemble all the good ideas from each edition into one and through this synthesis arrive at an ideal edition? Quite apart from the legal implications, some are opposed to mixed editions because the authorship of the editor is at stake. But how much importance should be given to authorship? Obviously the comments by Alban Berg carry more weight than those of later editors. It is also a fact that all the editors were assisted in one way or another. For instance Deryck Cooke initially used the corrupt Jokl edition for the 1960 broadcast and was later helped by Berthold Goldschmidt, David Matthews and Colin Matthews. Posthumously his edition was further improved by input from Kurt Sanderling, Simon Rattle and Theodore Bloomfield. Berthold Goldschmidt annotated Cooke's first edition which was used for the Berlin première in 1964, pencilling in some important decisions that found their way into the printed edition and into the conducting score.[36] This is not to belittle Cooke – most of the decisions are very much his in any case – but it puts the unassailability of an editor into perspective. Involvement with the editions of Mazzetti, Wheeler and Barshai has demonstrated to the present author that every editor is keen to know what others have done. The amount of 'borrowing' depends on the scruples of the editor, and, at the risk of charges of plagiarism, it would seem common sense to 'borrow' a good solution. The final results will vary between those editions that are just as defensible as Cooke's, but which contain 'borrowed' elements, and those based on wholly independent decisions. The latter are unlikely to be more successful because they will inevitably contain a number of errors or misinterpretations avoided by editors who compared other editions. A mix of all

---

[36] This score is located in the Akademie der Künste, Berlin. For details of Goldschmidt's involvement see Rothkamm, 2000b. For example, such decisions as the reading of the second voice in the F clef instead of G clef in bars 170–71 of the Adagio, and in the same movement the reading of: (a) the third note in second violin in bar 182 as F flat, and (b) the lowest trombone note on the third beat of bar 183 as E flat instead of D, may well have originated from Goldschmidt.

editions would necessarily be the work of consensus: extreme ideas, some good and much bad, would be avoided. Perhaps all listeners should be able to concoct the ideal edition themselves with the help of a scholarly edition of all the autograph material such as that planned by the present author.

Reviewing 'performing versions'

As stated earlier the performing versions now available are by Rudolf Barshai, Clinton Carpenter, Deryck Cooke et al., Remo Mazzetti, Giuseppe Mazzuca and Nicola Samale, and Joe Wheeler. Hans Wollschläger withdrew a seventh version and Barry Guerrero is considering an eighth. Carpenter began his initial versions of all five movements in 1946; Wheeler started in 1953, Wollschläger in 1957 and Cooke in 1959. These editions, conceived just thirteen years apart, were nevertheless worked on independently. Yet after the famous Cooke broadcast in 1960, Wheeler and Carpenter subsequently corrected mistakes from their scores. Editors of the Symphony are consequently indebted to Cooke.

Most editors have in fact spent years 'perfecting' their performing versions and consequently cannot help but think that they have captured Mahler's spirit best. Most of them have had the opportunity for repeated performances over several years, and have therefore been able to correct misconceptions or wrong notes, and to trim down superfluous instrumentation especially in the percussion sections. The editing process resembles Mahler's own: after a stage of thickening the texture, the stage of thinning out and simplification sets in. As a result editors probably produce at least three scores on their path to presumed perfection. According to David Matthews (1991, p. 60): 'From the late 1960s until the publication of the score in 1976, we collaborated on the extensive revision of the score which Deryck had already begun.' Wheeler, Carpenter, Mazzetti and Barshai also produced several versions.[37] The most glaring infelicities having been removed from each edition, we now have six completed versions that differ slightly on very many occasions but which do not offer hugely different conceptions of the work. This is because the work is horizontally uninterrupted and because Mahler ordered all movements and the sections within those movements. Colin Matthews (1995/1996, p. 309) has argued that the coda of the Adagio and Scherzo in F sharp minor might have gone through major revisions (probably reductions), that the recapitulation of 'Purgatorio' may have been extended and varied, and that the last two movements have bars that may or may

---

[37] It seems likely that editors consistently (re)work and perfect the same score rather than starting from scratch with each new attempt. However, in the pre-xerox era editors were compelled to rewrite by hand, just as Mahler did. This process sometimes led to bigger changes (for example those in Wheeler's third and fourth editions).

not have been included in the finished work.[38] Thus the similarities between the editions will always far outweigh the differences. How many of those uninitiated into this work would thus be able to tell whether the score sounds unfinished and inferior in comparison with Mahler's completed scores? How many listeners would be able to discriminate between the performing versions or between successful and poor performances of different versions? Only the 'arrangement' by Carpenter would probably have the 'honour' of being recognized.

Deryck Cooke

Cooke was initially given detailed assistance by the composer and conductor Berthold Goldschmidt, who acted as translator and as mediator between Cooke, Alma Mahler and Erwin Ratz. At a later stage Cooke welcomed the additional involvement of the young composers Colin and David Matthews.[39] Cooke's edition has been widely praised for its faithfulness to the manuscript, its transparency and its overall balance.[40] David Matthews (1991, p. 61) claims that 'The elusive Mahlerian sound, which we all could hear when we looked at the bare notes of the score, was extremely difficult to achieve in practice, but I think that finally we did go a long way to achieving it.' Nevertheless the Scherzo in F sharp minor and the climaxes in the Scherzo in E minor and Finale have been regarded as too thinly orchestrated, raising the question of whether a still better performing version was possible. The result was that ensuing versions were at their most daring in these very sections. However, even the most brilliant ideas in other editions do not mitigate their weaker choices. David Matthews claims that the Cooke team would have welcomed an even better edition, but doubted that this would be possible.[41] Scrupulous interpretation of the manuscript coupled with fine musical taste has earned the Cooke edition its deserved acclaim.

Analysis of the score disproves the contention that one is listening to Cooke rather than Mahler in this performing version. To give just one example: Cooke wrote a counterpoint in small print in the trumpet part beginning at bar 347 of the Scherzo in F sharp minor. The manuscript and Cooke's notes clarify that the entire counterpoint apart from the last bar is Mahler's and is taken from RF30. Similarly in bars 387 and 389 of the Scherzo in E minor Cooke writes a counterpoint in the cellos that is not in the SS, but exists, as Cooke explained, on

---

[38] Although no one has yet considered a major rethink of Mahler's concept, it would be instructive if Matthews were to provide a comprehensive discussion of these issues.

[39] For a detailed study of Cooke and his assistants see Rothkamm, 2000b.

[40] Fellow editors Mazzetti and Barshai, the conductors Rattle, Chailly and Sanderling and many Mahler scholars are among those who have rated it highly. The first full public performance of Cooke's performing version took place on 13 August 1964, conducted by Berthold Goldschmidt.

[41] Personal communication with the author.

the second setting of page VIII:[42] thus these notes are not Cooke's but Mahler's own.

Somewhat more contentious is the question of whether one should heed indications that are in the SS but not in the OD. In bar 81 of the Adagio Cooke doubled the second violins with the oboe as indicated only in the SS. As for the issue of 'filling in', Cooke modestly claimed that his edition was merely a 'performing version of the draft' but this does not mean that he never made additions. For example in bars 325–30 of the Scherzo in F sharp minor he writes an unobtrusive counterpoint in the first violins. In bar 352 of the Scherzo in E minor he writes the last two notes for the horns as A–G sharp, thus giving them a logical conclusion. He is at his most daring in bars 260–61 of the Finale, where he adds a counterpoint in the clarinets in whole tones.

In terms of dynamics, Cooke sometimes indicates a reduction to *pp* to good effect: the *pp* section in bars 416–39 of the Scherzo in F sharp minor seems particularly appropriate, although no dynamics were indicated by Mahler either in the OD or on RF22 and 36. The same holds true for the *pp* in bars 335–48 of the Finale. Here Mahler wrote just the principal voice without harmony or dynamics. Cooke's *pp* scoring for mostly strings and harp at this recapitulation renders the *ff* in bar 352 far more effective.

Joseph Wheeler

Until 1997 only amateurs performed this edition. As a consequence numerous mistakes remained in the score, and confidence in Wheeler as an editor was seriously undermined. However, in 1997 the Colorado Mahlerfest, with Stan Ruttenberg as president and Robert Olson as principal conductor, decided to play a version of the Wheeler edition in which the numerous wrong notes had been corrected by Olson with the assistance of Remo Mazzetti and the present author. Recorded with Jerry Bruck as the sound engineer, it was released on CD by the Colorado Mahlerfest in 1997.[43] Olson later recorded this revised Wheeler edition in May–June 2000 with the Polish National Radio Symphony Orchestra.[44] However, this time Olson reinstated some of those dubious choices that had been removed in 1997 – more out of respect for Wheeler than from conviction, although Wheeler may well have agreed with most of the 1997 corrections. The recording is very well produced and, with the removal of many mistakes and the deletion of superfluous percussion, it can justifiably be regarded as the definitive Wheeler performance. Remo Mazzetti was so enamoured with it that he even contemplated withdrawing his own edition, and although he did not do so he

---

[42] It so happens that Mahler wrote two pages numbered VIII not only for the SS of the Adagio but also for the SS of the Scherzo in E minor.

[43] The CD is available only through the Mahlerfest (Stan Ruttenberg).

[44] Naxos, 8.554811.

continued to revise his own work as a result. Mazzetti's view (1997) that Wheeler's choices are as legitimate as Cooke's is open to debate. For example Wheeler is alone in omitting Mahler's insertion of bars 77–81 in 'Purgatorio' and in choosing – in reaction to Cooke – the fast opening for the Finale. With the elimination of much superfluous percussion the 1997 version is left with a 'conservative' orchestration.

Clinton Carpenter

Carpenter's version, given its world première on 8 April 1983 by the semi-professional Civic Orchestra of Chicago conducted by Gordon Peters, represents the most liberal approach to the Tenth Symphony. The Brabant and Gelders Orchestra under Theodore Bloomfield played his edition professionally in Utrecht in 1986. Harold Farberman's performance with the Philharmonica Hungarica was released on CD (originally on the now defunct Golden Strings label, see below), and the BBC broadcast the version on 11 November 2000 with the Bournemouth Symphony Orchestra under Andrew Litton. He later repeated this with the Dallas Orchestra.

Carpenter often goes beyond the limits that many would draw. He tried to be bold because he thought Cooke's edition did not sound 'finished', but his additions – undertaken without regard for the German saying 'in der Beschränkung zeigt sich der Meister' ['the master is revealed through limitations'] – tend to distract from Mahler's music. The Litton performance gives one the consistent impression of being lulled to sleep and then rudely awakened. Carpenter tried too hard to make something 'happen' on each page of the score. The piece thus lurches from one drama to another, giving the listener insufficient time to digest what is heard, and offering no clue about Mahler's real climaxes.

Remo Mazzetti

The Dutch Radio Philharmonic Orchestra under Gaetano Delogu premièred the Mazzetti edition in Utrecht (the first three movements in November 1986 and the complete work in February 1989). A CD with the St Louis Orchestra under Leonard Slatkin then appeared in 1995.[45] Mazzetti further revised his version after this, his work on it partly coinciding with his reacquaintance with the revised Wheeler version. This later version supersedes the previous version and has been recorded by the Cincinnati Symphony Orchestra under Jésus López Cobos.[46] The Mazzetti performing version largely adopts the solutions of the Cooke team, and is therefore similar in its melodic and harmonic structure

---

45   RCA Victor Red Seal 09026 68190 2.
46   Telarc, 2000, CD-80565.

although of course the instrumentation is different. The doublings are subtly divided over different instruments but the ends of the fourth and fifth movements – criticized in the Cooke edition for being too thinly orchestrated – sometimes lack the continuity of a voice in the same instrument, making the musical discourse difficult to follow. This problem was also encountered by Barshai and by Mazzuca and Samale.

Rudolf Barshai

Barshai heard Hermann Scherchen's LP recording of the Adagio in Russia during the 1950s. A lifelong fascination was born. Shostakovich told him that Mahler's Tenth still awaited him.[47] Barshai went on to conduct the Cooke version and was dissatisfied with a number of its decisions. The arrival of his own performing version was therefore just a matter of time. He tried out his version in Ljubljana in October 2000, then in St Petersburg in December 2000 and in Verona in May 2001. After the Verona performance he confided that he could reorchestrate the entire work. He presented the work again, this time considerably thinned out, on a two-week tour with the Junge Deutsche Philharmonie in September 2001.[48]

Queries regarding the manuscript and previous performing versions discussed by Barshai and the present author are noted in Bernd Feuchtner's draft foreword to Barshai's score, due to be published by Universal Edition. The advice offered on the manuscript was not structural, and Barshai's eventual decisions were his own. Feuchtner writes:

> The goal of the Barshai score is to keep as close as possible to Mahler's manuscript. [Yet] in cases of doubt, Barshai's decisions were rarely based on scholarly analysis, which could easily have resulted in misinterpretations of the artistic process, but principally on his own subjective reaction as to whether something was suitable for Mahler's music or not. And the fact that Mahler had done something similar in another place or even another symphony rather constitutes an argument against opting for analogy: for if any composer purposely avoided any form of repetition, then it was surely Gustav Mahler.[49]

---

[47] This and subsequent comments by Barshai were made in personal communication with the author.

[48] This orchestra's Berlin performance served as the basis for the CD released on Brilliant Classics, 92205 – 1 + 2, together with the earlier recorded Fifth Symphony.

[49] 'Das Ziel der Bearbeitung von Rudolf Barshai ist es, Mahlers Manuskript möglichst nahe zu kommen. ... [Aber d]as Kriterium für die Entscheidung in Zweifelsfragen war niemals die wissenschaftliche Analyse, die im künstlerischen Prozess viele Fehler nach sich ziehen würde, sondern allein das persönliche Gespür, ob etwas zu Mahler passt. Und daß er etwas an einer anderen Stelle oder gar in einer anderen Symphonie ebenso gemacht hat, ist eher ein argument gegen den Analogieschluß: wenn ein Komponist bewußt jede Wiederholung vermieden hat, dann Gustav Mahler'. (Translation by Susan Perkins)

It would seem well-nigh impossible to keep 'as closely as possible to Mahler's manuscript' without at the same time at least looking for analogies. In fact the main task for both scholar and editor should surely be to look for analogous passages in Mahler's OD, SS, draft SS and even in his other symphonies. Barshai would of course agree that it is necessary to check, through continual comparison with previous drafts and analogous passages, whether one is reading the right notes. What is meant here is that he felt free to overrule certain generally accepted interpretations of the manuscript. Since Barshai has for years thought deeply about how this work should sound (see Feuchtner, 1999), the idea that scholarly analysis results in misinterpretation of the artistic process is surely to be regarded as an overstatement. The first step for any editor is to apply common sense to the consideration of what was written. Only then is the editor free – up to a point – to interpret and to make additions or changes as he or she sees fit. After all, it is Cooke's scrupulous interpretation of the manuscript (albeit with much expert assistance), rather than his orchestration, on which the success and standing of his edition are based.

There are several instances where the Barshai edition disagrees, in some cases justifiably, with Cooke's choices. The first example is the last semiquaver in bar 101 of the Adagio. In the OD Mahler wrote an unclear E flat and G (concert-pitch A flat and C) in the first and second horns. In the SS he wrote concert-pitch A natural which forms a parallel octave with the A in the cello. Alban Berg also commented on this point: 'Wouldn't this reading be possible or something like it! That would also be thematic and the parallel octave in cello would be avoided' ['Wäre nicht folgende Lesart möglich [musical notation inserted] oder so ähnlich! Das wäre auch thematisch und die parallelen Oktaven in den Anfangs[?]stimmen [Vlc.] wären vermieden'].[50] The familiar chromatic line in the horn sounds strong and the parallel octave with solo cello probably went unnoticed or was silently accepted. Although it avoids the parallel octave, Barshai's solution of E flat–G may take some getting used to. The second example concerns the penultimate bar of 'Purgatorio'. Here Mahler wrote the chord B flat4–E5–G5. Cooke notates this in the diplomatic transcription included in his edition but chose not to score it (see Cooke, 1989, pp. 76 and 173). In electronic communication, the Matthews brothers conceded that the placing of the G clef at the end of bar 168 does not make sense for the harp (it has already ascended to this clef halfway through the bar). The presence of an additional accent for this high chord in the SS is further proof of the accuracy of the present author's reading. Barshai decided to use the chord in his edition, scored on the first quaver for trumpets and celesta, while three clarinets sustain the chord in its next inversion (E5–G5–B flat5), doubled by horns one

---

[50] Alban Berg's notes, which Cooke read, are housed in the Alban Berg Archiv at the Österreichische Nationalbibliothek.

octave lower. However, he also read the last three bass notes of this bar as C–D *natural*–B flat as in the 1924 scores (Schalk, Mengelberg and Dopper, and Zemlinsky). To make this fit he controversially deleted the D flat from the descending arpeggio in the harp part, thus changing Mahler's own notation. The newly found sketch page (BSB Mus. ms. 22747 [1]) omitted the B flat major part of the recapitulation, bars 154–59, starting the coda in bar 159 still with five flats in place, thus implying that from bar 159 to the end Mahler was thinking in the minor mode. The third example is bar 83 at the end of the introduction to the Finale where Barshai, assuming that Mahler wrote a big crescendo, uses a tutti *ff* for the whole bar, although the manuscript indicates nothing of the sort. In the fourth place, contrary to the accepted reading of the chords in bar 95 of 'Purgatorio' and bar 83 of the Finale as D–*E flat*–G–B flat, Barshai replaced E flat with E natural. His contention that the Allegro moderato from bar 84 of the Finale also begins with an E flat, and thus removes its effect when already used, is a valid one, but not strong enough grounds to override the E flat in the chord. Barshai felt that an E flat triad over a pedal D sounded too dark, but in those very bars Mahler wrote 'Todesverkündigen' in the sketch and 'Tod! Verk!' in the SS. Finally in bar 390 of the Finale Barshai chose to read a leading-note E sharp rather than a tonic-note F sharp in the bass. Other editors assume that Mahler accidentally wrote the note too low, resulting in the E sharp. The analogous passage of Mahler's first draft in B flat does read tonic B flat. Barshai prefers to delay the use of the final tonic F sharp to the last three bars, and is not concerned that such an extremely low leading note appears nowhere else in the piece.

Despite Barshai's belief that excessive dynamic accents often impair the formal clarity of a musical work, he sometimes chooses to burden the ends of musical phrases in his instrumentation of the Tenth with a full orchestral tutti including brass and percussion, as for example in bar 83 of the Finale. Other examples are found in bars 115–22 and 244–47 of the Scherzo in E minor. These bridges to the ensuing waltz music would be more appropriately served with lighter orchestration without Barshai's percussion (bass drum, timpani, cymbal, tam-tam, triangle and glockenspiel).

Barshai dislikes the simple G chord with open fifths in bar 339 of the Finale, and contemplated reading the chord as G–D, F sharp–B–F sharp. The manuscript of the Tenth shows that when Mahler uses two combined staves F and G clefs are intended, spelling the chord as G–D, D–G–D. Only when Mahler was sketching a motif did he sometimes write four trials one underneath another. In such a case the same clef is understood. Barshai finally agreed with the reading of the chord as G–D, D–G–D.

Far from being mere philological hair-splitting, the above questions concern crucial matters of content. There is all the more need for considerable caution when overriding what Mahler seemed to have written and in accepting the assumption that 'scholarly analysis could easily result in misinterpretations of the artistic process'. Subjectivism on the part of the editor could perhaps result even more easily in such misinterpretations.

Barshai's commitment to this music is very genuine. As a conductor and string player he is able to communicate his intentions directly to an orchestra, sometimes taking a viola to demonstrate a particular phrasing. Which of the other editors could do this? The quality of Barshai's scoring in, for example, the Scherzo in F sharp minor suggests that he would be the best editor for strings. His weakest points are when he feels it necessary to enhance Cooke's effects. The sudden use of many solo voices at the end of the Scherzo in E minor and Finale seems out of balance with the huge preceding climaxes, and yet he could have used a real tutti *pp* more often. Some attribute Barshai's rather more robust orchestration – for example his use of the xylophone at the beginning of the Scherzo in E minor – to his predilection for Mahler's Sixth Symphony.

It is probably too early to decide whether his edition is generally superior to Cooke's. The latter's expertise in many parts of the Scherzo in E minor and Finale would in any case be hard to match. If Barshai were to minimize his 'alternative' reading of the manuscript and sometimes opt for leaner textures his edition would be an even worthier rival to Cooke's. His recording certainly compares favourably with others.

Giuseppe Mazzuca and Nicola Samale

A new version by Giuseppe Mazzuca and Nicola Samale – best known for their edition of the Finale of Bruckner's Ninth Symphony – was premièred in the Teatro Morlacchi in Perugia, Italy, on 22 September 2001 by the Vienna Symphony Orchestra under Martin Sieghart. From listening to this version it was noticeable that the editors did not simply copy Cooke but took account of the other versions as well. Their use of the extreme low E flat in the tuba in bar 194 of the Adagio – the beginning of the Chorale – as well as the chord B flat–E–G in the penultimate bar of 'Purgatorio' would suggest that the editors heard the Barshai edition in Verona, but this could be coincidence. The following comments are based on experience of the live performance and on examination of the as yet unrevised and unpublished score.

The first violins are again in the high register in bars 20–21 of the Adagio (see above and Bouwman, 2001, p. 48, for discussion of Mahler's probable intention to use the lower register). In bars 36–37 the flutes are missing, as indicated in the SS. As in Barshai's edition, bars 139–40 have a new counterpoint in the cellos. In bar 150 the violas are doubled by the trumpet; in view of the problems of ensemble it may be better that the violas be left to play alone at this point. The second oboe note in bar 154 is wrong, moving to F sharp instead of E natural. The last semiquaver of bar 158 in the first violins should be E sharp instead of F sharp, as in the SS and OD. In bar 164 only the chords B–G sharp and D–B (concert pitch) are added in the clarinets instead of the usual, more complex counterpoint (see Ex. 18.1). Like Barshai the editors reject Cooke's explanation that Mahler miscopied the second voice into the second violin part in bars 170–71 (see Bouwman, 2001, p. 47). In bar 172 the horn F is placed on the second beat as in all previous drafts. A bass drum roll is added in bars 195–97, and in bar 198 G flat is chosen instead of G natural in horns and trumpets.[51] The first quaver G sharp in second violin bar 226 should be E sharp.

The Scherzo in F sharp minor contains many small trills added by the editors (for example the flute trill on F sharp in bars 54–57), and these become more frequent towards the end of the movement. In bars 137–41 the trumpet imitates the violin motif at a distance of two crotchets, although there is no indication of this in Mahler's manuscript. While the bass note in bar 145 of the Cooke score is D, here the editors opt for the E natural written in RF17. The upbeat to the trio remains (Barshai removed this). The counterpoint in bars 347–52 is derived from the fourth system of RF30 and is therefore Mahler's. The editors copy only bars 347–48 for the trumpet (as Cooke did) and give the rest to the second violins. They even copy Mahler's phrasing (three slurs over six quavers) in bar 350. Cooke probably felt the second violins were too weak to compete with the full woodwind section and gave the entire counterpoint to the trumpet, omitting the three slurs. In bar 428 a rather fussy counterpoint is added in the flutes, distracting from the main voice. The change to an 'Alla Breve' time signature for the fermata note three bars before the end may be superfluous but demonstrates the editors' attention to detail since that is in fact what Mahler wrote.

In bars 35–41 of 'Purgatorio' the block chords are copied in the violas, and trills are added on the second beat. In bars 154–59 these same block chords are given to clarinets and also supplied with trills on the second beat. As in the editions of Mengelberg and Barshai, in bar 67 the horns repeat the motif from bars 26–28. In bar 144 the melody is given to bassoon as in the Mazzetti version, but in bar 145 it is once again given to oboe as in the opening section. In bar 169 a treble chord B flat4–E5–G5 is added, scored for three clarinets, three oboes and two flutes, as was suggested to Barshai by the present author. However, the editors add a C5 to the chord which is not in the manuscript.[52] The final bass notes are C–D flat–B flat as in the Cooke edition and most of the others.

Like Barshai the editors decide to omit the encircled notes in bars 178–79 of the Scherzo in E minor. It is not clear why C6 is used in the second violin in bar 261 instead of E6. Again, as with Barshai, the counterpoint seen on Mahler's second setting of page VIII is ignored in bars 387 and 389. However, in bars 424–27 the editors add a rather saccharine new counterpoint in the clarinet and

---

[51] This is a frequent point of discussion. The resurfaced SS page (BSB 22744 [15]) hints towards G natural but is very unclear.

[52] Barshai uses the next inversion of the chord: E5–G5–B flat5.

one for second violin in bars 428–31. In bars 438 and 440[53] the editors add repeated triplets in the trumpets, and further repeated brass notes in bars 442–43, in both cases following Barshai. Similarly, like Barshai, they omit the counterpoint derived from an analogous passage that Cooke added in bars 482–85, where Mahler wrote only the principal line.

The tuba as used by Cooke and Barshai would seem to be the most effective instrument for the bass opening of the Finale. Even when doubled by harp – as in Mazzetti's edition – and reinforced as it is here with the bass clarinet playing the last three notes, the double bass does not give sufficient 'edge' to the sound.[54] Mazzuca and Samale wisely refrain from cluttering up the flute solo from bar 29 onwards. In bars 45–46, again like Barshai, they do not use the prescribed alternative that Mahler wrote one staff lower. In view of the ineffective resulting counterpoint, Mahler's 'simple' alternative is preferable. Berthold Goldschmidt's suggested tremolo in the viola in bars 73 and 75 is adopted here (Barshai uses six horns at this point).

In bar 90 the editors double the main voice an octave higher in woodwind, and add trills. Perhaps it would be more appropriate to reserve this exuberance for later in the allegro section. In bars 280–81 the manuscript has some unexpected rests as well as a tentative extra bar line. Most editors have assumed that Mahler's additional bar indicated a continuation of the solo A in the trumpet, as in the Adagio. Curiously the performance had a general pause at this point but the score does not, perhaps suggesting some last-minute changes on the part of the editors or conductor. The editors decide to adopt Wheeler's curious ritardando in bars 249–50, here termed 'breiter'. In bar 292 Mahler's indication for trumpet and horn is overruled through an almost imperceptible switch to strings. In bar 323, as in Wheeler's version, the flute, rather than Cooke's second violin, again has the solo. I do not personally like the switch at the end to strings (bars 286–92) and then to oboe (bar 326). In bars 366–72, the woodwinds take over from the strings. In performance the woodwinds unfortunately sounded weaker than the first violins, and the solution of Cooke and Barshai is more effective. At bar 376 the editors use an *f* dynamic on the second beat. Cooke, Barshai and Mazzetti evidently would consider this to be too late, given that they interpret the first note of bar 368 as the dynamic climax of this passage. Carpenter and Guerrero nevertheless support Mazzuca and Samale in having the climax at the later point.

---

[53] All bar numbers given are those in the Cooke version. In the Mazzuca and Samale score bars 440 and 442 are equivalent to bars 438 and 440 in Cooke's score.

[54] Even if the double basses sound Mahlerian there seems little point in using them if the listener always misses the first bars because of the softness of the instruments. Barshai temporarily contemplated using two double bassoons and one bassoon to play this low melody, but then rejected the idea and switched to two muted tubas. The combination of tuba, double bassoon and double basses has not yet been tried.

Hans Wollschläger

Wollschläger edited the Adagio unchanged, apart from some small instrumental retouchings, in Detmold in January 1957, and orchestrated the Scherzo in F sharp minor with completions in April 1957.[55] His original manuscript of the latter movement, currently housed at the IGMG in Vienna, like that of the Scherzo in E minor, consists only of a transcription of the sketches, with accompanying remarks by Erwin Ratz. The editing of 'Purgatorio', carried out in April 1958 to May 1959 in 'a free structure instrumentation' ['freie Struktur-Instrumenta-tion'],[56] was the last to be completed. This movement is absent from the other originals housed in the IGMG. According to Wollschläger the Scherzo in E minor is an orchestration with completions and changes. Yet the title page in the IGMG describes it only as a synopsis of the texts. The Finale is a full-blown performing version, and was completed on 28 July 1957. Wollschläger drew up his version in what he calls 'youthful enthusiasm'[57] but then rejected it because, he says, he came to the conclusion that a masterpiece even in the form of a fragment must not be tampered with. It has been suggested that he was persuaded by Erwin Ratz – then the director of the IGMG who himself was not in favour of tampering with the manuscript that Mahler left behind – to abandon further efforts at making a 'performing version'. Yet correspondence between them shows that Wollschläger was just as extreme when it came to concern for preserving the privacy of Mahler's legacy. Curiously, he confided in a letter to Deryck Cooke that he could not stop himself adding more and more to the score and that in fact Mahler's legacy was in better hands with Cooke. Barshai met Wollschläger in Bamberg in summer 2001 when he performed his version with the Junge Deutsche Philharmonie, and the two editors expressed interest in studying each other's manuscripts.

An examination of bars 390–400 of the Finale will give a representative example of Wollschläger's insight into the interpretation of the manuscript. In bars 390–91, where Barshai read the bass notes as E sharp–F sharp and Cooke as F sharp–F sharp, Wollschläger omits these notes completely, leaving the tenor voice D–C sharp as the lowest voice. In bars 392–93 he overlooked the F clef indicated by Mahler and gave the notes scored by Cooke for the cello to the first and second violins, obviously in G clef. He felt he had to ascribe the final big 'sigh' in bar 394 to the horns, now reading these notes in F clef. Technically it could be maintained that the notes were written in F clef, yet because Mahler had started to write 'Lan[gsam]' in the top staff of page 10 of the manuscript, he wrote the notes in question one staff lower. The absence of a G clef at this point

---

[55] I am grateful to Hans Wollschläger for providing this and subsequent information regarding his work on the manuscript.

[56] In other words a full-blown orchestration.

[57] Personal communication with the author.

does not mean that the notes were to be read in F clef. In the original B-flat ending of the symphony these notes do appear in the top staff, confirming the assumption that the big 'sigh' was written in G clef. If Wollschläger had continued work on the manuscript he would presumably have corrected this misreading.

Barry Guerrero

This American scholar has not yet written his version, but provides the following account of his views on the manuscript[58] (the comments of the present author are in square brackets or given as footnotes):

> **Adagio:** I would leave the orchestration much the way it is in Cooke, possibly adding a bass roll at the end of bar 57, tam-tam in bar 194 and a bass roll in bar 198, but not too loud. The percussion additions should be subtle.[59]
>
> **Scherzo in F sharp minor:** this has been orchestrated badly [by Mahler and Cooke]. Horns and strings are simply not convincing. Wheeler is completely wrong here: too heavy and cumbersome, much heavy brass and percussion. Think of clarity as in the Rondo-Burleske [of the Ninth Symphony] or of Stravinsky or even Shostakovich. The motor elements should be much more wind-orientated, with the melody broken up and fragmented more between the various solo winds and combinations. At the beginning I would use all four bassoons instead of the clunky sounding horns. I would add trills on the minims of bars 2 and 4. Where the grace note leads to a minim, that could be doubled by a single horn. I would try unison flutes until the second half of bar 4. At that point I might switch back to oboes, but drop them down an octave. I would leave the violins out till the first big trio section! In bars 17–20 I would change the metre to 2/4. The horns have strong accents here. From bar 23 the basses and cellos should play chugging semiquavers just as they do near the end of the movement [from bar 492]. Tremolos in basses are unclear. I would vary the orchestration of the falling octave: in bar 43 use clarinets, possibly also low oboes, instead of horns [indicated by Mahler]. Also at bar 43 I would not use the high oboes and violins in unison – that is very uncharacteristic for Mahler [and yet the oboes are indicated by the composer]. At bar 55 add glockenspiel. In the second half of bar 60 replace horn by bass clarinet. In bar 83 I might take the melody away from the oboes and give it to flutes or clarinets instead. Then when the trills happen in the lower parts, I would give that to the oboes instead. From bar 93 use glockenspiel again. I consider the weakest moment in the entire Cooke version, and every subsequent version as well, to be right after bar 478 [Guerrero is in fact referring to the upbeat to bar 478]. The two pick-up notes there should be loud. The orchestra should re-enter like gang busters and not sneak back in. I would double those two pick-up notes, plus the down-beat note, with timpani and with bass drum

---

[58] The information was received in personal communication with the author, who is grateful to Guerrero for permission to publish his comments.

[59] Most of these ideas have already been realized in previous versions such as those of Mazzetti and Cooke et al./Sanderling.

on the first beat. Tuba and trombones should play that bass line, not just low strings. [Cooke and Barshai use cellos, double basses and one trombone. Thicker instrumentation would possibly further undermine the accuracy.] At bars 485 and 491 timpani should double the bass line. Again I would re-work the ending. Mazzuca & Samale have done the best job with the ending so far. Mine would nevertheless be an improvement. Wheeler's idea to add a Rute is fine, but I would use it at bar 492, and then phase it out as the trumpets begin to work their way up (and thus direct our attention towards what they are doing).

'Purgatorio' & Scherzo in E minor: in the standard Cooke version these are quite good, although just a little more reinforcement of the climaxes is needed. At the last outburst [of the Scherzo in E minor] I would place a cymbal crash on the down beat, place a timpani roll underneath the high solo trumpets, and then place a *forte* tam-tam stroke where the trombones come in with their grinding dissonance. A softer tam-tam stroke would follow a few bars later as the harmony becomes even more weird and twisted. From there to the start of the fifth movement, the tempo should be much slower.

Finale: for the opening I would use a set of deep bells somewhere between bars 18 and 21, and possibly off-stage cowbells for the very ending of the Symphony – way off in the distance. [Of the drum strokes at the beginning:] the bass drum will do – one off stage and, for the last blow, one on stage. It should be a solid *f*, not *ff*. I really rather like the roll that Chailly uses but I would not try that myself. I feel that the reprise of the first movement's expressionistic climax [from bar 275] (anti-climax, really – more like sinking into the abyss) should be greatly reinforced with percussion. Like David Hurwitz [Guerrero's adviser/assistant] I'm also not satisfied with how the climax is set up. It needs to be far more frightening and horrific. I would add tons of percussion but more importantly I would do much more with the return of the Symphony's opening motto [from bar 284]. I would have that played with trumpets and trombones in octaves – with a solid *f* dynamic. When you get to the top of the phrase, that would segue into unison horns in the upper octave giving way to the strings just a few bars later. Once the motto gets back down it would sound exactly the same as at the beginning of the Symphony. I would also get rid of the dissonant trumpet descant as it adds absolutely nothing [this is clearly marked by Mahler].

After the Symphony's opening motto, I would re-orchestrate the following chorale for brass and get rid of most of the woodwinds. An E-flat clarinet or piccolo would still be needed on the real high part, and contra bassoon for the low. I am speaking specifically about where the big tam-tam smash exists in the Cooke version [bar 267], and the music begins slowly to sink into the abyss. Again, I agree with both Carpenter and Mazzuca/Samale that bars 376–79 should be loud not soft. The music cries out for it to be loud there – one last final climax in the major. Mazzuca/Samale is really convincing at that spot. Again listen to what Mazzuca/Samale do with all the string-dominated material after the reprise of the first movement's (anti-) climax. Cooke (especially under Rattle) and Barshai both just sit on that material as though it were doing nothing, and are totally bloodless. That simply cannot be right. The concluding eight or nine minutes of the Symphony need to be vastly more passionate than they usually are.

A note on tempi and the drum strokes in the Finale

Mahler had not yet fully differentiated the tempi in his drafts. Yet the balancing of tempi is a major consideration for editor, conductor and listener alike. Slow music would obviously be conducted and orchestrated differently from fast music, and within each movement there are also changes of tempo. For example the juxtaposition and gradual merging of the Andante and Adagio tempi in the first movement are only achieved after careful balancing. In the first movement the crotchet pulse of the Andante should be distinctly faster than that of the Adagio, the unaccompanied viola melodies being only slightly slower than the accompanied version from bar 32 onwards. If the Andante is started too slow the Adagio has to move with a slow quaver pulse.

The tempi of both Scherzos and their contrasting trios also have to be weighed very carefully. If it is assumed that their main tempi are fast, the editor should probably use a lighter and more transparent orchestration and not burden the music with large amounts of added counterpoint or thickened textures. Barshai, however, argues that Mahler always wrote for the best ensembles and that therefore even a thick orchestration could work as long as it is nimbly and elegantly played.[60]

Broadcasts and CD recordings set the example for the future conductor. In the years since 1960, Goldschmidt and Ormandy began with fairly fast tempi, and then Wyn Morris and Sanderling introduced slower ones.[61] Truly divergent tempo choices became less and less frequent. Carpenter clearly felt the music at a slower tempo and orchestrated accordingly. Harold Farberman's recording of this 'arrangement', however, largely ignored its slower tempi.[62] The actuality of the sound made Farberman choose faster tempi. Nevertheless the tempi chosen by conductors of this work vary no more than those chosen for 'completed' works by Mahler.

Sometimes editors varied their tempo markings even more in response to another editor. For example in his third edition Wheeler initially wrote 'tempo giusto' for the introduction to the Finale – in other words 'work the tempo out for yourself'. After hearing the Cooke edition Wheeler changed this to 'allegretto (crotchet in tempo of end of fourth movement, rather held back)'. At the end of his fourth edition Wheeler wrote:

> In another version of this work, Deryck Cooke has considered that this Introduction is <u>slow</u>: while, in the absence of any tempo marking, this is a

---

[60] Personal communication with the author.

[61] Goldschmidt gave the première at the 1964 Proms in London on 13 August with the London Symphony Orchestra. Ormandy, Philadelphia Orchestra, 1965, Columbia 335/735; Morris, New Philharmonia, 1972, Philips 6700-067; Sanderling, Berlin Symphony Orchestra, 1979, Eterna 8 27435/Ars Vivendi 2100225 LC 7082.

[62] Philharmonica Hungarica, 1996, Deutsche Schallplatten Berlin, DS 1044-2.

possible and indeed inspiring interpretation of the Ms., I feel that the preceding Scherzo, cut off by the Bass Drum, is trying to start again, and the Adagio has, so to speak, to overcome the efforts of the Devil to go on dancing.

Whether Wheeler's response can be regarded as inspired is a matter of opinion. A case can be made for taking the crotchet of the Scherzo in E minor as equal to the somewhat held-back quaver, rather than crotchet, of the Finale. A similar example is the tempo of the Scherzo in F sharp minor. Carpenter is probably alone in choosing 'in gemächlicher Bewegung, ohne Hast'. Mazzetti disagreed with this and initially wrote 'Schnelle Viertel. (Sempre Allegro assai)', but was eventually persuaded by the present author to drop 'assai'.

In his recent award-winning recording of the Cooke edition with the Berlin Philharmonic, Simon Rattle evidently tried to milk maximum emotion from the piece, sometimes at the expense of an overall balance.[63] His initial Andante tempo is on the slow slide and although the Adagio as a whole makes frequent effective use of rubato, some of the fast sections, especially in the Scherzo in F sharp minor, seem almost out of control. This performance was broadcast live on 25 September 1999 and subsequently released, with repair takes, as a CD shortly before other well-received performances by Chailly and the Concertgebouw Orchestra.[64] Chailly takes a more sober approach and is more balanced in tempi and emotion, but as a result is possibly less exciting for some. Unfortunately, with the appearance of the successful Rattle recording, none of these performances is to be released on CD. Instead we have Chailly's first CD with the Berlin Radio Symphony Orchestra (a recording that the conductor still values), which was reissued in 1995.[65] The novelty of Chailly's latest performance of the Cooke edition is the implementation of Eduard Reeser's idea to precede the drum beat in the introduction of the Finale with a short roll rather than to retain a single stroke. Some vehemently oppose this, but to others – including the present author – it has a sense of 'rightness' despite Alma's reference to a single stroke. The extra-musical connotation of the New York fireman's cortège is nevertheless important in relation to the acoustic aspect of the completely muffled drum, which has been a continual problem for many editors. The present author has never heard or seen that the drum was actually completely muffled as specified by Mahler. He did not write 'big drum' or specify its diameter. Cooke initially considered Mahler's *sf* to be *ff*. Carpenter stuck to *p*. Barshai decided to place the drum in the far distance.

---

[63] EMI Classics, 1999, 7243 5 56972 2 6.

[64] In 2001 Chailly gave a number of performances of the work in Amsterdam, London and Lucerne, and again in June 2002 in Amsterdam. The second performance in Amsterdam was broadcast.

[65] Decca, recorded 1986, 444 872-2DX2.

Conclusion: pro and contra

There is still opposition to a 'completion' or 'performing version of the draft' of
this work. There were even objections to the publication of the facsimile. Bruno
Walter made strong efforts to persuade Alma not to publish anything on the
Tenth. Some doubt the sincerity of the editors, accusing them of seeking easy
fame and money. But certain efforts to protect Mahler's unfinished legacy are of
equally dubious sincerity. Mathias Hansen asserted that however fascinating
Mahler's manuscript for a Tenth Symphony looks, a finished Tenth will never
exist:

> For Mahler the road from draft to final result is an act of composition in
> which no subsequent arrangers should or could be involved. Therefore they
> should simply be satisfied with reinforcements and doublings of the given
> material. In a score they can merely present what, for Mahler, signified the
> starting point of the developing materials: that which would only have been
> built up through, for example, the technique of variation. Such an unavoid-
> able limitation must forgo Mahler's multi-perspectivism, the perilous,
> graduated journey of his music as it develops into distinctive new forms of
> emotional certainty – and all that remains is the certainty of an over-
> simplification that leads to exaggeration. To avoid any misunder-standings:
> this is not the fault of the subjective shortcomings of the arrangers, but of the
> inevitable absence of the composer's imagination. It so happens that this is
> not at the disposal of the arrangers in spite of their respect – or rather
> precisely because of the burden of respect.   (Hansen, 1991, p. 53)[66]

This statement gives the impression that any 'completion' would necessarily be
a fraud, the editor's attempt to realize the incomplete a futile exercise because of
an imposed lack of compositional imagination. But should the German saying 'in
der Beschränkung zeigt sich der Meister', used above in connection with
Carpenter's edition, not also apply to editorial intervention? Hansen's claim that
the material left behind by Mahler is the starting point – and no more – of his
development of the materials is possibly even harder to prove than Cooke's claim

---

66 'Für Mahler ist der Weg vom Entwurf zum Resultat ein Kompositionsakt, auf
den sich spätere Bearbeiter nicht einlassen dürfen und können. Sie müssen daher,
vereinfacht gesagt, sich mit Verstärkungen, mit Verdopplungen des gegebenen Materials
begnügen; sie können nur das in eine Partitur projizieren, was bei Mahler den
Ausgangspunkt für Materialentfaltung bedeutet hätte, was etwa durch die
Variantentechnik erst strukturiert worden wäre. Solch unausweichliche Beschränkung
muß die Vielsichtigkeit Mahlers, muß die gefahrvolle Gradwanderung seiner Musik, die
sich zu einer eigenen, neuartigen Bewegungsform von Sicherheit entfaltet, verfehlen –
und es bleibt die Sicherheit der Simplifizierung, die in die Vergrößerung mündet. Das ist,
um keine Mißverständnisse aufkommen zu lassen, nicht einem subjektiven Versagen der
Bearbeiter anzulasten, sondern der unumgänglichen Abwesenheit von kompositorischer
Imagination. Sie steht nun einmal den Bearbeitern nicht zu Verfügung, bei alle Pietät
oder gerade wegen des Zwangs zur Pietät.'

that the 'sketch contains the whole essence of what the composer has to say' (1961, p. 353). Paul Banks writes:

> I believe that the real significance of any debate about completions is not the possibility that any definite conclusions about their validity might be reached, but the extent to which it encourages us to re-examine the basis of aesthetic experience and critical judgement.
>
> (1991, p. 15)

Those for and against would find common ground with regard to the status of the unfinished and the editor's input only if they were to study all sketches and drafts of the manuscript without prejudice.[67] Only when this has been done will an objective evaluation of an editor's input be possible, and opinions become a little more constructive than an instinctive 'hands-off' or 'against love there can be no final argument' (Matthews, 1991, p. 73).[68]

We can all make up our own minds as to whether the unfinished manuscript pages for Mahler's Tenth Symphony should lead to 'performing versions' and, if so, whether these versions are satisfactory when actually performed. Six 'performing versions' are now available. Most have already been recorded more than once. Apart from certain obvious features, it remains very difficult to differentiate between the editions. Although it is essential to compare each edition carefully with all the drafts of Mahler's manuscript, as well as to compare the different solutions chosen by the editors, only the Cooke score is available to purchase, making an assessment of the others difficult. The other versions are for hire at their respective publishing houses. The Wheeler version will probably be for sale in an edition from the Colorado Mahlerfest. The facsimile editions have long been sold out and are not complete. Because of this the present author is currently planning to edit diplomatic, chronological and user-friendly transcriptions of all the extant manuscript material of the Tenth Symphony as a contribution to the never-ending fascination with Mahler's final, unfinished work.[69]

---

[67] For some, even perusing the facsimile is seen as prying into Mahler's personal property. For others, this led to a lifelong fascination and desire to hear a realized form of the 'work'.

[68] The implication of this statement is that only critics of the work have reason at their disposal, and that love for the music obscures this quality.

[69] For details of this plan see Bouwman, 2001. Parallel to the author's work, Steven Coburn's recently completed thesis (2002) discusses four basic topics: (1) the reformulation of the layers of chronology; (2) Mahler's traditional construction of form and his progressive complicating of this; (3) the hypothesis of multi-tonic complexes, in line with the work of Robert Bailey and Christopher O. Lewis (1984), but in contrast with the views of Steven Bruns (1989); and (4) the hypothesis that aspects of Mahler's life are encoded into the music itself.

Appendix

Markings and inscriptions in those books of the Alma Mahler-Werfel Collection numbered (1)–(25) in the catalogue in Chapter 3

(1) Richard Dehmel, *Erlösungen. Gedichte und Sprüche*

Page number(s) and text	Marking[1]
Complete texts of poems: 24, 'Das alte Lied'; 38, 'Erleuchtung'; 43, 'Leises Lied'; 44–46, 'Frühlingsgebet'; 105, 'Ruf'; 107–8, 'Die Busse'; 130–31, 'Die Seemannsfrau'; 136, 'Ansturm'; 143, 'Narzissen'; 208, 'Wiegenlied'; 217, 'Auf See'; 249–51, 'Nachruf an Nietzsche'; 310, 'Letzte Bitte'	a) pencil: either I, O∼,), or └
173: last two lines of 'Vergleiche'	
Titles of poems: 41, 'Die Rose'; 100, 'Deine Nähe'; 171, 'Landung'; 196, 'Spruch in die Ehe'	either — — or **x**
299–308: above text of 'Eine Lebensmesse Dichtung für Musik. (Dem Componisten Conrad Ansorge)'	inscription, probably in Alma's hand: 'VORGETRAGEN VOM DICHTER AM 6 MÄRZ 1904'
309: above text of 'Nach einem Regen'	inscription, probably in Alma's hand: 'VORGETRAGEN VOM DICHTER AM 6 MÄRZ 1904'
'Nach einem Regen'	⊂

---

[1] Key to symbols: I vertical line in margin; II double vertical line in margin; III triple vertical line in margin; IIII quadruple vertical line in margin (further multiple vertical lines as marked);) curved upright line in margin;)) double curved upright line in margin; — — underlining of text; = double underlining of text; ≡ triple underlining of text; ∼ underlining of text with wavy line; ≈ double underlining of text with wavy line; └ square bracket around text; ⊂ curved bracket around text; { this type of curled bracket against text; [this type of bracket against text; / diagonal line in margin; // double diagonal line in margin; X crossed diagonal lines in margin; **x** small cross in margin; + upright cross in margin; * asterisk in margin; O encircling of text; O O double encircling of text; O∼ encircling of text with wavy line; ≠ text crossed through; S vertical wavy line in margin; ⌐ horizontal wavy line in margin; —I horizontal line in margin; ? question mark in margin; ! exclamation mark in margin; V V-shaped sign in margin; ∧ inverted V-shaped sign in margin; ⊤ or ⊥ signs used to denote an insertion in text; √ tick in margin.

495

Complete texts of poems: 53, 'Jetzt und immer'; 95, 'Frühlingsglück' [5-note musical theme notated above this poem in the top right-hand corner of p. 95]; 106, 'Geständnis'; 129, 'Stimme des Abends'; 146–47, 'Lobgesang'; 296, 'Pfingstlied'

b) red-brown pencil:
either I, **S**,), or ∟

(2) Eckermann, *Gespräche mit Goethe in den letzten Jahren seines Lebens* 1. Bd. 2. Bd.

Page number(s) and text	Marking
	) (light-blue ink)
	Pencil (unless otherwise indicated):
1823	
Thursday 19 June: 'So war nun meine Existenz ... verschiedener Art' ['Thus my subsistence ... various sorts']²	—
Thursday 18 September: poetic creative processes; '"Nehmen Sie sich in Acht ... nichts daran verloren"' ['"Beware ... lost nothing"']; '"Es ist aber jetzt keine Zeit ... Schritt gelten"' ['"Past is the time ... a goal"']; '"Machen Sie vorderhand ... Zeitschriften"' ['"... If at present ... periodicals"'];	—
'" Die Welt ist so groß ... halte ich nichts"' ['"The world is so great ... out of the air"']	—
'"Bei einem großen ... scheitert man"' ['"With a great poem ... shipwreck"']	=
'Ich sagte Goethen ... etwas Gutes' ['I told Goethe ... something good']	//
'"Besonders warne ich ... selten reif"' ['I especially warn you ... seldom ripe']	X
'"Ferner ... zustande kommen"' ['"Further ... accomplished"']	
'"Bei einem gegebenen ... nach seiner Weise"' ['"With a given ... his own fashion"']	—
'"Ja ich rate ... nach seiner Weise"' ['"Indeed, I advise ... his own fashion"']	—
Tuesday 21 October: 'Ich fragte darauf Goethe ... der Pflanze hineinsieht' ['I then asked Goethe ... inner life of the plant']	—
Saturday 25 October: '"Was zwanzig Jahre ... so ward es nichts"' ['"What has kept ... failure"']	—
'"Geist und irgend Poesie ... hervorlockten"' ['"Intellect ... poetic feeling"']	—
Monday 3 November: '"Die wenigsten Künstler ... malen!"' ['"Very few artists ... painted?"']; '"Das müßte schlimm sein ... Ewigkeit"' [It would be a pity ... eternity"];	—
'"Das müßte schlimm sein"'; '"wenn Sie das nicht sollten"'; '"Beharren Sie nur dabei"' ['"It would be a pity"'; '"if it were not so"'; '"Only persist in this"']	≠
Friday 14 November: Schiller's *Wallenstein*; '"Es geht mir mit Schiller ... nichts helfen konnten"' ['"I have ... profit him"']; '"Es war nicht Schillers Sache ... durchgesprochen hat"' ['"It was not Schiller's plan ... scene after scene"']	—

² Translations taken from J. W. Goethe, *Conversations with Eckermann* (1823–32), trans. John Oxenford (San Francisco: North Point Press, 1984).

"'Dagegen war es ... vollendet war'" ['"On the other hand ... completed"']

Sunday 16 November: "'Zugleich ... als möglich'" ['"It is ... exaggeration"']

1824

Friday 2 January: resistance to public criticism; "'Jenes ungestörte ... unverhüllt entgegen!'" ['"That undisturbed ... original nature?"']

"'Wer sich heutzutage ... ist verloren'" ['"He who does not ... is lost"']

Sunday 4 January: "'Man war im Grunde ... heutigen Tag'" ['"People were never ... present day"']

"'Man braucht nur den *Egmont* ... zu gelten'" ['"We need only read *Egmont* ... of the people"']

Tuesday 27 January: abstention from public business as means of increasing creative output; "'Der Verlust ist Schmerzlich ... sie nicht wie ich'" ['"The loss is painful ... without their being able to learn mine"']

Wednesday 25 February: 'Goethe zeigte mir heute ... "gemischten Welt kommen"' ['Today, Goethe showed me ... "mixed society"']

"'In dem, was ich selber ... unmöglich gewesen'" ['"For myself ... impossible"']

"'immer als Royalist behauptet'" ['"always been a royalist"']

"'Die Beschäftigung mit Unsterblichkeitsideen ... bessere Gedanken'" ['"This preoccupation with immortality ... better thoughts"']

Thursday 26 February: *Goetz von Berlichingen* and artistic anticipation; "'Ich schrieb meinen *Götz von Berlichingen* ... Antizipation besitzen'" ['"I wrote *Goetz von Berlichingen* ... anticipation"']

"'*Goetz von Berlichingen*'"; "'von zweiundzwanzig'" ['"*Goetz von Berlichingen*"; "at two-and-twenty"']

"'Antizipation'" ['"Anticipation"']

"'Überhaupt ... Persiflage geworden'" ['"Generally ... persiflage"']

"'Allerdings ... z. B. zu sagen'" ['"Certainly ... but the lines"']

[In the same paragraph]: "'wie'" "'wie'" "'wie'" ['"how" "how"']

above "'Es ist aber', sagte ich 'im ganzen Faust keine Zeile'" ['"Yet", said I, "every line of *Faust* bears marks"']

"'Mag sein ... nicht wahrnehmen'" ['"Perhaps so ... phenomena"']

Saturday 28 February: "'Es gibt ... das Höchste geleistet'" ['"There are ... accomplished"']

"'Die Manier ... zustande kommen'" ['"Mannerism ... produced"']

Sunday 29 February: "'Die Konstitution in Frankreich ... geleitet worden'" ['"The constitution of France ... directed by such means"']

"'Rhein mit der Donau'" ['"Rhine with the Danube"']

Monday 22 March: resting in the shade of oak trees; "'Bei großer Sommerhitze ... fuhren zurück'" ['"I know ... to the house"'] [Includes the following sentence: ['"ich sitze hier gerne an warmen Sommertagen nach Tische, wo denn auf diesen Wiesen und auf dem ganzen Park umher oft eine Stille herrscht, von der die Alten sagen würden: daß der Pan schlafe'" ['"In hot summer days, I like to sit here after dinner; and often over the

Marginal annotations:
= =
—
— —
= (faint, thick pencil strokes)
—
) (light-blue ink)
— (light-blue ink)
—
=
S
—
inscription not in Mahler's hand
= =
? (in margin)
=
— —

meadows and the whole park such stillness reigns, that the ancients would say: "Pan sleeps"'"]

Tuesday 30 March: Hamlet, *Zauberflöte* and German public; "'Es wird schwer halten ... an die Dornen'" ["'It will be very difficult ... he goes to the thorns'"] / —

Wahlverwandtschaften; "'Deshalb steht auch der Lafontaine ... lassen können'" ["'La Fontaine, too, ... let each other alone'"] —

Tieck and Shakespeare as great talents; "'Tieck ist ... zu verehren habe'" ["'Tieck is ... reverence'"] = —

Sunday 2 May: "'Und dann ... sich stellen wie Sie wollen'" ["'And then ... whether you like it or not'"] |

"'Er sprach darauf besonders viel über die Farbenlehre ... schlechte Erbschaft zugefallen'" ["'' He talked a great deal about his theory of colours ... bad inheritance!'"] | (very thick)

"'Wir sprachen darauf ... oder Schüsseln'" ["'We then talked of ... pots or dishes'"]

Wednesday 24 November: difference between German and French literature and increasing interest in German literature among French writers; "'Das Gespräch wendete ... nach außen zu wenden'" ["'We then talked of ... without for means'"] ⊂ |

"'Besonders aber ist ... das Rechte'" ["'But, especially ... the Frenchman'"] | (very thick)

subjectivity and objectivity in young German poets; "'Wir sprachen darauf über unsere eigene Literatur ... nicht zu denken'" ["'We then talked about our own literature ... never thought of'"] **X** (in both margins)

Friday 3 December: "'Und noch heutzutage ... nicht gemäß ist'" ["'And in our own day ... not suited to you'"] —

Thursday 9 December: "'Goethe erzählte mir darauf ... einen Spaß zu machen suchen'" ["'He then told me ... a good turn'"] —

1825

Tuesday 18 January: the true power of poetry; "'Das aber die wahre Kraft ... in der Irre'" ["'Nobody dreams ... much mistaken'"]; Byron and *Faust*, Scott and *Egmont*; "'Ich habe ... zu loben als zu tadeln'" ["'The greater part ... praised than censured'"]; Schiller; "'Er griff in einen großen Gegenstand ... auf der Bühne kein Glück machen'" ["'He seized boldly ... cannot succeed on the stage'"] — —

Thursday 24 February: Euripides and Shakespeare; "'Goethe gab mir recht ... durch Erzählung'" ["'Goethe agreed with me ... by narration'"] — —

Byron's rejection of the hereditary and patriotic; his perpetual negation; "'Daß er sich vom Herkömmlichen ... reine Freude finde'" ["'Not only did he ... finds pure joy'"]; his unreflective inspiration; "'Aber alles ... wissen nicht wie'" ["'But where he will create ... how it was done'"]; his injurious aristocratic rank; "'Der hohe Stand ... in den mittleren Ständen finden'" ["'His high rank ... in the middle classes'"] = = =

Tuesday 22 March: "'Ich sah in schöne Augen ... zu Bette zu halten'" ["I saw in beautiful eyes ... "in bed —

vertical inscription against both marked passages:
'Auch Stendhal' probably not in Mahler's hand

vertical light-blue ink inscription in margin: 'und Tolstoi?' probably not in Mahler's hand

to-day"']; '"Aber ich suchte auch ... einen Guten Tag zu machen"' ['"But I also sought to raise ...
a merry day with them"']; '"Sehr viel", erwiderte Goethe ... "was ich ihr schuldig war"'
['"A great deal ... what I owed to it"'] |

Thursday 14 April: '"Sein ganzes Metier ... sich vorzugsweise eigne"' ['"His whole profession ... he was
adapted"'] | —

Wednesday 20 April: '"Und so sehe ich ... von ganzen Jahrtausenden"' ['"Thus I am ever convinced ...
thousands of years"']   ? (light-blue ink in margin)

Wednesday 27 April: '"Zelters Brief ... als Blume gewähren kann"' ['"Zelter's letter ... nature can produce"']
'"Nun heißt es wieder ... als die seinigen"' ['"It is further said ... better appointed than his"']; '"Soll ich
denn also ... Besten ist"' ['"If then I must ... common weal"'] | (light-blue ink)

Sunday 1 May: Homer, Euripides; '"Wir sprachen über den Bogen des Odysseus ... eine große Zeit!"' ['"We
spoke about the bow of Ulysses ... Euripides!"']
Sophocles; '"Hatten die Stücke des Euripides ... Euripides selber!"' ['"If the pieces of Euripides ...
Euripides himself?"'] | (light-blue ink)

Thursday 12 May: '"Nun streitet sich ... streiten können"' ['"For twenty years ... dispute"'] | (light-blue ink)
Wednesday 15 October: '"Bisher glaubte die Welt ... daran zu glauben"' ['"Till lately ...believe them"'] || (light-blue ink)
'"Und dann! ... verschiedene Dinge"' ['"After all ... different things"'] | (light-blue ink)
'"Sobald wir ... ihren Glanz breiten"' ['"If we grant freedom ... hidden sun"']   = ∪

1826

Sunday evening 29 January: '"Wenn einer singen ... in Manier zugrunde geht"' ['"If a person learns to sing ...
ruined by mannerism"'];   )
'"Ich will Ihnen ... objectiver Natur waren"' ['"I will now tell you ... objective nature"'] |
'"Das Gespräch lenkte sich ... in ihrer Wahrheit zeichnete"' ['"The conversation now turned ... just as they
were"']   )
'"Nein", sagte Goethe ... "geht nicht hinein"' ['"No", said Goethe ... "stay away, as I do"'] |
Thursday 16 February: 'Wir kamen auf Napoleon ... "das war alles"' ['We then talked of Napoleon ... "that
was all"']
'"Wir Deutschen ... der Gegenstand liegt zu entfernt"' ['"We Germans ... too far off"']

Easter Day 26 March: 'Goethe war heute ... Lord Byron' ['To-day at dinner ... Lord Byron']   ? inscription above question mark: 'und Kleist'
Wednesday 26 July: the symbolic nature of theatrical literature, e.g. Molière's *Tartuffe*; 'Diesen Abend ... "eine
Exposition ist!"' ['This evening ... "the first scene!"'] |
Within this passage: 'Ich fragte ... "eine Exposition ist!"' ['I asked ... "the first scene!"'] |
Wednesday 8 November: Byron and *Macbeth*; '"Ja", sagte Goethe ... sich mochte gedacht haben' ['"Yes",
said Goethe ... Goethe's meaning']   ≡
   |

499

Wednesday 29 November: Delacroix's *Faust* lithographs; '"Ja", sagte ich ... ihre Imagination hinausgehend finden!"' ['"Yes", said I ... passing his imagination!"']

Within this passage: '"Herr Delacroix"' ["M. Delacroix"]

Monday 11 December: Humboldt; '"Was ist das für ein Mann! ... Jahre verlebt"' ['"What a man he is ... lived for years"']

Wednesday 13 December: talent and Mozart, Leonardo da Vinci; '"Man sieht ... aus der Welt verschwunden"' ['"We see ... vanished from the world"']

Italienische Reise: 'Ich sagte, daß ich dieser Tage ... "nichts von Bedeutung"' ['I said I had lately ... "nothing of importance"']

Wednesday 20 December: *Farbenlehre* discussion; 'Ich erzählte Goethen nach Tisch ... "in seiner Blöße darzustellen"' ['I told Goethe after dinner ... "expose it in its nudity"']

1827
Sunday 14 January: Zelter's song *Um Mitternacht*; 'Nach einer Pause ... "etwas Ewiges, Unverwüstliches"' ['After a pause ... "in the melody!"']

Within this passage: '"Es hat in der Melodie etwas Ewiges"' ['"There is something eternal ... in the melody"']

'"Nachdem die Gesellschaft ... meinen eigenen Schriften!"' ['"After the party ... my own writings!"']

Monday evening 15 January: progress of *Wanderjahre*. *Faust* Part II: 'Nach Vollendung ... "Kraft des Augenblicks"' ['After the completion ... "strength at the moment"']

Thursday evening 18 January: 'Der Löwe ist ... Frommer Sinn und Melodie'. 'The lion ... the tyrant of the wood']: botanical simile for the novel; '"Um für den Gang ... etwas schreiben will"' ['"As a similitude ... to write anything"']

visual-art simile for *Wanderjahre*; '"Die übrigen einzelnen Erzählungen ... schriftstellerischen Produktionen"' ['"The single tales ... literary productions"']

nature in literature, Schiller and Byron; '"Aber weil mein früheres Landschaftszeichnen ... so hat er genug"' ['"but, because my early drawings of landscapes ... he has enough"']

'"Ich bin bei meinen Reisen ... zu behandeln gewußt"' ['"I have, on my journeys ... to treat me"']

Sunday evening 21 January: Solger's letter to Tieck on *Wahlverwandtschaften*; 'Folgerungen bewunderten"' ['"He is not so happy ... sequence of the reasoning"']; '"In seinen philosophischen Untersuchungen ... "Hoch vor allen ... freilich sehr schön"' ['"High above all ... really very fine"']

Monday evening 29 January: imminent publication of *Helena*; discussion of turning it into an opera; Meyerbeer; '"Es ist die *Helena* ... Änderung nicht machen dürfen"' ['"This", said he, "is *Helena* ... the intended alteration"']

Within this passage: '"dem Eingeweihten ... Sängerinnen besetzt werden müssen"' ['"the higher import ... male and female"']

Marginal marks (top to bottom): — = — — — **?** (light-blue ink) —— (light-blue ink) / — — — = — — — **X** — —

Passage	Marking
"sowie nachher im Teile der Oper'"; "'besetzt werden müssen'" ["'and the operatic part must be sustained'"]	–
"'Da sieht man'", sagte Goethe ... "schwere Sache'" ["'There you see'", said Goethe ... "difficult matters'"]	X
'Hieran knüpften ... "als wäre es was'" ['Some reflections ... "as if it were something'"]	–
Wednesday 31 January: unnamed Chinese novel compared to *Hermann und Dorothea*; "'Chinesischen Roman ... ganz das Gegenteil sind?'" ['"Chinese novel! ... exactly the contrary?"']; "'Einer macht es ein wenig besser ... diese Epoche zu beschleunigen'" ['"One makes it a little better ... hasten its approach"'] value of ancient Greeks as literary model compared to Calderón and *Nibelungen*; "Aber auch bei solcher ... uns daraus aneignen'" ["'But, while we thus ... so far as it goes'"]	IIIII /// (below last line of this passage)
"Manzoni ... mein *Egmont*" ["'Manzoni ... my *Egmont*'"]	=
"'Und wozu wären denn die Poeten ... nicht verstanden'" ["'What would be the use of poets ... not have understood him'"]	I
Euripides, Aeschylus and Sophocles (*Philoctetes* and *Phaethon*); "Darin", fuhr Goethe fort ... "unnütze Arbeit sein'" ["'Here, again'", continued Goethe ... useless task'"]	I (both margins, though only last two sentences marked in right margin) –
Within this passage: "'haben wir jetzt an den Philokteten ... und am besten'" ["'a fine example in Philoctetes ... Sophocles'"]	I
"Aber die Art ... Zug von Belvedere war es aber wider nicht'" ["'But the manner of doing ... Belvedere'"]	))
"Ich habe sie dieser Tage ... kann ich nicht loben'" ["'I have not touched it of late ... I cannot commend'"]	III
Thursday evening 1 February: "Vielleicht", sagte Goethe ... das Ganze'" ["'Perhaps'", said Goethe ... the whole'"]	///
"Die griechische Tragödie ... heiterer Natur ist'" ["'The Greek tragedy ... lies at the foundation'"]	) I
"Sie mögen recht haben ... und anwendet'" ["'You may be right ... by analogy'"]	I (very faint) I
"'Und dann, um von den Schülern ... die Farben lehre geschrieben'" ["'Then, the scholars ... theory of colours'"]	I
'Unter den Deutschen ... "Verwirrung wieder oben auf" [' Among the Germans ... "before we are aware"']	I
"So rütteln sie jetzt ... das ist das beste'" ["'Thus they are now pulling to pieces ... let others go as they please'"]	) I
Wednesday 7 February: 'Goethe schalt heute ... "auf die Pfaffen" ['To-day Goethe spoke severely ... "against the priests"']	I (very thick) I
Wednesday 21 February: 'Bei Goethe zu Tisch ... "Unternehmungsgeiste vorbehalten'" ['Dined with Goethe ... "enterprising spirit"']	I
"'bedeutende Handelsstädte ... fünfzig Jahre auszuhalten'" ["'important commercial towns ... fifty years more for the purpose'"]	
Wednesday 28 March: discussion of Sophocles' *Oedipus*, *Antigone* and *Philoctetes*; "'Hierbei'", sagte Goethe ... ihn zeugen könnte'"; ["'Here'", said Goethe ... nobody to beget one'"]; "Wir sprachen darauf über Sophokles ... sein Metier wie einer'" ["'We conversed further on Sophocles ... understood his craft thoroughly'"]; "'Die Ähnlichkeit mit dem Philoktet ... Körperlichkeit zu gewinnen'" ["'The resemblance to ...'"]	

501

Passage	Marginal marking
Philoctetes ... fullness for the piece'"]	
Within these passages: "'Ajax'", "'Hercules'"	
"'Sophokles ging aber bei seinen Stücken ... und folgen mußte'" ["'But Sophocles ... obliged to follow'"];	— — (dark-blue ink)
"'Wenn Polyneikes ... des Toten umherschleppen'" ["'When Polyneices ... from the dead body'"]	= =
"'Denn", sagte sie ... "ihn zeugen könnte'" ["'For', says she ... "nobody to beget one"'"]	≡
"'gar zu sehr als ein dialektisches Kalkül erscheint'" ["'to savour too much of dialectical calculation'"];	/
"'In beiden Stücken ... körperlichen Gebrechen leidend'" ["'In each piece ... bodily infirmities'"];	
"'Ich kenne und liebe Molière ... ein Ton des feinen Umgangs'" ["'I have known and loved Molière ... tone of good society'"]	S (light-blue ink)
"'Ein Dichter aber, den Sokrates ... als auf den Knien'" ["'A poet whom Socrates ... upon his knees'"]	I (light-blue ink)
Sunday 1 April: "'Durch Gott selber ... begabten Gemütern'" ["'Through God himself ... gifted minds'"]	) (light-blue ink)
"'Von Corneille ... zum Fürsten machen würde'" ["'From Corneille ... make a prince of him'"]	I (light-blue ink, both margins)
"'er ihn zum Fürsten machen würde'" ["'he would make a prince of him'"]	— — (light-blue ink)
recommendation to study Molière, Shakespeare; "'Man studiere nicht ... immer die Griechen'" ["'Not contemporaries ... always the Greeks'"]	=
Within this passage: "'aber vor allen Dingen die alten Griechen und immer die Griechen'" ["'but, above all things, the old Greeks, and always the Greeks'"]	— — (light-blue ink), followed by !!! (light-blue ink)
Wednesday 11 April: "'Diesen Zustand der Atmosphäre ... nicht hinreichen'" ["'This state of the atmosphere ... insufficient to fathom'"]	S (light-blue ink)
"'Ihr müßtet wie ich ... kaum eines Weiteren'" ["'You ought like me ... anything further'"]; "'Lessing hält sich ... Resultate habe ich ausgesprochen'" ["'Lessing ... I have discovered'"]	I
Wednesday 18 April: "'Wächst sie endlich ... in Erstaunen zu setzen'" ["'If, lastly ... creates astonishment'"]	I
Within this passage; "'man von ihr sage: es walte in ihr etwas, das fähig sei, uns in Erstaunen zu setzen'" ["'one can say of it, 'There is in that oak something that creates astonishment''"]	I
"'Du hast im Grunde recht ... die Vernunft des Autors wider herausfindet'" ["'You are right ... the author's reason'"]	I
discussion of Rubens landscape and Macbeth; artist's relation to nature; "'Es ist der mächtige Schatten ... ihre eigenen Gesetze hat'" ["'But this dark ground ... laws of its own'"]	I vertical inscription in margin: 'Kokoschka'
"'Der Künstler hat ... geradezu von der Natur abgeschrieben'" ["'The artist has ... exactly from Nature'"];	=
"'Ich habe Kinder aufgesäugt usw.'" ["'I have given suck, etc.'"]; "'Er hat keine Kinder! usw.'" ["'He has no children!'"]	=
"'Diese Worte des Macduff ... wieder anschauen und genießen'" ["'These words of Macduff ... with the same spirit'"]	I
"'Shakespeare läßt den Macbeth ... bedeutend zu sein'" ["'Shakespeare does not make Macbeth ... significant for the moment'"]	II (some crossing of lines)
Tuesday 24 April: "'August Wilhelm von Schlegel ist hier ... kosmetischer Mittel'" ["'August Wilhelm von	S

Schlegel is here ... cosmetic means'"]	Vertical inscription 'Schindler [illegible word]' in margin
Thursday 3 May: "'Ich habe gar nichts dawider ... auf einsamen Wege durchzuhelfen'" ['I have nothing to oppose to this ... our solitary way'"] on the poor reception of German folk poetry'; "'Allein was so davon lebendig geworden ... Stellen des Tasso sangen!'" ["'But which of these so lives among us ... Italian fishermen!'"]	L (light-blue ink); vertical pencil inscription 'Werfel!' in margin
Sunday 6 May: "'Von allem diesem erzählte ich Schillern ... sein bewundernswürdiges Gedicht schreb'" ['I related all this to Schiller ... his admirable play'"]	S (light-blue ink)
'Wir freuen uns ... zu bringen gesucht' ['We were pleased ... to represent by it']	I (light-blue ink)
Within this passage: "auf den *Tasso*'" ["upon *Tasso*'"]	I (light-blue ink)
"'Idee?'' sagte Goethe, – "'das ich nicht wüßte!'" ["'Idea!' said Goethe, "as if I knew anything about it'"]	! (written after this passage in light-blue ink)
"'Wollte ich jedoch einmal ... desto besser'" ["'If I still wished ... the better it is'"]	I (light-blue ink)
Within this passage: "'wären etwa meine *Wahlverwandschaften*'" ["'is probably my *Wahlverwandschaften*'"]	— (light-blue ink)
Thursday 5 July: "'Als der Kanzler und Coudray gingen ... die Toten erreicht haben'" ["'When the Chancellor and Coudray departed ... reached the body'"]	III
"'Ich habe den Roderik Random ... Ich versprach dieses zu tun'" ["'I have often heard the praises of Roderick Random ... I promised to do so'"]	I
'Wir sprachen darauf über die beiden Foskari ... Frauen zeichne' ['We then spoke of the Two Foscari ... excellent women']	x (light-blue ink)
Within this passage: 'beiden Foskari' ['Two Foscari']	— (light-blue ink)
"'Seine Frauen ... Homer alles vorweggenommen'" ["'His women ... the most prudent'"]	I
"'Ich konnte als Repräsentanten ... ich will es euch nicht verraten'" ["'I could not ... I will not tell you how'"]	I
Within this passage: "'der gegenwärtige Tag selbst'" ["'the present day itself'"]	— (light-blue ink)
"'Allerdings'', sagte ich ... zu Hause ist und sein mag und soll'" ["'Certainly', said I ... always should be, at home'"]	I (light-blue ink)
"'Ich freute mich dieses bedeutenden Wortes und merkte es mir'" ["'I rejoiced at this important saying and bore it in mind'"]	≠ (light-blue ink; possible misplaced underlining)
Monday evening 9 July: 'Ich fand Goethe allein ... zubereitet habe' ['I found Goethe alone ... a large piece of him']	I (light-blue ink)
Within this passage: 'und sich ein gutes Stück davon zubereitet habe' ['and dressed a large piece of him']	— (light-blue ink)
"'Mich wundert'' ... dem Menschen sei' ["'I wonder'' ... like men']	I (light-blue ink)
"'Mir ist für die Franzosen ... noch nicht sehr weit gebracht'" ["'I have no fears for the French ... indirect mode'"]	I
Within this passage: "'Hans, zieh mir die Steifel aus! ... noch nicht sehr weit gebracht'" ["'Hans, pull off him'"]	I (in both margins)

my boots ... indirect mode'"]

Passage	Marginal mark
Sunday 15 July: 'Goethe fuhr fort, die englischen Zeitungen zu lesen ... Fouqué' ['Goethe continued reading the English newspapers ... Fouqué']	≠ (diagonal line through paragraph)
"'Jene haften zu sehr am Realen ... mit großem Geiste'" ["'They [the French] stick too much to the real ... upon this point'"]	IIIII (some lines diagonally joined)
Within this passage: "'immer Aristokraten'" ["'always aristocrats'"]	— — (light-blue ink)
Wednesday 18 July: "'Ich habe Ihnen zu verkündigen ... durchaus vollkommen ist'" ["'I must announce to you ... absolutely perfect'"]	I (light-blue ink)
Saturday 21 July: "'Sie wissen, Aristoteles sagt vom Trauerspiele, es müsse Furcht erregen, wenn es gut sein solle'" ["'You know Aristotle says of tragedy, 'It must excite fear, if it is to be good'"]	— — (light-blue ink)
"'wenn Wir ein moralisches Übel ... im Leser oder Zuschauer'" ["'a moral evil ... in reader or spectator'"]	x (light-blue ink)
"'Zweitens ist ihm die katholische Religion ... revolutionären Reibungen'" ["'Secondly, the Catholic religion ... revolutionary collisions'"]	) (with two oblique strokes through it)
Within this passage: "'die er als Protestant nicht gehabt haben würde'" ["'that he could not have had as a Protestant'"]	— — (light-blue ink)
Monday 23 July: 'Ich ging ihm daher entgegen ... anderer Art verhandelt wurden' ['I therefore went to meet him ... subjects of another kind']	S (light-blue ink)
Within this passage: "'Ich sagte Ihnen doch neulich ... unerträglich werden'" ["'I told you lately ... a dry chronicle'"]	=
Wednesday 25 July: "'Ich habe mir die Freiheit genommen ... eine Familie für sich'" ["'I have taken the liberty ... family of her own'"]	I
Monday 24 September: Goethe berates younger poets for their negativity; 'Mit Goethe nach Berka ... poetisch zu Sinne'" ["'I went with Goethe to Berka ... 'weakness to deal with'"]	I (very thick)
'Ich verlebte darauf mit Goethe ... diese Einleitung' ['I passed, afterwards, with Goethe ... this introduction']	I (light-blue ink)
Within this passage: 'des "Faust"' ['of *Faust*']	— — (light-blue ink)
Wednesday 26 September: "'Wenn man von dieser Höhe ... über diesem Berge fliegt' ["'Looking down from this height ... fly over this mountain?'"]	=
Sunday 7 October: "'Wir waren, wie gesagt ... fataler Geruch strömte'" ["'We were, as I have said ... a drawer near me'"]	I
"'Als ich sie öffnete ... allerlei Erinnerungen und Gesprächen'" ["'When I opened it ... conversations and recollections'"]	=
"'Ich hatte", sagte ich ... "wieder zu den andern'" ["'I had", said I ... "back to the others'"]	≠ (diagonal line through paragraphs)
"'Dieses Ihr Knabenereignis ... Zukunft gestattet ist'" ["'This boyish adventure ... is accorded it'"]	) (light-blue ink)
"'Wir haben alle etwas von elektrischen ... Hausgenossen triebe'" ["'We all have some electrical ... rest of the household'"]	I

Mark	Entry
| (light-blue ink)	"'sie werden unwillkürlich ... Zeichen und Wunder!'" ["'they are involuntarily ... signs and wonders!'"]
| (light-blue ink)	"Die Straße war ... nicht getäuscht hatte" ["'The street was ... invisible influence'"]
|	*Jena, Monday 8 October:* "Alle diese äußeren Dinge ... und in Erstaunen zu setzen'" ["'All these outward things ... from the humming bird to the ostrich – is astonishing'"]
| (light-blue ink)	"so hat man wiederum zu bewundern ... so wäre damit manches Rätsel gelöst'" ["'we must still wonder that Nature ... unravel many enigmas'"]
≠ (diagonal line through paragraph)	"'und man könnte mit Überzeugung sagen ... die ihn anrufen'" ["'and it could be said ... call upon Him'"]
| (light-blue ink)	"'Ich hatte im vorigen Sommer ... von den alten Rotkehlchen füttern ließen'" ["'Last summer ... by the old robins!'"]
	"'Das ist einer der besten ... Moses und die Propheten'" ["'That is one of the best ... Moses and the prophets'"]

1828

Mark	Entry
S	*Tuesday 11 March:* reference to *Tristram Shandy* and Napoleon; genius and artistic productivity: Dürer, Holbein, Mozart, Oken, Humboldt; 'Ich bin seit mehreren Wochen ... "und der so gut bedient wäre!'" ['For several weeks ... "and who would be so well served?"']
|	entelechy; 'Ich konnte nicht umhin einige hochstehende deutsche Männer zu erwähnen ... "besonderer Produktivität wahrnehmen'" ['I could not forbear mentioning some Germans of high standing ... "singular productiveness"'];
	Goethe himself (*Geschwister, Clavigo, Divan, Faust*); 'Ich hatte in meinem Leben eine Zeit ... noch nicht verwirrt haben'" ["'There was a time when ... the trifles of daily life'"]
|	Shakespeare (*Hamlet*); "'Sodann aber giebt es eine Produktivität ... lieber zu vertändeln und zu verschlafen'" ["'However, there is a productiveness ... all unproductive days and hours'"]
|	inspiration of wine; "'Ich war in meinem Leben sehr oft in dem Fall ... was dem einen nützt, schadet dem andern'" ["'I have often been unable ... what is useful to one is prejudicial to another'"]
‖‖‖ (almost merged into one thick line)	the misfortunes of middle age; the mission of extraordinary men; "'Überhaupt', fuhr Goethe fort ... Goethe reichte mir seine liebe Hand, und ich ging' ["'You will find", continued Goethe ... Goethe gave me his dear hand, and I departed']
‖	Within this passage: "'Der Mensch muß wieder ruiniert werden!'" ["'Man must be ruined again!'"]
≠ (diagonal line through paragraph)	*Wednesday 12 March:* "'Ihr Traum ist sehr artig ... wider frisch und froh auf den Füßen'" ["'That is a very pretty dream ... fresh and joyful'"]
"	"'Mir gehen oft ähnliche Gedanken durch den Kopf ... nicht so gar schlecht stehe'" ["'I have often thought so ... not in such a desperate plight'"]
"	"'Ich habe in Sterne gelesen ... im Kriege mit ihnen wolle ausrichten'" ["'I have been reading Sterne ... with them in battle'"]
"	"'Ich habe sie ein Jahr vor der Waterlooschlacht ... keine Gebrechen der Väter'" ["'I saw them in Brussels

... ancestral failing'"]

"'empfinde ich oft eine kleines Grauen ... nichts übrigbleibt als der Philister'" ["'I often feel a slight shudder ... nothing remains but the Philistine'"]

Sunday 15 June: 'Der junge Goethe wird hinausgerufen ... "es ist ja kaum vier Uhr!"' ['Young Goethe was called out ... "it is scarcely four o'clock"']

Thursday 11 September: '"Schiller erscheint hier ... zu freier Ausdehnung Raum geben"' ["'Schiller appears here ... gives us room to expand"']

Friday 3 October: Scott's Fair Maid of Perth; "Aber nicht war", fuhr Goethe heiter fort ... indem sie über den Tisch neigend ihm die Hand drückte' ["'But", continued Goethe, with animation ... leaning over the table to press his hand']

Tuesday 7 October: "'Ich bewundere wirklich die Einrichtung ... und das Stück ganz anders anfangen lassen'" ["'I really admire ... and have begun the piece quite otherwise'"]; "'sie habe statt eines einzigen armseligen Paares ... nichts Besseres zu thun haben'" ["she has, instead of one paltry pair ... nothing better to do'"]

"Die heilige Schrift ... durch Herrn von Martius zu Widersprüchen angeregt'" ["'Holy writ ... excited by von Martius to argument'"]

Wednesday 8 October: 'Tieck mit Gemahlin und Töchtern ... in den Vorzimmern mit ihnen zusammen'" ['Tieck, returning from a journey ... in the anteroom'"]

Thursday 9 October: "'Doch wir wollen uns nicht ... zuerst publizierten Romane nur gleichkäme'" ["'But', he continued ... "that first-published novel'"]
Within this passage: '"'Waverley'"'

Saturday 11 October: Goethe acknowledges positively the unpopularity of his works; "'liebes Kind", sagte er ... 'in ähnlichen Richtungen begriffen sind'" ["'My dear young friend', said he ... "whose aims are like my own'"]

Monday 20 October: '"Dante erscheint uns groß ... nur Intention geblieben ist'" ["'Dante seems to us great ... external obstacles'"]

Wednesday 22 October: 'Heute war bei Tische ... "in der Wirklichkeit anzutreffen sind"' ['To-day at dinner ... "than could be found in reality"']

Thursday 23 October: 'Goethe stand auf ... "Sie sehen, Humboldt, es ist aus mit mir!"' ['Goethe went to his desk ... "You see, Humboldt, it is all over with me!"']

"'wie er jetzt viel Tröstliches ... eine menschenfreundliche Lehre'" ["'he now found much consolation ... It is a human doctrine'"]

"Ja, so war er! ... daß ich recht habe'" ["'Yes, such he was! ... that I am right'"]

'Wir sprachen sodann über die Einheit Deutschlands ... "eine einzige große Residenz habe"' ['We then spoke of the unity of Germany ... "a single great capital"']

"Man hat einen Staat wohl einem lebendigen Körper mit vielen Gliedern verglichen ... von denen Licht und Leben ausginge?'" ["'A state has been justly compared to a living body with many limbs ... whence light

Entry	Marginal mark
and life might proceed?'"]	
Tuesday 18 November: "'Goethe sprach von einem neuen Stück ... unserer neuesten Litteratoren zu klassifizieren haben'" ["'Goethe spoke of a new article ... our most modern literati'"]	I (very thick)
Within this passage: "'Es giebt Leute unter den Poeten ... aus dem Sinne schlägt'" ["'There are people ... drive from his mind'"]	—
"'neuesten'" ["'most modern'"]	— inscription: 'allerneuesten!' written underneath
	—
1829	
Monday 9 February: "'Wahlverwandtschaften'"	—
Tuesday 10 February: 'Über den Zustand damaliger Kultur ... die nicht bestehen konnte' ['We talked of the state of culture ... worthy to remain']	I
Within this passage: 'Aberglaube, daß er nicht hinkomme, wenn jemand darum wisse'" ['the superstitious fancy that he would not succeed if anyone knew about it']; "'Der Faust' entstand mit meinem 'Werther'"' ["'Faust' sprang up at the same time as *Werther*"]	— (light-blue ink)
'Er ist dagegen' ['but he opposed it']	—
Wednesday 11 February: 'Über den Ort ... Herrn von Reutern' ['With respect to the place ... Herr von Reutern']	I
Thursday 12 February: 'Goethe liest mir ... "in goldenen Buchstaben ausgestellt haben"' ['Goethe read me ... "in golden letters, to my annoyance"']	I
'Mathematiker Lagrange' ['mathematician Lagrange']	
"'er ist zu sehr mit italienischen Theatern verflochten'" ["'he is too much engaged with the Italian theatres'"]	≡ (light-blue ink) inscription: 'wo ist ____ [illegible word]?' written after this sentence
"'Alles Große und Gescheite ... einzelner Vorzüglicher sein'" ["'All that is great ... few eminent individuals'"]	III (all diagonally joined)
Friday 13 February: "'von vielem habe ich eine Ahnung ... in welchem sich die Kräfte konzentrieren'" ["'much I know ... in which the powers are concentrated'"]	I
"'Man muß alt werden ... Erstarrten, daß er es nutze'" ["'You must be old ... the already fixed, that it may make use of it'"]	I
Sunday 15 February: 'Goethe empfing mich ... der Farbenlehre' ['Goethe received me ... the *Theory of Colours*']	≠ (diagonal line through paragraph)
Tuesday 17 February: 'Viel über den "Großkophta" gesprochen ... "auf den breitesten Weg des Gartens tritt"' ['We talked a great deal about Goethe's *Grosskophta* ... "the broadest walk of the garden"']	S
"'In der deutschen Philosophie ... nicht viel mehr zu wünschenhaben'" ["'In the German philosophy ... in German philosophy'"]	S (light-blue ink)
Wednesday 18 February: "'wenn ihn das Urphänomen ... wohin er noch etwas zeichnen soll'" ["'if the primary phenomenon ... he can inscribe anything'"]	S

Thursday 19 February: 'Artaria'; 'Hof' ['Artaria'; 'court']

'"Es ist in vielfacher Hinsicht ... das Ganze nicht verletzen darf"' ['"For many reasons ... without compromising the whole"']

'"Auch will mir scheinen ... macht den Eindruck"' ['"It seems to me ... makes the impression"']

'"Man möchte auf Sie schelten ... Freiheit gegeben"' ['"You may be blamed ... so important a matter"']

'"und so gerieten wir unvermutet ... unter die subjectiven Erscheinungen"' ['"and we fell unadvisedly ... the subjective phenomena"']

'Der auf dem Schnee gesehen ... sehr konsequent zurechtlegt' ['The blue shadow ... Mont Blanc']

'Als ich nun ... Wie ich aber zu diesem Aperçu gelangte, will ich sagen' ['When of late ... I will explain']

'Aus den Fenstern ... das Blau unverändert zu sehen blieb' ['The windows of my apartment ... the blue remained unaltered']; 'Ich blickte noch einmal ... sobald der Anlaß nur gegeben ist' ['I looked once more ... the blue readily appears to us in it']; 'Allein sie waren ebenfalls nicht blau ... oder Mondlicht' ['Again, they were not blue ... moonlight']; 'Daß das Licht des anbrechenden Tages ... eins dem andern' ['That the dawning day ... he and Juliet']; 'Das Licht vom Auge des Geistes ... kommen zum Auge in einem bläulichen Ton' ['Light, as seen by the mind's eye ... a bluish tone']; 'Man lege in der Dämmerung ... wurde das unangenehmste Gemisch entstehen' ['Place a sheet of white paper ... the most unpleasant mixture would arise']

Within these passages: 'Diese Lehre fand ich ... eine objective Grundlage stattfinde und zu beachten sei' ['Now, on a careful observation ... objective foundation here also']

'Daß das Licht des anbrechenden Tages ... eins dem andern' ['That the dawning day ... he and Juliet']

'erscheint blaß' ['appears pale']

'Doch stehe noch Folgendes zu weiterer Bestätigung' ['The following may serve as a further confirmation']

Friday 20 February: '"Es geht uns wie den Weibern ... sind sie wieder schwanger!"' ['"It is with us as with wives ... in the family-way again!"']

Between last sentence of previous section ('Goethe spricht viel Gutes von Göttling' ['Goethe speaks very well of Göttling']) and first sentence of following section:

Monday 23 March: '"Ich habe unter meinen Papieren ein Blatt gefunden ... wo ich die Baukunst eine ersterrte Musik nenne"' ['"I have found a paper of mine among some others ... in which I call architecture 'petrified music'"']

'"die Stimmung, die von der Baukunst ausgeht, kommt dem Effekt der Musik nahe"' ['"the tone of mind produced by architecture approaches the effect of music"']

Thursday 2 April: '"Das Klassische nenne ich das Gesunde, und das Romantische das Kranke"' ['"I call the classic healthy, the romantic sickly"']

Friday 10 April: 'Ich erquickte mich darauf ... "nur als Phrase bedienen"' ['I now refreshed myself ... "as

---

Margin annotations:

| —

‖

≠ (diagonal line through paragraph)

"   "

"   "

/

| —

?

≠ (diagonal line through paragraphs)

"   "

"   "

"   "

"   "

illegible word written diagonally in margin

? (tilted at a backwards angle)

| —

inscription after this sentence: 'wo ist der Seele?'

| inscription above this passage: '+ Geborene Musik'

~ (across page)

x (after end of this sentence)

|— ? (cf. GMB: 137; SLGM: 155)

|

508

mere phrases'"]

Wednesday 15 April: "'Wir sprachen über Leute ... der verborgte Vorrat erschöpft ist'" ["'We talked of people ... the liquid treasure is exhausted'"] |

Tuesday 1 September: mind-body question; Fichte, Kant, limits of human intellect; philosophy of immortality; African slave trade; "'Die Periode des Zweifels ... welches er zu erlangen wußte'" ["'The period of doubt ... and to obtain'"] |

Sunday 20 December: 'Bei Goethe zu Tische ... "bei gesünderer Lebensweise noch länger halten können"' ['Dined with Goethe ... "if he had lived in a healthier way"'] "'Geht nur", sagte Goethe ... über den Knaben Lenker'] "'Pray, no more about the public" ... the Boy Lenker']   L |

1830

Wednesday 17 February: 'Von seinen "Wahlverwandtschaften" ... der Geschichte in Sesenheim' ['Of his *Wahlverwandtschaften* ... the Sesenheim story'] Within this passage: 'wie er erlebt worden' ['just as he had experienced it']   II (light-blue ink in left margin) III (light-blue ink in right margin)   I (light-blue ink, after the end of this sentence)

Sunday 7 March: "'Hierbei aber", sagte er ... daß die Pferde abbestellt wurden'" ["'I have shown ..." ... the horses were countermanded']   II (diagonally joined)

Sunday 14 March: "'Man hat Ihnen vorgeworfen" ... "so wird es um alle gut gehen"' ["'You have been reproached" ... "it will prove well with all"'] "'Und wenn noch die borniertre Masse ... war meiner Nature gemäß'" ["'And if it were only the narrow-minded masses ... was comfortable to my nature'"]   II |

Eckermann's account after Goethe's third letter of Wednesday 12 October: 'Am 20. November nachmittags ... und in den öden Feldern' ['On the afternoon of the 20th November ... and in desert fields'] Within this passage: 'Am 20. November nachmittags' ['On the afternoon of the 20th November'] 'Abends an Table-d'hôte ... sein einziger Sohn in Italien am Schlage gestorben sei' ['In the evening, at the table d'hôte ... his only son had died of paralysis in Italy']   I (right margin) | | I (left margin)

1831

Wednesday 21 December: 'Allein wie er in völliger Kraft ... seinen unersetzlichen Verlust zu beweinen hatte' ['But, as he was daily before my eyes ... his irreparable loss'] Within this passage: '22. März 1832'   ! | |

(3) *Goethes Werke*, hrsg. **Im Auftrage der Großherzogin Sophie von Sachsen: IV/20 Briefe. Januar 1808 – Juni 1809**

Page number(s) and text	Marking
	Pencil:
250: 'December'; 'Das Wunderhorn, das ich sehr schätze, ist keinesweges unmittelbar und augenblicklich aus dem Boden entsprungen. Es geziemte denen, die sich mit solchen Dingen abgeben, die Geschichte solcher Erscheinungen zu erforschen. Ferner gehört der Verfasser zu den eingebildeten Neulingen, die gegen das was sie Ästhetik nennen sich auflehnen, damit nur ihre Orakelsprüche als etwas erscheinen sollen. Nicht daß ich alles verwerfe, was die neue Zeit lebhafter als die ältere treibt, aber wie verdrießlich ist es erprobte Maximen des Urtheils von solchen verworfen zu sehen, die in jeder Äußerung zeigen, daß sie weder von Gehalt noch von Behandlung eines Kunstwerks den wahren Begriff haben'	[
Within this passage: 'Das Wunderhorn … entsprungen'	x
'denn ich muß gestehen, daß ich nur den geringsten Theil der Blätter gelesen habe'	x

(4) *Goethes sämtliche Werke. Jubiläums-Ausgabe in 40 Bänden*, hrsg. **Eduard von der Hellen, 1 Gedichte (I)**

Page number(s) and text	Marking
	a) pencil:
49–50: 3rd and 5th verses of 'An Lottchen'	!
82: 5th verse of 'Generalbeichte'	! (long)
83: 'Ein anderes' whole text	! (left of two vertical lines)
206: no. 6 of 'Venezianische Epigramme' whole text	!
	b) dark-purple ink:
63–64: 1st verse of 'Wanderers Nachtlied'	‖
65–66: 'An den Mond' title	! (very thick)
„ whole text	∟
„ 'Selig, wer sich vor der Welt/Ohne Haß verschließt' (in 7th verse)	!
„ final verse	—
	‖
	c) purple ink:
83: 'Ein anderes' whole text	! (right of two vertical lines)

(5) *Goethes sämtliche Werke. Jubiläums-Ausgabe in 40 Bänden, hrsg. Eduard von der Hellen, 2 Gedichte (II)*

Page number(s) and text	Marking
	a) dark-blue ink:
162: 'Genialisch Treiben' whole text	─
252–53: 'Urworte. Orpisch' ('Dämon') 1st verse	=
" 2nd verse	‖
	b) purple ink:
163: 'Hypochonder' title and whole text	O
167: 'Das Beste' title and whole text	O~
199–204: 'Paria' whole text	─
213: 'Ungeduld' whole text	V
240–41: 'Wiederfinden' whole text	─
244–45: 'Eins und Alles' whole text	V and l
246: 'Parabase' whole text	─

(6) *Goethes sämtliche Werke. Jubiläums-Ausgabe in 40 Bänden, hrsg. Eduard von der Hellen, 3 Gedichte (III)*

Page number(s) and text	Marking
	a) pencil:
275: 'Veni Creator Spiritus', against title	inscription 'S. 381' ═ (possibly in Mahler's hand)
381: footnote describing Goethe's interest in the Latin hymn	V (in both margins)
	b) purple ink:
275–76: 'Veni Creator Spiritus' whole text	─

(7) *Goethes sämtliche Werke. Jubiläums-Ausgabe in 40 Bänden*, hrsg. **Eduard von der Hellen, 4 Gedichte (IV)**

Page number(s) and text	Marking
	a) light-blue ink:
3–7: 'Gott, Gemüt und Welt' lines 15–20	I and **V**
" lines 30–32, 78–82, 87–88, 103–10	**V**
between lines 66 and 67	?
11–17: 'Sprichtwörtlich' lines 83–84, 93–94, 147–50, 218–22, 237–38	**V**
37: 'Zahme Xenien I' lines 109–12, beginning 'Nichts vom Vergänglichen'	**V**
129: Zahme Xenien IX' lines 810–13	**V**
	b) purple ink:
24: 'Sprichtwörtlich' lines 422–56	_
60: 'Zahme Xenien III' lines 748–51	!!!
75: 'Zahme Xenien IV' lines 1161–64	_
" lines 1179–82	=
" at end of poem	inscription, probably in Alma's hand: 'original bei Siegfried Ochs'[3]
95: 'Zahme Xenien VI' lines 1714–21	_
	c) dark-blue ink:
242: 'Anhang. Maximen und Reflexionen', lines 22–26 'Jüdisches Wesen. Energie der Grund von allem. Unmittelbare Zwecke. Keiner, auch nur der kleinste, geringste Jude, der nicht entschiedenes Bestreben verriete, und zwar ein irdisches, zeitliches, augenblickliches. Judensprache hat etwas Pathetisches'	**!!** (same hand as purple exclamation marks in b) above)

---

[3]   I am grateful to Herta Blaukopf for pointing out that Ochs visited Alma in Vienna in 1915 and gave her a Goethe autograph as a gift (ML: 76; ABL: 81).

512

(8) *Goethes sämtliche Werke. Jubiläums-Ausgabe in 40 Bänden*, hrsg. Eduard von der Hellen, 5 *West-östlicher Divan*

Page number(s) and text	Marking
	a) purple ink:
6: 'Freisinn' from 'Moganni Nameh. Buch des Sängers'; 'Laßt mich nur auf meinem Sattel gelten! … Stets blickend in die Höh'	)
76: 'Suleika' from 'Suleika Nameh. Buch Suleika'; 'Volk und Knecht und Überwinder … Wenn man bliebe, was man ist'	‖
	b) pencil:
16: 'Selige Sehnsucht' from 'Moganni Nameh. Buch des Sängers'; 1st verse: 'Sagt es niemand, nur den Weisen … Das nach Flammentod sich sehnet'	[
5th verse: 'Und so lang' du das nicht hast … Auf der dunklen Erde'	[

(9) *Goethes sämtliche Werke. Jubiläums-Ausgabe in 40 Bänden*, hrsg. Eduard von der Hellen, 14 *Faust (II)*

Page number(s) and text	Marking
	pencil:
206: Act 3, inner courtyard of a castle, surrounded with ornate fantastic buildings of the Middle Ages; Panthalis: 'Nicht nur Verdienst, auch Treue wahrt uns die Person' ['in merit not alone/But in our loyalties we keep our personal life'][4]	— —
Alle: 'Ewig lebendige Natur/Macht auf uns Geister, Wir auf sie vollgültigen Anspruch' ['Nature eternal asserts/Claim on us spirits, As on her we call with full warrant']	I and S (very short)
256: Act 5, Deep Night; Lynceus the keeper of the tower: 'Zum Sehen geboren, Zum Schauen bestellt … Von der Zugluft angefacht' ['A look-out born, Employed for my sight … Fanned to fury by the breeze']	I
260: Act 5, midnight; Faust in the palace: 'Ein düstres Reimwort folgte: Tod … Da wär's der Mühe wert, ein Mensch zu sein' ['And chiming with it came the sound of *Death* … I'd know at last the worth of being man']	I
261–62: Act 5, midnight; Faust: 'Ich bin nur durch die Welt gerannt … Er, unbefriedigt jeden Augenblick!' ['My way has been to scour the whole world through … He finds them who is never satisfied']	I
Within this passage: after 'Nach drüben ist die Aussicht uns verrannt' ['And what's beyond is barred from human ken']	L

---

4 Translations taken from Goethe, *Faust Part Two*, trans. P. Wayne (Harmondsworth: Penguin, 1959).

'Tor, wer dorthin die Augen blinzelnd richtet ... Was braucht er in die Ewigkeit zu schweifen!' ['Fool, fool is he who blinks at clouds on high ... Why haunt eternity with dim surmise?']

263: Act 5, midnight; Care: 'Soll er gehen, soll er kommen? ... Er verliert sich immer tiefer' ['Come or go? Or in, or out? ... Ever straying, ever thwarted']

264: Act 5, midnight; Faust (blinded): 'Auf strenges Ordnen, raschen Fleiß ... Genügt ein Geist für tausend Hände' ['Quick diligence, firm discipline ... A thousand hands need but one mind']

265: Act 5, the great outer-court of the palace; Mephistopheles: 'Wie man's für] unsre [Väter tat]' ['[As for] our [sires they used to do]']

267: Act 5, the great outer-court of the palace; Faust: 'Gemeindrang' ['All [...] join']
'Das ist der Weisheit letzter Schluß ... Genieß' ich jetzt den höchsten Augenblick' ['Here wisdom speaks its final word and true ... I take my joy, my highest moment this']
Within this passage: 'Freiheit' ['freedom']
'Auf freiem Grund mit freiem Volke stehn ... Genieß' ich jetzt den höchsten Augenblick' ['Standing on freedom's soil, a people free ... I take my joy, my highest moment this']
'Verweile doch, du bist so schön!' ['Linger you now, you are so fair!']

268: Act 5, burial scene; Lemur (solo): 'Wer hat den Saal so schlecht versorgt? ... [Lemuren:] Der Gläubiger sind so viele' ['Who was it made the room so vile? ... So many claim a share']

269: Act 5, burial scene; Mephistopheles: 'Sonst mit den letzten Atem fuhr sie aus ... Die Elemente, die sich hassen' ['Time was, the soul with last breath left the house ... Until the elements, each other hating']

270: Act 5, burial scene; Mephistopheles: 'Und in dem Siedequalm das Hintergrundes ... So viel Erschrecklichstes im engsten Raum!' ['See, in the seething fume of that dread maw ... In smallest space will greatest horrors teem']
'Nun, wanstige Schuften mit den Feuerbacken! ... hier unten lauert, ob's wie Phosphor gleißt' ['Now, big-paunched rascals, you whose cheeks are burning ... Look out for streak of phosphor here below']
'Nun, wanstige Schuften mit den Feuerbacken! ... Dann fort mit ihr im Feuerwirbelsturm!' ['Now, big-paunched rascals, you whose cheeks are burning ... Then bear her off in fiery whirling storm']

271: Act 5, burial scene; the host of heaven: 'Folget, Gesandte ... Des weilenden Zugs!' ['Follow, blest envoys ... Breath of delight']
Mephistopheles: 'Mißtöne hör' ich, garstiges Geklimper ... Ist ihrer Andacht eben recht' ['Jangling I hear, a foul discordant noise ... Finds in their worshipping its proper place']

272: Act 5, burial scene; chorus of angels: 'Blüten, die seligen ... Überall Tag!' ['Blest blossoms acclaiming ... To throngs of light']

273: Act 5, burial scene; chorus of angels: 'Was euch nicht angehört ... Dringt es gewaltig ein' ['Things ill-

x (with right diagonal extending into first line of this passage)

+

| and ***** (latter in right margin)

≠ (replaced with inscription (not in Mahler's hand): 'deren' written both above deleted word and in brackets in margin)

)

— —

|

— — (linking the curved line and vertical line on either margin, possibly indicating a cut-off point)

√

X (lines joined at the bottom)

X

!

inverse **S**-shaped line

?

|

|

| (in both margins)

fitting cease … Comes the assault too nigh']
Within this passage: 'Dürft ihr nicht leiden'; 'Dringt es gewaltig ein' ['Think not to bear them']; ['Comes the assault too nigh'] — — (linking the two vertical lines in both margins, creating a possible bracket)

274: Act 5, burial scene; Mephistopheles: 'Was halt mich ab, daß ich nicht fluchen darf? … Sie kommen mir doch gar zu lieblich vor!' ['What weighs upon me, that I cannot curse? … These miscreants who have had my hate and wrath'] | (possibly !)

'Ihr schönen Kinder, laßt mich wissen … O näheret euch, o gönnt mir einen Blick!' ['You sons of beauty, tell me, as I meet you … Draw nearer, pray you, granting me one glance'] ! (possibly l)

275: Act 5, burial scene; Mephistopheles: 'anständig-nackter' ['with decency [appear] more nude'] — —

276: Act 5, burial scene; Mephistopheles: 'Ein großer Aufwand, schmählich! ist vertan' ['And wrecked a deep-laid scheme in shameful sort'] — — (with short S in both margins)

276–77: Act 5, mountain-gorges, forest, cliff, wilderness; chorus and echo: 'Waldung, sie schwankt heran … [Pater ecstaticus:] Ewiger Liebe Kern' ['Forest branches swaying … Immortal love's core'] S

283–84: Act 5, mountain-gorges, forest, cliff, wilderness; Magna Peccatrix (Luke 7: 36): 'Bei der Liebe, die den Füßen … [Zu Drei:] Dein Verzeihen angemessen!' ['By the love that gave its tears … Thy divine forgiving grace'] C

Anhang aus dem Nachlaß

293–94: last line of poem 'Abschied'; '[Des Zeitengeists] gewaltig freches Toben' — — and ! (at end of line)

(10) *Goethes sämtliche Werke. Jubiläums-Ausgabe in 40 Bänden*, hrsg. Eduard von der Hellen, 26 *Italienische Reise (I)*

Page number(s) and text	Marking
	a) blue-purple pencil:
8: Karlsbad bis auf den Brenner, München, den 6. September 1786; 'Nun soll … in meiner Seele geworden ist!'	l
40–41: Verona bis Venedig, Verona, den 16. September 1786; 'Doch nur in der frühesten Zeit … zum besten zu haben',	ll
'und die übrige Masse … wie ungeheuer das Ganze sei'	l
46: Verona bis Venedig, Verona, den 16. September 1786; 'Die schönsten Stellungen … wo so schöner Raum wäre'	l
52: Verona bis Venedig, Verona, den 17. September 1786; 'Ein solches Übergefühl … selbst noch ehrwürdig'	ll
54: Verona bis Venedig, Verona, den 17. September 1786; 'ein so hohes Alter erreicht'	inscription after this sentence: 'Skalingengräber?' [Skalingergräben?'] not

Page number(s) and text	Marking
	in Mahler's hand
88: Venedig 1786, den 5. Oktober; 'Wissen wir doch ... sich zu sein dünkten'	)
92: Venedig 1786, den 7. Oktober, Abends; 'Heute früh war ich ... hat diese Zeremonie viele Freude gemacht'	))
	b) blue ink:
120: Ferrara bis Rom 1786, [Bologna], den 19. Oktober abends; 'So sprach mich eine Beschneidung ... an der Ausfahrung'	— —
	c) pencil:
6: Karlsbad bis auf den Brenner, Regensburg, den 5. September 1786; 'Als Dekoration ist nun Gold ... und angezogen werde'	)
9: Karlsbad bis auf den Brenner, Mittenwald, den 7. September Abends; 'Nach Walchensee ... sorgfältig zu ihren Füßen'		
14–15: Karlsbad bis auf den Brenner, Auf dem Brenner, den 8. September abends; 'Betrachten wir die Gebirge ... von einer unsichtbaren Hand ganz eigentlich abgesponnen'	{
56: Verona bis Venedig, Vicenza, den 19. September; 'denn man verdient wenig Dank ... wenn alles ist, wie es ist'	)
65: Verona bis Venedig, Padua, den 27. September; 'und was ist Beschauen ohne Denken?'	— —
'Hier in dieser neu mir entgegentretenden Mannigfaltigkeit ... scheint mir völlig gleich'	— —
73: Venedig 1786, den 29. September, Michaelistag Abends; 'Von Venedig ... wie es mir entgegenkömmt'	— —
118: Ferrara bis Rom 1786, Bologna, den 19. Oktober Abends; 'aber es geht mit der Kunst wie mit dem Leben: je weiter man hineinkommt, je breiter wird sie'	— —
377: Sizilien 1787. Sonntag den 13. und Montag den 14. Mai 1787; 'mir aber, dem von Jugend auf Anarchie verdrießlicher gewesen als der Tod selbst'	— — !

(11) Goethes sämtliche Werke. Jubiläums-Ausgabe in 40 Bänden, hrsg. Eduard von der Hellen, 27 Italienische Reise (II)

Page number(s) and text	Marking
	a) blue ink:
4: Neapel 1787, An Herder, Neapel, den 17. Mai 1787; 'Ich bin freilich ... bei der seinigen zu hoffen'		
Within this passage: 'unter den Millionen Welten'	— —
'Laß mich meinen Gedanken ... alles Manierierte'		
10–11: Neapel 1787, Neapel, Sonnabend den 26. Mai 1787; 'das himmlische in das Säkulum ... ihren Gott wiedergeben soll'	!
'Er befindet sich zum Beispiel ... die genauste Prüfung zugesteht'	)

Page number(s) and text	Marking
12–13: Neapel 1787, Neapel, Sonnabend den 26. Mai 1787; 'In einem kurzen Wahlspruch … bildet sich ein Hypochondrist'	|
Neapel 1787, Neapel, den 27. Mai 1787; 'Hamilton und seine Schöne … ihre musikalischen und melischen Talente'	|
37: Philipp Neri, der Humoristische Heilige; 'In solch einem enthusiastischen Momente … seiner Gefühle veranlassen'	)
47: Philipp Neri, der Humoristische Heilige; 'Diese und dergleichen Gaben … mit erstaunenswürdiger Energie hervortun konnten'	) (with dot beneath, possibly forming a type of exclamation mark)
81: Rom 1787, Dienstag, den 31. Juli; 'Michel Angelo und Raphael'; 'auf Leonard da Vinci'	— —
83: Rom 1787, Neapel, den 17. Mai 1787; 'daß in demjenigen Organ der Pflanze … in einen peinlich süßen Zustand versetzt'	|
Within this passage: 'Vorwärts und rückwärts … eins ohne das andere nicht denken darf'	)) (of indeterminate shape)
153: Rom 1787, Rom, den 10. November; 'Daß mein Egmont Beifall erhält … wie das vorige war'	|
16: Neapel 1787, Neapel, den 27. Mai 1787; 'Auch, muß ich selbst sagen … einer des andern humaner Krankenwärter sein werde'	b) pencil: III
156: Rom 1787, Bericht, November; 'Schubart'	— — ?
158: Rom 1787, Bericht, November; 'und man hätte zuletzt die Theriaksbüchsen des Doktors … als Mozart auftrat'	!
Within this passage: 'als Mozart auftrat'	— —

(12) *Hölderlins gesammelte Dichtungen in zwei Bänden. 1. Bd. Gedichte*

Page number(s) and text	Marking
	Pencil:
49: final verse of 'Die Unsterblichkeit der Seele'; 'So singt ihn nach, ihr Menschengeschlechte! nach … Himmelsentzückungen meine Größe'	|
129: first verse of 'Hymne an die Liebe (Umarbeitung vom 'Lied der Liebe'); 'Froh der süßen Augenweide … Frei und froh, wie wir, sich freun!'	|
160–61: 'Dem Sonnengott'; 'Wo bist du? trunken dämmert die Seele mir … Leben und Geist sich in uns entzündet'	|
161: 'Sonnenuntergang'; 'Wo bist du? trunken dämmert die Seele mir … Die ihn noch ehren, hinweggegangen'	|

(13) Gottfried Keller, *Gesammelte Gedichte I*

Page number(s) and text	Marking
	Pencil:
68: 'Herbstlied', part of 4th and 5th verses; 'Wo Thränen er durch Leid erpreßt … Der scheut noch weniger den Tod!'	|
120: 'Die Goethe-Pedanten', part of 1st verse; 'Wer spricht von Ordnung, wo die Berge wanken?/Wer spricht von Anmut, während die Gedanken/Noch schutzlos irren mit zerrauftem Haar?'	/
Within this passage: 'die Gedanken/Noch schutzlos irren mit zerrauftem Haar?'	
121: 'An A. A. L. Follen', verses 3 and 4; 'Uns mangelt des Gefühles edle Feinheit … Entsagend dumpf der Ehre und dem Rechten!'	|
125: 'Den Zweifellosen', part of 6th verse; 'Wie wenig ist's, was ihr im Busen hegt/Da ihr so satt hier, so vergnüglich seid!'	/
216: 'Becherlied', part of 3rd verse; 'Sie glüht bewegend Herz um Herz … Doch alles lebt im Liede fort'	|
Individual words, p. 135: 'bekleiben'	— — and ?
146: 'Sommersternenächten', 165: 'Span', 166: 'zweifärbig'	— —

(14) Graf Hermann von Keyserling, *Unsterblichkeit. Eine Kritik der Beziehung zwischen Naturgeschehen und menschlicher Vorstellungswelt*

Page number(s) and text	Marking
	a) pencil:
1: 'Vorwort zur zweiten Auflage'; the supra-personal continuation of the self; 'und so dauert der einzelne Mensch ... ein Überpersönliches'	I
succession and simultaneity of existence; 'Aber die Einheit des Lebens ... auch in der Simultaneität'	x
3: 'Vorrede' (dated 1907); the value of great men; 'daß sie gelebt, nicht auf dem, was sie getan haben'	— —
4: 'Vorrede'; Plato's immortality lies in the questions and directions of his thought; 'Sie bezieht sich nicht ... heute überstiegen'	I
6: 'Vorrede'; the immortality of great thinkers lies in the method of their thought, not the ideas themselves; the inevitable progress of science and philosophy; 'Die Unsterblichkeit großer Denker ... daß die Wissenschaft fortschreitet?'	I
7: 'Vorrede'; Meister Eckhart and pioneering thought; 'folglich kommt es auch im geistigen Schaffen ... wie Meister Eckhart sich ausdrückt'	I
9: 'Vorrede'; the greatest ideas stand at the boundaries of the ungraspable; 'Das Tiefste ist immer das ... ungeheuer Rätsel vermitteln'	I
18: 'Einführung'; contrast between European and Oriental traditions; 'mit welcher der Europäer ... andauernde Genüge zu finden?'	I
19: 'Einführung'; 'white' people's desire for physical nourishment makes them forget about life itself; 'der Weiße vergesse ... an dieser Bemerkung'	II
19: 'Einführung'; references in footnote 2 to Lionel Giles's *Musings of a Chinese Mystic, Selections from the Philosophy of Chuang Tzŭ* and *The Sayings of Lao Tzŭ*	I
20–21: 'Einführung'; contrast between European drive to achieve and Indian contemplation; '1st Europas geschäftiges Lebensideal ... verachtet oder vergaß?'; Japanese view of moral inferiority of 'white' races; 'Der Japaner ... zu ihm dringt'; fetishism of worshipping man-made gods: 'man glaubt ... selber erschaffen hat'; footnote 1 reference to Max Müller, *Theosophy or Psychological Religion*, p. 383	I
26: 'Über den Unsterblichkeitsglauben überhaupt'; human vanity and animal life contrasted; 'Nur die menschliche Eitelkeit ... der übrigen Tiere verschieden wäre'; the role of human intellect; 'Doch ist der Mensch ... so sicheren Instinkte'	I
30–31: 'Über den Unsterblichkeitsglauben überhaupt'; Confucius on life after death; '"Bejahe ich die Voraussetzung ... Zeugen deines Tuns wären"'	I
footnote 1 reference to H. Oldenberg, *Buddha*, p. 320 ff.	x
32: 'Über den Unsterblichkeitsglauben überhaupt'; footnote 1 reference to E. Rohde, *Psyche* I, p. 278	x

519

34–35: 'Über den Unsterblichkeitsglauben überhaupt'; the last hours of Kant's life; 'oder an das Verhalten Kants ... den Aufgaben des Lebens zuwandte'; words do not have just a single meaning; 'Man sollte doch endlich begreifen ... Inhalt verbinden'

42: 'Über den Unsterblichkeitsglauben überhaupt'; the difficulty of understanding the Chinese religious mentality; 'was einem völlig fremd ist ... die Einbildungskraft ist Erinnerung'

54: 'Über den Unsterblichkeitsglauben überhaupt'; Indian rejection of concrete representations of God; 'Und das tiefsinnige Indervolk ... sind alle Pfade der Rede aufgehoben'

64: 'Über den Unsterblichkeitsglauben überhaupt'; footnote 1 reference to quote from Paul Mongrés, *Sant' Ilario*, Leipzig, 1897, p. 305

67: 'Über den Unsterblichkeitsglauben überhaupt'; Greek view of immortality; 'Bei den Griechen ... kritische Philosophie nicht offenbaren'

91: 'Todesgedanken'; the psychology of desire; 'Daß ich etwas will ... mit rechten Dingen zugehen'

95: 'Todesgedanken'; the aesthetic 'truth' of death; 'Im letzten Augenblicke ... in der Wirklichkeit'; the necessity of boundaries in life; 'Das Grenzenlose entgeht überall dem Bewußtsein ... durch das Nicht-Sein umrahmt'; 'Der Ausdruck ... andererseits das Sein' death as the artistic form of life; 'Der Tod ist wirklich ... ein Paradoxon'

98: 'Todesgedanken'; the valuing of great people only after death; 'und bei Christus ... angefeindet und unterschätzt'
Within this passage: 'Im Verstorbensein allein liegt schon ein solches Verdienst, daß jeder Tote im gleichen Grade überschatzt wird, wie der Lebende angefeindet und unterschätzt'
advantageous for geniuses not to be well known; 'Um die Psychologie ... *en robe de chambre nie*'

99: 'Todesgedanken'; idealizing the reputation of the deceased; 'Und da die Hoffnung ... dem Ideal entsprechend deuten'; 'Wie erleichtert atmet ... unbedingt gelten gelassen'

100: 'Todesgedanken'; idealizing the reputation of the deceased (Goethe); 'Nun ist aus ihm ... sich selbst hinausgewachsen'; 'So führen denn ... am Leben zu sein'; 'Welcher ist nun der tiefste ... gibt es keine scharfe Grenzlinie'
'Ähnliche Gründe ... ihrem Wesen nach unbegrenzt'

102: 'Todesgedanken'; how the dead become living; 'Und daraus folgt ... die Toten die Lebendigen sind'

118: 'Das Problem des Glaubens'; belief as a metaphor for existence; 'forderten Eigenschaften ... deren einer dem Sein des Subjektes'

126: 'Das Problem des Glaubens'; the necessity of productive activity; 'anstatt sich fortreißen zu lassen ... negiert er zugleich sich selbst'

136: 'Dauer und Ewigkeit'; relationship between past and present; 'Und wenn dieser mir manchmal ... nicht folgen kann'
'In dauernder Gegenwart ... begrabe ich den vorhergehenden'

inscription in hand 1 in right margin (in both margins, right margin only up to 'Leben in Beziehung')

137: 'Dauer und Ewigkeit'; relationship between past and present; 'Wo ich dauernd … Das Leben steht nicht still' =

Within this passage: 'Eher als daß man sagen könnte … ließe sich behaupten' ?

'Beweist am deutlichsten … in sie hineingetragen' ?

'Auch ein Stern … Notwendigkeit zugrunde' —

138–9: 'Dauer und Ewigkeit'; life, creativity, Goethe and *Werther*; 'er dauert, muß er sich verändern … er erschöpfte sich in der Gegenwart' |

Within this passage: 'alles Endzweck' —

140–41: 'Dauer und Ewigkeit'; the qualitative rather than quantitative difference between stages of life; 'qualitativ verschiedener Zustände … eine Vorbereitung zum Tode'; 'Darum ist es ebenso willkürlich als sinnlos … so will es der Rhythmus des Lebens' —

Within this passage: 'Ist ein Lebenstempo ein langsames … der Rhythmus des Lebens' ?

'Wer hingegen den absoluten Wert … nichts beharrt' =

142: 'Dauer und Ewigkeit'; death as the 'keynote' of the 'symphony'; 'Wir wähnen als die Gleichen … zum Grundton diene' —

143: 'Dauer und Ewigkeit'; individuality as what connects one's being with the outside world; 'was ich jetzt bin … ist die Vergangenheit tot' —

'Sogar mein rückgreifendes Verantwortlichkeitsgefühl … gar nichts gemein zu haben' | (inscription in hand 1 in margin)

151–53: 'Dauer und Ewigkeit'; the rarity of immediacy of feeling; 'glaubt der Mensch … zur Konvention geworden ist' |

human desire for eternity; 'Der Mensch will die Ewigkeit … Nun wollen sie ewig zusammen sein' | (in both margins)

Within this passage: 'denn die Zeit … im unendlichen Augenblicke beschlossen' —

154: 'Dauer und Ewigkeit'; the migration of birds as sign of divine intention; 'und daß doch diese Speise … unterhalten könnten?' —

156: 'Dauer und Ewigkeit'; the opposition between eternity and individuality; 'Reflektieren wir rein logisch … die Ewigkeit verneint sie' —

159–60: 'Dauer und Ewigkeit'; mankind's desire for immortality; 'Das beharrende Ich … zu leben, ist gar nicht möglich' =

168: 'Das Bewußtsein'; no form of existence is superior; 'und ist der Sinn des Lebens … keiner Existenzform ein absoluter Vorzug innewohnt?' ∧ (I only for last three lines)

169–70: 'Das Bewußtsein'; instinct acts quicker than reflection; 'alle subalternen Reaktionen … zum Automatismus der Seerose wieder zurück' —

170: 'Das Bewußtsein'; the nature of mental functions; 'So ist's auch mit den geistigen Funktionen … Vorstellungen gelangen' ?

171: 'Das Bewußtsein'; the will to life; 'Wenn der Wille zum Leben … das Unzulängliche …' —

177: 'Mensch und Menschheit'; only doubt leads to knowledge (e.g. Hume and Kant); 'Aller geistige

Fortschritt ... das Transzendente erreichbar sei?'

'Wer vor Kant ... Ungewisse hinausragen'

Text	Mark
179: 'Mensch und Menschheit'; moral anarchy; 'dem Gebot der Entsagung ... die Moral der Anarchie'	==
180: 'Mensch und Menschheit'; the problem of the moral critic; 'Das eigentliche Problem ... keinem Zweifel'	x
184: 'Mensch und Menschheit'; footnote 1 reference to H. Oldenberg, *Buddha*, p. 160	I
185: 'Mensch und Menschheit'; the pre-eminence of Christianity; 'Es ist nämlich unbestreitbar ... schon längst entdeckt'	x
186–87: 'Mensch und Menschheit'; European thought dominated by Christianity; 'Man gebe sich hierüber ... auf den Individualismus verzichten'	x
194: 'Mensch und Menschheit'; the elevation of the individual personality; 'Deswegen ist auch ... immer größerer Mannigfaltigkeit differenziert' development of racial difference; Christianity valuing the individual personality; 'Mit dem Christentum ... orientiert war'	X
... the individual personality takes place at the expense of the whole and of the chosen ones; 'gibt diesem Einzelnen ... man übt zugleich ethischen Selbstmord'	X followed by **x**
202: 'Mensch und Menschheit'; the extreme individuality of creative artists such as Wagner or Nietzsche; 'den schaffenden Künstler ... der Idee seiner Kunst'	I and **!**
203: 'Mensch und Menschheit'; the artist's duty to mankind; 'Jeder Künstler ... um so gebieterischer' 'von ihren Ansprüchen ... seine Aufgabe zu erfüllen'	I
205: 'Mensch und Menschheit'; the purpose of life; 'so ist es ... einziger Zweck' 'Wohl ist das Leben sein eigener, einziger Zweck, nicht aber die Person'	==
209: 'Mensch und Menschheit'; the man of great ideas as against the limited egoist; 'der eine geistige Existenz ... vor allem das Kind'	I
210: 'Mensch und Menschheit'; knowing oneself through understanding oneself; 'Jedenfalls kennen wir uns selbst ... als Überwertung der eigenen Person'	?
224: 'Mensch und Menschheit'; great people using their life as a means to a higher end; 'Ja, er bescheidet sich gern ... ihm die Menschheit übertrug'	I
226: 'Mensch und Menschheit'; the artist transcending his limitations; '"So bin ich nun einmal" ... nur in so weit bist Du ein Wert'	IIII
246–47: 'Individuum und Leben'; the grotesque negation of life; male–female relations; the eternal feminine; 'jede Weltanschauung ... um diesen ihren Zweck zu erreichen'	⌐ and **!**
248: 'Individuum und Leben'; footnotes 1 and 2 references to Carl Ernst von Baer, *Ueber das allgemeinste Gesetz der Natur in aller Entwickelung* (St Petersburg, 1864) and *Welche Ansicht der lebenden Natur ist die richtige?* (Berlin, 1882); Darwin and Spencer on sexual function and growth	I; inscription in hand 2 in margin : 'G.'
253: 'Individuum und Leben'; footnote 1 reference to Th. Boveri, *Das Problem der Befruchtung* (Jena, 1902), p. 32	I; diagonal inscription in hand 2 on p. 246: 'Gottesanbeterin' [?]
258: 'Individuum und Leben'; individualism and the whole in bee colonies; 'trotz ausgesprochenster Individualisierung ... Maeterlincks wundervollen Bienenroman'	I; L; x

Within this passage: 'Sir John Lubbocks' L

259: 'Individuum und Leben'; physical and mental phenomena; 'Die physischen Phänomene … ins Reich der Natur' I

261: 'Individuum und Leben'; social formations are an artifice; 'Nicht anders verhält es sich mit den sozialen Gebilden der Menschen … wie die Sixtinische Madonna zur Zoologie gehört'; the artist creates for mankind; 'Gehen wir jetzt daran … sich selbst heraus erschöpfend zu verstehen' I

263: 'Individuum und Leben'; the monstrous phenomenon that every step forward takes us nearer to our grave (reference to *Faust*); 'alle Gegenwart in die endlose … den Tod schon im Herzen trägt'; 'Haltlos jagen wir in die Zukunft … mit dem objektiven Weltgeschehen übereinstimmen' III and ‼

264: 'Individuum und Leben'; the sorrow of death (quotes from Goethe and Dante); 'Jedesmal, wo sich mein Geist von den reinen … Haft Verurteilen' I

265: 'Individuum und Leben'; the pathos of death; 'wie nur irgendein durch Liebeslied gebrochenes Frauenherz … echten Glückes' III

266: 'Individuum und Leben'; we must not subdue the immediacy of personal experience; 'aus dieser Überlegung … wird brünstig ersehnt' I

269: 'Individuum und Leben'; consciousness is an expensive gift; 'Was die Menschen … erhöbe sie empörten Widerspruch' I

all life processes are purposeful; 'zweckmäßig', 'zielstrebig' — —

270–71: 'Individuum und Leben'; teleological processes in nature: 'Diese Finalität entspricht … schreibt Maeterlinck "ont le sentiment confus qu'un hazard"' I

272: 'Individuum und Leben'; we all live for the future in different ways; 'Und die dumpfe Masse der Menschen … die Liebe zur Ewigkeit' I

Within this passage: 'die Liebe zur Ewigkeit' — — (≡ 'Liebe zur Ewigkeit')

275: 'Individuum und Leben'; life is a process of becoming without final aim; 'In allem Konkreten … das Konkrete überhaupt verleugnen' I

Nietzsche's ideas on individuality more accurate than Schopenhauer's (quote from *Der Wille zur Macht*); 'So urteilt gar mancher Naturphilosoph … "mit den Aufgaben aller Zukünfte der Kette"' — —

276: 'Individuum und Leben'; 'Zweck des Lebens ist das Leben selbst'; 'Oder präziser ausgedrückt, according to Nietzsche, the ego is more than a singularity in the links of a chain; 'Oder präziser ausgedrückt, wofern zwischen Individuum und Gattung kein wesentlicher Unterschied besteht' X

'der Augenblick ist die einzige Realität', 'wer ihn erschöpft, erfaßt die Ewigkeit' — —

280: 'Individuum und Leben'; 'Wo sich das Individuum der Art zu opfern scheint, lebt es in Wirklichkeit sich selbst. Denn das Wesen, das Ich ist mit der begrenzten Person nicht identisch' X

282–83: the highest value of the individual lies in his mortality; 'Will ich leben … Der Tod ist überwunden' I

Back pages: above a review of the book in the *Freie Glocke*, Leipzig inscription, possibly in hand 1
Advertisement for Elias Metschnikoff, *Beiträge zu einer optimischen Weltauffassung* (München: J. F. X

Lehmanns Verlag, n.d.) (chapters include 'Pessimismus und Optimismus' and 'Goethe und Faust')

	b) purple ink:
145: 'Dauer und Ewigkeit'; 'das Bewußtsein eines beharrenden Seins geht auf ein Ueberpersönliches; alles Persönliche gehört dem wechselvollen Werden der Phänomene an'	– –
146: 'Dauer und Ewigkeit'; consciousness is a mixture of impressions and memories; 'jedem neuen Stadium … Eindrücken und Erinnerungen'	)
Within this passage: 'Daher hängt die Stimmung, die das Gewesene in mir auslöst, in Wirklichkeit nicht vom Gewesenen ab, sondern davon, wer ich jetzt bin'	x (at beginning and end of passage)
147: 'Dauer und Ewigkeit'; past and present; 'Die Vergangenheit ist ihrem Wesen nach unpersönlich, alles Persönliche betrifft ausschließlich die Gegenwart'	I

(15) Friedrich Nietzsche, *Werke* 1. Bd. *Die Geburt der Tragödie. Unzeitgemässe Betrachtungen*

Page number(s) and text	Marking
Unzeitgemässe Betrachtungen	a) purple ink:
285: 'Vom Nutzen und Nachteil der Historie', section 1; 'Bei dem kleinsten aber und bei dem grössten Glücke … er wird wie der rechte Schüler Heraclit's zuletzt kaum mehr wagen […]' ['In the case of the smallest or of the greatest happiness … like a true pupil of Heraclitus, he would in the end hardly dare […]']⁵	I
286–87: 'Vom Nutzen und Nachteil der Historie', section 1; 'Um diesen Grad und durch ihn dann die Grenze zu bestimmen … eines Volkes und einer Cultur nöthig' ['To determine this degree, and therewith the boundary … *of a people and of a culture*']	I
290: 'Vom Nutzen und Nachteil der Historie', section 1; '[…] unhistorischen Zustande vorher begehrt und erstrebt zu haben … wenn ihr Werth auch sonst unberechenbar gross wäre' ['having first desired and striven for it in an unhistorical condition such as that described … they must still be unworthy of this love']	I
296: 'Vom Nutzen und Nachteil der Historie', section 2; 'Zumeist winkt ihm kein Lohn, wenn nicht der Ruhm … in der Forderung einer monumentalischen Historie ausspricht' ['Mostly there is no reward beckoning him on, unless it be fame … the demand for a *monumental* history']	I
297: 'Vom Nutzen und Nachteil der Historie', section 2; '[…] Betrachtung so beseligt fühlen … nachdem es längst ihrer Verachtung preisgegeben war' ['gaining strength through reflecting on past greatness … after	X

⁵ Translations taken from Friedrich Nietzsche, *Untimely Meditations*, ed. D. Breazeale, trans. R.J. Hollingdale (Cambridge: Cambridge University Press, 1997).

Page number(s) and text	Marking
having for long been the object of their contempt'] Within this passage: 'Doch nur das, was sie als Schlacke' ['Only the dross'] 'Aber eines wird leben, das Monogramm ihres eigensten Wesens ... der Geschlechter und die Vergänglichkeit' ['But one thing will live, the monogram of their most essential being ... of generations and the transitoriness of things']	—
300: 'Vom Nutzen und Nachteil der Historie', section 2; 'Nehmen wir das einfachste und häufigste Beispiel ... welche allein aus jener Historie wahrhaft […]' ['Let us take the simplest and most frequent example ... that history in a true […]']	::
301: 'Vom Nutzen und Nachteil der Historie', section 2; '[…] lernen und das Erlernte in eine erhöhte Praxis umzusetzen vermögen ... sogar das Privilegium des "guten Geschmacks"' ['[…] of transforming what they have learned into a more elevated practice ... determining what is "good taste"']	::
302: 'Vom Nutzen und Nachteil der Historie', section 2; 'lasst die Todten die Lebendigen begraben' ['let the dead bury the living']	.
317: 'Vom Nutzen und Nachteil der Historie', section 2; 'Was soll noch gehofft, noch gelaubt werden ... mit unzugänglicher Innerlichkeit auseinanderfällt!' ['What is there left to hope for or believe in ... with an inaccessible inwardness on the other!']	—
325: 'Vom Nutzen und Nachteil der Historie', section 5; 'Sind die Persönlichkeit erst in der geschilderten Weise zu ewiger Subjectlosigkeit oder, wie man sagt, Objectivität ausgeblasen ... sofort sieht der ausgehölte Bildungsmensch über das Werk hinweg und fragt nach der Historie des Autors' ['If the personality is emptied in the manner described and has become eternally subjectless or, as it is usually put, objective ... the hollowed-out cultivated man at once looks beyond the work and asks about the history of its author']	!!!!! (beginning large and becoming progressively smaller) b) pencil: —
553: 'Richard Wagner in Bayreuth', section 8; 'Wer würdig ist, zu wissen, was damals in ihm vorgieng, worüber er in dem heiligsten Dunkel seiner Seele mit sich Zwiesprache pflog – es sind nicht Viele dessen würdig: der höre, schaue und erlebe Tristan und Isolde, das eigentliche *opus metaphysicum* aller Kunst' ['He who is worthy to know what took place in him then, what he was accustomed to discuss with himself in the darkest sanctuary of his soul – not many are worthy of it – let him hear, behold and experience *Tristan und Isolde*, the actual *opus metaphysicum* of all art']	

(16) Friedrich Nietzsche, *Werke* 2. Bd. *Menschliches, Allzumenschliches. Ein Buch für freie Geister I*

Page number(s) and text	Marking
376: 'Man alone with himself', aphorism 550; 'Schnur der Dankbarkeit. – Es giebt sclavische Seelen, welche	Pencil: —

die Erkenntlichkeit für erwiesenen Wohlthaten so weit treiben, dass sie sich mit der Schnur der Dankbarkeit selbst erdrosslen' ['Cord of gratitude. – There are slavish souls who go so far in readiness to acknowledge favours done them that they choke themselves with the cord of gratitude']⁶

388–89: 'Man alone with himself', aphorism 599; 'Lebensalter der Anmassung ... ein unverbesserlicher Narr der Eitelkeit' ['Age of presumption ... an incorrigible fool of vanity for the rest of one's life'] — III → II

392–93: 'Man alone with himself', aphorism 609; 'Lebensalter und Wahrheit ... mit der Miene der Einfalt zu sagen pflegt' ['Age and truth ... with an air of simplicity'] — I

aphorism 610; 'Die Menschen als schlechte Dichter ... einen Reim zu finden' ['Men as bad poets ... finding a rhyme'] — I

396–97: 'Man alone with himself', aphorism 616; 'Der Gegenwart entfremdet ... welche sie nie verlassen haben' ['Estranged from the present ... those who have never left it'] — I

399: 'Man alone with himself', aphorism 623; 'Tiefe Menschen ... noch Gegenwärtigkeit des Geistes zu haben' ['Deep men ... their presence of mind almost deserts them'] — I

410–11: 'Man alone with himself', aphorism 635; 'Desshalb sollte jetzt Jedermann mindestens eine Wissenschaft von Grund aus kennen gelernt haben ... und dass allein eine geringe Minderheit Gewissheit will' ['It is for this reason that everyone now should have acquired a thorough knowledge of at least one science ... only a small minority want *certainty*'] — I

(17) Friedrich Nietzsche, *Werke* 3. *Bd. Menschliches, Allzumenschliches. Ein Buch für freie Geister II*

Page number(s) and text	Marking
259: 'Part Two. The Wanderer and His Shadow', aphorism 115; 'Welche Gegenden dauernd erfreuen ... Und vielleicht gestattet diese Regel eine gleichnisshafte Anwendung auf den Menschen' [*'Which regions give lasting pleasure* ... And perhaps this rule may also be applied metaphorically to men']	a) purple ink: O~ (semi-erased)
358–59: 'Part Two. The Wanderer and His Shadow', aphorism 308; 'Am Mittag. – Wem ein thätiger und stürmereicher Morgen des Lebens beschieden war ... fast unheimlich und krankhaft, aber nicht unangenehm' [*'At noon.* – He who has been granted an active and storm-filled morning of life ... almost uncanny and morbid, but not unpleasant']	b) heavy, dark pencil: IIII (all linked diagonally) (cf. Barham, 1998: 462–63 for a discussion of the possible significance of this aphorism for Mahler)

⁶ Translations taken from Friedrich Nietzsche, *Human, All Too Human*, trans. R.J. Hollingdale (Cambridge: Cambridge University Press, 1996).

Within this passage: '[überfällt um] den Mittag des Lebens eine seltsame Ruhesucht' ['overcome] at the noontide of life by a strange longing for Repose']

'Er fühlt sich glücklich dabei, aber es ist ein schweres, schweres Glück' ['He feels happy as he gazes, but it is a heavy, heavy happiness']

'Da endlich erhebt sich der Wind in den Bäumen ... als selbst der Morgen war' ['Then at length the wind rises in the trees ... even than the morning']

'Den eigentlich thätigen Menschen ... aber nicht unangenehm' ['To truly active men ... but not unpleasant']

above no. 308 and at top of p. 359

	—	—
⌐	at end of sentence
≠	(crossed diagonal lines through passage)
≠	(horizontal lines through text)
≣	(quadruple underlining in dark pencil all joined diagonally, and stretching across width of page)
| and)	

364: 'Part Two. The Wanderer and His Shadow', aphorism 322; 'Tod. – Durch die sichere Aussicht auf den Tod ... durch den das ganze Leben widerlich wird!' ['Death. – The certain prospect of death ... through which all life is made repulsive!']

(18) Friedrich Nietzsche, *Werke* 5. Bd. *Die fröhliche Wissenschaft*

Page number(s) and text	Marking
30: 'Jest, Ruse and Revenge. A Prelude in Rhyme', no. 62; *'Ecce Homo.* Ja! Ich weiss, woher ich stamme!/Ungesättigt gleich der Flamme/Glühe und verzehr' ich mich./Licht wird Alles, was ich fasse,/Kohle Alles, was ich lasse:/Flamme bin ich sicherlich!' [*'Ecce Homo.* Yes, I know where I'm related./Like the flame, unquenched, unsated,/I consume myself and glow:/All's turned to light I lay my hand on,/All to coal that I abandon./Yes, I am a flame, I know!']⁷	a) purple ink: O
78–79: 'Book One', aphorism 42; 'Arbeit und Langeweile ... im Gegensatz zu der widrigen Plötzlichkeit des europäischen Giftes, des Alkohols' [*'Work and Ennui.* ... in contrast to the obnoxious suddenness of the European poison, alcohol']	I
88: 'Book One', aphorism 54; below last line 'und eben damit die Dauer des Traumes aufrecht zu erhalten' ['and thereby *the duration of the dream*']	inscription in hand 1: 'Harmonische Band [?] in die Vergangenheit G M'
89: 'Book One', aphorism 55; 'Sondern dass die Leidenschaft, die den Edlen befällt ... in welcher der Edelsinn auf Erden sich offenbart' ['But that the passion which seizes the noble man ... in which nobility of character	S S inscription in hand 1, written at end of this passage: 'OSSI' (possibly a

---

7 Translations taken from Friedrich Nietzsche, *Joyful Wisdom*, trans. T. Common, P.V. Cohn & M.D. Petre (New York: Frederick Ungar, 1960).

527

will reveal itself on earth']

Within this passage: 'eine Tapferkeit ohne den Willen zur Ehre' ['a bravery without the desire for honour']

90: 'Book One', aphorism 56; 'Diese junge Welt verlangt, von Aussen her solle ... mein Glück an die Wand zu malen' ['This young world desires that there should arrive or appear *from the outside* ... my *happiness* on the wall']

95: 'Book Two', aphorism 59; 'Wir Künstler!' ... Oh diesen Menschen von ehedem haben verstanden zu träumen und hatten nicht' ['*We Artists!* ... Oh, those men of former times understood how to *dream* and did not']

Within this passage: 'Wir Künstler' ['*We Artists!* ... it twitches impatiently, and glances, as we have said, contemptuously at nature']

96: 'Book Two', aphorism 59; 'und auch wir Menschen von heute verstehen es noch viel zu gut ... sondern als unsere Ebenen, als unserer Sicherheiten!' ['and we men of the present day also still understand it too well ... but as our plains, as our places of safety!']

98: 'Book Two', aphorism 62; 'Liebe. – Die Liebe vergiebt dem Geliebten sogar die Begierde' ['*Love.* – Love pardons even the passion of the beloved']

99: 'Book Two', aphorism 65; 'Hingebung. ... eine sehr schwermüthige Geschichte!' ['*Devotedness.* ... a very melancholy story!']

86: 'Book One', aphorism 51; 'Wahrheitssinn. ... denn dort hat die Tapferkeit ihr Recht verloren' ['*Sense for Truth*. ... for bravery has there lost its right']

87–88: 'Book One', aphorism 54; 'Das Bewusstsein Scheine. ... und eben damit die Dauer des Traumes aufrecht zu erhalten' ['*The Consciousness of Appearance*. ... and thereby *the duration of the dream*']

Within this passage: 'dichtet, fortliebt, forhasst, fortschliesst' ['continues to meditate, love, hate and reason']

89: 'Book One', aphorism 55; 'in welcher der Edelsinn auf Erden sich offenbart' ['in which nobility of character will reveal itself on earth']

94: 'Book Two', aphorism 58; '[einzusehen, dass unsäglich mehr daran liegt,] wie die Dinge heissen, als was sie sind' ['[to perceive that unspeakably more depends upon] *what things are called*, than on what they are']

95: 'Book Two', aphorism 59; 'Das "Naturgesetz" klang ihm schon wie eine Verleumdung Gottes' ['The "law of nature" sounded to him as blasphemy against God']

'im Grunde hätte er gar zu gern alle Mechanik auf moralische Willens- und Willküracte zurückgeführt gesehn' ['in truth he would too willingly have seen the whole of mechanics traced back to moral acts of volition and arbitrariness']

96: 'Book Two', aphorism 59; 'zu lieben, zu hassen, zu begehren, überhaupt zu empfinden – sofort kommt der Geist und die Kraft des Traumes über uns' ['to love, to hate, to desire, and in general to feel, – immediately']

---

diminutive of Oskar [Kokoschkal])

≈   L and |

| (crossing the previous line)

|

≠ (two crossed diagonal lines)

O O

b) thick black pencil:

|

|

illegible inscription in hand 2 above this passage (top of p. 88)

inscription in hand 2 below this passage: 'es ist auch so!! G K'

— —

— —

! at end of this passage

— — (faint under the first six words, then bolder)

528

the spirit and the power of the dream come over us']

98: 'Book Two', aphorisms 62 and 63; between the two texts
aphorism 63: 'Das Weib in der Musik' ['Woman in music'], against text

99: 'Book Two', aphorism 65

169: 'Book Three', aphorism 134: 'Die Pessimisten als Opfer. ... die Wirkungen der Kellerluft und des Ofengiftes in deutschen Wohnräumen' ['Pessimists as Victims. ... is essentially a cold-weather complaint']

202: 'Book Three', aphorism 255: 'Nachahmer. ... A: "Also –?"' ['Imitators. ... A: "Consequently –?"']

205: 'Book Three', aphorisms 274 and 275: "Was ist die das Menschlichste? – Jemandem Scham ersparen' ['What dost thou think most humane? – To spare a person shame']; 'Was ist das Siegel der erreichten Freiheit? – Sich nicht mehr vor sich selber schämen' ['What is the Seal of Attained Liberty? – To be no longer ashamed of oneself']

214: 'Book Four. Sanctus Januarius', aphorism 283; '283' 'Vorbereitende Menschen. ... und ihrer Folgen willen' ['Pioneers. ... and their consequences'] 'Denn, glaubt es mir! ... sie [die Erkenntnis] wird herrschen und besitzen wollen, und ihr mit ihr!' [' For believe me! ... she [knowledge] means to *rule* and *possess*, and you with her!']

225: 'Book Four. Sanctus Januarius', aphorism 294; 'Daher ist es gekommen dass so wenig Vornehmheit unter den Menschen zu finden ist ... und sonnenlicht um uns sein' ['*That is the cause* why there is so little nobility to be found among men ... and sunshine around us']

233: 'Book Four. Sanctus Januarius', aphorism 303; 'Aber sie sind geübt und erfinderisch ... Hier ist ein ganz anderer Mensch' ['But they are skilled and inventive ... Here is quite a different man']

235: 'Book Four. Sanctus Januarius', aphorism 305; 'bewaffnet gegen sich selber, scharfen und misstrauischen Auges ... von aller weiteren Belehrung!' ['armed against himself, with sharp distrustful eye ... from all further *instruction!*']

246: 'Book Four. Sanctus Januarius', aphorism 325; 'Willen in sich fühlt, grosse Schmerzen zuzufügen? ... das ist gross, das gehört zur Grösse' ['will *to inflict* great pain? ... that is great, that belongs to greatness']

320: 'Book Five. We Fearless Ones', aphorism 367; 'Wie man zuerst bei Kunstwerken zu unterscheiden hat. ['*How one has to Distinguish first of all in Works of Art*. ... ob er vom Auge des Zeugen aus nach seinem werdenden Kunstwerke' ... Whether he looks at his growing work of art']

323: 'Book Five. We Fearless Ones', aphorism 369; 'ein Solcher, der von Nichts als von Schwangerschaften ... Niemand kennt sein Kind schlechter als seine Eltern' ['one who no longer knows or hears of anything except pregnancies ... nobody knows a child worse than its parents']

325: 'Book Five. We Fearless Ones', aphorism 370 (entitled '*What is Romanticism?*'); 'ebenso eine tragische Ansicht und Einsicht in das Leben ... Einschliessung in optimische Horizonte' ['require a tragic view and insight into life ... imprisonment within optimistic horizons']

inscription in hand 2: 'Wagner!'
inscription in hand 2: 'Sch[openhauer ?] !'
≠ (two crossed diagonal lines)

c) pencil:
I (very faint, possibly purple)
III (almost merged into one thick line)
—
—
— —
=
=
—

I (very faint, possibly purple)

—

I (very faint, possibly purple)

—

—

) (partly I)

Within this passage: '[bei ihm] erscheint das Böse [, Unsinnige und Hässliche gleichsam] erlaubt, in Folge eines Ü[berschusses von zeugenden,] Befruchtenden [Kräften]' ['[With him] evil [, senselessness and ugliness] seem [as it were] licensed, in consequence of the o[verflowing plenitude of procreative,] fructifying [power]'], '[einen Gott, der ganz eigentlich ein] Gott für [Kranke, ein "Heiland" wäre]' ['[a God who is specially the] God of [the sick, a "saviour"]'], '[ebenso auch] die Logik, [die begriffliche Verständlichkeit das Daseins – denn die Logik beruhigt, giebt Vertrauen]' ['[similarly he would have need of] logic, [the abstract intelligibility of existence – for logic soothes and gives confidence]'], '[kurz eine gewisse warme furchtabwehrende Enge und Einschliessung] in optimische Horizonte' ['[in short he would need a certain warm, fear-dispelling narrowness and imprisonment] within optimistic horizons']

327: 'Book Five. We Fearless Ones', aphorism 370; '[eine Kunst] dieses Ursprungs wird immer eine Apotheosenkunst sein ... [(]den dionysischen Pessimismus)' ['[art] of this origin will always be an art of apotheosis ... [(]Dionysian pessimism)']

	Marking
(Within this passage ...)	—
	"
	"
	"
	"
327	—

(19) Friedrich Nietzsche, *Werke* 7. Bd. *Jenseits von Gut und Böse. Zur Genealogie der Moral*

Page number(s) and text	Marking
	a) pencil:
Jenseits von Gut und Böse	
14: 'Part One. On the Prejudices of Philosophers', section 6; 'Allmählich hat sich mir herausgestellt ... die ganze Pflanze gewachsen ist' ['Gradually it has become clear to me ... the whole plant had grown'][8]	—
16: 'Part One. On the Prejudices of Philosophers', section 7; 'versteckt sass und dreihundert Bücher schrieb ... Kam es dahinter?' ['sat, hidden away ... Did they find out?']	—
16–17: 'Part One. On the Prejudices of Philosophers', section 9; '"Gemäss der Natur" wollt ihr leben? ... wie könntet ihr's denn nicht?' ['"According to nature" you want to *live*? ... how could you *not* do that?']	—
23: 'Part One. On the Prejudices of Philosophers', section 13; 'Die Physiologen sollten sich besinnen, den Selbsterhaltungstrieb als kardinalen Trieb eines organischen Wesens anzusetzen' ['Physiologists should think before putting down the instinct of self-preservation as the cardinal instinct of an organic being']	—
25: 'Part One. On the Prejudices of Philosophers', section 15; 'Sensualismus mindestens somit als regulative Hypothese ... Folglich ist die Aussenwelt nicht das Werk unsrer Organe –?' ['Sensualism, therefore, at least as a regulative hypothesis ... Consequently, the external world is not the work of our organs –?'] Within this passage: 'Folglich ist die Aussenwelt nicht das Werk unsrer Organe –?' ['Consequently, the external world is not the work of our organs –?']	—

---

8 Translations taken from *Basic Writings of Nietzsche*, trans. & ed. Walter Kaufmann (New York: Modern Library, 1968).

27: 'Part One. On the Prejudices of Philosophers', section 17; 'nämlich, dass ein Gedanke kommt, wenn "er" will, und nicht wenn "ich" will' ['namely, that a thought comes when "it" wishes, and not when "I" wish']

44–45: 'Part Two. The Free Spirit', section 26; er ist zur Erkenntnis nicht gemacht ... Erleichterterm seiner Aufgabe' ['he was not made ... helps for his task']

51: 'Part Two. The Free Spirit', section 31; 'Jugend ist an sich schon etwas Fälschendes ... dass auch dies Alles noch – Jugend war!' ['after all, youth in itself has something of forgery ... that all this, too – was still youth']

61: 'Part Two. The Free Spirit', section 40; 'die Feinheit seiner Scham will es so ... in den Herzen und Köpfen seiner Freunde herum wandelt' ['the refinement of his shame would want it that way ... through the hearts and heads of his friends']

61: 'Part Two. The Free Spirit', section 41; 'man muss sich selbst seine Proben geben ... Nicht an einem Vaterlande hängen bleiben' ['One has to test oneself ... Not to remain stuck to a fatherland']

62: 'Part Two. The Free Spirit', section 41; 'und sei es das leidenste und hülfbedürftigste ... ein Zufall hat blicken lassen' ['not even if it suffers most and needs help most ... some accident allowed us to look'] 'sich zu bewahren' ['to conserve oneself']

63: 'Part Two. The Free Spirit', section 43; 'man muss den schlechten Geschmack von sich abthun ... [alles Seltene für die Seltenen]' ['One must shed the bad taste ... [all that is rare for the rare]']

Within this passage: '"Gut" ist nicht mehr gut, wenn der Nachbar es in den Mund nimmt' ['"Good" is no longer good when one's neighbour mouths it']
'Zuletzt muss es so stehn ... die Abgründe für die Tiefen' ['In the end it must be ... abysses for the profound']
'alles Seltene für die Seltenen' ['all that is rare for the rare']

93: 'Part Four. Epigrams and Interludes', section 67; 'Die Liebe zu Einem ... Auch die Liebe zu Gott' ['Love of one ... The love of God, too']

Within this passage: 'Auch die Liebe zu Gott' ['The love of God, too']

94: 'Part Four. Epigrams and Interludes', section 72; 'Nicht die Stärke ... die hohen Menschen' ['Not the intensity ... high men']

97: 'Part Four. Epigrams and Interludes', section 92; 'Wer hat nicht ... himself ... geopfert? –' ['Who has not ... himself once? –']

Within this passage: 'Ruf schon einmal' ['reputation [...] once']

101: 'Part Four. Epigrams and Interludes', section 116; 'Dir grossen Epochen ... als unser Bestes umzutaufen' ['The great epochs ... as what is best in us']

section 120; 'Die Sinnlichkeit ... leicht auszureissen ist' ['Sensuality ... easily torn up']

104: 'Part Four. Epigrams and Interludes', section 136; 'Der Eine sucht einen Geburtshelfer ... ein gutes Gespräch' ['One seeks a midwife ... a good conversation']

Margin annotations:
— │
│
│
│ (both margins, right margin purple ink superimposed) ////
└ (around beginning of this sentence, implying the highlighting of the rest of this section)
│
│ (in both margins)
— │
— │
│ and └
‖
— │
‼
│

⌐

|

b) purple ink:

|

| (right margin, superimposed on pencil)

|

‼

O

?

[illegible inscription above text

|

|

| and O

⊂

|

|

|

108: 'Part Four. Epigrams and Interludes', section 168; 'Das Christenthum gab dem Eros Gift zu trinken ... zum Laster' [' Christianity gave Eros poison to drink ... a vice']

110: 'Part Four. Epigrams and Interludes', section 183; '"Nicht dass du mir belogst ... erschüttert' ['"Not that you lied to me ... shaken me"']

27: 'Part One. On the Prejudices of Philosophers', section 17; 'Was den Aberglauben der Logiker betrifft ... und gehört nicht zum Vorgange selbst' ['With regard to the superstitions of logicians ... and does not belong to the process itself']

61–62: 'Part Two. The Free Spirit', section 41; 'Man muss sich selbst seine Proben geben ... Nicht an einem Vaterlande bleiben' ['One has to test oneself ... Not to remain stuck to a fatherland'] 'und sei es das leidenste und hülfbedürftigste ... bis zum Laster treiben' ['not even if it suffers most and needs help most ... into a vice']

94: 'Part Four. Epigrams and Interludes', section 68; '"Das habe ich gethan" ... giebt das Gedächtniss nach' ['"I have done that" ... memory yields'] section 70; 'Hat man Charakter ... wieder kommt' [' If one has character ... repeatedly']

95: 'Part Four. Epigrams and Interludes', section 74; 'Ein Mensch mit Genie ... Reinlichkeit' ['A man with spirit ... cleanliness'] section 76; 'Unter friedlichen Umständen ... über sich selber her' ['Under peaceful conditions ... upon himself']

96: 'Part Four. Epigrams and Interludes', section 82; '"Mitleiden mit Allen" ... mein Herr Nachbar! –' ['"Pity for all" ... my dear neighbour! –']

102: 'Part Four. Epigrams and Interludes', section 125; 'Wenn wir über Jemanden umlernen müssen ... die er uns damit macht' ['When we have to change our mind about a person ... very much against him'] section 126; 'Ein Volk ist der Umschweif der Natur ... und um dann um sie herum zu kommen' ['A people is a detour of nature ... and then to get around them']

110: 'Part Four. Epigrams and Interludes', section 185; '"Er missfällt mir" ... so geantwortet?' [' "I don't like him" ... answered that way?']

210: 'Part Eight. Peoples and Fatherlands', section 244; 'vom Auslande her ... dass man über sie selten völlig Unrecht hat' [' in which he [Goethe] deprecates ... one is rarely completely wrong about them'] 'die Widerspruchs-Natur im Grunde der deutschen Seele aufgiebt (welche Hegel in System gebracht, Richard Wagner zuletzt noch in Musik gesetzt hat) ... rechtfertig sich leider zu oft in Deutschland' ['the contradictory nature at the bottom of the German soul (brought into a system by Hegel and finally set to music by Richard Wagner) ... unfortunately justified all too often in Germany']

213: 'Part Eight. Peoples and Fatherlands', section 245; 'die unter wirklichen Musikern wenig in Betracht kam. Anders stand es mit Felix Mendelssohn ... als der schöne Zwischenfall der deutschen Musik' ['that was not considered seriously by genuine musicians. It is different with Felix Mendelssohn ... as the beautiful *intermezzo* of German music']

220–21: 'Part Eight. Peoples and Fatherlands', section 251; 'diese Zukunft macht, mit den Juden ... einer neuen über Europa regierende Kaste' ['for this future, take into account the Jews ... a new caste that will rule Europe'] I

222: 'Part Eight. Peoples and Fatherlands', section 252; 'Rasse, dass sie streng zum Christenthume halt ... er hat das Christenthum eben noch nöthiger' ['race that it clings firmly to Christianity ... they stand more in *need* of Christianity'] I

229–30: 'Part Eight. Peoples and Fatherlands', section 256; 'Bei allen tieferen und umfänglicheren Menschen ... ob es in der Wagnerischen Kunst etwas schlechthin Deutsches giebt' ['In all the more profound and comprehensive men ... whether there is in Wagner's art anything outright German']) → I

c) blue pencil:

64: 'Part Two. The Free Spirit', section 44; 'wir freien Geister! – die Schuldigkeit ... wo und wie bisher die Pflanze "Mensch" am [...]' ['we free spirits – to sweep away ... where and how the plant "man" [...]'] IIIII (some lines crossed, or linked diagonally)

d) red pencil:

126–27: 'Part Five. Natural History of Morals', section 195; 'Die Juden – ein Volk "geboren zur Sklaverei" ... mit ihm beginnt der Sklaven-Aufstand in der Moral' ['The Jews – a people "born for slavery" ... they mark the beginning of the slave rebellion in morals'] I

212: 'Part Eight. Peoples and Fatherlands', section 245; 'aber wer darf zweifeln, dass es noch früher mit dem Verstehen] und Schmecken Beethoven's vorbei sein wird! ... und endlich vor Napoleon beinahe angebetet hatte' ['but who may doubt that the understanding] and taste for Beethoven will go long before that! ... and finally almost worshipped before Napoleon'] I

218–19: 'Part Eight. Peoples and Fatherlands', sections 250 and 251; 'unendlicher Bedeutungen, die ganze Romantik ... Ein Denker, der die Zukunft Europa's auf seinem Gewissen hat, wird, bei allen Entwürfen, welche er bei sich über [...]' ['infinite meanings, the whole romanticism ... A thinker who has the development of Europe on his conscience will, in all his projects [...]'] I (leading into the similar, purple markings on pp. 220–21)

Within this passage: 'Man muss es in den Kauf nehmen ... ([...] diese Sybel und Treitschke und ihre dick verbundenen Köpfe an –)' ['It must be taken into the bargain ... ([...] these Sybels and Treitschkes and their thickly bandaged heads!)'] II

Within this passage: 'Man muss es in den Kauf nehmen ... bald die Wagnerianische, bald die teutonische, bald die preussische' ['It must be taken into the bargain ... now the Wagnerian, now the Teutonic, now the Prussian'] III

Zur Genealogie der Moral

a) purple ink:

348: *'Second Essay.* "Guilt", "Bad Conscience", and the Like', section 3; 'vielleicht ist sogar nichts furchtbarer und unheimlicher ... (zum Beispiel die Castration)' ['perhaps indeed there was nothing more fearful and uncanny ... (castration, for example)']
Within this passage: '"nur was nicht aufhört, weh zu thun, bleibt im Gedächtniss" – das ist ein Hauptsatz aus der allerältesten (leider auch allerlängsten) Psychologie auf Erden' ['"only that which never ceases to *hurt* stays in the memory" – this is a main clause of the oldest (unhappily also the most Enduring) psychology on earth'] — I

— II

350: *'Second Essay.* "Guilt", "Bad Conscience", and the Like', section 3; '[...] und Vorgänge behält man endlich fünf, sechs, "ich will nicht" im Gedächtnisse ... auf dem Grunde aller "guten Dinge"! ...' ['[...] and procedures one finally remembers five or six "I will not's" ... at the bottom of all "good things"!'] — IIII

379: *'Second Essay.* "Guilt", "Bad Conscience", and the Like', section 16; 'sie ist nicht leicht zu Gehör zu bringen und will lange bedacht ... und des Friedens eingeschlossen fand' ['it may sound rather strange ... within the walls of society and peace'] — I

'Nicht anders als es den Wasserthieren ... entwerthet und "ausgehängt"' ['The situation that faced sea animals ... disvalued and "suspended"'] — S

'eine entsetzliche Schwere lag auf ihnen ... ihnen zu Willen sein' ['a dreadful heaviness lay upon them ... to humour them'] — I
Within this passage: 'auf ihr "Bewusstsein" ... ihnen zu Willen sein' ['to their "consciousness" ... to humour them'] — II

394: *'Second Essay.* "Guilt", "Bad Conscience", and the Like', section 23; 'Dergestalt dienten damals die Götter dazu ... wie es vornehmer ist, die Schuld ...' ['In this way the gods served in those days ... what is *nobler*, the guilt'] — II

399: *'Third Essay.* What is the Meaning of Ascetic Ideals?', section 1; 'Was bedeuten asketische Ideale? ... im Kampf mit dem langsamen Schmerz und der Langenweile' ['What is the meaning of ascetic ideals? ... the struggle against slow pain and boredom'] —)) (crossing over)

b) red pencil:

312–13: 'First Essay. "Good and Evil", "Good and Bad"', section 7; ' – Man wird bereits errathen haben ... weil er – siegreich gewesen ist ...' ['One will have divined already ... because it – has been victorious'] — I

317: 'First Essay. "Good and Evil", "Good and Bad"', section 10; ' – Der Sklavenaufstand in der Moral beginnt damit ... des niedren Volks' ['The slave revolt in morality begins when ... of the lower orders'] — I (and √ at top of page)

336–37: 'First Essay. "Good and Evil", "Good and Bad"', section 16; '[...] Völker, etwa die Chinesen oder die Deutschen ... Napoleon, diese Synthese von Unmensch und Übermensch ...' ['[...] nations – the Chinese or the Germans, for instance ... Napoleon, this synthesis of the *inhuman* and *superhuman*'] —)
Within this passage: 'und nicht nur in Rom ... oder zahm werden will' ['and not only in Rome ... or desires — II (linked diagonally)

534

to become tame']

'die Wiederherstellung auch der alten Grabesruhe des klassischen Rom ... brach unter den volksthümlichen Ressentiments-Instinkten zusammen' ['the restoration too of the ancient sepulchral repose of classical Rome ... collapsed beneath the popular instincts of *ressentiment*']   =

337: 'First Essay. "Good and Evil", "Good and Bad"', section 17; 'War es damit vorbei? ... was ich gerade mit jener gefährlichen [...]' ['Was that the end of it? ... what the aim of that dangerous [...]']   =

Within this passage: 'War es damit vorbei? ... nachzudenken, weiter zu denken' ['Was that the end of it? ... to reflect and pursue his train of thought']   )

(20) Friedrich Nietzsche, *Werke* 8. Bd. *Der Fall Wagner. Götzen-Dämmerung. Nietzsche contra Wagner. Der Wille zur Macht I* (I. Buch: *Der Antichrist*). *Dichtungen*

Page number(s) and text	Marking
Götzen-Dämmerung	
136–37: 'Skirmishes of an Untimely Man', section 25; 'Mit Menschen fürlieb nehmen ... mit denen man nicht "fürlieb nimmt" ... ' ['To put up with people ... with whom one does not "put up"'][9]	a) pencil: ⏐
137: 'Skirmishes of an Untimely Man', section 26; 'Wir schätzen uns nicht genug mehr, wenn wir uns mittheilen ... Aus einer Moral für Taubstumme und andre Philosophen' ['We no longer esteem ourselves sufficiently when we communicate ourselves ... Out of a morality for deaf-mutes and other philosophers']	⏐
138: 'Skirmishes of an Untimely Man', section 29; 'Aus einer Doctor-Promotion ... über den Staats-Beamten als Erscheinung' ['From a doctoral examination ... over the civil servant as phenomenon']	⏐
172–73: 'What I owe to the Ancients', section 4; '"[...] nothwendig zur Festfeier, und hielt es als einen unentbehrlich Theil des Gottesdienst fest ... es warf Koth auf den Anfang, auf die Voraussetzung unsres Lebens ...' ['"[...] necessary part of the festival and therefore it was maintained as an indispensable feature of the religious service" ... it threw *filth* on the origin, on the presupposition of our life']	b) red pencil: ⏐
Nietzsche contra Wagner	
208: 'Epilogue', section 2; 'Vor Allem: eine Kunst für Künstler, nur für Künstler!' ['Above all, an art for Artists!']	a) pencil: — ⏐

[9] Translations taken from *The Portable Nietzsche*, ed. & trans. Walter Kaufmann (New York & London: Penguin, 1976).

artists, *for artists only!*']

Der Wille zur Macht I (I. Buch: *Der Antichrist*)

a) pencil:

213: 'Preface. Revaluation of All Values'; 'Dies Buch gehört den Wenigsten ... seine Kraft, seine Begeisterung [...]' ['This book belongs to the very few ... keeping our strength, our *enthusiasm* [...]']
—

218: 'First Book: The Antichrist. Attempt at a Critique of Christianity', section 1; 'ein Ja, ein Nein, eine gerade Linie, ein Ziel ...' ['a Yes, a No, a straight line, a goal']
—

section 2; 'Was ist gut? ... Was ist schädlicher, als irgend ein Laster? – Das Mitleiden der That mit allen Missrathnen und Schwachen – das Christenthum...' ['What is good? ... What is more harmful than any vice? Active pity for all the failures and all the weak: Christianity']

253: 'First Book: The Antichrist. Attempt at a Critique of Christianity', section 30; below bottom paragraph of page 'Dies sind die zwei physiologischen Realitäten ... und Nervenkraft, bleibt [...]' ['These are the two *physiological realities* ... and nervous energy [...]']
inscription in hand 1, not Mahler's

263: First Book: The Antichrist. Attempt at a Critique of Christianity', section 38; ' – Ich unterdrücke an dieser Stelle einen Seufzer nicht. Es giebt Tage, wo mich ein Gefühl heimsucht, schwärzer als die schwärzeste Melancholie – die Menschen-Verachtung' ['At this point I do not suppress a sigh. There are days when I am afflicted with a feeling blacker than the blackest melancholy – *contempt of man*']
inscription in hand 2, not Mahler's

264–65: 'First Book: The Antichrist. Attempt at a Critique of Christianity', section 38; 'Selbst bei dem bescheidensten Anspruch auf Rechtschaffenheit ... dass es keinen "Gott" mehr giebt, keinen "Sünder", keinen "Erlöser"' ['If we have even the smallest claim to integrity ... that there is no longer any "God", any "sinner", any "Redeemer"']
?

'prachtvoll als Ausdruck der Selbstsucht und [...]' ['magnificent as an expression of the selfishness [...]'] at top of p. 265, above the previous underlined passage

281: 'First Book: The Antichrist. Attempt at a Critique of Christianity', section 46; at top of page above concluding lines 'Einen Judenhandel Ernst zu nehmen ... "was ist Wahrheit!"...' ['To take a Jewish affair seriously ... "What is truth?"']
—
inscription, possibly in hand 2

287: 'First Book: The Antichrist. Attempt at a Critique of Christianity', section 51; at bottom of page, below the following: 'die "innere Welt" des religiösen Menschen sieht der "inneren Welt" der Überreizten und Erschöpften zum Verwechseln ähnlich; die "höchsten" Zustände, welche das [...]' ['the "inner world" of the religious man looks exactly like the "inner world" of the overexcited and the exhausted; the "highest" states that [...]']
inscription, possibly in hand 2:   'ekelhaft!'

293: 'First Book: The Antichrist. Attempt at a Critique of Christianity', section 53; 'Gerade das war die welthistorische Dummheit aller Verfolger ... Zarathustra' ['This was precisely the world-historical stupidity of all persecutors .... *Zarathustra*']
inscription in hand 1

302–4: 'First Book: The Antichrist. Attempt at a Critique of Christianity', section 57; '[...] oder ein
—
—

536

pessimistischer Blick, ein Auge, das verhässlicht ... Der Anarchist und der Christ sind Einer Herkunft' ['[…] or a pessimistic glance ... The anarchist and the Christian have the same origin']

(21) Friedrich Nietzsche, *Werke* 2. Abtheilung 7. Bd. Nachgelassene Werke von Friedrich Nietzsche. *Ecce Homo. Der Wille zur Macht*, erstes und zweites Buch

Page number(s) and text	Marking
Ecce Homo	a) thick, faint pencil: I
11–13: 'Why I Am So Wise', section 2; 'Abgerechnet nämlich, dass ich ein *décadent* bin ... Wohlan, ich bin das Gegenstück eines *décadent*: denn ich beschrieb eben mich' ['Apart from the fact that I am a decadent ... Well then, I am the *opposite* of a decadent, for I have just described *myself*']¹⁰ Within this passage: 'Er reagirt auf alle Art Reize langsam ... denn ich beschrieb eben mich' ['he reacts slowly to all kinds of stimuli ... for I have just described myself']	) and I
19: 'Why I Am So Wise', section 6; 'Das Begriff jener tiefe Physiolog Buddha ... so redet die Physiologie' ['This was comprehended by that profound physiologist, the Buddha ... thus speaks physiology']	II and / (crossing through double lines)
28: 'Why I Am So Clever', section 1; 'Aber die deutsche Küche überhaupt – was hat sie nicht Alles auf dem Gewissen! ... Der deutsche Geist ist eine Indigestion, er wird mit Nichts fertig' ['But German cuisine quite generally – what doesn't it have on its conscience? ... The German spirit is an indigestion: it does not finish with anything']	b) thick, red ink: I
14: Why I Am So Wise', section 3; 'Letztere lebte ihre ganze Jugend ... das grosse Ja zum Leben nicht eingerechnet' ['The latter lived all her youth ... the great Yes to life']	c) pencil: inscription in Alma's hand vertically along the left margin: 'Ich bin frei von den Menschen – fühle im Innersten, wie ich in jedem Moment überall hingehen könnte – denn nichts spricht jetzt so stark auf mich ein, als die Natur. Und [?] die Menschen lieben mich – ich aber bin unabhängig' (transcribed by Herta Blaukopf). Inscription in hand 2 at top of page, dated at bottom of page 'Breitenstein im Somer 16'

---

10 Translations taken from *Basic Writings of Nietzsche*, trans. & ed. Walter Kaufmann (New York: Modern Library, 1968).

30–31: 'Why I Am So Clever', section 2; '[Der animalische *vigor* ist nie gross genug] bei ihm geworden … und selbst heroisch angelegte Eingeweide zu entmuthigen' ['[His animal vigour has never] become [great enough] for him … even inherently heroic, intestines']

'und bei einer kurzen Reise schon, etwa von Turin nach Mailand … viele Unglücks-Orte für meine Physiologie' ['and even during a short journey, say, from Turin to Milan … so many disastrous places for my physiology']

33: 'Why I Am So Clever', section 3; 'ich würde mich hüten, Jemanden in meiner Nähe reden oder gar denken zu lassen … Man muss dem Zufall, dem Reiz von aussen her so viel als möglich aus dem Wege gehn' ['I'd beware of letting anyone near me talk, much less think … One must avoid chance and outside stimuli as much as possible']

36: 'Why I Am So Clever', section 4; 'Wenn ich einen Blick in meinen Zarathustra geworfen habe, gehe ich eine halbe Stunde im Zimmer auf und ab, unfähig, über einen unerträglichen Krampf von Schluchzen Herr zu werden' ['When I have looked into my *Zarathustra*, I walk up and down in my room for half an hour, unable to master an unbearable fit of sobbing']

38: 'Why I Am So Clever', section 5; 'jene hochfliegende und hoch emporreissende Art von Künstlern wie Delacroix, wie Berlioz … Charles Baudelaire … jener typische *décadent*, in dem sich ein ganzes Geschlecht von Artisten wiedererkannt hat – er war vielleicht auch der letzte' ['that high-flying and yet rousing manner of artists like Delacroix, like Berlioz … Charles Baudelaire … that typical decadent in whom a whole tribe of artists recognized themselves – and perhaps he was also the last']

39: 'Why I Am So Clever', section 6; 'Denn ich war verurtheilt zu Deutschen … Dies Werk [*Tristan*] ist durchaus das *non plus ultra* Wagner's; er erholte sich von ihm mit den Meistersingern und dem Ring' ['For I was *condemned* to Germans … This work [*Tristan*] is emphatically Wagner's *non plus ultra*; with the *Meistersinger* and the *Ring* he recuperated from it']

42: 'Why I Am So Clever', section 8; 'Man kann, bloss in der beständigen Noth der Abwehr … keine Stacheln zu haben, sondern offne Hände' ['Merely through the constant need to ward off … not to have quills but open hands']

43: 'Why I Am So Clever', section 9; 'An dieser Stelle ist nicht mehr zu umgehn … sogar die oberste Klugheit zum Ausdruck' ['At this point the real answer to the question … even the supreme prudence']

45: 'Why I Am So Clever', section 9; '[…] Obhut zeigte sich in dem Maasse stark … eine weite Zukunft! – wie auf ein glattes Meer hinaus' ['[…] *protection* manifested itself to such a high degree … an *ample* future! – as upon calm seas']

'kein Verlangen kräuselt sich auf ihm' ['there is no ripple of desire']

'ich selber will nicht anders werden' ['I myself do not want to become different']

—

—

—

v

/

—

—

—

! inscription, probably in Alma's hand, at top of the page above this passage: 'auch ich will'

– – inscription, probably in Alma's hand, in left margin: 'S. S. 14', presumably referring to the inscription cited above.

– –

538

46–47: 'Why I Am So Clever', section 10; ' – Man wird mich fragen, warum ich eigentlich alle diese kleinen und nach herkömmlichem Urtheil … die ganze Casuistik der Selbstsucht' ['One will ask me why on earth I've been relating all these small things … the whole casuistry of selfishness']   I

'ich bin selbst in Zeiten schwerer Krankheit nicht krankhaft geworden … wenn es das Schwerste von mir verlangte' ['even in periods of severe sickness I never became pathological … when it made the hardest demands on me']   I

'Man darf keine Nerven haben'; 'leiden ist ein Einwand' ['One must not have any nerves'; 'Suffering […] is [also] an objection']   – –

'ich habe immer nur an der "Vielsamkeit" gelitten … hat man mich je darüber betrübt gesehn?' ['I have suffered only from "multitudes" … has anyone ever seen me saddened on that account?']   X

52: 'Why I Write Such Good Books', section 1; '[…] halben des Darwinismus verdächtigt … ist darin wiedererkannt worden' ['[…] suspected me of Darwinism on that account … has been read into it']   =

64: 'The Birth of Tragedy', section 2; 'Die Erkenntnis, das Jasagen zur Realität, ist für den Starken … sondern sich in dem Wort "dionysisch" begreift' ['Knowledge, saying Yes to reality, is just as necessary for the strong … but comprehends himself in the word "Dionysian"']   )

65: 'The Birth of Tragedy', section 3; at top of page above passage beginning '"jene Lust, die auch noch die Lust am Vernichten in sich schliesst"' ['"that joy which includes even joy in destroying"']   L implying the highlighting of the rest of section 3, ending 'die fast alle ihre grundsätzlichen Vorstellungen von Heraklit geerbt hat, Spuren davon. –' ['and the Stoics inherited almost all of their principal notions from Heraclitus']

Within this passage: 'Die Bejahung des Vergehens und Vernichtens … was bisher gedacht worden ist' ['The affirmation of passing away and destroying … than anything else thought to date']   I inscription in Greek above this line

98: 'Thus Spoke Zarathustra. A Book for All and None', section 7; 'Ich kenne das Glück des Nehmenden nicht; und oft träumte mir davon, dass Stehlen noch seliger sein müsse als Nehmen' ['I do not know the happiness of those who receive; and I have often dreamed that even stealing must be more blessed than receiving']   I

'Sie nehmen von mir: aber rühre ich noch an ihre Seele? Eine Kluft ist zwischen Nehmen und Geben; und die kleinste Kluft ist am letzten zu überbrücken' ['They receive from me, but do I touch their souls? There is a cleft between giving and receiving; and the narrowest cleft is the last to be bridged']   I

Der Wille zur Macht

321: aphorism 244 (Nov. 1887–March 1888); 'Gehen wir von der Erfahrung aus, von jedem Falle … was der "Gott der Liebe" seinen Gläubigen für Tendenzen eingiebt' ['Judging from experience, from every instance   a) pencil: inscription in hand 2

539

... what tendencies the "God of Love" inspires in his believers']¹¹

'An sich hat ja Wissen und Weisheit keinen Werth ... einen hohen Unwerth darstellte' ['Knowledge and wisdom in themselves have no value ... represent a great disvalue']

Within this passage: 'keinen Werth' ['no value']; 'Ziel haben' ['be in possession of the goal']; '[es könnte] ein Ziel [geben]' ['[there *could* be] a Goal']

| | inscription, possibly in hand 2: 'alter Schacherer' |
| | — |

(22) Friedrich Nietzsche, *Morgenröthe. Gedanken über die moralischen Vorurtheile*

Page number(s) and text	Marking
112–15: Book II, section 114; 'Von der Erkenntnis des Leidenden ... In diesem Zustande kann man nicht Musik hören, ohne zu weinen' ['On the knowledge acquired through suffering ... In this condition one cannot hear music without weeping']¹² Within this passage: 'Pessimismus' ['pessimism']	a) thick black pencil: **S** —
176: Book III, section 184; 'Der Staat als Erzeugniss der Anarchisten ... ist zu jung und entzückend für sie, als dass sie nicht Alles um seinetwillen litten' ['The state as a product of the anarchists ... is too new and delightful for them not to suffer anything for its sake']	I
204: Book III, section 206; 'Dagegen die Pfeife der socialistischen Rattenfänger immer im Ohre tönt ... den Ort so lange wechseln, als noch irgend ein Zeichen von Sclaverei mir winkt' ['If, on the other hand, you have always in your ears the flutings of the Socialist pied-pipers ... to keep moving from place to place for just as long as any sign of slavery seems to threaten me']	I
128–29: Book II, section 129; 'Der angebliche Kampf der Motive ... eine der folgenreichsten und für die Entwicklung der Moral verhängnissvollsten Verwechselungen!' ['Alleged conflict of motives ... a confusion itself very rich in consequences and one highly fateful for the evolution of morality!']	b) pencil: I and ⌐ I
181–83: Book III, sections 191 and 192; 'Bessere Menschen! ... wie die Freigeister anderer Völker' ['Better People! ... as did the free-spirits of other nations'] Within this passage: section 192; 'Da steht Pascal, in der Vereinigung von Gluth, Geist und Redlichkeit' ['There stands Pascal, in unity of fervour, spirit and honesty']	III (with diagonal cross lines)
'hat dabei jene jüdische Zudringlichkeit, welche Paulus gegen Gott hat, abgstreift' ['has at the same time	IIIIIII (with diagonal cross lines, very thick)

---

¹¹ Translations taken from Friedrich Nietzsche, *The Will to Power*, ed. W. Kaufmann, trans. W. Kaufmann & R.J. Hollingdale (New York: Vintage, 1968).

¹² Translations taken from Friedrich Nietzsche, *Daybreak: Thoughts on the Prejudices of Morality*, ed. M. Clark & B. Leiter, trans. R.J. Hollingdale (Cambridge: Cambridge University Press, 1997).

put off that Jewish importunity which Paul evidenced towards his God']

Within this passage: 'Zudringlichkeit' 'gegen Gott' ['importunity' 'towards [his] God']	— —
'Und in Port Royal kam zum letzten Male das grosse christliche Gelehrtenthum zum Blühen' ['And in Port-Royal the great world of Christian scholarship saw its last efflorescence']	III (with diagonal cross lines)
191: Book III, section 198; 'Seinem Volke den Rang geben ... Lehrer und deren Nachkommen' ['Those who determine their nation's rank ... teachers and their descendants who have done it']	I
193: Book III, section 201; 'Zukunft des Adels ... hohen physischen Kraft zu wahren weiss' ['Future of the aristocracy ... in possession of high physical strength']	I
224: Book IV, section 235; 'Dank abweisen ... Diess beleidigt tief—und warum?' ['Refusing gratitude ... To do so is very wounding—and why?']	I
section 238; 'Das Streben nach Anmuth ... strenge Sitten und peinliche "Lebensberufe" zurück' ['The striving for charm ... stern customs and demanding "life-tasks"']	I
225: Book IV, section 239; 'Wink für Moralisten ... ein guter Mensch werden.—und jetzt!' ['Hint for moralists ... a good man for the sake of his art—. And now!']	I
307: Book V, section 452; 'Ungeduld ... So wird ein Fehler des Charakters zur Schule des Genie's' ['Impatience ... Thus a defect of character becomes a school of genius']	c) purple ink: I

(23) Arthur Schopenhauer, *Sämtliche Werke in zwölf Bänden. Zweiter Bd. Die Welt als Wille und Vorstellung 1. und 2. Buch*

Page number(s) and text	Marking
	All pencil:
13: from 'Vorrede zur ersten Auflage: 'gebe ich mit innigem Ernst ...geringeschätzt wird' ['I part with the book with deep seriousness .... disparaged as trivial'][13]	)
Within this passage: 'wo sie als paradox ... geringeschätzt wird'	— —
14: from 'Vorrede zur zweiten Auflage'; 'weil ich fortwährend das Falsche ... ihrer selbst wegen betrieben werden' ['for I constantly saw the false .... The object itself must always be pursued for its own sake']	I
33–34; first book §3; 'Der Hauptunterschied ... bestimmenden Teile ist' ['The chief distinction ... determine each other *ad infinitum*']	I and **S**
Within this passage: 'Phantasma' ['phantasm']	ǂ

---

13 Translations taken from Arthur Schopenhauer, *The World as Will and Idea*, trans. R.B. Haldane & J. Kemp (London: Routledge & Kegan Paul, 1964).

541

34: 'und für diese haben wir die Zeit erkannt ... Folgen ihres Inhalts' ['we have found to be time ... consequences of their content']
Within this passage: 'seinen Vater, vertilgt hat' ['effaced', 'its generator'])

34: 'bejammerte', 'ewigen Fluß der Dinge', 'immerdar Werdende' ['laments', 'eternal flux of things', 'ever becoming'] — —

35: 'oder auch dem hingeworfenen Strick ... Satze des Grundes' ['or the stray piece of rope ... principle of sufficient reason'] —

§4; 'fūllt sie den Raum, füllt sie die Zeit' ['does it fill space and time'] — — (marginal note: 'DU SIEHST ZUM RAUM WIRD HIER DIE ZEIT')

36: 'eben wie die Zeit, eben wie der Raum' ['as in the case of time and space'] — —

39: 'Aber wie mit dem Eintritt der Sonne ... ist nicht die Anschauung' ['But as with the rising of the sun ... is not perception'] —

127: §16; 'Lehren der Veden, des Platon, des Christentums und Kants' ['the doctrines of the Vedas, of Plato, of Christianity, and of Kant'] —

129: 'd.h. man soll leben mit gehöriger Kenntnis des Hergangs der Dinge ... die Welt und das Leben nicht kannte' ['that is, one ought to live with a due knowledge of the transitory nature of things ... did not know the world and life'] ?

(24) Eugène Delacroix, *Mein Tagebuch*

Page number(s) and text	Marking
	a) blue–purple ink:
35: the modern character of art reflected in Beethoven; 'dass uns Mozart ... dass sich in ihm [Beethoven] der moderne Charakter der Kunst tatsächlich mehr spiegelt' Within this passage: 'dass Beethoven der spätere ist'	|
50–51: discussing the logic of music's harmony and counterpoint with Chopin; the relationship between the art and science of music; comparison of Mozart and Beethoven; Berlioz and Ingres; 'Tagsüber sprachen wir über Musik ... Auf Ingres und seine Schule anzuwenden'	| and)
59–60: comparison of architects with painters, poets and musicians; 'Ein Architekt, der wirklich alle Bedingungen seiner Kunst erfüllt ... wir dieser seiner Bestimmung'	|
78: the greatness of Chopin; 'Wenn auch ein Teil der Werke dieses Mannes ... er vielleicht kaum der Versuchung widerstanden'	)

542

202–3: masterpieces which are the product of youth; 'sind die, welche in ihrem Leben … muss man das Vertrauen'

Fashionably popular pieces compared with true masterpieces whose deeper value emerges with time; 'Es gibt sehr talentvolle Menschen … um später wieder ans Licht zu kommen'

The hope that those whose work is despised during their lifetime receive their reward in another sphere; 'Man muss hoffen … in einer anderen Sphäre finden werden'

Other similar markings located against text describing; Chopin and Mickiewicz; claim that humour and seriousness should not be mixed; the Beethoven symphony as too long; young artists' taste for the bizarre.

b) pencil:
|
vertical inscription in margin 'Salome?' possibly in Mahler's or Alma's hand
S

(25) Ernst Jentsch, *Musik und Nerven II. Das musikalische Gefühl*

Page number(s) and text	Marking
	a) pencil:
2: 'Die Formen der Gefühlzustände'; 'Phantasietätigkeit' at bottom of page	— ‖ inscription in hand 1 (not Mahler's)
4: 'Die Formen der Gefühlzustände'; between 'Diese Anschauungsweise, die parallelistische' and 'besagt also, dass die Einzelheiten beider Erscheinungsreihen, die der physischen und der psychischen, einenander in gewisser Weise entsprechen, ohne indes identisch zu sein'	⊤ denoting insertion; inscription against same mark in margin in hand 2 (not Mahler's, possibly Werfel's): 'ist ganz un-naturwissenschaftlich!'
physical and mental anomalies and abnormalities; 'und geistige Anomalien … abnormen morphologischen Eigenschaften sein müssen'	‖ inscription in margin in hand 3 (not Mahler's, possibly Alma's): 'Ohren!' ≡
28: 'Die Wirkungen der akustischen und rhythmischen Reize'; musical vibrations; 'Wenn der Dichter sagt: "Wenn das Gewölbe widerschallt/Fühlt man erst recht des Basses Grundgewalt" … Die musikalischen Erschütterungen'	‖ and ⊂ inscriptions in margin in hand 2
31–33: 'Das musikalische Empfinden'; physiological as well as psychological origins of emotion; 'Was für unsere vorliegende Betrachtung … denn die früher allgemein gültige' 'Besonders wesentlich ist dabei … sondern gleichzeitig ein körperlicher Zustand sein müsse' Within this passage: 'gleichzeitig'	‖
33: 'Das musikalische Empfinden'; 'Die spezifische Wirkung der musikalischen Kunst kann dagegen, wie gesehen wurde, sehr unabhängig von Vorstellungselementen sein (sie muss es nicht)'	≡
36–37: 'Das musikalische Empfinden'; the release of psychological tension; 'Es handelt sich hier … der assoziativen Verknüpfung "Lärm"'	— ‖
	‖ inscription in margin in hand 2

543

	inscription in margin in hand 2
the understanding of music as sensual excitation; 'Meint man hier mit "Musik" … eines bestimmten Individuums musikalisch zu fühlen'	I inscription in margin in hand 2: 'klingt oft wie moderne Symph. mir lieber, als ein Werkelallein'
fairground noise; 'Wenn man z. B. einen Jahrmarktstrubel … was elementare Musikwirkung ist'	inscription in margin in hand 2
38–39: 'Das musikalische Empfinden'; a barrier should not be set up between the sensual and reflective aspects of music; 'Trotz dieser deutlichen Zweiteilung … Schranke zu errichten' the argument whether musical form and content should be demarcated; 'wie der sterile Streit, ob "Form" und "Inhalt" in der Musik sich genau abgrenzen lasse' Within this passage: 'sterile' 'Das intakte und komplette Tongehör ist wichtig, aber keine absolute Vorbedingung für das musikalische Fühlen'	–– and ⊥ L
40–41: 'Das musikalische Empfinden'; the physiology of amusia; 'Die "Amusie" kann sich also von vielerlei Ursachen herschreiben … noch nachträglich angebahnt werden kann' 'Auch bei andern psychophysischen Vorgängen ändert die Einsicht in den Zusammenhang ja nichts an der subjektiven Wahrnehmung' musical stimuli can evoke abnormal conditions; 'Hervorzurufen sind derartige abnorme Zustände … unbestimmter Art'	inscription in margin in hand 3: 'also Hoffnung!' I (thick) I (thick)
42: 'Das musikalische Empfinden'; the affectiveness of music; 'Ganz ähnlich verfährt die Psyche des musikalisch Empfindenden … ein ähnlich beschaffenes Vorstellungsbild zu gestalten' the fantasy of the listener; 'Man engt auf diese Weise die Phantasietätigkeit des Höreres … gar nichts einfallen würde'	III inscription in margin in hand 3: 'also unechtheit [sic] von Programmusik' I
Within this passage: 'phantasiearmen Kunstadepten'	––
45: 'Das musikalische Empfinden'; 'Eine Gruppe von musikalischen Gebilden, welche dieser Synthese besonders gut zugänglich sind, bildet die musikalische Darstellung von Bewegungen aller Art von der Stampfmühle bis zum Spinnrad, wobei die Imitation mittels des Rhythmus sehr erleichtert wird'	I (pencil and purple pencil superimposed)
48: 'Das musikalische Empfinden'; intention and inspiration of composers; 'Ob die Intention des Werks … in der Musik vorkommen'	I inscription in margin in hand 1
49: 'Das musikalische Empfinden'; only the strongly predisposed can tolerate continuous playing of music; 'Die musikalische Schöpfungen sind in der Dauer … immer wieder von neuem fesseln'	I inscription in margin in hand 3: 'Erklärung [?] für meine Ungelehrsamkeit in Toblach!'
Within this passage: 'den Durchschnitt der', 'Nur der starker Präf[disponierte]' bottom of page, above footnotes, after discussion of orchestral music's means of expression	inscription in margin in hand 3: 'Abschieben!'
54: 'Das musikalische Empfinden'; the effect of music on perception; 'Die Wirkungsweise der Musik … der unmittelbaren musikalischen Empfindung des Hörers nichts zu tun'	–– inscription in margin in hand 1

544

57: 'Das musikalische Empfinden'; harmonic effects; 'deshalb gut die "leeren" Konsonanzen ... stehender harmonischer Effekte'

inscription in margin in hand 2 referring to 'Bohème'
|

59: 'Das musikalische Empfinden'; the profundity of music; 'der Musik die Erhebung über die Sinnenwelt ... ihren Platz in der menschlichen Kulturgeschichte zu behaupten' Beethoven's belief that music has more to reveal than some science and philosophy: 'Und so ist es denn gut ... als manche Wissenschaft und manche Philosophie'

X

63: 'Über das musikalische Geniessen'; 'Man nehme z. B. an, es handle sich um einen Fiebernden, der irgend welche tönenden Geräusche der Umgebung zu wirren Musikbildern vervollständigt'

[inscription in margin in hand 2

65: 'Über das musikalische Geniessen'; on the 'beautiful'; 'Man könnte beinahe frei nach Carl Lange ... die unser Organismus erfährt'

[inscription in margin in hand 2: 'Man sollte meinen, dass dies selbstverständlich ist. Siehe dagegen Hanslick-Beckmesser-Melodei [sic]'

'wenn z. B. ein kleines gänzlich unmusikalisches Kind über eine Klaviatur gerät, ist man eigentlich berechtigt, von Musikalisch-Hässlichem zu sprechen ... Behandlung eines Instruments beleidigt' Within this passage: 'beleidigt'

inscription in margin in hand 2

66: 'Über das musikalische Geniessen'; 'Das menschliche Leben, wie es auf dem grössten Teil der erde heute noch ist, könnte ohne die hohe Kunst auskommen, ohne primitive Musik und Gesang dagegen oft nicht'

| —

72: 'Das pathologische musikalische Fühlen'; mind-body relation; 'zumal die Verbindung von Leib und Seele eine ausserordentlich enge, wahre Durchdringung eine ungemein innige ist' Within this passage: 'Leib und Seele'

L

75: 'Das pathologische musikalische Fühlen'; 'Eine weitere häufige Erschöpfungserscheinung ist auch das lästige hartnäckige Sichaufdrängen von Melodien, Motiven, Refrains gegen den Willen des Betroffenen ("musikalische Zwangsvorstellungen")'

inscription in margin in hand 2

88: 'Die musikalische Anlage'; relation between musicality and hair growth; 'Zu denjenigen Degenerationszeichen ... die ursprüngliche Beschaffenheit des Haarwuchses erlaubt'

~ | inscription in margin in hand 2: 'Prater!'

95: 'Die musikalische Anlage'; final paragraph of book: thanks are due to the creative artist; 'Nicht mit dem puren Intellekte ... so wissen wir uns mit seinem Urheber in Hinblick auf den Endzweck unseres Strebens im Einklänge, in der Aufgabe der Veredelung des Menschengeschlechts'

inscription in margin in hand 1: 'erinnerst Du Dich an einer Abend-Discussion in Savoy?' [NB on their last trip to New York, Mahler and Alma stayed at the Savoy Hotel from 25 October 1910 until April 1911] inscription below this passage in hand 3: 'also doch – Zweck der Christusse! ——— '

24–25: 'Die Wirkungen der akustischen und rhythmischen Reize'; the physiological effects of musical stimuli; 'Ja, gewisse dieser Einwirkungen fallen sogar bei grösserem musikalischen Verständnisse geringer aus als in der Norm'

b) purple pencil:
| inscription in margin in hand 2

'Man kann aus diesem Beispiele ersehen, wie es grade das tiefere Verständnis ist, das in harmonischer Beziehung in der Duldsamkeit vorausgeht'	| inscription in margin in hand 2
the use of the ear to keep tempo; between 'so zieht auch der Musiker das Ohr zur Taktkontrolle vor, wie der Gebrauch des Metronoms' and 'beweist'	T denoting insertion; inscription against same mark in margin in hand 2 (mixture of pencil and purple pencil)
49: 'Das musikalische Empfinden'; the artist often does not fully grasp the significance of his creation after the event; '[dass das Werk seinem Schöpfer nachmals als] etwas ihm fremdes, ihm selbst unbegreifliches [erscheinen kann, von] dem er nicht recht weiss, wie er dazu gekommen [ist, und dessen Kommentar er] gern dem Kunstkritiker überlässt'	— inscriptions in margin in hand 2: 'Das sehr oft' (against first underlined passage); 'das weniger' (against third underlined passage)
52–53: 'Das musikalische Empfinden'; the blunting effect of repetitive music; 'Allerdings kommt hier dazu, dass der physiologische Effekt namentlich gegen das Ende der Leistung oft möglichst in die Höhe getrieben werden soll'	inscription in margin in hand 2: 'Applaus-treiben!!'
with 'higher' music, emotional identification and gratification come with repeated hearings and study; 'Je naïver das Verständnis ist, um so weniger ist ihm meistens grade mit den Meisterwerken der Kunst gedient'	inscription in margin in hand 2, including the following: 'das Erlebnis mit Mahler's "schwerstem Lied" (der Gefangene im Turm" [sic] [reference to *Wunderhorn* song 'Lied des Verfolgten im Turm']
	|
the physiological theory of affects; 'Nach der alten Theorie … äusserlich wahrnehmbare Affektzeichen aufzuweisen hat' the intensity of feeling engendered by music; '[wird man erwarten können, dass ausgesprochenes musikalisches Gefühl einen gewissen Intensitätsgrad besitzen, nach aussen wenigstens] etwas hervortreten [muss, um als solches bezeichnet zu werden]'	— — inscription in margin in hand 2 referring to *Tristan*
'[Einen guten Einblick, ob und in wie weit affective Teilnahme an einer musikalischen Darbietung vorhanden war, gewinnt man zuweilen auch, wenn diese] unvermutet abgebrochen [wurde]'	— —
59: 'Das musikalische Empfinden'; the relationship between musical emotion and materialism; '[Auch die Vertreter der materialistischen Weltanschauung, welche gegenwärtig noch vielfach] als Postulat der exakten Wissenschaft [angesehen wird]' at bottom of page	— — inscription above this phrase in hand 2: 'mit Recht'; * * after the underlined phrase * and inscription in hand 2
84: 'Die musikalische Anlage'; the development of musical ability through practice and heredity; 'Gegenwärtig ware aber niemand mehr imstande, den Musiksinn etwa auf erstere Weise selber zu erwerben, sondern man hat ihn eben oder man hat ihn nicht'	) inscription in margin in hand 2: 'Warum nicht?'
'[Freilich kann er, wenn er vorhanden ist, sehr vervollkommnet werden, aber schaffen lässt er sich in der kurzen Spanne] eines [menschlichen Lebens in seiner jetzigen Form vom Individuum selbst nicht]'	— — inscription in margin in hand 2
87: 'Die musikalische Anlage'; inherited musical ability; 'eine oder die andere Generation überspringen, [doch kann auch der Repräsentant dieser eine gute Disposition besessen haben]'	— — inscription in margin in hand 2: 'Mendel!'
'[Nach mehreren Geschlechterfolgen verschwindet dann das Talent aus der Familie oder es wird] durch ein	— — inscription in margin in hand 2:

anderes ersetzt' between 'Kumulierung des Talents durch Zuchtwahl kommt' and 'vor'	'Nicht spezifisch Begabung' ⊥ denoting insertion; inscription against same mark in margin in hand 2: 'nicht'
'[Die Vererbung findet nicht in der Weise statt, dass etwa das Talent] in einer bestimmten Form [den Nachkommen weitergegeben wird]'	— inscription in margin in hand 2: 'Doch auch das! Siehe meine Unterscheidung in spezifische und Nicht spezifische Talente'
'So kann, wenn der Ascendent z. B. an schwerer Migräne leidet, der Descendent zwar von dieser frei sein, dafür aber etwa eine convulsive Anlage erhalten, die jener nicht besass'	| inscription in margin in hand 2
88: 'Die musikalische Anlage'; relation between musicality and hair growth; 'Zu denjenigen Degerationszeichen, welche speziell mit der musikalischen Anlage häufiger vergesellschaftet sind, gehört die abnorme Fülle des Haupthaars'	| inscription in margin in hand 2 leading from this highlighted passage to the next
'Für Nichtmediziner ist es vielleicht angebracht, an dieser Stelle zu bemerken, dass die sogenannte Kahlköpfigkeit eine Krankheit des Haarbodens oder eine Folge anderer Krankheiten ist'	|
89: 'Die musikalische Anlage'; 'Es [das Tongehör] verfeinert, wo die musikalische Anlage vorhanden ist, oft wieder gleichzeitig das musikalische Verständnis, kann dieses jedoch nicht erschaffen, und es gibt Individuen mit sehr feinem Tongehör, die gar kein musikalisches Verständnis besitzen'	inscription in margin in hand 2: 'hier sehr unklar'
94: 'Die musikalische Anlage'; music and the gifted mind; 'dass ein vielseitig begabter und gebildeter Geist auch besonders vielen neues in neuer ansprechender Form zu vermitteln gehabt habe. Dies träfe für eine Reihe Fälle zu, aber nicht für alle'	| inscription in margin in hand 2

547

Bibliography

Abbate, Carolyn (1991), *Unsung Voices: Opera and Musical Narrative in the Nineteenth Century*, Princeton: Princeton University Press.

Adler, Guido (1916), *Gustav Mahler*, Vienna: Universal Edition.

—— ([1916] 1982), *Gustav Mahler*, in Reilly, 1982, pp. 15–73.

Adorno, Theodor (1960), *Mahler. Eine musikalische Physiognomik*, Frankfurt: Suhrkamp.

—— (1970–86), *Gesammelte Schriften in zwanzig Bänden*, ed. Rolf Tiedemann in collaboration with Gretel Adorno, Susan Buck-Morss & Klaus Schultz, Frankfurt: Suhrkamp.

—— (1984), *Aesthetic Theory*, trans. C. Lenhardt, London: Routledge & Kegan Paul.

—— (1992a), *Mahler: A Musical Physiognomy*, trans. E. Jephcott, Chicago: University of Chicago Press.

—— (1992b), 'Mahler: Centenary Address, Vienna 1960', in Adorno, 1992c, pp. 81–110.

—— (1992c), *Quasi una Fantasia: Essays on Modern Music*, trans. R. Livingstone, London: Verso.

Agawu, V. Kofi (1986), 'Tonal Strategy in the First Movement of Mahler's Tenth Symphony', *19th-Century Music*, 9 (3), 222–33.

—— (1991), *Playing with Signs: A Semiotic Interpretation of Classic Music*, Princeton: Princeton University Press.

—— (1997), 'Prolonged Counterpoint in Mahler', in Hefling, 1997, pp. 217–47.

Ames, Katrine (1990), 'An Affair to Remember', *Newsweek*, 29 October, 79.

Anon. (1913a), review of Mahler's Eighth Symphony, *Die Zeit*, 15 March, signed 'mg' [possibly Max Graf].

Anon. (1913b), 'Die "Sinfonie der Tausend"', *Schlesische Zeitung*, 10 September, signed '—r.'.

Anon. (1924), 'Das Jüdische bei Gustav Mahler', *Halbjahr Israelisches Familienblatt*, 24 January [unsigned]; clipping from the Steininger Collection, Geheimes Staatsarchiv, Preussischer Kulturbesitz, Berlin.

Aprahamian, Felix (ed.) (1967), *Essays on Music: An Anthology from* The Listener, London: Cassell & Co.

Aspetsberger, Friedbert & Partsch, Erich Wolfgang (eds) (2002), *Mahler-Gespräche. Rezeptionsfragen – literarischer Horizont – musikalische Darstellung*, Innsbruck: Studien Verlag.

Bahr, Hermann (1890), 'Die Moderne', *Moderne Dichtung*, 1 (1), 1 January, 13–15.

Bahr-Mildenburg, Anna (1921), *Erinnerungen*, Vienna & Berlin: Wiener Literarische Anstalt.

Bal, Mieke (1997), *Narratology: Introduction to the Theory of Narrative*, 2nd edn, Toronto: University of Toronto Press.

Banks, Paul (1987), 'Mahler 2: Some Answers?', *Musical Times*, 128, April, 203–6.

—— (1989), 'Aspects of Mahler's Fifth Symphony: Performance Practice and Interpretation', *Musical Times*, 130, May, 258–65.

—— (1991), 'Mahler and the Ethics of Completing Unfinished Works of Art', in Op de Coul, 1991, pp. 4–16.

Banks, Paul & Mitchell, Donald (1980), 'Gustav Mahler' in Sadie, 1980, vol. 11, pp. 505–31.

Barham, Jeremy (1992), 'Gustav Mahler and the Philosophy of Schopenhauer and Nietzsche', unpublished MMus thesis, University of Surrey.

—— (1998), 'Mahler's Third Symphony and the Philosophy of Gustav Fechner: Interdisciplinary Approaches to Criticism, Analysis and Interpretation', unpublished PhD thesis, University of Surrey.

Barry, Barbara (1993), 'The Hidden Program in Mahler's Fifth Symphony', *Musical Quarterly*, 77 (1), spring, 47–66.

Barthes, Roland (1967), *Elements of Semiology*, trans. A. Lavers & C. Smith, New York: Hill and Wang.

—— (1974), *S/Z: An Essay*, trans. R. Miller, New York: Hill and Wang.

—— (1977), *Image–Music–Text*, ed. and trans. S. Heath, London: Fontana Press.

Barzun, Jacques (1990), 'Literature in Liszt's Mind and Work', in Sullivan, 1990, pp. 206–23.

Batka, Richard (1910), 'Das Jüdische bei Gustav Mahler', *Kunstwart*, 23 (20), 97–98.

Bauer-Lechner, Natalie (MS), *Mahleriana*, unpublished manuscript housed in the collection of Henry-Louis de La Grange, Bibliothèque Musicale Gustav Mahler, Paris.

—— (1923), *Erinnerungen an Gustav Mahler*, Vienna: E.P. Tal.

Bekker, Paul (1918), *Die Symphonie von Beethoven bis Mahler*, Berlin: Schuster & Loeffler. [Rev. repr. in *Neue Musik. Gesammelten Schriften*, Stuttgart & Berlin: Deutsche Verlags-Anstalt, 1923.]

—— ([1921] 1969), *Gustav Mahlers Sinfonien*, Berlin: Schuster & Loeffler, repr. Tutzing: Schneider.

Benjamin, Walter (1996), *Selected Writings. Vol. 1: 1913–1926*, Bullock, Marcus & Jennings, Michael W. (eds), Cambridge & London: The Belknap Press of Harvard University Press.

Berke, Dietrich & Hanemann, Dorothea (eds) (1987), *Alte Musik als ästhetische Gegenwart. Kongreßbericht Stuttgart 1985*, Kassel: Bärenreiter.

Berl, Heinrich (1923), 'Zum Problem einer jüdischen Musik', *Der Jude. Eine Monatsschrift*, 7 (5), May, 309–20.

—— (1926), *Das Judentum in der Musik*, Stuttgart, Berlin & Leipzig: Deutsche Verlags-Anstalt.

Bernstein, Leonard (1986), *Der kleine Trommler. Essay über die Musik und das Leben Gustav Mahlers*, ZDF television programme, 8 May 1986, broadcast simultaneously by the BBC and Israel Television, Tel Aviv.

Blaukopf, Herta (ed.) (1983), *Gustav Mahler. Unbekannte Briefe*, Vienna: Zsolnay.

—— (ed.) (1984), *Gustav Mahler–Richard Strauss: Correspondence, 1888–1911*, trans. E. Jephcott, London: Faber & Faber.

—— (ed.) (1986), *Mahler's Unknown Letters*, trans. R. Stokes, London: Victor Gollancz.

—— (1988), 'Frankfurt, a Wrongly Established Date and Physical Science', *News About Mahler Research*, 20, 3–5.

—— (ed.) (1996), *Gustav Mahler Briefe*, 2nd edn, Vienna: Zsolnay.

—— (2002), '"Bücher fresse ich immer mehr und mehr". Gustav Mahler als Leser', in Aspetsberger & Partsch, pp. 96–116.

Blaukopf, Kurt (1969), *Gustav Mahler oder der Zeitgenosse der Zukunft*, Vienna, Munich & Zürich: Fritz Molden.

—— (1973), *Gustav Mahler*, trans. I. Goodwin, London: Allen Lane.

—— (ed.) (1976a), *Mahler. Sein Leben, sein Werk und seine Welt in zeitgenössischen Bildern und Texten*, Vienna: Universal Edition.

—— (ed.) (1976b), *Mahler: A Documentary Study*, with contributions from Zoltan Roman, trans. P. Baker, S. Flatauer, P.R.J. Ford, D. Loman & G. Watkins, London: Thames and Hudson.

Blaukopf, Kurt & Blaukopf, Herta (eds) (1991), *Mahler: His Life, Work and World*, with contributions from Zoltan Roman, trans. P. Baker, S. Flatauer, P.R.J. Ford, D. Loman, G. Watkins & K. Williams, London: Thames and Hudson.

Blessinger, Karl (1920), *Die Überwindung von musikalischen Impotenz*, Stuttgart: B. Filser.

—— (1939), *Mendelssohn, Meyerbeer, Mahler. Drei Kapitel Judentum in der Musik als Schlüssel zur Musikgeschichte des 19. Jahrhunderts*, Die Kulturpolitischereihe, vol. 9, Berlin: Bernhard Hahnefeld.

—— (1944), *Judentum und Musik. Ein Beitrag zur Kultur- und Rassenpolitik*, Berlin: Hahnefeld.

Bloch, Ernst (1923), 'Mahler, Strauss, Bruckner', *Die Musik*, 15 (9), June, 664–70.

Bloomfield, Theodor (1991), 'The Scores of the Four Versions of Mahler's Tenth Symphony Seen from the Perspective of a Conductor', in Op de Coul, 1991, pp. 106–25.

Bontinck, Irmgard & Brusatti, Otto (eds) (1975), *Festschrift Kurt Blaukopf*, Vienna: Universal Edition.

Botstein, Leon (2002), 'Whose Gustav Mahler? Reception, Interpretation, and History', in Painter, 2002, pp. 1–53.

Bouwman, Frans (2001), 'Editing Mahler 10: Unfinished Business', *Musical Times*, 142, 43–51.

Brandenburg, Sieghard (ed.) (1998), *Haydn, Mozart & Beethoven: Studies in the Music of the Classical Period: Essays in Honour of Alan Tyson*, Oxford & New York: Oxford University Press.

Březina, Aleš (ed.) (1996), *Prager Musikleben zu Beginn des 20. Jahrhunderts*, *Jahrbuch der Bohuslav Martinů-Stiftung*, 1, Bern: Peter Lang.

Broch, Hermann (2001), *Hofmannsthal und seine Zeit. Eine Studie*, Frankfurt: Suhrkamp.

Brod, Max (1920), 'Gustav Mahlers jüdische Melodien', *Musikblätter des Anbruch*, 2, 378–79.

—— (1961), *Gustav Mahler. Beispiel einer deutsch-jüdischen Symbiose*, Frankfurt: Ner-Tamid Verlag.

Bruns, Steven (1989), 'Mahler's Motivically Expanded Tonality: An Analytical Study of the Adagio of the Tenth Symphony', unpublished PhD thesis, University of Wisconsin–Madison.

Brzoska, Matthias & Heinemann, Michael (eds) (2001), *Die Geschichte der Musik in 3 Bänden*, Laaber: Laaber Verlag.

Buhler, James (1996), '"Breakthrough" as Critique of Form: The Finale of Mahler's First Symphony', *19th-Century Music*, 20 (2), 125–43.

Burnham, Scott (1995), *Beethoven Hero*, Princeton: Princeton University Press.

—— (2001), 'How Music Matters: Poetic Content Revisited', in Cook & Everist, 2001, pp. 193–216.

Cardus, Neville (1965), *Gustav Mahler: His Mind and His Music. Vol. 1: The First Five Symphonies*, London: Gollancz.

Chanan, Michael (1971a), 'Mahler in Venice?', *Music & Musicians*, June, 26–28.

—— (1971b), 'Death in Venice', *Art International*, 15 (7), September, 31–32 & 57.

Chatman, Seymour (1978), *Story and Discourse: Narrative Structure in Fiction and Film*, Ithaca: Cornell University Press.

—— (1981), 'What Novels can do that Films can't (and Vice Versa)', in Mitchell, 1981, pp. 117–36.

Chesterman, Robert (ed.) (1976), *Conversations with Conductors*, London: Robson Books.

Christy, Nicholas, Christy, Beverly C., & Wood, Barry C. (1970), 'Gustav Mahler and his Illnesses', *Transactions of the American Clinical and Climatological Association*, 82, 200–17.

Coburn, Steven (2002), 'Mahler's Tenth Symphony: Form and Genesis', unpublished PhD thesis, New York University.

Cone, Edward T. (1968), *Musical Form and Musical Performance*, New York: W.W. Norton.

—— (1982), 'Schubert's Promissory Note: An Exercise in Musical Hermeneutics', *19th-Century Music*, 5 (3), 233–41.

Cook, Nicholas & Everist, Mark (eds) (2001), *Rethinking Music*, Oxford & New York: Oxford University Press.

Cooke, Deryck (1961), 'Mahler's Tenth Symphony: Artistic Morality and Musical Reality', *Musical Times*, 102 (June), 351–54.

—— (1967), 'Mahler's Unfinished Symphony', in Aprahamian, 1967, pp. 146–50.

—— (1980), *Gustav Mahler: An Introduction to his Music*, London: Faber Music.

—— (1976), *Gustav Mahler: A Performing Version of the Draft for the Tenth Symphony*, New York: Associated Music Publishers/London: Faber Music.

—— (1989), *Gustav Mahler. A Performing Version of the Draft for the Tenth Symphony*, 2nd edn, London: Faber Music.

Cooke, Mervyn (ed.) (1995), *Donald Mitchell: Cradles of the New. Writings on Music 1951–1991*, London: Faber & Faber.

Coudenhove-Kalergi, Richard Nicolaus von (1932), *Revolution durch Technik*, Vienna & Leipzig: Paneuropa.

Culler, Jonathan (1981), *The Pursuit of Signs: Semiotics, Literature, Deconstruction*, Ithaca: Cornell University Press/London: Routledge & Kegan Paul.

Culshaw, John (1982), *Putting the Record Straight*, New York: Viking.

Dahlhaus, Carl (1982), *Esthetics of Music*, trans. W. Austin, Cambridge: Cambridge University Press.

Danuser, Hermann (1975), 'Zu den Programmen von Mahlers frühen Symphonien', *Melos/Neue Zeitschrift für Musik*, 1 (Jan.–Feb.), 14–18.

—— (1986), *Gustav Mahler. Das Lied von der Erde*, Munich: Fink.

—— (1988), 'Funktionen von Natur in der Musik Gustav Mahlers', *Österreichische Musikzeitschrift*, 43 (11), 602–13.

—— (1991), *Gustav Mahler und seine Zeit*, Laaber: Laaber Verlag.

—— (ed.) (1992), *Gustav Mahler. Wege der Forschung*, Darmstadt: Wissenschaftliche Buchgesellschaft.

Darcy, Warren (2001), 'Rotational Form, Teleological Genesis, and Fantasy Projection in the Slow Movement of Mahler's Sixth Symphony', *19th-Century Music* 25 (1), 49–74.

Decsey, Ernst (1911), 'Stunden mit Mahler', *Die Musik*, 10 (18), 352–56, & 10 (21), 143–53.

Del Mar, Norman (1980), *Mahler's Sixth Symphony: A Study*, London: Eulenburg Books.

Dibelius, Ulrich (1971), 'Mahlers zweite Existenz. Seine Symphonien auf Schallplatten', *Hi-Fi Stereophonie*, 10 (5), 347–54.

Diether, Jack (1960a), 'Music Mourns van Beinum and Adler', *Chord and Discord*, 2 (9), 32–34.

—— (1960b), 'Bruckner & Mahler in the First Years of the Stereo Disc – June 1960', *Chord and Discord*, 2 (9), 100–112.

—— (1963), 'The Facts Concerning Mahler's Tenth Symphony [Foreword]', *Chord and Discord*, 2 (10), 3–8.

—— (1969), 'Notes on Some Mahler Juvenilia', *Chord and Discord*, 3 (1), 3–100.

—— (1971), 'The All-Purpose Adagietto', *The Villager*, 15 July.

Eckstein, Friedrich (1936), *'Alte unnennbare Tage!' Erinnerungen aus siebzig Lehr- und Wanderjahren*, Vienna: Reichner.

Eggebrecht, Hans Heinrich (1982a), *Die Musik Gustav Mahlers*, Munich: Piper.

—— (1982b), 'Dichtung, Symphonie, Programmusik. I. Symphonische Dichtung', *Archiv für Musikwissenschaft*, 39, 223–33.

Ehlers, Paul (1908), review of the Prague première of Mahler's Seventh Symphony, *Der Sammler*, 131, 29 October, 8.

Eichenauer, Richard ([1932] 1937), *Musik und Rasse*, 2nd edn, Munich: J.F. Lehmanns Verlag.

Ekdahl Davidson, Audrey & Davidson, Clifford (eds) (1985), *Sacra/Profana: Studies in Sacred and Secular Music for Johannes Riedel*, Minneapolis: Friends of Minnesota Music.

Engel, Gabriel (1932), *Gustav Mahler, Song Symphonist*, New York: Bruckner Society of America.

Erben, Karel Jaromír (1864), *Prostonárodní české písně a říkadla* [*Popular Czech Songs and Sayings*], Prague: Jaroslav Pospíšil.

Erlich, Victor (1965), *Russian Formalism: History, Doctrine*, The Hague: Mouton.

Ermers, Max (1932), *Victor Adler. Aufstieg und Grösse einer sozialistischen Partei*, Vienna: Epstein.

Fallows, David (1980), 'Adagietto', in Sadie, 1980, vol. 1, p. 88.

Feder, Stuart (1978), 'Gustav Mahler Dying', *International Review of Psychoanalysis*, 5, 125–48.

Feuchtner, Bernd (1999), 'Der Teufel tanzt es mit mir. Mahlers Zehnte-Fragment läßt uns keine Ruhe. Rudolf Barshais neue Aufführungsversion', *Frankfurter Allgemeine Zeitung*, 2 June, feuilleton.

Filler, Susan (1977), 'Editorial Problems in Symphonies of Gustav Mahler: A Study of the Sources of the Third and Tenth Symphonies', unpublished PhD dissertation, Northwestern University.

—— (1984), 'Mahler's Sketches for a Scherzo in c minor and a Presto in F major', *College Music Symposium*, 24, 69–80.

—— (1990), 'Mahler in the Medical Literature', *News About Mahler Research*, 23, March, 8–13.

—— (1991), 'Manuscript and Performing Versions of Mahler's Tenth Symphony', in Op de Coul, 1991, pp. 36–50.

—— (1997), 'The Missing Mahler: Alois (Hans) in Chicago', in Weiß, 1997, pp. 39–45.

Fischer, Jens Malte (1997), 'Gustav Mahler und das "Judentum in der Musik"', *Merkur*, 51 (8), 665–80. [Rev. version in Fischer, *Jahrhundertdämmerung. Ansichten eines anderen Fin de siècle* (Vienna: Paul Zsolnay, 2000), pp. 131–58.]

Floros, Constantin (1981), 'Weltanschauung und Symphonik', in Klein, 1981, pp. 29–39.

—— (1985), *Gustav Mahler III. Die Symphonien*, Wiesbaden: Breitkopf & Härtel.

—— (1987a), *Gustav Mahler I. Die geistige Welt Gustav Mahlers in systematischer Darstellung*, 2nd edn, Wiesbaden: Breitkopf & Härtel.

—— (1987b), *Gustav Mahler II. Mahler und die Symphonik des 19. Jahrhunderts in neuer Deutung*, 2nd edn, Wiesbaden: Breitkopf & Härtel.

—— (1991), 'Aspekte der Programmatik bei Mahler', in Vogt, 1991, pp. 436–44.

—— (1994), *Gustav Mahler: The Symphonies*, trans. V. Wicker, Aldershot: Scolar Press.

Flothuis, Marius (1991), 'Dürfen und können wir ein unvollständig überliefertes Werk ergänzen?', in Op de Coul, 1991, pp. 17–25.

Foerster, Josef Bohuslav (1922), 'Gustav Mahler in Hamburg', *Prager Presse*, 2 April–2 July.

—— (1955), *Der Pilger. Erinnerungen eines Musikers*, Prague: Artia.

Forte, Allen (1984), 'Middleground Motives in the Adagietto of Mahler's Fifth Symphony', *19th-Century Music*, 8 (2), 153–63.

Franklin, Peter (1977), 'The Gestation of Mahler's Third Symphony', *Music & Letters*, 58 (4), pp. 439–46.

—— (ed.) (1980), *Recollections of Gustav Mahler by Natalie Bauer-Lechner*, trans. D. Newlin, London: Faber Music.

—— (1991), *Mahler Symphony No. 3*, Cambridge: Cambridge University Press.

—— (2002), 'A Soldier's Sweetheart's Mother's Tale? Mahler's Gendered Musical Discourse', in Painter, 2002, pp. 111–25.

Friedmann, Aron (1908), *Der synagogale Gesang*, 2nd edn, Berlin: Peters.

Fülöp, Peter (1995), *Mahler Discography*, New York: The Kaplan Foundation.

Gartenberg, Egon (1978), *Mahler: The Man and his Music*, New York: Schirmer Books.

Genette, Gérard (1980), *Narrative Discourse: An Essay in Method*, trans. J.E. Lewin, Ithaca: Cornell University Press.

—— (1997), *Paratexts: Thresholds of Interpretation*, trans. J.E. Lewin, Cambridge: Cambridge University Press.

Gerigk, Herbert & Stengel, Theo (1940), *Lexikon der Juden in der Musik*, Berlin. [Repr. in Weisseweiler, 1999.]

Gerstenberg, Walter, LaRue, Jan & Rehm, Wolfgang (eds) (1963), *Festschrift Otto Erich Deutsch: Zum 80. Geburtstag am 5. September 1963*, Kassel: Bärenreiter.

Giroud, Françoise (1991), *Alma Mahler or the Art of Being Loved*, Oxford: Oxford University Press.

Glanz, Christian (ed.) (1999), *Wien 1897. Kulturgeschichtliches Profil eines Epochenjahres*, Frankfurt: Peter Lang.

Godde, Christoph & Lonitz, Henri (eds) (1995), *Bruno Walter. Gesammelte Briefe*, Frankfurt: Suhrkamp.

Gradenwitz, Peter (1961), *Die Musikgeschichte Israels. Von den biblischen Anfängen bis zum modernen Staat*, Kassel: Bärenreiter.

Greene, David (1984), *Mahler, Consciousness and Temporality*, New York & London: Gordon and Breach.

Hall, David (1993), 'Encounters with Kubelik', *Stagebill*, spring, 8–14, Chicago: Chicago Symphony Orchestra.

Hansen, Mathias (ed.) (1985), *Gustav Mahler Briefe*, Leipzig: Reclam.

—— (1991), 'Fragment und Vollendung. Mahlers X. in der Perspektive der IX. Sinfonie', in Op de Coul, 1991, pp. 51–59.

Harris, Ellen T. (1990), 'Das Verhältnis von Lautstärke und Stimmlage im Barockgesang', in Marx, 1990, vol. 3, pp. 157–71.

Hatten, Robert S. (1994), *Musical Meaning in Beethoven: Markedness, Correlation, and Interpretation*, Bloomington & Indianapolis: University of Indiana Press.

Hefling, Stephen (1981), 'Variations *in nuce*: A Study of Mahler Sketches and a Comment on Sketch Studies', in Klein, 1981, pp. 102–26.

—— (1983), 'The Road not Taken: Mahler's *Rübezahl*', *Yale University Library Gazette*, 57, 145–70.

—— (1988), 'Mahler's "Todtenfeier" and the Problem of Program Music', *19th-Century Music*, 12 (1), 153–63.

—— (1992), '*Das Lied von der Erde*: Mahler's Symphony for Voices and Orchestra – or Piano', *Journal of Musicology*, 10, 293–340.

—— (ed.) (1997), *Mahler Studies*, Cambridge: Cambridge University Press.

—— (2000), *Mahler: Das Lied von der Erde*, Cambridge: Cambridge University Press.

Heinsheimer, Hans & Stefan, Paul (eds) (1926), *25 Jahre neue Musik. Jahrbuch 1926 der Universal-Edition*, Vienna: Universal Edition.

Herf, Jeffrey (1984), *Reactionary Modernism: Technology, Culture and Politics in Weimar and the Third Reich*, Cambridge: Cambridge University Press.

Heyworth, Peter (ed.) (1985), *Conversations with Klemperer*, London: Faber & Faber.

Hilmar-Voit, Renate (ed.) (1991), *Symphonische Entwürfe*, Tutzing: Hans Schneider. [Facsimile edition of Mahler's manuscripts of the Scherzo in C minor and the Presto in F major.]

—— (ed.) (1998), *Des Knaben Wunderhorn. Gesänge für eine Singstimme mit Orchesterbegleitung*, *Kritische Gesamtausgabe* vol. 14/2, Vienna: Universal Edition.

Hirsch, Eric D. Jnr. (1967), 'Objective Interpretation', Appendix 1 in Hirsch, *Validity in Interpretation*, New Haven & London: Yale University Press.

Hirschfeld, Robert [r. h.] (1907), 'Feuilleton. Konzerte', *Wiener Abendpost*, 10 January.

Hofmannsthal, Hugo von (1893), 'Gabriele d'Annunzio', *Frankfurter Zeitung*, 37 (219), 9 August, morning edn, 1–3.

Hopkins, Robert (1983), 'Secondary Parameters and Closure in the Symphonies of Gustav Mahler', unpublished PhD thesis, University of Pennsylvania.

—— (1990), *Closure and Mahler's Music: The Role of Secondary Parameters*, Philadelphia: University of Pennsylvania Press.

Hruschka, Alois & Toischer, Wendelin (1891), *Deutsche Volkslieder aus Böhmen*, Prague: Verlag des Deutschen Vereins zur Verbreitung gemeinnütziger Kenntnisse.

Isaacs, Reginald (1983–84), *Walter Gropius. Der Mensch und sein Werk*, 2 vols, trans. G.G. Meerwein, Berlin: Mann.

Istel, Edgar (ed.) (1910), *Mahlers Symphonien, erläutert mit Notenbeispielen*, Berlin: Schlesinger.

Johnson, Douglas (1998), 'Deconstructing Beethoven's Sketchbooks', in Brandenburg, 1998, pp. 225–35.

Johnson, Julian (1999a), *Webern and the Transformation of Nature*, Cambridge: Cambridge University Press.

—— (1999b), 'The Sound of Nature? Mahler, Klimt and the Changing Representation of Nature in Early Viennese Modernism', in Glanz, 1999, pp. 189–204.

Jones, Ernest (1953–57), *Sigmund Freud: Life and Work*, 3 vols, London: The Hogarth Press.

Jongbloed, Jan (1991), 'Mahler's Tenth Symphony: The Order of Composition of its Movements', in Op de Coul, 1991, pp. 143–53.

Jülg, Hans-Peter (1986), *Gustav Mahlers Sechste Symphonie*, Munich & Salzburg: Musikverlag Emil Katzbichler.

Kaplan, Gilbert (1986a), *Gustav Mahler: Symphony No. 2 in C minor 'Resurrection' Facsimile*, New York: The Kaplan Foundation.

—— (1986b), 'How Mahler Performed his Second Symphony', *Musical Times*, 127, May, 266–71.

—— (ed.) (1995), *The Mahler Album*, New York: The Kaplan Foundation/ Thames and Hudson.

Kaplan, Richard (1981), 'The Interaction of Diatonic Collections in the Adagio of Mahler's Tenth Symphony', *In Theory Only*, 6 (1), 29–39.

—— (1984), 'Sonata Form in the Orchestral Works of Liszt: The Revolutionary Reconsidered', *19th-Century Music*, 8 (2), 142–52.

—— (1992), 'The Finale of Mahler's First: Cyclicism, Narrative, and the "Footsteps of the Giant"', paper presented at the Annual Meeting of the American Musicological Society, Pittsburgh, 6 November 1992.

—— (1996), 'Temporal Fusion and Climax in the Symphonies of Mahler', *Journal of Musicology*, 14, 213–32.

Karbusicky, Vladimir (1978), *Gustav Mahler und seine Umwelt*, Impulse der Forschung, vol. 28, Darmstadt: Wissenschaftliche Buchgesellschaft.

—— (1996a), *Mahler in Hamburg. Chronik einer Freundschaft*, Hamburg: Bockel Verlag.

—— (1996b), 'Gustav Mahlers Beziehung zur tschechischen Musik', in Březina, 1996, pp. 77–92.

—— (1998), 'Zur Philosophie der kosmischen und irdischen Harmonie in der Musik', in Kolleritsch, 1998, pp. 142–76.

Karpath, Ludwig (1934), *Begegnung mit dem Genius*, Vienna: Fiba.

Kater, Michael (1997), *The Twisted Muse: Musicians and their Music in the Third Reich*, Oxford: Oxford University Press.

Kauders, Albert (1907), Feuilleton 'Gustav Mahlers Sechste Symphonie', *Fremdenblatt*, Vienna, 5 January.

Kaufmann, Walter (1974), 'Translator's Introduction', in Nietzsche ([1887] 1974), pp. 3–26.

Keegan, Susanne (1991), *The Bride of the Wind: The Life of Alma Mahler*, London: Secker & Warburg.

Kennedy, Michael (1974), *Mahler*, London: Dent. [2nd edn, 1990.]

Killian, Herbert (ed.) (1984), *Gustav Mahler. Erinnerungen von Natalie Bauer-Lechner*, Hamburg: Karl Dieter Wagner.

Kinderman, William & Krebs, Harald (eds) (1996), *The Second Practice of Nineteenth-Century Tonality,* Lincoln: University of Nebraska Press.

Klein, Rudolf (ed.) (1981), *Gustav Mahler Kolloquium 1979*, Beiträge der Österreichischen Gesellschaft für Musik, 2, Kassel: Bärenreiter.

Klemperer, Otto (1960), *Erinnerungen an Gustav Mahler*, Zürich: Atlantis.

Klose, Friedrich (1927), *Meine Lehrjahre bei Bruckner. Erinnerungen und Betrachtungen*, Regensburg: Deutsche Musikbücherei.

Knittel, Kay (1995), '"Ein hypermoderner Dirigent": Mahler and Anti-Semitism in *Fin-de-Siècle* Vienna', *19th-Century Music*, 18 (3), 257–76.

Kolleritsch, Otto (ed.) (1998), *Das gebrochene Glücksversprechen*, Studien zur Wertungsforschung, vol. 33, Vienna & Graz: Universal Edition.

Korngold, Julius (1907), 'Feuilleton', *Neue Freie Presse*, Vienna, 8 January.

Kramer, Lawrence (1990), *Music as Cultural Practice: 1800–1900*, Berkeley & Los Angeles: University of California Press.

Kraus, Karl (1959), *Worte in Versen*, Munich: Kösel.

Kravitt, Edward F. (1978), 'Mahler's Dirges for his Death: February 24, 1901', *Musical Quarterly*, 64, 329–53.

—— (1988), 'The "Lieder" of Alma Maria Schindler-Mahler', *Music Review*, 49, 190–204.

Krebs, Dieter (1997), *Gustav Mahlers Erste Symphonie. Form und Gehalt*, Musikwissenschaftliche Schriften, vol. 31, Munich: Musikverlag Katzbichler.

Krenek, Ernst (1941), 'Gustav Mahler', in Walter, 1941, pp. 155–220.

Kropfinger, Klaus (1985), 'Gerettete Herausforderung. Mahlers 4. Symphonie – Mengelbergs Interpretation', in Stephan, 1985, pp. 111–75.

Krummacher, Friedhelm (1990), '"Die wenigen Blätter" und "die Sämtlichen Keime". Über Mahlers Skizzen zum Kopfsatz der III. Symphonie', in Kuckertz et al., 1990, pp. 347–63.

Kubik, Reinhold (2001), 'Unnoticed Sources to Mahler's Fifth Symphony', *News About Mahler Research*, 45 (autumn), 5–12.

Kuckertz, Josef et al. (eds) (1990), *Neue Musik und Tradition. Festschrift Rudolph Stephan zum 65. Geburtstag*, Laaber: Laaber Verlag.

Kühn, Hellmut & Quander, Georg (eds) (1982), *Gustav Mahler: Ein Lesebuch mit Bildern*, Zürich: Orell Füssli.

La Grange, Henry-Louis de (1973), *Mahler. Vol. 1*, New York: Garden City.

—— (1974), *Mahler. Vol. 1*, London: Gollancz.

—— (1979), *Gustav Mahler: Chronique d'une vie. Vol. I: Vers la gloire (1860–1900)*, Paris: Fayard.

—— (1983), *Gustav Mahler: Chronique d'une vie. Vol. II: L'Âge d'or de Vienne (1900–1907)*, Paris: Fayard.

—— (1984), *Gustav Mahler: Chronique d'une vie. Vol. III: Le Génie foudroyé (1907–1911)*, Paris: Fayard.

—— (ed.) (1986), *Colloque International Gustav Mahler, 25–27 Jan. 1985*, Paris: L'Association Gustav Mahler.

—— (1991), 'The Tenth Symphony: Purgatory or Catharsis?', in Op de Coul, 1991, pp. 154–64.

—— (1995), *Gustav Mahler. Vol. 2. Vienna: The Years of Challenge (1897–1904)*, Oxford: Oxford University Press.

—— (1999), *Gustav Mahler. Vol. 3. Vienna: Triumph and Disillusion (1904–1907)*, Oxford: Oxford University Press.

La Grange, Henry-Louis de & Weiß, Günther (eds) (1995), *Ein Glück ohne Ruh'. Die Briefe Gustav Mahlers an Alma*, Berlin: Siedler.

Landau, Ludwig (1936), 'Das jüdische Element bei Gustav Mahler. Zum 25. Todestage–18. Mai 1936', *Der Morgen*, 12, 67–73.

Lange, Friedrich Albert (1873–75), *Geschichte des Materialismus und Kritik seiner Bedeutung in der Gegenwart*, 2nd edn, Iserlohn: J. Baedeker.

Lea, Henry A. (1985), *Gustav Mahler, Man on the Margin*, Bonn: Bouvier Verlag Herbert Grundmann.

Lebrecht, Norman (1987), *Mahler Remembered*, London: Faber & Faber.

—— (1990a), 'The Variability of Mahler's Performances', *Musical Times*, 131, June, 302–4.

—— (1990b), *Gustav Mahler im Spiegel seiner Zeit – Portraitiert von Zeitgenossen*, Zürich & St Gallen: M & T Verlag.

—— (1993), *Gustav Mahler. Erinnerungen seiner Zeitgenossen*, Mainz: Schott/Munich: Piper.

Leur, Truus de (1997), 'Amsterdam: A Courageous Community', in Mitchell & Straub, 1997, pp. 76–101.

Levy, David (1986), 'Gustav Mahler and Emanuel Libman: Bacterial Endocarditis in 1911', *British Medical Journal*, 293, 1628–31.

Lewis, Christopher O. (1984), *Tonal Coherence in Mahler's Ninth Symphony*, Ann Arbor: UMI Research Press.

—— (1996), 'The Mind's Chronology: Narrative Times and Harmonic Disruption in Postromantic Music', in Kinderman & Krebs, 1996, pp. 114–49.

Litterscheid, Richard (1936), 'Mendelssohn, Mahler und wir', *Die Musik*, 26 (6), March, 413–17.

Louis, Rudolf (1905), *Anton Bruckner*, Munich & Leipzig: Georg Müller.

—— (1909), *Die deutsche Musik der Gegenwart*, Munich & Leipzig: Georg Müller.

McClatchie, Stephen (1996), 'The 1889 Version of Mahler's First Symphony: A New Manuscript Source', *19th-Century Music*, 20 (2), 99–124.

McGrath, William J. (1974), *Dionysian Art and Populist Politics in Austria*, New Haven: Yale University Press.

—— (1981), 'Mahler and Freud: The Dream of the Stately House', in Klein, 1981, pp. 40–51.

Machatzke, Martin (ed.) (1987), *Gerhart Hauptmann. Tagebücher 1897 bis 1905*, Berlin: Propyläen.

Mádl, Karel B. (ed.) (1906), *Špalíček [Little Booklet]*, Prague: Verlag Jan Otto.

Mahler, Alma (1910), *Fünf Lieder*, Vienna: Universal Edition.

—— (1915), *Vier Lieder*, Vienna: Universal Edition.

—— (ed.) (1924), *Gustav Mahler Briefe 1879–1911*, Vienna: Paul Zsolnay.

—— (1940), *Gustav Mahler: Erinnerungen und Briefe*, Amsterdam: Allert de Lange.

—— (1971), *Gustav Mahler: Erinnerungen und Briefe*, ed. Donald Mitchell, Frankfurt, Berlin & Vienna: Propyläen.

—— (1990), *Gustav Mahler. Memories and Letters*, ed. Donald Mitchell & Knud Martner, trans. B. Creighton, London: Sphere Books.

Mahler, Gustav (1924), *Zehnte Symphonie*, Berlin, Vienna, Leipzig: Paul Zsolnay. [First of the two facsimiles of Mahler's manuscript of the Tenth Symphony.]

—— (1995), *Facsimile Edition of the Seventh Symphony*, 2 vols (Commentary and Facsimile), Amsterdam: Rosbeek Publishers.

Mahler-Werfel, Alma (1959), *And the Bridge is Love*, in collaboration with E.B. Ashton, London: Hutchinson. [Also published in New York: Harcourt, Brace & Co., 1958]

—— ([1960] 2000), *Mein Leben*, Frankfurt: Fischer Taschenbuch.

—— (1997), *Tagebuch-Suiten 1898–1902*, ed. Antony Beaumont & Susanne Rode-Breymann, Frankfurt: S. Fischer.

—— (1998), *Diaries 1898–1902*, selected & trans. A. Beaumont, London: Faber & Faber.

Malloch, William (1964), *I Remember Mahler* (programme broadcast on KPFK, Los Angeles, 7 July 1964); NYP *The Mahler Broadcasts 1948–1982* CD, 1998, Nos 11 & 12.

Martner, Knud (ed.) (1979), *Selected Letters of Gustav Mahler*, trans. E. Wilkins, E. Kaiser & B. Hopkins, London: Faber and Faber.

—— (1985), *Gustav Mahler im Konzertsaal. Eine Dokumentation seiner Konzerttätigkeit 1870–1911*, Copenhagen: privately published.

—— (1991), 'Purgatorio: An Attempt for a New Interpretation', in Op de Coul, 1991, pp. 214–16.

Martner, Knud & Becqué, Robert (1977), 'Zwölf unbekannte Briefe Gustav Mahlers an Ludwig Strecker', *Archiv für Musikwissenschaft*, 34, 287–97.

Marx, Hans Joachim (ed.) (1990), *Aufführungspraxis der Händel-Oper. Veröffentlichungen der Internationalen Händel-Akademie Karlsruhe*, Laaber: Laaber Verlag.

Matter, Jean (1959), *Mahler le Démoniaque*, Lausanne: Foma.

Matthews, Colin (1974), 'Mahler at Work: Some Observations on the Ninth and Tenth Symphony Sketches', *Soundings*, 4, 76–82.

—— (1989), *Mahler at Work: Aspects of the Creative Process*, New York & London: Garland Publishing.

—— (1995/1996), 'The Tenth Symphony and Artistic Morality', *Muziek & Wetenschap*, 5 (3), 303–19.

Matthews, David (1991), 'Deryck Cooke's Performing Version of Mahler's Tenth Symphony: My Own Involvement, some Notes on the Evolution of the Score and some Ethical Problems', in Op de Coul, 1991, pp. 60–73.

—— (1999), 'The Sixth Symphony', in Mitchell & Nicholson, 1999, pp. 366–75.

Maus, Fred E. (1991), 'Music as Narrative', *Indiana Theory Review*, 12, 1–34.

Mazzetti, Remo Jr. (1997), 'A Mahler 10 for the Ages: An Appreciation of Joe Wheeler's Realisation', booklet notes accompanying the CD recording of Wheeler's version of Mahler's Tenth Symphony, Colorado Mahlerfest, conducted by Robert Olson.

Metzger, Heinz-Klaus & Riehn, Rainer (eds) (1989), *Muzik-Konzepte. Sonderband: Gustav Mahler*, Munich: edition text + kritik.

—— (eds) (1999), *Musik-Konzepte 106. Gustav Mahler Durchgesetzt?*, Munich: edition text + kritik.

Meylan, Claude (ed.) (2000), *William Ritter chevalier de Gustav Mahler. Écrits, correspondance, documents*, Berne: Peter Lang.

Micznik, Vera (1987), 'Is Mahler's music autobiographical? A Re-appraisal', *Revue Mahler Review*, 1 (February), 47–63.

—— (1989), 'Meaning in Gustav Mahler's Music: A Historical and Analytical Study Focusing on the Ninth Symphony', unpublished PhD thesis, State University of New York at Stony Brook.

—— (1994), 'Mahler and "the Power of Genre"', *Journal of Musicology*, 12, 117–51.

—— (1999), 'The Absolute Limitations of Programme Music: The Case of Liszt's *Die Ideale*', *Music & Letters*, 80 (2), May, 207–40.

—— (2001), 'Music and Narrative Revisited: Degrees of Narrativity in Beethoven and Mahler', *Journal of the Royal Musical Association*, 126 (2), 193–249.

Mitchell, Donald (1958), *Gustav Mahler: The Early Years*, London: Rockliff.

—— (1975), *Gustav Mahler: The Wunderhorn Years*, London: Faber.

—— (1980), *Gustav Mahler: The Early Years*, Banks, Paul & Matthews, David (eds), rev. edn, Berkeley & Los Angeles: University of California Press.

—— (1985), *Gustav Mahler: Vol. III: Songs and Symphonies of Life and Death*, London: Faber & Faber.

—— (1990), 'Mahler's "Orchestral" Orchestral Songs', paper presented at Rondom Mahler II Congress and Workshop, Rotterdam, 10–13 May.

—— (1995) 'Mahler and Nature: Landscape into Music', in Cooke, 1995, pp. 162–74.

—— (1999), 'Eternity or Nothingness? Mahler's Fifth Symphony', in Mitchell & Nicholson, 1999, pp. 236–325.

Mitchell, Donald & Nicholson, Andrew (eds) (1999), *The Mahler Companion*, Oxford: Oxford University Press.

Mitchell, Donald & Straub, Henriette (eds) (1997), *New Sounds, New Century: Mahler's Fifth Symphony (1901–2), with a History of Performances by the Royal Concertgebouw Orchestra (1906–97)*, Bussum: THOTH/Amsterdam, Royal Concertgebouw Orchestra.

Mitchell, W.J. Thomas (ed.) (1981), *On Narrative*, Chicago & London: University of Chicago Press.

Moens-Haenen, Greta (1987), 'Vibrato im Barock', in Berke & Hanemann, 1987, vol. 2, pp. 380–87.

Monelle, Raymond (2000), *The Sense of Music: Semiotic Essays*, Princeton: Princeton University Press.

Monson, Karen (1984), *Alma Mahler, Muse to Genius*, London: Collins.

Morgan, Robert (1996), 'Modular Form in Mahler', Paper presented at the International Conference 'Austria 996–1996: Music in a Changing Society', Ottawa, 6 January 1996.

Moser, Hans Joachim (1943), *Musiklexicon*, 2nd edn, Berlin: Hesse.

Mosse, George L. (1964), *The Crisis of German Ideology: Intellectual Origins of the Third Reich*, New York: Grosset and Dunlap.

Mozart, Leopold ([1787] 1968), *Versuch einer gründlichen Violinschule*, 3rd edn, Augsburg, repr. in facsimile, Leipzig: VEB Deutscher Verlag für Musik.

—— ([1787] 1985), *A Treatise on the Fundamental Principles of Violin Playing*, trans. E. Knocker, 2nd edn, Oxford & New York: Oxford University Press.

Muntz, Maximilian (1899), review of Mahler's Second Symphony, *Deutsche Zeitung*, 10 April.

Murphy, Edward (1975), 'Sonata-rondo Form in the Symphonies of Gustav Mahler', *Music Review*, 36 (1), 54–62.

—— (1986), 'Unusual Forms in Mahler's Fifth Symphony', *Music Review*, 47 (2), 101–9.

Nadel, Arno (1923), 'Jüdische Musik', *Der Jude*, 7 (4), 227–36.

Namenwirth, Simon M. (1985), 'Polemics Galore: The Critical Reception of Mahler's Eighth Symphony', in Ekdahl Davidson & Davidson, 1985, pp. 3–19.

Nattiez, Jean-Jacques (1990), 'Can One Speak of Narrativity in Music?', *Journal of the Royal Musical Association*, 115 (2), 240–57.

Neufeld, Ernest (1913), Lecture on Mahler's Eighth Symphony reported in Anon., 1913b.

Newcomb, Anthony (1992), 'Narrative Archetypes in Mahler's Ninth Symphony', in Scher, 1992, pp. 118–36.

Newlin, Dika (ed.) (1950), *Style and Idea*, New York: Philosophical Library.

—— (1979), *Bruckner, Mahler, Schoenberg*, London: Marion Boyars.

Niemann, Walter (1913), *Die Musik seit Richard Wagner*, Berlin & Leipzig: Schuster & Loeffler.

Nietzsche, Friedrich ([1887] 1974), *The Gay Science*, trans. W. Kaufmann, New York: Vintage Books.

Nikkels, Eveline (1991), 'Ist Mahlers Zehnte Symphonie ein Lied vom Tode?', in Op de Coul, 1991, pp. 165–72.

Nikkels, Eveline & Becqué, Robert (eds) (1992), *A 'Mass' for the Masses: Proceedings of the Mahler VIII Symposium, Amsterdam 1988*, Rijswijk, The Netherlands: Nijgh & Van Ditmar.

Notley, Margaret (1999), 'Late-Nineteenth-Century Chamber Music and the Cult of the Classical Adagio', *19th-Century Music*, 23 (1), 33–61.

Olsen, Morten S. [Solvik, Morten] (1992), 'Culture and the Creative Imagination: The Genesis of Gustav Mahler's Third Symphony', unpublished PhD thesis, University of Pennsylvania.

Op de Coul, Paul (ed.) (1991), *Fragment or Completion? Proceedings of the Mahler X Symposium Utrecht 1986*, The Hague: Nijgh & Van Ditmar.

Oxaal, Ivar, Pollak, Michael, & Botz, Gerhard (eds) (1987), *Jews, Anti-Semitism and Culture in Vienna*, London & New York: Routledge & Kegan Paul.

Painter, Karen (ed.) (2002), *Mahler and his World*, Princeton: Princeton University Press.

Painter, Karen & Varwig, Bettina (trans. & eds) (2002), 'Mahler's German-Language Critics', in Painter, 2002, pp. 265–378.

Pfohl, Ferdinand (1973), *Eindrücke und Erinnerungen aus den Hamburger Jahren*, ed. Knud Martner, Hamburg: Karl Dieter Wagner.

Pople, Anthony (ed.) (1994), *Theory, Analysis and Meaning in Music*, Cambridge: Cambridge University Press.

Prawer, Siegbert (ed. & trans.) (1964), *The Penguin Book of Lieder*, Harmondsworth: Penguin.

Prince, Gerald (1982), *Narratology: The Form and Functioning of Narrative*, Berlin, New York & Amsterdam: Mouton.

—— (1987), *A Dictionary of Narratology*, Lincoln: University of Nebraska Press.

Pringsheim, Klaus (1960), 'Erinnerungen an Gustav Mahler', *Neue Zürcher Zeitung*, 184, Wednesday 6 July, 6–7.

Pulzer, Peter (1988), *The Rise of Political Anti-Semitism in Germany and Austria*, Cambridge, Mass.: Harvard University Press.

Ratner, Leonard G. (1980), *Classic Music: Expression, Form, and Style*, New York: Schirmer.

Ratz, Erwin (ed.) (1967), *Zehnte Symphonie. Faksimile nach der Handschrift*, Munich: Walter Ricke/Meran: Laurin. [Second of the two facsimiles of Mahler's manuscript of the Tenth Symphony.]

Redlich, Hans Ferdinand (1920), 'Die Welt der V., VI. und VII. Sinfonien', *Musikblätter des Anbruch*, 2 (7–8 [1. u. 2. April-Heft]), 265–68.

—— (1963), 'Mahler's Enigmatic Sixth', in Gerstenberg, LaRue & Rehm, 1963, pp. 250–56.

—— (1966), 'Gustav Mahler: Probleme einer kritischen Gesamtausgabe', *Die Musikforschung*, 14, 378–401.

—— (1968), 'Gustav Mahler. Symphonie VI', in Redlich, Hans Ferdinand (ed.) (1968), Gustav Mahler, *Symphony No. 6*, Mainz: Ernst Eulenburg, pp. iii–xxvii.

Reeser, Eduard (1980), *Gustav Mahler und Holland. Briefe*, Vienna: Bibliothek der Internationalen Gustav Mahler Gesellschaft.

—— (1997), 'Gustav Mahlers letzte Melodie', in Weiß, 1997, pp. 223–39.

Reich, Willi (ed.) (1958), *Gustav Mahler. Im eigenen Wort – Im Worte der Freunde*, Zürich: Verlag der Arche.

Reilly, Edward (1982), *Gustav Mahler and Guido Adler: Records of a Friendship*, Cambridge: Cambridge University Press.

—— (1986), 'A Re-examination of the Manuscripts of Mahler's Third Symphony', in La Grange, 1986, pp. 62–72.

—— (1993), 'Sketches, Text Sources, Dating of Manuscripts: Unanswered Questions', *News About Mahler Research*, 30, 3–9.

—— (1995/1996), 'Mahler's Manuscripts and What they can Tell us: An Informal Consideration', *Muziek & Wetenschap*, 5 (3), 363–83.

Revers, Peter (2000), *Mahlers Lieder. Ein musikalischer Werkführer*, Munich: C.H. Beck.

Richolson-Sollitt, Edna (n.d. [1934]), *Mengelberg spreekt*, The Hague: Kruseman.

Riezler, Walter (1910), 'Rundschau. Gustav Mahlers Achte Symphonie', *Süddeutsche Monatshefte*, 7 (2), November, 604–6.

Rimmon-Kenan, Shlomith (1983), *Narrative Fiction: Contemporary Poetics*, London & New York: Routledge.

Ritter, William (1906), *Études d'art étranger*, Paris: Mercure de France.

Roller, Alfred (1922), *Die Bildnisse von Gustav Mahler*, Leipzig & Vienna: E.P. Tal.

Roman, Zoltan (1975), 'Aesthetic Symbiosis and Structural Metaphor in Mahler's *Das Lied von der Erde*', in Bontinck & Brusatti, 1975, pp. 110–19.

—— (1991), *Gustav Mahler and Hungary*, Budapest: Akadémiai Kiadó.

Rosenzweig, Alfred (1933), 'Wie Mahler seine "Achte" plante. Die erste handschriftliche Skizze', *Der Wiener Tag*, 3607, 4 June, 27–28.

Rothkamm, Jörg (1999), 'Wann entstand Mahlers Zehnte Symphonie?', in Metzger & Riehn, 1999, pp. 100–122.

—— (2000a), 'Wer komponierte die unter Alma Mahlers veröffentlichten Lieder? Unbekannte Briefe der Komponistin zur Revision ihrer Werke im Jahre 1910', *Die Musikforschung*, 53 (4), 432–45.

—— (2000b), *Berthold Goldschmidt und Gustav Mahler. Zur Entstehung von Deryck Cookes Konzertfassung der X. Symphonie*, Heister, Hans-Werner & Petersen, Peter (eds), *Musik im 'Dritten Reich' und im Exil*, vol. 6, Hamburg: von Bockel.

—— (2003), *Gustav Mahlers Zehnte Symphonie. Entstehung, Analyse, Reception*, Frankfurt: Peter Lang.

Rowley, H.H. (1965), *Apokalyptik. Ihre Form und Bedeutung zur biblischen Zeit. Eine Studie über jüdische und christliche Apokalypsen vom Buch Daniel bis zur geheimen Offenbarung*, trans. I. & R. Pesch, Einsiedeln: Benziger.

Rubin, Ruth (1963), *Voices of a People: Yiddish Folk Song*, New York & London: Thomas Yoseloff. [Rev. edn, Chicago: University of Illinois Press, 2000.]

Rychetský Jiři (1987), '"Eits a binkel Kasi (Hrasi)"', *News About Mahler Research*, 17, April, 7–8.

—— (1989) 'Mahler's Favourite Song', *Musical Times*, 130, December, 729.

Ryding, Erik & Pechefsky, Rebecca (2001), *Bruno Walter: A World Elsewhere*, New Haven: Yale University Press.

Sachs, Joseph (1937), *Beauty and the Jew*, London: Edward Goldston.

Sadie, Stanley (ed.) (1980), *The New Grove Dictionary of Music and Musicians*, London: Macmillan.

—— (ed.) (2001), *The New Grove Dictionary of Music and Musicians*, 2nd edn, London: Macmillan.

Salten, Felix (1924), 'Mahler', in Salten, 1924, *Geister der Zeit. Erlebnisse*, Vienna: Paul Zsolnay, pp. 59–75.

Samuels, Robert (1994), 'Music as Text: Mahler, Schumann and Issues in Analysis', in Pople, 1994, pp. 152–63.

—— (1995), *Mahler's Sixth Symphony: A Study in Musical Semiotics*, Cambridge: Cambridge University Press.

Schadendorff, Mirjam (1995), *Humor als Formkonzept in der Musik Gustav Mahlers*, Stuttgart: Metzler.

Scharlitt, Bernard (1920), 'Gespräch mit Mahler', *Musikblätter des Anbruch*, 2 (7–8), (*Sonderheft Gustav Mahler*), 309–10.

Scheichl, Sigurd P. (1987), 'Contexts and Nuances of Anti-Jewish Language: Were all the "Antisemites" Antisemites?', in Oxaal, Pollak & Botz, 1987, pp. 89–110.

Scher, Steven Paul (ed.) (1992), *Music and Text: Critical Inquiries*, Cambridge: Cambridge University Press.

Scherzinger, Martin (1995), 'The Finale of Mahler's Seventh Symphony: A Deconstructive Reading', *Music Analysis*, 14, 69–88.

Schiedermair, Ludwig (1901), *Gustav Mahler. Eine biographisch-kritische Würdigung*, Leipzig: Hermann Seemann Nachfolger.

Schlüter, Wolfgang (1983), 'Studien zur Rezeptionsgeschichte der Symphonik Gustav Mahler', unpublished PhD thesis, Technische Universität, Berlin.

—— (1989), 'Die Wunde Mahler. Zur Rezeption seiner Sinfonien', in Metzger & Riehn (eds), 1989, pp. 7–149.

Schmierer, Elisabeth (1991), *Die Orchesterlieder Gustav Mahlers*, Kassel & London: Bärenreiter.

—— (1988), 'The Expression of Humour in Mahler's *Wunderhorn-Lieder*', unpublished paper presented at the International Musicological Symposium, Melbourne.

—— (2001), 'Liedästhetik im 19. Jahrhundert und Mahlers Orchesterlieder', in Brzoska & Heinemann, 2001, vol. 3, pp. 85–105.

Schoenberg, Arnold (1912/1948), 'Gustav Mahler', lecture MS, rev. & partly trans. Schoenberg, 1948. [Published in Stein, 1975, pp. 449–72, and Newlin, 1950, pp. 7–36.]

—— (1935), 'Speech on the Jewish Situation', in Stein, 1975, pp. 502–5.

Schubart, Christian Friedrich Daniel ([1806] 1969), *Ideen zu einer Ästhetik der Tonkunst*, Vienna, repr. Hildesheim: Verlag Georg Olms.

Schumann, Otto (1940), *Geschichte der deutschen Musik*, Leipzig: Bibliographisches Institut.

Seidl, Arthur ([1900] 1920), *Moderner Geist in der deutschen Tonkunst*, Regensburg: Gustav Bosse.

Seiffert, Wolf-Dieter (1993), 'Punkt und Strich bei Mozart', paper presented at the 11th Internationaler Kongreß der Gesellschaft für Musikforschung in Freiburg im Breisgau, 1 October 1993.

Sine, Nadine (1983), 'The Evolution of Symphonic Worlds: Tonality in the Symphonies of Gustav Mahler, with Emphasis on the First, Third, and Fifth', unpublished PhD thesis, New York University.

Sipe, Thomas (1993), 'Mahler and the "Novelization" of the Symphony', paper presented at the American Musicological Society Annual Meeting, Montréal, 3–7 November 1993.

Sombart, Werner ([1911] 1982), *Jews and Modern Capitalism*, trans. M. Epstein, introd. S.Z. Klausner, New Brunswick: Transaction Books.

Specht, Richard (1905), *Gustav Mahler*, Berlin: Gose und Tetzlaff.

—— (1906), *Gustav Mahler, Sechste Symphonie. Thematischer Führer*, Leipzig: Kahnt.

—— (1913), *Gustav Mahler*, Berlin: Schuster & Loeffler.

—— (1918), *Gustav Mahler*, rev. edn, Berlin: Schuster & Loeffler.

—— (1919), *Das Wiener Operntheater. Erinnerung auf 50 Jahren*, Vienna: Paul Knepler.

—— (1922), *Gustav Mahler*, Berlin: Schuster & Loeffler.

Sponheuer, Bernd (1992), 'Dissonante Stimmigkeit. Eine rezeptions-geschichtliche Studie zum dritten Satz der Mahlerschen Ersten', in Danuser, 1992, pp. 159–90.

Stadler, Friedrich (ed.) (1997), *Wissenschaft als Kunst. Österreichs Beitrag zur Moderne*, Vienna & New York: Springer Verlag.

Stefan, Paul (1910), 'Zur Uraufführung der VIII. Symphonie von Gustav Mahler in München', *Neue Musik-Zeitung*, 31 (24), 489–91.

—— (1912), *Gustav Mahler. Eine Studie über Persönlichkeit und Werk*, 4th edn, Munich: Piper.

—— (1913), *Gustav Mahler: A Study of his Personality and Work*, trans. T.E. Clark, New York: G. Schirmer.

—— (1923), *Mahler für Jedermann*, Vienna & Leipzig: Wila.

Stein, Erwin (1929), 'Eine unbekannte Ausgabe letzter Hand von Mahlers IV. Symphonie', *Pult und Takstock*, 6, 31–32. [English translation, 'The Unknown Last Version of Mahler's Fourth Symphony', in Stein, 1953, pp. 31–33.]

—— (1953), *Orpheus in New Guises*, New York: Rockliff.

Stein, Leonard (ed.) (1975), *Style and Idea. Selected Writings of Arnold Schoenberg*, trans. L. Black, London: Faber & Faber.

Stephan, Rudolf (ed.) (1979a), *Gustav Mahler. Werk und Interpretation. Autographe, Partituren, Dokumente*, Cologne: Arno Volk.

—— (1979b), *Gustav Mahler. II. Symphonie c-moll*, Meisterwerke der Musik, vol. 21, Munich: Fink.

—— (1985), *Mahler-Interpretation. Aspekte zum Werk und Wirken von Gustav Mahler*, Mainz: Schott.

Stolzing, Josef (1912), 'Die Symphonie der Tausend', unidentified review, dated 18 May, of a Berlin performance of Mahler's Eighth Symphony; from the Steininger Sammlung, Geheimes Staatsarchiv, Preussischer Kulturbesitz, Berlin.

Strasser, Otto (1974), *Und dafür wird man noch bezahlt. Mein Leben mit den Wiener Philharmonikern*, Vienna: Paul Neff Verlag.

Sullivan, Jack (ed.) (1990), *Words on Music from Addison to Barzun*, Athens: Ohio University Press.

Swarowsky, Hans (1979), *Wahrung der Gestalt*, ed. M. Huss, Vienna: Universal Edition.

Tarabová, Milada (1937), *Z přednášek J.B. Foerstra, lektora na Karlově universitě, 1929–1936* [*From the Lectures of J.B. Foerster at the Charles University, 1929–1936*], Prague: Foerster Society.

Taylor, Virginia Sue (1988), 'The Harp in Mahler's "Klangfarbengruppe"', unpublished PhD thesis, Washington University.

Tibbe, Monika (1971), *Über die Verwendung von Liedern und Liedelementen in instrumentalen Symphoniesätzen Gustav Mahlers*, Munich: Katzbichler.

Urban, Erich (1927), untitled article on recent performances of Mahler's First and Fourth Symphonies, and Bruckner's Second Symphony, *Berliner Zeitung am Mittag*, early March [?].

Vill, Susanne (1979), *Vermittlungsformen verbalisierter und musikalischer Inhalte in der Musik Gustav Mahlers*, Tutzing: Schneider.

Vodnoy, Robert (1993), 'Tempo and Structure in Gustav Mahler's Symphony No. 5: A Search for Unity, Continuity and Organization', unpublished DMA thesis, Indiana University.

Vogt, Matthias Theodor (ed.) (1991), *Das Gustav-Mahler-Fest, Hamburg 1989. Bericht über den Internationalen Gustav-Mahler-Kongreß*, Kassel: Bärenreiter.

Walter, Bruno (1912), 'Mahlers Weg. Ein Erinnerungsblatt', *Der Merker*, 3 (5), 166–71.

—— (1936), *Gustav Mahler*, Vienna: Herbert Reichner.

—— (1937), *Gustav Mahler*, trans. J. Galston, London: Kegan Paul, Trench, Trubner & Co.

—— (1941), *Gustav Mahler*, New York: Vienna House.

—— (1947), *Theme and Variations*, trans. J. Galston, London: Hamish Hamilton.

—— ([1958] 1990), *Gustav Mahler*, trans. L. Walter Lindt, London: Quartet Books.

Webster, James (1980), 'Sonata form', in Sadie, 1980, vol. 17, pp. 497–508.

Weigl, Karl (1910), 'Gustav Mahler. VI. Symphonie in A moll', in Istel, 1910, pp. 103–24.

Weiner, Marc A. (1993), *Undertones of Insurrection: Music, Politics, and the Social Sphere in the Modern German Narrative*, Lincoln: University of Nebraska Press.

Weiß, Günther (ed.) (1997), *Neue Mahleriana: Essays in Honour of Henry-Louis de La Grange on his Seventieth Birthday*, Berne: Peter Lang.

Weisseweiler, Eva, (1999), *Ausgemerzt! Das Lexikon der Juden in der Musik und seine mörderischen Folgen*, Cologne: Dittrich.

Weißman, Adolf (1922), *Die Musik in der Weltkrise*, Stuttgart & Berlin: Deutsche Verlagsanstalt, trans. M.M. Bozman as *The Problems of Modern Music*, London: Dent, 1925.

—— (1926), 'Rasse und Nationalität in der Musik', in Heinsheimer & Stefan, 1926, pp. 86–105.

Wellesz, Egon (1960), 'Gustav Mahler und die Wiener Oper. Festrede', *Neue Deutsche Rundschau*, 71 (2), 255–61.

Wellesz, Egon & Wellesz, Emmy (1981), *Egon Wellesz. Leben und Werk*, Vienna: Paul Zsolnay.

Wessling, Bernd (1974), *Gustav Mahler. Ein prophetisches Leben*, Hamburg: Hoffmann & Campe Verlag.

White, Hayden (1981), 'The Value of Narrativity in the Representation of Reality', in Mitchell, 1981, pp. 1–24.

Wildhagen, Christian (2000), *Die* Achte Symphonie *von Gustav Mahler. Konzeption einer universalen Symphonik*, Frankfurt: Peter Lang.

Wilkens, Sander (1988), 'Mahler's Trieste Conduction [*sic*] Score: An Unknown Source to the History of the Fifth Symphony', *News About Mahler Research*, 19, March, 11–14.

—— (1989), *Gustav Mahlers Fünfte Symphonie. Quellen und Instrumentationsprozess*, Frankfurt: Peters.

Williamson, John (1986), 'The Structural Premises of Mahler's Introductions: Prolegomena to an Analysis of the First Movement of the Seventh Symphony', *Music Analysis*, 5 (1), 29–57.

—— (1997), 'Dissonance and Middleground Prolongations in Mahler's Late Music', in Hefling, 1997, pp. 248–70.

Willnauer, Franz (1993), *Gustav Mahler und die Wiener Oper*, Vienna: Löcker.

Wistrich, Robert (1990), *Between Redemption and Perdition: Modern Antisemitism and Jewish Identity*, London & New York: Routledge.

Worbs, Hans Christoph (1960), *Gustav Mahler*, Berlin Halensee: Max Hesse.

—— (n.d.), *Gustav Mahler*, The Hague: H.J. Dieben.

Wunberg, Gotthart (ed.) (1981), *Die Wiener Moderne*, Stuttgart: Philipp Reclam Jun.

Ziegler, Hans S. (ed.) (1939), *Entartete Musik. Eine Abrechnung*, Düsseldorf: Völkischer Verlag.

Zschorlich, Paul (1927), 'Der "ungefüge" Bruckner und Mahlers Hohngelächter', *Deutsche Zeitung*, 12 March.

Zychowicz, James L. (1988), 'Sketches and Drafts of Gustav Mahler 1892–1901: The Sources of the Fourth Symphony', unpublished PhD thesis, University of Cincinnati.

—— (1994), 'Music Manuscripts in the Bibliothèque Musicale Gustav Mahler, Paris', *Fontes Artis Musicae*, 41 (3), July–September, 279–95.

—— (2000), *Mahler's Fourth Symphony*, Studies in Musical Genesis and Structure, Oxford: Oxford University Press.

Index